W9-CJC-927

The Wind Won't Know Me

The Wind Won't Know Me

A History of
the Navajo-Hopi
Land Dispute

EMILY BENEDEK

Alfred A. Knopf New York 1992

THIS IS A BORZOI BOOK
PUBLISHED BY ALFRED A. KNOPF, INC.

Copyright © 1992 by Emily Benedek
Published in the United States by Alfred A. Knopf, Inc., New York,
and simultaneously in Canada by Random House of Canada Limited, Toronto.
Distributed by Random House, Inc., New York.

Grateful acknowledgment is made to the following for permission to reprint previously published and unpublished material:
Frances Collin, Literary Agent: Excerpts from *The Running Narrative of the Organization of the Hopi Tribe of Indians, 1936,* unpublished journal of Oliver La Farge. The La Farge Collection, Harry Ransom Humanities Research Center, the University of Texas at Austin. Reprinted by permission of Frances Collin, Literary Agent.
The University of Arizona Press: Excerpts from *Me and Mine: The Life of Helen Sekaquaptewa* as told to Louise Udall. Copyright © 1969 by the Arizona Board of Regents. Reprinted by permission.
The University of New Mexico Press: Excerpts from *The Second Long Walk: The Navajo-Hopi Land Dispute* by Jerry Kammer. Copyright © 1980 by The University of New Mexico Press. Reprinted by permission.
The following photographs were taken by Kenji Kawano: insert pages v, x (bottom), xi (bottom), xii, xiii, and xiv (top). All remaining photographs were taken by John Running.
Library of Congress Cataloging-in-Publication Data
Benedek, Emily.
The wind won't know me: a history of the Navajo-Hopi land dispute
by Emily Benedek.—1st ed.
p. cm.
Includes index.
ISBN 0-394-55429-9
1. Navajo Indians—Land tenure.   2. Hopi Indians—Land tenure.
3. Navajo Indians—Government relations.   4. Hopi Indians—
Government relations.   I. Title.
E99.N3B453   1992
979.1'35004972—dc20   92-52892
CIP
Manufactured in the United States of America
First Edition

FOR MY PARENTS

and for all parents and grandparents who
fight for what is precious to them

The wind won't know me there.
The Holy People won't know me.
And I won't know the Holy People.
And there's no one left who can
   tell me.

AN OLD NAVAJO WOMAN

Contents

Spring 1986

Acknowledgments

This book grew out of a story I reported for *Newsweek*, "Two Tribes, One Land," in 1985. Many people at *Newsweek* were helpful to me, and I would like especially to thank the following: Peter McGrath, who approved the idea; Aric Press, who wrote a fine story based on my research; Bob Rivard (now at the San Antonio *Light*), who sent me off to Arizona; and David Gates, who wrote a follow-up and has been a generous friend for many years.

I am grateful to Robert Gottlieb for signing up this book at Knopf and to Lee Goerner for taking it on.

Thanks also to my editor, Ann Close, who inherited this book and let the people in it burn a place in her thoughts. I am grateful also for the help of her assistant, Ann Kraybill. Heartfelt thanks to Karen Leh for her conscientious and astute work as production editor of this book.

Thanks to Kris Dahl, Gordon Kato, and Dorothea Herrey at ICM.

Many people participated in this project; to those who prefer to remain unnamed, I thank you here. Thanks also to Sandra Massetto, Dick Ivey, David Aberle, Jim Hildebrandt, Bob Lomadafkie, Alma Dodson, John Running, Sam Minkler, Courtney Hoblock, Lee Phillips, Sara Aleman, Phyllis Hogan, Jon Norstog, John Craddock, David Williams, Hollis Whitson, Jay Levi, Edgar Cahn, Jonathan Cahn, the late David Shaw-Serdar, Percy Deal, Leroy Morgan, John McCain, and Ron Faich for their help and encouragement. And of course, great thanks to the Tsos, the Hatathlies, the Bedonies, and Abbott Sekaquaptewa for allowing me into their lives at such a critical time and sharing with me their thoughts and feelings.

I owe a debt to John Redhouse for his work *Geopolitics of the Navajo Hopi Land Dispute*, which documents the role of energy interests in this dispute. I also owe a heavy debt to Jerry Kammer, whose book, *The Second Long Walk*, and whose coverage of the dispute in the 1970s for the

Gallup Independent were of immense help in the writing of this book. Also I would like to thank Tim Coulter, who produced *Report to the Hopi Kikmongwis* for the Indian Law Resource Center in Washington. That document was invaluable to me. Also thanks to librarians at the Museum of Northern Arizona Library, the Special Collections Department of the University of Arizona, and the Heard Museum Library.

Many thanks to my friend Michelle Hammer for her friendship, humor, and editorial advice.

And finally, I would like to thank Jeffry J. Andresen, M.D., a man who honors the imagination and understands the language of the heart. He showed me what this book is really about. For him, these lines from T. S. Eliot:

> We shall not cease from exploration
> And the end of all our exploring
> Will be to arrive where we started
> And know the place for the first time.
> Through the unknown, remembered gate
> When the last of earth left to discover
> Is that which was the beginning. . . .

Summer 1985

I am well known among the hills, among the ditches, rivers, streams, plants. I have touched them in various ways and they have touched me the same. There is no place but here.

ASDZAA YAZHI BEDONI, NAVAJO

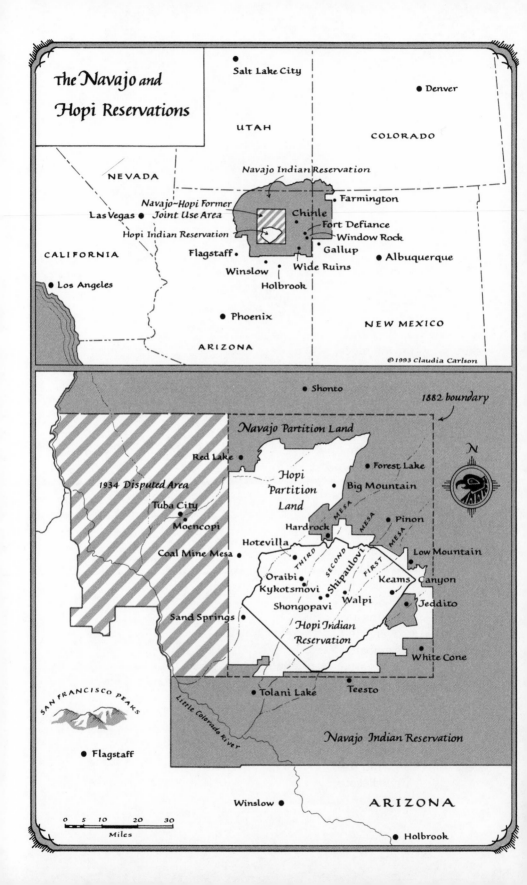

The Sun Dance,
Big Mountain

A young Navajo dances in the center of the sun dance arbor. His red skirt hangs low on his hips. Bracelets of sage grass encircle his wrists and ankles. After three days of dancing without food or water, only a bitter sage tea to sip, his long, slim frame is emaciated. His black hair falls past his shoulders onto skin burned deep red by the beating sun.

On the dancer's chest are two small wounds made earlier in the day by Leonard Crow Dog, the leader of this once outlawed ceremony. The two cuts carry pegs pushed through the skin and muscle like needles in a stitch. From the pegs, ropes loop up into a brightly festooned cottonwood tree, which is set in the center of the arbor. The dancer stares into the tree and prays. He prays for a vision to help him transcend his pain.

Suddenly, the rope connecting the pegs in his breast to the tree is yanked tight. The dancer is lifted into the air by his skin. Back arched into a half moon, he twists, flails his arms and legs in an attempt to break free. He starts to dance again as the rope is pulled higher. The young man flaps eight feet from the ground before the skin, dry as rawhide, breaks, and he falls to the earth. Blood trickles down his chest as he picks himself up and runs a victory lap around the arbor. His face is rapturous. His ordeal is over. He has purified himself and in so doing has offered strength to the embattled Navajos, the people of this land.

The sun dance arbor encircles a flat, dirt dance area tucked into a hollow of red slate hills in the remote area of Big Mountain, a long, flat mesa on the Navajo Indian reservation in northeastern Arizona. Beneath juniper boughs, which shade the arbor ring, a half-dozen men sit around a skin drum and intone the thick chants of old Sioux songs layered with the deep beat of the drum and the cry of a single voice, much higher, desperate, like wind traveling through a rocky pass. At the arbor's western end, Clyde Bellecourt, a former leader of the American Indian Movement, prepares to break his ties. He has been pierced in the muscles of his upper back. Leonard Crow Dog attaches two ropes to the pegs lodged between his shoulder blades. Hanging from the ropes are a half-dozen buffalo skulls. The skulls, tied one after the other, trail ten feet behind Bellecourt on the red earth.

Around him in the arbor dance two hundred Indians who step foot to foot in parallel rows, bent forward slightly at the waist, clutching eagle feathers in their hands, breathing in and out through whistles of eagle bone. They are weary. Many lift their feet only a few inches from the ground; some dancers, trying to fight their fatigue, hoist their legs in exaggerated steps, folding and unfolding their bodies in a last spasm of endurance. The men's chests, backs, and arms are covered by round spots of mutilated skin that mark sun dances past. Many dancers wear eagle feathers standing in their hair. Some carry staffs of animal heads.

The dancers move in lines, hip to hip. The women dance in their own lines beside the men. Women from Big Mountain who are in their sixties and seventies dance next to the young ones. Their jaws are set, their bare feet now oblivious to the burning sand. Katherine Smith is one of the . elderly women dancing here. In 1979, she loaded up her rifle and shot into the air over a work crew erecting a barbed wire fence through her land. Since then, she has been carted off to jail and prosecuted for per-forming the familiar tasks of her life—caring for her animals and tending to her home. She has watched as her precious sheep herd was reduced in size. Yet she remains steadfastly certain of one thing: she will never leave this land. Her face is calm, knowing; a smile settles about her eyes.

The drum beats faster as Clyde Bellecourt takes his first step forward, struggling to move the heavy buffalo skulls. The pegs pull away from his back, and the blood again starts a slow course down to his hips. He shouts and starts to run around the arbor, dragging his burden. The other sun dancers continue their steps to the beat of the drum and the shriek of eagle-bone whistles. Bellecourt drags the arbor once, grunting with the effort, blood trickling down to the top of his skirt. His skin is pellucid; the toll of the ordeal shows in the lines of his face. After another half lap, the outside peg pulls away, breaking the strip of muscle and skin. The skulls rattle along the red ground beneath the sun, which beats relentlessly on the dancers. Some have dry heaves. Others are near delir-ium. Without warning, a dancer jumps on the string of skulls, wrenching the remaining peg from Bellecourt's back. The whistles peal above the frenzied singers and Bellecourt bounds around the circle.

The air smells of blood and the cloying perfume of burning sweet grass here in this rugged land in the Navajo chapter of Hardrock. (The Navajo Nation is divided into 109 rural communities called chapters. Every chapter operates like a local government with its own officials, and each sends representatives to the Tribal Council, the primary governing body of the tribe, in the capital of Window Rock.)

The elderly men and women of this area, whose gnarled brown hands and wrinkled faces resemble the tough, twisted branches of the juniper and piñon trees that dot the landscape, have been ordered by the federal government to leave this place, their sheep, the burial places of their dead to settle a boundary dispute with their neighbors, the Hopis.

But the people said no. And they knew they had to muster the spirit of the old days to win this battle. Indians from across the country sit in the shade of the arbor, as do white supporters in their own segregated areas, where they are patrolled by young militant Indians dressed in paramilitary gear with knives strapped to their legs. No food or drink is allowed in the arbor, shoes must be removed, and spectators are forbidden from crossing the eastern entrance. A quick tap on the shoulder from one of the young Indian guards sends an errant Anglo quickly back to his place. Navajos from other parts of the reservation watch with a mixture of curiosity and fear, for this is not a Navajo ceremony. Navajos don't believe in the letting of blood.

This ceremony was originally a Plains Indian rite intended to renew the people's communion with the sun, the wind, the earth, and the gods. As in other sacrificial rites, the offering of flesh is intended to secure the positive regard of the supernaturals. The sun dance is also an offering to the gathered humans: the Blackfeet teach that the rigors of the ceremony are not intended to showcase an Indian's bravery or his ability to withstand pain, but rather to show his spiritual strength by his ability to transcend pain. This strength he offers as a gift to his people. This is a ritual for which the Indians here today have prepared for many months, and which they will feel for many weeks after it is over. But this is also a spectacle designed to bring attention to a land and a people that usually remain out of sight of the Anglo world. Many of the dancers are urban Indians, in whose faces one sees the marks of other races: black, white, and yellow. They have fought battles for Indian rights on reservations and on the streets of major cities. Part of their battle is to find their own Indianness. The Navajos of this area are very different. They don't need to search for what is Indian. In one of the remotest areas of the United States, they live their lives much as their grandparents did a hundred years ago.

After breaking his ties, Bellecourt is helped beneath the shade of juniper boughs at the western edge of the arbor, which has been set aside as a resting place. He is given a sip of sage tea, and salve is dabbed on his wounds. He falls onto the blankets beneath a banner that reads REMEMBER WOUNDED KNEE, a salute to another time when tribes of Indians gathered to gain spiritual strength for a final battle against the white man. It was in 1890, after a Paiute Indian named Wovoka had a vision that the white men would be washed away by a flood, the buffalo would return to the Plains, and the Indian dead would arise with the flowers of the next spring. Wovoka created the Ghost Dance, which the near-defeated Plains Indians took up with great hope and passionate energy. Small and large camps within the once great Sioux Nation danced through the fall and winter of 1890, convinced that the end of the world was imminent, that their pain and humiliation would soon end. So great was their faith that they didn't even rise up against the U.S. government when their leader, Sitting Bull, was killed while in captivity.

However, in the dead of winter, their dreams of freedom finally met up with the harsh reality of the Seventh Cavalry. A band of Indians on its way to Pine Ridge, South Dakota, was intercepted at Wounded Knee Creek. Three hundred men, women, children, and elderlies were killed by Hotchkiss guns before noon the next day. The battle of Wounded Knee signaled the end of the nineteenth-century Indian Wars. The Indians at Big Mountain are reaching back to the inspiration of the old ways, but praying that their struggle will have a very different outcome.

Leonard Crow Dog wears two long braids. His red skirt hangs beneath a great strong belly. He is a fearsome man with a lofty bearing who has learned the rituals of the sun dance from Fool's Crow, one of those who revived the dance in the 1950s. Crow Dog is about to pierce a young dancer. The man asks for the pegs to be placed in his arms. He is a Navajo from this area and he wants to test himself severely. The drum beats, the chanters wail, and the man silently receives his cuts. He is hitched by ropes to a horse, which sidesteps and rears, spooked by the dancers and the banners fluttering in the tree. As four men hold the dancer, a bareback rider lets out a screech and drives the horse at a gallop toward the eastern exit, ripping the pegs from the Indian's arms.

Away from the sickening heat and fatigue of the sun dance arbor, spectators putter around camps of tents, trucks, and RVs among the dry, juniper-dotted hills. Navajo ladies—the elderly Navajo women refer to each other as "ladies"—prepare breakfast in small cookshacks, frying potatoes with onion and egg and flapping fry bread into pans of bubbling lard. Kee Shay, a tall, gangly Navajo man on whose land the camp has been built, walks up to the ladies and jokes with them. He picks up a large hunting knife from the counter. "What's a man's knife doing here in a woman's kitchen?" he asks in Navajo, a guttural language that is marked with glottal stops and aspirations whose sounds seem to hop and fall naturally over the shapes of the high desert. The women are dressed in the garb that is now considered traditional, but was in fact picked up from Anglo frontier women. They wear full, silky pleated skirts and cotton or velveteen blouses decorated with silver and turquoise jewelry, socks, and sturdy shoes. Their hair is neatly pulled back in a figure eight–shaped bun and tied with white yarn. They giggle shyly at Kee Shay's question and repeat the joke among themselves. Kee Shay smiles and strides on, his mouth twisted into its peculiar northwest-southeast slant. He checks the water barrel, which is refilled several times a day by trucks carrying water from the nearest tap—fifteen miles away —and heads up to the sun dance arbor. Navajos passing him put out their hands respectfully for a shake. He is a quiet man and an elder statesman of the area. Although he has given permission for this ceremony to be held on his land, his feelings about it are mixed. Navajos don't believe in bloodletting, he reminds himself over and over. But in a brave last effort to preserve their way of life here, the people are reaching out to foreign ways, ways that are taboo.

Hand-lettered signs are stuck in the ground beside dirt roads that have been cut quickly by the treads of hundreds of vehicles. They designate Indian camps and non-Indian camps. Unlike the signs of segregation that have only recently disappeared from the border towns, these signs have been placed by the young Indians who patrol the area. The recently radicalized people of Big Mountain have declared this area the Sovereign Dine Nation. Dine is what the Navajos call themselves. It means "The People." Fed up with their tribal government's failure to reverse the white man's law, the people of this rough, isolated land, more than a hundred miles away from the Navajo capital, have seceded from the Navajo Nation and are taking the law into their own hands. In their desperation, the people here are turning not only to alien Indian ways but also to the alien ways of white people and political activism in a last attempt to save what is precious to them.

Many of the Navajos attending the sun dance here live in other parts of the sprawling 25,000-square-mile reservation and are not affected by the law that is forcing the people of this area to move. Others are indeed affected by the law, but live in different chapters like Teesto and Coal Mine Mesa, whose residents have not become as outspoken and militant as the people here. Most even view the radicalism of the Big Mountain Navajos with suspicion, since there is little precedent for political agitation among the Navajos. Families lounge around their pickups gossiping, visiting with friends. Like the summer squaw dances, this is a social occasion as much as a ritual, a chance for people to gather from their remote camps and see old friends and relatives. Many people would just as soon not watch too much of the ceremony.

There is a break in the dancing and Kee Shay makes a brief announcement that reflects his apprehension. He says in Navajo, "Our friend Leonard Crow Dog and his fellow Sioux brothers offered to come here and have a sun dance to help out the people faced with relocation. We could not deny their offer of friendship." Kee Shay's message is translated into English, the only language all the dancers know.

When the sun turns for the horizon, the rocky slopes glinting brilliant gold, the dancers take their final steps and retire to the camp of tipis set up near the arbor. In the shadows of the old Plains dwellings, dancers untie their hair and talk quietly among themselves as they change into regular clothes. Some wander back to the camp. Others enter the sweat lodges. None eat or drink. Some will not sleep, but will attend a peyote meeting until dawn.

Away from the dancers, however, the observers eat, gather around campfires, prepare to sleep under the chunky stars. A quarter mile away from the sun dance camp, lawyer Lew Gurwitz places his bedroll in a small clearing within the section marked NON-INDIAN. He is the biggest reason there is a resistance here. Gurwitz, a tall, burly man, wears his flowing white hair shoulder length. A native of Boston, who still speaks with a broad Boston accent, Gurwitz bears a resemblance to Marlon Brando and is sometimes mistaken for an Indian. He wears jeans, denim shirt, a turquoise ring, Hopi silver bracelet, and frequently ties a bandana around his head. He has been active in Indian affairs for fifteen years, representing American Indian Movement (AIM) activists in court and organizing grass roots support groups.

Gurwitz came out here after the passage of a 1974 law that devised a Solomonic solution to the finding of a U.S. court that a large piece of land was jointly owned by the Navajos and Hopis. The law, the 1974 Navajo-Hopi Indian Land Settlement Act, authorized the division of the jointly owned land into two equal pieces and authorized the relocation of all Indians who found themselves on the wrong side of the line. The sides are now known as the Hopi Partition Lands and the Navajo Partition Lands. Most of the people being asked to move are Navajos, about ten thousand of them. One hundred Hopis found themselves on Navajo land. "There's going to be a war," Gurwitz says, rolling out a sleeping bag. "It may be a short war. But these people have said, and they mean it, 'You'll have to drag me dead out of my hogan.' And there are people around the country who'll stand beside them and fight."

The fourth and final day of the sun dance nears an end. The last dancers break their ties and take their victory laps. All the pegs are gone from the dancers' bodies. Most of the scars have begun to heal. There is a feeling here of a cleansing, a contentment, fatigue born of great accomplishment. The ceremony is marred only momentarily when a white observer, caught up in the frenzy, jumps into the sun dance arbor and runs a lap as the dancers take their final steps. He moves with his shoulders hunched and his neck jutted forward as if he were in the clutches of a demon. Leonard Crow Dog picks up the microphone and shouts, "Whitey, whitey, get out of the arbor." The words jar the dry, hot air and shatter the fragile sense of mutual purpose that has grown here. Crow Dog repeats himself until someone finally waves the semidelirious man back under the canopy with the rest of the counterculture spectators. A murmur of disapproval snakes through the Indians in the crowd.

After the melee settles, the closing ceremonies begin with a prayer from Thomas Banyacya, a Hopi man who does not believe the Navajos should move to resolve the land dispute with his tribe. He represents a significant number of traditional Hopi people who do not recognize the authority of the Hopi Tribal Council, which wants to divide the land and move the Navajos, and which they believe is a puppet of the U.S. government and does not represent them. They have thrown their lot in with the Navajo resistance. Banyacya, a short, round man who wears his hair pulled back in a bun with a filmy red kerchief about his forehead, sprinkles corn pollen on the ground. He intones a Hopi prayer, then in English says, "We must not forget who we are. We are red men who live on our red land. We have difficult times ahead and we mustn't forget our traditional ways, our ceremonies, our sings, dances, and prayer. We must call on the Great Spirit to help us protect our land."

More speeches are made and traditional Indian giveaways offered. One family commemorates the birth of a son and distributes Pendleton blankets and bolts of cloth to relatives. Kee Shay is offered a gift in thanks for the use of his land. Ironically, the money that bought the gifts was provided by white supporters. It galls the Indians that white people are allowed to watch this sacred ceremony, but they know they need the white man's sympathy. A sensitive peace exists between the Indians here and their white supporters, but beneath the relations, and evident at any perturbation, is Indian anger, Anglo guilt.

Trying to channel the former and milk the latter is Lew Gurwitz. Except for a few years as a criminal attorney, Gurwitz has devoted his career to Indian issues. He represented the AIM militants who occupied the South Dakota hamlet of Wounded Knee in 1973 to protest treatment of the Sioux, and helped the unsuccessful defense team of Leonard Peltier, who was tried and convicted of the June 1975 murders of two FBI agents on the Pine Ridge Reservation. In 1979, when Gurwitz was representing Peltier on charges resulting from a prison break, he met a few elderly ladies from Big Mountain who had traveled to Los Angeles to pray for Peltier. Roberta Blackgoat, Pauline Whitesinger, and Alice Benally, three matriarchs of Big Mountain, introduced themselves to Gurwitz. Two years later, Larry Anderson, a Navajo and then an AIM activist, contacted Gurwitz and told him the ladies wanted to know if he'd come out and help them fight relocation. Gurwitz said he would.

In January 1982, Gurwitz traveled to the National Lawyers Guild convention in Santa Fe with Larry Anderson. The National Lawyers Guild was the first racially integrated lawyers' group in the country. It was founded in 1937 by left-wing attorneys as an alternative to the American Bar Association. The conventions offer opportunities to attend workshops and network with attorneys of like mind, and at one of them Gurwitz and Anderson met a young law student named Lee Brooke

Phillips. Before the convention was over, the three had formed the Big Mountain Legal Defense/Offense Committee, which they created in the same spirit as the Wounded Knee Legal Defense/Offense Committee. They wanted to create a grass roots campaign whose purpose would be publicizing the little-understood government plan to relocate thousands of Navajo people for the purpose of clearing an area of land determined by a court of law to belong to the Hopis. More disturbing, BMLDOC would argue, is that the Hopis, ancient village dwellers, would likely never move out to the rough grasslands the Navajos have called home for hundreds of years.

After the Guild meeting, Phillips returned to Ohio State Law School and Gurwitz and Anderson drove back to Big Mountain. They arrived near the place where the sun dance arbor now stands. There was only the start of a small shack, so Gurwitz and Anderson met outside with some of the area residents. Kee Shay was there, quiet, intense, troubled about the future for the two wives and two households he supports in old Navajo fashion. Alice Benally, an angry and fiercely determined grandmother, sat on a blanket with her knees folded beneath her as did Ruth Benally, another grandmother, strikingly beautiful and shy; Roberta Blackgoat, a high-spirited woman with an unfailing sense of humor; and stoic Jane Biakeddy. A prayer was said, and the people told Gurwitz of the upheaval that had come to their world. They told him of the sudden arrival of fences through their land. As Roberta has explained it, "The fencing is hurting our Mother Earth. Having pins pushing in her, like when a little split gets into your finger, the fencing hurts our Mother Earth." They told Gurwitz that their sheep herds had been reduced so far that they could no longer support themselves. They told him that new rules prevented them from rebuilding their decaying hogans—the round, one-room buildings with hemispherical roofs that are the Navajos' traditional dwellings. They told him they needed help.

The following summer, Lee Phillips was between his second and third years of law school. He arrived in Arizona with little idea of what he would see, let alone where he would stay. He landed in Phoenix to temperatures over 110 degrees. "I thought I'd arrived in hell," he recalled. The 140-mile drive north to Flagstaff and up to an elevation of 7,000 feet reassured him. The temperature cooled and pine forests enveloped him. Flagstaff is one of the largest towns bordering the Navajo reservation, which is the size of West Virginia. (The Hopi reservation is inside the Navajo reservation, approximately one fifth its size, and completely surrounded by Navajo land.) Flagstaff is also the home of the Navajo and Hopi Indian Relocation Commission (the Commission), the federal agency created to move the thousands of Navajos and the one hundred Hopis who found themselves on the wrong side of the newly drawn boundary line.

For months, Phillips slept on the couch of a local Flagstaff attorney named Michael Stuhff, who was then representing two Navajo women, Katherine Smith and Ruth Benally, who had illegally constructed new hogans on their land. That summer, Phillips and Gurwitz "tried to figure out what the hell was going on," as Gurwitz put it, sorting through reams of court and government documents, trying to understand the law, the history, and build a plan of attack. Gurwitz reestablished his media and congressional contacts and made new ones. The two lawyers began to advise Navajos how to fight the law they didn't understand.

The Navajo tribal government was following a completely different tack at that point. Reeling from huge fines imposed on it for not enforcing livestock reduction and a building ban on the disputed land, the tribe, unable actively to thwart the law anymore, and unwilling to support the measure, withdrew, and left the affected Navajos to fend for themselves. "It was clear to the people of Big Mountain from the gitgo that Peter MacDonald [their tribal chairman at that time] was not representing their interests," recalled Gurwitz. And Michael Stuhff was not a political activist. He had a "straight" practice, according to Gurwitz, and the people of Big Mountain wanted to make a political statement. That is what Gurwitz and Phillips set out to do.

The next summer, Lee Phillips passed the Arizona bar exam and moved back to Flagstaff to stay. In the summer of 1985, at the time of the sun dance, Phillips was on the second year of a community law fellowship, working out of the Coconino County Legal Aid office. His work for the Navajos was done after hours and free of charge.

Here at the sun dance, Phillips is dressed in fatigues and wears sunglasses with leather-laced blinders and a red bandana wrapped around his head. He has baleful eyes, a straggly beard, and chestnut brown hair. After seeing scores of traditional Navajo families relocated at government expense into border towns only to be ruined by culture shock and the droves of unscrupulous real estate agents and loan officers who prey on them, Phillips was determined to do everything he could to stop the relocation program. Three years after his first visit to the Navajo reservation, Phillips enjoys an easy repartee with many of the resisters, who have come to depend on him for advice and help, and some, for friendship.

One of the first Navajos Phillips met when he came to Arizona, Dennis Bedonie, sits on his bedroll in the fading light, in the non-Indian section of the sun dance camp with Gurwitz and Phillips. He quietly prepares some peyote, which to him and other members of the Native American Church, a pan-Indian religion, is a sacred substance. Dennis has mixed feelings about the sun dance and the Navajos' decision to accept a ceremony from an alien religion. He and Phillips and Gurwitz sit in front of the glowing coals of a fire. The fulsome smells of the sun dance are no longer present in their nostrils. The pristine desert air surrounds them; there is no noise but the crackle of the fire. "This may be a sign of desperation," Dennis says slowly. "The people are showing a willingness to stand up and defend the land." What that may mean one year from now, July 1986, when the government has set a deadline date for the relocation program, is unclear. Hundreds of families still live here.

In an attempt to avoid a violent turn to the struggle, Gurwitz was trying to promote change through the political system. He had just returned from a lobbying trip to Washington, where he sensed a new openness. "We are going to recommend to [current Navajo chairman Peterson] Zah to push repeal of the law even though we know his advisers tell him repeal is impossible," he said. "But we think it is possible. Congress still doesn't fully understand what's going on out here."

While in Washington, Gurwitz made full use of a report from the House Appropriations Committee that excoriated the Relocation Commission. Gurwitz said, "What this report shows and something we're trying to push with people in Congress right now is that when this bill was presented to them in 1974, there were misrepresentations about the amount of money that would be expended, the number of people who would be affected, the ability to move people, and that sort of thing. And now that we have the information available, it shows that Congress should take another look at this and see if it's worth two billion dollars to take people from self-sufficient independence into the chaos and welfare status they'll have out here."

Gurwitz was determined to make sure it wasn't easier for Congress to shut its eyes to the matter. "We have a very unique situation," he said. "We have a real people's lobby going on that's funded by nobody, just the people themselves. We have people contacting every congressional and senatorial office in Washington and not just bitching and moaning but saying, 'Here are the facts.' It's incredible how unenlightened most of the people on the Hill are in terms of this piece of legislation."

Gurwitz had presented a dramatic argument to Congress and to Navajo supporters in the budding grass roots movement. He claimed the law was a "genocidal policy" contrived to remove the Navajos from their land to make room for the strip mining of coal. "Peabody Coal will support any proposal to get the people off the land," he said, referring to a company that operates two strip mines on Black Mesa, an "island in the sky" that holds nineteen billion tons of coal. Gurwitz and Phillips argued that energy interests had fueled the dispute and they postulated that an intertribal conflict had been created by a consortium of energy companies in the early 1970s to remove Indians living atop the massive coal deposits whose outlines just happened to run perilously close to the land dispute boundaries. "It is much easier for Peabody Coal Company to move in and strip-mine once the people are off the land, so they get them off the land under the pretense of a land dispute," Gurwitz said. This idea caught on with the Navajos and the traditional Hopis, and if you ask someone from the area why they are being asked to leave, they will say, "The energy companies want to dig out the minerals from Mother Earth."

No conspiracy on the part of the coal companies has been proved, but energy interests certainly played a role in the battle. And Gurwitz did not hesitate to arouse outrage in whatever way he could. Though his first question to legislators was, "Why are we spending all this money to take these people's independence from them?" he was also prepared to follow up with other arguments. He said, "That's why we developed these secondary and tertiary views—the coal, the energy, the destruction of the Southwest, the water, and the money. There are a dozen reasons why you want to oppose the further implementation of this bill. And I think we're starting to spread that message along on the Hill.

"It takes five, six, seven years to build a movement in this country," he continued. "The movement is now built. Everywhere I go in the country, people know what Big Mountain is. This thing is just starting to build right now. We're getting more press. The more publicity we build, the less chance that Congress or Goldwater will be able to get away with this." Barry Goldwater, in 1985 in his last term as U.S. senator, presented a formidable obstacle to the forces who would encourage change. He was the strongest and most effective supporter of land partition and relocation in Congress, and as the senior senator of the state in question, he almost singlehandedly controlled the issue in Congress by virtue of a custom known as senatorial courtesy.

Gurwitz is a big-hearted man who is deeply moved by the Navajos' way of life and their quiet determination not to be absorbed by the world around them. He ekes out a living with fees from speaking engagements and funds from a private philanthropist. He sleeps on floors and often enough his meals consist of potatoes wrapped in fry bread. He is a devoted radical. "The biggest danger the Indians present to the United States is freedom," he says. "How the hell could the government get people to work in factories and offices when the Indians were hunting, fishing, living peaceful lives in harmony with the land? Back when General William Tecumseh Sherman came out west, he sent a letter back east. It said that we have to destroy the Indian tribes because they can never be integrated into our society. And they can't be integrated because they don't understand greed." For the next year, Lew Gurwitz and Lee Phillips will lead a motley crew of militant Indians, traditional Navajo grandmothers, Hopi religious stalwarts, and counterculture whites in a final battle against integration and assimilation of one of the most traditional groups of Indians remaining in America.

(2)

The Hatathlies,
Coal Mine Mesa

A three-quarter moon shivers high over the outline of volcanic peaks. It is just before dawn in Coal Mine Mesa. Jack Hatathlie, a Navajo and the father-in-law of Dennis Bedonie, who camped with Lew Gurwitz and Lee Phillips at the sun dance, steps out the door of his cinder block house and picks his way across the brown, lumpy grassland that stretches in every direction, uninterrupted by man-made shapes except the shacks, hogans, and livestock corrals of his own camp. Jack steps up to the outhouse and swings the door shut behind him. When he emerges, he carries a flute. His daughter Brenda, the youngest of his eleven children, likes to play the instrument where no one can see her. But when her little cousins taunt her, she runs out of the privy to chase them, and in her pique, leaves the instrument behind.

For the moment, Jack's mind is not on his children, but on the dark night, when the wind howls ferociously across the canyon, the dogs bellow, and unidentifiable lights flicker. His relatives have warned him about skinwalkers and witching in Coal Mine Mesa. One of his sons has left his wife and three children, another son suffers grand mal seizures, and his wife is exhausted by severe headaches. It is about his wife that he worries now. A seer told them that she needed a particular ceremony, and he must find a medicine man who knows the right song, who will sit up through the night with her in a hogan and draw a sand painting that will restore balance to her life.

Jack's hair is cut short, razored up the back of his head, a style he adopted while working on a track maintenance crew for the Sante Fe railroad. He wears an orange baseball cap decorated with lines of glass beads. He is tall and barrel-chested and his eyes and mouth crinkle easily into a smile.

The Hatathlie camp is at the end of a short dirt track that runs straight off State Highway 264, the road that connects the eastern and western sides of the Navajo reservation, and which, in the middle of its run, links the Hopi villages across their three mesas. The Hatathlies live just on the Hopi side of the Hopi Partition Lands (HPL). Coal Mine is inhabited completely by Navajos; it is Hopi land in name only.

The Hatathlie camp is made up of a four-room cinder block house, three hogans, a corral and run-in shed for the horses, an outhouse, and a basketball hoop with backboard. In a dip a little way from the house is a sweat lodge, and thirty-foot poles used to make a tipi for peyote meetings are stacked on a trailer. A stone hogan and a log hogan stand empty. Because of a 1972 building freeze, the Navajos on Hopi land are forbidden to repair their houses without Hopi permission, and the Hopis have not granted permission to the Hatathlies or most other Navajos for repairs. The mud hogan also needs repair, but it is still used for sings. When the family comes home for ceremonies, they sleep sitting up on the couches in the house, or in their trucks, because of the lack of housing.

Jack enters the house and crosses the worn linoleum of the living room. In four strides he is past the fifty-gallon drum that serves as a wood-burning stove, past two green plaid couches and into the kitchen, which has a table, assorted old dinette chairs, a dry sink, broken propane refrigerator, and propane stove. Bessie sits at the table, her face blank, inscrutable. Her head has ached for several weeks now. A couple of sheep legs—hoof, bone to the knee, and wool, ready to be singed and cooked underground—lie on the table before her. Jack tells her in Navajo that he is going to look for the medicine man. Bessie murmurs a few words, struggles to her feet, and walks into the living room, where she sits on one of the couches. She wears a velveteen blouse, full cotton skirt that falls to midcalf, and moccasins. She lets her hair down from its bun, or tsiyeel, and brushes it. Although Bessie, a strong, solid woman, looks older than her fifty-six years, her lush, waist-length hair has barely a strand of gray. Slowly, with great pain, she winds her hair back up and ties it behind her neck with a clump of white yarn in which two pink shells—talismans for good health she received in a ceremony as a young mother—are tied.

Before setting out, Jack decides to cleanse the truck of malevolent spirits. He's not sure the truck has been contaminated in any way, but as a precaution, he burns some cedar and offers up good, for good is stronger than evil in the Navajo world. With an eagle feather, he cajoles the smoke toward the truck parked in front of the house. Jack holds the ignition key out before him and, working the eagle feather like a sculptor's tool, swirls the smoke over it. Then he claps some of the smoke with his open palms against his chest, inhaling deeply.

Outside, daylight spills around the horizon as the sun begins its quick exchange with the moon, and a hem of blue lifts the night away from

Navajoland. Flat tornadoes of ocher clouds, whipped like tide eddies in the sand, are left floating motionless beneath the roof of the sky. Like fossils suddenly exposed on a long-submerged rock, the still streaks of cloud are the only clues to the night's unrest.

Jack and Bessie climb into the four-wheel-drive vehicle and head east along a dirt road that parallels Highway 264, which connects Coal Mine Mesa with the bustling Navajo town of Tuba City thirty miles to the west and with the ancient villages of the neighboring Hopi tribe at an equal distance to the east. Jack drives along the rangeland, through shallow washes, up slate hills, past occasional Navajo camps. It is vast, desolate, empty land, but Jack and Bessie notice plants and changes imperceptible to an outsider. Jack motions excitedly toward a small pile of rocks he noticed the day before while he was looking for the medicine man. He doesn't know who left the marker or what it signifies. He passes a cliff rose plant and reaches out the window to pull off a stem. The soft petals of the flowers are packed into rags and used as diapers. The flowers absorb urine and keep the baby from chafing. He points to a juniper bush, from which branches are cut and boiled into a brew to help women recover from childbirth.

After straining over a small mountain of red rock, which sets the vehicle at a frightening angle and tests its tires over small boulders, Jack turns toward a hogan cut into a dip in the hillside. A man standing outside sees the vehicle and hurries into the house. Jack pulls up to the front door and beeps his horn. The house is still, no one emerges. A sheep corral is cut into the side of a red-rock butte and fenced with bits of mattress springs and scrap car parts. Clotheslines are heavy with garments. Several lines are hung with nothing but blue jeans. Jack beeps the horn again. A little girl appears at the door. Jack shouts in Navajo, "Go get that man we just saw run into the house." The girl disappears and a middle-aged man steps hesitantly to the door, peers at the vehicle, then breaks into a smile when he recognizes Jack, his clan relative. He walks over to the driver's side and shakes hands with Jack and Bessie. "I didn't know who you were," he says, smiling. "I saw the new vehicle, I thought it was BIA."

These Navajos use the term BIA, the acronym for the Bureau of Indian Affairs, to refer to governmental Washington, to Anglo law, to any member of Anglo officialdom, or anyone who looks like one. Navajos see many "BIA" out on the reservation. Relocation officials travel out to count heads, or to persuade Navajos to sign up for a new house. Officials come out to complain about illegal construction. Missionaries travel across the reservation looking for potential Mormons or Baptists. And real BIA officials drive about in official government vehicles to count and impound sheep. These are the most dreaded. It is better simply to pretend one is not home than to deal with the livestock officials.

As the man chats with Jack, other family members stream out of the ancient one-room hogan. After a few minutes, Jack heads on. The truck rattles along a dirt track for a couple of miles until Jack pulls up to a camp of houses. He stops in front of a mud hogan. Smoke wafts from the center smoke hole. Jack and Bessie wait in the car. After ten minutes, an old man with a straggly gray ponytail and blue jeans that hang from his bony hips emerges. Jack walks to him and greets him formally. The old man tells Jack the medicine man is out, but will be back shortly. Jack returns to the truck, and in ten minutes, just as the old man predicted, the medicine man pulls up to the hogan in a green Ford Ranger.

Jack walks over to the burly short-haired man who steps from the truck. They confer for a few moments and duck into the hogan. Inside, beneath the heavy log roof beams layered like a spiraling conch shell, they share some tobacco, drink coffee. Bessie waits silently in the car. After fifteen minutes, Jack comes out of the hogan alone and steps up into the truck. He wonders whether there's anyone left who knows the prayer. The young men are not learning all the songs from the elders, and many old medicine men are going to their graves with untold prayers. After pulling away and turning toward home, he tells Bessie that the medicine man doesn't know how to do the particular sand painting they want. "Maybe the medicine man in Red Lake knows it," he tells her. "I knew his dad, his dad knew many things."

Bessie wakes before dawn. She turns to look at Jack, who is asleep beside her. His shirt has tangled over his belt buckle. Bessie fixes it and rises quietly from bed. She is also fully dressed. She thinks it strange that her daughter Ella, who is married to Dennis Bedonie, has taken on the white people's way of sleeping in nightclothes.

Bessie slips on her shoes, scoops a pinch of ceremonial cornmeal from a pouch and walks outside. The clear, frosty air surprises her into taking a deep breath. The sky is still black, the moon high over the horizon. She walks past the sheep corral where her skeleton flock of six sheep and goats huddle together, up the hill to the east of the house where her herds, hundreds of animals, used to rest in the early morning sun, glinting like a cotton field.

To the southwest, past the sheep, rising from the horizon like a totem, a god-mark, are the San Francisco Peaks, three ancient volcanic cones sacred to the Navajos and the Hopis. Bessie can just make out their outlines in the moonlight. From every vantage in this area of the reservation and all the way to Flagstaff, where they sit, the Peaks loom, a living presence, over which gather the storm clouds that the Hopis and Navajos pray will bring them rain. On many days, the clouds will form, rage, darken, and then disappear, sprinkling the precious rain elsewhere. Sometimes, glorious days, the wind will carry the clouds to them, to the cornfields, where they will open up and sustain the thirsty plants. The Peaks are always in the minds of these Indians. According to the Hopis, their gods, the Kachinas, winter on the mountaintops. And for the Navajos, the Peaks mark the western boundary of their land, Dinetah. They are an anchor, a beacon, a sign of home.

Bessie sprinkles the cornmeal in an arc, out in front of her and high over her head. She was taught as a little girl that if she wanted something good in life, she must get up early in the morning to pray. At dawn the gods are coming toward the west. As the Holy People head toward her, she will come face to face with them and they'll listen to her prayers, take pity on her, and help. And after they come face to face with her, they will enter her hogan, whose door always faces east, and look around. Her grandfather taught her that if everything is neat and put away, the gods will say, "This person is poor, this person should have something nice." But if the hogan is messy with dirt and piles of clothes here and there, they will think she has a lot of material things and they won't help her.

On the eastern horizon, the sun is rising. Jets of white light shoot through the clouds in a starburst. As she watches, the sky opens around the laboring globe like a buckskin pouch whose lips are swollen by the light, first red, then citron, then yellow as the sun fills the bag. When the pouch is full, the roof of the sky lifts and the bag disappears. The early morning is delicate, soft. Breezes range over the land carrying smells of sweet grasses, female rain. Bessie savors it, prays again, as she was taught and as she taught her children.

The first thing you should pray for is to offer thanks for your life, she taught Ella, her eldest. Always thank the Holy People for the life they gave you on this earth. Then you thank them for your parents and your family and then you give thanks for your sheep, the livestock, and the land. And you always ask for understanding, knowledge, and wisdom. You need those things when you grow up. If you don't have them, how are you going to think? When you get older and get into trouble, when you have problems, you're going to have to be strong to solve them.

Bessie needs all the strength she can gather. She has been told, as have her neighbors at Big Mountain in the northeast and Teesto in the southeast, to move from the land she and her ancestors have lived on for generations. She has been told, over and over, that the land on which she stands, over which she roamed as a little girl following her herds, belongs to the neighboring Hopi tribe. She has been told that the reservations have been divided by new lines, and that her house falls on the Hopi side of the line. These words still make no sense to her.

Bessie prays again, closes her eyes, and thinks of the miles of pasture she crisscrossed with her herds. Never once did she see a Hopi living on the land. "I sit here and think about these things," she tells her daughter

Ella. "I listen to the radio and hear about what they're doing in Washington. And I try to understand why they're doing it. I wonder if they realize they're destroying people's lives, their way of thinking and their lives.

"This is our home, this is where we have always been. This is where the Creator put us with the plants and the livestock. We cannot live anywhere else," she says. "How can you be given a day, a month to move, and yet there's no place for you to go?"

Bessie's mother died when she was three years old. The land and the sheep became her parents. Bessie didn't know what sickened her mother until much later, when she learned that people who coughed up bright splotches of blood suffered from tuberculosis. After Bessie's mother died, her father moved in with one of his other wives. But this wife already had many children, and there was no room for Bessie, so she lived with her grandfather until she was eight. Then she and her sister went off on their own with the sheep. They drove the animals from summer pastures to winter fields, from Badger Springs to Blue Canyon and through the area of Coal Mine where she now lives. As Bessie and her sister herded, they learned where all the wild foods and springs were, they knew the hollows and ridges, where eagles nested and where herbs grew. They gathered wild potatoes and onions, they picked wildflowers and ate the pollen. They caught cicadas and pulled off the sections behind their heads and ate them. And down in the canyon, where they kept the livestock in the winter, they dug up a particular clay that could be eaten and they picked seeds from juniper trees. By the time she was married, Bessie knew every inch of the territory, she had made countless offerings, and her memories were associated less with people than with places in the vast, fragile, difficult land. After she married Jack, they continued to move with the sheep over these lands, always on the lookout for the best seasonal pastures, moving between three different hogans. They finally settled down where they now live, by the water tank on the hill known as "the place where you take the saddle off your horse."

Bessie taught her daughters what she had learned about her livestock. She told Ella, "When I am gone, the sheep will be your mother and father. They will provide for you and they will teach you. With your livestock, you will learn patience, endurance, and perseverance. Your sheep should be your everyday thought. Every waking moment you have when you're with us should be about sheep, where to take them to eat, which water hole to take them to. The sheep should be your first priority."

But now, Bessie has very few livestock to pass on to her children. The Navajos and their sheep became too numerous for the desert. In the 1930s, when scientists feared that overgrazing would turn the Southwest into another dust bowl, the government instituted the first of what were to be many livestock reductions. Flocks of thousands of animals were reduced to hundreds. Now, because of further reductions implemented as a result of the land dispute, Bessie's hundreds have been reduced to a handful, even though the land can now support more. A Navajo family needs at least three hundred head of sheep to be self-sufficient.

When Bessie gets back inside, she begins breakfast by stirring a pot of watery mutton stew. She bought the meat for this stew from a neighbor; she doesn't have enough animals to butcher. After the Hopis' rights to half the disputed land were established in court, the Hopis complained their half was being destroyed by Navajo sheep. A federal judge ordered the Navajos to reduce their flocks while waiting for the government to build them new houses away from the disputed land. Bessie was compelled to sell eighty percent of her sheep. The same judge ordered a freeze on new Navajo construction in the area. Hogans have only a short life and must be frequently rebuilt, so year after year since the freeze was ordered in 1972, Navajo hogans have fallen into disrepair.

Bessie empties Blue Bird flour from a gunny sack into a Tupperware bowl and adds salt, baking powder, and water. She kneads it into a ball and gets a pan of lard heating on the propane stove. She pulls the dough into small pieces, whacks them into flat round shapes a foot in diameter, and drops them into the sizzling fat. She flips the browning rounds with tongs and when they're done, drops them on a plastic plate. Bessie scoops water from a barrel into an enamel coffeepot, adds coffee, and puts it to boil.

As the smells wend their way out of the kitchen into the two bedrooms, the family stirs, and one by one, the children walk into the living room and sit on one of the two sofas, two armchairs, and two logs that serve as chairs. School photos and pictures of two of Bessie's children in military uniform hang on the walls near the ceiling. Three rifles are racked on the wall; an arrangement of arrows tied with bits of leather, a talisman from a ceremony, is nailed over the front door.

All but five of Bessie's children still live with her, and all of them return to her house for months on end, responding to a need of most Navajos, even the most assimilated, to return home to the land for long periods. Bessie watches them as they walk into the living room. The younger ones were not brought up the same way as the eldest. She didn't have the sheep with which to teach them, and she knew they would be living in a different world by the time they grew up. They watch movies, go to school, get wage-earning jobs. Brenda, eleven, the flute player, is chubby and shy, and she often reads books while hanging off the edge of her mother's bed. She gets up off the mattresses the girls sleep on in the second bedroom, enters the living room, and sits in the chair nearest the kitchen. She turns her face down to her chest. Levonne, fourteen, rail thin, eager to please, picks up a small stretcher on which she is beading a hat band. She smiles shyly, revealing deep dimples in her cheeks. Theresa, nicknamed Budge, a stunning sixteen-year-old, is expecting a baby. She has been acting petulant because Bessie has told her not to see her boyfriend anymore. He is a close clan relative and the coming baby will be born for and into the same clan. This is a grave embarrassment to Bessie. Budge sits down, picks up a copy of *Self* magazine, and flips through it. Felix, twenty, who has slept on the couch, goes outside to find the horses. He suffers from periodic seizures, which not only frighten them all, but leave Felix exhausted and sore for days afterward. Bessie wonders if he has those fits because he fell off the horses too many times. Felix's umbilical cord was tied to a horse's tail to make him livestock-minded, and he takes care of the horses and cattle. Glenn, twenty-four, scored very high on math tests at school and went on to college at Arizona State University on a scholarship. After one year he returned home, unable to withstand the pressure of living in the city. Freddy, twenty-six, is a member of the Arizona National Guard, and also works part time at the Page power plant, where his father works as a custodian. Bessie has a second son with the same name, whom they call Fred. He is twenty-one, lives in Page, and works at the Lake Powell marina. She has nicknames for most of her kids because she wasn't able to name them herself. All of her children except Brenda, the youngest, were named by the Anglo nurses at the Indian hospital. Most Navajo-speaking mothers don't have English names picked out, so the nurses routinely fill out the birth certificates with their own choice of names. It was the nurses who gave the name Fred to two of Bessie's sons.

Jack gets up from bed and enters the kitchen. He and Bessie serve themselves stew, take a piece of fry bread, and sit on plastic chairs by the table. After their parents begin to eat, the children file in, take a bowl of stew, a piece of fry bread, and return to their places. They eat silently, completely absorbed in their food, dipping the bread in the stew, sucking every morsel of meat from the bones.

Before the livestock reductions, Bessie's kids didn't have time for a big breakfast. She woke them at dawn and sent them out to run several times around the cornfield while shouting so as to make their lungs grow strong. Then one of them would track the horses, unhobble them, and lead them home. Another milked the goats and brought the milk in to Bessie. Breakfast then was just boiled milk and bread, or maybe some blue cornmeal mixed with milk. The little girls, Ella, Lula, and Lenore, now married and living off the reservation with their families, wore traditional skirts and blouses, their hair pulled back in buns. Every morning, they brought the flock to the windmill. If it was summertime, and the well was going dry, they'd have to be the first ones to get their flock to water.

Bessie taught them how to herd on horseback. Ella rode in front of her mother and Lula stayed wrapped in a cradleboard tied to the side of the saddle. Jack was off working on the railroad then, and Bessie had to mind the animals and the kids. When Ella was five, Bessie sent her out with the sheep herself or with her little sister, giving them a bag of roasted corn nuts to eat, and Bessie stayed in with her other babies. Sometimes they got hungry and tired and came home crying, but they learned to be responsible—they learned to care for the animals and put their flocks' needs ahead of their own.

Bessie looks up from her stew and sees that the boys have finished. One of them heads out to the privy with a roll of toilet paper. "Got a little treaty paper," he jokes, the joke that's not so funny, the joke that every Indian tribe shares.

The Navajos signed many treaties with the United States. One of them stuck. It was signed in 1868 and marked the end of the Navajos' four-year incarceration at Fort Sumner, on the Pecos River in the New Mexico Territory, where they had been marched, along with the Mescalero Apaches, to Bosque Redondo, a reservation set up to rid the Southwest of raiding Indians. Kit Carson did the job of tracking down the Navajos, burning their fields and crops and chopping down their fruit trees until, in the middle of the winter of 1864, the Navajos, starving, with little clothing, surrendered and marched to the Bosque. The government wanted to assimilate the Navajos and Apaches, stop their warring ways and make them peaceful farmers like the New Mexico Pueblos. But the government had chosen an area for the new reservation that was unfit for farming. The area had no firewood, poor soil, and brackish water that sickened the Indians. After four years, during which time half the population died, the experiment was abandoned. Pestilence had prevented the crops from producing, and corrupt suppliers led to food shortages that killed many Navajos and Apaches. Finally, the government called for settlement talks. When the Navajos were asked where they would like their reservation to be, Barboncito, one of the Navajo leaders, said, "We do not want to go to the right or left, but straight back to our own country. . . . Our grandfathers had no idea of living in any other country but our own," he told them, explaining why settling them in Arkansas or Oklahoma was impossible. He explained to U.S. peace commissioners that First Woman had told the Navajos after the Creation that they should never move beyond the area bounded by the four sacred mountains—to the north, the La Plata mountains of Colorado; to the south, Mount Taylor in central New Mexico; to the west, the San Francisco Peaks in Flagstaff; and to the east, the Sierra Blancas in Colorado and Pelado Peak, twenty miles east of Jemez, New Mexico.

Barconcito told the white men that despite all they had learned at the Bosque, despite their labor in the fields, their failures and unhappiness proved they were not meant to live outside their own land. He recalled how rich the Navajos were back home, how there were sheep in every direction, bountiful crops and clear water, and how the medicine men could gather the correct herbs to heal their patients. He said he hated his life now, having to walk to the commissary for food like a child.

Barboncito had his way, and a reservation was set aside for the Navajos back in Arizona and New Mexico. However, it encompassed only a tenth of their former land. It straddled the New Mexico–Arizona border and reached up to the Colorado-Utah state lines. Most Navajos had no idea where the boundaries of this piece of land began or ended, and they simply wandered back to their old homes and met up with the bands that had eluded capture. The Navajos were a changed people, however. The first winter, they subsisted on government rations. The next year, they were issued 14,000 sheep and 1,000 goats. Raiding of white settlers, for the most part, stopped, and the Navajos devoted themselves to farming and herding their flocks.

They had learned many new things during captivity. They learned how to farm with irrigation, they learned silversmithing, they learned how far one could travel with a wagon. Their new survival skills lessened their inclination to raid and steal—activities that were condoned by Navajo teachings. Their diet had changed, they had developed a taste for beef and coffee, and they had discarded their old skins and woven blankets for modern clothing. Men adopted wide-legged cotton pants and the women wore the long full skirts and blouses they had admired on the frontier women.

The Navajos were overjoyed to be back home, to Dinetah, the land of the Dine. On their trek back from the Bosque, after fording the Rio Grande, they caught sight of Mount Taylor, the southernmost of their sacred mountains. One old man said, "When we saw the top of the mountain from Albuquerque, we wondered if it was our mountain, and we felt like talking to the ground, we loved it so, and some of the old men and women cried with joy when they reached their homes." After surviving a few difficult winters, the Navajos thrived and multiplied. They followed their sheep in every direction and quickly grew out of their treaty reservation. The U.S. government accommodated their growth by adding pieces to their reservation until it stretched into three states and completely encircled the Hopis.

Unbeknownst to the Navajos, in 1882 the U.S. government withdrew a rectangle of land from the public domain for the use of their neighbors, the Hopis. Nothing marked the boundaries of their own reservation, and nothing marked the bounds of the Hopi reservation. The Navajos continued to expand into unused territory. Bessie's ancestors settled around the Hopis at Coal Mine Mesa, herding their animals to better pastures, all the while unaware the land had been assigned to the Hopis on a map somewhere far off in Washington.

.   .   .

Bessie watches Glenn and Freddy put on their wide-brimmed cowboy hats, leave the house, and get into the red "duelly," Jack's oversized new pickup truck, which has four wheels on the rear axle. The boys head southwest to Billy Yazzie's house. They haul a livestock trailer behind them and joke about Billy Yazzie on the way over. They call him the Navajo Clint Eastwood. He is tall, well built, with piercing eyes and a narrow, straight nose. After they arrive, Glenn pauses to chat with Vida Mae, Billy's daughter, a slim girl with thick, long hair cut short around her face and a strong, direct look like her father's. Freddy and Glenn negotiate with Billy for the use of his tractor to till their cornfield. They agree on a price, Billy drives the tractor up into the livestock trailer, and climbs in the truck with the boys.

When they get back to the Hatathlies' camp, Felix is digging post holes around the perimeter of the cornfield. The existing fence, constructed of various poles, logs, sticks, and wire, is half standing, half on the ground. Felix was told by the doctors not to engage in strenuous work for fear it might trigger another seizure, but he feels he is a burden to his parents if he doesn't work. He struggles to set a huge post into the ground. Billy Yazzie rolls the tractor into the field and sets the rotors, then stops. The entire family is poised around the field behind the house. They are all thinking the same thing. Somehow, without a discussion, the decision to go ahead and prepare the cornfield for next summer has been made. They till the field twice every year—after the harvest in late summer, and in the spring—but the Hatathlies are not sure what will happen less than a year from now, July 1986, when they are supposed to be relocated from this land.

Billy walks up to Jack and says, "Why do you want me to work for you and take all that money that you're going to pay me to plow your field when they're going to evict you in July?" Jack is quiet for a few moments, then he replies slowly in Navajo, "Well, you know the government's always saying that, the government's always passing this or that law. I'm sure there's not that many jails to house all the people out here. We're just going to have to live like before, planning things and not even thinking about July 1986. Life's just going to go on." Billy turns, adjusts his cowboy hat, walks back to the red tractor, mounts it, and puts it in gear. The tractor bobs up and down over the irregular ground, peeling back the sandy soil in straight lines, back and forth, preparing the soil to receive the winter snow.

(3)

The Complicated World
of the Hopis

Twenty miles east of the Hatathlies' camp, surrounded on all sides by
the Navajo reservation, live the Hopis, about 4,500 of them, in villages
scattered over the tops of three bony fingers of Black Mesa, a slightly
hollowed tabletop plateau that rises six hundred feet from the rolling,
arid plain below. The Hopis are an ancient people; they have lived on
the mesas for over a thousand years. One of their villages, Oraibi, which
dates from A.D. 900, is considered the oldest continuously inhabited town
in North America. Although there are about ten thousand Hopis, more
than half of the tribal members live off the reservation for reasons of
employment, better housing, and freedom from the intense scrutiny
common to such a small community.

The fourteen Hopi villages consist of stone houses, many of them
built from the same timbers and rocks that made up different, smaller
dwellings hundreds of years ago. Over the years, houses have fallen
apart, were rebuilt, enlarged. Some of the clan houses hold religious
paraphernalia in underground chambers and secret rooms that have been
maintained for generations. The older structures have small rooms and
are several chambers high. Most are huddled at the edges of the mesa,
looking out over the sweeping pastel plains below. The views are vast,
spectacular; from the tops of the mesas, one can see fifty miles in every
direction, can see interlopers long before they reach the mesas.

The villages are a strange mix of old and new. Modern cement-block
houses stand beside crumbling, stone dwellings. New vehicles are
parked beside some houses, piles of coal lie in three-walled bins beside
others. The air is acrid with the smell of burning coal. Television anten-
nas poke from the flat roofs of some dwellings. Outhouses cling to the
cliff edges, perched between brick ovens in which Hopis bake bread.
Children and bony dogs run the streets as they did a hundred years ago;
small grocery stores, sometimes one room of a house, offer video rentals.

Leroy Morgan, a thirty-two-year-old Navajo from White Cone, a town twenty-five miles southeast of First Mesa, drives north from Navajoland to the Hopi village of Hotevilla. He is looking for David Monongye, a traditional Hopi who strenuously objects to the Hopi Tribal Council, which over the years has usurped power from the hands of the religious priests and village elders. Leroy quickly passes over the boundary line onto Hopi land. He points to a barbed wire fence indistinguishable from the others that keep livestock from straying onto the highway. Yet he knows it is the fence separating the Navajo and Hopi Partition Lands. "That's the fence," he says grimly. Wherever he is, Leroy knows where the fence runs. He can always pick it out. The fence has taken on a personality and become a character itself in the drama of this dispute.

Ahead in the distance lie the three Hopi mesas, stretching east and west as far as one can see. Their steep walls loom darkly from the plains below. There are no dwellings dotting the plains as there are on Navajo-land, because the Hopis live on the mesa tops. Navajo defenders like to say that the dispute is about human rights versus real estate, since the Hopis are not likely to live on the land but just graze animals on it. And few will even do that, since the majority of Hopis are not so inclined.

Leroy points to two Navajo boys riding horses just on the Navajo side of the fence. The horses pick their way over a narrow trail, with the children slumped into the saddles, wearing Walkmans. "I used to herd sheep on horseback," he says. "But look at those kids. They're on their horses with Walkmans grooving to Def Leppard and groups like that." Leroy giggles, then his face becomes serious, inscrutable.

As Leroy approaches the bottom of Second Mesa, signs advertising craft shops appear along the highway. Leroy drives up Second Mesa, over its top, down its flank, and west to Third Mesa, the westernmost prong. He climbs up to Third Mesa, rising through the jagged rocks. He points up to the outhouses perched against the sky like sentinels and says, "Sometimes Navajos call the Hopis cliffshitters because their out-houses are pushed right up to the edges of the mesas." He laughs.

He turns off the road toward the mesa edge to the village of Hotevilla. Leroy parks his vehicle and walks to the plaza, which is marked by several kivas, or underground prayer chambers, indicated by the pole ladders sticking up out of their entry holes. On all sides of the dirt plaza are small, ragged stone houses with glass windows and wooden doors. Leroy walks up to one of the homes, swings open the screen door, and walks in. The kitchen is spacious, clean, the floor covered with scraps of linoleum. A very old man, short, skinny, with heavy white hair in bangs and straight sidelocks, sits upright on a chair. He stares toward Leroy without seeing. An elderly woman sits near the window, unmoving, gazing out, and a younger woman in her fifties walks to the door from another room to greet Leroy.

The Hopi woman says Yat'ee, the Navajo greeting. Leroy laughs in surprise, shakes her hand, and responds in English because he does not know the Hopi greeting. He wears Wrangler jeans, a plaid flannel shirt, and a brightly beaded belt buckle. His hair is long and wound up into a tsiyeel. His head is covered with a flat-brimmed stovepipe hat, which he leaves on. Leroy tells the woman that he is here to see Grandfather David. The woman sighs, shows Leroy to a bench along the wall. She mumbles that many people have been to see David in the past week. David can't hear most of this or see it, for he is blind and hard of hearing. He is almost a hundred. Leroy shakes David's hand and tells him he is with a journalist who wants to know about the land dispute. The old man straightens and smiles. He is handsome still, his straight nose and cheekbones strong, his wiry frame agile as a boy's. Leroy tells David his name, where he is from, his clan. He has to repeat himself slowly, loudly for David to hear. When he is finished, David smiles again, begins to speak quietly, in English. "The older people know they are friends with the Navajos," he says, staring straight ahead. "We trade with them. We buy their wood and their mutton and they buy our peaches and piki [a flaky bread made of blue cornmeal]." He pauses, adjusts the black-framed glasses parked uselessly on his nose. "The young people don't know it. They want to fight with them. But it's not like that."

David explains that the younger generation has been taught to hate the Navajos, even though their parents and grandparents once lived side by side with them in relative peace. Hopis who want to compete in the white world and earn salaries and run cattle and develop industry have forgotten the old ways, are disobeying the religious laws and ignoring the prophecies. David still meets with other elders and priests in village meetings, during which they try to continue to lead their people, try to fulfill their traditional roles. But today, their authority is eroding. Children are educated in white schools rather than at home according to the Hopi way. Kids are learning more about the Anglo culture than about their own. And the Tribal Council, lured by federal money, the modern world, jobs, and the realities of Washington and the free market, is less and less inclined to follow the old ways.

"We ask the Tribal Council to come to our meetings," says David. "They don't come. We have our own ceremonies, our own ways. But the Hopi Tribal Council is destroying our way of life. They're taking it away from us."

David falls silent. The younger woman is puttering around a large stove. The old lady by the window pushes her empty wheelchair back and forth before her. David continues to sit erect, but he closes his eyes. Then he says, "The Tribal Councils of Navajo and Hopi are together. They don't tell the people what's going on. If something sounds good, they'll sign a paper. They never want to talk to old people. When old people go down to talk, the Council members go away, say they're busy."

Grandfather David again becomes quiet. The woman by the stove says, "He's tired. Every day the white newspapers come here." Leroy nods, sits for a few moments, then gets up. He walks out to the car, removes a bag of apples and a container of salt from the seat, and carries them back into the house. He hands them to the woman, who nods, and places the goods on the table. David speaks up from his chair, says, "What it is, they want to dig out a lot of minerals that are underground. That's what the so-called land dispute is about."

Leroy drives to a nearby grocery store for a can of soda. A chubby young Hopi man and his wife operate the one-room canteen, which sells canned goods, soda, candy, and snacks. The young man chats with Leroy, asks where he is from. After he learns that Leroy has visited David, he says that David is his grandfather. He doesn't say whether or not he agrees with David's worldview, but makes it clear that most Hopis don't involve themselves in politics at all. "That isn't the Hopi way," he says. "The Hopi way is to stay quiet if you don't like the way things are being run."

One thing Hopis do do is gossip. And they gossip particularly about people who are at all different from the norm. David travels frequently to speak before groups of white people, and there are Hopis who believe he is paid large sums of money to do so. The young man says, "You know, I don't know if he gets anything. He says he doesn't, but that's what people say." The young man doesn't volunteer his name, in fact indicates great apprehension about speaking out at all. He fears he will be the subject of gossip, perhaps retribution, if he expresses himself. When asked how much his life is affected by the doings of the Tribal Council, the young man answers, "We don't listen to the Tribal Council." He becomes extremely agitated, however, when recounting an incident that had recently taken place out on the Navajo Partition Lands. He tells Leroy that a group of Hopis had journeyed out to capture an eaglet for a Hopi ritual sacrifice. The nesting ground was on the Navajo half of the disputed land. When the Hopis arrived at the site, they were met by a group of Navajos who prevented them from passing onto the land. "That isn't right," says the Hopi man, waving his hands in the air. "It is our religion to capture the eagles." His face becomes very red. "That just isn't right," he says again.

Leroy tells him that the Navajos subject to relocation feel as threatened about the loss of their way of life as he feels about the eaglet incident. The man looks at Leroy blankly. "We don't know much about that," he says, seemingly ignorant of the land dispute or the Navajos' despair.

"If you felt the Tribal Council were doing something that hurt the

Navajos, if you felt that relocation was wrong, would you speak up?" asks Leroy. The man shakes his head with a look of surprise. "We would not do anything," he says matter of factly.

Ivan Sidney sits behind his desk in the office of the Hopi Tribal Chairman. He is a small, barrel-chested man with thick, straight black hair that is streaked with gray and cut in a pageboy shape. On his desk is a coffee cup marked Arizona State Police, a memento of his four years as a state patrolman. He subsequently served nine years as chief of the Hopi police before he was elected Hopi tribal chairman in 1983.

Sidney pounds his fist on his desk, leans forward in his chair, and says heatedly, "This is very discouraging to me. I wish this tribe was big enough and strong enough to hire a good public relations agent to go and do a good job in telling our side of the story." He pauses, lays out his unhappiness with a terse, not quite grammatical account of the indignities visited upon him by the Navajos. "I'm just frustrated with this whole thing. I had some newspeople from Colorado spent two days in Big Mountain. They said they herded sheep with Katherine Smith, Biakeddy. I can name all of them who everybody talks to. They're pretty good actresses now. They know what to say. They spent two days up there and then came to see me and said, 'We're in a hurry, do you have fifteen minutes?' That's not fair."

Sidney has other gripes. He is angry that David Monongye and Thomas Banyacya continue to speak out against the Tribal Council. "I don't know if you're coming out here to talk to David and Thomas and all that. When I pick up your [white] newspapers, it looks like Navajos are all standing strong and over here you've got David saying one thing, Thomas saying one thing, the tribal chairman saying one thing. It looks divided over here. And it looks bad on the outside."

Sidney twists in his seat, clasps his hands at his waist, "I was elected [chairman with] sixty-one percent of the vote. That means the other part didn't vote for me. But, like with Reagan, not everybody voted for him, but right now, he's their president."

Truth be told, Sidney won with 51 percent of the vote, squeaking by his opponent, Abbott Sekaquaptewa, by 42 votes, 908–866. But the Hopis never really took to the idea of a tribal government, and voting numbers have historically been low. According to 1980 census figures, there are a total of 8,287 Hopis living in seven states. Sidney's 908 votes comprise 10 percent of the population. Counting only the Hopis who live on the reservation, who number 4,562, Sidney received 19 percent.

Nevertheless, having won the election (which Sekaquaptewa challenged, claiming that Sidney's victory margin consisted of unregistered voters), Sidney wants some respect. "If Thomas or David oppose," says Sidney, "they should come to me. That's how we need to carry this issue, because if you go out there, eighty percent of the Hopis are going to tell you that if we have disagreements we should talk it out among ourselves. So far, the indication that I've got from the Hopi villages is that they're all unified. There's only just one or two Hopis opposing. Thomas is out there as one Hopi speaking one opinion. He has been used all these years to interpret what the elders are saying."

Ivan Sidney has repeatedly been criticized in the local press for not having control over his Tribal Council and not being able to achieve a quorum. The Hopi constitution established nineteen seats on the Council, including the chairman and vice-chairman. In the summer of 1985, four of the fourteen villages were not sending any representatives because they didn't believe in the tribal government. And elected representatives from First Mesa could not be seated because they hadn't been approved by the Kikmongwi, or high religious priest, as is required by the Hopi constitution. When the vice-chairman was arrested on a drunk driving charge and took a leave of absence, the Council did not have a quorum, could not have a quorum, even if every member was in attendance.

The Hopis have historically resisted the concept of a Tribal Council. Each village considers itself an independent entity. Its residents are members of different clans, each has slightly different clan stories, and even the language differs across the mesas. Just three years after the Tribal Council was created and put in place by the U.S. government in 1936, it failed to achieve a quorum. Even John Collier, who was a proponent of Indian self-government, admitted in 1963, eighteen years after leaving his post as Indian commissioner, that the Hopi Council had "never worked" because it had failed to take into account "the conscious and unconscious motivations and accompanying resistances of the several diverse Hopi societies."

Yet in 1955, under pressure from Washington, the Hopi government was reconstituted. But tension between the so-called progressive and traditional factions has persisted. No one really knows the extent of Hopi opposition to the modern government, because Hopis traditionally show their disapproval by remaining silent. This characteristic has angered many old Navajos who wonder why their friends the Hopis won't speak out against relocation.

It is incumbent upon Chairman Sidney to dispel the perception of disagreement among the Hopis and to promote the idea that the Hopis approve of the relocation program. He acknowledges that many Hopis do not understand the details of the law. "However, every Hopi knows that all of this land is Hopi land," he says. "We got this land from the Supreme Being to be the overseers of this land. And every Hopi knows the borders of what is Hopi land. They know that the Navajos came here very recently. That is what really the law is trying to say. That this is Hopi land."

Chairman Sidney has messages on his desk from other news organizations requesting interviews about the land dispute. He knows he is losing the battle of images, that his tribe is perceived as the bully by insisting that old Navajos must be removed from their homes. He realizes the irony here; the Hopis have been portrayed through history as a gentle, peace-loving people who abhor conflict and physical aggression, while the Navajos have been described as aggressive marauders. He wishes there were some way to illustrate the injustices he feels the Hopis have suffered at the hands of the Navajos. "If we had cameras and newspapers, especially in the late 1700s, 1800s when there were attacks on Hopis by Navajos, I think the Hopis would have been the ones saying, 'We're suffering.' You'd see Hopis being dragged off their land."

(4)

The Law:
Healing v. Jones

Stewart Udall, the freshman congressman from Arizona, was only vaguely aware that a problem existed between the Navajo and Hopi Indians. In 1955, during his first race for the U.S. House of Representatives, he remembers driving up to the Hopi villages and getting stuck in a muddy wash. Udall's impression was that "the Hopis were grouped on the mesas in their villages and that the grazing land was up there." He didn't see any Navajos, so had no reason to believe the two tribes' use of the area overlapped significantly.

"My thought was that this was like a quiet title dispute only in a large scale," he says now. "The issue was settling where the boundary was and that if that was done, there were no human problems. It was probably a matter of livestock, you know. They'd build a fence and then the livestock wouldn't roam."

In 1958, after being approached by lawyers from both tribes, he agreed to introduce a bill into Congress to allow the two tribes to sue one another for their proper share of the area in dispute. Twenty-two years later, after serving as Secretary of the Interior under John F. Kennedy and living away from Arizona, Udall returned home. He was shocked to find that the little boundary dispute and the lawsuit that grew out of his bill had become the largest relocation of civilians in the United States since the internment of Japanese-Americans during World War II. He recalls, "I realized there was this three-man commission, they were spending a quarter of a billion dollars, were moving people around. I couldn't believe it."

Udall learned it wasn't simply an issue of determining a boundary line between the two tribes. The dispute involved 1.8 million acres that the tribes had come to share. The Navajos lived on it, scattered miles apart from each other with their flocks of sheep, and the Hopis grazed cattle on it, planted cornfields on it, gathered wood from it, and traveled over it to visit shrines and collect eaglets. Few Hopis lived on the land, for they are a Pueblo people whose religious observances require them to live in or near their villages on the mesa tops. Yet they have a strong relationship with the land. Throughout the tribe's historic and prehistoric wanderings, the Hopis crisscrossed northern Arizona, establishing villages, meeting up with other peoples, moving on. These places now have historical as well as religious significance to the Hopis, and periodic return to the sites is important for the devout. The number of religious faithful, however, has diminished steadily in the thirty years that the land issue has been argued in American courts.

The Navajos' attachment to the land is more immediate than the Hopis'. Their hogans are built on it. Their ancestors' bones lie in it, their own umbilical cords have been buried in their animal corrals or beneath the women's looms. Asking the Navajos to leave means asking them to abandon the repository of their memories, the land which they have learned to master, the sites through which they communicate with their gods.

The present tangle of legal battles and personal tragedies that has grown from this dispute can be traced not to a conflict between the Navajo and Hopi Indians but, sadly, to a battle of wills between a white Indian agent and two other white men over Indian education. In 1882, agent J. H. Fleming became exasperated by the interference of two Anglos, E. H. Merritt and Dr. J. Sullivan, in his attempts to improve the Hopi children's attendance at boarding school. The majority of Hopis were violently opposed to sending their children away to white schools, one of which was 175 miles away in Albuquerque, New Mexico. Sending their children off to learn vocational skills made little sense to the blanket-clad Hopis; there were no jobs on the reservation. Even worse than the separation from their children for months and years at a time was the knowledge that the children were not learning the Hopi way; future priests were away at government-run boarding schools during the years they should be learning the sacred ceremonies; girls were learning modern hygiene and how to press clothes instead of learning to grind corn, make piki bread, and prepare materials for their future wedding ceremonies.

Messrs. Merritt and Sullivan helped the Hopis oppose the government's program. And the Hopi agent found to his dismay that he was unable to evict the meddlesome whites because the Hopi lands were public lands, never withdrawn from the public domain as a reservation. On November 11, 1882, Fleming wrote to the Commissioner of Indian Affairs and threatened to quit if he couldn't get rid of the two Anglos. Officials in the Washington office of the BIA were perturbed by his threat, and one day after receiving Fleming's letter, Commissioner Hiram Price telegraphed Fleming and asked him to outline boundaries "for a reservation that will include Moqui [Hopi] villages and agency large enough to meet all needful purposes and no larger." He did so, and on December 16, the President of the United States, Chester A. Arthur, signed an executive order setting aside a rectangle of land in Arizona that measured seventy miles north to south and fifty-five miles east to west, "for the use and occupancy of the Moquis and such other Indians as the Secretary of the Interior may see fit to settle thereon."

As soon as Fleming received President Arthur's executive order, he requested that the troops at Fort Wingate evict Merritt and Sullivan. Ten days later, having rid himself of the thorn that had plagued him, Fleming resigned. In his haste to expel the whites, however, Fleming had set the stage for this tragic conflict. Reaching for quick and easy boundaries, Fleming had drawn a neat rectangle that fell precisely within 1 degree of latitude and 1 degree of longitude. Within the boundary of the new Hopi reservation, however, lived three hundred to six hundred Navajos, herding their sheep, tending their cornfields, traveling between winter and summer pastures; eighteen hundred Hopis lived on the mesas in 1882. The day President Arthur set aside land for the Hopi reservation, at least one out of six of its inhabitants were Navajos, and the Navajo culture was entering a vital, prolific period in its history. Fifty years later, within the Hopi boundaries, Navajos would outnumber Hopis three to one.

In the period following their release from Fort Sumner in 1868, the Navajos prospered and their sheep multiplied. The western movement of whites pushed the Navajos from New Mexico into Arizona and around the Hopis. The United States increased the initial area it had set aside in 1868 for the Navajos by several more executive order areas until, by 1934, the Navajo reservation completely surrounded the Hopi 1882 Executive Order Area. The Navajo population continued to grow, however, and rather than face the politically unpopular task of returning more white-controlled land to the Indians, the Interior Department encouraged the Navajos to squeeze in around the Hopis. It was the hope of the Indian Affairs office that the two tribes "would become so friendly and cooperative as to enable them to live in the same country without any jurisdictional or other differences."

The Hopis complained almost immediately about the Navajos' presence within the newly drawn Hopi borders. For the most part, the Navajo trespasses were minor, and likely the result of competition over limited water and grazing areas. A Hopi BIA agent reported in 1884 that "quite frequently trifling quarrels arise between members of the two tribes; these are usually caused by careless herding of the young Navajos, who allow their herds to overrun these outlying [Hopi] gardens. . . . The best of good feeling generally exists between these tribes; they constantly mingle together at festivals, dances, etc. . . . [The Hopi] barters his surplus melons and peaches with his old pastoral neighbors for their mutton."

Interior officials did not know what to do about the complaints and offered suggestions ranging from the view that the Navajos within the reservation had rights of occupancy equal to the Hopis', to the view that the reservation was set aside exclusively for the Hopis. Some even argued the intention was to create a joint use reservation.

In 1888, six years after the creation of the Executive Order Area, Hopis complained to Indian Affairs agents that their crops and grazing areas on the lowlands just surrounding the mesas were still being overrun by Navajos. The Secretary of the Interior asked the Secretary of War to send a company of troops to the area "to remove all Navajo Indians found trespassing with their herds and flocks on the Moqui reservation and to notify them that their depredations must cease and that they must keep within their own reservation." The military expedition reached the reservation in December. Since it was winter, the Navajos were not moving their flocks near the Hopis, and the soldiers felt that requiring the Navajos to pack up and move with the snow and cold coming on would constitute an undue hardship. Instead, they warned the Navajos not to go within twelve miles of the Hopis. The next year, the Hopis complained again and another detachment of troops was sent. Again, the soldiers arrived in December, and again, Navajo herds were not found near the Hopis. The troops again left the area without removing the Navajos. Instead, they met with several Navajo bands and ordered them not to bother the Hopis. The cavalry had been instructed not to anger the Navajos; memories of Fort Sumner were still fresh in the Navajos' minds. The troops also noted that no boundary markers existed. It was easy to see how Navajo sheepherders could stray onto Hopi land.

In the first few months of 1891, the Navajo agent, the School Commissioner, a settler named Thomas V. Keam, and Special Agent George W. Parker decided to mark a boundary sixteen miles in radius from the central Hopi village of Mishongnovi. This would form a clear boundary within which the Navajos were not to pass. These four men marked the line with stone mounds and monuments. It became known as the Parker-Keam line. The land within the line, though it included most of the land the Hopis actually used, was only about a third of the land set aside for the Hopis by the 1882 Executive Order.

The Hopis still asserted their rights to the entire 1882 area. From 1927 to 1932, attempts were made to divide the reservation between the two tribes. Interior officials vacillated between two competing desires: to keep the Navajos away from the Hopis, and not to anger the Navajos by moving them. The government's inaction seemed to be exacerbated by the fact that Indian agents admired the industriousness of the Navajos and were highly critical of the Hopis' lackadaisical attitude toward animal husbandry and establishing a presence on the land. The agents clearly felt that the Hopis wouldn't use the land even if the Navajos were removed from it. A superintendent of the Hopi agency wrote that a tribal member "should not be permitted to eject an industrious (if disobedient) neighbor and then allow the land to waste and his sheep to decline in filthy mesa corrals while he indulges in snake dances, basket dances, clown dances, and the ten thousand other displays he uses as an excuse why he should not be on the range." Another agent explained why the Hopis would never leave their mesa villages: "They are strictly a community people and their dances, religious customs, and ceremonials cannot exist without their living as such. Neither can the Hopi exist without the dances and ceremonials, and this, to a large degree, explains why they have not prospered parallel to their neighbors, the Navajo." Nevertheless, the Hopis, who in fact claimed sovereignty over a much larger swath of northern Arizona than the 1882 executive-order area, were not about to relinquish one bit of the smaller piece given them by the U.S. government. The Hopis wanted it whether or not they planned to use it in ways the government could appreciate.

In 1934, the Indian Reorganization Act was passed. Known as the "New Deal for Indians," it called for the writing of tribal constitutions and the creation of tribal governments. Part of the Act called for conservation methods to protect Indian land from misuse and exploitation by whites. For Navajos and Hopis, this meant soil conservation and livestock control. Silt buildup at the base of the Hoover Dam was blamed on erosion of the reservations. The control of livestock was accomplished by the creation of grazing districts, which also provided a convenient administrative remedy to the encroachment of Navajo stock into Hopi land. Hopi livestock permits were distributed in one area, known as District 6, whose boundaries followed generally the Parker-Keam line. The rest of the 1882 land was divided into Navajo grazing areas. The Hopis were not happy with this division since it limited them to only part of their 1882 reservation. The establishment of District 6 was, in effect, the first partition of the land between Hopis and Navajos, although the Commissioner for Indian Affairs told the Hopis it would not compromise their rights to the rest of the 1882 reservation. District 6 was enlarged and the final boundary was set in 1943. A survey in 1965 revealed the total area to be 650,013 acres. At that time, approximately one hundred Navajo families were living within the boundaries of District 6. They were expelled. Many of them moved just outside the District 6 boundary and now face relocation a second time.

Udall's 1958 statute, Public Law (PL) 85-547, authorized the two tribes, through their respective tribal chairmen, to defend or commence an action against each other before a special three-judge panel of the U.S. District Court of Arizona. The action would proceed "for the purpose of determining the rights and interests of said parties in and to said lands and quieting title thereto in the tribes or Indians establishing such claims pursuant to such Executive Order as may be just and fair in law and equity." Nine days after it was passed, the Hopi chairman filed a friendly lawsuit against the chairman of the Navajo tribe. The case, known as *Healing v. Jones,* after the Hopi and Navajo tribal chairmen, Dewey Healing and Paul Jones, was later referred to as "the greatest title problem of the West." The Navajo Tribal Council was as naïve as Stewart Udall regarding the impact of this lawsuit; it passed a resolution asking Congress to advance money to the Hopis to help them pay for their part of the litigation.

The special panel of judges was convened in 1960 in Prescott, Arizona, to hear the case. The Hopis argued that the entire 2.5-million-acre 1882 Executive Order Area should be set aside for their exclusive use. The Navajos, contending that they were the "other Indians" the Secretary had settled on the 1882 area, argued that they had exclusive interest in all land except District 6. The court issued its decision in 1962, and determined that the Hopi Tribe, subject to the trust title of the United States, "has the exclusive right and interest, both as to the surface and subsurface, including all resources," to District 6. The court further found that the Hopi and Navajo tribes, subject to the trust title of the United States, "have joint, undivided and equal rights and interest both as to the surface and subsurface, including all resources" of the land of the 1882 area outside of District 6. The case was appealed to the U.S. Supreme Court, which affirmed the lower court's decision on June 3, 1963. The justices agreed that District 6 belonged to the Hopis and that both tribes had equal interests in the 1.8 million acres that comprised the rest of the 1882 area, leaving more unanswered questions than had existed before the case was heard.

Abbott Sekaquaptewa backs his battered pickup off the curb beside his stone house in the Hopi village of Kykotsmovi. He grinds into gear and at the end of the crescent-shaped street he turns into the grocery store lot. He stops the car, slides his metal crutches to the ground, and slowly lowers his body between them.

Abbott sets the walking sticks out in front of him and undulates forward, pushing his body and legs up toward his arms and then setting his sticks again like a daddy longlegs negotiating a foreign trail. A severe case of arthritis left him crippled as a boy. He has an artificial hip, most of his vertebrae except for those at his neck are fused, and all of his joints continue to degenerate, though slowly now. Abbott's upper body is long and muscled; his legs are short and splayed over his crippled feet. Despite his crablike figure, Abbott is a handsome man. His face is open, his eyes are expressive. He is familiar with his own people as well as with the white man, and he is not afraid to reveal himself. Abbott, unlike many Hopis, speaks forthrightly about his dreams for his people, and is an unwavering supporter of Navajo relocation. Yet he is also one of the most open-minded Hopis and is a walking encyclopedia on the land dispute, although his position is very partisan.

Abbott walks past the gas pumps and two large pickups filled with Navajos. This grocery is a customary stop for Navajos heading home toward Big Mountain, which lies due north over bone-shattering dirt roads. The Navajos look off into the distance as Abbott hobbles by. They know who he is: for the Navajos subject to relocation, Abbott is the symbol of their misery. He is the man who, with the aid of a devoted lawyer and the support of Arizona's venerable Senator Barry Goldwater, successfully lobbied for the passage of Public Law 93-531, the 1974 statute designed to return half of the 1882 area to the Hopis. Based on the findings of the 1962 *Healing v. Jones* decision, it authorized partition of the 1882 area and the relocation of ten thousand Navajos and one hundred Hopis from their homes. Yet if they were forced to speak, the Navajos would be respectful. Here in Indian country, Abbott is an elder, and therefore worthy of respect, although the Navajos' respect for him is mixed with fear. They fear his power, they wonder if he is aided by supernaturals.

Abbott, fifty-six, buys a copy of the *Arizona Republic*. An elderly Hopi man nods to him, and the young cashier acts as it she doesn't know who he is, though she does. Abbott is out of power now. After twelve years as tribal chairman, he was narrowly defeated by thirty-eight-year-old Ivan Sidney in 1983, two years ago. At Hopi, as on the Navajo reservation, most of the jobs available are tribal jobs, and loyalty to the sitting chairman is required for employment. At the store or in the few Hopi eating establishments, Abbott will be ignored by his political enemies and consulted on various matters by his supporters. The community is so small and gossip so rampant that some Hopis are hesitant even to acknowledge a member of an opposing faction.

Abbott leaves the store and calls out a deep-voiced halloo to a wiry Hopi man with short-cropped hair and a baseball cap. It is his neighbor, just in from checking his cattle, which graze down off the mesas within District 6. He and Abbott move a few feet away from a couple of old Navajo ladies waiting for rides home. Abbott's neighbor draws pictures in the air with his hands as he tells Abbott that one of his cows was stolen and butchered by Navajos. He hadn't seen the theft himself, but was told of it by one of his friends, who witnessed the scene while out tending his cornfield. The friend watched helplessly while the group of Navajos killed the cow, loaded it into a truck, and drove it to their camp. The Hopi man had followed the Navajos and watched them butcher the cow and divide up the meat. Abbott's neighbor says he informed the BIA police—even drove the police to the Navajo camp and showed them the carcass. The police took no action.

Abbott commiserates with his friend, then struggles back to his truck.

"We were given the land around the mesas by the giver of the breath of life," he says slowly, pulling himself onto the seat, trying to control his anger. "And it was given to us for good reasons. We need those lands for our culture, our religious life, our sense of belonging. Hopi people feel they have a purpose for being here on this earth. They have been called on to maintain a stewardship over Mother Earth. It's a very solemn kind of thing and their responsibility is terminated only when the source of that authority is ready to take it back, and that's the giver of the breath of life, the divine power."

Abbott starts the truck and pulls out of the parking lot. He heads down to the bottom of the mesa, past stone houses and small orchards. Kykotsmovi is a relatively new Hopi town, created at the turn of the century by Hopis who wanted to be closer to the government-run school.

"The natural environment doesn't belong to the Hopis," says Abbott. "They belong to it—they are a part of it, therefore they respect the things of nature—or they did. But now, there are some doubts that are being created among the younger people because of two things—they're not learning these things from the elders, or the elders aren't teaching them these things anymore. And at the same time they're going to school in a high-tech world that teaches them technology but not the knowledge of life. So, these cultural things, spiritual things, ceremonial things are beginning to erode."

Abbott stops at the bottom of the village, turns north on Highway 264 and heads up to the top of Third Mesa. The car moves through a passage of ocher rock blasted from the mesa to accommodate the roadway. Thousands of rocks have tumbled from the top of the mesa and rolled down the steep walls, skidding to a stop in the ravines. Abbott looks toward the smoky horizon of pastel mesas that rise thirty miles to the south. Abbott calls them the Hopi Buttes, but the Navajos who live on the rolling plains beneath the strange lumps call the area Teesto. As a result of the bill whose passage Abbott vigorously lobbied for, Teesto is now part of the land being returned to the Hopis, the HPL. Abbott looks toward the buttes and explains his passion to preserve a land base for his people within the 180,000-member Navajo Nation. "Unless things are done to protect Hopi as Hopi," he says, "the Navajo Tribe will swallow up the Hopi Tribe. And it's only a matter of time. Hopi society will become a part of Navajo society. There will be no more Hopi society. It's like throwing ten gallons of white paint into 180 gallons of blue paint. It's going to look real blue by the time you get through fixing it up. That's the reality."

For almost a decade after the special panel of judges ruled in 1962 that the Navajos and Hopis had joint, undivided, and equal rights to the 1882 area outside of District 6, the land was administered as a joint use area, an arrangement the Hopis found highly unsatisfactory. The Navajos not only lived on it, but their livestock foraged all the available grass, leaving no room for Hopi livestock. Although the Hopis had won half the land from the decision of *Healing v. Jones,* they had yet to assert control over their half. Eight years after the 1962 *Healing* decision, in 1970, the Hopis petitioned the district court in Tucson to allow them to enjoy their rights as cotenants. After a lengthy court battle that made its way to the U.S. Supreme Court, the Navajos were ordered in 1972 by a Writ of Assistance and Order of Compliance to take steps to allow the Hopis to use half the land. The Navajos were ordered to reduce their sheep to half the carrying capacity of the land, and since range specialists had determined that the land was severely overgrazed, the Navajos were ordered to reduce their flocks by an average of ninety percent. They were also ordered to halt any new construction in the Joint Use Area. Two years later, in 1974, a more permanent solution was crafted by Congress. The Navajo-Hopi Indian Land Settlement Act, PL 93-531, was passed. It ordered the drawing of a line of partition dividing the Joint Use Area in half, and that all Indians who found themselves on the wrong side of the line be moved. The law also authorized the establishment of a relocation commission to supervise the moves.

As Abbott drives across the Hopi mesas, it is eleven years after the passage of the Act, and the Navajos are still not all moved from the HPL, and the three hundred families that remain have vowed to fight. The area that Abbott calls the Hopi Buttes and that the Navajos call Teesto is still dotted with hogans and livestock corrals. Some Navajos have chosen to move in accordance with the government program and have left their abandoned homes behind. Others took their hogans with them, leaving behind nothing but foundations. Other Navajos remain with reduced herds and under the construction freeze.

It would seem that the Hopis had gained the upper hand over the Navajos through the Settlement Act, regaining the use of 900,000 acres of land, causing the removal of hundreds of uneducated, Navajo-speaking families. But Abbott Sekaquaptewa maintains the strong belief that the Hopis are still at great risk of cultural domination from both the Navajos and the U.S. government. "It's as if we were *nothing,*" he says vehemently about his neighbor's livestock theft. "The Hopis don't amount to anything. We don't influence the government, violations like this have no meaning to anybody. We're just a nonentity. That really does something to you. I wouldn't be surprised if it wasn't at the bottom of all the alcoholism—a plain giving up on the part of the younger people."

Sekaquaptewa doesn't believe that the decline of Hopi traditional life is irreversible. "I think the way to do it is to stop threatening the culture," he says. "It's constantly being threatened with the deprivation of its land base and the Hopi peoples' sacred places, the loss of their culture, and being relegated to a state of insignificance as nonentities. If they're not under that threat, I think they'll be able to retain their cultural lives for a long time. But if somebody's always coming in, trying to steal their masks and sacred things or just not being their advocates—or when something happens it's done to the Hopis and they always take the other guy's side, even though the other guy's wrong. If somebody's always trying to take away the Hopis' land base that they established many years ago for good reason. If these things didn't exist, I think the society could rejuvenate itself and develop to a degree where we could really contribute more to other societies than we're doing now.

"There are reasons why we're threatened with this thing now," he goes on. "There were not any Navajos in the area, as far as we know, until about 150 years ago. Now, they'll say they've been here forever. But that's not really true. But, today, the San Francisco Peaks are their traditional shrine, even though they didn't know about them until about 150 years ago. Their spirits live on a mountain they didn't have over 150 years ago. In other words, our shrines have become their shrines. Our beliefs have become their beliefs. Our traditions have become their traditions. And this constant taking away from our culture and making it their own culture bothers us. And then on top of that, non-Indians come in and swallow that hook, line, and sinker, like it was always that way when the Hopis know they have only borrowed it within the last 150 years. It's this experience that bothers us. This is what we're offended by. Some of them even make prayer feathers now. I can't make prayer feathers because I'm not a priesthood person—you have to be a priest in order to make prayer feathers. So here I'm a Hopi and I can't make prayer feathers but some Navajo in Ganado can make prayer feathers. These kinds of things. . . ."

Eight miles to the north of Kykotsmovi, Abbott passes Hotevilla, the village in which he was born, the same village that is home to David Monongye—Grandfather David, who opposes the tribal council that Abbott once led—who was a childhood playmate of Abbott's mother. Abbott takes a turn onto a small graded road toward his family's ranch, twelve miles southwest of Hotevilla, and six miles from Howell Mesa, where Bessie Hatathlie herded sheep as a child.

Abbott spent a full year bedridden in hospitals in Phoenix and Winslow when he was a teenager. An old janitor from the hospital saw Abbott years later, after Abbott had become chairman of the Hopi Tribe, and told him, "I was so afraid for you. I used to see you in your room struggling day after day for your life. After a while, I stopped looking in, because I was afraid you wouldn't make it."

But Abbott did make it. And the inner strength that helped him leave the hospital forty years ago still burns in him now, and in many ways, is the source of the fight still left in the Hopi Tribe. "I guess living through things like that makes you real tough," says Abbott, who is almost completely self-taught, from English to history to electronics to law. He wears a battered Stetson "Gunslinger" hat jauntily over his wavy graying hair. "I learned never to give up. I'm not sure that's the best answer, but that's the one I learned.

"Domination, the tendency of people to come here and want to dominate, control, and own us is at the bottom of Hopi history. We as Hopis have not been able to deal with that. We can't deal with it. That's what we want to throw off."

(5)

A Brief History
of the Hopis

The Hopis are a people of law. The Navajos are a people of opportunity.
The Hopis are rule-bound, religious, and self-righteous. The Navajos are
adventurers and improvisers; throughout their history, they have enthusiastically embraced new ideas and skills and turned them into something uniquely their own. Navajo life is far freer and allows far more
individual expression than does life at Hopi.

The Hopis, although they consider themselves superior to the Navajos, are also jealous of them, jealous of their freedom. They are infuriated
to see the Navajos profit from their own initiative. The Navajos learned
weaving from the Pueblo people and went on to develop weaving into
an art form far surpassing that of their teachers. Much of Navajo ceremonialism was learned from the Pueblos with whom the Navajos had
intermarried. Says one anthropologist, "Learning is the wrong word. The
Navajos *took* from their Pueblo relatives the skeleton of a mythology and
the details of a complicated ritual, and on these they built a structure
Wagnerian in its grandeur."

This quality elicits nothing but scorn from the Hopis. Who came first,
who has primacy, holds more importance for the Hopis than who has
elevated a skill or a ceremony to the greatest heights. The Hopis condescendingly attribute the Navajos' success to qualities like aggression.
Says Abbott, "The Navajos are aggressive. They're materialistic. Everything they encounter they try to control and exploit and use to their
advantage. Their value system is directed that way. It's not the same as
the Hopi system."

But the Hopis also resent their own tribesmen who lift themselves up
from the common lot. Abbott's family was driven out of the village of
Hotevilla because his parents adopted certain modern ways. And they
prospered. The children were ridiculed, called "bahanas" or white men.
Anyone who dares to be different at Hopi feels the full brunt of societal

disapproval, and the scorn is directed with all the energy of the self-righteous. Abbott acknowledges this. "Hopi means different things," he says. "It means peaceful, good person, well-behaved person, yes, but its religious meaning is *righteous*. We have a 'we're better than you' attitude, and we call ourselves Hopi even though we do bad things to each other. We bicker, we're jealous, we can't get together to put up a common front against the outside."

Knowledge of these qualities has led observers at times to take some of the Hopis' complaints less than seriously. Nevertheless, the Hopis have bravely maintained the hope that they and their values would be protected by the U.S. government. The Hopis have at times been shocked to learn that the Bureau of Indian Affairs isn't as sensitive to the Hopi sense of right and wrong as they are themselves. Abbott says, "I think over the years the BIA found some of the Hopi complaints to be very petty—not realizing the legal right or the moral right. A lot of times they were more interested in carrying out Bureau programs and weren't very interested in what the Indians thought."

But the Hopis often couldn't make it clear exactly what they thought. Because each of the fourteen Hopi villages considers itself an autonomous unit and because clans within the villages compete for authority on certain matters, it is often difficult to come to a consensus. Here is a joke told by Hopis: A Navajo walks along and accidentally bumps up against a magic lantern and a genie pops out. The genie tells the Navajo he has three wishes. The Navajo says, "I want to be the richest man in the world." And the genie makes it happen. Then the Navajo says, "I want to look like the richest man in the world." And the genie gives him a three-piece suit. Then the Navajo says, "And I don't want to work a day in my life." And the genie makes him a Navajo again. Then a Hopi walks down the road and accidentally bumps the lantern. The genie jumps out and tells the Hopi he has three wishes. For the last fifteen years, the Hopis have been trying to figure out what to ask the genie for.

The conflict between the Hopis and Navajos, which emerged as a battle over land, is at bottom a cultural conflict between neighbors with different values and habits. The Hopis feel intruded upon by the Navajos, borrowed from, cast aside, and not protected by the U.S. government. The Navajos are bewildered that the government could ask them to move from their homes to make room for the Hopis when they know the Hopis will not live on the land they vacate. To understand the layers of hostility and frustration that have fueled this dispute for a century, it is essential to understand the history of how the two tribes came to inhabit the same piece of land, what pressures the tribes encountered over those years, and how, as cultural units, they resolved those tensions. Although modern ways have somewhat changed the lives of Hopis and Navajos alike, both tribes have maintained their essential character. Like farming people and their less-settled neighbors around the world, Navajos and Hopis look at the world very differently and hold each other up in many ways as models of what not to be.

And as in other old disputes over land in Northern Ireland and in the Middle East, ancient disagreements still color modern dialogue—if dialogue exists at all. Slights become feuds that become myth or history. People who should be allies become enemies. Every fact, every incident is magnified by time, by longing, by familiarity, and above all, by the unforgettable fantasy of returning home, returning to better days.

The Hopis are an ancient people whose roots in the Four Corners area (where the states of Colorado, Arizona, New Mexico, and Utah meet at a point) predate the Navajos' by hundreds of years. For almost a thousand years, the Hopis have lived a demanding and intricate way of life peculiarly adapted to their world atop the harsh, dry, wind-whipped mesas. Their stone houses are almost invisible on the mesa tops, clinging there through extremes of weather as if they were anchored to the very center of the earth. And in spirit and in ceremony, the Hopis maintain a connection with the center of the earth, for they believe that they are the earth's caretakers, and with the successful performance of their ceremonial cycle, the world will remain in balance, the gods will be appeased, and rain will come. Kachinas, humans dressed as ancestral spirits, dance in hand-woven kilts, headdresses, feathers, and fronds, believing they are sending messages to the real Kachinas, who live beyond in the spirit world. They stamp and chant in rhythms Hopis believe resonate with the earth's vibratory center, and a visitor to the magnificent, profound displays finds it hard to disbelieve. Hopi songs are eerie, guttural, earthly; the sounds seem to be formed with little interference from the mouth but rather to have their origins deep inside the short, gnarled people, to pass directly through them from the bowels of the mesas.

Tradition tells the Hopis that they have risen through three worlds, each of which was destroyed when man, created perfect, allowed his will to topple him from grace. In each world, the Hopis explored their basest behaviors and came to know themselves thoroughly. They emerged into this, the fourth world, from the west, where the third world had become a watery mass. Here, they were sent on their way through migrations outlined to them by Massau, god of fire and death. They were told to separate by clan groups and crisscross the world through the four directions, forming the sign of a swastika, until they returned to their designated home, the center of the universe, at the appearance of a great star. Their brother, Bahana, the white man, was to go east. He carried a tablet with him which he would show the Hopis on his return. He was to rejoin his lost brothers at a designated time, at which point he would right all wrongs, and conduct a purification that would herald the Hopis' next or fifth world.

The migrations, as other more familiar tales of exodus, tested the Hopi people and defined their faith. In the most extreme of circumstances, wandering without a permanent home, the different clan groups told stories and developed ceremonies to protect themselves and encourage the positive regard of the gods. Like other creation myths, the literal meaning of the Hopi legends can be mined for clues about the locations of their wanderings.

It has long been surmised that American Indians migrated across the Bering Strait from Asia in waves, each pushing the next farther south, and that this all happened relatively recently—no more than ten thousand years ago. However, some argue that people have been in the Americas for at least 25,000 years and perhaps twice that, and that they had the opportunity to migrate south and north and east and west and then back again, filling the continents. The Hopi legends suggest that the prehistoric ancestors of the Hopis didn't arrive in North America via the Bering Strait at all, but traveled across the ocean from the west in boats, moving from island to island, from a continent now lost, for they are told, "Down on the bottom of the seas lie all the proud cities . . . and the worldly treasures corrupted with evil. . . . But the day will come, if you preserve the memory and the meaning of your Emergence, when these stepping stones will emerge again to prove the truth you speak."

The Creation story can also be read as a mystical allegory for man's passage through different developmental stages until he finally rises through the last opening, emerging from the underworld to full consciousness. "It is a Road of Life he has traveled by his own free will, exhausting every capacity for good or evil, that he may know himself at last."

Science shows us that the final destination of the Hopis, the center of the universe, fell in a most convenient place, because on the towering, sandstone-bottomed mesas, the Hopis had found an area of permanent springs. The three narrow mesas on which the Hopis settled were cut from Black Mesa by the ephemeral runoff of the Tusayan washes (Oraibi Wash, Dinnebito Wash, Wepo Wash, Polacca Wash, and Jeddito Wash), which pull sand and silt down off the mesa to the valley bottom below and toward the Little Colorado River. The winds then blow the sand back up against the mesa bottoms, where it serves to hold moisture and reduce rainfall runoff. The Hopis can then plant crops in the moist sand, where they are not affected by cycles of erosion as badly as crops in nearby areas. Windbreaks of brush are constructed to try to keep the sand from blowing away, and crops with deep roots, such as strains of beans and maize and fruit trees, have been developed by the Hopis to thrive in the high desert.

The area of the mesas is generally believed to have been occupied by humans for more than ten thousand years, and although it is still unclear whether the ruins of villages in the area that are fifteen and sixteen hundred years old were lived in by direct ancestors of the Hopis, anthropologists have shown that "the cultural remains present a clear, uninterrupted, logical development culminating in the life, general technology, architecture, and agricultural and ceremonial practices to be seen on the three Hopi mesas today."

Ten thousand years ago, the Southwest was wetter than it is now and the bands of hunter-gatherers who roamed the vast area enjoyed the use of shallow lakes, were shaded by pine and spruce stands, and shared their lives with a varied fauna including mammoths, deer, rabbits, horses, antelope, sloths, and turtles. Until 5000 B.C., the area underwent cycles of increased moisture and drought, leading eventually to an overall decrease in moisture until it became the familiar land the Hopis know: an arid land of steep sandstone plateaus, deep vertical-walled box canyons, with occasional stands of piñon and juniper.

In 2000 B.C., population in the Southwest was sparse and made up of small egalitarian bands of close kinship groups moving frequently to take advantage of water supplies, plants, and building materials. They ate grass seed, small rodents and birds, insects, piñon nuts, and berries. These people did not build permanent structures, but probably lived in natural shelters or windbreaks made from branches. Because these hunter-gatherers were always on the move for new supplies of food, fuel, and other materials, they could not carry any more than was necessary and therefore could not accumulate wealth.

The present Hopi culture retains many features of its hunter-gatherer past, which anthropologists believe had three basic economic propositions. First, food production was based on division of labor according to sex. Men did the hunting and women the gathering and child care. (Today, there is little wild game, but Hopi men usually take charge of the livestock and farming while the women cook and take care of the children). Second, food was consumed immediately after it was found and was shared within the kinship group. And finally, any extra food was distributed according to clan ties. The Hopis tried every season to harvest and save enough food to last three years in case of drought. Today—although supermarkets prevent starvation if the drought clings —harvested food is distributed among clan members, and obligations to family and closely related clans are taken very seriously. This makes private business among Hopis difficult. An individual shop owner, for example, will feel obligated to provide for relatives if they are in need. Also, great pressure is brought to bear on Hopis who become wealthy. They are ridiculed and gossiped about until they are reduced to the common level.

Humans have lived as hunter-gatherers for most of their history. This kind of human organization "has been judged the most stable and hence the most successful form of economic and social adaptation that mankind has achieved." However, between 2000 and 1000 B.C. that most stable of adaptations began to change in the Southwest, when the agriculture introduced a thousand years previously by people from Mexico began to influence the hunter-gatherers. Farming caught on very slowly. For hundreds of years, hunter-gatherer bands probably planted small plots of maize and squash, then left them untended during hunting forays. Whatever had survived the pestilence of rodents and insects would be harvested in the fall. It was not until a thousand years after the first corn plots began to influence patterns of life that agriculture became the subsistence base. Around A.D. 500, along the banks of the Salt and Gila rivers, agriculture was the basis for the development of at least one town of fifty inhabitants, and two hundred years later, large-scale irrigation was in use.

Hopi is a Uto-Aztecan language, and linguistic analysis suggests that expansion of the Mesoamerican culture, along with the first ears of maize, may have reached the Four Corners area around 3000 B.C. when the Desert culture—identified by the use of basketry, flat milling stones, and food of seeds and small desert animals—was becoming what is today known as Anasazi culture. The name Anasazi was taken from a Navajo term thought to mean "ancient people" but which can also be translated as "enemy ancestors." The Anasazi are known for the magnificent cliff dwellings they built in the Southwest at such sites now known as Montezuma Castle, Chaco Canyon, Canyon de Chelly, and Mesa Verde. Between A.D. 600 and 1000, agricultural activities became more intensive, and the Anasazi depended less on hunting and gathering. They built fantastic villages hidden up in protected shelves of canyon walls. No one knows why they began to depend more on farming and hence to become more sedentary, but it has been suggested that population increases in the area may have reduced available forage. And as population centers grew and food production increased, people became increasingly sedentary and built permanent structures. Then their populations increased further, leading to the need for more food production.

The architecture, methods of ceramic construction, and design styles of the Anasazi were greatly influenced by Mesoamerican traditions. One anthropologist surmises that the Hopis were a renegade group of religious cultists who separated from the Mayan, Toltec, and Aztec peoples and made their way north, slowly, through many wanderings, to the Four Corners region. Petroglyphic traces of their migrations through the larger Anasazi settlements are numerous, and those petroglyphs are now considered sacred remains of the clan migrations. However, Hopi legends maintain, in a bit of "the tail wagging the dog," that the Aztec, Mayan, and Toltec people were Hopi clans who failed to complete their prescribed religious tasks and migrations.

Mysteriously, around A.D. 1200, the magnificent cliff dwellings of the Anasazi were abandoned all through the area that is now Arizona, Colorado, and New Mexico. It is not clear why; perhaps drought, perhaps disease or dietary problems, perhaps invasion by other tribes. There is evidence that dental decay and iron-deficiency anemia are more prevalent among populations dependent on agriculture as opposed to those who supplement their food harvests with gathered foods. Also, some hypothesize that major drought periods that drove away foraging animals and led to cycles of crop failures were followed by torrential rains that washed away the topsoil and then caused erosion and deep arroyo cutting. People moved into larger and larger communities for survival, thereby putting a greater stress on the arable land, until the system finally broke down and the survivors moved away. They collected in two areas, which are now the lands of the Hopi and the Zuni.

Before the large influx of the Anasazis in the mid-thirteenth century from what is now Flagstaff and along the Colorado River, the Hopi ancestors lived in small groups of pueblos and farmsteads. However, for a hundred years between 1250 and the middle of the fourteenth century, towns of from five hundred to a thousand people sprang up in Hopi country as the Anasazi fled their cliff dwellings. The increased size of settlements as well as the artifacts found there indicate that the incoming people profoundly influenced the existing culture. The people who arrived on the Hopi mesas had a strong sense of their own identities, as did the different groups of Hopi clans who had already organized themselves into small villages. There was assimilation of sorts, yet some of the newcomers established their own villages—for example, on Antelope Mesa, east of First Mesa, the easternmost of the three mesas the Hopis now inhabit. By the time the Spanish arrived, it is believed, most of the newcomers were fully assimilated into Hopi towns. Hopi legends tell that newcomers were asked to prove their religious worth before being admitted to a village. Once a group of arrivals could demonstrate their particular powers with the gods, they were given a place to settle and certain responsibilities in maintaining the religious cycle, whose purpose was unrelentingly crucial: achieving the positive regard of the gods to ensure rainfall in a land of low and irregular precipitation.

The Hopis may have been less affected by the drought that drove the newcomers from their former homes because of their permanent springs. But they also had the advantage of an unusual planting strategy, which they still practice today—hedging their bets against disaster by making use of all the planting techniques available to them, such as planting in the valleys of streams that overflow after torrential rains or planting in the areas where water overflows the mouths of arroyos. Forms of irrigation were also used in prehistoric times as they are today; crops are grown in terraces and watered by hand or with the use of ditches. In another measure to maximize the chance of success with unpredictable weather, the Hopis cultivate small plots over a great area, to take advantage of different conditions. One anthropologist concluded, "Had the Spanish not interrupted developments in the area, most of the Colorado Plateau would probably have been repopulated by peoples using a strategy such as this one."

The Hopis did not build huge settlements like the Anasazis'. Perhaps they understood that small communities were the only ones possible in the unpredictable and dry highlands, and it was a natural outgrowth of their strategy to hedge their bets. Or perhaps the Hopis' independence of spirit and the heterogeneous makeup of its different villages militated against centralization.

The Hopis believe that the clans were sent on different migrations with the ultimate purpose of settling together in one place. However, the migrations were marked by constant splits and quarrels, causing clans to separate and go their own way. This became "the principal motif of all the [Hopi] migration legends—a quarrel between two brothers in the same clan or between the leaders of two clans, each challenging the power of the other's deity and ceremony with his own, causing another split." This tendency for groups to divide over quarrels rather than compromise or fight persists at Hopi today. The idea of decision by a majority has no meaning to the Hopis. The elder religious priests are consulted in matters of religion and their word is obeyed. In secular matters, the village leaders or clan leaders are given the final word. But there is always disagreement about which individual is in the right position to have the final word.

From the fourteenth through the sixteenth centuries, the Hopis' remarkable agricultural techniques, their highly developed pottery and mural paintings, as well as their utilization of coal distinguished them, along with the Rio Grande Pueblos and the Zuni-Acoma peoples as "one of the three major centers of Pueblo life." The Hopis' fierce independence and devotion to the performance of their ceremonial cycles helped them repel the influence of the Spanish, who had a terrible effect on many of the other native southwestern people.

In 1528, Alvar Núñez Cabeza de Vaca was shipwrecked on the Texas coast. He and his three companions traveled near to what is now El Paso, and there heard of prosperous farming communities along the Rio Grande. The information he sent back to Spain was the first the Europeans had received about the Pueblo people. Eleven years later, Esteban, a black man who had been shipwrecked along with Cabeza de Vaca, journeyed back to the New World with Fray Marcos de Niza. Accompanied by Indian servants, the group traveled in search of riches northwest to the legendary Seven Cities of Cíbola, just west of the continental divide and on the eastern side of the present-day Arizona–New Mexico

border, the land of the Zuni Indian villages. Esteban was killed on entering the southernmost village and Fray Marcos beat a hasty retreat, but
not before claiming the area the possession of the king of Spain. On the
basis of the friar's "enthusiastic if exaggerated report to the viceroy," an
expedition set forth the next year, 1540, led by Francisco Vásquez de
Coronado, in search of riches. Their goal was to conquer what are now
the pueblos of Zuni, Acoma, and Hopi.

Coronado was already in Mexico, where the Spanish, seven years
earlier, had completed their conquest of the Aztec Empire. In 1540, he
marched through Cíbola in search of the seven fabled cities of gold with
a cavalry, infantry, and artillery numbering three hundred men in full
battle dress, one thousand horses, and six hundred pack animals, and
six Franciscan friars prepared to missionize and see that "the conquest
might be Christian and apostolic and not a butchery." They conquered
the southernmost village and turned it into their headquarters, but didn't
find the gold and silver they were after. So Coronado sent his standard
bearer Pedro de Tovar north with seventeen mounted soldiers, some foot
soldiers, and the friar Juan de Padilla, to the area they called Tusayan—
Hopi—where seven more villages were said to stand. Like the Aztecs
and the Mayas, whose legends included the myth of a returning white
being, the Hopis believed in the return of the Bahana, or white brother.
Historians have long surmised that the Vikings appeared in North America in the eleventh century, and the widespread myth of the bearded
white man is so common it suggests that the Indians had seen whites
before the Spanish. Whatever the origin, the Hopis had been expecting
Bahana, who was now twenty years late. The legends even told them
where to meet him if he was on time (the bottom of Third Mesa), if he
was five years late (Yellow Rock), or ten years late (Pointed Rock), fifteen
years late (Cross Fields), or twenty years late (below Oraibi).

According to the account of Castañeda, chronicler of the Coronado
expedition, the Hopis awoke to find the Spaniards camped below their
village of Awatovi. Thinking they might have encountered Bahana at
last, though it was not the appointed meeting place, the Hopis descended from the town toward the camp and sprinkled a line of sacred
cornmeal across the path before the Spanish. The Spanish didn't understand the Hopis' warning not to cross the line. The tension increased
until a Hopi man hit one of the Spaniards' horses on the cheek of the
bridle, whereupon Friar Juan muttered, "To tell the truth, I do not know
why we came here." The men took this as a call to arms and charged the
expectant Hopis, shouting their battle cry of "Santiago!" They drove the
Hopis into their village with swords and lances. The Hopis then came
out with offerings of woven cotton cloth, piñon nuts, corn, turquoise,
and skins, which Tovar received before starting off for the other Hopi
towns.

Hopi scholar Frank Waters describes the legendary Hopi account of what happened after Tovar accepted their gifts. Still thinking Bahana had arrived, the Hopis steered Tovar and his men to Oraibi to meet the clan chiefs at the bottom of the village, the appointed meeting place if Bahana were twenty years late. There, they sprinkled four lines of cornmeal on the ground. Then the "Bear Clan leader stepped up to the barrier and extended his hand, palm up, to the leader of the white men. If he was indeed the true Pahana, the Hopis knew he would extend his own hand, palm down, to form the *nakwach*, the ancient symbol of brotherhood. Tovar instead curtly commanded one of his men to drop a gift into the Bear Clan chief's hand, believing that the Indian wanted a present of some kind. Instantly all the Hopi chiefs knew that Pahana had forgotten the ancient agreement made between their peoples at the time of their separation."

According to tradition, the Hopis then fed Tovar and his troops and tried to explain what Bahana may have forgotten, that at this appointed time, each side was to make a thorough examination of the other's ways and expose the wrongs and inconsistencies. After the examination, the two would again live together and reestablish the worldly unity they'd had before they were sent out on their tests and migrations.

But the Spaniards hadn't remembered, and soon left for the Grand Canyon, for they were looking for a waterway to the "South Sea" or Gulf of California. Over the next fifty years, the Spanish tried to assert control over the Pueblo lands they had taken possession of for the king. However, they never found the wealth they sought, nor did they find a trail from the ledge of the canyon to the Colorado River below for their sea route south, and in 1608 the Council of Indies recommended that the Spanish abandon New Mexico because it was an "extravagant and unprofitable possession."

Though the adventurers were disappointed with their find, the priests weren't, and they remained to begin the work of conversion. The first mission at Hopi was built at Awatovi in 1629. This village, the easternmost outpost at Hopi and one of the largest villages, was the point of contact with eastern tribes like the Zuni, Acoma, and Rio Grande Pueblos, who brought trade objects to Hopi from three ancient trade routes extending to the Gulf of Mexico and Texas, Southern California, and the Baja California–Mexico area. These routes connected the Hopis with the Mojave, Hualapai, and Havasupai tribes as well as the Pimas and Papagos (now Tohono O'odham). One anthropologist points out that as a result of its location and commercial importance, Awatovi had "a cosmopolitan, sophisticated flavor far surpassing that of the other villages. Hence, it would not only be more receptive to new ideas, but would in turn be responsible for introducing many innovations to the several other Hopi towns—for, although the purpose of this inter-tribal trade was to barter material objects, it should be kept in mind that an equally important transfer of ideas, language, and other nonmaterial culture took place."

The friars had thus picked a most propitious town in which to begin their travails. After resisting at first, the people of Awatovi converted, supposedly after a Franciscan friar named Francisco Porras restored the sight of a blind boy by laying a cross over his eyes. By 1674, missions had been built as well, by obedient Hopi labor, in Oraibi and Shongopavi. Smaller churches, or *visitas*, were built at Walpi and Mishongnovi. At Awatovi, the new church was built directly over the main kiva so as to demonstrate the "superposition" of Christianity over Hopi religion. Hopi religious paraphernalia was destroyed and "the finest examples of Hopi kiva murals," which decorated the walls, were obliterated when the kiva was filled to the roof with clean sand. The Hopis dragged logs from forty to one hundred miles away for the construction of the church, and Hopis today point out long cylindrical hollows in the rock near Oraibi, supposedly caused by the dragging of heavy timbers. The Hopis also modified their own pottery styles and made pottery plates with European foot lips and bowls for the refectories and painted murals on the walls. However, the rains didn't come after the Hopis were prevented from conducting their dances, and the Hopis tried to practice their religion in secret away from the villages. Some even left Hopi and migrated to the Rio Grande. The Hopis who remained became increasingly resentful of the heavy-handed ways of the priests. As Frank Waters writes,

Enforced labor not only built the church but supplied all the needs of the priests. Tradition recalls that one *padre* would not drink water from any of the springs around Oraibi; he demanded that a runner bring his water from White Sand Spring near Moencopi, fifty miles away. The *padres'* illicit relations with young Hopi girls were common in all villages, and the punishment given Hopis for sacrilege and insubordination added to the growing resentment. It is recorded that at Oraibi in 1655, when friar Salvador de Guerra caught a Hopi in "an act of idolatry," he thrashed the Hopi in the presence of the whole village till he was bathed in blood, and then poured over him burning turpentine.

The Spanish eventually occupied most of the twenty-odd Rio Grande pueblos, as well as those of Zuni to the west and Hopi to the northwest. During the occupation, there were sporadic uprisings, but the Spanish managed, through brutal reprisals, to keep the Indians subservient to their secular and religious rule. However, by 1680, the Pueblos had had enough. In a coordinated effort, the Indians struck, killing twenty-one missionaries and four hundred colonists. The Pueblos destroyed the churches, government records, even "vented their fury on the hens, the sheep, the fruit trees of Castile, and even upon the wheat." The Spaniards who escaped death fled to Mexico, where they remained for over a decade. At Hopi, four priests were killed and the churches dismantled.

Soon after the revolt, many Pueblo people feared retaliatory raids from the Spanish, and large numbers of Rio Grande Pueblos moved to Hopi seeking refuge. Two new villages were built to accommodate them, Hano on First Mesa and Payupki on Second Mesa. Others sought refuge with the Navajos and the Apaches. Over the next twenty years, Spanish attempts to reconvert the Pueblos were strenuously resisted, but native populations fell as the result of battle deaths and starvation. Many villages emptied as people traveled west; some villages split and fought each other over conversion. New alliances sprung up between Indian tribes to fight the common enemy, the Spanish. The Hopi leaders received help from the Navajos, Utes, and Havasupais. Once again, as in the great Anasazi migrations of the mid-thirteenth century, and immediately following the Pueblo Revolt, Hopi served as a refuge for people in times of need; some stayed and became a permanent part of Hopi, like the Tewas of Hano, while others returned home once better times arrived, like the Southern Tiwas who had settled the village of Payupki on Second Mesa. It was also during this period that for security reasons, the Hopis moved the villages of Walpi, Mishongnovi, and Shongopavi up to the mesa tops from their former locations at the cliff bottoms near the springs.

The Hopis remained virtually undisturbed by the Spanish until 1700 when Padre Juan Garaycoechea was accepted at Awatovi and baptized seventy-three Hopi children. (In the previous year, there is evidence that a delegation of Christianized Hopis, probably from Awatovi, journeyed to Santa Fe to ask for missionaries. Perhaps fearing a Spanish attack—for the Spanish had reconquered the Rio Grande Pueblos by 1699—these Hopis had offered to rebuild their mission.) Perhaps Christianity was allowed back at Awatovi and none of the other Hopi villages because of the miracle of the blind boy's return to sight accomplished earlier by Father Francisco Porras (though Porras was poisoned at Awatovi four years after the supposed miracle). Whatever the reason, the reacceptance by the Awatovis of the hated church infuriated the other Hopi villages and would lead to an act of internecine violence that would become a permanent part of the Hopi soul.

After baptizing the children, the Franciscan father left Hopi for Zuni. Another delegation of Hopis traveled to Santa Fe, and offered a plan for religious tolerance and peace. They would respect the Spanish ways if the Spanish respected theirs. Neither would try to convert the other. Governor Cubero of New Mexico sent them away with a firm no.

So the Hopis took matters into their own hands. Not only were the other Hopi villages infuriated by the reappearance of the Spanish and their church at Awatovi, but more important perhaps, the Awatovis possessed certain clans that were essential to the ceremonial cycle, and their loss to Christianity would threaten the security of all the Hopis. The Awatovi chief himself traveled to Oraibi to urge that the unfaithful among his people be punished.

The leaders of Oraibi, Mishongnovi, Shongopavi, and Walpi gathered and decided to attack the Christian converts. One evening in fall, when all the Awatovi men were in the kivas preparing for the first great ceremony in the cycle, the attack began. The warriors pulled up the kiva ladders and shot arrows down into the chambers. They then threw down torches and chili peppers, which the villagers had grown after taking a liking to the Spanish import. Men not on the kiva were chased down, tortured, murdered, dismembered, and left in a heap at the bottom of Mishongnovi, now known as Death Mound or Maschomo. Awatovi was burned and the women were divided up and taken by the different villages. The next day, the Hopis returned to Awatovi and crushed every remaining artifact, leaving the village to melt back into the earth. The remains are still visible.

There are stories that some Awatovis had been forewarned, and had left the night before, saying they were embarking on a hunting expedition. The next morning they looked over their shoulders and saw smoke rising from their village. The surviving Awatovis headed to Canyon de Chelly, where some of their clans had once lived, but eventually moved back to the area and some intermarried with the Navajos in what is now the Teesto area. Navajos of the Red Tobacco clan trace their ancestors to the survivors of Awatovi. Many years later, some individuals returned to Hopi.

But the Hopis had successfully repelled the Catholic Church, and they kept it away for over a hundred years. The Kachinas had triumphed, and the Hopis perhaps could be called "the most famous 'apostates' in the history of Spanish Christianity." The Hopis had tried out European life and rejected it, and decisively reasserted their right to their own ways. In 1706, the Hopis made even plainer their determination not to allow back the church, when they attacked Zuni "in order to keep the Spanish mission program from extending to their villages."

The one-hundred-year period around the Pueblo Revolt of 1680 was a highly significant one for the Hopi people. Serving as a refuge for their cousins among the Pueblos, the villages grew and their identities became further differentiated. According to Albert Yava, a Hopi-Tewa, "The people of the Hopi villages didn't think of themselves as belonging to the same tribe. They considered themselves to be Walpis, Mishongnovis, Shongopavis, Oraibis and so on. The village was their nationality, you might say." This is an important point, for it will have bearing on the U.S. government's later attempts to form a single governmental entity to represent the Hopis.

Also during this period, the "Little People of Peace" as the Hopis like to be known, showed their fierce determination to remain independent; they also showed their skills at war. Commenting on the Pueblo auxiliary soldiers who later, in the mid-1700s, teamed up with the Spanish to fight Apache, Navajo, Ute, and Comanche raiders, one anthropologist writes,

> The stereotype of the Pueblo Indian as nonaggressive and essentially peaceful lacks validity. In fact, the historical record furnishes ample evidence of assertive personality characteristics and warlike propensities of the Pueblos. The first Spanish explorers refer to intervillage conflict, particularly among the Piro and between Pecos and its neighbors, that indicates war was an accepted feature of Pueblo life. Instances of Indian resistance to Spanish domination, culminating in the Revolt of 1680, as well as the Awatovi massacre by the Hopi, further aid in dispelling the image of the Pueblos as passive and docile people.

This is a significant observation, because later, the Hopi Tribe would argue that the Navajos forcefully occupied parts of the 1882 reservation, taking advantage of the Hopis' aversion to violence. The argument that the peaceful Hopis had been overwhelmed by the "marauding Navajos" is a powerful one that the Hopis use to their advantage. But as we have seen, the Hopis proved themselves worthy and brave soldiers, not hesitant to fight for what they believed, even if it meant slaughtering members of their own people.

Frank Waters, in *Book of the Hopi*, writes that the pressures that culminated in the destruction of Awatovi drove the Hopis to undo themselves.

> For the Hopis were a People of Peace, dedicated since their Emergence to a universal plan of Creation which ever sought to maintain in unbroken harmony the lives of every entity—mineral, plant, animal, and man. Now, in one act of unrestrained hate and violence, they had committed a fratricidal crime of mass murder that nullified their own faith and stamped forever an ineradicable guilt upon the heart of every Hopi. It revealed for the first time a hidden and immeasurable chasm between Hopi religious perfectionism and its attainment in human terms. Never again could the Hopis justify their supreme religious idealism as a faith more workable than others. Awatovi revealed also a schizophrenic rift that was to keep widening. The principal motif of all the migration legends, as we have seen, was a quarrel between two brothers in the same clan or between the leaders of two clans, resulting in a split, a separation, or the formation of a new clan. These were minor breaches that did not impede the full unification of all the clans at their final, ordained place of settlement. But now for the first time we see with the destruction of Awatovi a major split among inhabitants of whole villages, a rent in the web of Hopi brotherhood.

The violent schisms within Hopi society had just started; although they wouldn't involve murder, the Hopis would suffer ever more regularly from painful splits over the question of religious purity, with an increasing minority maintaining a rigid Hopi observance, and the majority adapting to what they found useful among the influences of the outside world. The imposition of American authority over the Hopis in the early twentieth century occasioned an additional round of dramatic splits in Hopi society, including the ruptures of two villages, Oraibi and Hotevilla, permanently dividing Hopis who remained faithful to tradition and those who accepted the American-sponsored form of tribal government.

(6)

A Brief History
of the Navajos

Hopi legends tell of the arrival at the mesas of a bedraggled, long-haired stranger dressed in skins and woven plant fibers. They fed him and were kind to him. Soon, there were more of these strangers, similarly poverty-stricken, similarly ill clad. Modern Hopi versions of the story place the arrival of these wandering people, the Navajos, around the time of the arrival of the Spanish in the mid-1500s.

Both the Navajos and their cousins the Apaches are of Athapaskan linguistic stock and are believed to have begun their migrations from Canada's Northwest Territory in a large group or in small bands about a thousand years ago. The Athapaskans were a people who hunted and fished and lived among the lakes and streams of the north woods. As one anthropologist describes them, "They led a wandering life, with little organized government. Their ceremonies were only the few, irregular ones which called the wild game. Their medicine men were solitary visionaries, with no established ritual."

The Athapaskans lived in variants of the pole hut wherever they went. In the north, a conical shape was made by leaning poles together; the structure was then covered with any available material. In Canada it was birch bark. When the Athapaskans reached the Plains, it was buffalo hide. Early Navajos lived in dwellings almost unchanged from the shelters of their distant ancestors. The original Navajo forked-pole hogan, now referred to as a male hogan, is made much like the Athapaskan hut but covered with mud. The female hogan, the most popular hogan today, is shaped like an igloo and made of mud or wood or cement block.

The typical Athapaskan dwelling deteriorated quickly and archaeological remains, if they are found, are difficult to date, even with dendrochronology. It may be that precursors of the Navajos entered the Southwest hundreds of years before the Spanish entry. Archaeological sites to support that theory have not been found. The earliest known site remains widely attributed to Navajos are near Gobernador Knob, in northern New Mexico, and have been dated to 1541. The northwestern corner of New Mexico is filled with archaic Navajo place names, especially in Gobernador Canyon, and events in ancient Navajo legends are located in this area. Three out of the four mountains or ranges within which the Navajos define Dinetah are in this general vicinity. The fourth, the San Francisco Peaks in Flagstaff, Arizona, is far removed from the other three, suggesting that the Navajos first settled in the eastern area of their traditional homeland and then expanded westward.

Some Navajo myths, however, describe a group of Navajos exploring Dinetah from the west to the north. Another song indicates a great familiarity with the land, which the Navajos crisscrossed many times: "They started to walking from there toward the west to Hole in the Ground. They kept walking to Swallow's Nest . . . then to House under the Rock Spreads Out. Then to Mistletoe Hangs. Then Dead Tree Stands Up. Then to Possessing Fish. Then to Red House. Then to Lake with Weeds on Surface. . . ." Although these place names aren't now known, the Navajos maintain that their ancestors carefully scouted old Dinetah, that they did "walk over every stone in it before they settled down."

Anthropologists do not agree on either the route the Athapaskans took into the Southwest or the date of their arrival. Some think the Athapaskans entered the Southwest along the mountains of the Rockies, others believe they traveled south to the Great Plains and then west, while others believe the Athapaskans entered the Southwest from the northern plains. Other theories that combine these routes are also prevalent. The date of entry is also in question, some believing that the Athapaskans arrived in A.D. 800 to 1000, others 1200 to 1400, while still others believe they arrived after the Spanish.

It is not clear whether the Athapaskan people played any role in the abandonment of the large Anasazi communities from about A.D. 1250 to A.D. 1350, but there is evidence they occupied the villages soon after they became empty. Anthropologist Homer Aschmann doesn't think the Athapaskans entered the land of the Pueblos by invasion as is commonly believed; rather, he suggests that Apachean "expansion was really an *Unterwanderung,* the poorest people seeking ecological niches that the established residents had neglected because of their unattractiveness." David Wilcox argues that the newcomers claimed those unwanted niches only after first securing permission from the Pueblos. He suggests that the first interactions between these people were "largely based on a network of cautiously amicable social and economic arrangements. The plainsmen wintered near their patron-clients, trading bison products for maize and cotton goods." Soon, the Athapaskans settled permanently near their Pueblo neighbors and made new trade and territorial arrangements with them. Wilcox suggests that the products offered by the newcomers were beneficial to the Pueblo dwellers, whose economic system was experiencing "shrinkage and inward collapse" as more and more people lived in large centers and began to depend more heavily on agriculture for their food.

The first historical reference to what may have been close relatives of the Navajos was made by Coronado, who, in 1541 on one of his *entradas*, found Indians in what is now Kansas, "living in skin tents like Arabs." Plains elements are present in Navajo ceremonies, suggesting that some proto-Navajo bands at one time lived in the Plains area. A buffalo village is mentioned in a shooting chant, and in one of the Navajos' oldest ceremonies, the Enemy Way, a special rattle must be made from a buffalo scrotum.

In 1583, while Antonio de Espejo journeyed to Hopi looking for a lake of gold, his group mentioned meeting what may have been Navajos, whom they referred to as "Indios serranos," or mountain Indians, near Mount Taylor. These Indians were semisedentary. They grew corn, which they made into tortillas, but they also hunted in areas far away from their base camp. They traded meat, hides, alum, and salt to the Pueblo tribes, with some of whom, like the Acomas, they were closely allied. One of Espejo's men recorded an elaborate ceremony between these "Querechos," or wandering Indians, and some Tewa emissaries, in which they both used a feather-tipped bow as a peace symbol and shared a smoke with a cane cigarette, indicating a mingling of ceremonial cultures.

The meeting of these people with the Spaniards was friendly at first, but after Espejo had made his way to Hopi and was on his way back to the Rio Grande, he was attacked by the Querechos and the Acomas at Acoma. The Indians' assault was conducted to secure the freedom of some servants. One of them was a Querecho woman given to Francisco Barreto by a Hopi. This account indicated "that the Querechos were found from as far west as the Hopi pueblos, where Barreto had obtained the girl, to Mount Taylor," locating the Navajos, in the days of the early Spanish explorers, in the general area of Dinetah. It is also interesting to note that the trade or sale of slaves, which was endemic during this period, was engaged in by the Pueblos as well as the "wild" tribes.

It is not clear when the Navajos and their cousins the Apaches became fully differentiated, but their separation may have begun when several bands of hunter-gatherers (the Navajo forebears) dropped out of the continuing Athapaskan migration and settled into a more sedentary life of farming. In 1630, Fray Alonso de Benevides, the Custodian of Missions of New Mexico, noted two distinct groups of Apacheans; one, the "wild" group, people of the hunt who never farmed and who later became the Apaches, and the other, the "Apaches of Navajo," who were "very great farmers." The Navajos, slowly becoming more sedentary, likely had also begun to learn some of the Pueblos' astonishingly complex and colorful religious rituals. Soon, the Navajos' origin myth explained that they too emerged from previous worlds, out from Mother Earth, like the stories of their new, highly developed neighbors, the Hopis.

The Navajos were known by many names. The Hopis called them Tavusahs, or head pounders, because they killed their enemies by crushing their heads with a stone. As we have seen, the early Spanish explorers referred to various non-Pueblo bands of Indians as Querechos, or wandering Indians. Later, they adopted the Tewa word Apachu, which means enemies or strangers, to refer to the Apachean tribes. In 1626, a Franciscan friar was told by the Tewas of a people who lived between Jemez and the Utes whom they called Apaches de Navaju, from the Tewa *navahu*, a compound of *nava*, or field, and *hu*, or wide arroyo, to form a word meaning "a large arroyo in which there are cultivated fields." The Spanish then used the term to refer to the Indians living south of the San Juan River. It is not clear just how far they were dispersed, but when Coronado entered the area in 1540, it is likely the Navajos stretched south to Acoma and west to the Hopi villages, the general area of the Navajo reservation today. The Apaches de Navaju came to be known to the Spanish as the people of the "large planted fields." Benevides reported they were called this because of their farming ability (*muy grandes labradores*). The Navajos, we have seen, had a very simple name for themselves: Dine, or the People. A people in transition, the Navajos presented different faces to the foreigners they met.

The Navajos' stories, gods, and language changed as they settled in new environments and learned from the Pueblos. Yet reminders of their past in the wilds of Canada still remain in their language. The Navajo words for gourd dipper mean "horn spoon" to the Athapaskans of British Columbia. The flight of an owl is described by the Navajos with a word that in the north means to paddle a canoe. Embedded in their language are also traces of their interaction with the Pueblos: the word for corn, which they have now eaten for hundreds of years, means "food of the strangers."

Navajos today still retain customs characteristic of northern Indians. They desperately fear the dead and their possessions and will abandon a hogan in which someone has died. The Navajos practice mother-in-law avoidance, as do other Athapaskans. A traditional Navajo man will not stay in the room of his mother-in-law, nor speak to her directly. This "age-old device for keeping peace in the family" has been referred to by some as the origin of the mother-in-law joke.

By the time the Spanish arrived, however, the Navajo culture was "highly composite." Through marriage to Pueblo women taken in raids, or through intermarriage with whole clans that fled the Pueblos just after the Pueblo uprising (1680–1700), they incorporated skills of the Pueblos into their own culture. "The name Navajo, then, really applies to a mixture of northern nomads with village farmers. The culture of the group has shown what might well be thought of as hybrid vigor. On the basis of Pueblo ceremonial traits has been built a magnificent structure, using many elements from other areas and enlivening them all with a superb imagination."

As early in 1525, raiding had become a problem in the Southwest. The Spanish promised to help the Pueblos east of the Rio Grande defend themselves from raids by Apaches and Comanches. However, their presence on the scene only exacerbated the raiding. The 2,500 Spanish settlers in the New Mexico territory provided choice targets for the theft of livestock and crops. The Pueblo villages were also fine targets. Because they were required to pay tribute to Spain, they had become more productive.

The raiding problem was further complicated by the Spanish, who, desirous of labor for their farms, developed a slave trade. They provoked disagreements with the Apaches for the purpose of capturing them as slaves, and they undertook slave-hunting expeditions and bought slaves from the Apaches and Comanches whom those tribes had captured from tribes farther to the east. This stimulated further raiding and retaliatory attacks in the area.

Although the Hopis were subject to Ute and Apache raids from the north, they liked even less the entry of the Navajos, though they were farmers and more sedentary than many of the other non-Pueblo tribes. What was irritating about the Navajos was that they were moving in and, apparently, staying.

Although the Hopis like to point out their cultural superiority to the Navajos, the Hopis were at one time also hunter-gatherers, and the present Hopi culture retains many features of its hunter-gatherer past. Anthropologist Ruth Underhill notes that Hopi ceremonialism still retains vestiges of the shaman, or visionary, which is typical of hunter-gatherer societies. "The Pueblos have not discarded the . . . shaman. Instead, they have organized both the shamans and their spirit helpers into societies, which function, like their other groups, with appointed leaders and standardized ritual. Taos and Hopi, at the two ends of the Pueblo country, retain the individual shaman who, as usual, lives in the shadow of sorcery." The Hopis have "many marks of the desert food gatherer" about them.

Although Navajos and Hopis share a hunter-gatherer past, and both arrived in the Southwest after extensive migrations and interaction with other groups, they came from very different peoples and histories. The Hopis are descendants of the highly sophisticated community-living Anasazi. The Hopi clans followed different routes during their wanderings, arrived on the mesas at different times, and have different interpretations of their now collective tales and religion. These disparate people are joined together on the mesa tops by the intricate year-long ceremonial cycle that involves each village and clan as an indispensable member in the survival of all. The Hopis are essentially theocratic, governed by laws and prophecies, desiring peace, but aggressive when their way of life is threatened. They are fiercely religious, wracked by internal frictions exacerbated by a hostile climate, and always trying to repress their own physical aggression.

The Navajos are descendants of simple people with an adventuresome spirit whose relatives in the north, called Tlingit and Haida, became skilled totem and canoe builders. Other Athapaskans have joined with Eskimos by the Bering Sea, some have become associated with the Sahaptin tribes in Oregon, and still others have adopted the basketmaking and White Deer dance of the Yurok in California. Writes Underhill, "In fact, these colonizing northerners remind one of the Norsemen in the Old World, even though their travel was by land and not by sea. Over and over again, European history tells of the movements of the Scandinavians into Britain, France, or Italy. Each time, the wanderers learned the customs of the new country and took their place among its foremost citizens, as Saxons, Normans, or Varangians. So the Athapaskans of the north woods poured their vigor into Indian cultures up and down western North America."

After the Pueblo Revolt of 1680, the thousands of Pueblo Indians who joined the Navajos and Apaches to escape the Spaniards' brutal attempts at reconquest brought along with them small flocks of the sheep, goats, cattle, and horses that the Spanish had left behind. Both the Pueblo people and the livestock had a tremendous influence on the Navajo bands. It has been suggested that one fourth of the Navajo population at the end of the seventeenth century were Pueblo refugees. One anthropologist writes, "Undoubtedly, among the refugees were not only simple folk, but there must have been many highly trained Pueblo religious leaders—of secret curing associations, hunter associations, and warrior associations. Thus, regardless of possible earlier cultural contacts during the *Dinetah* phase, the greater cultural synthesis and the Puebloization of the Navajo may have taken place with the actual mingling of people. This therefore is the most probable moment in Navajo history when Apachean-Pueblo in-laws became fully acknowledged children of Mother Earth through the myth of emergence." Also, at this time, the Apachean hunter gods began to be represented as masked dancers, known to the Navajos as "Yeis," in the style of the Hopi Kachinas. It is thought that at this time the art of weaving was developed, or revived, among the Navajos.

The introduction of herd animals provided the economic basis for the cultural transformation from a hunter society to a society of herders and farmers. Today, Navajos will tell you that the Holy People gave them sheep, they are so central to their culture. To Navajos, sheep are like money in the bank. Writes Underhill, "To the Navajo, this new property which could move under its own power was a miracle—no more tedious foot journeys of a few miles a day, with the baggage carried on the backs of women! Now all the goods could be loaded on horses, and the whole family could ride, even the baby in its cradleboard hanging to the saddle. Their food, in the form of sheep, could follow behind, and so could their clothing, in the form of wool on the sheep's backs. No urban urge to town building could stand against such a mobile invitation."

With sheep, the Navajos were self-sufficient. Every bit of the sheep was (and is still) eaten—even stomachs and intestines and brains—or used for clothing and bedding. The Navajos' love for the woolly herds led them to raid the Spanish and the Pueblos for more. It is said that after raiding a flock, they made sure to leave a few ewes so the flock would grow and be ready for them to raid again in a year. The Navajos quickly learned the advantages of the horse, which increased their contacts with other groups and also generated the necessity for saddles, bridles, and ropes, which in turn increased trading needs and eventually led to the development of new crafts. For the first time, it was easy for Navajos to meet in large groups for ceremonial and political purposes.

Accompanying the growing herds of livestock between the best seasonal pastures led the Navajos to a new pattern of behavior called transhumance—a seasonal shifting between abodes. Some Navajos still are transhumant—moving with their flocks between summer and winter homes—but because of overcrowding on the reservation, most have settled down on one homesite. A common misconception about the Navajos, perhaps arising from their differences from the Pueblos and their relatively late arrival in the Southwest at a more primitive state of development, is that the Navajos are—or were, in the historical period—nomadic. Harvard anthropologist Clyde Kluckhohn made particular note of this in *The Navaho*:

> Navaho "nomadism"—at least during any historical period—is a myth, and it is most unfortunate that through popular writings this myth has become so deeply rooted in the notions which educated people have of the Navahos. The very fact that clan names are mainly place names suggests that sedentary groupings were the rule. The horse made the Navaho mobile, to be sure, but the shiftings were confined, in most cases, to well-defined areas. Once a family had moved into a new region, one or more dwellings would be built in places which became fixed centers of family life for many years. While actual buildings were often destroyed or abandoned because of deaths or for other reasons, the new ones erected would seldom be very far off. Within the range claimed by a particular family group, the number of desirable sites was limited by the necessity for protection from the weather and scarcity of wood and water.

The Navajos made full use of the livestock with which they had been blessed. They used the wool to spin yarn, which they then dyed and wove into blankets. The increased food supply allowed the population to increase, and the steady source of goods for trade and sale allowed the Navajos to purchase metal tools and enter the world of capitalist economics.

The Navajos traded meat and hides for corn and fruit from the Pueblo people, and they raided as well. The two activities were not mutually exclusive. Certain Navajo families might refrain from raiding friends or relatives in certain pueblos, but they felt no hesitancy in raiding other Pueblo neighbors.

Raiding was an economic enterprise, the purpose of which was to acquire livestock, food, and servants. It was undertaken by small groups for a particular reason. A different kind of raid was made in retaliation for prisoners taken from the Navajos. After 1700, raiding and warfare became the way of life for many of the southwest tribes. The Navajos fell prey to the Comanches and the Utes, who stole from their farm plots and also stole women and children for sale to the Spaniards. The Navajos retaliated against the Spanish, and took Spanish female captives, from whom emerged a Navajo clan called the Mexican clan. The Navajos also continued to raid Pueblo tribes, including the Hopis and the Jemez. The Navajos previously had welcomed large numbers of Jemez people into their bands and even created a new clan, the Coyote Pass clan, which was made up of Jemez women and their descendants. But even this relationship did not protect the Jemez from raids.

Although older Navajos, the "ricos" who had accumulated huge herds of sheep, tried to stop the raiding and make peace with the Spaniards, younger men trying to build up herds did not heed the advice of the older headmen. The raiding generally accelerated from the early 1700s until the United States took over the government of the region through the Treaty of Guadalupe Hidalgo in the mid-1800s. By this time, the Navajos were clearly differentiated from the Apache tribes, but were in no sense a cohesive tribe. They lived in bands of from ten to forty families, each of which had its customary territory for livestock and farming. Two or more bands might join together for a raid, but "the temporary associations resulted in no permanent wider organization."

Navajo raiding increased dramatically between 1800 and 1820, and by 1840, Navajos "ran wild" in northwest New Mexico. "Warfare had definitely begun to rise to a place of great importance in Navajo culture." The raids infuriated the white settlers in New Mexico and in retaliation, they raided the Navajos for slaves. By 1860, it is estimated that New Mexicans held 5,000 to 6,000 Navajo slaves.

Both the New Mexicans and the Pueblos were desperate to stop the Navajo raiding. At first, the United States tried to sign treaties with the Navajos. This was unsuccessful, in large measure because the Navajos had no central authority. The government soon realized that treaties signed with one headman were not binding on bands led by other men. Between 1846 and 1850, twenty thousand horses and mules, as well as eight hundred thousand sheep and cattle were reported stolen in the northwestern corner of New Mexico.

The U.S. War Department decided that something had to be done, and military posts were set up at Fort Defiance. Instead of bowing to the show of force and the Anglo alliance against them with the Utes, Zunis, Hopis, other Pueblos, and even the friendly Mount Taylor Navajos (known to other Navajos as "Enemy Navajos"), the Navajos decided to fight back. The Anglos' strength seemed to wane for a couple of years when the U.S. cavalry was diverted to the Civil War. The Navajos, unaware of the war to the east, thought they had prevailed. But the Navajos met their match in Colonel Kit Carson, and as we have seen, they returned from Bosque Redondo in 1868 a changed people.

(7)

The Tsos, Mosquito Springs

It is hard to imagine the silence near Mae Tso's hogan. It is not what you might expect—a soft quiet with rolling breezes and distant splashes of sound. Rather it is an angry silence, a deafening silence, a silence so loud you are compelled to cup your hands over your ears. For your ears hammer violently in the absence of sound, much as your eyes will fire, dark in place of light, against your eyelids if you carelessly stare at the sun.

Mae Tso lives about twenty miles northeast of Bessie Hatathlie, deep toward Tohatchie Canyon, in an area called Teesyatoh or Mosquito Springs. Her house is miles from a paved road and an hour or so from the Dinnebito Trading Post, where she goes to pick up her mail every week. Her land is as familiar to her as the faces of her eight children, for she grew up here and has herded sheep over these grasslands for almost fifty years. Her parents live nearby, as do her sisters and aunts and her grandmother, Jenny Manybeads, a bent, scant-toothed woman with long snow-white hair and almost one hundred winters under her belt. In all directions, yellow, sparse grasses grow on softly rolling land that falls, just beyond the Tsos' privy, into a steep canyon.

These days, the silence of Mae's land is frequently broken by visitors, both white and Indian. Several times a month a stranger will bump over the washboard dirt tracks that lead to her hamlet to hear what she has to say. These people are journalists, sympathetic members of Christian groups, lawyers, or do-gooders. Mae is usually sitting behind her loom under the cottonwood tree. She gets up, smiles shyly, wrings her hands, and speaks with such heartbreaking lucidity that few drive away unmoved.

Mae's ordeal began one day in 1977 when a storm blew quickly over the canyon. The horses trotted home, swinging their heads and blowing air from their nostrils as the winds built behind them. The sheep herded themselves, baaing and shaking their bells around their necks as they bumped along in a tawny, woolly herd and into their corral of twisted juniper boughs.

Mae and her husband, Askie, and their eldest daughter, Betty, were away at a relative's squaw dance. Inside the log house, three of Mae's sons, Larry, nineteen, Earl, fourteen, and Hoskie, seven, were preparing a dinner of beans with pieces of sheep fat, lazy bread, and coffee. Lazy bread is cooked in the oven, like biscuits. If their mother had been there, she would have fashioned the dough into flat round shapes and roasted them over the fire or fried them in lard. But the boys followed the easier recipe and dropped the dough in teaspoon shapes onto a pan in the oven. The stove, which sat on the dirt floor of the cabin, ran off a butane tank. Before the boys could begin to eat in the dim light of a kerosene lantern, a bolt of lightning brightened the shadowed room and the boys were knocked to the floor. Hoskie, the youngest, found himself under a bed. A rank smell of scorched wood filled their nostrils. As their eyes readjusted to the dark, they saw that their house was in a shambles. The roof and one and a half sides were gone. The rest of it lay open like a broken eggshell.

The boys were hysterical with fear, as it is taboo for Navajos to be anywhere near a lightning strike. Without thinking, they ran several miles to their grandpa's house and told him the story. He welcomed them and sat them in front of the stove, but slowly the boys realized they had done a dangerous thing. They had brought the infection of the lightning strike with them and spread it to all the people staying at their grandfather's.

Later that night, returning home from the squaw dance, Mae and Askie saw that something terrible had happened to their house. In the glare of the headlights they saw logs lying on the ground every which way. After checking for the boys, they drove to the house of Mae's father, Sam Wilson. All night the adults sat up in the round hogan and discussed what should be done. Betty, who was then nine, listened from a corner, where she lay curled up on a sheepskin beneath a blanket, frightened into silence. The family members finally fell asleep, exhausted, on sheepskins on the dirt floor, around the wood-burning stove.

The next day Mae and Askie went out in search of a medicine man to perform a sing for them. They were successful, and almost immediately they began a ceremony at the destroyed house. All the relatives were there who had been infected—Sam Wilson, his wife, Blanche, and the uncles and aunts who lived in the same camp. Betty remembers the prayers and songs lasting most of the day. The medicine man had a large bucket of plants which he set to smoldering. He carried the smoking greens past the blown-apart house and around the property. Then all the people walked through the smoke themselves.

That ceremony cleansed them of the immediate danger, but according to Navajo belief, the family was obliged to abandon the house that had received the strike. But when the Tsos applied to the Navajo Tribe for assistance in acquiring materials for a new house, they received unexpected news. They were told that they couldn't rebuild their house because the land on which they lived now belonged to their neighbors, the Hopis.

The Tsos had heard something about a law that partitioned a large rectangle of land around them between the two neighboring tribes. Public Law 93-531 had been discussed in meetings at their chapter house. But it had seemed so distant, yet another law come down from "Washindone"—the Navajo word for the District of Columbia, the government, and the Great White Father. And there weren't any Hopis living nearby, so what, the Tsos wondered, would their village-dwelling neighbors ever do with the land? But being told they couldn't rebuild their home to conform to the laws of the Holy People came as a shock to Mae, who speaks Navajo and understands only the rudimentary English she picked up at the Hardrock Mission school before she ran away from the third grade in 1945.

Mae's great-grandmother had been taken prisoner by Kit Carson and marched to Bosque Redondo. But she escaped and found her way back to relatives who were hiding near the Hopi villages. She was a member of the Flowing Water Together–Mexican clan, whose clan stories tell them they are descended from a little girl who emerged from the juncture of the San Juan and Colorado Rivers. According to the story, the spiritual people placed the clan on the area that is now Black Mesa and instructed them to be its caretakers. She married and had children and, in the Navajo way, buried the umbilical cords of her children in the ground near the sheep corral. Mae's grandmother, Jenny Manybeads, and her mother, Blanche Wilson, did the same.

As Mae contemplated her choices in rebuilding her home, she was teetering on the edge of a tangle of history in which she would become an outspoken participant. She and her family and hundreds of others would find out, in various ways, with varying degrees of accuracy, what that law created in 1974 really meant. Mae, a shy, intensely loyal and emotional woman, would become one of her people's strongest spokespersons. It would cost her her health and almost her marriage. But to Mae, the choice was clear. The land was hers and it held everything she knew. She would fight to the death.

In the years after the lightning strike in 1977, as Mae and Askie tried to replace their home, they were shown maps and pictures of the rectangle of land that President Chester A. Arthur had designated as the Hopi area one hundred years ago. And they were shown a line that had been finalized in 1977 after negotiation between the tribes, which zigzagged through the rectangle and divided it into two halves, one for Navajos and one for Hopis. They saw that their house fell on the Hopi side. This sudden division of lands between the tribes that had coexisted as long as Mae and her relatives could remember shook Mae and her family to its core. Her father said in 1978, "This dispute, what has it done? It has hurt our feelings and our hearts and our livelihoods. What are we going to live on in the future? Sometimes I sit up late at night and smoke my pipe and think about it, because it hurts all over."

The Navajo culture is matrilineal and matrilocal. Land and property pass down through female heirs, and husbands move into the wife's family after marriage. Although Navajos don't own the land they live on, each family has a "customary use area" in which they live, graze their animals, and grow crops. So the area in Tohatchie Canyon where Mae and her family live is considered hers, and is near the customary use areas of her maternal relatives. But Askie's mother lived on land that had become part of the Navajo Partition Lands (NPL). So when the tribe told Mae she couldn't rebuild on the HPL because a federal judge had issued a ban on new construction there, she decided they would try to build over on her husband's mother's land. First, they had to apply for a homesite lease. That had to be approved by the families in the area, because the Tsos would, in effect, be moving onto their customary use area. After the homesite lease was approved and the Tsos again applied for assistance to the tribe for building materials, Percy Deal, a clan relative of the Tsos and a chapter official, told them that since they were planning to leave the HPL, they should apply for relocation benefits, authorized as part of the 1974 Act to qualifying families. A modern house would be built for them by the newly formed Navajo and Hopi Indian Relocation Commission. The Tsos thought about it and decided to go ahead and apply for relocation benefits.

Meanwhile, the family was still living in a small hogan, and the log cabin they had rebuilt from the one that had been struck by lightning. But they weren't supposed to be anywhere near the lightning strike and they felt increasing pressure to move. The house they had rebuilt was made of the lightning-damaged logs and others that were rotting. The house was not sturdy and the family was afraid it might collapse in high winds. The Tsos decided not to wait for the relocation house. Pride was a part; they didn't want to go to the government for help. They decided to build a hogan themselves. They hauled materials over to the area of their homesite lease on the NPL. Between tending a cornfield at home, and Askie's work assignments for the Santa Fe Railroad, they began to build. But as soon as they put part of the walls up, someone tore them down. After repairing the damage, the Tsos returned to their new homesite and found their materials scattered. They took this as a sign they were not wanted. Even though the people who were most likely tearing down the house were Askie's relatives, the Tsos decided to heed the warnings that they were not welcome. "We would have been like a road sign," says Betty. "We would have been just sitting there like a road sign that you can see from a distance. The people would have looked upon us like we were intruders. We would be taking up space where their livestock would have been."

The Navajo Tribe has sixteen million acres of reservation land, a chunk about the size of a medium-size state, and during the many debates in Congress over how to resettle the Navajos who found themselves on Hopi land, there was much talk of all the free land available for them to be resettled on. There was in fact very little land on the reservation that was habitable and not already claimed. Said anthropologist David Aberle before the House Indian Subcommittee, "I think it is important to keep in mind that the Navajo Reservation is a paradox. It is an area of low population density which is severely overcrowded and has been for decades. The kind of free land that has been talked about simply does not exist." Because of the poor condition of the land, many hundreds of acres are needed to support even a few livestock. And in the remote areas of the disputed land, livestock is still a major economic activity. Although the actions of Askie's relatives seem uncharitable, they reflect the family's knowledge that the balance they had struck with survival was fragile, and likely threatened if another family moved onto their grazing land.

So the Tsos decided to build a new hogan back on their original property. A hogan is a symbol of all that is Navajo. The hemispheric hogan represents the shape of the Navajo universe—that is, the land between their four sacred mountains. "The hogan has four main posts, which represent the four sacred mountains," Mae explains. "The two doorway posts represent two other mountains [Huerfano Mountain and Gobernador Knob]. The top of the hogan represents the Father Sky. The bottom part is Mother Earth. Between these two are all living things. In the middle of the hogan is a place for the fire. In our ceremony, all our songs and prayers are within the hogan. Because the hogan represents all creations, all the teachings are also there."

Following the Navajo rule that a house hit by lightning must be rebuilt away from the strike, the Tsos built the new hogan a little way north of their camp. They made it a modern-type hogan, with cinder blocks on the bottom and logs on top. They had only started when Navajo tribal officials came by and told them they were not allowed to construct any new dwellings in the area.

But the Tsos continued. They didn't know what else to do. The demands of the growing family and the rules of their gods were in conflict with the new law from "Washindone." Soon, Mae started receiving official letters in the mail, telling her to stop the construction. One day, when Mae was away from home attending a school board meeting, the Navajo Tribe came and tore down the structure.

It is a day that is not spoken of by the Tsos. Betty believes her father was at home at the time, but has never asked him directly. "I think from the beginning, my father wasn't sure what to do. He believed that the law was the law but it was a horrible way of taking someone's possession, and [relocation] was a horrible way of dealing with someone." Her father never spoke of the day when officials from his own tribe came to dismantle his house.

Soon afterward, Mae went down to Tucson to a trial. She and several ladies from Big Mountain were being sued for violating restrictions insisted upon by the Hopis. Mae was confused in Tucson—all the streets bewildered her, as did the substance of the proceedings. She and the other women were represented by the Navajo Tribe. And they all lost. When Mae returned from Tucson, she was ill for several months. She had pains in her chest and headaches. Betty blames the Navajo Tribe. "My mother was sick for a long time. The Navajo Tribe hurt their own people that way, mentally."

The Tsos' housing situation wasn't getting any better. Mae and Askie had eight children and one of their eldest boys had a wife and baby; they were all crowded into one hogan and the damaged log cabin. Askie again decided they would take matters into their own hands. It had been six years since the lightning strike. "Our roof was leaking," says Betty, "and the logs where it was in the ground were rotting. Sooner or later it would have just fallen over or collapsed in. So for those reasons, we just went ahead with the construction without the approval of both tribes. When my parents were first talking about constructing the new house, they were going to defend it whether it was from the Navajo Tribe or the Hopi Tribe, whoever came by. Because there was no way we could continue to live in our old hogan and our log cabin. It was not safe."

In the summer of 1983, they all moved into the log house and they tore the hogan down. They rebuilt it again with cinder blocks at the bottom to prevent rotting and logs on top. It is octagonal and approximately twenty-five feet in diameter. It has a dirt floor and glass windows. They moved the structure a few feet to the south, just to avoid the termites and ants that had lived in the base of the old hogan. Officials from both tribes carefully observed this work. Betty says, "At the beginning, they used to park a little ways from us and take pictures and not even come up to the house and ask us anything. Then, after a while, they started coming up to the house and telling us not to build our house. And then they would take pictures of it."

Percy Deal came over and said to Askie, "Uncle, you are breaking the law. Tear down your house." The two are clan uncles. The Navajos usually identify relatives by their clan affiliation rather than their blood tie. And Askie replied, "Uncle, why should I tear down my house? The old one was not safe to live in. Where shall I put my family?" They continued the work. Askie bought new materials and salvaged as much as he could from the old cabin. His brothers and nephews helped with the construction.

By this time the idea of moving had become unthinkable. Mae's family had lived in the same area for five generations. Worse, Mae had now seen tragedy befall relatives who had ignored their Navajo ways and moved from their land. Mae's sister and brother-in-law Coleen and Hugh Yazzie relocated to Flagstaff, lost their house, and had been reduced to begging for help. Unacquainted with taxes, electricity, and water bills that built up without ceasing, with uncertain income and none of the backup systems the reservation offered during tough times, the Yazzies fell increasingly into debt. Coleen worked as a maid. Her husband lost his job after he started drinking heavily. They eventually gave their relocation house to an unscrupulous real estate agent who traded it for a rental interest in a Utah property and some cash. The agent had purchased many relocation houses from troubled Navajos in the same way. The Navajos, completely unfamiliar with deeds or mortgages or partial ownership, were as helpless as sheep led to slaughter. The Tsos felt that relocating must be wrong if it led their relatives to such an unspeakable end. For not only had the Yazzies sold their land—the government actually hung signs on vacated hogans reading PROPERTY U.S. GOVERNMENT —but they had also lost what the government had given them in compensation, and were now homeless.

So accepting a relocation house had become out of the question for the Tsos. They were convinced that relocation would ruin them. The whole idea made no sense, and it conjured fears of a huge void, sadness, loneliness, and sheep hunger. Mae's friend Pauline Whitesinger puts it this way: "In our traditional tongue there is no word for relocation. To move away means to disappear and never be seen again."

In August 1985, Mae sits on a steel-springed double bed in her one-room house. Betty sits beside her and absently strokes her mother's hands. To the right of the bed is a Formica table and chairs and a small stove that runs off bottled gas. Extra-large sacks of flour, potatoes, and dry cat food are propped on the floor. The Tsos joke they are the only family on the reservation that buys food for their cats. Unlike most reservation felines, which are half-dead balls of bones and fur, the Tsos' cats are sleek and muscular.

A red cooler rests on the table. It holds perishables, though it functions only if a visitor happens to bring some ice or cold sodas. On a chair near the front door is a bar of soap and a pan of murky water that serves as a washbasin for the family for the day. The floor is dirt.

In the other half of the house, shelves and trunks separate sheepskin pallets on which the children sleep. The Tsos are relatively well off, since Askie has a job with the track maintenance crew of the Santa Fe Railroad.

And Mae is an accomplished weaver and her rugs fetch good prices. Yet even Navajos with steady incomes live in conditions that Anglos would find quite inadequate—entire families in a single room, most sleeping on the floor, no electricity or running water. Most Navajos, however, feel that a small house or hogan is perfectly suited to life on the range; it is easy to heat. And for people whose schedules are governed by their flocks—early to bed, early to rise—it is not important to stay up late with the aid of electric lights. In fact, many older Navajos cannot stand sleeping in multiroom houses. They have been soothed within the womblike hogans for their entire lives. The angular shapes of houses and furniture unsettle them.

But younger Navajos, who have lived in boarding schools or off the reservation with Anglo families, sometimes find the return from modern life difficult. Mae's son Earl has improvised by hooking up an old black and white television to the battery of the pickup truck. His favorite program is "Miami Vice," which he rushes home to watch on Friday nights. The cement hogan, in which Earl and his brother Sam sleep, is dominated by the television, a huge boom box, and a collection of heavy-metal tapes.

Askie is away with the railroad; he is usually gone for six or seven weeks at a time. The youngest children are at school. This house, which the family started last year, after rebuilding the hogan, still needs a ceiling, floor, and insulation. The outside is finished only with tar paper. When they have the money, the Tsos will add outside boards and a floor. However, it will likely stand as it is for years. Mae leans back upon pillows fluffed up against the round metal headboard. Earl and Sam wander in and out of the house and eventually sit on the bed, leaning against her protectively. Sam is strikingly handsome and wears dark aviator glasses. He is spending most of his time at the Big Mountain survival camp, a shack built near the sun dance grounds to house visitors and young men like him who are devoted to fixing it up, walking patrols, and warning locals of intruders like BIA vans or Hopi police. Earl stays at home and minds the sheep and the horses. His wife left him recently and took their young son and daughter with her. Earl has struggled with alcohol problems. His face is perpetually fixed in an angry scowl.

Mae wears a simple blouse pinned at the neck with a turquoise brooch, pleated skirt, and sturdy shoes. She has darkened, oval-shaped glasses and her long black hair is pulled into a tsiyeel. The dusk is falling and the light in the house is dim. Mae speaks quietly in Navajo. She pushes stray strands of hair back into place and smiles painfully, shyly. Sometimes she looks at the floor. At other times, she gets excited and cuts half-moon shapes in the air to illustrate her words. Then she pins her hands together in her lap, and looks up with a girlish expectancy. The children listen quietly. When Mae has finished, Betty begins to translate into English.

One day in 1983, Betty narrates, Mae was home weaving under the tree beside their house. Askie was back from the railroad, resting beside her on a blanket, leaning against the house. At the time, they were still living in the log cabin that had been struck by lightning. They had seen their first attempts to build a hogan over on the NPL scuttled by self-protective relatives. And they had watched the fruits of their second attempt pulled down by the Navajo Tribe. However, their new hogan was almost completed. All it needed was a roof, and no one from either tribe had tried to stop them this time. Timothy and Calvin, Mae's youngest boys, were out herding sheep. The older children were at school or at work. The day was peaceful, the sun high, and the quiet comforting to Mae, who finds it difficult to tolerate the noise of Flagstaff or Winslow for even a day's shopping.

As Mae was weaving, one of the boys appeared at the hogan, out of breath, shouting, so Mae could hardly understand him. "They took the horses," he said. "The horses are loaded in the trailers. The police took the horses." Mae and Askie jumped into their truck and raced to the area where the boys had been. They caught sight of a police vehicle and a livestock truck ahead, and they chased them over the dirt track, then to the graded road, and finally to the tar road. At Howell Mesa, near the Hatathlies', Mae and Askie pulled in front of the trucks and forced them to stop. Mae shouted at the officers and the officers shouted back, but the three Indians in police uniforms all spoke different languages and none understood Navajo. Mae says one of them, a woman, came over and pulled Mae from her truck. Mae was shouting, "Why are you taking the horses?" but no one could understand. In frustration, Mae stood in front of the police truck and lifted the hood. She shouted in Navajo, over and over, asking them where they were taking her horses. Then, Mae says, one of the officers showed her his badge and shoved her out of the way. The stock trailer then drove off past them. In fury, Mae grabbed the female officer by the hair. Askie shouted at her to let go and tried to untwine her fingers. Mae then tried to kick the officer. She picked up a handful of dirt, threw it in the woman's face, and shouted, "If you really wanted the land, you wouldn't wipe the dirt from your face." The woman, whom Mae assumed was Hopi, didn't understand a word that Mae said, and wiped the dirt from her eyes.

The two other officers in the truck surrounded Mae. Mae shouted at Askie to get back in their pickup and go home to the kids. They tried to grab him, but he ran to the truck and got away. The two male officers grabbed Mae. She fought back. "They were so big and fat," she said. She twisted her arm and pulled away. But one of them hit her in the back and she fell down to the ground and blacked out. Mae was forty-six when this happened two years ago. She still gets a pain in her back, she says today.

When she came to, they put her in the truck. One, whom she thought was a Papago, sat next to her and sat on her skirt. He kept pushing against her, and she was furious at him for sitting so close. They took her to the Hopi village of Oraibi and then transferred her to a patrol car, which took her to the jail at Keams Canyon. They took her glasses away from her and told her to take off her hair tie, but she refused. She wouldn't tell them her name, but they found it on a scrap of paper in her pocket. They brought her before an investigator and he told her she'd done wrong to the government. It was a white man, a BIA law enforcement officer. He kept asking her to tell him why she did what she did. "Why do you attack your government?" "Why do you act disrespectfully to your government?" "Why do you break the law?" She replied that she'd been pleading for years with her own tribal government in an attempt to save her land, her home, her memories. Her own people would not help her. Why should she speak to him?

She refused to answer his questions and they took her back to her cell and gave her jail clothes, which included pants. She told them that all her life she'd been taught to wear skirts. A Navajo kept saying to her, "Take off your skirt." She just looked at him. Then he started yelling at her to change her clothes. She finally told him to be quiet, that his mother wore a skirt too. He gave up and walked away, muttering that she must be mentally retarded.

Meanwhile, Askie had gone to his aunt's house and made a phone call to Percy Deal. Percy called the jail and spoke to Mae. After she told him her story, she was taken back to her cell. She had a lot on her mind. She still had a sharp pain in her back and her heart ached. She felt that her heart must be broken. She thought about the people on the land, then the officials. She thought of the elderly people and Barry Goldwater, whom she saw as the evil wind behind the law. How would other people handle this if it happened to them, she wondered. What about the widows? She thought how she pleaded with the leaders against relocation. She went to meetings against relocation. She went to meetings about relocation. She tried to offer alternative ideas. She thought of how she fought to make things better. By resisting, she was put in jail. She had pleaded with the leaders before acting on her own and it hadn't worked. Now she was fighting back. At that point, Mae started hearing things and then she fainted.

When she woke up, she was in the hospital. She heard someone calling her name. She saw a doctor and nurses and two nurse's aides. She was still furious. "Why don't you just leave me there?" she yelled at them. "Why didn't you just eat me?" A Navajo nurse tried to soothe her. She told Mae they were there to help her, they weren't tribal officials. Mae calmed down and they gave her an IV. The doctor stayed with her. She spent the night there and a man—a doctor or nurse, she didn't know—stayed with her the whole night. The next day she felt stronger, but they gave her medication that made her drowsy. They told her she had suffered a heart attack.

Eventually, an officer came by and told her she had to go back to jail. Before she left, she was given a couple of shots, tranquilizers, she thought. Then she left with the officers without handcuffs. She felt numb. She heard ringing in her ears. Her eyes were dry and she was really sleepy. Back at the police station she was taken to a room with a table in it. She fell asleep, slumped against the table. Someone came by later to take her to a hearing. She saw Percy there. She couldn't hear anything, could only see people's mouths moving. She left with Percy and got her things back from the jailkeeper.

Percy drove her home. When she got close, she could see the horses out grazing near the house. She was so relieved she fell asleep in the truck. They didn't disturb her, left her sleeping in the truck. Larry, Mae's eldest son, a police officer in Tuba City, rounded up the kids from school and brought them home. They stayed with Mae for a week until she felt well enough to do her chores. Sam, who was working at Basha's Supermarket in Tuba City, went home also. Slowly she got stronger and felt better. Today, she is relieved that the rangers haven't returned. "Maybe they're ashamed," says Mae. "They should be."

The Tsos do not have livestock permits for their horses, so the BIA was attempting to impound them for being illegal animals on the range. The Tsos feel that they should not be required to pay for permits for animals that were given to them by the Holy People and which the Navajos were instructed by their gods to take care of. Says Mae, "When the BIA shows us that they make the rains fall and the grass grow, then we'll consider paying them for livestock permits."

The incidents with the horses and the tearing down of their hogan have made the Tsos militant resisters of relocation. "We're going to stay," says Mae. "We'll see what the outcome will be." Mae doesn't understand why the Hopis want the land, nor does she believe the tales of marauding Navajos. "There was no trouble between the two tribes," she says. "I pity them for what is happening today, but I still love my friends who are Hopi. We know people, Hopis, who live in the villages. They don't like the relocation, but they don't know how to stop it. There is a woman, a medicine woman from Oraibi, who told us not to move, she was a Holy Lady, Mina Lansa. I attended meetings at David Monongye's house where I heard of Mina Lansa's words." Mae feels that the traditional people of both tribes know that relocation is not the answer to their problems. Mae feels that the white culture, as it has influenced both tribal councils, is making the Indian people forget their ways and their own laws and tempting them with the fruits of the modern world, which she rejects. "I haven't broken any laws," she says. "We have our own laws, the laws of the people between the four sacred mountains, so I am not afraid. I have faith that God will look out for us."

Mae doesn't think about politics or tactics. She knows simple truths. About this she speaks plainly. She told her daughter later, "Our Creator has placed us here on the land even before the white man came. The Creator placed us without boundaries. There was no such thing as Navajo or Hopi land. We were all placed to live in balance with every living being; everything that was created on Mother Earth. Life is a circle. Our roots are way down deep and how can you pull someone's culture, their way of life, their religion out; when you try to do that by relocating the people, our relatives, they suffer in many ways. When you have relocated our relatives, you have taken them away from who they are, what they are made of. The young children, both male and female—who's going to teach them about how the Dine people have emerged on Mother Earth? Who's going to tell them the meaning of Mother Earth? How will our stories, our teachings, be passed on to the future generations? Because of these things, we have chosen not to relocate."

Night has grown about the Tsos' house. The sky reaches down about it like a huge hogan, a gigantic womb. The stars are so bright, so large, and so numerous it seems they must tumble in the windows, into the canyon, onto the animals. The sheep rumble and patter in the corral, the rooster pecks at anyone tramping to the privy, the horses are tied to a tree.

Two visitors arrived, earlier in the day, along with lawyer Lee Phillips, to see Mae. Part of the underside of their rented car was ripped from its moorings as the car bucked over the rough dirt roads. They investigated the damage and tied the damaged part to the engine with a bicycle book strap.

On the way to Mae's, the visitors stopped at the grocery in Kykotsmovi for some food to bring as a gift. They bought a chicken and some beef ribs, tomatoes, cucumbers, and cans of soda pop. After speaking with Mae about the land dispute the guests bring out the food they have brought and begin to prepare it. They want to clean the chicken and they ask Betty for some water. They are puzzled when she brings a small bowl of water. They dip the chicken pieces into the bowl, wiggle them around, ask for more water. Betty brings another bowl. The process goes on and she is asked for another bowl, which she brings, looking tenser each trip. The visitors turn the chicken over in the bowls, the fat and skin and water making a greasy slop. Then the visitors, who have taken over the kitchen with great enthusiasm—to their credit, they want to provide a feast to this family who has moved them so much with their words— suggest they broil the chicken and ribs over a flame. Betty and her brothers speak in Navajo. Time passes. No wood is brought. After some small talk, Betty pulls Lee Phillips aside. He returns to the house and tells the visitors that the Tsos are out of firewood. He suggests that Betty fry the chicken in lard. The visitors, slowly sensing they are disrupting the order here, back off. Betty quickly heats up a fry pan and cooks the chicken. The ribs are put aside for another day. The cucumbers and tomatoes are sliced.

The food is eaten quickly. After the meal, the room feels crowded, and the visitors hardly seem to fit. Earl and Sam walk outside and over to the hogan. In a few minutes, the sounds of drumming and the eerie wail of chanting float across the grasses. The visitors walk out into the sweet summer air. All around them are soft shadows and far-reaching darkness. They make their way to the hogan by the light of the moon and the fist-size stars. They peer in the door. In the golden light of a kerosene lamp, they see the boys sitting close to one another, legs crossed, the drum between them. Earl beats a regular, furious beat, and the two sing. They appear lost in their chants, haunting songs of times long gone. The visitors listen for several minutes, then step away, letting the flap fall silently across the hogan door.

They return to the house, beneath the rich, bright sky, breathing deeply of the full air. Lee Phillips steps out and whispers to them that the Tsos have run out of water. In a rush, they realize why the washing of the chicken was so difficult, and caused such an odd feeling. They hurry to their car, remove two gallon containers of water, and bring them inside the house. They decide it is time to go, tonight, before they further disturb this world they know so little about.

Fall 1985

We original native people know
what the supreme law of the land
is. It is the Great Spirit. It is not
written down. Hopi people don't
want fencing, they don't want livestock permits. Those laws are from
Washington. I tell white people
across the country that this is their
law, from their congressmen.
"With your taxes and your votes,"
I tell them, "you are doing this to
us." It is like a hatchet. This is a
genocide bill. We have no place to
go. If the bill goes, the land will fall
to mineral development. If this
happens, we will all find ourselves
with our bedrooms on our backs.
The law is doing this to all native
peoples.

—THOMAS BANYACYA, HOPI

(8)

The Hatathlies and
the Old Ways

Jack Hatathlie laces up his shoes at the kitchen table. He is preparing to
return to his job at the Navajo Power Plant in Page, about a hundred
miles northwest of Coal Mine Mesa, where he has worked as a custodian
for fifteen years. The Navajo plant (some call it un-Navajo) is one of two
huge generating stations that burn coal mined from Black Mesa, a towering tabletop of piñon and juniper that encloses nineteen billion tons of
coal. The 1,500-foot-high mesa is sacred to traditional Hopis and Navajos,
who fought unsuccessfully to keep it from being strip-mined.

Jack has held wage jobs for many years. He worked for the Santa Fe
Southern Pacific Railroad as a member of the track crew; he worked at
the Navajo Army Depot in Bellemont, Arizona, digging bunkers; and
now he works at Page. He has lived apart from his family for extended
periods. When he was assigned to track crews in Needles, California, he
was away from home for periods up to six months. When he worked in
Flagstaff, he found a little house on the south side of town in which he
could stay with his family during the week. They returned to the reservation for weekends.

Even before the recent livestock reductions made on the HPL at the
insistence of the Hopis, Jack knew he couldn't support his family on
livestock alone. Although some Navajos in other parts of the reservation
—who are not subject to such severe restrictions—manage to subsist
with livestock and the food they grow in their cornfields, it has been
almost sixty years since a million Navajo sheep roamed over the Southwest and provided the Navajo with a good income.

Livestock provide food and wool for clothing, and they are a highly
liquid asset; but livestock are also family. Children are given animals at
birth, and no matter how many months or years later, they will be able
to pick their sheep and goats out from the rest of the herd. Sheep are
butchered for ceremonies or sold for money, and Navajos remember

each and every transaction, whose sheep was chosen and for what purpose. And herds reflect the family, because they are composed of animals belonging to the family members. The sight of a herd has a consistent and profound effect on Navajos; one is hard-pressed to find a Navajo who doesn't break into a delighted smile at the sight of a sheep herd.

During the 1930s, hundreds of thousands of horses, cattle, and sheep were killed or transported off the reservation by the U.S. government in an attempt to reduce erosion and prevent the development of another dust bowl. Navajo livestock had increased from 20,000 sheep in 1868 to over a million in 1928. (The human population had grown from 15,000 to 40,000 in the same period.) By 1940, the livestock had been reduced to 620,000, and by 1952, to 433,000. Anthropologist David Aberle calculated the loss as follows: "In percentage terms, Navajos had lost 80 percent of their per capita holdings if 1930 is used as a base."

The government agents paid for stock that could not be consumed, but in a particularly grisly episode, they shot 3,500 goats and let them rot in the sun rather than bear the expense of transporting them off the reservation. It was a desecration to the Navajos, who believed the overgrazing had nothing to do with an overabundance of animals, but was simply the result of insufficient rain. And they were convinced the rains weren't coming because the people had disobeyed their gods by selling their sheep. "Before stock reduction, it rained all the time," one man recalled. "There was a lot of livestock everywhere, and it rained and rained. Then, when [Indian Commissioner] John Collier put a blockade on livestock, the rain ceased altogether. Before that you could see livestock everywhere, and it rained continuously. You could see the golden blossoms of sunflowers growing for miles and miles around. Much grass grew. Pigweed grass grew thickly everywhere you looked."

John Collier underestimated the psychological impact the livestock reductions would have on the Navajos, but later wrote, "In my long life of social effort and struggle, I have not experienced among any other Indian group, or any group whatsoever, an anxiety-ridden and anguished hostility even approaching to that which the Navajos were undergoing." Former tribal chairman Sam Ankeah, who served between 1946 and 1954, called the livestock reductions of the 1930s "the most devastating experience in [Navajo] history since the imprisonment at Fort Sumner."

Jack is a responsible man. He does not drink, and has not since he was a young man and got drunk at a squaw dance and fell asleep by a campfire. During the night, he rolled onto the fire and burned his back. He shows the scars to his children and grandchildren and warns them against the evils of alcohol. He shows them the scars on his back and calls them the stains of wine.

Jack has worked in strange places and with white people for most of his life, yet he feels at home in only one place, Coal Mine Mesa. His salary, $24,000, makes his family income five times higher than most of those who live near him, even though it supports as many as fifteen people. Nevertheless, it is difficult for him to live all week around a blasting, belching plant whose operation violates many of his beliefs about the land. During the week in Page, he works the night shift, plays an occasional game of cards with some other Navajos, and returns to a small trailer. Sometimes, he keeps a horse there to ride. "When I come home from Page," he says in Navajo, "I eat and sleep a lot better. I visit people, I haul wood and water, bring the horses back in the mornings. I keep myself busy all the time and I don't notice the time until I have to go back to work. I've spent so many years working at Page, and I still haven't gotten used to being away from home."

Bessie sets some stew before him. He soaks a piece of roasted bread in the broth. "My umbilical cord is buried here on the land near Crow Spring. It is buried in a sheep corral. It was buried in a sheep corral so that I would like and make a living with livestock. I used to herd sheep a lot when I was young. All the boys are like that. We also, as parents, did that for our children. Some of their umbilical cords are buried in the sheep corral. Only one of them, his umbilical cord is tied to a horse's tail. As for a girl, her umbilical cord is buried where the loom is standing. This is done so she will like and work at the loom."

Jack and Bessie believe they will not survive away from their land. "We belong here," says Jack, matter-of-factly. "Our way of life is here. Maybe if we tell them about our way of life, maybe they'll understand us. They should try to understand native people. All native people have their own teachings and way of life."

Jack and Bessie make daily offerings to the sun and to the earth. When Bessie gathers a plant to make dye for her wool, she offers a prayer in exchange. When she and Jack leave Coal Mine and pass over the Little Colorado, she makes an offering to assure them of a safe journey. In making these offerings, she communicates with the gods. The offering places are channels to the Holy People, and as she visits the places, the gods keep track of her. The gods can't hear her from just anywhere. She believes that in different areas of the reservation there are different gods, and if she should move from her home, she would lose touch with the gods that have guided her throughout her life. In a new place, the gods might not hear her at all. Jack says, "Our offering places are sacred to us, and the spiritual beings take care of us. By performing our ceremonies and offerings we are allowed to die of old age. That's how it was before us; our forefathers are buried here on this land. Why should we leave them behind? If we leave our offering places and our burial sites we will not be able to survive. We know what the land is like, the spiritual beings know us here. If we go away from here we'll die of loneliness and hunger. We won't be able to eat or sleep."

Jack is ready to head back to Page. He rises and walks to his truck. He blows the horn to scatter the goats gathered in front of his vehicle. Felix appears over the hill on horseback, chasing the other horse to the corral.

Jack reaches the end of the rutted drive and turns onto Highway 264 just as his twenty-eight-year-old daughter Genny drives in. Genny lives with her twin three-year-old sons, Toshone and Alshone, on the Northern Arizona University campus in Flagstaff, a hundred miles south, while she finishes up a degree in social work. She beeps the horn of her beat-up green pickup and waves. Genny pulls up in front of the house and the twins jump out. Toshone grabs one of the sheepdog puppies and carries it into the house upside down. Alshone runs like a dervish after a duck with a piece of rope he finds on the grass.

Genny's brother Glenn sits on a box in front of the three-quarter-ton flatbed which Bessie uses to haul water. He is installing new brake pads. Next to him on the ground is a brake kit he bought for $140. He has lost some of the parts, but he can't afford to buy a new kit. He stares at the brakes, trying to figure out how to fix them.

Behind the house are other car bodies, one on blocks, others working their way into the earth. Alshone and Toshone play under a camper shell. They are pretending to run a peyote meeting. Alshone beats on the bottom of a baby seat with a stick and lets out a quavering wail. The twins burst into hysterical giggles. They run crazily to the sheep corral, swinging their sticks, chasing after the goats nearby. They tie each other up with rope and play horse and rider, then they take off for the outhouse. Alshone goes inside and closes the door. Toshone pulls down his pants and crouches against the outside wall. When he is done, he shows off his production and picks up the puppy sitting nearby, which has so far survived the twins' assault by going limp as a rag doll.

Genny finds her mother on one of the sofas, suffering through another migraine headache. She leads Bessie into her bedroom and onto the steel-springed bed. There are two bureaus and a loom in the room, and the wall over the bed is hung with graduation pictures of her children, a beaver skin, and several medicine bags. Genny massages her mother's head and neck and speaks to her soothingly in Navajo.

Bessie's daughter Ella is also here, and she walks over to her mother's bureau, opens a drawer and gently lifts out some eagle feathers mounted into beaded handles. "This one's my dad's," she says, lifting up a grand feather that he uses for peyote ceremonies. "The eagle is the bird that flies higher than all the others and closer to the gods," says Ella. "So it is the most sacred, and it brings messages to the gods with its feathers." She lifts up some smaller feathers. "These belong to my brothers. And this is a grandfather peyote button." She opens a small silver box and reveals a hard round peyote button. Ella walks over to the closet and takes down a painted box. "We got this from a friend who is a Pacific Northwest Indian. He made it for us. These are my mom's." Inside are three turquoise brooches, rings, and a necklace. "The gods told Navajos to wear turquoise so they could recognize them," she says. Ella touches the jewelry and carefully puts it away. These things are the family riches, but their value lies in their religious significance. The feathers are used for formal ceremonies and informal blessings, as when Jack blessed his truck before setting off to find the medicine man. The peyote button is a symbol, not unlike a rosary for Catholics. And the turquoise is an identification as well as a sign of wealth and blessing.

"My mom used to tell us that when there was a fog in the winter not to run around and make a lot of noise because Mother Earth and the Creator were mating," says Ella. "And in the springtime, the Earth would give birth to beautiful plants and flowers. And she taught us that a man should take care of his wife like the Creator takes care of Mother Earth. He should decorate her with turquoise and shell like Mother Earth is decorated with flowers in the spring."

Ella turns to leave, points out one more thing, her mother's closet. "That's where my mom keeps her skirts," she says. "The kids aren't supposed to mess around in there, but Brenda often sits in there reading. She's there whenever she's not in the outhouse practicing her flute."

Ella hears the sound of an engine by the road. She walks outside. A yellow school bus stops at the end of the Hatathlies' driveway, and Brenda, Levonne, and Budge debark and head up the drive, their books pressed to their chests, like schoolgirls anywhere, wearing high-top sneakers and jeans. The twins run toward them screaming, dragging the puppy. Budge scolds them half seriously, then bursts into laughter. Her pregnancy is now quite apparent. She and Levonne both have easy smiles and deep dimples. Bessie calls Budge "the strong type" because of her sturdy build and strength. Levonne is a sylph and naturally drawn to children. She lifts Toshone high in the air. All three girls are exceptionally beautiful, with bright eyes, lips so precise they seem cut from marble, fine, straight noses. Alshone runs up to Brenda and manages to irritate her instantly. She runs off to the house and into her mother's closet.

Genny is still massaging her mother. She has been at it for over an hour. Bessie gestures toward a black leather handbag and Ella passes it to her. Bessie pulls out an envelope with a return address of the U.S. Government Bureau of Indian Affairs. She hands it to Ella. Ella opens it, reads it carefully, then translates. She tells her mother that the letter states she has two days to pay $106 for her livestock permit. The permit allows her six goats, four cattle, and two horses. They speak in Navajo.

Bessie tells Ella she has already gone to the Coal Mine Mesa chapter house to seek an extension.

Each of the 109 chapters on the Navajo reservation has a name, a meeting place or chapter house, chapter officials, and delegates to the Navajo Tribal Council, which meets in Window Rock and is the tribe's governing body. The chapter meetings are like town meetings, the chapter houses like community centers, with showers, meeting rooms, and offices for the chapter officials, who look after the needs of the people of their chapter. Money is also distributed by the tribe into programs through the chapter houses, such as ten-day weaving projects, irrigation projects, or fruit tree plantings.

The Coal Mine Mesa chapter house is very close to Bessie's land and directly adjacent to the Hopi ranger station, where the Hopis keep their eye out for unpermitted livestock and illegal Navajo home repair, so it is hard for the Hatathlies to remain out of the Hopis' sight. Bessie has also gone to see Larry Nez, a neighbor and a Princeton graduate who works for the tribal government. He was not able to help her get an extension either. Ella hands back the letter. It carries a cheerful red poinsettia stamp. Because Bessie is unfamiliar with the poinsettia and its significance as a symbol of Christmas, she misses the irony of its appearance on her letter from the BIA.

As Genny rubs her mother's head and neck, Bessie rolls her eyes. She wears thick glasses that exaggerate her prominent cheekbones. She looks exhausted. She puts the letter back into her handbag. In the bag is a thick wad of letters tied up with a rubber band. They are all letters from the government. They mean nothing to her until her children translate them for her, and even then, most often, they make no sense.

"I think my mother has really changed since five years," Ella observes. "I don't see her the way she used to be when we were growing up. My mother used to sing all the time. A lot of people used to call her the singing lady. When she was weaving, especially, she would sing songs about growing up or herding sheep. She would sing about horses, she would sing squaw dance social songs, she would sing her weaving songs. When she was herding sheep, too, she would sing all the time. When she was teaching me how to track horses or get the horses together in one place, she would sing all the time while I was following her. Sometimes she went after the sheep in the afternoons and I stayed home with the kids. I got lonely sometimes and I climbed up on top of the summer shack. Pretty soon, I'd hear her singing. And then I knew she was pretty near.

"Maybe it's because of relocation. She hardly shows expression anymore. She doesn't laugh like she used to. Sometimes, way into the night she'll be sitting in the living room spinning wool, thinking about something."

Bessie has lost the largest asset she had to pass on to her children: land and animals. Sometimes she cries thinking about having nothing to give to Ella, her heir. From her own mother she received a large flock. But now she has nothing to pass on, nothing to give her children for the future. With a flock of six sheep, she can't even butcher a sheep when her children come home. The animals are now pets. One little goat lost its mother a few months ago, and Bessie bottle-fed it. It followed her all around the house and slept curled up on the couch. Jack thought the kid was crazy thinking it was human, and he chased it out of the house when he came home. It stood at the door and cried, and when Bessie walked by, it took a piece of her skirt in its mouth and followed her. Bessie did nothing to keep it out of the house. It lay beside her when she wove. Then, one day, as suddenly as its mother had died, the little goat was stolen, or disappeared. No one knows who took it, a Navajo or a Hopi.

"Sometimes I see my mom wandering up on the hill and sometimes she'll be over by the corral, and the sheep aren't there," says Ella. "The few goats we have left will be wandering around the house. She goes to the places where the sheep used to gather, where they used to sleep. And I think she thinks about these things when she's out there. Now, it seems that she's got nothing to hope for. All the things that she taught us are gone. Gone with the sheep."

Bessie raised Ella, her firstborn, in the traditional Navajo way—herding sheep, tracking horses, weaving, making bread, and cooking mutton stew. Today, after spending her high school years living with a Mormon family in California, then returning to the reservation with her first boy, Kimo, after his father was killed flying a plane in the Vietnam War, she is a few credits away from a college degree at Northern Arizona University. Ella, at thirty-three, has accomplished what few Indians have. She lives and excels in the white world, yet she remains devoted to her parents, her home on the reservation, and the old ways. She must make compromises, however. Because she wants her children to receive good educations in white schools, they are not learning their own language. But the children—Buzz, twelve, Nell, six, and Kimo, fifteen—still feel a great tie to their grandparents, the livestock, and the land, and have formed ambivalent bonds in the Anglo world. Buzz angrily asks Ella why the white people do things like tell his grandma to move. He tells her he hates white people. "I tried to tell him," says Ella, "that it's not the white people that are doing it, it's their laws."

"People are scared of the law," Ella says, walking out of her apartment in the married student housing of the university's Flagstaff campus. It is dawn. Her kittenish daughter Nell prances along beside her clutching a blond Cabbage Patch doll in a cradleboard Ella made for it. "The law can do anything. We need to have faith that the Creator will take care of us. Navajos are losing their faith. They're just believing what's happening in the white man's world. That's very frustrating for me." Ella and Nell head around the corner to Genny's apartment. Nell is an adorable child, seductive, manipulative, and absolutely charming. Her long hair is pulled away from her face in two French braids and held with beaded barrettes. She wears small turquoise earrings, pink pants, pink top with a fashionable, oversize button, and a pink winter jacket.

Ella and her sister are driving up to Coal Mine in Genny's green truck. "The land is our mother," says Ella. "She feeds us and provides for us. Selling your life, that's what you're doing when you're relocating," she says. "You sell your land and whatever you believe in, your parents' religion. You're even selling the bones of your relatives. Because when I confront the Holy People that travel every morning from the east, I don't want to confront them with the knowledge that I sold the land and my beliefs. I don't want it on my conscience that I sold everything they put down for us way back in the beginning of time. Even if people come in there and force us to move, I'm not willing to take any money for it. I know I can make it in the white man's world, paying bills, paying for my apartment."

Genny is in the truck already, waiting for Ella. She has close-set eyes, high cheekbones, a square chin. Her face is proud and defiant and she is the only Hatathlie daughter who wears her hair long and unstyled. Today she has it in one braid pulled over her right shoulder.

Ella resembles her father; her face is broad, with wide-set, vulnerable eyes that see ambivalence and paradox where her sister sees black and white. Ella can be expansive about her deepest thoughts, yet can as easily purse her sculpted, full lips and withdraw. Her permed hair is short, feathered about her face, and, she shyly admits, dyed brown.

Both Ella and Genny are fiercely devoted to their parents. In some ways, Genny has chosen a less traditional way of life. She works, and she is a single mother. Genny believes the only way to succeed in life is to beat the system, a philosophy Ella does not embrace. For her part, Ella's traditional upbringing has become more central to her since she returned to the reservation in the 1970s. Her high school years were spent in California with her Mormon foster parents. (Many Navajo and Hopi parents enroll their children in Mormon foster parent programs to offer them a good education and better opportunities.) Ella opted to remain in the white world after high school when she married a Mexican-American. After his death in Vietnam, she returned to her mother's home with her newborn son. Her return to Navajo ways was made plain by her marriage to Dennis Bedonie several years later, which was arranged, in the traditional fashion, by her grandmother. Now, Ella finds strength and guidance in the old ways, and her devotion to her family is simple and basic. She is the eldest daughter and, in the Navajo way, guardian of her parents' welfare. She has inherited many traditional responsibilities and is trying to fulfill them while bringing up her own children in a dual world.

Ella, Genny, and Nell set out from Flagstaff this fall morning and head north on Route 89 to Tuba City. On weekends this road is the province of pickup trucks filled with Navajo families coming to Flagstaff to shop. The cabs are jammed with four and five people; frequently an old grandma or some grandkids ride in the bed of the truck. At night, the road belongs to long-distance truckers driving eighteen-wheelers north to Page, Glen Canyon Dam, and Utah, south to Flagstaff and Phoenix. The white and amber lights that run the lengths of the semis blink along the black ribbon of tarmac like a string of Christmas lights hanging between the pink hills of the reservation to the north.

Genny and Ella get on the road just as daylight approaches, the sky grows pastel and vague, and the cloud formations of the early morning disappear as the sky opens. The underbellies of new cumulus puffs blaze as the sun mounts over the horizon. The landscape is as forgiving as a Grant Wood painting. Piñon and juniper trees stand like lollipops on the rolling hills. Even the stiff plains grass looks soft as a wheat field in the early morning light. Strands of electrical wires dip between the transmission towers, which appear to be giant Kachina dolls marching across the land. The electricity sizzles through the wires like droves of cicadas. Sometimes sparks fly through the wires over the mud and log hogans beneath. The source of some of the electricity in these lines is coal dug from Black Mesa on the Navajo reservation. Yet the hogans underneath the wires—in fact, most hogans on the reservation—don't share in the bounty, and have no electricity.

Sixty miles north of Flagstaff, Genny turns east on Route 160 and climbs northeast to Tuba City. The landscape is parched and lunar. Ridges and vast, barren valleys reveal the area as the ocean bed it once was. The swirling red dust makes the horizon pink; there are no animals here or hogans. A tourist might think he was on Mars until he sees, near Moenavi, a hand-painted sign that reads DINOSAUR TRACKS. Inevitably, there is a station wagon parked just after the turnoff and an Anglo family dressed in vacation wear gathered around their vehicle.

Up a rise, and Genny enters Tuba City. On the left is a Chevron station. On the right is a large gravel parking lot. Tucked into the western end of the lot is the Tuba City Truck Stop. Up the street is the new high school, post office, and a new tribal office building. Tuba City is part of the Navajo reservation and has grown right up to the boundaries of the Hopi village of Moencopi, which is an island separated by forty miles from the other Hopi villages, another unfortunate consequence of the

1882 executive-order reservation, which failed to include the village within its bounds. Moencopi, which is located at the mouth of a huge wash, is blessed with permanent springs, a longer growing season, and warmer temperatures (because of lower altitude) than the other Hopi villages. It was originally the site of farms tended by Hopis from Oraibi. Hopi men (who ran there from Oraibi) camped at Moencopi for several days during harvest, but didn't settle the area until soon after the Mormons settled Tuba City, about 1876. The close existence of Navajo and Hopi settlements here reflects the history of the tribes' contacts—tentative arrangements based on reciprocal trading and colored by apprehension of foreign ways. Until Anglo lawyers for the tribes initiated attempts to identify boundaries, living arrangements and trading arrangements were made on a small scale, family by family, as they are still, informally, by members of the two tribes. When Abbott Sekaquaptewa's family moved out to their ranch in District 6 near Hotevilla, his parents bought a hogan there from a Navajo man. When the Sekaquaptewas returned to the village for any reason, they hired a Navajo to tend their cattle. These ties are still the mainstay of commerce between tribal members.

The Truck Stop is run by a Hopi family. The front wall is glass, so patrons can watch the comings and goings in town. The walls are decorated with sports trophies and pictures of souped-up cars with oversize wheels. The cafe serves Navajo (Hopi) tacos—a piece of fry bread covered with beans, cheese, lettuce, and tomato—hominy stew, hamburgers, and fried chicken. The cafe is usually filled with Navajos, Hopis, and Anglos, all of whom get along in their relief of finding a place to wash and eat.

A huge livestock truck is parked in the lot. It belongs to Ray, a white sheep trader. Ella stops the car and tells Nell to go ask Ray the price of the lambs. Nell runs over, tips her head to speak to the craggy, lean man, and runs back, legs akimbo, rolling her eyes. "Got no little lambs today," she says matter-of-factly. Then, "Ray's truck smells *horrible.*" She bursts into giggles. Ella laughs and says, "That Ray, he's never going to find himself a wife, a white woman, because he always smells like mutton."

Across the street, continuing west beyond the Chevron station, a macadam road lined with cottonwood trees planted by government agents and missionaries after the turn of the century leads to the BIA compound. The community of boxy stone houses with Victorian porches, two-story administrative offices, and schools beneath a canopy of mature trees in the middle of the red, dusty desert, appears like a Hollywood back lot. Its functions are as byzantine as its appearance is mystifying, but Navajos go to school here, apply for money and social programs here, and are treated at the Indian Health Service hospital.

Ella points out the trailer where her husband Dennis used to work when they lived at her mother's in the early seventies. She heads away from the compound to the swap meet, a field of dirt and grass that is now covered with hundreds of pickups. Navajos sell all manner of things from booths and the backs of their trucks—old clothes, furniture, hideous lamps and shoes, as well as beaded items, jewelry, and pottery. Ella and Jenny walk carefully past each booth, greeting relatives and friends, fingering jewelry, beads. One woman sells Navajo hair brushes, thick batches of stiff grasses, and stirring sticks, a dozen smooth, straight twigs used to stir cornmeal mush and considered an indispensable item in a Navajo woman's house. Ella gently fingers the sticks, turns them over, feels their weight, and judges how much money she has in her pocket. She reluctantly puts the sticks back.

Ella sees her mother beside the red truck, selling fry bread. Ella greets her with a formal handshake. Bessie tells her she received a letter from Kimo, Ella's eldest son who is living with Ella's sister Lula in California this year. Kimo wrote to say he was trying to get a part-time job at school so he could send his grandma money. He wrote, "My mom never tells me anything about what is going on out there, but I have dreams about it all the time and I know there are a lot of things going on and that you're having a hard time." Kimo told Bessie she could sell his cows if she had to, but he suggested that maybe she'd better keep one in case he ever gets married and needs a cow to pay the bride price. He enclosed a five-dollar bill in the note. Bessie tells Ella she came to the swap meet so she could spend the five dollars. They both laugh.

Ella moves on toward a small woman with tightly permed hair who is selling bread at a small stand. Ella puts out her hand and they shake. Rita is Hopi, a longtime friend who plants a cornfield a couple of miles from the Hatathlies' camp and has done so for as long as Ella can remember. They catch up on news and Rita says, "Why don't you come on up to visit anymore?" Ella says, "Oh, I don't know," and laughs. Nell tugs on her mother's hand. She begs her mom for a pop, perhaps sensing her mother's discomfort. Ella says goodbye to Rita, not mentioning what's uppermost in her mind—the land dispute and relocation. She does not want to bring it up, because she knows it is painful for Hopis who have Navajo friends, but she doesn't understand how her Hopi friends can remain quiet, can support their Tribal Council's efforts to move the Navajos. She walks on to a stand where mutton sandwiches are sold.

Ella supports her family with the stipend she receives as part of her scholarship from the Navajo Tribe. She also does beadwork and sells it through a trader in Flagstaff. Her husband, Dennis, who finished his sociology degree at NAU a few months ago, has yet to find a job, so money is always in short supply. Some days they have only one meal. Ella peels a dollar from her pocket and drops it, crinkled, on the counter, as if she had just removed a dirty bandage from her finger.

The vendor lifts a slice of mutton from the grill and places it on a piece of roasted bread. She sets a roasted green chile next to the meat. She hands the sandwich to Ella and draws a sweating Coke from a cooler. Ella picks at the meat and offers to share with Genny, who has rejoined them. Ella sees Genny has purchased some stirring sticks herself. She traded them for some barrettes she beaded.

They climb back in the truck and Genny heads east again toward Coal Mine Mesa. As soon as she passes the Tuba City Truck Stop she is in the Hopi village of Moencopi, actually two villages, a modern village with a new Mormon church close to the road and a traditional village of stone houses on the cliffs above the ancient Hopi farm sites in Moencopi Wash.

Moencopi Wash was cut over the years by torrential flash floods that occur during the biannual monsoons. The ingenious Hopi farmers still fill the great twisting canyon and its moisture-holding soil with plots of melons, beans, corn, and peaches, as well as turban squash, safflowers, and sorghum, which were introduced by the Mormons, whose nineteenth-century colony in Tuba City is now gone.

As they approach Coal Mine Mesa, which is halfway between Moencopi and Third Mesa, Genny breaks into a smile, looks around at the vast expanse of rolling grassland, takes a deep breath. "I feel relaxed as soon as I get near home," she says. "Out here, you can go anywhere, nobody will bother you. You can stop and make an offering wherever you'd like. In Flagstaff there are stop signs and lights that tell you when to walk and where you can go. People who live in Flagstaff are always running around, jogging or exercising to release tension. In Coal Mine, you don't need to do that."

The twins have been staying with their grandma, whom Genny regularly uses as a babysitter. They run helter skelter out of the house when they see their mother pull up. They are handsome, spirited boys dressed in matching sweatsuits and sneakers that close with a Velcro flap. "You're a dead man," Genny teases Toshone, looking at his shoes, which are placed on the wrong feet. She says this because Navajos place the shoes on dead bodies on the wrong feet, so their spirits can't track their way back from the spirit world. Toshone looks shyly down at his shoes, then up at his mom and bursts into giggles. He runs off toward the goats, which are resting near the stone hogan, and scatters them, yelping, waving his arms.

Ella's brother Freddy and his girlfriend, Bea, are back from Page, where they have been staying in Jack's trailer. Freddy is as graceful as a dancer and moves sensuously, with an awareness of his body that is not apparent in his brothers. His face is mobile and expressive. Bea is short and thin, with bright, wounded eyes.

Freddy has to report to National Guard duty tomorrow, and Bea is cutting his hair. He sits on the edge of his mother's bed; she sits behind him using a manual clipper. After she trims the back of his neck and over his ears, she gets a basin of water and washes his hair, gently, slowly. They seem completely absorbed in each other.

When she is finished, Bea begins to polish Freddy's black boots. Freddy gathers together the pieces of his camouflage outfit, tries to push out the wrinkles and then decides he'll iron it when he gets to Ella's place in Flagstaff this evening. He hangs the pieces, including a cap, in a plastic garment bag and places the bag in the cab of the truck.

Bessie arrives home soon after her daughters and places a pot of beans on the top of the fifty-gallon barrel that, cut in half, serves as a wood-burning stove in the living room. A door has been snipped out of the barrel in front and hangs by a wire. Bessie shoves some wood chips inside, stokes up the fire, and pulls the metal cutout back over the hole. A stovepipe leads the smoke out the front wall of the house. All the windows in the house are broken, but the Hatathlies have not been given permission by the Hopis to repair them, so the windows are boarded up to keep the house warm.

Freddy comes back from the truck with a Coke he left there to stay chilled. Bessie opens the stove door and props one end of a metal grate on top of the barrel, the other end on its cement base. She places flat circles of dough on the grate and roasts several pieces of bread. She pulls the beans from the stove and places the pot on the floor beside some plastic bowls and utensils. Genny and Ella serve themselves beans. Bea unwraps a Butterfinger candy bar and sits cross-legged on the sofa, eating it corner by corner, savoring every bite, turning the bar like a baton. It is dark save for the glow from the fire. The twins sit in a chair and look at the pictures in *The Little Engine That Could*.

Ella leaves soon after dinner. In the car, on the way home, Ella says, "When I was small, I don't remember ever going to the store. I don't remember having a lot of things that people have today, like candy, pop, and all that stuff. I think people just lived on what they harvested during the fall.

"When we came back from herding in the afternoon, my mom would make pancakes with blue cornmeal and milk. Other times my mom would make bread in the morning, and in the evening we'd milk the goats again and just soak the bread in the milk. And then in the afternoon, when we were out herding someplace, and we were hungry, sometimes my sister would just grab a goat and we would take turns lying under it, and milk the milk into our mouths."

Ella was taught to gather the same wild food her mother learned of when she was a girl, herding sheep in the same area. "There were always a lot of things we could gather," she says. "Sometimes we'd gather wild onions, we'd gather wild potatoes, we used to gather these flowers—I don't know what they're called, they're red. We used to pick a lot of those and then pick the pollen from it, the insides. We used to gather these bugs too, cicadas, that's what we used to gather, and there was a certain part in the back of the neck, just a little part—you could take it off, break it, and you could eat that part. A lot of times, too, you could get bees, wild bees, catch them, and there was a little sac inside you could get, and you used to eat that. I guess it was honey or pollen in it. And sometimes we used to gather those and feed them to our dogs and they used to make the dogs mean." Ella laughs, a happy, tinkling laugh. Her speech is mesmerizing, the circular rhythms of Navajo protruding into her English to make her sentences free of time, soothing as lullabies.

"There was always a lot of things you could eat when you were herding sheep. A lot of times we used to go down to the canyon and there was a sort of clay you could find down there that you could eat too. And we gathered a lot of seeds too with my mother and she would grind these seeds and make bread or she would use them for seasoning in soups, too.

"And I think the first fruit I became aware of was apples and peaches. The Hopis used to come in their wagons and they would bring them. My mom used to dry the apples or we used to put them in an ash pit and we used to cook them like that, like baked apples. To dry apples, you just cut them, slice them, and put them out in the sun. Then you put them in flour bags, twenty-five-pound flour bags. My mom had a way of drying canteloupe, too. She used to cut them in strips and hang them on a pole and dry them.

"Watermelon seeds had that milky taste to them. In the springtime we had a juniper tree down in the canyon, and we used to eat juniper seeds from there and my mom also used to tell us not to eat them because I guess at one time it was struck by lightning. And you don't bother things that are struck by lightning, but we used to eat those things from the lightning. We ate the pumpkin seeds raw. There were a lot of things you could eat. Most of the time, people lived on corn. They either ground it, dried it, or they used it in a variety of ways, making bread or making cornmeal mush. That's how they lived, just like that.

"There was a root you could dig up that was rubbery, that you could chew like chewing gum. And there were, like mint leaves you could find. You could chew those mint leaves or you could put it in your soup. A lot of the sheep like mint leaves too. Sometimes my mom would dry out a lot of those and she would bring it out to the sheep during the winter."

Ella explains that in the afternoons, after they came home, the chores with the sheep continued. The herd was taken to the windmill and water and the horses were hobbled while the sheep took their afternoon naps. Then house chores were done with one eye on the sheep, who could get up and wander away, defenseless prey for wolves.

In the evenings, wood had to be chopped, water hauled inside. After eating, Ella's mom took out her bag of wool. Says Ella, "We would card until we fell asleep. My mom would be spinning or weaving all night. Sometimes she would be telling us stories that go along with our legends, or she would tell us stories about her grandfather or what happened when she was small.

"In the morning, especially if we stayed up real late carding wool, we would cry when my mom would chase us up and send us outside to run. We'd always have to run every morning. We'd have to run a half mile or a mile and when you're running you're supposed to yell to strengthen your lungs. And then when we came back, she'd have the cornmeal and we'd have our prayers.

"My younger sisters don't do that anymore. I look at them. In the morning they sleep late. My mom has to constantly tell them to do this and that. Sometimes they talk back to my mom. They don't card wool anymore; it seems like they hardly have any chores except washing dishes and bringing in the water.

"They really don't have any responsibilities. To me, they're lazy. My mom used to tell me, if you sleep late, the sun's way up there and you're still sleeping. You get up grouchy and mean. You don't feel like eating, you feel sick. If you get up early in the morning, you run and have your prayers. That's why it's always important to get up early.

"She used to tell us, when we would be crying, that she's not being mean to us, she just wants us to have a good life, to think about the future, so that we can always be strong. She says, 'You're going to have to endure things because you live in a cruel world, in the white man's world. You're going to have to be strong to live in his world, strong so you don't run after the things he values.'

"I think that's really true. I think back on it. I think about the kind of life I had and compare it with my sisters'. I feel good about the life I had. I'm glad my mom did that to me. There was never a time my mom told me to do something twice. If she did, she gave me a whipping and so I learned early in life that you shouldn't talk back to your mom or your dad. If they want something done, you should do it right there.

"Every day was a lecture. Every time we ate there was a lecture. Every time I cooked I did something wrong, burned the bread or burned the soup, or I didn't make my broth right for the soup. Or I made soup and maybe the potatoes were too hard. And making the pour-in cake sometimes I would make it too dry. My dad would lecture me and tell me I had to prepare for the future.

"Everything was planning for the future because 'one of these days you're going to get married and have children and you're going to bring shame into the family if you can't do these things in front of your mother-in-law, so they can be proud of you and give us credit for raising you the right way.' He used to tell me that.

"I used to hate it. My mom was always telling me I was doing something wrong and I must be really stupid because it's the same lecture over and over all the time. I used to dread it. And my mom would tell me the stories that went with the stirring sticks and why you should always have stirring sticks and a grinding stone and brushes and all those kinds of things.

"I used to think, I don't need all these things. I'm not going to live like this. I'm going to live in a house with a white picket fence, the white man's way."

The sky floats above her, deep blue, grand, vast, infinitely far away. Smoky curls of clouds ring the horizon, rolling, turning, lit by the moon.

Nell stands in front of her grandma's house. She looks at the stars, which are as big as songbirds in the early winter sky. "What are the stars made of?" she asks. Then, "What are UFOs?" and "Where do they land when they fall?" A plane passes overhead, the lights barely visible. "What is it like to ride in an airplane?" she asks. "Does it tickle?" What does she mean, tickle? "Like it feels when you go over a bump in the car," she answers. "Tickle in your tummy."

It is cold. Animal and plant sounds whisper from gouged canyons and endless, tired grasslands. When Ella was a child and a plane passed overhead, Bessie would awaken the children and tell them to go out and look at the strange apparition. Neither Bessie nor her children had any thoughts of actually flying in one of the iron birds.

Where Nell now stands, wondering what it would be like in an airplane, Bessie once stood, trying to catch a sunbeam in a fragment of mirror to signal her kids away from the road. Tourists would often stop and ask the little girls—who, thirty years ago, wore traditional skirts and velveteen tops—to pose with their sheep for pictures. The children liked to do it because the tourists sometimes gave them some coins in return. "We asked them for money," Ella recalled, giggling. But Bessie didn't like this game and she flashed at them to come home.

Today, Bessie's headaches are still bad; Jack hasn't been able to find a medicine man to perform the ceremony she needs. She has gone to another diagnostician,· a stargazer, who looked into a crystal and identified her illness. The stargazer suggested another, more commonplace ceremony for Bessie, which the family plans to arrange for next weekend.

Dennis and Ella, who have come up from Flagstaff for the day to visit, say good night and speed along Route 264 toward home. Along the black stretch of road a mile from the Hatathlies' house, Dennis and Ella are surprised to notice a family walking in the pitch dark on the shoulder of the road. Dennis slows down after Ella recognizes some of his relatives. The family—three women, two adolescent boys, and a baby—approach the vehicle, and quietly climb in. Two of the women sit in the back, squatting gratefully atop a spare tire. They are silent for most of the ride, crouching without complaint. Once they reach Tuba City, one of the boys directs Dennis through winding dirt paths to a small clearing. There is not exactly a structure, but a roof covering a dugout at the edge of a small wood.

Dennis and Ella walk with them down into the cave. There is one room, illuminated with a kerosene lantern. The walls are mud, reinforced with two-by-fours. The floor is covered with mats and sleeping materials. The family appears awkward, embarrassed about their shelter. They have moved away from their home in Coal Mine Mesa and are awaiting relocation. Almost twelve hundred families are in similar circumstances —they have moved from the HPL because they can no longer support themselves or house their families as a result of the livestock reductions and building freeze, and have found temporary lodging with family or, like these people, in a shack in Tuba City. Most years in its appropriations package, the Relocation Commission has been directed to spend its money only to move people like Bessie and Jack, who are still living on the HPL. This policy conforms with the Hopis' wishes—to focus on clearing the HPL. The people who have voluntarily removed themselves, and are certified for a relocation house, are waiting, waiting—some, like this family, in desperate straits. This is a little-known effect of the law, but twelve hundred families—about 4,800 people—have been stranded now in this situation. Nell steps closer to her mother and grips her Cabbage Patch doll. After a brief visit, the Bedonies leave.

They drive on in silence. On their way through Tuba south to Flagstaff, they pass a gathering of police cars and flares. Dennis slows, spots a relative, asks what happened. He is told that a man, drunk, walked into the road and was hit by a car. A half mile down the road, Dennis approaches another accident scene. A second man has been hit and killed. It is Saturday night in Tuba City and alcohol is taking its lethal toll.

A few days later, Bessie Hatathlie lights a kerosene lamp that spits like a furious cat. Nell sits on a couch in her grandma's living room with her Aunt Budge's newborn baby, Valene, in her lap. Nell holds the baby quite professionally and calls the little one her new baby sister. The baby is her clan sister, though by blood she is her first cousin. Budge sits across the room. She has arranged a supply of Pampers in a hanging diaper bag behind her, and has placed cans of evaporated milk out on the windowsill. Her attitude toward the baby is detached, bored. She is waiting for her boyfriend, Stanley, to come by.

Levonne does her homework by the kerosene lamp. It is almost impossible to make out the words of her text in the bad light, but that is the best light in the hogan, and the children must all compete for it. Bessie walks in from the kitchen with some dough. She tears off handfuls and flaps them into flat rounds and sets them on the improvised grill. She roasts a few pieces of bread and stirs a pot of red beans that has been simmering on the top of the barrel stove. Everybody serves himself some of the redolent soup.

Ella and Bessie speak together in Navajo. Their mood is somber, they eat slowly, carefully, savoring each bite of the simple meal. The light from the fire flickers on their faces and warms their skin. They finish their food and then begin to talk.

Bessie finally had a sing, and the headaches that had immobilized her disappeared for a few days. But the day before yesterday, she felt the tension creeping back into her neck. She is worried about Felix, who suffered another round of seizures, and who was denied disability payments by the Social Security office. Bessie pulls a letter from her pocketbook and shows it to Ella. Ella reads it and tells her Felix has been denied disability because he missed an appointment with a Flagstaff doctor for an examination. Felix had had another seizure on the day of the appointment and his dad had taken him to a Hopi medicine man instead.

"When I ask my mom about relocation, she never really talks about it," Ella says later. "But tonight she talked about it. I told her I thought my sister Lula applied for relocation benefits and I think they're going to tag the stone house." Ella's cousin at the Relocation Commission told her that Lula had been corresponding with the Commission. Every adult head of household that is certified for relocation by the Commission must identify a dwelling on the HPL that is his or hers. After he or she relocates, the government tags and condemns the dwelling. Of the Hatathlies' four dwellings—an old mud hogan that the family has torn down, moved around, and rebuilt for thirty-five years; a log hogan that is unlivable because of rot and disrepair; a stone hogan in which Glenn and his girlfriend Vida Mae now stay; and the main house—only two are habitable. If Lula should relocate, the stone hogan would be tagged and condemned, reducing the available housing to one dwelling.

The act of relocating not only removes a family member from the household, but it also eliminates a dwelling from the base camp, most of which are in tatters as a result of the ten-year-old building freeze. One unexpected result of the Commission's regulations is that when a head of household relocates—and his or her former hogan tagged by the government—it removes a dwelling from the mother's camp that she or another family member might have used. "Because my mother gave us those homes, I don't think it's right that we get paid for them," says Ella. "We get paid for the houses that she gave us, and they remove them one by one, until nothing is left and they come to take my mom off forcibly. It's not right."

Bessie attended a chapter meeting recently, and relocation was the subject of discussion. They discussed the New Lands, whose selection had just been completed by the tribe. When the Navajo-Hopi Indian Land Settlement Act, PL 93-531, was passed in 1974, Congress authorized the Navajo Tribe to purchase some land to help make up for the land they were losing to the Hopis. Though they would lose 900,000 acres of the HPL, Congress only authorized the tribe to purchase an additional 250,000 acres. The families moved off of the 900,000 acres would presumably be moved to the 250,000 acres. The additional land, it was thought, "would solve the problem."

The Navajo Tribe made a speedy selection. But the land it chose caused an immediate and angry uproar. The tribe selected a piece of land known as the Arizona Strip, which was separated from the rest of Arizona by the Colorado River and the Grand Canyon. It so happened that the Arizona Strip was a rugged piece of wilderness much prized by Anglo deer hunters and a few families of Mormon ranchers. The Arizona Save the Strip Committee was formed, and immense pressure was brought on Congress to prevent the Navajos from buying the land. It took six years, but finally, in 1980, Congress passed amendments to PL 93-531 that prevented the Navajos from choosing this piece of land. In recompense, the amendments authorized the transfer of 250,000 acres of land to the Navajos free of charge, and also provided for the Navajos to purchase another 150,000 acres to be taken in trust by the Secretary of the Interior as part of the Navajo reservation. Under the 1980 amendments, the tribe would thus gain 400,000 acres to replace the 900,000 lost.

However, the sad consequence of the six-year delay is that the Navajos who relocated during those years either had to secure an on-reservation homesite lease, which, as we have seen with the Tsos, is problematic, or were compelled to move off the reservation. So most relocatees wound up moving to border towns, where they did not fare well. After the Relocation Commission realized that more than half the relocatees had lost their homes in the first few years of relocation, they placed minimum income requirements on Navajos allowed to move to the border towns. And the Commission also limited their ability to encumber the homes with debt.

The tribe's second land selections were made in 1983. They included 371,400 acres adjacent to the southeast boundary of the reservation near the towns of Sanders and Chambers, Arizona. The land was acquired through a complicated series of land exchanges and were made available to the Commission in 1986—eleven years after the Settlement Act was passed and nine years after the first relocation.

Though the ranches that make up the New Lands were chosen by the tribe, the Navajos subject to relocation are not happy about moving there. They say the land is unfamiliar to them. And they are worried about the water supply because of a much publicized uranium tailings spill in 1979 that sent record amounts of radioactive waste gushing down the Puerco River, which runs through part of the New Lands. Not only that, the people know it is very dry down there, because some of them have grazed their cattle on two ranches owned by the tribe nearby. Where is the water to support all the families and their livestock?

"Those people over there at the meeting," says Ella, "couldn't figure out how you could be given a day, given a month to move, and yet there's no place for you to go. My mom said a lot of people don't want to move to the New Lands, they want to stay close to Tuba City, to their relatives and children."

Ella tells her mother she thinks the Commission will probably put her in a big community housing development like the one that had been built at Tuba City for the "low rent people." Bessie is discouraged. She doesn't know what to believe. It seems like the stories coming from the Relocation Commission change all the time.

"You know," says Ella, "I once told my mom that in court you can be given a life sentence, to stay until you die in jail, or they can electrocute you, and I described how they do that. And she said to me, 'You know that's similar to what the relocation bill is doing. It's like a life sentence. Maybe we're being given a sentence for killing those Hopis a long time ago, when we used to fight them.' She said, 'Every day I sit here and think about these things. And I sit here trying to figure out why they're doing it.' "

Bessie does not understand the white people's way of collecting money through taxes to pay for projects that affect people other than themselves or family. Navajos take care of their own; they don't take care of strangers. Bessie tells Ella, "When I hear working people are putting up the money for Navajos to move, I wonder if these people realize that they're destroying our lives, our way of thinking and our lives."

Both Ella and her mother have been troubled with bad dreams, which suggests to Ella that their life is out of balance. And she points to the fact that they are constantly spending money for ceremonies to cure specific ills, their livestock isn't doing well, and wolves have come out in broad daylight and eaten two sheep out of the pen. She tells Bessie she thinks they should have a stargazer come and tell them what is at the root of their problems, and that Jack should lead them all in a peyote meeting.

Ella tells Bessie that she plans to call her sisters in California and ask them to save about a hundred dollars so they can all pitch in for some ceremonies that they need. Ella says, "You know those arrows over our front door, on the inside? Well, they were put there four years ago. Every four years, you're supposed to have a renewal sing for them. I told my mom she should have it done soon. It costs from eight hundred to a thousand dollars. Those things, the jewelry that is passed down, we shouldn't pawn for money or for food. We've been doing that. I told her we shouldn't be doing that. We also used to have a Beauty Way for my mom every four years on Mother's Day. Between those years we'd have a peyote ceremony for her. We haven't done that. We should have a Beauty Way for her to put her back in harmony with nature and everything around her."

Of course, all these ceremonies must take place on the reservation. They require a hogan, a lot of space, and relatives and friends who can bring sheep to butcher. Some of the ceremonies take as many as nine days. To feed all the relatives, this requires many sheep. It is unthinkable to have such a ceremony in a town. Where could it be held? At whose hogan? In the squaw dance, or Enemy Way, ceremonial objects must be carried on horseback from one location to another. Bonfires are made, herbs picked, and offerings made. Even on the New Lands, patterns established for hundreds of years would be broken, relatives would live in different proximity to one another, certain medicines might be unavailable.

Bessie says to Ella sadly, "It seems all of my children are different. They're different from the way they used to be. It seems like they're always sick or they're worried about something. As a mother, I know there's something wrong with my children. Just by looking at you, I know there's something wrong."

But, even as Ella and Bessie face the stresses of illness and aggravation, unsettling news, and of course the ever present specter of the July 1986 deadline, there is some good news. Glenn has decided to marry Vida Mae, daughter of their neighbor Billy Yazzie, the "Navajo Clint Eastwood." Or rather, Vida Mae's mother has decided Glenn will marry Vida Mae. She thinks that they've been living together long enough to warrant a wedding.

Apparently Glenn learned of all this after Vida Mae's mother paid a visit to Bessie and announced the bride price. This visit was her way of telling Bessie what she expected. The price was set at five hundred dollars and a cow. Ella asks her mother what Glenn thinks about all this. He recently took a test to qualify for a three-month training course in computers, and he scored at the top of the group, missing only one question on the exam. He has always been good at science and math and he looks forward to the course. Bessie laughs and says, "I told him he has to come up with the five hundred dollars himself and he's got to come up with a cow himself. He told me he was going to ask Vida Mae if he could borrow one of her cows for the bride price." Bessie laughs out loud, the first laugh Ella has heard from her in weeks.

Hatathlie means singer, or medicine man. Jack Hatathlie comes from a family of medicine men, and he himself is a roadman for the Native American Church. The Hatathlies are also known for their swift runners.

In their youth, Jack's grandfather and uncles competed against the Hopis in footraces. Says Ella, "My grandfather knows a lot about running. He'd initiate runners, give them medicine, say prayers over them, sometimes teach them the songs. He'd grind up butterfly wings and turn it into an ointment to help them run faster." They ran for prizes of melons, peaches, corn, or pieces of silver.

Although they raced for fun, they also ran to procure food for the family. After the stock reductions in the 1930s, Jack and his relatives would get together in a pack and run up to Hopi in the winter to steal horses for food. Navajos don't like the taste of beef in the winter. They think the cattle taste different than they do in summer with fresh grass in their bellies. Navajos didn't want to kill their own horses, so thirty years ago when this activity went on, Navajos who needed meat sometimes captured and killed a Hopi horse.

"They'd run out at dusk, isolate a horse and chase it down to the Navajo reservation, shoot it and butcher it, and divide up the meat," Ella explains. "A lot of Navajos used to raid the villages up there in the old days, especially in the winter for horsemeat."

The Navajos did not perceive this as morally reprehensible. Ella matter-of-factly describes her father's raiding without a word of condemnation or self-examination. "Raiding was common in my dad's younger age," she says. "That was happening when I was growing up." Having livestock was so important that all else—such as how the livestock were obtained—was irrelevant.

John Ladd, a student of the Navajo, writes, "The Navajo 'economic theory' assumes that there is a potential abundance of goods, and that through cooperation the amount of goods will be increased for everyone; in other words, they would deny the basic assumption upon which much of our own economic theory depends, namely, the scarcity of goods."

The Navajo assumption of bounty—and the denial of the possibility of scarcity—coupled with a cultural responsibility to care for the clan, leads the Navajos to a troublesome belief that taking someone else's animal to feed their own relatives is fine. Navajo religion even supports raiding. Says Friedrich Abel, a German writer and student of the Navajo, "[The Navajos have] no Christian moral concept of sin [regarding theft]. In fact, the Navajo religion grew up to support and protect raiding. This was a source of wealth and comfort. Stealing was like taking animals from the woods."

Sometimes Navajos even steal from each other, but will rarely steal from a clan relative. One old man in Teesto knows someone is stealing the odd sheep from his herd. He has taken to leaving his shotgun by the front door. Yet he is not completely convinced he wants to catch the thief, and never seems to get to the gun in time. Says the man, "I think I know who it is. He's having trouble feeding his family."

The stealing that took place during Ella's youth has slowed. Ella remembers when her family began butchering its own animals in the winter. "One of our horses was slaughtered in the winter. We also killed our cows for meat during the winter. Then we divided the meat up to the ones who had families—me, my mom, my sister." Even Abbott Sekaquaptewa, the most vocal Hopi on the subject of Navajo stealing, acknowledges that the theft has declined over the past thirty-five years. He says, "In my lifetime, [it was] not so bad. There have been bad things that happened." Yet he is nevertheless infuriated by any thefts, most recently by the theft of his friend's cow.

Stealing, no matter how acceptable to the Navajos or how they rationalized it, drove—and drives—the Hopis wild. "It's as if we were *nothing!*" cries Abbott over and over, burning with hurt and indignation. Abbott is further infuriated that BIA officials seem to have little interest in pursuing the perpetrators. This makes Abbott feel that the Navajos have tremendous power over the Hopis.

"If nobody does anything about it," Abbott says, "they're going to do it again. They know they can get away with it. The only way, psychologically speaking, I survive is I remember the tradition that says at the beginning of the migrations, the gods lifted up a number of ears of corn. One was long and beautiful, just perfect. Another one was good but not as good. Another was still less. And then there was a short, stubby ear of blue corn of very poor quality. These different grades of corn, so to speak, they were put out and they represented a life way. And the people, the various people had a choice of what they would select. And the Navajos selected the longest, most perfect ear of corn. And the Hopis selected the shortest. That signified the Navajos would experience all the material things in this life. They would have everything, but it didn't guarantee anything into another existence. It could all end here.

"Whereas the short, stubby corn was of poor quality, but it was hardy and it would last and although it represented a life of hardship it would last into the next world and could earn the Hopi people an existence in the next world.

"I remember that and that way it helps me to be able to deal with problems [such as] when nobody does anything about their violations. And I think to myself, see, that's what tradition says they're going to be like. They're going to experience everything to their advantage in this world. That's what's happening here."

Abbott's experience with the Navajos began when his family moved full time to its ranch on District 6 to run cattle and farm. His mother, Helen, describes in a book about her life, *Me and Mine*, the troubles the family had with the Navajos:

Our ranch was right on the border of the Hopi-Navajo Reservations. There had always been animosity between the people of these tribes, and we had lots of trouble with our Navajo neighbors. The wagon road that the Navajos traveled going to Oraibi to trade passed right by our garden, and many times they stopped and helped themselves to the melons, fruits, and vegetables. If they traveled on horseback their trail passed right in front of our house, and nothing was safe. We sometimes went into the village for a few days and on our return we would find the door broken in, food taken, and things generally scattered about. How could we remedy this? We decided we had to do something about it. It would be best to make friends with those who passed our way. We said to them, "If you are hungry and you find us gone, you are welcome to use the stove to cook your food. If you are cold, come in and make a fire and get warm. If you are tired, you may rest in our beds (they nearly always carried their own blankets). But when you go, please leave things as you found them, and leave the door closed and let us be friends." It worked. Once Emory was asked, "Did you ever find anyone in your bed?" His immediate response was, "Yes, and it wasn't Goldilocks."

There were good ones among our Navajo neighbors. It was the bad ones that gave us the trouble. The honest ones came to trade their meat for our melons and fruit. Once when we were away, a certain Navajo man came, left some meat, took some of our garden stuff, and left a note saying he had taken what he thought was a fair trade. It was, and I always respected that man.

The Sekaquaptewas were better off than most Navajos and Hopis; they actually had things that could be stolen. But the Navajos were not the only ones to steal from them. Helen reports that she was robbed by her own people in the early years of her marriage in Hotevilla: "I had the first real store-bought diapers and very soft little blankets and safety pins in Hotevilla. Very often, after I had washed them, some diapers or maybe a blanket would be missing from the clothesline."

There were all kinds of problems with livestock. The Hatathlies had a somewhat rambunctious bull who tended to wander off in amorous pursuit of Hopi cows. The Hopis didn't much like this. Ella explains, "We used to have a bull named Bullshit. And he always liked the cows over in District 6. He used to wander over there and we used to always have to bring him back. And the rangers would always come over to our house and tell us that Bullshit was in District 6 again. He would just lie down and wouldn't move [when the Hopis tried to chase him away]. If we weren't home, they used to leave a note on our door, a note with a cow and a six and a fence at the bottom so my parents would know he's over there again. 'Oh, Bullshit's over here again,' [they'd say]. 'We don't want Bullshit mating with our cattle, you know, he's a poor breed.' They used to say that about him."

Finally, a Hopi got so fed up, he beat the bull with a whip. Recalls Ella, "One time they beat him up really bad because he just lay down and wouldn't move. And I guess this other Hopi guy came by later and fed him some herbs, I guess for his injuries on his back because his back was all swollen from the whipping. So we went over there and got him back. My parents thought he was a big problem so they sold him, sold him at the auction."

The Sekaquaptewas themselves got in trouble when animals strayed into Hopi cornfields. Helen Sekaquaptewa recalls that whenever a Hopi in the area had his corn trampled, he blamed it on her husband. "If horses ate the corn," she recalls, "Emory's horses were always blamed."

These incidents reveal inevitable conflicts between farmers and herdsmen who inhabit the same land. And they also suggest that part of the problem here is poverty. People in need—Hopis and Navajos—at times stole food and clothing.

Nevertheless, payback from the Navajos has become Abbott's lifelong obsession. As one anthropologist put it, "Chairman Abbott Sekaquaptewa burns with a commitment to Hopi ethnicity and a passion for unremitting vengeance against the Navajo." To Abbott, the petty thefts are symbols of a larger reality, which is that the Hopi are completely encircled by another tribe—and one that is twenty times larger.

Not all Hopis are as angered by the Navajo presence as is Abbott. One forty-seven-year-old Hopi man, Jim, who didn't want his name used for fear of retaliation from the Hopi tribal government, says, "There was never any problem between the Hopi and Navajo people. The trouble is between the tribal governments. The government is what's messing it up. . . . Why move people who are already settled for a long time? It's not right, at least in my opinion."

This man grew up out on a ranch away from the villages and had daily contact with the Navajos who lived near him. He didn't have the same experiences the Sekaquaptewas describe. He says, "I lived out there. The Navajos came around, we would talk, they would do something wrong, we'd tell them, and they'd come back and apologize. . . . We used to trade with the Navajos, talk to them, go to squaw dances, all peaceful. Now since the land dispute, we don't ever trade with them."

Jim feels that the Hopis who say it is the Navajos' presence that keeps them from living out on the land are kidding themselves. He says, "Right now, there's a lot of Hopis talking about the [HPL], but they're not about to move [out there]. They're building around [the First Mesa village of] Polacca. . . . I know what my grandfather and great-uncles told me. The Hopis won't go down to the land. They don't know how to chop wood any more, no one can herd sheep. Many years back, they say the Hopis are supposed to build houses where there are springs way off the reservation. But they didn't. That's why the land dispute is coming in. Our grandfathers told us the Navajo would come in because the Hopis are too lazy to live out there. . . . It's really the Hopis' own fault. Now they're depending on the government and the lawyers to work for them. My grandfather knew a long time ago it was going to happen."

Jim feels the Hopis will never move out on the land. "The Hopis are just too chicken to be living out there. . . . Hopis live up here because they have good things like TV. They're not going to go out there on the land and start again unless they have money." He smiles and adds, "I wouldn't mind moving if they built me a house and gave me running water and electricity."

The real events of Navajo-Hopi history are made up of stories of people like Helen Sekaquaptewa and Rita (the Hopi who has a cornfield near the Hatathlies) and Jim. Each story has its own character, problems, and history. These stories and their possible solutions—increased understanding between individuals such as that fostered by Helen Sekaquaptewa and Jim, better law enforcement, more lands for the Hopis elsewhere—were ignored or dismissed in the confusion generated by the congressional debate over partition of the land and exaggerations that the Hopi Tribe faced destruction from without.

The disagreements between the Navajo and Hopi people are largely the inevitable strains that exist between poor people of different cultures living in an area of limited resources. Those differences have been distorted into racial stereotypes—the peaceful, village-dwelling Hopis who abhor violence versus the implacable, thieving Navajos. Those stereotypes have been generated and maintained by the legal process (one strong incentive being the millions of dollars in legal fees that have been generated and are still being generated at government expense) and the realities of media coverage.

Through a fluke of history, Congress decided to fashion a massive program—one requiring hundreds of millions of dollars and the relocation of ten thousand people—that reduced the stories and the incidents and characters to numbers and sides of a fence. No one would similarly advocate solving inner-city problems by relocating entire ethnic groups so as to reduce cultural misunderstandings and thefts of food.

The consequences are far-reaching. The relocation is forcing into the modern world a pocket of Navajos who are some of the most traditional Indians in the country, while the potential benefit to the Hopis remains unclear. The antagonism that has grown between the tribes is now preventing their working together on urgent, shared issues such as alcoholism, unemployment, education, and economic development.

(9)

The American Assault
on the Hopi Spirit

For the past five hundred years the Hopis have been beset—by Spaniards eager for native riches and heathen souls, by hit and run raids from Utes, Apaches, and Navajos, and by insistent missionaries of all stripes. But no intrusion has worked to destroy the Hopi spirit as successfully as the United States government's attempts to force a democratic, representative government on the autocratic Hopi villages. What remains today of Hopi culture and religion after that onslaught is tenuous, distorted, like the pulse of life a body tries to send through the shreds of tendon and bone that connect it with a severed limb. Oliver LaFarge, a student of the Indian and a Pulitzer Prize–winning author, who was hired by the BIA to convince the Hopis to adopt a constitution and representative government, wrote in his journal in 1936: "The Hopis have been operated on by everyone, official and unofficial, from Coronado through Kit Carson and General Scott to Oliver La Farge. In almost every case they have suffered for it. They still stand almost where they did, but they are slightly cracking. Why they should ever trust *any* white man is a mystery to me." Since those lines were written, the crack has deepened and spread. What remains is a thousand-year-old society fragmented by its people's responses to the imposition of U.S. government programs on a civilization whose own religion, social organization, and economics were shaped over a millennium specifically to meet the demands of its difficult environment. At first, the Hopis reacted in one of two ways to the government bureaucrats who began trooping across the mesas in the late nineteenth century. They submitted or they opposed the newcomers. Then, in a style typical of Hopi society, these two groups fragmented. Among those who complied with the government's plans were those who passively went along and others who embraced the new ways by imitating the worst qualities of the occupiers. Other Hopis rebelled, and under the pressure of their futile fight, divided again and again, growing more bitter and disillusioned with each new government effort to change them.

The tragic result of this conflict is that what was truly Hopi—the conviction within each individual that he or she played a singular and essential role not only in the perpetuation of the tribe, but in the maintenance of the earth's harmony—began to crumble, and with it the Hopi culture as it had existed for hundreds of years. Within a generation after tribal government was imposed in 1936, Hopi priests began dying without successors, and Hopi ways, tied inextricably to the performance of elaborate ceremonies, disappeared with them. Some Hopis tried to find meaning in their loss by invoking prophecies of the Purification, the day that Bahana—the lost white brother—would come and right all wrongs and send Hopis into the next world. To them, the dying out of tradition was a fateful sign; thus they did nothing to stop it.

Others interpreted Hopi myth in such a way as to support the establishment of modern, white-sponsored tribal government in place of the Hopi religious hierarchy by suggesting that the trappings of ritual were meant to disappear until the religion became something more Anglicized. Abbott Sekaquaptewa is among current adherents of this interpretation. Says he, "As I understand it, the Kachina ceremonies will die after a while. And then our religious life will come to just praying from the heart with the cornmeal only. And then even [the cornmeal] would die out, so it's just prayer. That's part of the prophecy." That idea was palatable to Christianized Hopis, like Abbott, who was once a Mormon.

This latter interpretation was viewed bitterly by the traditional faction, whose members perceived it as a way for Hopis with no hereditary leadership roles to gain power they never could have enjoyed under the traditional system. The traditionals fought relentlessly against those who wanted to change Hopi society. Many have died now, and the traditional ways with them. Of the fourteen Hopi villages, only one, Shongopavi, can complete its entire religious cycle.

At the turn of the century, Oraibi was a village of one thousand with an active ceremonial life. Now, it is a decrepit shell of crumbling rocks and timber. Fewer than several dozen families live in warrens of rooms hidden among scores of empty houses, dwellings that were abandoned by Oraibis during two massive departures from the village in 1906 and 1907. The descendant of the last Kikmongwi—the village's top religious leader—lives in a house near the highway, where he greets tourists and tells them the village rules. Stanley Bahnimptewa, a former Mormon convert, asks guests to sign a log book, peers at them through ominously tinted glasses, and warns them not to take pictures, make sketches, use any recording devices, or touch any religious offerings, such as the small greasewood plants hung with feathers and talismans that dot the perimeter of the village like flares set by hopeful survivors.

To understand why the "progressive" Hopis who supported the BIA-established Tribal Council, the *Healing v. Jones* litigation, and partition of the former Joint Use Area so burned for the return of their land, and to understand why an equal number of Hopi "traditionals" were ineffective in stopping plans to relocate their Navajo neighbors, one must understand the modern history of the Hopis.

The Hopi culture remained virtually unchanged from the time of the Spanish explorers to the mid-1850s. The Hopis successfully repelled those who would undo them and stuck to their ancient ways. They ousted the Catholic priests during the Pueblo Revolt and even slaughtered members of their own tribe who returned to Catholicism. In part, the Hopis survived by passive resistance. One of the ways they used this technique was in adopting the outer trappings of life suggested by their occupiers and keeping their traditions secret. Hopis have long imitated the dress of outsiders while maintaining their traditional blankets and hair whorls for ceremonial purposes. (Most contemporary Hopi women wear the cotton housedresses and full-length aprons popular with Anglo women in the 1950s. Most Hopi men wear pants and shirts and have their hair cut short.)

Toward the end of the nineteenth century, however, forces began to gather that changed Hopi life forever. As Abbott Sekaquaptewa says, "The traditional enemy of the Hopi are the Utes, who would cross the San Juan River on raiding forays down into this country. This was happening a long time ago, before the Spanish. The raids came from the north and that's the reason why my clan—the Eagle clan—were the protectors, and we were assigned clan lands on the northern perimeter —that's what the first line of defense was. There's no clan land beyond that. At a certain point, [the Utes] began to get cut off by the Spaniards and the Anglos. After that, the Apaches were raiding from the south— they'd come up on raiding forays and then they'd retreat. And the Hopis would have running battles with the Apaches going down the Oraibi Valley and those valleys between the mesas. Then, after 1840, the Navajos, who were being pressured from the east, started raiding the Hopis, which is what they were doing to the settlers and other tribes.

"But the difference between the Ute raids, the Apache raids, and the Navajo raids is, the Utes and Apaches conducted hit and run raids. The Navajos settled in."

The Navajo presence around the Hopis increased after the Navajos' release from Fort Sumner in 1868. The returning Navajos joined up with Navajo bands that had eluded capture, and, responding to pressure from Anglo settlements, moved into empty territory around the mesas. They no longer raided on the grand scale they had before. Some of the bands that had not been incarcerated at Fort Sumner continued to raid, however, and Navajo leaders like Barboncito had little control over them. But for the most part, the raiding was reduced to pilfering crops and the occasional theft of livestock, like the theft of Hopi horses in winter that Ella described taking place in her youth. Yet, where rain is unpredictable and sometimes not forthcoming, every vegetable and every cow may be vital to a family's survival, and the thefts angered and depressed the Hopis. For some Hopis, like Abbott Sekaquaptewa, the actual loss was less biting than the affront of his neighbors not sharing his moral values.

He says, "I lived out on the land with my parents. And my father had Navajo friends and they were his friends. They'd come and help him with the harvest, or when we went to the village for ceremonial things, they'd herd sheep for us. But they showed an inability to keep hands off —a melon or a pumpkin or some beans—even your friends, acknowledged friends. If I thought so little of you that I did those things to you, what would that do to you?

"To the Hopis, there's a right and wrong. And what the Navajos do is wrong in Hopi culture. But we're expected to tolerate it because in that culture, it's all right to do it. Why can't it be the other way? Since it's our property, they should respect it. We're expected to live according to *their* beliefs and *their* ways and say nothing. We become subject to them and their ways. That's domination. And that's hard for people to survive, at least for me. It's hard to survive."

In 1881, the transcontinental railroad was completed, and it ran sixty miles to the south of the Hopis. This brought white people into the Hopi world. In 1858, a colony of Mormons settled in Moencopi, Oraibi's breadbasket. Like the Spanish friars who felt it their duty to convert the Indians to Catholicism, so the Mormons believed they had a special responsibility to shape the souls of the Indians. Mormons believe that Indians were once a tribe of Israel which traveled to North America from Palestine in 600 B.C. Following God's instructions, they built a civilization here, but fell to baser ways. Their skin became dark. Mormons believe, however, that if the Indians accept the church, their skins will again become "white and delightsome." Mormons therefore proselytize very actively on Indian reservations. A former church leader even suggested that Indian children on Mormon placement in Utah indeed became more light-skinned after receiving Mormon care, education, and music lessons. Many Indians were upset at the suggestion that their skin color was a curse, and they pointed out that Indian children on placement in Utah spend less time in the sun than they do on the reservation.

The Mormons, searching for a place upon which to create their heavenly civilization on earth, were interested in settling the land near the Hopis. Jacob Hamblin, a Mormon apostle, impressed a Hopi named Tuvi, who was cast out of Oraibi because he was suspected of witchcraft. Hamblin took Tuvi and his wife to St. George's, Utah, where they were awed by the flour mills and cotton gins. Tuvi's wife, Talasnimka, was

Abbott's mother's great-aunt. She returned from Utah after a year wearing "a cotton dress and a bonnet and, like Marco Polo, she brought back 'things'—yeast, a coffeepot, a dishpan, and a Dutch oven," recalls Abbott's mother, Helen.

The gifts and the glimpses of white civilization convinced Tuvi to give Hamblin permission to plant crops near him. He established Tuba City, naming it for Tuvi. But in 1879, other Mormon settlers arrived with whom Tuvi was not familiar. He complained to a BIA agent, who wrote the following to the Commissioner of Indian Affairs in 1879:

> Tu-bee, formerly a chief of the Oraibi Village, is here and complains that the Mormons are intruding upon their farming lands at Moen Kappi and interfering with their planting. He states that his father planted there when he was a boy as well as many other Oraibies and that it is their ground. At Moen-av-ee eight miles above, in the same Cañon they had another place of planting where they lived during the summer. A few years ago Jacob Hamlin, one of the Mormon Apostles, came in there and asked permission to plant that season and water his stock, which was granted. In the spring when the Indians returned to plant, as usual, they found other Mormons in possession and when they attempted to go to work, the Mormons said, Oh, no! we have bought this place from Mr. Hamlin and you can't plant here. . . . I would respectfully inquire whether there is not some law by which the Indians can be protected in their rights to lands, which they have cultivated for a century or more?

The Commissioner answered the agent by stating that under United States law, the Hopis had no recognized legal right to their lands, which were, in effect, public lands. This is of course the same answer that Agent J. H. Fleming received three years later, when he complained to the Commissioner of Indian Affairs that whites were meddling in his schooling program. Fleming's inquiries eventually led to the creation of the 1882 Executive Order Area, which was incorrectly drawn on two counts: the boundary encompassed hundreds of Navajo families, and it failed to include the Hopi satellite villages of Moencopi and Moenavi. Fleming apparently thought the Mormons had permanently driven the Hopis out of the farming areas, and seemed willing to accept that fact. He wrote, "The lands most desirable for the Moquis & which were cultivated by them 8 or 10 years ago, have been taken up by the Mormons & others, so that such as is embraced in the prescribed boundaries, is only that which they have been cultivating within the past few years." This statement further supports the view that Fleming's interest in creating the 1882 area was not to protect Hopi land from intruders, but simply to relieve himself of the irritation of the two white meddlers.

The Spanish, though they were guilty of brutal religious incursions into Indian life, didn't question the Pueblo Indians' rights to their land; they provided land grants to each Pueblo tribe. Nor did the Mexicans question Pueblo land rights after Spain ceded to them the territory of New Mexico in the early nineteenth century. The treaty between Spain and Mexico specifically noted the Pueblo Indians' rights to their land. And the Americans at least promised to guarantee Pueblo land rights when the United States signed the Treaty of Guadalupe Hidalgo at the conclusion of the Mexican War in 1848. Nevertheless, the Commissioner of Indian Affairs determined in 1879—only thirty years after the signing of the treaty—that Hopi lands were public lands of the United States.

Even in the mid-1950s, the Hopis had no vested rights to the 1882 reservation. As stated by a court finding, "An unconfirmed executive order creating an Indian reservation conveys no right of use or occupancy to the beneficiaries beyond the pleasure of Congress or the President. . . . Such use and occupancy may be terminated by the unilateral action of the United States without legal liability for compensation." The Hopis were tenants at will of the government. No vesting of rights occurred until the Congress passed PL 85-547 on July 22, 1958, the statute that allowed the Navajos and Hopis to sue each other over property rights to the 1882 area.

It was not the first time that land had been given to Indians and then taken away. Indeed it was part of a long tradition begun by British settlers, who, constantly moving westward and with an insatiable appetite for land, simply broke treaties made by the British government that had guaranteed lands to the tribes. "Throughout the period preceding the formation of the United States," wrote historian Edward H. Spicer,

> the British failed to conceive of an empire which should include the Indians as an integral part of its citizenship. As the settlers pushed westward, the result was the growth of a territory inhabited almost entirely by Europeans with a few persisting Indian communities. To be sure, some individuals and groups of Indians remained as a backwash of conquest within the borders of the British colonies, but where they existed there was no recognition of their land rights or local government and no systematic efforts were made to incorporate them as citizens. They existed merely as objects of charity with doubtful human status. At the shifting boundaries of European expansion the British government continued to try to settle the border warfare by negotiating new treaties and dealing with the tribes as foreign nations.

The Americans adopted the British approach in 1776. They dealt with Indian tribes as foreign nations, yet they didn't promise them any rights to land. The purpose of treaties was simply to agree to peace; they did not guarantee that whites could not settle on Indian lands or travel through them. According to Spicer, "This curious paradox—recognition by the Anglos of the Indians as a political unit capable of making binding treaties but without rights in the land where they lived—provided no basis whatever for mutual adjustment of interests; it constituted a sort of reversal of the Spanish policy which recognized the land rights of Indians but not their political independence of Spain."

The Hopis took the Treaty of Guadalupe Hidalgo so seriously that common myth holds that the Hopis were present at the signing. They say that "the treaty was sealed by words which were sacred bonds and by ceremonial smoking, which was a signature put into the ether with smoke." One Hopi described the seriousness of the signing as follows:

> About the destruction. The warning was given to the United States by the Hopis that if it, as a power and spiritual nation, disregarded this promise of the ceremonial signature of the smoking, then the destruction will fall on this nation because of the disobedience to the Creator's promise in the beginning. Since Spain has experienced defeat from Mexico and is no longer a power in the Western Hemisphere, and now Mexico being defeated by the United States, so if the United States continues to have no respect and disregards the ceremonial smoking promise of honesty of "word of bond" between men, then this country is worshipping a false God. And justice will come for sure. So on this basis the Hopi holds title to this land superior to the United States with all the written documents.

The United States failed to acknowledge this "word of bond," and almost immediately violated the terms of the treaty and assumed absolute sovereignty over Hopi lands. The rights of the Hopis to the land on which they'd lived for more than a thousand years was dissolved. The Hopis are very proud that they never made a two-party treaty with the United States because they never were at war with it, nor were ever conquered by it. In 1949 a group of traditional Hopis sent a letter to Harry Truman confirming their pride and determination to remain a sovereign nation:

> We are still a sovereign nation. Our flag still flies throughout our land (the flag of our ancient ruins). We have never abandoned our sovereignty to any foreign power or nation. We've been self-governing people long before any white man came to our shores. What Great Spirit made and planned no power on earth can change it.

The ultimate law-abiding people, the Hopis believed their rights under the Treaty of Guadalupe Hidalgo would be respected, and they were bewildered by the U.S. government's self-serving reinterpretations of past agreements. As Vine Deloria put it,

> The idea of the treaty became so sacred to Indians that even today, more than a century after most of the treaties were made, Indians still refer to the provisions as if the agreement were made last week. The treaty, for most tribes, was a sacred pledge made by one people to

another and required no more than the integrity of each party for enforcement. That the United States quickly insisted that the treaties should be interpreted rigidly as strictly legal documents has galled succeeding generations of Indians and made permanent peace between Indians and the federal government impossible.

Although the Hatathlies and others jokingly refer to toilet paper as "treaty paper," their quips reflect the painful disappointment which Deloria describes. Ella says that when news of relocation first began to trickle across the reservation, the Navajos thought they would be protected from removal by their own treaty rights with the United States, much as the Hopis thought their land rights would be protected by the Treaty of Guadalupe Hidalgo. She says, "When the law was passed in 1974, no one really believed it would be carried out. I mean, they're always passing laws in Washington and it takes a long time to affect us. Also, people kept saying they were protected by the treaty. Forcing people off the reservation or away from their homes had to be in violation of their treaty rights." They found to their dismay that it was not.

During the period between 1850 and 1934, United States policy toward Indians underwent several changes of direction. Instead of dealing with them as foreign, separate nations, the U.S. government decided it would try to "civilize" the Indians. One means was to send Indian children to school, the other was outlined in the Allotment Act of 1887, also known as the Dawes Act, which attempted to eliminate communally held lands and divide Indian land into individually owned, family homesteads.

The assumption held by the original thirteen American states was that Indians "would gradually be absorbed into the general population." This didn't happen, and islands of lands were set aside for the eastern tribes within the boundaries of the colonies. After the French and Indian War, the idea of a separate "Indian country" was conceived. And after 1830, the idea of removing Indians to western lands, a concept suggested by Thomas Jefferson, became law. In 1850, because of the immense numbers of white settlers headed west who wanted to take the land set aside for the Indians (and did), a new reservation policy brought back the idea of islands of Indian land surrounded by privately owned or government land.

Allotment was a logical next step in the government's policy during the so-called reservation period, which was marked by "a tendency to further minimize the functions of tribal leaders and tribal institutions and to continually strengthen the position of the Government representative and his subordinates, and to improve effectiveness of their programs to break down traditional patterns within the Indian communities."

The Allotment Act further eroded the historical patterns of tribal organization. The intent was to turn Indians into land-owning, tax-paying citizens. "It is plainly the ultimate purpose of the bill," according to the 1888 annual report of the Board of Indian Commissioners, "to abrogate the Indian tribal organization, to abolish the reservation system and to place the Indians on equal footing with other citizens of the country." However, Indians have traditionally thought of land in terms of community rather than individual use. The idea of allotments caught on slowly with them but was quickly understood by the whites as an opportunity to acquire Indian lands. Few Indians decided to farm their allotments, so in 1891, provision was made for them to lease their lands to whites.

The Curtis Act of 1898 further extended the effects of allotment and provided for the incorporation of towns, the abolition of tribal courts, and increased jurisdiction of the United States courts. The Curtis and Dawes Acts, for example, led directly to the breakup of the Five Civilized Tribes. The most devastating effect, however, arose from the provision that authorized the U.S. government to purchase from the tribes any land not claimed for allotments. The government then sold these "excess" lands. From 1881 to 1900, Indian land holdings were reduced by half—from 155,632,312 acres to 77,865,373 acres. By 1934, Indians held only 48 million acres. "Furthermore," according to a 1934 Commissioner's report to Congress, "that part of the allotted lands which has been lost is the most valuable part of the residual lands; taking all Indian-owned lands into account, nearly one-half, or nearly 20,000,000 acres, are desert or semidesert lands."

Allotment was ended in 1934, after two thirds of Indian land holdings had been lost to white settlers. According to the government's own analysis, the purpose of the Allotment Act was to "replace tribal culture with white civilization." "Progress" was thought more likely under the rules of "white individualism" than under the tribal system, and the government felt that assimilation—its ultimate solution to the Indian problem—was least expensively accomplished through allotment.

The Hopis knew little about the British or the Americans or their plans for Indians until the mid-nineteenth century. During the 1850s and 1860s, a variety of U.S. government surveyors and administrators began to journey to the Hopi mesas. The Hopis believed they would be protected by these white men, who paid them for supplies and services rather than taking them, as had their predecessors, the Spanish. Soon, some Hopis began to believe that the Americans were the lost white brother, the Bahana of their myths, as they had once thought of the Spanish.

Other Hopis were not so sure this white man was Bahana either. One Hopi, Tuwahoyimwa, said,

These first white government people treat us like fierce tribe because they been taught that all Indians are warlike people and you must treat them in rough way to have them understand. Our people know it was predicted that the white man would come in one of two ways. One with understanding and love, treating us with respect when we meet. The other with force and terrible manner, showing us he had lost his good religion. When we were treated unkindly by the government men, our religious leaders began to be suspicious. Is this who was foretold would come with understanding and love? The elders who kept our sacred documents realized that something was wrong with the white man's belief. We, the people, began to check into his manner and conduct. Some of the white people were good, like Miss Skeets, who would come into our homes and take care of our illness without considering us a dirty Indian. They accepted us as humans with feelings, also. But different were those who had other concept of us Hopis.

Divisions grew between those who thought the Americans were Bahana and those who didn't. The split eventually shifted from a subject of religious debate to a political struggle between those who accepted government programs and those who didn't. The most dramatic response to the imposition of U.S. government rule at Hopi took place in the village of Oraibi and emerged as a conflict between the "Hostiles" and the "Friendlies"—so named by the United States Indian agents. The chief complaint against the government was its deportation of Hopi children to school in Keams Canyon, a lengthy trip for Hopis on Second and Third Mesas. Hostile parents hid their children from the soldiers who came to take them away. Among the children who were hidden were Abbott's mother, Helen, and father, Emory.

Helen, though from a Hostile family, eventually developed an appreciation of the advantages that white life could offer, and she took comfort in the teachings of the Mormons, which she found similar in many ways to Hopi religion. She recalls—with more humor and goodwill than most Hopis can conjure—the attempts to hide Hopi children from the soldiers, in an autobiography that she wrote with the help of Louise Udall, a Mormon friend and mother of U.S. Representative Morris Udall and former Interior Secretary Stewart Udall. By the time she was of school age, a day school had been built just off Third Mesa. This reduced the Hopis' resistance somewhat to sending their children to school. Helen recalls,

When we were five or six years of age, we, with our parents (Hostiles) became involved with the school officials, assisted by the Navajo policemen, in a serious and rather desperate game of hide-and-seek, where little Hopi boys and girls were the forfeit in the game. Every day the school principal sent out a truant officer, and many times he himself went with the officer, going to Hopi homes to take the children to school. The Navajo policemen who assisted in finding hidden children were dressed in old army uniforms, and they wore regular cavalry hats over their long hair, done up in a knot. This made quite a picture—especially the traditional hair style with a white man's hat. It had not been customary for Indians to wear hats up to that time.

When September came there was no peace for us. Early in the morning, from our houses on the mesa, we could see the principal and the officer start out from the school, walking up the trail to "get" the children. Hostile parents tried every day in different ways to hide us from them, for once you were caught, you lost the game. You were discovered and listed and you had to go to school and not hide any more. I was finally caught and went to the Oraibi day school one session, when I was about six years old, but not before many times outwitting Mr. Schoolman.

Sometimes, after a very early breakfast, somebody's grandmother would take a lunch and go with a group of eight to twelve little girls and hide them in the cornfields away out from the village. On another day another grandmother would go in the other direction over the hills among the cedars where we would play in the ravine, have our lunch and come back home in the afternoon. Men would be out with little boys playing this game of hide-and-seek. . . .

I don't remember for sure just how I came to be "caught." Maybe both my mother and myself got a little tired of getting up early every morning and running off to hide all day. She probably thought to herself, "Oh, let them get her. I am tired of this. It is wearing me down." The hide-and-seek game continued through September, but with October, the colder weather was on the schoolman's side.

So, one morning, I was "caught." Even then, it was the rule among mothers not to let the children go voluntarily. As the policeman reached to take me by the arm, my mother put her arm around me. Tradition required that it appear that I was forced into school. I was escorted down off the mesa to the schoolhouse, along with several other children. First, each was given a bath by one of the Indian women who worked at the school. Baths were given in the kitchen in a round, galvanized tub. Then we were clothed in cotton underwear, cotton dresses, and long black stockings and heavy shoes, furnished by the government. Each week we had a bath and a complete change of clothing. We were permitted to wear the clothes home each day, but my mother took off the clothes of the detested white man as soon as I got home, until it was time to go to school the next day.

Although the Friendlies were rewarded for their cooperation with much-prized axes, hoes, shovels, and rakes, the Hostile faction refused to be bribed, even with such alluring implements. The Hostile parents instructed their children not to pick up their pencils in school. "If you do," Helen Sekaquaptewa recalls being told, "it means you give consent to what they want you to do. Don't do it." The children of the Friendlies quickly adopted an attitude of entitlement and superiority. They shunned the children of the Hostiles in the playground and called them names. Walking up the mesa toward home at the end of the day, they ran ahead and pelted the Hostile children with rocks.

In 1894, nineteen Hopi men were thrown in jail for refusing to send their children to school. At the same time the government was forcing Hopis to educate their children in the white ways, it was also trying to implement the Allotment Act. This proved too much even for the Friend- lies. The Hopis universally resisted. They pulled out surveying stakes as soon as the surveyors left. The ancient division of lands among the Hopi clans was too strong a tenet of Hopi life for any Hopi to tolerate losing. It has even been suggested that the Hopis' successful resistance saved other nearby tribes from allotment. According to one anthropologist, "The Third Mesa Hopis' resistance appears to have saved not only the Hopi but also the other Pueblos, the Navaho, the Mescalero, White River and San Carlos Apache, and the Papago, from allotment and its disas- trous consequences."

The pressures on the Hopis to become Anglicized exploded in vio- lence at Oraibi. The precipitating events began when Loloma, the Oraibi chief, undertook a journey to Washington, ostensibly to discuss the Hopis' objections to Navajo encroachment. The trip had been arranged by Thomas Keam, the Anglo settler and trader (who earlier had helped draw the Parker-Keam line, the Hopi exclusive use area, whose general boundaries were later adjusted and renamed District 6). On June 16, 1890, five Hopi chiefs, Loloma, Hononi from Shungopavi, Sima and Ahn- awita from Walpi, and Tom Polacca from Hano, who acted as interpreter, left for Washington.

Once there, the Hopis were advised that they could better ward off the Navajos if they moved down from the mesas and settled out on the land as the Navajos did. The chiefs listened to this, but knew it was impossible for the Hopis to leave the shrines and the kivas that were dug underneath the ancient villages, and in which their essential religious functions were performed.

The Indian Affairs agents who had encouraged the Hopis, as early as 1886, to move away from their villages down to the land below to farm and run livestock couldn't understand why the Hopis clung to the mesa tops, and they communicated this to Washington. One agent, Inspector H. S. Traylor, reported that Navajo encroachment into Hopi territory was the Hopis' own fault. He wrote, seemingly unable to comprehend the Hopis' apparent lack of desire to fight, that the Hopi is "the most pitiable and contemptible coward who now lives upon the face of the earth." He went on, "Were he otherwise than the coward that he is, he would prefer to die fighting rather than to surrender the resources of his territory to an enemy."

The agents also thought the terrible poverty at Hopi could only be remedied by pushing the Indians down onto the surrounding land, but the government's policy of encouraging the Hopis away from the mesas only exacerbated problems with the Navajos. In the late 1920s and early 1930s the Hopis finally started moving down, but they ran into the Navajos at the water and best grazing areas. Even in 1917, there was some Hopi movement to the outlying areas, because one old Navajo woman, who lived near Beautiful Mountain, where her family had developed a spring, testified that she "heard the rumble of Hopi hoes" and moved away from them across the Dinnebito Wash.

The visit of the five chiefs to Washington, though it provided no formal guarantees about the Navajos, made a great impression on Loloma. After seeing how many white people lived in the vast areas between Hopi and Washington, he was convinced that the Hopis could never prevail in a conflict. When they returned home, the five chiefs shocked the Hopis by indicating their support for the government programs. They cooperated more with the school administrators and even some missionaries. Loloma took his son and nephew to school and even moved a few miles out of Oraibi to Flute Spring to look after his herds as a gesture of faith to the Americans. He tried to persuade others to do likewise. Upon his return, he even claimed the white man was Bahana. His fellow villagers were overwhelmed. About half supported him, the other half thought he was sadly wrong about the white man. The latter rallied behind Lomahongyoma, a Hostile, who reminded Loloma that Bahana was supposed to speak Hopi and possess the other halves of the sacred tablets. The Americans met neither qualification.

For years, the divisions at Oraibi festered. In 1899, the Hostile faction built a new kiva and determined to hold their own version of the important ceremonies. This caused great anxiety among the people, for this duplication divided families along clan and ceremonial lines and not only made it difficult to find enough people to fill the roles of the ceremonial duties, it augured more bad times. In 1898, the Hopis had been decimated by a smallpox epidemic that reduced their numbers to 1,832.

Loloma died at the turn of the century and passed his position as village chief on to Tewaquaptewa. Eventually, Lomahongyoma turned his leadership of the Hostile faction over to Yukioma. In 1904, Yukioma asked about thirty Hostiles from Shongopavi to move into Oraibi. They were assigned houses in the village and given farm land in Bear clan holdings. Lomahongyoma, as head of the powerful Spider clan, authorized these assignments, though it was a direct challenge to Tewaquaptewa, who was a member of the Bear clan. Oraibi was in an uproar. In 1906, Tewaquaptewa complained to the Superintendent at Keams Canyon. The official told Tewaquaptewa that the people from Shongopavi had no right to remain in Oraibi and if he wanted to expel them, Washington would help. Rather than accept white help just yet, Tewaquap-tewa instead sent to Moencopi for friendly reinforcements. He wanted to have the problem settled before the August snake dance, and planned to expel the Shongopavi emigrés during the days preceding the ceremony. The village was restless, waiting for the inevitable. Guns were cleaned, knives sharpened, and bows made. On the morning of September 7, Tewaquaptewa and some of his supporters walked over to Yukioma's house. Tewaquaptewa's spokesman requested three times that the Shon-gopavi people leave. Yukioma's people refused and a terrible argument broke out. In the afternoon, the feuding groups milled about on a flat ground slightly northwest of the village. At a certain point, Yukioma shouted and drew an east–west line in the sand with his big toe. He and his people lined up on the north side. Tewaquaptewa and his followers lined up with their backs toward Oraibi on the south side. Yukioma stepped over the line and acknowledged to Tewaquaptewa that if he was pushed back over the line, he and his people would leave Oraibi. The two sides formed in fan shapes and started pushing. Yukioma was lifted high in the air by the force. He was bruised and pushed so hard he had to fight for air. Finally, after several hours, he was pushed over the line. Someone watching from the roof of a house fell off in excitement. "It is done!" Yukioma cried. Later, someone scratched these words on a rock at the point of the struggle: "Well it have to be done this way now that when you pass me over this LINE it will be DONE, Sept. 8, 1906." Next to the sentence is a carved bear claw, mark of Tewaquaptewa's Bear clan and a drawing of Massau, god of Yukioma's Fire clan.

Yukioma and about three hundred of his people left Oraibi that day and walked eight miles north. They stopped at a spring and founded the new village of Hotevilla. It was to be a cold and hungry winter, however. Two troops of cavalry arrived at Oraibi a month after the split. Seeing that the problem had been solved without them, they rode on to Hote-villa, where they rounded up the Shongopavis and escorted them home. Yukioma and others were arrested and taken to Fort Wingate. The women were left to fend for themselves in the crude shelters that had been built before the men were arrested. Helen Sekaquaptewa and her family were among those who wintered in the new village of Hotevilla. She recalls,

> Days dragged, each augmenting the misery of the exiles in their im-provised shelters; the cold increased, and each day decreased the hope of going back to their comfortable houses in Oraibi. The need of better shelter was urgent. There was neither time nor manpower to quarry sandstone and gather the other materials to build proper Hopi houses. The men went to work with axes chopping cedars and preparing to build hogans like those of the Navajos—poles standing upright, lean-ing to the center, and cracks filled with mud. In a few weeks with all hands helping there were forty to fifty hogans ready for use.

We were not accustomed to the Navajo way of cooking and heating with an open fire in the middle of the floor and the smoke going out of a hole in the center of the roof. Nearly every day a house or something in it would catch fire. Everyone kept a container with water on hand, and when the alarm was given everyone ran to help. Even *I* remember grabbing my little bottle of water and running to put out the fires. The hogans were pretty well finished before "they" [the white people] took the men away.

That winter, after Yukioma's return, a breakaway faction of the Hotevilla group returned to Oraibi. They were subjected to much ridicule and harassment and in October 1907 left again. They traveled a mile southwest of Oraibi and founded Bacavi Village.

Yukioma was taken to Washington in the hopes he would acknowledge the benefits of the white man's ways, as had Loloma. But it didn't work. "Not even the size of President Taft impressed the old spider-like Hopi prophet," according to Agent Leo Crane, who neither liked nor understood the Hopis. "Youkeoma returned as sullen and determined as before . . . and sat down in his warren of a pueblo amid the sand and the garbage, to await whatever the white man might see fit to do about it."

Crane remained determined that Hopi children go to school. Although Yukioma recited the entire Creation myth to Crane to convince him that the children should not be taken away from their religious duties and teachings at home, Crane sent troops into Hotevilla. In 1911, Crane wrote,

I do not know how many houses there are in Hotevilla, but I crawled into every filthy nook and hole of the place, most of them blind traps, half-underground. And I discovered Hopi children in all sorts of hiding places, and through their fright found them in various conditions of cleanliness. It was not an agreeable job; not the sort of work that a sentimentalist would care for. . . . By midday the wagons had trundled away from Hotevilla with 51 girls and 18 boys . . . nearly all [of whom] had trachoma. It was winter, and not one of those children had clothing above rags; some were nude. During the journey of 45 miles to the Agency many ragged garments went to pieces; the blankets provided became very necessary as wrappings before the children reached their destinations.

The children attended the Agency school at Keams Canyon for four years without returning home. According to Crane, they then elected to go to the Phoenix Indian School. Their parents wouldn't recognize them when they returned home with short hair, different names, and a new language, ill equipped for their life at Hopi, and still unsuited for life in the white man's world.

A year later, Crane had a school built at Hotevilla—the village created by Hostiles at such desperately high cost to avoid the Anglo influences that had penetrated Oraibi. Crane was relentless in his determination to break the Hopi will. When Yukioma protested again against sending the Hotevilla children to school, Crane locked him up. "I shall go home sometime," Yukioma told Crane sagely. "Washington may send another Agent to replace you, or you may return to your own people, as all men do. Or you may be dismissed by the government. Those things have happened before. White men come into the desert; but the Hopi, who came up from the Underworld, remain. You have been here a long time now—seven winters—much longer than the others. And too—you may die."

When Leo Crane returned to Hopi for a visit in 1921, two years after he had left his job as an agent, he found his old nemesis Yukioma had allowed himself to be locked up again rather than submit to the ways of the white man that he knew were wrong for his people. "He was squatted on the floor, sifting a pan of flour for the prison-mess, his old trade." Yukioma was telling the Hopi legends again from start to finish. Crane observed him, "a deluded old savage, possessed by the witches and kachinas of his clan, living in a lost world of fable . . . the last of the Hopi caciques." Agent Crane had broken a strong and brave old man.

The Americans weren't content with Loloma's successor as chief of Oraibi. The Commissioner of Indian Affairs decided that before Tewaquaptewa could actually lead Oraibi, he had to learn the English language and become acquainted with American customs. He and a man from Moencopi were packed up with their families and sent to Sherman Institute in Riverside, California. The government's idea was to subdue Tewaquaptewa completely and turn him into a cooperative functionary. The plan failed and Tewaquaptewa was terribly embittered by his experience. When he returned to Oraibi he found that many of his people had succumbed to the promises of Mennonite missionaries and converted to Christianity. Not only that, many Oraibis had moved down to New Oraibi, or Kiakochomovi (now Kykotsmovi), to be closer to the trading posts, schools, and water.

Tewaquaptewa became more rigid and idiosyncratic as the years went on. As Oraibi lost its population, it also lost its ceremonies. Tewaquaptewa was dying and his village was dying with him. In the last years of his life, he alienated many Oraibis, became nearly blind from trachoma, and scratched out a living carving Kachina dolls and selling them to white tourists. He died in 1960, requesting that his religious paraphernalia be buried with him. His adopted son and intended heir, Stanley Bahnimptewa, lived in Los Angeles, where he wished to remain. Eventually, Tewaquaptewa's adopted daughter, Mina Lansa, took over as Kikmongwi and Thomas Banyacya, David Monongye, and Mina's husband, John Lansa, traveled to Los Angeles to persuade Stanley to give over his hereditary rights to Mina. Stanley agreed to do so on a temporary basis.

Mina and John Lansa, Thomas Banyacya, and Grandfather David Monongye became the most outspoken of a new traditionalist movement, which tried desperately to turn back the tide and resist the U.S. government's efforts to do away with the Hopi system. They bitterly fought the Hopi Tribal Council once it had been established and filled with Hopis cooperative with the U.S. government, and lent their support to the Navajos subject to relocation.

Although the intrusiveness of the Americans was the precipitating factor in the Oraibi split, the essential problem was a truly Hopi one—a struggle for power between two religious groups at Oraibi, the familiar cause of division among the Hopis. As anthropologist Mischa Titiev wrote, "Loloma's receptiveness to American influence provided a *casus belli*, but . . . the primary division of the village resulted from the splitting of the weak phratry tie that had held two strong clans together." And Commissioner of Indian Affairs Francis E. Leupp wrote, "It is believed by not a few persons who know these Indians well, that their division grew wholly out of the internal political dissensions of the tribe; that one of the factions conceived the device of declaring itself friendly to the United States Government, not because it felt so especially, but because it believed that by such a declaration it could win the favor of the Government and obtain an invincible ally in its struggle with the other faction."

Oraibi was ruined by the quarrel. And the effect on the tribe was devastating. Frank Waters writes,

> The Oraibi split, followed by the Hotevilla split, thus helplessly followed the pattern of Hopi disunity set during the clan migrations. It was not marked by bloodshed as had been the destruction of Awatovi. But it was as tragically disastrous to a people now thinned by disease, encroached upon by the ever-increasing Navajos, and demoralized by government restrictions and control. If ever the Hopis needed to be consolidated by unity of purpose and endeavor into an integrated tribal whole, it was now. Instead, the inherent faults and weaknesses of their clan system cracked under the cumulative strain into a rupture that could not be healed.
>
> The Oraibi split was more than a social schism between two factions. It was a psychological wound no Hopi can forget, that bleeds afresh whenever he talks. In Yukioma's avowed retreat back into the prehistoric ruins of the past, back into mythology, we read the retrogression of a living tradition unable to confront the future. And even this retrogression was a failure.

The Hopi religious spirit and ceremonial life was changed irrevocably by the determined, programmatic efforts of the Americans to "civilize" them. And the Americans were aided in their efforts by the Hopis' cultural tendency toward division in the face of religious conflict. During this time, another aspect of Hopi religious life became clearer: religious leaders, rather than fighting to maintain Hopi ways, gave up and decided that their ceremonial knowledge and paraphernalia should die with them. The evocation of the Purification is now heard frequently at Hopi—"when the Purification comes" is a refrain, an explanation, a hope. "When the Purification comes," all wrongs will be righted and the Hopis will move into the next world. This belief in divine intercession keeps traditional-minded Hopis—except in extraordinary circumstances —from speaking out against wrongs in this world.

In the early 1930s, the United States reversed decades of Indian policy that had attempted to assimilate the Indians and turn them into land-owning farmers. The Congress passed in 1934 the Indian Reorganization Act (IRA). It was, ostensibly, the "New Deal" brought to Indian country. The Act provided for the tribes to form their own governments and write their own constitutions. Its ambitions were lofty; however, in practice, the new program failed to meet its stated objectives. Largely because of a lack of qualified Bureau of Indian Affairs personnel, the philosophy and goals of the Act itself were perverted in their implementation. Many tribes were not prepared to write their own constitutions, for example, and simply accepted documents prepared for them. And the communal orientation of many tribes was in conflict with some of the principles of the Act.

Oliver LaFarge, an anthropologist who was known and liked by the Pueblo people among whom he had traveled, was assigned the task of convincing the Hopis to adopt the IRA and a constitution. The traditional Hopi leaders made it immediately clear that they felt there was little need for a new form of government since their own village government was well in place. Nevertheless, Indian Commissioner John Collier was very eager for the tribes to accept the IRA, and he made a personal visit to Hopi in 1936 to urge them to take advantage of the chance to form their own government quickly, before, he warned them, Washington had a chance to change its mind. He also suggested that the Hopis' problem with Navajo encroachment would be solved by the IRA: "I do not mean to say, and I am not saying, that the Hopis and Navajos are rivals at all, but I am saying that there are some things which need to be settled by the two tribes and they cannot be settled until both tribes are organized. In the meantime the Hopis are going to get the bad end of the deal if they stay unorganized."

Collier's emissary LaFarge knew from his earlier visit in 1934 that the Hopi Tribe was divided into factions, which he called "Smarties, Christians, Progressives, and Conservatives." The last two were LaFarge's names for the Friendlies and the Hostiles respectively. He estimated that these two groups existed in about equal numbers and he warned in a report to Collier that the lines between them "are not clearly drawn and need not be. They are the people in each village who, from temperament, tradition, or training, welcome, or oppose, improvements in way of living, etc., etc., within a universally accepted framework of Hopi-ism. These are the people to whom the term 'ka-Hopi', 'not Hopi,' implies everything ugly, violent, untrue."

The other two groups, the Smarties and the Christians, made up the ka-Hopi group, and according to LaFarge's estimates, represented "a total of between 4 percent and 7 percent (let us say 120 to 250 at the outside) of the total population [and] are cordially hated by the remaining 3,000-odd. Due to their vocalism, command of English, and skill at manipulation, they have managed to get themselves in disproportionate numbers onto every representative group which has been formed."

The Smarties were mostly young men who were well-educated. "Some of them wear long hair and affect to be very devout Hopis, others try to act like white men. . . . They include individuals who will steal, and sell, sacred objects from kivas; bright youths who are more than ready to become informants for ethnologists and other students and who will invent what they don't know. They are, in the main, smooth and of good address, and with *one* exception, the only Indians I have ever known who ran after me and fussed over me because I was famous."

During his 1934 fact-finding visit to Hopi, LaFarge had estimated the Christians at about a hundred. He perceived that they spoke to please their listeners and felt that their main interest was in increasing their own influence. LaFarge pointed out two Hopis, Otto Lomavitu and Byron Adams, both of whom would be important figures in the Hopi Tribal Council, and said Lomavitu misrepresented himself as from Oraibi and "made a speech very much in pro of old Hopi ways. In the same way, Adams of Polacca protested . . . against commercialization of sacred Hopi rituals. The same individuals go up on the mesas and assure the Hopis that they are going directly to hell, where all their forebears now are, for following these same ways and practicing these same ceremonies."

LaFarge was convinced early on of the difficulty in organizing the Hopis. Most importantly, he wrote in 1934, "We must take account of the separatism, reaching in ancient times to actual warfare, between villages. A decision will have to be made as to how binding the action of a council of the whole can be upon each village." He also warned against "allowing the Christian and Smarty of Ka-Hopi Progressives to speak for the majority." He insisted that use of these people as interpreters must be "abandoned."

When Oliver LaFarge returned to Hopi in 1936 to campaign for passage of the IRA, he kept a journal, in which he wrote his impressions and thoughts about the Hopis. He worked and recorded from June 1 to

September 11, 1936, and he routinely ignored the advice he had written to himself during his previous stay. His objectives had changed. Whereas he had first come to study and observe, his job now was to convince the Hopis to mark an X next to the Yes box on the upcoming ballot.

LaFarge felt that he was best received at First Mesa, where the Tewas lived in a village called Hano next to the Hopi villages of Walpi and Sichomovi. (Ivan Sidney, the current Hopi chairman, is from First Mesa and of Tewa parentage; the Tewas have long been active in the Tribal Council.) "The name Hopi means peaceful," wrote LaFarge. "They abhor war and physical violence. Wherefore they quarrel constantly and the talking never ceases. In this respect the Tewas, who will punch a man's head for him, are a great relief."

The Hopis' "good manners and friendly approach are from the lips out," he wrote. "They are intensely suspicious, and great harbourers of the memory of wrongs received." He went on, "The Hopis fight with words and sheer endurance, and consider nothing ever settled unless it is settled in their favour. Right, justice, reason, and plain fact do not affect them unless violently brought home, and even then they will still grieve over it and hope for a rearrangement, a generation or more later." He urged the Hopis to adopt the IRA. "I told them that of course, they could not get back all that land. But they should have more than now, and the right to push the Navajos out of what was given to them. And their eagle hunting territories, beyond should be protected." LaFarge now seemed to favor the settling of Hopi problems through the U.S. system and he quickly forgot the warnings he had earlier offered John Collier, that the "Smarties" seemed to have undue influence in dealings with the white man, over and against the desires of the majority of people, and that the idea of a council of the whole was anathema to Hopi culture and tribal organization.

In October 1936, the Hopis cast their votes on reorganization. Ballots marked in favor of the measure tallied 651, and there were 104 votes against. Only one third of those Hopis eligible to vote cast a Yes for reorganization. The rest voted No or abstained from voting. Even though LaFarge knew that the Hopis express opposition by abstention, he made no objection when the BIA recognized the vote as an approval of the new tribal government. LaFarge himself acknowledged, at the time of the campaign, "It is alien to [the Hopis] to settle matters out of hand by majority vote. Such a vote leaves a dissatisfied minority, which makes them very uneasy. Their natural way of doing is to discuss among themselves at great length and group by group until public opinion as a whole has settled overwhelmingly in one direction. . . . Opposition is expressed by abstention. Those who are against something stay away from meetings at which it is to be discussed and generally refuse to vote on it."

After the election, LaFarge admitted in his journals that the abstentions should have been counted as negative votes. He had trouble explaining to the Hopis how the U.S. government had decided to consider the Hopi vote affirmative. "No amount of explaining could convince conservative Hopis that it was right that their failure to vote against the Reorganization Act had not been counted as so many negative votes."

When the Tribal Council came into being, as could have been expected, people from the "Smarty" group dominated its ranks. Byron Adams, who LaFarge noted in his 1934 letter to Collier had good motives but devious means, later became tribal chairman. LaFarge wrote to the BIA warning them of Adams, whom he described as "deeply dishonest, self-seeking, slick" and "a low character and one of the villains of the piece."

The village of Kykotsmovi, which was later to become the location of the tribal headquarters and the Hopi capital, was typical of the Smarties. "Here at Kiakuchomovi is all the meanness, stinginess, smartness, retentive memory of evil received, and distrust of the Hopi, and very little of the redeeming features. A Hopi taken out of the Hopi Road is a shell of a man."

Just those Hopis whom LaFarge had found least admirable were those who filled the ranks of the Tribal Council, for the Conservatives (as traditionalists) would not take part, nor many of the Progressives. LaFarge predicted that the Conservatives wouldn't be able to stand their ground in the face of the Smarties and the pressures of the outside world. The Progressives would prevail against them, yet although he played a large role in thrusting the Progressives into Hopi political life, he didn't seem to like them and he perceived they had lost their values. He observed, "These people, whose way of life has been materially improved by white contact, and who through their friendly approach to officials probably get more than their fair share of the jobs, retain the same violent sense of grievance against the government as the more conservative Hopi villages. Having partially lost the basic Hopi values, they retain the characteristic materialism, self-seeking smugness and quarrelsomeness, which with their somewhat confused progressivism makes them the least attractive group to deal with." LaFarge seemed to have forgotten that he told the Hopis soon after his arrival not to worry about preserving Hopi traditions because the IRA would protect them. He had said, "In this organization lay the means which the government itself provided for protecting the Hopi way."

At the start of his stay at Hopi, LaFarge seemed much more approving of the Conservatives. "They were strictly business, sincere, reasonable. These and Chimopavi [Shongopavi], the conservatives, are the best to deal with I've met so far. In the end, they will accept or reject for sound reasons of their commonweal. I wish they were all like these hostiles!"

LaFarge was impressed by the depth of the Hostiles' religious conviction. He wrote, "Entirely governed by their religion, which has many admirable aspects, they are magnificently stubborn in their determination to live according to the Hopi path, and will face death and destruction, imprisonment, anything, to stand by their ideals and their gods. Through this they achieve real sincerity and strength. Once set, they make good friends. Their dance forms and their other work show them to be artists and craftsmen. They are very hard workers."

But by the end of his stay, LaFarge was bitterly disappointed by the Hostiles' determination not to reorganize. And he wrote disapprovingly of them in his journal, calling them "gutless," and criticizing them for their "rigid attitude of hostility to the government" coupled with "grabbing every benefit and free handout which comes their way, and yelling for more."

After the excitement was over and LaFarge was about to return to his own home, he realized that what he had worked so diligently to bring about at Hopi was in fact ka-Hopi, not Hopi. The Tribal Council had *not* been approved by a majority of the Hopis, and the people who would eventually sit on the Council represented the most ostracized and confused members of the tribe. Putting them in the position of making decisions for the whole, most of whom were determined to continue being Hopis and shied away from voicing objections, was tantamount to booby-trapping the tribe. Perhaps he eventually understood the hubris that allowed him to force an alien government on a people with a highly developed and effective system of their own. In a final note to his *Running Narrative*, penned on the last day he was in Hopi country, LaFarge bared his motivations:

> The main theme I have in mind is the white man's burden. I have thought of it often in the past fifteen years, in different ways. It is a snare and a delusion, it is also a reality and something not to be ducked. I sat on my porch in the moonlight one warm night shortly before the Flute Ceremony, with a forbidden and quite strong drink of rye whiskey and water beside me. I had the evening clear, I was tired, I aimed for nine o'clock bed. I smoked my pipe and sipped and looked at the moon. I heard some girls laugh together, the high, rather silly laughter of adolescents in a group, I heard a woman speak and laugh, I heard a man go by on horseback, singing, I heard voices, I saw the lights on top of the mesa, and faintly caught the shred of a song from up there. I heard cars moving. All these sounds and the lights tired me. With each observation I felt the weight again. They can play and laugh, but I am planning their futures. I carry them. There is no rest for me while I am aware of their presences.
>
> I thought then, and faced the facts about this Constitution. The Hopis are going to organize, first, because John Collier and a number of other people decided to put through a new Indian law, the Reor-

ganization Act (Wheeler-Howard Act). The Indians didn't think this up. We did. Collier, Kohn, Cutting, Thomas, Wheeler, Harper, myself . . . so many others. They accepted it when they had their referendum last year, because Hutton put it across, just as the Jicarillas did because Graves and Wirt and I decided they should, and the Navajos rejected it because the missionaries and the Indian Rights Association worked against it. We came among these people, they didn't ask us, and as a result, they are our wards. It's not any inherent lack of capacity, it's the cold fact of cultural adjustment.

Charlotte Westwood [an attorney from the Solicitor's office], spoke to me about the fact that I said all the right things "this is your decision, it is up to you" and so forth, but that my manner was paternal and authoritarian. Sure it was. Why duck the facts? We bring to these Indians a question which their experience cannot comprehend, a question which includes a worldview and a grasp of that utterly alien, mind-wracking concept, Anglo-Saxon rule by majority vote, with everything that follows in the train of that.

The Hopis will accept a constitution which includes self-government and the best transition into our democratic system I could devise, because Edwin Marks [Hotevilla school principal] and Lorenzo Hubbell [trader at Oraibi] and Alexander G. Hutton [BIA Agency Superintendent] and I decided they should. Primarily the decision was mine; the others upheld my hands. . . . That is the white man's burden; to undo despite the lack of comprehension of his wards, the harm that he himself has done.

This anthropologist, who in the privacy of a quiet evening could admit his fears about his own paternalism and overreaching, nevertheless continued to defend the legitimacy of the Hopi vote on reorganization. In a letter to John Collier a week before the above entry, he wrote, "Progressives and Conservatives alike are agreed upon the document thus formed." The Kikmongwi of Oraibi quickly complained about the Progressive influence in the new Hopi government, and in response, LaFarge wrote to a U.S. senator a letter "which discounted the protest and which characterized the traditionals as an insignificant minority under the leadership of a man . . .'not quite sane.' "

From its inception, the Tribal Council was boycotted by several villages. Its quorum troubles were so severe that in early 1939 "the Washington office of the BIA was drafting and considering proposed amendments to the Hopi Constitution to overcome the problem the Hopi Tribal Council was having in making a quorum at its meetings." In 1943, the Council disbanded. It was reorganized in 1950 and remained more or less nonfunctional until 1955, when the BIA officially recognized it again as the Hopis' representative body, though there was still considerable opposition to it. Frank Waters observed in 1963, "The tribal council is a complete and abject failure, a white concept of democratic self-government operating against the traditional background of Hopi belief and custom, and dividing the people into irreconcilable factions."

The idea of secular leaders was completely alien to the Hopis. The religious leaders were the ones whose role was to help solve problems, lead the Hopis through their complicated rituals, and choose their own successors. Their responsibilities, however, were narrowly defined, and there were many leaders. As one anthropologist put it, "Hopi political organization is difficult to characterize, because authority is phrased in ritual rather than secular terms and is not concentrated in any single position."

As anthropologist Mischa Titiev observed,

On the whole, the village chief is looked upon rather as a guide and an advisor than an executive; and as an interpreter of Hopi tradition rather than as a legislator. A chief's word is respected and his opinion usually sought on any vital matter, but there is virtually no provision for his active participation in government. No compulsion is brought to bear on those who do not care to consult the chief on matters that do not come directly under his personal supervision, and he lacks the power to enforce such decisions as he may render. A man may dance Katcina or not as he sees fit; he may join a secret society or not as he pleases; participation in community work is largely voluntary; and there is scarcely an activity that is not optional rather than compulsory. Even if the head of a very important ceremony were to allow it to lapse, there is little to hinder him and no mechanism to punish him. The policy of the "state" is one of nearly completely laissez-faire, and the phrase "pi um I" (It's up to you) may well be the motto of Hopi society.

The U.S. government could not deal with such a convoluted system. It needed an entity that would say, "It's up to us." Uppermost was the BIA's interest in helping energy companies sign exploration leases. By 1950, more than twenty oil companies were corresponding with the BIA superintendent over his progress in reorganizing a Hopi Tribal Council that could grant rights so that they could proceed with mineral exploration. The 1882 area had become one of the hottest untested sources of oil and coal in the nation.

(10)

Coal

"There's a lot of minerals under the earth here, that's what this land dispute is all about," says Bessie Hatathlie. And she is right. If high quality, easily recoverable coal had not been found under Black Mesa, it is unlikely that a massive relocation of Navajo sheepherders would ever have been contemplated. Although the Hopis repeatedly insisted to intruders—be they Apaches, Utes, Navajos, or Anglos—that Hopi land was inviolable, those claims were effectively ignored by the U.S. government until the Hopis' interests overlapped those of a very powerful group—the energy industry.

Coal was discovered under Black Mesa in 1909. The first investigation of the area, performed by the U.S. Geological Survey, estimated that the rolling mesa held 8 billion tons of recoverable coal. Sixty years later, the Arizona Bureau of Mines theorized that there could be as much as 21 billion tons hidden beneath the forested plateau. Black Mesa was predicted to be one of the world's biggest energy centers. Further studies suggested that huge supplies of oil, natural gas, and uranium also underlay the area. Strangely enough, the massive folds of the ancient strata holding these minerals lay almost precisely beneath the rectangular boundaries of the Hopi 1882 Executive Order Area.

In 1933, the supervisor of the Bureau of Indian Affairs in Keams Canyon was asked to identify who controlled the mineral rights in the 1882 area. The Commissioner of Indian Affairs in Washington answered by stating "it would appear" that both tribes shared the mineral rights. The companies that had initiated the request were not satisfied by that answer, and in the early 1940s, in response to further pressure from the energy industry, the Hopi BIA superintendent again asked the Commissioner to clarify the matter. Felix Cohen, the Solicitor General of the United States, issued a seminal opinion entitled "Ownership of the Mineral Estate in the Hopi Executive Order Area" in 1946. Cohen determined that the two tribes held coextensive rights to the minerals in the 1882 area.

Thus began the political reality of the land dispute. It was not repeated Hopi complaints about Navajo encroachment onto uninhabited 1882-area lands that drove the government to action. It was the pressure of oil and gas companies to determine ownership of the area.

One more element was needed for the battle over the 1882 area to go forward: lawyers. Conveniently enough, in 1946 the U.S. Congress created the Indian Claims Commission to hear claims from Indian tribes of the U.S. government's unlawful taking of land. The Claims Commission was not authorized to return land to Indians, but only to compensate them with money, after which it would extinguish the tribes' historical claims. The monetary value of the land was to be determined as of the date of taking—usually fifty to a hundred years prior to the claim. This, of course, reduced the government's liability. Although the tribes didn't stand to get what they wanted from this program—land—attorneys stood to gain a great deal. The act provided that lawyers could receive up to 10 percent of the value of the compensation paid the tribes. One estimate suggests that white lawyers earned a total of $60 million by extinguishing Indian claims to their ancestral lands.

In 1947, two lawyers applied to the nation's largest Indian tribe, the Navajos, for the combined post of claims attorney and general counsel. Norman Littell of Arlington, Virginia, a former assistant attorney general under Roosevelt, was eventually chosen over John Boyden of Salt Lake City. Boyden promptly approached the Hopis. Although the Interior Department was prepared to approve his contract, his appointment could not be ratified by the Hopi Tribal Council, because it no longer existed.

In order to secure approval to become the tribe's claims attorney, John Boyden made the rounds of the villages, trying to drum up support. Boyden knew a little about Indians and Indian law. His law partner, Charles Wilkinson, had been a partial author of the Indian Land Claims Act. Boyden himself had served as U.S. Attorney in Utah from 1933 to 1946, where he had represented the government in several Indian cases, during which time he had "developed a close working relationship with reservation superintendents and other BIA personnel in the Southwest." Before setting out to persuade the Hopis to confirm him as their claims attorney, he had twice traveled to the Washington Bureau headquarters, prepared a possible contract with the Solicitor's office and the BIA, and assured himself that the Hopis had a legitimate claim of taking. However, as might be expected, five traditional villages—Oraibi, Shongopavi, Hotevilla, Mishongnovi, and Lower Moencopi—refused to consider his application.

With no Council to ratify his selection, Boyden resorted to treachery to convince the Hopis to hire him. During recorded meetings with the Hopi villages, Boyden tried to curry favor by suggesting that the Hopis might recover land through the claims process, though he knew very well that the Claims Commission was only authorized to make monetary awards. When it was time to vote, Boyden received a nominal number of Yes votes from the progressive villages of Shipaulavi, First Mesa, Kykotsmovi, and Upper Moencopi. As an example of the kind of support Boyden was shown, in Shipaulavi, population 116, Boyden received 9 votes. The BIA, not entirely convinced by similar numbers of Yes votes cast in the other villages, nevertheless rationalized that the vote of the progressive villages, scant though it was, should be considered more significant than the negative vote of the traditional villages, since the total population of the progressive villages outnumbered that of the traditional by 1,615 to 1,413. The BIA, armed with that argument, recommended approval of the contract. The Indian Law Resource Center, after conducting an investigation of the claims petition for the Hopi traditionalists in 1979, concluded: "In this play on numbers, a few poorly attended village meetings were characterized as a full-scale referendum of resident Hopis. Despite the fact that . . . traditional Hopi government was again ignored or avoided, and despite the fact that a false hope of possible return of land was being offered, Boyden's contract to represent the Hopis as their claims attorney was approved in Washington on July 27, 1951."

Boyden's initial interest in working for the tribe was clearly pecuniary (the law creating the Indian Claims Commission became known as the Lawyers Welfare Act because it proved so lucrative for attorneys). And Boyden had his eye on additional sources of revenue from the tiny Hopi Tribe. A memorandum of a meeting between the BIA and Boyden not long after his claims contract was approved shows that Boyden had mineral development on his mind. The memo states, "[Boyden] pointed out that remuneration for his services will depend largely on working out solutions to many of the Hopi problems to such a point that oil leases will provide funds." The BIA realized that pursuing mineral development would require a functioning tribal council. There was also something else: "Further than this problem," the memo continued, "but one not considered impossible of solution is the Hopis' traditional reluctance to disturb the land. However, it is believed that they will probably accept drilling when it is realized that nearby drilling operations may drain away their oil." The Hopis' deep and abiding beliefs about their land were considered here an obstacle that could be pushed aside as soon as the Hopis found themselves trapped in a situation not of their own making. Boyden made it clear that in order to avoid confronting the Hopis' reluctance to disturb their land, he didn't recommend reconstituting the Council just yet; first he wanted to stack it with members who would vote with him. The BIA concurred and, at Boyden's urging, approved his contract as general attorney on May 29, 1952. Boyden now was the tribe's claims attorney *and* general legal representative, though he was bitterly opposed by the Hopi traditionalists, who made their displeasure evident in repeated, clear, and moving communications with the BIA and the courts. Boyden successfully worked to defray the effect of this opposition. The traditionalists rallied support among whites sympathetic to their cause. This was the government's reply to one of them: "The Bureau of Indian Affairs is not unsympathetic to the views expressed by these 'traditionalist' leaders of the Hopi people who have a strong and deeply rooted desire to cling to their ancestral ways of life. However, there is a question as to how far we can go in satisfying their desires within the framework of national law and policy."

Boyden was a Mormon and therefore subscribed to the belief that Indians were a lost tribe of Israel that had abandoned its religious laws. Perhaps in part as a result of his religious convictions, Boyden's representation of the Hopis quickly developed a messianic flavor. Mormonism was particularly attractive to some Hopis because of the similarities in the origin myths of the two religions, and many of the members of the Hopi Tribal Council in its early days were Mormon converts.

Six days after the approval of his claims contract, Boyden filed a land claim. In the action, the Hopis claimed their aboriginal land reached up to the San Juan River in the north, followed the Colorado and the Little Colorado in the west, over along the Puerco River in the south, and over to the Arizona–New Mexico border in the east—generally the area of the Navajo reservation in Arizona.

Boyden also set about determining the Hopi rights to the mineral estate in the 1882 area. He challenged the Solicitor General's opinion that the Navajos and Hopis had coextensive rights, and in 1955, filed a brief claiming that the opinion was in error. He further argued that the Hopis' claim of exclusive rights to the mineral estate should be decided separately from the issue of the Navajos' rights to graze livestock on the area.

The Navajo attorney Norman Littell replied to Boyden's brief by criticizing his "novel attempt to sever horizontally the interests in lands held by two Indian tribes respectively, recognizing surface rights in one tribe and subsurface mineral rights in another." He suggested that this approach might have something to do with "the exciting new prospects for uranium and oil and gas development." The BIA and the University of Arizona College of Mines had just completed a three-volume report on mineral resources on the Hopi and Navajo reservations. It mentioned the possibility of extracting coal and producing electric power "within the foreseeable future."

Littell suggested that the tribes sue each other over their respective rights in the area, with the objective being the drawing of a boundary between the two tribes. (This was completely separate from the case

Boyden brought before the Land Claims Commission.) Boyden agreed, and the two attorneys received permission from their respective tribal councils to ask Congress for the authorizing legislation, which Stewart Udall, as we have seen, obligingly introduced in the House in 1958. By this time, the Hopi Tribal Council, in spite of dogged objections from the traditionalists, had been resurrected in some form. (So few villages sent representatives that the absence of just one participating member would leave the Council without a quorum.)

Littell seemed so eager for the suit to go forward that he encouraged the government to loan the Hopis the money to pay counsel. He then suggested that the government take as collateral the mineral estate of the 1882 area. He proposed that the Interior Department actually begin mineral extraction in the disputed area, place the revenues into a fund, and draw money from it to pay the Hopis' legal expenses. At the end of the trial, he proposed, the money could be distributed between the two tribes. No thought was given to the number of Navajos who might have to be moved to make room for the strip mining, or whether or not the Navajo and Hopi people wanted coal mined from the mesa they both held sacred.

Congress, in its infinite wisdom, struck from the bill Littell's suggestion that the Interior Department advance the Hopis enough money to litigate, as well as his proposition that the Interior Department lease mineral rights within the disputed area as collateral for the loan. Even after the 1962 *Healing v. Jones* decision, which determined that Hopis and Navajos had "joint, undivided and equal" rights to the surface and subsurface of the 1882 area outside of District 6, the Navajo tribal attorney appeared blinded by the prospect of mineral development. He told the Navajo Tribal Council that *Healing* had been a victory of sorts. Said he, "Never until now did the Navajos own title even though they had used and occupied most of the Executive Order Area. No leases or mineral exploration could be made by either tribe. As soon as administrative details are worked out, the oil and gas exploration by companies which have long waited to get into the territory can commence and known coal deposits may be developed."

Immediately after the establishment of the Joint Use Area (JUA)—that land outside of District 6 and within the 1882 boundaries that the *Healing* court determined was jointly owned by the tribes—Commissioner of Indian Affairs Philleo Nash called for meetings to decide how the area would be administered. One of the first meetings took place at the Valley Ho Hotel in Scottsdale on August 6 and 7, 1963. The Navajos immediately staked out their position: they would buy the land from the Hopis, and the Hopis could use the money to buy public land outside the reservation to make up for their loss. The Navajos argued that the JUA was completely inhabited by Navajos, and wasn't inhabited—nor had ever

been significantly inhabited—by Hopis. The Hopis dismissed the suggestion out of hand. They wanted their half of the JUA. Norman Littell
summed up the situation by saying, "What has evolved is a clear picture
of the irresistible force meeting the immovable body." The irresistible
force of the Navajos spread over the land with their sheep was head to
head with the immovable Hopis, whose culture and religion told them
that they were placed on the land to take care of it for all mankind.

The question was raised about whether the two tribes could settle the
issue of the subsurface rights first, so as to allow the mineral companies
to begin exploratory drilling right away. But the Hopis wanted the Navajos off one half of the JUA. And Boyden announced he would try to
prevent mineral extraction until the Hopis' half was vacated. Then Boyden revealed his trump card. He acknowledged that the oil companies
had put great pressure on the Hopis to resolve the issue of ownership.
He said he was counting on the lobbying help of the oil companies to
win his clients possession of half of the land. "Now, if we just go ahead
and do this," said Boyden about agreeing to the subsurface development,
"then the matter of partition is of no interest at all to the oil companies,
but if . . . partition was holding up the oil development the oil companies would be awfully interested in getting the legislation in. It is just
practical."

The energy companies' interest in the area set the machinery of the
partition in gear. Without their pressure, the land dispute might have
remained simply a simmering local problem between tribes, as it had for
the previous seventy-five years. Some observers of the land dispute
maintain that the energy companies, working in concert with lawmakers,
BIA officials, and tribal attorneys, *created* the concept of the land dispute.
They argue that the energy companies would have found it very difficult
to relocate Indians from their homelands for the purpose of clearing it for
strip mining. But if the Navajos were removed for another reason—
returning the land to Hopi control—then the land would be cleared
without any political fuss for the energy companies.

Partition of the JUA was desirable for the mineral companies for another reason: they would rather that the coal-rich lands were owned by
the Hopis because they preferred to deal with that tribe. In the early
1970s, the Hopis were actively courting energy companies while Navajo
chairman Peter MacDonald "was speaking against them." MacDonald,
who was trying to establish greater Navajo control over the tribe's resources, was asked in 1980 whether coal interests played a part in the
land partition. He answered, "Definitely. I think not just the fact that
there is coal and possibly uranium and oil in that area, but also my
position, a strong position against the energy companies, were factors.
In other words, one thing was to get the resources and the land, as much
of it as possible, through partitioning it and taking it away from the

Navajos. That's one objective, I feel, with the energy companies. The other was to punish me and the Navajo tribe for refusing to let the energy companies steal our resources again. So it was a double-barreled attack."

There is no convincing evidence of a broad-based conspiracy behind the land dispute. The Hopis' unhappiness with the Navajo presence on the land is well established in the historical record. It is more accurate to say that the energy interests provided the Hopi lawyer with an extremely powerful tool with which to bring attention to the problem, and ammunition with which to push for partition. Without the noise and sense of urgency created by the possibilities of mineral development, it is possible that a different solution to the land issue may have been undertaken. And without the possibilities of mineral development, the tribal attorney may have been less motivated to drag the Hopi Tribe into legal battles that have cost millions of dollars. Between 1974 and 1986 alone, the government reimbursed the tribes $5 million in legal fees, probably a fraction of the sums the tribes themselves paid to their lawyers.

In the period following the 1962 *Healing v. Jones* decision, there was tremendous excitement not only about the coal under Black Mesa, but also over the potential for oil. Black Mesa was called "one of the hottest untested areas in the entire country." The executive director of the Arizona Oil and Gas Conservation Commission announced that oilmen "have been licking their chops" for years over the area. And the *Oil and Gas Journal* crowed that "the ripest wildcat target in the United States for 1965 is going to be the Black Mesa basin of Arizona, still one of the largest unexplored basins in the country."

In the late 1960s and early 1970s, coal companies envisioned the Four Corners area as the center of a huge grid of six coal-fired power plants which would feed the fast-growing metropolitan areas of the Southwest. But plans went beyond the six massive plants. In 1974, a consortium of the Texas Eastern Transmission Company and Southern California Gas, called WESCO, began active negotiation with the Navajo Tribe about plans to build coal gasification plants on Navajo reservation land in New Mexico. Eventually four coal-fired plants were built. The coal gasification idea fizzled. However, it is clear that the energy-generating potential of the Four Corners area was of great interest at the time, and the energy crisis of the 1970s focused even more attention on cheap Indian coal.

Although there is no evidence that members of Congress were lobbied directly by energy interests during the discussion of partition legislation, and although there is no evidence available to support the suggestion that there was an organized attempt on the part of coal and oil companies to move the Navajos off the land, the power of the energy companies was never too far in the background throughout discussions of the land dispute. Several participants in the governmental process even went on to work for the interested parties. Harrison Loesch was a proponent of partition and relocation when he served as the Interior Department's liaison to the Bureau of Indian Affairs in 1974, and he also worked on the partition legislation in 1974 as the Senate Interior Committee Minority Counsel. In 1976, he became a Peabody Coal vice-president. Wayne Owens, the author of the partition bill passed into law in 1974, went to work in John Boyden's law firm in 1976. Jerry Verkler, a staff director of the Senate Interior Committee while the bill was being considered, and who worked vigorously to get the law passed, was hired by a member of WEST (Western Energy Supply and Transmission Associates), an association of twenty-three utility companies, local power authorities, and the Bureau of Reclamation, which was the developer and future operator of the coal-fired power plants planned for the Four Corners area.

Leon Berger, a former executive director of the Relocation Commission, summed it up: "We all know there is coal in the area. And we all know that originally, when the overall design of the master plans for power plants in that area were being contemplated . . . that they would have needed a tremendous amount of coal. And that's common knowledge. Also common knowledge that the Hopi would have been easier to deal with than the Navajo in terms of the mining of coal. Also common knowledge that if you're mining coal out there, you would have to have not too many people. And you put all that together and Harrison Loesch going to work for Peabody and people have alleged it is all part of a big conspiracy. Suspicious-looking ingredients there, but during the time I was involved with it, I saw nothing to say 'Aha! this is it.' "

Rather, it appeared that the dispute was driven by the interests of several parties. Mineral development had been very much on the mind of the Navajos' own attorney, Norman Littell, and, of course, John Boyden's payment was dependent on mineral revenue. After the *Healing* decision, the Hopi Council signed exploration leases with several oil companies. The tribe received $3 million for exploration contracts and bonuses. In a twist of fate mirroring the thick folds of tertiary marine sediment that apparently hid the oil far beneath the reach of the drilling rigs, all the holes came up dry.

Boyden billed the tribe $780,000 for the work he'd done on the *Healing* case. The Tribal Council, convened to approve his fee, concurred with the request of one of its members, who, in a burst of magnanimity, suggested that the tribe pay him an additional $220,000 and make him a millionaire.

The battle over the 1882 area proved advantageous for the Navajo lawyer as well. Although his risky litigiousness led ultimately to the displacement of thousands of Navajos, Norman Littell sued the Navajos for $2.8 million, or 10 percent of the value of half of the 1882 area he had "recovered" for the tribe. He settled for $795,000 in 1980 after a protracted battle. George Vlassis, a bearded, tough-talking lawyer with a sharp wit who became the Navajos' general counsel in 1972, asks, "Now, how is it that the lawyers for both tribes got contracts to represent the individual tribes that allowed for a fee of 10 percent of the value they won? Unheard of. They categorized this case as a claims case. A claims case is brought by an Indian tribe against the federal government, not [another tribe]. . . . How did that ever happen? Nobody has any answers to that. It should never have taken place."

And that's not the end of the shenanigans. Little did the Hopi Council members know that while representing the tribe in negotiations over oil leases with Aztec Oil and Gas, Boyden was also working for Aztec. Nor did they know later that Boyden represented the Hopi Council while one of his law partners represented Peabody in its intended merger with Kennecott Copper. (The government refused to approve the merger and Peabody was later sold to a consortium including the Bechtel Corporation.)

Peter MacDonald was the first Navajo leader to push for higher royalties and more control over mineral production on Navajo land. The royalties paid to the Navajos and Hopis in the early days were scandalously low. The Navajos were receiving from 20 to 35 cents a ton in the 1970s on coal that was worth $7 a ton to the companies that were stripmining it. Comparable coal is purchased for $1.50 a ton and more from others.

The Navajos and Hopis had also agreed to the cheap sale of an even more precious commodity: water. The Peabody mine at Black Mesa sends coal slurry to the Mojave plant in Bullhead City via a 273.6-mile-long pipeline that uses 2,000 to 4,500 gallons of water per minute, about 3,200 acre-feet per year drawn from deep wells of precious water. Navajos and Hopis complain that groundwater wells in the area have dried up since the water began being pumped for the coal slurry. The Hopis are paid $1.67 per acre-foot for the water. The Navajos negotiated a better deal— they get $5 an acre-foot.

The tribal councils in the early days were not sophisticated enough to manage the tribes' resources properly. In fact, even in the early 1970s, the Hopi Tribal Council was highly influenced by the energy companies courting it. In a *Washington Post* article, freelance writer Mark Panitch stated,

> The relationship between the Hopi council and the power companies became almost symbiotic. On the one hand, [then Tribal Council chairman Clarence] Hamilton speeches written by Evans [& Associates] would be distributed through the public relations machinery of twenty-three major western utilities. On the other hand, these utilities would tell their customers, often through local media contacts, that the Hopis were "good Indians" who wouldn't shut off the juice that

ran their air conditioners. . . . The Hopi rapidly took on the aura of the underdog who just wanted to help his white brother. Some of the Navajo, on the other hand, were saying threatening things about closing down polluting power plants and requiring expensive reclamation of strip-mined lands.

The tribal councils' inadequacy in representing their own interests flows directly from their history and the BIA's desire to use them primarily to approve mineral exploration leases. As we have seen, the Hopi Tribal Council was forced back into existence in 1955 for the purpose of approving energy leases. Other tribal councils had been created for the openly acknowledged purpose of approving Anglo mineral prospecting on Indian land. As far back as the turn of the century, the calling of a Navajo council to approve a mineral prospecting lease "was a routine and even casual event. The local agent would issue a call for all adult males to convene at the agency's headquarters on a given date. . . . Once a council had been held, the Indians disbanded."

These Navajo councils were called under the authority of an 1891 law authorizing mineral exploration on certain Indian lands. On the Navajo reservation, in response to requests made under that law, Navajos from the San Juan or Shiprock areas were called to a council to "rubber stamp an agreement authorizing such exploration."

The Navajos eventually wised up to this practice, which allowed them, under certain circumstances, a five percent royalty. In 1921, when a subsidiary of Standard Oil struck pay dirt, the council voted 75–0 against the approval of an oil lease. The BIA adjourned that council and reconvened new councils until it found one that would approve the lease. In 1923, the BIA found a council that would vote its leasing authority to the BIA itself. This in fact was the first act of the nascent Navajo Tribal Council—to transfer its leasing authority to the BIA. (The Navajos voted against reorganization under the IRA. To this day, the tribe doesn't have a constitution.) One historian suggests the Navajos agreed to this transfer of authority because, in return, they were promised "government aid in securing new lands" for their rapidly increasing tribe.

When lured with the promise of land, Indians have historically relinquished control of their destinies and placed their futures in the hands of the white man. For land, Indians will give up just about anything. Says Larry Nez, a Navajo and a Princeton graduate, about the Navajo-Hopi land dispute, "This is a fight where land is more important than people. I think that would be true for any Indian tribe at any time in history."

(11)

Public Law 93-531:
The Settlement Act

Although the *Healing v. Jones* decision determined the tribes' respective rights to the 1882 area, it obviously did not proffer a solution to the problem that the jointly owned land was almost completely inhabited by Navajos.

Soon after the *Healing* decision and the establishment of the Joint Use Area, the Navajos and Hopis met with Commissioner of Indian Affairs Philleo Nash to decide the future of the JUA. Abbott Sekaquaptewa was the Hopis' chief spokesman, and, after steadfastly refusing to sell the Navajos any part of the JUA, he set about trying to move Navajo livestock off the range to make room for Hopi animals.

Sekaquaptewa's intense interest in getting more grazing land has not been shared by many of his people. Albert Yava, a Hopi-Tewa, wrote in his book *Big Falling Snow*: "The well-off Hopi has special interests. If he owns a lot of cattle for example, that land we have been contesting with the Navajos is much more important to him than to a poor family in Shipaulovi. The average Hopi isn't going to benefit very much from the land settlement."

The Sekaquaptewas are certainly not average. The family is extraordinary. Abbott's father, Emory, was a BIA-appointed tribal judge and one of the first chairmen of the Hopi Tribal Council. Emory was industrious, entrepreneurial. In the 1920s he bought his own horses and wagon and worked as a "freighter" for the Lorenzo Hubbell Trading Post at Oraibi, hauling supplies from the railroad in Winslow and Flagstaff back to Hopi. While still a student at the Phoenix Indian School in the first decade of the twentieth century, he worked at the school's power plant. On the side, he repaired cars, and in the summers, supplied students as hired hands for Anglo farmers at harvest time. He later held other jobs in power plant maintenance and construction for the government. He also was a diligent and devoted farmer and livestock owner.

Today, one can see the large cottonwood trees Emory planted to provide shade for his cattle near the ranch. His success and perseverance with Anglo ways was unusual for Hopis at the time. The family also set itself apart by adopting Christianity. Emory and Helen became Mormon converts.

Emory and Helen shocked their families with their modern ways. Although they agreed to a Hopi wedding to please Helen's traditional family, they were also married by a minister and received a wedding license from the state. This so displeased Helen's family that the young couple was compelled to move away from the mesas. This would not be the last time that the couple's appreciation of white ways would cause problems for them among their people. After they moved back to the reservation into a house in Hotevilla in 1920, they again felt the disapproving gaze of less prosperous and more traditional Hopis. Helen recalls,

> Our lives were a combination of what we thought was the good of both cultures, the Hopi way and what we had learned at school. Whenever we departed from the traditions, our neighbors would scorn us. They were greatly offended because we were friendly with the government workers, the teachers, and the nurses, and even let them come into our house. . . . When I went to the spring for water, nearly every time I would meet a woman on the trail or at the spring who would bawl me out about something; even the clothes I wore on my back were taboo. I didn't wear the traditional dress. I did not enter wholeheartedly into all of the community social and religious events. Good traditional Hopi women sit all day in the plaza, maybe several days at a time, watching the dances. They have so many that I begrudged the time. I would rather stay at home and care for my house, or read, which I often did. I was aware that my neighbors were talking about me, laughing at me, mimicking, and generally belittling me all the time.

Eventually, in 1935, this pressure led the family to move out to the ranch they had established on Emory's family's clan land southwest of Hotevilla, and later still, to build a house in Kykotsmovi, the location of the tribal government headquarters.

The Sekaquaptewas' children were as extraordinary as their parents. One son, Wayne, who died in 1979, ran a successful crafts cooperative, and was co-owner of a company that ran the Hopi Cultural Center—a complex that includes a motel, restaurant, and museum. He also published a Hopi newspaper called *Qua Toqti* (The Eagle's Cry). Another son, Emory, Jr., attended law school at Brigham Young University and now teaches anthropology at the University of Arizona. Abbott was a representative to the tribal council from New Oraibi in the early 1950s, and of course later served as chairman.

Abbott Sekaquaptewa has made a profound mark on the Hopis' future. Though a fervent defender of Hopi ethnicity, Sekaquaptewa adopted, as did his parents but not all his brothers, the distinctly un-Hopi custom of living out on the land and running livestock. His love of the land and determination to carry on the family tradition established by his father has compelled Abbott to persist over several decades, through several court cases and exhausting congressional battles until his and his fellow Hopis' patrimony was secured and extended by law.

As tribal chairman, Sekaquaptewa represented a minority of Hopis— those few who raised cattle, supported economic development including mineral exploitation, and who maintained a burning desire to teach the Navajos a lesson about right and wrong. Anthropologist Richard Clemmer believes that Sekaquaptewa's energy and determination do not just reflect his own personal qualities, but can also be understood in a broader framework:

> When the tribal council was instituted, it almost immediately became a kind of unsanctioned fraternity whose members were the uninitiated and the disaffected. Those who converted to Christianity in the early part of the century effectively removed themselves from participation in most of the religious societies. Only the Kachina society, into which every Hopi youngster is initiated—except for those chosen for the Powamu society—remained open to them. Their descendants have been in the awkward position of knowing comparatively less about Hopi traditions than Hopis who are initiated into societies beyond the Kachina societies, and it is these descendants of early Christian converts who have always dominated the tribal council. Only through the council can the uninitiated obtain legitimacy for political action and for political interpretations of Hopi history and culture, and, of course, that legitimacy rests in large part upon the economic and political ties which the council maintains with outside interests such as the U.S. government and lease customers.

Clemmer believes the Sekaquaptewas, who have had such a profound influence on Hopi life, present a telling example of how Hopis who were very different from the norm came to shape the Hopis' future:

> The Sekaquaptewa family is unusual, and the tribal council has proven to be an effective channel in which the family has expressed its Hopi identity without commitment to the full spectrum of traditional Hopi culture. For Hopis like the Sekaquaptewas, who have personal histories reflecting some detachment from Hopi village life, the council and other features of the interface between Hopi communities and the bureaucracy of the surrounding Euro-American satellite are important sources of influence, power, and self-fulfillment. The council is a source of upward mobility for those Hopis who do not have access to

traditional prestige positions because of their religious affiliation, their ideology, or their non-conformity to Hopi ways, but do not wish to wholly assimilate to United States culture. Above all, the council provides a channel through which to affect the Hopi destiny, which is such an important feature of Hopi mythic process.

In the meetings which immediately followed the *Healing* decision, Abbott Sekaquaptewa pushed relentlessly for Hopi possession of its share of the JUA. This desire reflected the feelings of almost every Hopi that the land was theirs. No Hopi would have relinquished the land. What is not clear is what most Hopis thought about what to do about the Navajos living on it. Abbott said the Hopis were not interested in any kind of shared reservation concept. His strategy was to employ the issue of grazing to regain the Hopis' use of half the land. He asked Commissioner Nash whether they could divide the JUA into Navajo and Hopi grazing districts. Nash said that the BIA had no authority to partition the land. Then Sekaquaptewa asked whether they could divide the whole area into one large grazing district that the two tribes would share equally. That would have amounted to the same thing—getting a large percentage of the Navajo stock off the range. Boyden made the Hopi position plain: "We feel that it is imperative and to the best interests of both tribes that immediate stock reductions . . . be had."

But Commissioner Nash understood that if the Navajo stock went, the Navajos would be next, because they had no other means of subsistence. And moving off all the Navajos was an unattractive alternative. As it had between 1882 and 1958, the Department of the Interior, which supervises Indian affairs, decided to do nothing but try to keep the peace. Twenty-three Secretaries of the Interior had come and gone without settling the conflict. The Joint Use Area became known in the musty halls of the Interior Department as the No Hope Area.

Sekaquaptewa knew that by getting rid of Navajo stock, he would eventually get rid of the Navajos. He tried different ways at different times, fighting BIA livestock regulations until he was successful at obtaining from the courts in 1972 a Writ of Assistance that ordered the Navajos to reduce their stock. In the end, this tactic was the most significant force in encouraging Navajos to move off the land and seek relocation assistance.

There is a peculiar irony to Sekaquaptewa's choice of the livestock issue as his strategy for winning back the use of the land. Stock raising is not a traditional Hopi activity. In fact, Abbott's grandfather warned him about relying on stock. Abbott recalls, "My grandfather used to say, 'Work very hard to raise cattle, be industrious so you can raise cattle, and benefit from the enjoyment of them because domesticated livestock do not belong to the Hopi, they belong to the Spaniards and one day the white man will come and take them back.' " Other Hopis believed this as well. Abbott explains that the Hopi BIA superintendent used stories about this tradition to encourage Hopis to sell their animals during the livestock reductions of the 1930s and 1940s.

The Navajos, on the other hand, though they got livestock at the same time and in the same way—from the Spaniards—believe they have had livestock from the beginning of time, that the Holy People gave stock to them. These myths reflect the relative importance of the animals in each culture.

Running cattle is barely economically feasible in Navajo and Hopi country. Abbott says, "I've never showed a profit in any of my ranching operations. It's always a good tax write-off."

Although ranching brings back no profit, is not a traditional Hopi activity, and Hopi stories foretell its end, Sekaquaptewa used the livestock issue as the wedge to dislodge the Navajos. Interestingly enough, it is the Navajo use of stock that has made them what they are today. Sheep is what brought large numbers of Navajos onto Hopi land. The success of the Navajo culture and its proliferation is tied to its successful use of sheep. Sheep is what made the Navajos independent. The Navajos took sheep raising from the Spaniards and elevated it to a high art. The sheep represent everything about the Navajos that the Hopis are jealous of and fear.

After it became clear to Boyden in 1963 that BIA Commissioner Nash was not going to move the Navajos, he got Colorado Representative Wayne Aspinall to sponsor a bill to partition the land. It went nowhere.

Negotiations between the tribes went on for seven years with little success. By 1970, Boyden was proceeding vigorously with a two-pronged attack—in the courts and in Congress. He convinced Arizona Representative Sam Steiger to sponsor another partition bill. At the same time, Boyden petitioned the district court in Tucson for the Writ of Assistance, claiming the government had failed to provide for Hopi possession of half the JUA. Judge Walsh, one of the *Healing* court's three judges, wrote that he didn't have the power to enforce the *Healing* decision and he dismissed the writ. The Ninth Circuit Court of Appeals, however, told Walsh he was wrong; he did have the power to grant such a Writ. The appellate court decision was confirmed by the U.S. Supreme Court, and in 1972, Judge Walsh heard the Hopis' claims about damage to the range. The Hopis presented the following facts: The BIA had determined the carrying capacity of the JUA in 1964 to be 22,036 "sheep units." According to a 1968 livestock count, there were animals equivalent to 88,484 sheep units on the JUA. The JUA was overstocked by 400 percent.

On October 14, 1972, Judge Walsh ordered the Navajos to allow the Hopis "full and peaceable possession of its undivided, one-half interest in and to said premises." Walsh set out specific steps. He commanded the Navajos to reduce their stock to one half the carrying capacity of the land within a year and a half. After that time, all existing livestock permits would be canceled and new ones issued. Then the Navajos and Hopis would each be permitted to graze animals at one half the carrying capacity of the land.

The reductions proved a tremendous assault on the Navajos' already tenuous attempts to subsist on the land. BIA figures showed that the 1,150 Navajo families on the JUA ran 63,000 sheep and goats, 5,000 horses, and 8,000 cattle, which the BIA calculated to equal 120,000 sheep units. The land was so badly damaged it could only carry 22,036 sheep units. In order to bring their animals to half the carrying capacity, the Navajos had to reduce their stock by 90 percent, leaving each family with 9.5 sheep units, enough for one cow and one horse, or nine sheep or goats.

To further provide the Hopis access to their half of the land, Judge Walsh forbade any new construction on the JUA unless it was approved by both tribes. The Navajos, who needed to repair or rebuild their hogans every few years, resisted the order, and the Navajo tribal government did little to enforce the decree. Boyden went back to the courts, and Judge Walsh found the Navajos in contempt. He fined the tribe $250 for each day the livestock numbered over the limits he had determined in the writ and for each day an illegally built structure remained standing.

"The Hopis had built up a lot of political steam," says a Washington lobbyist who had worked on the Senate Interior Committee at the time. "Boyden had set up a two-track system with the courts and Congress, and the Navajos were being caught between the two forces."

George Vlassis, the Navajos' general counsel, had just arrived in Window Rock, home of the tribal government. As he reviewed the tribe's legal activities, he realized that a time bomb was ticking that the Navajos weren't aware of. "The Navajo people didn't realize they'd lost something in *Healing v. Jones,*" he recalled in his Phoenix office in 1985. "It was like I was coming into the bottom of a well that was a hundred feet deep and I look up and I can't see daylight and that's the kind of hole they'd dug for themselves by not doing anything over the last ten years since the *Healing v. Jones* decision."

In the winter of 1973, Vlassis got his first glimpse of the work Boyden had undertaken. "The next extraordinary thing that happens," he said, was his meeting with Congressman Sam Steiger in Window Rock. Steiger was then the U.S. Representative from the Fourth District. Later, he was to be a special assistant to the notorious Arizona governor Evan Mecham, and he would be convicted of extortion for threatening a member of the state Board of Pardons and Paroles (a conviction that was later overturned). "Steiger arrives in Window Rock," said Vlassis, "where nobody ever goes by accident. And there's a council meeting. So Sam Steiger is standing on the steps of the Administration Building, fifty yards away from where the Tribal Council meets. And I come out of the meeting and walk over and ask him if he'd like to see the chairman or the Tribal Council or something. And he says, 'Yeah, well, in a minute here.' I say, 'What's up?' He says, 'Well, I got a bill here that I'd like to stick in the ear of the chairman of the tribe, a bill to give the Hopis the land they're entitled to, a partition bill.' He says, 'You know, it's been a matter of concern to Senator Goldwater for a long time. And it's a matter of concern to me too. And we don't seem to be able to get the issue resolved, so we have this bill.' And lo and behold, not only is there a copy of the bill, but there's a map in there showing how the land's going to be divided. And all the bill says is that here's the line. Navajos are on this side, Hopis are on the other, and the Navajos will have to get out. Period. And there's no money provided, no consideration of where the population is actually located."

Vlassis realized the Navajo Tribe had to "get on the horse and begin to get a legislative program together." But in Washington, he found that Boyden and the Hopis had gotten there first. Committee hearings had begun on the partition bill and John Boyden and Abbott Sekaquaptewa, who was preparing to run for tribal chairman, already had their campaign well underway. The Hopi position, set forth by Sekaquaptewa, was that the Hopis' survival as a people depended on their having a sufficient land base to protect them from the Navajos. Sekaquaptewa didn't suggest that the Hopis would suddenly move out to the land en masse, but he insisted that the way Hopis used the land—for wood gathering, eagle gathering, pilgrimages, and the collection of building materials—was irreconcilable with Navajo use: occupation. And he repeated inflammatory claims that without partition, the Navajos would continue to exact a bloody toll of dead and mutilated Hopis. The Navajos presented the issue as a conflict between human rights (Navajo rights) and real estate rights (Hopi rights). They argued that the Hopis would never live on the land and partition and relocation would replace already poverty-stricken Navajos with Hopi cows.

The Navajos responded by assembling a huge team of lobbyists, lawyers, and public relations people. In addition, eighty Navajos and a handful of Hopi traditionalists rolled into Washington in the summer of 1974 on a bus from Window Rock. But, according to reporter Jerry Kammer, the effect on the legislators was not what had been intended:

> While the Navajo representatives bustled about, the Hopis deliberately kept a low profile. Several of the lawyers in John Boyden's firm flew in from Salt Lake City and teamed up with two or three Hopis to make the rounds of Senate offices. The lawyers made a brief presentation of the land dispute's history, and the Hopis followed with a short speech asking for understanding and help. It was all very deft

and economical, and it contrasted stunningly with what the Navajo were doing. Some Senate aides found themselves resenting the Navajos. Their instincts told them there could be little moral force behind the Navajo position if it had to be presented by so many non-Indian professionals. Because it was so excessive and desperate, the Navajo effort backfired. . . .

Another plus for the Hopis was that Abbott Sekaquaptewa came across far better than Peter MacDonald. Senate aides later recalled Sekaquaptewa as intense but gracious, MacDonald as stuffy and arrogant. Sekaquaptewa was grateful to anyone who would listen to him and understood that he would often have to tell his story to legislative aides. MacDonald spoke condescendingly to aides, expecting to be ushered into the company of the senators. . . . The effect of Navajo lobbying ineptitude was to lose friends and disillusion people. It cheapened the story of the people of the JUA.

Sekaquaptewa had earlier told the House Subcommittee on Indian Affairs that the "relentless Navajo dominance and forcible occupation of Hopi land has become a creature of the night, a living nightmare." He complained of the "onslaught of Navajo trespasses and other excesses in the destruction of life and property that have been a way of life with them since their arrival on this land." He warned that the situation was urgent. "Violence and destruction are as common today as they have been historically in this conflict. It is not beyond imagination that open warfare will once again become the order of the day." The Hopi approach took advantage of common misperceptions of the Navajos to minimize the human costs of relocation. "It should be remembered that the Navajos are a nomadic people and are not settled in any one place," Abbott stated in his authoritative, convincing voice. "Even today, they are moving about. For a Navajo family to move and change their place of residence is not the tragedy that some would have us believe."

For their part, the Navajos floundered about, trying to demonstrate the misery relocation would cause. Vlassis described the Navajos' strategy: "We began to take larger delegations of Navajos in, because one thing we do have is a lot of Navajos. We prepared position papers so we could explain what all this was about, so even if we got thrown out, here was the stuff we left behind. And now we're getting a public record established on what the hell is going on here and how this is outrageous. So we go on with that and start to have congressional hearings. That's where things got pretty exciting because, among other things, we brought a delegation of Hopi traditionals including Mina Lansa, a priestess whom we met through some intermediaries like Thomas Banyacya. They said they wanted to go to Washington with us and express their views. So Thomas Banyacya calls and says the tribal government won't give them the money to go. I said well I think I can fix that, so I go back to Navajo, say these people are going to be invaluable for us in the hearing before Senators Fannin and Goldwater and the rest, because they're the real McCoy. So their way was paid with Navajo money. So we get to the hearings and Mina gets up and explains how they don't go for this pushing the Navajos out, that this bill is contrary to their wishes. Our friend Sam Steiger leans over and whispers in Goldwater's ear and I hear him say, 'Ask her who paid her way here.' She says matter of factly, 'The Navajos, that's who paid my way.' Then we hear a theatrical 'Aha! Now we understand what kind of scene we have here,' and that all makes sense from an Anglo point of view, that you've paid the witness, the witness is going to say what you want."

Vlassis felt that although the Navajos were finally getting heard, they weren't having much of an effect, basically "just making a nuisance of ourselves." As might have been expected, Abbott Sekaquaptewa inserted in earlier testimony a statement attempting to denigrate the significance of the Hopi traditional opposition. He said,

> The Navajo now seeks to recruit some self-styled traditional leaders from along the Hopi Tribe to support them in preventing a just and equitable settlement through this legislation. The opposition of this small faction in the tribe to everything beneficial that the tribal council has ever attempted is nothing new. They attempted the same tactics on me during my own administration and will continue to do so with each new tribal administration. All former chairmen of the Hopi Tribal Council have experienced similar opposition. The Congress should recognize that these traditionalists, in their opposition to the legislation on religious grounds, are grossly misrepresenting and confusing the Hopi religious principle of the salvation of man with the Hopi people's struggle for economic survival.

The Navajo Tribe, under Vlassis's direction, got serious and engaged the help of organized labor. Senator James Abourezk of South Dakota led a spirited fight to derail the partition and relocation legislation, but it was too late. Says one Interior lawyer who has worked on the case for ten years, "John Boyden set the groundwork so well, he had prepared the entire strategy so carefully and it was so clean that Abourezk didn't have a chance. I don't think anyone had a chance. Boyden had everything set for a decade. He was just waiting to move forward and lay down an unassailable attack." In addition, there wasn't much interest on the part of Congress to understand lives far off in Arizona. For one, Congress was absorbed in the Watergate revelations during the summer of 1974 when the Settlement Act was passed. Only three senators that summer listened to all the testimony offered to the Interior Committee; the other dozen were otherwise occupied. Moreover, said Abourezk, "Basically, Congress has no interest in Indians."

The complicated collision of two very different cultures sharing the same area of land was reduced to a propaganda war in testimony before congressmen who had neither the time nor the inclination to sort out fact from fiction. The Hopis tried to show that the Navajos were intransigent, lawless marauders, who deserved to be punished and removed from the land they had taken from their poor, small neighbors. The Hopis promoted the idea of a range war; of repeated mutilations and deaths of Hopi animals and people at the Navajos' hands. Abbott Sekaquaptewa's outrage at occasional Navajo pilfering became exaggerated in his presentations to Congress until the Navajos and Hopis were engaged in a war that threatened the existence of the Hopis. The Salt Lake City public relations firm, Evans and Associates, helped Sekaquaptewa formulate a strategy to convince Congress that *unless* the Navajos were moved, they would obliterate the Hopis. According to a reporter who covered the dispute, Evans and Associates (which also handled public relations for WEST, the energy consortium that was planning to develop the power grid) "virtually stage-managed a range war on the borders of the Hopi reservation." Navajo chairman Peter MacDonald said, "A routine problem of livestock trespassing on a neighbor's pasture has been expanded to depict an unreal situation of Hopi people living in terror of Navajos."

The Navajos pleaded for mercy, parading Navajos and Anglo experts to testify to the hardship and trauma of relocating people from a primitive culture. But the concepts were difficult—how does a white man living in Washington, D.C., begin to understand what it means to Bessie Hatathlie to be separated from the springs where the gods hear her prayers? Abbott Sekaquaptewa's stories of terror and humiliation at the hands of thieving, implacable Navajos were much easier to comprehend.

Thayer Scudder, a world-renowned expert on population relocation at California Institute of Technology, warned the Senate that relocation would not go easily. In a book he wrote later, *No Place to Go*, he stated: "The profound shock of compulsory relocation is much like the bereavement caused by the death of a parent, spouse or child." He also warned that relocation undermines a people's faith in themselves, in the family heads who are unable to protect them, and in local leaders. "Violence, alcohol abuse, and mental and physical illness are all too often intimately associated with forced removal." Scudder also warned that the fate of the Navajo would be worsened by their love of their land as well as the fact they'd lived under stressfully circumscribed conditions for years before moving.

Another question that was dismissed was the real problem of where the Navajos would be relocated. Again, the congressmen, led by Sekaquaptewa's and Boyden's brilliantly crafted and impressively defended statements, failed to understand why there was no room for the relocatees on the rest of the sprawling reservation. No matter that experts testified that overcrowding on seemingly vast areas of land, too, was a commonly misunderstood problem in relocations of pastoral people.

In spite of the facts presented, Arizona Senator Paul Fannin distributed a printed statement a month before the law was passed. It read, "It is not the will of this Congress or any of its members to disrupt the Navajo way of life or to create any economic, cultural, or social hardship on these Americans." And he and his fellow senator Barry Goldwater distributed a "Dear Colleague" letter warning their fellow senators not to be misled by the "emotional campaign put on by the Navajo Tribe to prevent the relocation of any Navajos living in the Joint Use Area. There is no relocation problem. This is a once in a lifetime opportunity for their families to better their living conditions as well as educational and job opportunities."

With the help of statements like these, PL 93-531, the Navajo-Hopi Indian Land Settlement Act, was passed on December 22, 1974. It authorized one last opportunity for the tribes to negotiate a compromise on the use of the JUA with the help of a federal mediator. If the effort failed, the mediator was authorized to help Navajo and Hopi negotiating teams determine a line for partition of the land, "so as to include the higher density population areas of each tribe within the portion of the lands partitioned to such tribe to minimize and avoid undo social, economic, and cultural disruption insofar as practicable." The Act gave the District Court for Arizona jurisdiction to partition the JUA according to the lines recommended by the mediator. Again, the tribes failed to compromise, and, in 1975, a line was drawn, which the mediator described as "a surveyor's nightmare." The line was adopted by Judge Walsh on February 10, 1977. The first relocation took place four months later.

Although the special court that heard *Healing v. Jones* did so according to what was "just and fair in law and equity," it did so according to Anglo-American concepts of law and equity. Mae Tso and Bessie Hatathlie understand a very different set of laws and equities. The judges and lawmakers, in turn, may have found it very hard to understand what Tso meant when she said, "All my decisions are clear when I walk on the land where I was born."

In Anglo-American law, if two parties jointly own an article, regardless of which party uses it or has paid the larger part of the purchase price, the parties own the article half and half. Therefore, after the court decided the two tribes had "joint, undivided and equal rights and interest" in the JUA, any legislative solution would be inclined to divide the land fifty-fifty.

In a *North Dakota Law Review* article that appeared while Congress was debating the partition bill, attorney Richard Schifter argued that this case should never have been sent through the court system; the rights to the JUA should have been settled by legislation "in such manner as would best serve the public interest" rather than "requiring the courts to wrestle with a multitude of legalisms and then having to face the possibly unintended consequences."

Schifter argued that the Indian Claims Commission and the U.S. Court of Claims, judicial bodies that have decided many issues of Indian title, "consistently have refused to apply to Indian tribal lands the common-law principle that joint interests are necessarily equal." Instead, they have considered "patterns of use and occupancy as the basis for quantifying the joint interests of Indian tribes." Population figures were also considered.

In this case, the Navajos on the Executive Order Area in 1958 numbered 8,800 and the Hopis 3,700. And as for use, in 1958, the Navajos lived all over the land. Most Hopis lived within District 6: "A few had homes, farms or grazing lands in adjoining districts in the 1882 reservation." The Hopi use was described by the *Healing* court as including "wood cutting and gathering, obtaining coal, gathering plants and plant products for medicinal, ceremonial, handicrafts and other purposes, visiting of ceremonial shrines, and a limited amount of hunting."

A legislative solution influenced by use, occupancy, and population would likely have given large parts of the JUA to the Navajos and compensated Hopis with other land. Since the Hopis' aboriginal land claim covers a vast area, there was public land available to offer the Hopis as an alternative.

However, the Settlement Act, which was based on *Healing's* concept of joint and equal ownership, ordered a fifty-fifty division of land. And this led to a division of land that provided the Hopis with more acreage per capita than the Navajos, even though the Navajos use the land for grazing and the Hopis live clustered in the villages. According to figures calculated by Navajo demographer Ron Faich, the Hopis have 342 acres per person on the Hopi reservation, while the Navajos have 121 acres per person on the Navajo reservation.

Schifter argued another compelling point: when Indian tribes have brought claims to the government of unlawful taking, and the takers of the property were white—no relocations of whites have ever been undertaken. As Schifter wrote before PL 93-531 was passed, "The enactment by Congress of a bill to partition the joint-interest area and expel Navajo residents represents a sharp departure from the approach employed in legislation such as the Pueblo Lands Act and the Alaska Native Claims Settlement Act. Congress would impose a burden on the members of the Navajo Tribe which in similar circumstances it has not seen fit to impose on non-Indians. Such action raises a serious question of invidious racial discrimination in violation of the Fifth Amendment."

Sam Steiger was asked in 1974 why the Congress was considering an approach it had not considered in situations where white settlers were living on Indian land. He made Schifter's point for him when he replied, "I would simply tell the gentleman that the distinction between that situation and this one is that in those instances, every one of those instances, we are dealing with non-Indians occupying, and believing they have a right in the lands. Here, we are dealing with two tribes. This is the distinction."

It now seems clear that the relocation program was rushed through Congress without an adequate understanding of the effects on the Navajos. In addition, the fairness of the Act as well as its adequacy as public policy have also been questioned in terms of its roots in the common-law principle of joint ownership. And it is clear, in the words of one of its chief promoters, that this legislation would never have been sought had the Hopis made a claim of taking against Anglo sheepherders.

There is some suggestion that the Navajos had a chance to win a solution other than a fifty-fifty division of land. A former Interior Affairs Committee member who worked on writing the law and is now a Washington lobbyist says that the Navajos had an opportunity to get a more advantageous law than they did. "I think the Navajos lost a golden opportunity to settle back in 1974," he said. He felt that the Senate Committee was open to the idea of "giving the Hopis a smaller portion of land and greater mineral rights," but MacDonald was not prepared to compromise. "Peter [MacDonald] thought he had the muscle to beat it. . . . I won't fault him on his decision . . . but I would have thought the Navajos would have realized the political realities and legal restraints."

After the bill was passed, and a partition line affirmed by the court, it was much more difficult for Congress to step in and alter the line. "[Back in 1974] we still had the whole expanse of land to deal with," said the former committee staff member. "It was a classic standoff," he continued. "We tried our hand and each side refused to give. The Navajos still thought they could beat the Hopis. Congress had the hot potato. It had to act. The courts were moving forward with writs of assistance and so forth. The Navajos acted intransigently through the years. And they wouldn't compromise when [the congressional] staff was ready to compromise. I think both sides left Congress no choice but to resolve it as it did. There was no eagerness on the part of Senate Committee members to deal with this. They would have preferred compromise." He added that had the Navajos indicated interest, the Committee would have imposed a solution different than a fifty-fifty partition of land. "The Navajo tribal government just wouldn't compromise. They wouldn't accept the fact of their defeat in court. They thought they could muscle their way out of it."

Tribal Councilman David Clark told reporter Jerry Kammer in 1980 that the relocation program was producing "unbelievable strain" on the Navajos: "They just break down and cry while I'm talking with them. All you have to do is touch it and it comes out. One of the expressions I hear a lot is that the government is tearing their hearts out while they're still alive. They say, 'I'm not an animal. I'm not a prisoner. But that's the way I'm being treated in my own country.' "

At Hopi in early 1980, workshops were held to discuss possible Hopi use of the HPL once all the Navajos had been removed. *Qua Toqti* reported that forty to fifty people attended the first, most of whom were tribal employees. The second workshop brought out ten people. The third workshop could only count two people interested in making use of the land to be vacated by the Navajos. An editorial accompanying the news report complained about weak response to a coupon distributed in the newspaper requesting ideas about how to use the land. After running the coupon for three weeks, the office received only three completed forms, including one from a Navajo.

(12)

Traditional Hopis
Try to Hold On

Thomas Banyacya marches from his home in Kykotsmovi a few yards down the street to the post office. The post office and the telephone are his lifelines to a world much larger than most of his neighbors enjoy. He gets mail and calls from San Francisco, Los Angeles, Sweden, Germany. He travels across the country giving lectures about the views of the Hopi traditionalists, whose ideas about the world, daily life, and the government differ quite dramatically from the ideas of the Hopis who run the tribal government from a collection of modern buildings a mile or so down the road.

Thomas receives a few envelopes, tucks them under his arm, and walks back home. Around him along the street are small stone houses, most of them well built, solid, charming. This village is relatively new, having been built in the 1920s. There is a general store and gas station across the street, behind which Abbott Sekaquaptewa lives with his mother, Helen, who is now past ninety.

Thomas's house is tucked into a small dip just off the main road across from a clapboard church whose white paint has vanished except for a few dull streaks. Hopis don't paint their houses, and whoever decided to paint the edifice has long departed with his paint. Thomas walks past a couple of old cars, a shed filled with junk, up a couple of stairs and through an aluminum screen door into a bright kitchen. He sits down at a picnic table covered with oil-cloth and prepares to recite the history of the world to a visitor. For that is what Thomas does. When he speaks to an outsider, someone who has come to see him about the Navajo-Hopi land dispute, he recites the history of the world, for only if you understand the Hopi history and point of view can you fully appreciate his present thoughts.

In 1948, during an extraordinary meeting of Hopi religious leaders, Thomas and three other men were chosen to spread the word of the old priests to the world. Usually secretive, keeping prophecies and predictions to themselves, the old leaders felt the world was in danger from modern ways and, bitterly opposed to the modern tribal council, decided it was time to let the world know what they thought. Thomas is now the only one of the four still alive. He takes his job very seriously, and travels around with the Big Mountain ladies speaking against relocation and acceptance of the white man's ways. He is viewed with jealousy and contempt by some Hopis, who think he is out for himself. Since he travels through the white world, some Hopis incorrectly surmise he is paid huge sums of money by the whites.

Thomas's wife, Fermina, a round-faced, plump woman in a cotton housedress and apron, places cookies and cupcakes on the table and pours tea. A bucket of dried peaches stands at the end of the table. Baked goods are stashed on every available ledge. The kitchen is filled with plants.

Thomas wears his hair pulled back into a bun like the Navajos' tsiyeel. He holds himself with great dignity while he delivers a monologue that is interrupted two or three times by the telephone, which he answers with an officious bark.

An anthropologist once noted, "When a Hopi wants to explain why he puts dog manure on his corn, he begins with the creation of the world, and takes half an hour to come down, via his maternal uncles, to the fact that rabbits will not molest corn thus treated. If you want to learn anything from a Hopi, you must be prepared to listen to the long prefaces." And so it is with Banyacya. The dissemination of this information is the purpose of his life.

Thomas Banyacya straightens on the bench. "Ivan Sidney [the Hopi tribal chairman] is looking to the government to solve the land problem in a government way," he says. "But the land belongs to all native people. The government comes in and violently takes land away from native people, or by legal tricks, by laying down certain laws and rules in their own terms. There is a Hopi prophecy that this would happen across the country and the last place it would happen would be the Navajo-Hopi area."

Banyacya mutters the words "Allotment Act, Dawes Act" with contempt. He refers to the government policy, begun in 1887 and ended in 1934, which encouraged the breakup of reservations into individually owned plots. "Those laws are very much against natural law, spiritual law," he says. "There was a prophecy that the white man would come and take the land from us one day. The Land Claims Commission, set up in 1946, was the beginning of the prophecy. Through land claims, the native people gave up their right to aboriginal land and got only money."

The Hopis received $5 million through the Land Claims Commission. To this day, the money, which has more than doubled, remains untouched in a bank account. Although some Hopis would like to make use of it, the majority objects vigorously to accepting money for their land.

"When the white brother comes," says Banyacya, sipping his tea, "the old leaders told us, he will bring many things. First a carriage pulled by animals. And we saw those. They were wagons. Then they told us the white brother would have carriages without animals. And he drove up to see us in automobiles. Then the white brother is going to build roads in every direction on our trails. One day you'll go down the road and you'll see water on the roads glistening. And soon we saw, on the black-top roads, the mirage of water on a hot day. Then you'll see cobwebs, which turned out to be telephone lines. Then they said, you'll have something where you'll be inside, doors and windows closed and be able to talk to people far away. These things were telephones and radios.

"Then they told us two world-shaking events will come. Those two events that were foretold were the First and Second World Wars. They said that in the second one, someone will reveal something old, the swastika symbol. And there will also be something so hot if dropped on earth will burn everything. This was the bomb that dropped on Hiroshima and Nagasaki. A lot of sickness will come about.

"In 1948, this was the first time we tell this story in public. We tell the younger son to tell the stories that have only been told in the kivas. We tell them so they can try to prevent the gourd with red hot ashes. We tell them that each invention he creates will lead many people away from natural teachings. Now, every year people want new cars. Finally you'll get a new car and be showing off to other people—that car's all messed up and no good anymore. Pretty soon you won't be taking care of your families or your children. You won't be able to control them. They'll become cruel. Soon, they'll fight cultural ceremonies and the spiritual ways.

"Someday, they told us, when people have the power to get to the moon. If [they get] there, they said, never bring anything from the moon down. You've already unbalanced nature too much. You are damming rivers, mining, tearing down mountains. The air is so dirty the sun will rise and set blood red from so much pollution. We used to have white sunsets. If you go up there and bring something down, there will be much more tidal waves, mountains blowing their tops, islands sinking. Nature will start warning us we're not taking care of it like we used to. Sooner or later, rain won't cover whole areas, we'll have spot rains where some places flood, and others will stay dry. The wind will become very destructive and will destroy everything that was built.

"The next thing, when a house is sent up there flying around, the world will be a terrible mess. People grabbing power, money, a good time. They will try to suppress others with police power. Fires will be started everywhere, little riots and little wars. When that has been fulfilled, maybe people will find out they shouldn't use them anymore for bad ways, so powerful, must turn power to good.

"In the Hopi legends, Hopi elders knew everything that would happen. We must send messages in every direction now. That gourd full of ashes is hanging over all of us today. The problem is how to get it down without hurting us all."

Thomas Banyacya takes another cup of tea and continues with his story. The sun is setting over the mesas and has cast a brilliant glow, rash as a bucket of gold paint splashed onto everything in sight. The dryness and the peculiar makeup of the air makes every object jump from its background. The quiet frames every noise.

"The BIA set up the Tribal Council, recognized them as leaders, never acknowledging the old leaders. The Kikmongwi has high powers. Through prayer and meditation, he can control the power. This is a spiritual center. This should be left in a natural state. The white man can't live here. Only people who know how to live on the land without destroying should be here.

"The reason the old leaders told us to bring these things to notice of the people is if they start moving in with force or legal tricks. For the Hopis, the white man means cleverness, justice, honesty, and truthfulness. If the white man does not bring these things there will be lying, corruption, like an apple decaying inside. The White House in the east will fall to the ground on its own corruption.

"They also told us there would be a house of mica standing on eastern lands where world leaders will gather and fix things that go wrong. We must make every attempt to knock on that door. If they open the door, we will bring them the message to clean up their own mess. If they don't open the door, we will keep knocking. We have made three attempts to knock on the door of the United Nations to talk about human rights and what has happened to all the native people of this country.

"The Bible tells of the same laws the Hopis follow. Do not kill, lie, steal. The Hopis are looking for the white person who will come and protect us. The Hopis are still looking at the sacred tablets, two are in Oraibi, and two are in Hotevilla. Someone, some white brother, took something from the people away. He must make that life real good, then come back for his brother whose skin is the color of Mother Earth. Together we will make our life real good. Everything is a circle, there is no end. As long as we follow the word of the Great Spirit we will not totally ruin our land. We will have a stronger generation to come. That's where we are now.

"We have tried to get the leader from the White House to come up here to sit down and meet with us face to face, heart to heart in a spiritual way. If the white brothers learn this or know this, they will be able to clean up this mess. If we don't change this mess, the powerful three purifiers will come and everything will be blown out. Cars won't move. Everything of metal will freeze. We'll be helpless when the purifiers come. We must clean it up first.

"The three purifiers are supposed to come from the eastern direction. I don't know what this means, an old man told me: 'Tomorrow morning, maybe for breakfast, the sky will darken, people will rain from the sky to earth—paratroopers—will come down. They'll destroy his people, take his stocks away. The purifier will know who's done wrong. They'll also know who's done right. Those who survive will be able to clean things up. People who don't listen, don't help, they'll be executed right there. People who stood by me, even though ridiculed, will be saved. The whole thing will become new again. Then other people will come from western direction after the purification from the east. If that happens, people will crawl upon the western side of the country like ants. When they come in, they won't be asking questions, they will be very severe, when they come to clean this mess up.'

"Then the old man said, 'The purifiers will come to find the people with long hair, the natural way. We promised to the Great Spirit, so that he will know when he sees us, who we are. All bad will be destroyed and the good gathered up by the Great Spirit. Land will be one, there will be no boundaries. The gentle rains will come again and there will be beautiful flowers and abundant food. It will be so good, in the beginning, that you will be able to drive far west without bringing any food. You will be able to pick it from the sides of the roads.'

"You pass all kinds of laws without asking us. You will make us landless, homeless people. This land is the only land we have. This is the land of the Great Spirit. European people can go back to their lands. Native people have no place to go. It may look so dark and hopeless, but one day, good people will come and they will realize it is necessary to protect nature and it is the native people who will take care of the land. Now, inventions destroy everything. What will happen here will happen everywhere. Sooner or later minorities will join together and the white people will be in the minority. It will be black people who clean these things up. They will be last to come together.

"The villages of Oraibi, Moencopi, Walpi, and Hotevilla still believe in traditional ways. Shongopavi and Mishongnovi have their own [traditional] system of life there. Shipaulavi branched from Shongopavi when the Catholic Mission was allowed in. Twenty years of drought and famine came as a result of this Catholic Mission that tried to interfere with Hopi life. Some of them fell for the white man's ways. After Oraibi split, some went to Kykotsmovi, a group left for Hotevilla, then ended up at Bacovi. Later, Upper Moencopi village was formed and is modern.

"Young people, without consulting elders, sent people to the Tribal

Council. First Mesa has no representative in the Council now. Today there is no quorum. Ivan Sidney has no authority to sign anything now. The traditional villages never sent representatives to the Council. They don't recognize it. They want to follow their own leaders. Oliver LaFarge realized this, that the Hopi traditional people must lead their people. The Tribal Council is a puppet. The BIA set up the government to confuse the people. The majority of Hopi traditional people never supported this.

"The native people hold [that] this land is common. The Great Spirit told us to take care of the land, each in our own way. When this law, PL 93-531 came, it came without the knowledge of the Hopi and Navajo people. They said it was the final solution to the problem they created themselves with the 1882 executive-order reservation and the land additions made to the Navajo reservation.

"John Boyden, who knew what was going on in Washington, told the Tribal Council, 'Don't you know the Navajos are taking land from you? If you give me the authority to go to court, you'll get the land back.' But Boyden and [Navajo attorney Norman] Littell were both out there deciding how to cut the land into two parts.

"Before the law was passed in Congress, it came out here. We had long arguments about how to share the land with the Navajos, even though we've been sharing it all this time. Sekaquaptewa and the other Mormons set up a propaganda war that we were involved in a range war. They tore down fences and then told congressmen the Navajos tore them down. There was no such war. It was just propaganda.

"The Hopi stockmen were asked to create some kind of incident. Hopi rangers out there tried to take some Navajo stock. Of course, there was an incident. They sent the Salt Lake City PR firm out there, and they really blasted this thing out. There was warring, fighting between the tribes then.

"That bill, 93-531, was never explained to the people. Relocation is only one part of it. Native people, if they knew what it said, would *all* reject it. The bill is no good because it sets an example for what the government can do to all other native people. Honor, justice, and fair play will be thrown out the window. The whole world will be upset. The U.N. has never been open to native people. All other people, including our so-called enemies, Russians, Cubans, are allowed in but the Hopi people have known for a long time that we must knock on the door a fourth time. If they don't answer, other people will come to purify this mess.

"Goldwater says repeal is too difficult. But if some senators came up here and saw what it's doing. If the Hopi and Navajo people can get together—not the leaders—and realize the danger—the only way is to ask for repeal."

The sun is now melting blood red over the horizon, and Thomas is tired from his recitation. He repeats himself, fiddles with his tea cup. Fermina, who has listened quietly, stands up and says, "It's not the Navajo or the Hopi people who wrote the law. We're not fighting. We're just struggling to maintain what we have here."

She quickly becomes agitated. "The U.S. government came in here and wrote laws for us. They just came here *yesterday*," she shouts, clenching her hand into a fist. "We've been here for thousands of years, and we made our covenant with the Great One. He put us here. The government told us we could be citizens. Citizens twice? This is our birthright. This is our heritage."

Her face contorts with anger. "Columbus came here and he called us savages, just animals. I was brought up in BIA schools and we are taught our whole culture was wrong. But many Hopi people have resisted Christianity and the new ways of the Tribal Council. And many Council people realize they've made mistakes, but they just can't drop their jobs, now that they are no longer self-sufficient." She stops, looks up at her visitors. "That's just what I think," she says, looking away and busying herself at the sink. By this time, Thomas has regained his strength. He repeats more prophecies, more wrongs.

He speaks with great energy and effort. Each time he retells the litany, he becomes stronger, he feels he is closer to convincing the white man of the coming danger. In the end, he says, "It has been told that when troubles come to the Four Corners area, it is close to the Purification. The spiritual leaders must teach others then. Then maybe the white people will realize it is not right, what they are doing, and they will use whatever means and powers they have to keep this land and this world in balance. If they don't, the purifiers will come, and many people will be killed, but the wrongs will be righted and we will start again."

"Shongopavi is the Vatican of the Hopi villages, the only village which still performs the full cycle of ceremonial dances," says Phyllis Hogan, an Anglo trader and herbalist, who apprenticed for eight years with a Hopi medicine man in the art of healing with herbs. Phyllis drives up Route 264 to Second Mesa, past a sacred spring that is protected by a new masonry wall and marked with a painted Hopi symbol. Just before the turnoff to Shongopavi, she passes a small rock house on the edge of the mesa overlooking the craggy canyon below. "That's the Peach House, which is used by the people who are high up in Hopi religious society," she says. It was once surrounded by peach trees, and was one of the first houses to have an orchard beside it. The trees have long since died. The house, though it is lived in, looks abandoned, as does much of Hopi.

Phyllis turns off the road onto a dirt path that leads to the village. Small cinder block houses and trailers are scattered on plots before the village proper. A huge butane tank stands upright outside the village. "That's where my friend Marvin hung himself," says Phyllis, pointing to a new house near the butane tank. "He married a woman from this village, but since he was from Hotevilla, he was denied initiation into one of the religious societies. He was fighting booze, but mostly, he couldn't bridge the gap between the Hopi and white worlds." Marvin was a gifted jeweler and Kachina carver whose work Phyllis sold in her Flagstaff store. She is currently displaying a set of abstract Kachina dolls she possessed when he died. The figures undulate with the curves of the cottonwood roots they were made from as if they were dancing or hesitating in the wind. The most haunting figure is that of a Spanish friar with a flat black hat.

Phyllis guides the truck carefully through several blocks of spare cinder block dwellings and approaches the older part of the village. Stone houses with flat roofs are clustered together in long rows. There are several kivas and two plazas in this village, and the older houses, some disintegrating, stand beside renovations and newer structures. The appearance is a hodgepodge of stone shacks huddled on the edge of the cliff. But there is a precise order to who lives where, because the houses are owned by the clans, and the religious leaders decide who lives in each house. We pass the demolished body of a 1950s Buick sedan. "That's Cyrus's car, and that's one of Cyrus's houses beside it," says Phyllis. Cyrus is a prominent Shongopavi resident and the Kikmongwi's right-hand man. "It's really his wife Marion's, but they live in another house most of the time."

Phyllis heads up to a spacious building by the edge of the western tip of the mesa. This is the home of Earl Pela, a spokesman for the man Shongopavis claim is the last legitimate Kikmongwi or chief priest, Grandfather Claude. Two of Earl's grandchildren come out to greet Phyllis. They say that Earl has just come back from a trip to Washington, and that he is tending his cornfield down in the wash. Two girls, one of whom identifies herself as Bonita and says she is in fifth grade, clamber barefoot into the car to guide Phyllis in a search for their grandpa.

They are not sure of the directions, but they recall being at the field before. All they remember is that it is in the wash. Phyllis figures they'll never find Earl's plot among all the other fields in the long, verdant Oraibi wash, but knowing that astonishing and unpredictable things happen out here, she decides to go ahead.

As Phyllis passes the village entrance, the girls chatter that their Auntie Stephanie is going out with a man named Jessie, who lives in the Peach House. They point to a small square cage atop a rock formation, where snakes are kept for the snake dance. And they gesture to some springs discernible only by the lone leafy trees that grow by them. The sight of these places excites them, makes them happy.

Phyllis descends down off Second Mesa. A couple of miles down Route 87 to Winslow, she leaves the tar route for a smooth, sandy dirt track that winds toward the green swath of the wash. She passes cornfields tucked into patches of land that mysteriously hold water, drives by small shacks where farmers sit and guard their fields, and passes large trees with overhanging branches and heavy leaves. All around are fields of bright green corn plants. It is as if she had suddenly entered the colored version of a black and white film. The girls are captivated by the foliage, which is more reminiscent of a Mississippi bayou than the high desert. "It would be nice to live down here," they say. They point this way and that as the dirt road winds along the wash. After several turns one of the girls says with certainty, "Here we are. This is his cornfield." Phyllis sees fresh car tracks. "Grandpa must have gotten a ride," they say. It is a long walk for an old man, even if he takes a shortcut down from the cliffs. It is a good hour and a half at a fast pace. Phyllis spots Earl's footprints leading down to the long cornfield, which is snuggled in a rich, red overflow basin. "There's his stick," one of the girls says. The other picks up the metal pole he uses to plant the corn kernels. It is propped beside a sage bush.

He isn't there, so Phyllis and the girls climb back up the path to a large floor-standing freezer. The girls lift the rocks off the top and open it up. Inside, they point out plastic containers of corn seeds, and a Gott thermos. They open the thermos, dip into the water with a plastic bowl, and drink thirstily. "There's Grandpa's hat," they exclaim, retrieving a blue cap from the bottom of the freezer. They close the thermos, shut the freezer top, and replace the rocks. Phyllis drives back up to the village, stopping at the Secakuku Trading Post for a pop. The girls see their aunt in a brown Pontiac, and go over to say hello.

On the way back up to the mesas, Bonita says that she goes to school in Winslow with Navajos and Hopis and Anglos. She says sometimes the Navajo kids have sad stories about relocating. "I get scared when I hear them," she says. "I feel bad for them." She stops for a moment, thinks. "But the bigger kids are ruining Hopiland," she says. "Marauding Navajos," she murmurs, as if a refrain from a familiar song.

Bonita pulls out of her pocket a necklace she found near her grandpa's house. It is a gold chain with an oval purple stone in front, and the clasp is stamped AVON. Bonita says she is selling it for ten dollars. She is hesitant to put it on herself. Phyllis tells her it is very pretty, that she should wear it. Bonita examines it carefully, then quietly puts it back in her pocket.

Earl is still not home. Six or seven young children, barefoot, dirty, clamber into the truck. They want to see how the windshield wipers work, whether the vent blows air. A hefty little boy of four, whom the others, giggling hysterically, call Fart Bubble, pulls out the truck's cigarette lighter, presses it to his lips, and inhales. He puts it back. A few minutes later, he pulls out the lighter again and repeats his mime of lighting a cigarette. He presses the lighter up to his moist lips and takes it away with a puzzled look. "Is it hot?" Phyllis asks, taking the lighter from him and touching her finger to the coils. She drops it with a cry. It is very hot. The little boy laughs, still a bit startled. He does not cry, he does not complain. Phyllis tells him he is a very brave boy and he smiles.

The children want to show Phyllis the edge of the cliff. As she walks over, two little boys from across the way trudge up from the edge, holding a freshly killed squirrel by the tail. They carry bows and arrows on their back, and the squirrel has a puncture wound on its shoulder. They proudly display the kill to their grandpa, who yells at them for going to the cliff. "There are snakes there," he scolds them.

Phyllis walks to the cliff, surrounded now by ten children. One little girl of seven or eight carries an infant brother. The kids scamper over the rocks, shouting and laughing. Fifty yards ahead are outhouses, about nine of them, perched at the edge of the mesa. The stench is bad, and garbage the Hopis have dumped over the side of the mesa is caught in bushes and between rocks. Bonita asks Phyllis to attach the necklace about her neck; Phyllis does so. Bonita's cousin teases her about it, but Bonita continues over the rocks with her head tilted self-consciously.

The rocks are slippery and the trash and outhouse vapors make it an unpleasant lookout. Phyllis heads back to the village to see Evangeline Talahaftewa, the matriarch of the Powamu society, and the most important female religious leader of the town. Phyllis trained with Evangeline's husband, Herbert, and after he died, she was asked by Evangeline to go through his medicine bundles and catalogue the contents—a rare honor. Earl's two granddaughters drive over too, but are hesitant to go in. They say they'll wait in the car.

Evangeline is sitting in her house, beginning to make a basket. She is a prize-winning basketmaker, and as head of the women's weaving society, decides who can and cannot be initiated into the society, and therefore, who can and cannot make Hopi baskets. Phyllis says Evangeline was the one who decided that Marvin, who hanged himself, could not join the Kachina society because he was from a different village. She is a short, heavyset woman with long gray hair that is braided and coiled at her neck. She has a cheery countenance and tells us to follow her to her daughter's house, since this one is a mess.

She and Phyllis walk across the top of a kiva, climbing a few steps up to the flat stone and gravel top, past the wide, tall ladder that leads down into the ceremonial chamber. It seems somewhat sacrilegious to do so, but Evangeline tramps right over it. This is one of the most important kivas, the home of sacred ceremonial items and traditions. Phyllis walks past a few new dwellings toward the eastern edge of the mesa, and enters the bright, open kitchen of a new cinder block house. She sits at a table covered with a checked, plastic cloth. Evangeline's daughter Bertha joins her. Bertha's husband, a famous Hopi silversmith, is in the back room, working at a small desk. Bertha is making fabric limbs for a Hopi doll. She sells dolls as well as baskets at art shows and fairs. Bertha holds up several rag dolls in plastic bags and tells Phyllis she will sell them for ninety dollars each. The whole family will take their wares to the Santa Fe Indian Market in August.

Evangeline is a traditional Hopi by virtue of her religious position, yet she talks like a defender of modernity. She says she doesn't know what Earl is up to, going to Washington, but she thinks that Thomas Banyacya has brainwashed him. She can't believe that Earl would join with people like Thomas who want to end relocation. Evangeline, though she occupies a high religious position, doesn't hesitate to criticize either Thomas or her village's Kikmongwi, Claude. In typical Hopi fashion, she keeps her own counsel. She also engages in a favorite Hopi pastime: vicious gossip. She and her daughter turn their attention to a confidant of Grandfather Claude. Then they talk about another villager, claim he is a thief and a boozer, and point out that he and his wife were kicked out of their village house after the police came once and confiscated stolen goods. The house is now inhabited by an old woman. But when she dies, they say, maybe Janice, a member of the Bear clan, will be allowed to move in. Unfortunately, Janice is married to a white man, and that might interfere with her plans. Meantime, Janice and her husband are trying to get approval to build a house on a small site at the entrance to the village. Evangeline is outraged that Janice has gotten the site, because she wants it for her own granddaughter. Evangeline points out that Janice and her husband have gotten Cyrus—Janice's uncle—on their side.

The talk turns to the Navajos. Bertha and Evangeline do little to hide their disgust. "We call them foxes," says Bertha. Evangeline says she bought a nice piece of meat from a Navajo lady and put it in the oven to roast. But as the heat began to work on the meat a horrible smell wafted from the stove and she had to throw the meat out. "And all my money gone, too. I didn't know the lady, or I would have gone to ask for my money back," she says.

Evangeline scowls as she works on the basket. She is coiling flat strands of dried grasses, piercing the central leather thong with a sharp pick and threading the flat piece through the holes. Her work is precise, neat, and strong. Every stitch is perfectly placed. Bertha reports that a Navajo came by with a truckload of yellow corn to sell one day and her neighbor bought some. Bertha went to her neighbor to ask for some. She was told it was tasteless, flat. "That Navajo probably found some old corn lying around someplace and loaded it into his truck," she says.

What disturbs them the most is that Navajos are crafting items that are traditionally Hopi. They feel the Navajos have no right to make baskets, since the Pueblos, back during the Navajos' migrations, taught them how to do it. In their minds, crafts are part of their religious tradition, and ownership of the idea has a great importance. They bitterly resent the Navajos' development of rug weaving. The Navajos learned weaving from the Hopis and have turned the craft into an art of their own. But that fact is irrelevant to the Hopis. The Hopis wove first, so they believe the craft belongs to them.

Evangeline and Bertha turn their attention next to village affairs. Old Grandfather Claude has decided that no electricity or plumbing will be brought into this part of the village. Bertha is irritated. She points to the kerosene lantern hanging over the table. "That white gas is expensive," she says. "Six dollars a gallon, and it only lasts about three nights, because we do our handwork at night." Bertha complains that some outside group is bringing in food for the village. She thinks Thomas Banyacya is responsible. She says the food is bad anyway. She thinks it must be surplus from stores sent in by one of the Anglo support groups. "It's just some stuff that other people don't want," she says. She says the vegetables were dry by the time they arrived at the village. She has been told another delivery will arrive tomorrow, and although she says she probably won't find anything good, she'll go over and look through it. She remembered once that a little boy came back with beautiful ripe tomatoes and cabbage and carrots. Everyone was envious. She asked her own little boy to go over and see if there was more, but her son refused. He said he didn't like to scavenge.

That talk reminds Bertha of a neighbor who has abandoned her children. They say the woman just drinks all day and leaves the children untended. Sometimes the kids come over and Bertha feeds them. Evangeline says she struggled to get them a Social Security check that would allow them to buy clothes. She finally succeeded and took the children to Winslow herself. She set aside half of the money for clothes, a quarter of the money for food, and a quarter for fuel. After buying the clothes, there was only a little money left and when she brought them to the food store they rushed from aisle to aisle pointing out things they liked. Evangeline said she felt sorry for them and bought more food than she should have. She used up the gas money.

She was only able to buy clothes for the children a couple of times before another member of the village decided she wanted a chance to spend the childrens' check for them.

The children were not the only ones abandoned by the alcoholic mother of the house. One night in March, during a period of bitter cold, the children's grandfather came to Bertha's door and asked Bertha whether she had any money for coal. He told her he had run out of fuel and it was freezing cold in the house. She went to her bag and opened her change purse. She told him she had four dollars. Coal "tops" cost two dollars each, and if he could find someone selling coal, he could buy two. Then he asked her if she had any piki, the flaky, Hopi bread made from blue cornmeal. She had a whole box of it, and she gave him onions too. She didn't have a sack for the onions, so he put them into his pockets. She asked him if he wanted the boys to help him home. He said no, he was all right, he would just follow the porch light. He thanked her and left. But somehow, in the cold and in his hunger, he followed the wrong light. He walked over the western edge of the mesa. The next morning, they found him at the bottom of the cliff, his arms embracing a large boulder. The piki was scattered all about him. Evangeline says they brought him back to her house and laid him on the floor. His arms were frozen in place, beseeching them. The onions still bulged in his pockets.

Phyllis gets up to go. When she reaches the car, the girls are gone. Phyllis is quiet, shaken. "When I first began to come up here," she says, "Herbert saved my life. I had been in a very bad car accident, and he is the most important bone doctor up here. It took a long time, but through manipulation and realignment and herbs, he got my vertebra back in place and away from the artery it was pinching. And then I began to learn from him and Evangeline and I thought I had met the holiest people in the world. I revered them. But now, listening to Evangeline speak, I'm turned cold as stone. There you have the most important matriarch probably of the entire Hopi society. And we heard not one word of compassion. All bitterness, petty jealousies, backbiting. The Hopis are killing themselves with their own frustrations and internal dissent. They turn it against the Navajos, who have a healthy, vibrant culture, who are growing and learning new things. They seem to despise the Navajos for adapting to new ways and learning new things. I'm very disillusioned."

Earl's great-grandson, Jefferson, the hefty boy who played with the lighter, meets Phyllis in front of Earl's house. He tells her Earl has returned. They push through a blanket serving as a screen door, and walk into a large kitchen, swept clean, whose perimeter is lined with old painted kitchen cabinets and chests of drawers.

Behind the kitchen is a partially enclosed sleeping and living area, and to the left, another room. Earl sits at the entrance to the second room, weaving. He wears a red headband knotted above his right ear. At Hopi, it is the men who weave. They make belts for ceremonial purposes as well as red and white striped wedding blankets. His hair is cut in bangs, with sidelocks cut at a level with his chin. His remaining hair is pulled back into a bun like the one the Navajos wear. Hopi men cut their hair this way for religious reasons. The bangs represent the clouds, the sidelocks the earth, and the long hair, the rain.

Earl sees Phyllis, gets up from the floor and walks over. He sports a short-sleeved khaki shirt and jeans. His leather loafers are cracked. He gives a big grin. Although he is in his seventies, his vibrancy and the good humor that spills from his eyes make him a stunningly handsome man. He is slight, about five feet tall, with a lively, boyish face.

He gestures to Phyllis to sit down at the kitchen table, placed beneath a window where a potted ivy grows in a plastic pot. The table is covered with oilcloth and surrounded by matching dinette chairs. Jefferson stands by a cabinet and points his finger up toward the top shelf. He stands silently, pointing, until his great-grandpa sees he is gesturing at the cereal boxes. Earl says to him in Hopi, then in English, "Wait, they will be back," referring to the women who will cook him a proper meal.

Earl sits down at the head of the table. He sits forward in his chair, intertwines his fingers. He speaks slowly, softly. He says there are some things he doesn't know, perhaps he'd better go get his friend Cyrus. Earl gets up and walks briskly out the door to look for Cyrus. Jefferson has found himself some peanut butter and leftover tortillas. He tells Phyllis he is in school, that he speaks only English at school, and that he is learning to do a Mexican dance. Earl returns, explains that Cyrus is tending his cornfield. "They don't learn Hopi," he says, referring to the little ones. "They learn English and the white man's ways in school." Earl shakes his head.

He says he would rather that somebody was with him, to correct him if he is wrong. He apologizes for his English. Unlike Evangeline, Earl is humble, respectful, and dedicated to speaking about only those things he is in a position to know. He doesn't gossip. The traditional Hopis take their words very seriously. If they don't know something, they defer to others. Members of a certain clan will tell their version of a story, and will warn a listener that it may be different from the story of another clan.

Traditional Hopi people like Earl tend to answer questions by telling a story or repeating a prophecy. The world as a whole exists on a continuum of time much longer than white people use. Everything has been foretold, and the Hopis wait for the predictions to come true. Events are not distinct or random, they are all part of a larger picture. Traditional Hopis consider the U.S. government a force that has persistently tried to push American ways on them. They have fought tenaciously against that influence, but have been worn down in the process. They have lost many people to the easier ways of modern life. Earl refers to the government as a person, as "he." "He kept working against us Hopis. Hopis always refuse everything that comes around at first." Earl says that the Hopis should never have accepted the livestock, the cattle that the white man brought—they should have waited, assessed the possible effects it would have. "The old people told us not to fall for the cattle," he says. "They will force us onto a small point." The small point was a diminution of the land they claimed as their own—the entire United States—and the old people were right, because with the livestock came grazing districts, and with grazing districts came boundaries and fences, and soon the Hopis were confined to District 6.

Says Earl, "The Hopis said the Navajos will get everything from the land. They accept everything right off." To the Hopis, accepting a new concept quickly is a mark of carelessness and a lack of respect for the old ways. Life as a traditional Hopi is torturous. It requires fasting and continence, long hours of praying and weaving in addition to farming. A traditional Hopi is often hungry and full of anxiety for the rainfall necessary to produce life from the sand. To be Hopi is to follow the path. To accept the new without due regard is ka-Hopi.

"The Navajos accepted the [Tribal] Council. Then they thought the Hopis would get one. But now, [Hopis] have a Tribal Council," Earl says, "planned over in Washington long time. They finally got to that point now. We tried to fight it."

The leaders of the village of Shongopavi met in 1936, after the creation of the Hopi Tribal Council. "All the traditional leaders had meetings up at the Kachina clan house," says Earl. "They asked each other about that, and they decide to send to Tribal Council Peter Navumsua, Talahaftewa's nephew, who was in the Gray Bear clan. Talahaftewa [Evangeline's husband] was Black Bear clan. He didn't want Peter to be in the Council. They keep asking each other and finally appoint Peter." They also chose a second delegate, Sammy, whom they called Sammy Babbitt, after the old trading family, the Babbitts of Flagstaff, because Sammy ran a grocery store. "Cyrus," says Earl about his friend, "he wasn't even initiated into anything, but he heard everything." He means that Cyrus did not occupy a priesthood position—and therefore could not speak with authority as a leader. Nevertheless, he was present throughout the deliberations. Although Earl has heard Cyrus tell his story countless times, he wishes that Cyrus were here so he could tell it all correctly. Earl says that finally they certified both to go to the Council meetings. And the old people met with them and talked to them about the old ways, and then sent them off.

"When the two came back," says Earl, "they think the white way. They're after the minerals. They want someone to be accepting everything.

"It was running for several years before they started the three judges in Prescott," says Earl, referring to the special three-judge court set up to hear *Healing v. Jones*. "No Kikmongwi was there," he says, "they just did it all themselves." Consequently, Earl and his fellow traditionalists do not recognize the outcome of that case. It is insignificant in their view of life, for an event of far greater importance is approaching. "If nobody follows the Kikmongwi, if they fall into the white man's life, then the

Kikmongwi and another man will have to come together and embrace each other." That other man is the white brother. "The Purification is coming," says Earl. "It is close. These people are all falling into the white man's life. There are just a few of us here."

Phyllis asks Earl if the natural disasters that we have experienced in the last few years are a result of the land dispute. Earl's face lights up and he smiles knowingly. "Hopi is supposed to be a peaceful people. Supposed to be respecting everything. The Tribal Council, the stock owners, are the very ones want to move the Navajos out. The traditional people can't move anybody out. They pray for everybody. Everybody is their son. We have disasters in nature because everything is upset.

"Abbott started it too early," says Earl. "It was not settled in proper way. The Hopi knows he owns the whole United States. That's how we understand. They renew the prophecies every year; it comes up during initiation. We don't write anything down like white people. We keep it in our heads."

Earl feels that any determination of boundaries made by the United States is meaningless. "We didn't settle in proper way. Didn't come together to settle who was here first." To the Hopis, this discussion is of utmost importance. They want the Navajos and the white people to acknowledge that the Hopis were here first. "The U.S. government thinks he is the first one here, that's why we have to settle it," says Earl. "The white man will have to listen because he has no land. The Navajos have no land either."

As far as any decisions made by the Tribal Council go, Earl feels they are invalid. "This is formed by the BIA," he says. "This council is the BIA's tool. It's not really helping the Hopis; it wants us to live like the white man and fight against our own people. That's what the government wants, they want to find somebody to accept everything." In Earl's view, which is shared by other Hopis who try to maintain the old ways, "only the people who have been initiated know their own way of life. A person who is initiated is called Hopi. . . . The ones who are not initiated want everything right off."

Earl doesn't feel that the relocation program is the answer. He objects to any solution that precedes a "proper settlement" where all parties sit down and establish who was there first. "We are not the ones been working against the Navajos, it's the Hopi Tribal Council," he says. "We are all involved with intermarriage" between Hopis and Navajos, says Earl. "It will be hard to move the Navajos." Ideally, he'd like the U.S. government to give back all the land to the Hopis and move "back to Europe." But he says the Hopis wouldn't force that solution. "If we settle things up in a proper way," he says, "we wouldn't move those white people out. They will be our neighbors, they will have to be good. They will work for the Hopis, because if we want to use our land, the white people know how to use tools, they use them really well. At that time, you can get half and half."

The Hopis believe that they were set down on this earth to keep it and protect it for all people. When they say they want the white people to work for them, it is not in the sense of master and slave. The Hopis simply believe that since they hold the fate of the earth in their hands, it is to everyone's benefit to cooperate, and the white men are uniquely able to help out with their technological skills.

Even if no one listens to the Hopis' proffered solution—and the traditionalists have tried repeatedly to get their message across to Congress, but Congress only wants to hear from one body at Hopi and it is the Tribal Council—Earl and his fellows don't despair. They are waiting for the white brother and the Purification, whose arrival they believe is imminent. "Somebody will come and write everything down," says Earl. "They will investigate, they will know everything."

Earl and Evangeline wait. They blunt their disapproval and disappointment with the solace that the end is near. They console themselves as their world changes around them that they are really not being called upon to speak out, to change anything, because any solution of this world is temporary. Earl is patient, positive; Evangeline is full of resentment. Two pieces of the puzzle of Hopi, cracking with the strain of internal and external pressures. Earl disapproves of Evangeline's behavior, saying, "In her position, she shouldn't hate anybody." He feels that denunciation and bad thoughts are not the Hopi way. "Those kind of people talking like that, they don't understand their knowledge. She doesn't know properly her way of life."

But even the betrayal of the Hopi way doesn't disturb his sense of the world. "Pretty soon it will all be put right," he says, nodding, smiling knowingly. "The Purification is coming."

(13)

Hope for Change:
The Morris-Clark Mission

The Navajo-Hopi land dispute generated three federal statutes, almost twenty federal lawsuits, and a dozen state court cases. It also brought about the creation of a new federal agency, the Navajo and Hopi Indian Relocation Commission, to carry out the relocation of the Navajo and Hopi families who found themselves living on the wrong side of the partition line.

By fall 1985, a decade after the Commission began its work, the agency had moved about a thousand Navajo families. Yet with only ten months to go before the July 6, 1986, deadline, the Commission had yet to build houses for the approximately 1,700 additional families that were certified as eligible. These families made up about 7,650 people, since the Commission estimated an average of 4.5 people per family. The Commission had completed only a third of its job.

The size of the relocation program had grown beyond all expectations. In 1974, it was thought that eight hundred families would have to be relocated. In the succeeding eleven years, the number had more than tripled. This is just one of the many problems that had not been properly anticipated. Cost was another. In 1974, Congress estimated relocation would cost $41 million. In 1985, the Commission estimated it would cost a total of $337 million to complete the job, a jump of 824 percent.

The task—to move about a hundred Hopis and thousands of Navajos—would have been difficult under the best of circumstances. Thayer Scudder, the expert on relocation of rural populations, studied the Navajo resettlement issue in 1978 and predicted four primary effects of relocation on the Navajos. He anticipated that it would undermine the people's faith in themselves: "They learn, to their humiliation, that they are unable to protect their most fundamental interests . . . [including] the preservation of their land (both for themselves and, of great importance, for their children), their homes, their system of livestock management with its associated lifestyle, and their links with the environment they were born to."

Scudder also predicted that the relocatees would become dependent on the agency that had moved them, in part because they had lost their self-respect and initiative. He also predicted that the stress and alienation fostered by the relocation would lead to the disruption of the family, in part because the influence of the family head would be undermined because of his or her incapacity to preserve the family's way of life. He predicted that depression, violence, illness, and substance abuse would all increase. Martin Topper, an anthropologist with the Indian Health Service, corroborated many of Scudder's predictions in a study of his own. He reported that relocatees have "eight times the mental health service utilization rate as non-relocatees."

Relocation would also alter relations between relocatees and other tribal members. Scudder anticipated that it would undercut the influence of local leaders, and set up conflicts between the relocatees, the hosts, and the outsiders. Relocatees who were settled on the reservation were compelled to move onto land that was already occupied and overgrazed, and their arrival would put stress on the existing services, like water, clinics, and schools.

All these dire predictions came to pass. But the relocation of Navajos and Hopis was burdened by even more than the usual difficulties expected with such a task. From the start, the Commission was staffed with political hacks who were astonishingly unqualified and ill prepared for their jobs. Where sensitivity, flexibility, and foresight were needed, the upper-level Commission staff was rigid, unimaginative, and defensive. Said Leon Berger, a former executive director of the Commission who resigned in protest over the Commission's direction, "The Commission's mentality is like that of the guards at Auschwitz. 'This is the law and we have to do it,' is what they say. The Commission is hiding behind the law. It has all the capacity in the world to deal with [the problems] correctly, but it is totally lacking in moral courage." One Interior official refers to the Commission as the "omission" for its lack of competence. Berger called the Commission "the epitome of the worst."

By fall 1985, Congress had become increasingly disgusted with the Commission's performance, and was beginning to take steps to relieve the agency of some of its authority. A 1985 report by the investigative arm of the House Appropriations Committee severely criticized the Commission for not providing adequate counseling, for managing by "trial and error," and for working toward "conflicting goals."

The Commission's failings had also been revealed in numerous media accounts, and by 1985, the Commission had become a lightning rod for criticism. Sara Aleman, chief of counseling at the Commission, was quoted in *Newsweek* in September 1985 as saying, "Counseling is a mis-

nomer, it's a set-up for failure." Sandra Massetto, one of the three commissioners, who distinguished herself from her colleagues by acting as
an advocate for the relocatees, called the Commission "a planning agency
with no plans."

The negative news reports led the other two commissioners to retal-
iate against the whistle blowers. Massetto's two colleagues, who consistently outvoted her, submitted a letter into her personnel file accusing
her of misfeasance and malfeasance of office, citing her comments to the
press. Aleman, the counseling chief, was fired after the *Newsweek* article
appeared. She had previously been demoted, along with other "malcon-
tents" who criticized the administration of the program. The internal
reorganization prompted job discrimination filings.

But the Commission's attempts to muzzle opposition couldn't erase
the facts. Many of the first relocatees had been directed by Commission
staff to a home builder which constructed prefabricated houses that literally cracked open and fell apart. At the time, the Commission had no
procedures in place for replacing or repairing faulty houses, and further,
did not begin inspecting new houses until three years after the home
purchases had begun.

The Commission's counseling program failed utterly. By 1985, more
than one third of the Navajos who had received relocation houses had
already sold them or lost them, and another thirty percent had seriously
encumbered their homes. Of those relocatees living in Coconino County
for more than thirty-six months, eighty-two percent had either sold their
houses or had put them up as collateral for loans greater than $10,000.
Said Lee Phillips, "There's a slaughter going on out here." Relocatees,
suddenly responsible for electricity payments, auto registration, taxes,
and water charges they had never before encountered, and many without steady employment, ran into financial trouble. They routinely put
their homes up as collateral for loans with astronomical interest rates,
and then ended up selling or trading the houses for small amounts of
cash, vehicles whose value or condition had been overstated, land that
was overvalued or encumbered (and not revealed as such), or "questionable, non-discounted third-party promissory note assignments." According to one investigation, "Although each sale took on its own
characteristics, there were also common threads. There was the trusted
real estate agent, who spoke their language, who learned of their financial plight, and appeared at the house to see if he could 'help.' There
were loans or offers of loans to tide the relocatees over the 'hard times,'
to get them back on their feet. The relocatees were told their houses
could be sold to generate cash, with a pickup truck and trailer thrown in
as part of the deal." The Arizona Department of Real Estate determined
that "a number of real estate licenses have been involved in fraudulent
practices while dealing with relocatee activity." As Thayer Scudder had

predicted, the relocatee victims returned to the Commission for help. The Commission turned them away, telling them they were no longer the agency's responsibility.

The relocatees who lost their homes this way did not fare well. Some wound up back on the reservation, humiliated, to stay with relatives who were already living in intolerably overcrowded conditions. The lucky ones found public housing; others turned to alcohol; some committed suicide. The relocatees' naïveté and lack of preparation for life off the reservation made failure a foregone conclusion. "The relocatee Indians are ill-prepared to move off-reservation," wrote a congressional observer, "but are forced to do so because of the outrageous conditions which exist on the former JUA. The relocatees literally have nowhere to go and are forced to move to town." These conditions were caused by the building freeze and livestock reductions ordered by Judge Walsh. The relocatees had nowhere to go because the Navajo Tribe's choice of the Arizona Strip for the so-called New Lands had been opposed by local Anglos, and new selections near Sanders, Arizona, had been held up by the complicated public land swaps necessary to secure them. Before the New Lands became available, six hundred families, approximately 2,496 individuals, had been moved to border towns.

Moreover, the Relocation Commission, which had been directed by law to "minimize the adverse social, economic and cultural aspects of relocation . . . and to avoid any repetition of the unfortunate results of a number of early official Indian relocation efforts," employed two people to offer postmove counseling to eight hundred families, so those moving to border towns could not rely on much help from the Commission to deal with their unfamiliar new world.

These facts did not go unnoticed in the Interior Department, though little could be done since the Relocation Commission was an independent agency in the executive branch and outside Interior's reach. But in January 1985, a rumbling began to be heard. The rumbling was indistinguishable to most people, but was thunderous to the dozens of souls locked away in various Washington offices who worried in one way or another about the Navajo-Hopi land dispute. William Clark was preparing to step down from his post as Secretary of the Interior, and he felt bad about leaving the issue unresolved. He decided to speak to the President about it.

The Interior Department, although it had few direct responsibilities in the relocation effort, was generally aware of the problems encountered in implementing PL 93-531. After the Hopis filed five separate suits against the Navajos and the United States seeking $143 million in damages, claiming loss of revenues from and damage to the HPL, Interior became increasingly concerned about its liability. The Field Solicitor's office in Phoenix sent a steady stream of messages to Interior about developments, and William Clark heard briefings on the subject during the weekly Monday morning meetings at Interior.

Moreover, the relocation fiasco seemed likely to be repeated in the Hopi suit against the Navajos over another huge chunk of land to the west of the 1882 area, known as the 1934 reservation area. The issue again was ownership of the land; a 1934 congressional act defining the Navajo reservation boundary reserved land in this area for Navajos "and such other Indians as are already settled there." (This language was slightly different from the problematic language in the 1882 Executive Order Area, which set aside land for the Hopis "and such other Indians as the Secretary of the Interior may see fit to settle thereon.") The 1974 Land Settlement Act, rather than coming up with a legislative solution to the disputed 1934 area, directed the tribes again to sue each other in federal district court to determine their respective rights to that land.

Before stepping down, William Clark discussed the situation with his old friend Ronald Reagan. Clark suggested he serve as the President's personal emissary to the two tribes in an attempt to get them to resolve their dispute through negotiation rather than to continue with the numerous lawsuits and the floundering relocation effort. "He felt when he went to Interior he had certain responsibilities, mainly cleaning up the problems created by [former Interior Secretary James] Watt, but the Indian problem was one of them," said Clark's trusted counselor Richard Morris, who was to do the legwork for Clark. "He had some personal concerns about the future of both tribes and, . . . having seen the failure of different government agencies to bring this to a resolution, [felt] that some effort should be made to . . . urge [the tribes] to settle their differences." Ronald Reagan agreed, and on February 8, Judge Clark hand-delivered letters from President Reagan to the two tribal chairmen at Keams Canyon, the old BIA compound at Hopi.

The President's letter noted that the present law had led to a great number of additional lawsuits "that have consumed both the time and resources of the Hopi Tribe and Navajo Nation, as well as of the federal government, with no real resolution of the underlying dispute being in sight." The President went on to explain that he saw an "important need for a speedy and final resolution of these issues so that old wounds may begin to heal and to minimize the hardships that are falling on individual members of the two tribes."

Because Judge Clark was no longer Secretary of the Interior, he was not in a position to initiate legislation or force a solution on the two tribes. The mission would not be aided by the presence of a cabinet-level emissary. President Reagan tried to add a little muscle to Clark's position, however, promising that if progress toward a settlement was not reached, the administration would take the matter into its own hands: "I am very hopeful of success in these negotiations," he wrote. "At the

BESSIE HATATHLIE OFFERS CORNMEAL TO THE HOLY PEOPLE.

BESSIE HATATHLIE

JACK HATATHLIE

THE SAN FRANCISCO PEAKS AS VIEWED FROM COAL MINE MESA

SNIPPING WOOL FROM A SHEEPSKIN

DENNIS AND ELLA BEDONIE IN THEIR TRAILER IN TUBA CITY

ANNIE BEGAY (ANNIE OAKLEY) IN HER TRUCK

KEE SHAY

JENNY MANYBEADS REACTS TO
BAD NEWS AT A HARDROCK
CHAPTER MEETING.

THE HOPI VILLAGE OF SHIPAULOVI

A HOPI CORN PLANT

ERNEST ELMER'S BEANS

ABBOTT SEKAQUAPTEWA IN HIS CORNFIELD

MOENCOPI WASH

ERNEST ELMER,
SON OF DAVID MONONGYE,
TENDS HIS BEANFIELD
NEAR HOTEVILLA.

THE HOPI VILLAGE OF MOENCOPI

GRANDFATHER DAVID MONONGYE

THOMAS BANYACYA

HOPI TRIBAL CHAIRMAN IVAN SIDNEY IN HIS OFFICE

NAVAJO TRIBAL CHAIRMAN PETERSON ZAH EXPLAINS THE
UDALL-MCCAIN BILL AT A HARDROCK CHAPTER MEETING.

THE RELOCATION COMMISSIONERS: (CLOCKWISE FROM LEFT) SANDRA MASSETTO,
HAWLEY ATKINSON, AND RALPH WATKINS

NAVAJO TRIBAL CHAIRMAN PETERSON ZAH, SENATOR BARRY GOLDWATER,
AND HOPI TRIBAL CHAIRMAN IVAN SIDNEY

PERCY DEAL HELPS MAE TSO
(LEFT) OUT OF A MEETING
WITH HOPI TRIBAL CHAIRMAN
IVAN SIDNEY.

BROS: THOMAS KATENAY,
TSO, WILLIE LONEWOLF SCOTT,
REGGIE DEER AFTER A HEARING
THE HOPI TRIBAL COURT

BESSIE YAZZIE IN FRONT OF HER PAMPERS-BOX HOUSE

MAE TSO'S CAMP

A NAVAJO COUPLE IN FRONT OF A TRADITIONAL HOGAN

A NAVAJO COUPLE IN FRONT OF THEIR RELOCATION HOME

same time, the tribes must realize that the present situation cannot be allowed to persist and that if movement is not made toward settlement of these issues, the Administration will promptly review the existing legislation and court orders and formulate a course of action that in our judgment is needed to resolve the matter. I strongly urge your full co-operation with Judge Clark."

The job fell on the shoulders of Richard Morris. Morris had been a senior research attorney for the California Supreme Court where Clark had served as a judge. Morris accompanied Clark to Washington in 1981 when Clark was appointed Undersecretary of State, and he continued as Clark's aide through his terms as director of the National Security Council and Secretary of the Interior.

Morris spent seven months meeting with Navajo residents of the HPL, the two tribal chairmen, Hopi villagers, and government officials. He distinguished himself with his quiet, unassuming manner and his desire to understand the positions of both tribes as well as the history and culture that had generated those positions. He was the first official from Washington to travel to the remote, windswept reservations since the 1974 law had been passed to see for himself and his government what the law had wreaked. Morris was sixty-nine years old when he took on the rough job, which required long and bone-shattering drives over unpaved roads. He weathered barbed comments from some Hopis that he should go back to Washington, and he felt the skepticism of the Navajos who had had their hopes raised many times before, and who, like the Hopis, didn't hold out much hope for relief from the men from "Washindone." Morris persisted and established a reputation among Navajos and government officials as a principled, honest man who was motivated to do what was right.

The Hopis of the tribal government objected to the very premise of Morris's mission. As far as they were concerned, the law was the law and the only issue remaining was getting the Navajos off the HPL. Ralph Regula, Republican representative from Ohio, explained why the Hopis felt so strongly this way: "It's *their* land. If you win a lawsuit from me for ten thousand dollars, you're not about to say, well, give me two thousand and we'll consider ourselves even. If you've got the ten thousand and the case has gone to the Supreme Court, which is the end of the line, and I have no further appeal, you're not going to say, Well, I'll be a nice girl and let you settle for two thousand." Regula, a member of the House Appropriations subcommittee that oversees the relocation program, added, "The land is theirs. It's theirs and they want it, bottom line. And we gotta do it. Gotta do it. They're not going to sell it, they're not gonna give it up. They want it and it's theirs."

Pat Dallas, one of Hopi chairman Ivan Sidney's close aides, made the Hopis' position clear in the spring of 1985: "We just want to see the law carried out. The Congress and the courts determined this is the way it should be. Morris is just another white man come into this area who doesn't know what's going on. The Navajo have a rope around his neck. He's seen ten Navajos for every Hopi." Dallas felt Morris was vulnerable to Navajo manipulation, and objected to Morris's visiting relocatees. "Like I say to everybody, I'm tired of you white people coming onto our land and trying to get something out of us without understanding where we come from and where we're going."

Dallas complained, "Most people do that, they get dragged around by the Navajo and they see nothing but hardship, nothing but emotion, nothing but what's going on today. They don't see beyond that, back into the 1850s, when the Navajos first came here. I've been told and told time and again about what happened in those days. And it's in our blood. We can't help how we feel. It's got to stop somewhere. Right now at this very minute they're out there probably, you know, stealing."

Morris quickly realized how difficult his task would be. He said, "The Hopis were not prepared to sit down to discuss issues. In their perception, these issues had been discussed and resolved before. They did not feel it productive to go through the same drill again."

But Morris quickly developed a strong sympathy for Navajos like Bessie Hatathlie who were being told to leave everything they knew. "I have tremendous compassion for those Navajos living on the HPL, those who have lived there forever. Even though the law gives this land to the Hopis, the Navajos are the people living there and identified with the land. The Great Spirit has given them responsibility for caring for that area. [Without it] there is no point in continuing on. They believe this. It is very difficult for the white people to understand."

This was not the first time that negotiations to avert or reduce relocation had been undertaken. The 1980 amendments specifically authorized the Commission to enter into negotiations concerning land exchanges or possible rental agreements. Those efforts, in part because of the ineptitude of the Commission, failed.

Negotiations had been tried in 1975 as well, as a result of the authorization in the 1974 act for a federal mediator to sit down with teams from the two tribes and try to work out an alternative to large-scale relocation. The Navajos had offered to buy the HPL from the Hopis, which the Hopis considered an insult and rejected out of hand. "Money disappears, land stays forever," they had said.

And, as we have seen, Indian Commissioner Philleo Nash and others had tried to guide the tribes toward negotiations between 1963, when *Healing v. Jones* was upheld by the Supreme Court, and 1974 when the Relocation Act was passed. In 1971, the Navajos offered the Hopis $18 million for the HPL, but were turned down.

The most promising opportunity for progress had appeared in 1983 when Ivan Sidney and Peterson Zah replaced bitter adversaries Abbott Sekaquaptewa and Peter MacDonald as chairmen of their respective tribes. Sidney and Zah had attended the Phoenix Indian School together, and even though Zah was ten years older, they had been friends. In April 1983, both traveled to Washington to tell Congress and the administration that they wanted more time to work things out together. "Let's take it away from the courts, away from the lawyers, away from the Congress," said Peterson Zah. "Ten presidents of the United States have tried to solve this. It has gone through eighteen or nineteen secretaries of the Interior. We've spent millions of dollars in lawyers' fees fighting each other and our people got to a state where they hate each other. Yet we're both minorities. We're both Native Americans. We shouldn't be fighting like this."

"I remember the great good feeling between them," recalled Representative Morris Udall about the period of time just after both were elected. "[Ivan] said to me, 'Pete and I are going to go out and sit under a tree and settle it.' It sort of had a poetic, loving context to it." During a reception at the Capitol celebrating the surprising turn of events, Ivan Sidney handed his friend Pete Zah a book on Hopi land and culture. "The book shows what we're trying to do," Sidney said. "We're trying to understand each other as people. Last week I went with him to a Navajo wedding. Pete Zah and I are both traditional Indians. The traditions teach that the sun goes down at the end of the day, and with it some of the bad memories. When the sun comes up, it's a new day. We believe this. We believe we can compromise."

Morris Udall, an Arizona Democrat and head of the House Interior Committee, had been very hopeful at that time. "I kept thinking that under the right auspices, like Jimmy Carter did at Camp David, that you could get a Begin and a Sadat type to come along," he remembered later. "But you can't get much closer to that than Zah, who in my judgment is willing to run some risks and put his political career on the line."

But the great promise of those early days was not to flower into meaningful discussions. Ivan Sidney did not realize how determinedly the Hopis would work to preserve the battles won. Despite Sidney's promises to settle the dispute with his old friend, the Hopi lawyers and the Tribal Council, over whom the lawyers had a good deal of influence, wouldn't let him do it.

At the end of the summer of 1983, on the advice of its attorneys, the Hopi Tribal Council passed "a series of resolutions designed to strip [Chairman] Sidney of his power, cut back on his travel, and reduce his influence with the federal government and the Navajo." Said Zah, "I actually believe the lawyers are afraid Ivan Sidney and I will settle some problems between our people. . . . And this means the lawyers will be out of millions in unnecessary fees."

Though the odds on reaching a settlement looked slim, Richard Morris was determined to try everything he could. He felt the relocation was wrong. He was impressed by figures which showed that after the partition, the Hopis, who lived in high-density villages, possessed 342 acres per person, while the Navajos had been left with 121 acres per person on which to live and graze their flocks. "The Hopis don't have to live on the land the way the Navajo live on the land. I doubt that in the immediate future there would be much change. So, basically, it's moving people off the land to make room for sheep. And I'm not sure the Hopis will even use the land for that. . . . If you look at it that way, [relocation] seems an unjust thing to do."

The land is rough, arid, sprawling. The land is everywhere, extending in all directions, occasionally rising into mesas or plunging into canyons until it disappears, at the horizon, into sky. Here, on the southwestern tip of the Navajo reservation, mounds of cinder a thousand feet high loom over fields of dry grasses, punctuating the landscape with strange, lunar forms. Cinder mined from these ancient volcanic hills has been paved into this road from Flagstaff to Leupp and on to Second Mesa, coloring it a deep vermilion.

To the north, the horizon is hazy with the pastel buttes of the painted desert. Sunflowers and snakeweed dot the grasslands. Framing the highway are the ever-present high-tension wires carrying electricity from Black Mesa to the white man. It is peaceful here. Old meets new with unspoken acquiescence, or perhaps it is simply surrender.

Lew Gurwitz heads up to the Big Mountain survival camp to meet with the Navajos and tell them what they can expect over the next ten months before the deadline. He passes Leupp, an ugly, modern reservation town marked by rows of trailers and one-story houses built in parallel rows with no yards. Four Navajo horsemen carrying lassos ride toward the miniature city with their flocks of sheep. A white mare stares at the passing traffic from the side of the road. There is invariably a dead dog in the twist of highway just before the brick elementary school.

"Zah will try to get a recommendation from Morris and Clark regarding land exchanges," says Gurwitz. "Then he'll try to get support in Congress for legislation." In the fall of 1985 the Navajo Tribe is still trying to regain possession of the HPL so as to eliminate the need for further relocation. In return, it plans to offer the Hopis the 250,000 acres of land it acquired near Chambers, Arizona, between 1983 and 1985 as part of PL 93-531, as amended, as well as some other land the tribe owns at the base of the San Francisco Peaks. But Gurwitz's group, the Big Mountain Legal Defense/Offense Committee (BMLDOC) is not supporting this plan. It wants to repeal the law, return the land to the status quo—"turn back the clock," as Stewart Udall puts it.

"We are going to recommend to Zah to push repeal of the law, even though we know his advisers tell him 'repeal is impossible,' " says Gurwitz.

Gurwitz and Lee Phillips feel compelled to advocate a complete repeal of the law, though the possibility of that, eleven years after its passage, is slim, if not impossible. But that is part of the alliance the group has struck with the traditional Hopis. The traditionalists object to any white law that affects life or land at Hopi, because they believe that the proper solution to the problems will only come at the time of the Purification. The coalition between the Navajo and Hopi elders is dependent on BMLDOC's fighting for repeal. This forces BMLDOC to take a radical position, and prevents it from compromising. And it has some usefulness for the Navajo Tribe. As Lee Phillips explains it, "We're out there fighting for the extreme left position, so the Navajo Tribe can come in closer to the center and look reasonable."

Gurwitz passes by the turnoff to Sand Springs and onto the Hopi Partition Lands. Ahead are glistening salmon- and rose-colored mesas, flat-topped hills jutting straight up from the sandy plains. Red dust has blown up about the bottom of the mesas and frozen into rock. The tops of the mesas are stratified with brilliant layers of red and orange. Abandoned hogans and shacks dot the countryside. The rangeland has recovered to a great extent and the grass is once again growing thick. There are no flocks or herds in sight. Navajos moved off this land, but Hopis have not replaced them. The Hopis have not even moved animals out. They have not been able to work out a permitting system among themselves; negotiations have been stalled by jealousy and interclan bitterness.

"Congress still doesn't fully understand what's going on out here," says Gurwitz. "The recent press coverage will raise people's consciousness on the issue. As we travel across the country, as we educate people, they are appalled. But the work of the [BMLDOC] office is to make contact with people to teach them and encourage them to write their congressmen. We tell them to argue that the relocation doesn't accomplish anything for the American people. The cost in U.S. dollars is too high, and it only produces human tragedy."

Gurwitz drives on for mile after mile, eventually climbing the long walls of the Hopi mesas toward Kykotsmovi and the general store. He fills up the tank with gas, buys some fruit and pop. He greets some Hopis, then heads on. The mesas are rocky, harsh. The villages are moribund fortresses perched high in the sky, placed so that Hopis can view intruders from every direction. One can see how a people positioned to see every traveler, every advancing cloud or dust storm can develop an eternal wariness, a worldview that is obsessed with protection. Standing on the mesa tops looking off to the buttes to the south or the San Francisco Peaks to the west, one has no doubt whatsoever why the Hopis would possess an intense desire to control the surrounding countryside. Small cornfields and peach orchards are tucked into clan land beside the road, struggling for every drop of moisture from the sandy soil, producing small quantities of precious vegetables and fruits. When resources are so scarce, the theft of even a dozen peaches by a Navajo is enough to throw an entire village into a panic.

Gurwitz heads off the mesa, leaves the paved road, and starts out north to the Dinnebito Trading Post over the shattering roads, past herds of Navajo sheep. Before Dinnebito, a stone house and mud hogan appear to the west, wedged into the side of a rock butte. Gurwitz points out the house and says it belongs to Henry King, a Navajo real estate agent who played a role in defrauding Navajos of their relocation homes. When Lee Phillips began investigating the scams, Henry King disappeared onto the reservation and escaped prosecution. It is said that Henry King's mother is a witch.

The trading post is crowded with trucks and Navajos come to pick up their mail and buy groceries and supplies. Dust devils whip in whirlwinds before the stock tanks and a small airplane tied to the ground that is owned by the Anglo proprietor of the store. As Gurwitz approaches Big Mountain, the scrub gets bigger, the trees taller. The hogans are tucked into hillsides and the stock corrals are made of wild twists of juniper logs and brush, like a vine of branches. Gnarled trees bend into the wind. The land seems so inhospitable, so difficult, it seems beyond comprehension that the government would pry loose people who cling so tenaciously to their lives here. And it seems equally incomprehensible that any other people would move here in their place.

Several miles up the twisting road stands the sign for the camp. "Big Mountain Survival Camp. No Guns, Drugs, Alcohol." Near it is the house of Kee Shay, the Big Mountain patriarch on whose land the camp is built. A couple of miles past Kee Shay's house the camp appears in view, with a dozen pickup trucks parked along the dirt paths before the roundhouse. The sun dance arbor stands a few hundred yards away. The "bros"—young Navajos from the area—patrol the environs with binoculars and guns in an AIM type of defense, against whom it's not clear, but most likely they're watching out for Hopi rangers who sometimes venture out in their panel trucks looking for unpermitted animals.

The residents of Big Mountain are gathered for the first of what will be monthly meetings from now, the fall of 1985, until the relocation deadline in July 1986. Roberta Blackgoat and several other women from the area stir vats of mutton stew and flip dough into sizzling pans of lard in the cookshack behind the survival camp. One woman slices blood sausage and another sets out a plate of roasted corn. Tin coffeepots roil. After eating, Lew Gurwitz leads the Navajos to the roundhouse. Lee

Phillips hangs back, looks at the stolid women and skinny men ambling past the beat-up trucks and cars. "Everything out here is a survivor," he says. "The people are small and bent like the trees, it's as if they grew out of the same spare land. The ladies' faces and hands are as hard and seasoned as the landscape."

Danny Blackgoat, the son of Roberta, one of the leaders of this resistance, sits up at the front of the room with a yellow legal pad in hand. Danny is over six feet tall, with dark skin and a powerful bearing. He wears a bandana about his forehead and a bear claw about his neck. It is dangerous for Navajos to see or be in touch with anything having to do with a bear. But Danny has earned the right to wear the bear claw by virtue of his struggles.

This is the first time Danny has led a meeting here on Kee Shay's property. Several years ago, Danny relocated, moved to Flagstaff into a modern house, and worked as a guidance counselor at Flagstaff High School. He appeared to be a model Navajo who successfully made it into the white world. But soon, the stress of living in town and the conflict of having sold his land sent Danny into a tailspin. He started to drink, then drink heavily, and soon his wife and children left him. It wasn't until he had lost everything, his family and his house, that he realized he had only one place to go and one fight to fight. He moved back to his mother's house, stopped drinking, and joined the resistance. Kee Shay, an unforgiving opponent of relocation, is somewhat skeptical of Danny's appearance here, but Roberta, Danny's mother, is a powerful figure in these parts, one of the most outspoken and effective resisters.

Roberta asks Kee Shay to offer a prayer, which he does in Navajo. Danny takes notes diligently on the yellow pad, and then translates into English. He is nervous. He swallows frequently. When the prayer has been translated, Gurwitz begins to speak. He informs the group that Leonard Peltier, the AIM member serving a federal prison term for the killing of two FBI agents, has been moved to Leavenworth into the general population. This is an improvement from the isolation unit at Marion Penitentiary. The ladies nod. Many of them participated in a prayer ceremony for Peltier in Los Angeles.

Then Gurwitz gets to the business at hand. He looks around at the ladies seated on colorful blankets, at the men sitting behind, at Kee Shay crouching near the roundhouse door, his mouth shearing his face at a diagonal. He is grim, serious, gaunt. "Washington has to realize there will be a change in the law. Richard Morris is upset with the Hopis, upset that they won't negotiate. He says if the Hopis don't bend, he will make the decision himself. He's talking about land exchanges to save Teesto, Coal Mine, and Big Mountain."

Some of the people understand the English. Most wait patiently for the translation, which will come at the end of Gurwitz's words. "They say there are only two hundred and fifty families left out here on the land. They think that out of the two hundred fifty, only eighty would have to move. Hopefully, they will come down to none, and then maybe the people who have left can move back."

This last claim—that perhaps Navajos would be permitted to move back to the HPL—is impossible and Gurwitz knows it. He is letting his desire to engage these Navajos, to encourage them to believe in him, get the better of his judgment. Gurwitz tells the gathering that there has been much press on the issue. The *Denver Post*, the *Dallas Morning News*, *Newsweek*, *Time*, and environmental groups are publicizing the issue. "In Washington, most offices now know something about the resistance, even though most were informed that it was a Hopi-Navajo dispute. But this is progress from the last time we were there when people hadn't heard of the land dispute."

Gurwitz tells them that the BMLDOC office in Flagstaff is generating hundreds of letters each week to congressional offices and to supporters across the country. "My belief now is that Richard Morris will recommend land exchanges. When the bill is presented to Congress, we hope that through letters, articles, and so forth, we will have enough strength to persuade Congress and influence the bill to expand it so nobody is forced to move and those forced to move will have a right to come back. We are trying to show that this is not a dispute between the Navajos and the Hopis—we will reveal the coal and the uranium interests—and that it has nothing to do with justice for the Hopi.

"I know, I understand, that as the pressure increases, it gets harder and harder to live on the land. That's why the BIA police come around, that's why there are negative editorials in the papers, why there are stories of arms caches, and PLO and Cuban influences. We must be strong now. The pressure is meant to intimidate us. If we can make them understand well enough, we will be able to persuade Congress of the wisdom and necessity of repealing the law.

"I hope this report will make you feel stronger and better because we're closer now. We must be careful as we approach the end, we can't make mistakes, because mistakes will work against us. We must be strong. They will try to separate us, turn us against each other. We must stick together to fight relocation."

The ladies shift as Danny turns back his yellow pages and begins to translate. The scent of burning cedar colors the air; the earthen floor is deep red, the Navajos are calm, heavy, steadfast as they listen to every word. Children run in and out of the roundhouse. When they approach their mothers or grandmothers, they nestle comfortably into their laps or arms. They get their hair combed or braided, they listen, then leave again. None cry. They appear completely secure in their mothers' love, self-reliant, content.

After the translation is finished, Lee Phillips says a few words on the report he submitted to Congress in an attempt to block further appropriations for the Commission. He half kneels, half crouches on the floor, his hand by his mouth. He looks up at the ladies with a combination of reverence and fear. He sounds so earnest, one listens for mendacious notes. The Navajo ladies seem puzzled by his demeanor. White men are supposed to be forceful and effective, not understanding.

Phillips also reports that he has filed two suits in Washington on behalf of the Navajo relocatees, suits aiming to stop relocation on the basis of its huge cost and apparent unworkableness. Phillips tells them about various cases of fraud against relocatees in Flagstaff, and what he has done to help the victims. He tells the Navajos that there is strife within the Commission. He suggests this is a good sign for them.

Kee Shay concludes the meeting. He speaks softly, with great authority, and with few words. He thanks Gurwitz for coming out, he thanks him for his report. He thanks both Lew and Lee for their efforts, and says that without Lew, no one would know about the resisters at Big Mountain. He also thanks Lee for helping the Navajos.

But he is worried about the final days, the forced relocation that is looming before them like a firewall. "Our children sign up without parental consent," he says, "without the knowledge of their parents. It's a known fact—please look out for it in your work. We agree with your plans for solidarity in the months ahead, but some of our young ones do not agree, not all let us know they are relocating." Kee Shay also is worried about the resistance in Teesto, which is accompanied by ever more aggressive and violent posturing.

When Gurwitz replies, he doesn't speak directly to the issue of violence. This is a sore point among the Navajos and members of BMLDOC. Some Navajos want to ensure that their struggle is peaceful. Others desire a fight, while Gurwitz and Lee plan to use the threat of violence as leverage. Gurwitz thanks the people who continue to struggle and resist, and he says that the people's prayers help him. "Please hold on," he pleads, "hold on for the next few months to see what the White House will say. I will fight with you until relocation is stopped, and until provision is made for your children to come back and live on the land with you."

Mae Tso picks up her blanket, folds it, smiles shyly at Lee and Lew, and shakes their hands. "I am not afraid," she says. "I haven't broken any law. My laws hold true within the four sacred mountains." Her friend Mina Lansa, the Hopi priestess who has since passed away, assured her that she should consider the land on which she lives as her own. "I have faith in God," she says. "We had a ceremony for Richard Morris. We prayed that he would see what is going on."

It seems he did.

. . .

Richard Morris tried desperately to understand. He had undertaken his first trip to Arizona at the end of February 1985, and had spent half a year traveling back and forth from Washington. Claudeen Bates-Arthur, attorney general of the Navajo Nation, observed that Morris "came out here and really tried to look at it under very difficult circumstances, and he's not a real aggressive person. He's a quiet, nice man who truly tried to look at the issue."

But even after months of effort, Morris wasn't able to bring the Hopis to the negotiating table. His original desire had been to accomplish land exchanges, in which the Hopis would relinquish some acreage of the HPL in return for land elsewhere. By June 1985, it appeared he had reached an impasse. The Hopis had made it clear that "they [would] *not* exchange one acre of HPL" and "[would] not enter into *any* agreement where that is the basis." In frustration, trying to find one point on which he could elicit a positive response from the Hopis, Morris asked at a public meeting, "Certainly, you would give up an acre of HPL land if I could give you—and I can't—but if I could give you the whole state of New Mexico?" The Hopis told him no. Morris explains, "As a matter of fact [one Hopi] said, 'Mr. Morris, we don't like New Mexico. But we won't give up an acre of the HPL for the whole state of Texas.' And nobody at that meeting dissented from that. They all seemed to be of that same view."

Since no one had contradicted the man, Morris assumed that all the Hopis in attendance felt the same way. But he wasn't sure. "I realize that those who disagree express their disagreement by not saying anything. That's part of the problem we confronted. It's very hard to determine a consensus of Hopi feelings. And I suppose that's why the whole time I was out there, the Council never had a quorum."

Richard Morris here confronted a most interesting collision of social and psychological facts of Hopi life. First is the Hopis' brilliant use of passivity to achieve their ends. With no quorum in the Council, no one could be blamed for making a mistake. As Abbott Sekaquaptewa himself puts it, "The Hopis are very, very good at passive resistance. They're stubborn as hell. They hang on and hang on and hang on."

Secondly, the meeting revealed to Morris that though every Hopi thinks for himself or herself, and the Hopi culture allows a great deal of individual freedom, there is at the same time a tremendous pressure to go along. Anthropologist Mischa Titiev put it this way: "The great emphasis on individual freedom of behavior is checked by a fear of nonconformity. 'It's up to you' is balanced by 'People say it isn't right.' So marked is the dread of running afoul of public opinion among the Hopi, living as they do in closely grouped communities where privacy is out of the question, that only a man of exceptional character dares to depart from conventional modes of behavior in any important respects."

Whether or not the Hopis were divided on the issue of giving up parts of the HPL is not clear. It is possible that a group of Hopis thought some compromise advisable. No one except the opposition traditionalists said anything to Morris to suggest a willingness to negotiate. But what was clear was that the Hopis' deep-seated disinclination to oppose the status quo made negotiation an almost impossible challenge. This, however, worked to the Hopis' advantage. Sandra Massetto, one of the relocation commissioners, put it, "If you were a Hopi, would you want to be known as the Hopi who gave up the land?"

Morris was never sure he had understood what the Hopis truly wanted. But the sum of what he had heard, and what he had not heard, was plain. "In the Hopi perception, it was not in their best interest to enter upon arrangements different from ones that exist now under PL 93-531. They thought that was their best bet to preserve their future and I thought that judgment was made in good faith by them."

Nevertheless, the idea of a comprehensive solution was gaining currency among concerned observers. The disputes were occupying much of the tribes' time and energy, and distracting them from economic development, social programs, and other matters. And the federal government was footing part of the bill for the prolonged, and very expensive, litigation. By the end of 1985, government reimbursement for legal fees for both tribes for lawsuits involving the 1882 and 1934 areas totaled $4.26 million. The tribes themselves had paid hefty additional sums.

Morris felt that the Hopis had every reason to negotiate, not the least of which was their advantageous position. He says, "The Hopis are in a position where they can demand concessions from the Navajos. Their bargaining position is perhaps stronger." For example, by giving up parts of the HPL, the Hopis could gain a corridor of land from the Hopi reservation to Moencopi, which is now an island on the Navajo reservation near Tuba City, as well as some valuable Navajo-owned land, including coal-bearing areas off the reservations, and cash. "Perhaps they could get more than they [would] give up," Morris said. "When I say that, I'm talking about material assets. And I suppose that's the Anglo way of looking at things. The Hopis look at things a little differently. They probably perceive they can't get more than they're giving up."

Navajo official Percy Deal recalled that one day in July 1985, Morris met with Ivan Sidney and his Council in the morning and, although discouraged about his seemingly fruitless efforts, went on to meet with a group of villagers in the afternoon. The second meeting had been interminable, the Hopis reciting prophecy and arguing heatedly among themselves. Percy Deal arrived to take Morris home. When he pulled up to the appointed meeting place, he heard shouting going on inside. Hopis were shouting at Morris. Deal heard Morris's voice rise. The arguments continued without break. Percy got a piece of paper, wrote Richard Morris's name on the outside and inside wrote, "I am here and am waiting for you." Morris came out almost immediately. Deal said, "I'll never forget the look on his face. He gave me a big smile and shook my hand and looked at me like a child does when his parents arrive. He looked so relieved, so happy. He told the Hopi security guy to put his bags in my truck. He had ridden out there in a fancy car with air conditioning and everything. And my truck was all beaten up, the bumper was falling off and the air conditioning was broken. But he couldn't wait to get in and drive away from there. He said to me, 'The Hopis are the most difficult and unreasonable people'."

To the Hopis, that comment reflects a painful truth: the white man and the Navajos will never understand them. J. C. Smythe, a former legislative assistant to the Hopis, says any discussion of the land as a commodity offends them deeply. "They see their mission, their whole life plan being torn away by these other groups. . . . Where the Hopis live is like the core of the universe. Spiritually and religiously, the land is inextricably linked to their existence. The land is like a child to them. That child is theirs to steward through life. They feel they've already given up half [the JUA] and they're complying with the law."

The idea of giving up any more of their land further violates the Hopis' sense of world order. And, Smythe suggests, the fact that they had only won half the land was still a sore point. Smythe asks rhetorically, "Did [the Hopi lawyers] ask the tribal members if they were willing to lose half the [1882 area] when the *Healing* case was filed? Did the Hopis know the consequences, the social impact [of *Healing v. Jones*]? I think they would have left it as the Joint Use Area; the risk of loss was too high. It was a heart-wrenching announcement to the Tribal Council when [the lawyers] told them that only half the land was won, or returned."

The possibility of Navajos living happily on the HPL under Hopi jurisdiction is about as likely as Palestinians singing the praises of Israeli rule of the West Bank. Smythe thinks the Morris venture was doomed from the outset. "The Council tried," he says. "They said, 'Okay, we'll try to work with Morris, another white man come out to solve an ancient dispute.' But it was done in such a way that was the antithesis of the Hopi way. It was done with time frames and demands and schedules.

"A way to work it," continues Smythe, "would be for a new [U.S.] President to come in and say, 'This is of highest priority.' He would then send a special emissary out who would stay with it for four years or eight years, live out there on the reservation, go to dances, make it a priority and spend the time. You don't do it in a couple of weeks. You don't look at it as a temporary issue. You don't look at the Middle East conflict as a short-term problem. Small victories are large ones and must endure."

One can imagine how even the most uncommon bureaucrat might find that task daunting.

For centuries, the Hopis have worked out the details of their survival.

The system they created to withstand the rigors of life in the high desert requires exhausting religious rites and a rigid social organization. Ways forged over thousands of years under the relentless heat and drought do not change quickly. The Hopis also know how slowly time passes, how long the cycles of nature endure. They have little faith in the short-term fixes of the Americans.

Moreover, they are constantly aware of being a small tribe surrounded by strangers. "They are so absorbed by their own anxieties of being surrounded by different people. When they drive to Winslow, they have to pass Navajos on their own land," says Smythe. "There is fear. Hopis tell their children, 'If you're bad, I'll send you to the Navajos.' The Hopi culture is complex and full of anxieties."

At the end of July, Morris and Clark decided to take one last stab at negotiation. Clark wrote to both chairmen on July 30, asking them to join him for a meeting at the White House. He reminded both that they had committed themselves "in good faith" to resolve their differences, and pointed out that so far no progress had been made. He acknowledged that the Hopis were unprepared to agree to any land exchanges, even those which would have given them "resources having values much greater than the resource value of the exchanged HPL." As a final effort, he asked the tribal chairmen to come prepared to discuss any possible alternative basis for discussion. He urged them to come without lawyers or staff, but encouraged them to secure the authority to negotiate for their tribal councils.

Since Clark no longer had a White House office, he borrowed the office of a National Security Council official. This was clearly not a high-level meeting and that message was probably not lost on the Hopis. However, Morris, convinced of the benefits of negotiation, had drafted a tentative memorandum of understanding and the outlines of a rental agreement whereby the Navajos acknowledged that the land belonged to the Hopis, with the proviso that the Hopis would allow some Navajos to remain on the HPL under Hopi jurisdiction. They sat down to talk. Zah had come with a modified version of the memorandum that he had been authorized to sign by the Navajo Tribal Council. Sidney, however, told Morris he didn't have the authority to sign anything. The meeting broke up without success. Two weeks later, Sidney contacted Morris and told him "the Hopis were unable to execute a memorandum of understanding, in part because on earlier occasions both the government and the Navajo had defaulted on other 'agreements.' "

Peterson Zah was very discouraged by the failure of the Clark initiative and irritated by the Hopis. "If Chairman Sidney knew from the outset that any compromise was unacceptable to his people, he should have said so and saved President Reagan, Judge Clark, and many other well-intentioned people a good deal of time and effort," he announced.

"Instead, for reasons I don't understand, he allowed the process to go forward with no intention to compromise." Ivan Sidney, reflecting on the failed effort, retorted, "Chairman Zah is saying, 'Sidney didn't agree to anything back there, why didn't he agree?' Well, simply because again we're the people who are going to give up something. We've been doing all the giving up. All these years." Not insignificantly, Sidney was facing an election in November against Abbott Sekaquaptewa, the man who had won the land for the Hopis. His ability to negotiate was further hampered by the realities of Hopi politics.

Richard Morris was saddened that the effort wasn't successful, but by October he had prepared a report of his efforts, which Judge Clark took to President Reagan. The report recommended further involvement by the administration, and sought the President's continued help. Acknowledging that the Hopis had the stronger legal case, Morris said he urged the President to consider that "compassion is more important than enforcing the current law."

Morris rejected the oft-repeated Hopi argument that today's Navajos in some way deserved to be punished for the historical depredations of Navajos against Hopis. "Whatever the conduct of Navajo a century ago," his report reads, "the Navajo now subject to relocation are not yet guilty of wrongdoing. If the Hopi were victims of federal inaction during the last century, surely today's traditionalist Navajo are victims of the relocation process as fashioned by the Congress."

The report recognized the advice of Federal District Court Judge Earl Carroll, who had asked the two chairmen and Morris to a meeting in his chambers in July 1985. "Judge Carroll urged the Tribes to embrace the President's initiative. He stated that legal proceedings then before his court would take years to resolve at costs of millions of dollars with likely unhappy results for each Tribe." Carroll told the tribes they "should not look to the Congress to solve their differences, as Congress and the Bureau of Indian Affairs had been, in part at least, the source of the problems; that the President's initiative, even if it resulted in only an agreement for binding arbitration, was an opportunity the Tribes should seize." Morris dryly concluded, "We, but not both Tribes, were persuaded by Judge Carroll's recommendations." Morris and Clark made one final suggestion of their own, that any negotiated settlement include the 1934 area and all other outstanding lawsuits so the tribes could move on and out of their legal morass. "Unless a comprehensive plan be thoughtfully developed and put in place," Morris wrote, "fundamental tribal disputes may persist for still another century."

A day after the report was filed, Morris was asked if he was pleased with it. "Pleased? I'd like to have been able to say a little bit more about our impressions, where the fault lies. We were cautioned not to." He said he thought it was a fair and honest report, and that "anyone who reads it will probably form some impression of who should give." He said that Interior was still interested in continuing negotiations and therefore wanted to preserve "some kind of credibility with both tribes." Yet he clearly felt the same frustration every other negotiator has felt: the Hopis will not compromise, will not even discuss the issues.

One thing Morris was convinced of: "Congress doesn't really know what's going on out there. Even the delegates from Arizona and New Mexico don't really know. I think we should be there and keep working to achieve an accommodation of the parties. It is too important to fail to [pursue] all our options."

Senator Barry Goldwater was one of the congressmen Morris believed did not really understand what relocation had wrought. Although Goldwater played a singular role in the dispute, he remained astonishingly ignorant throughout the years of "what's going on out there."

In the fall of 1985, in his last term as senator, after serving thirty-four years in the Senate and enjoying a much ballyhooed presidential run, Goldwater had no intention of leaving with a blotch on his record. As Lee Phillips put it, "Goldwater's pride has been deeply involved in this. The last thing he wants is his image tarnished in his last term." He did not want the relocation program tinkered with, in fact he thought it was too generous to the Navajos in the first place.

Goldwater had proffered his own partition bill in 1972. It did not provide any monetary help for the Navajos who would be obliged to move off the HPL. He said at the time, "I do not think we have to pay money to relocate Indians, when in the case of the Navajo they have 16 million acres . . . , literally tens of thousands of acres that are not being used."

Goldwater presented himself as an expert on Indians when he addressed the U.S. House of Representatives in 1973 in support of the partition bill then being discussed. He prefaced his remarks with a smattering of Indian history and lore, and his qualifications: "My interest in this matter has gone back, I guess, all the years of my life that I have known about it, and I remember the first time I visited the reservation, I was seven years old. And I was up there just a few weeks ago. . . . I have lived with both the Navajo and the Hopi, as Sam [Representative Steiger] explained. I operated a trading post at Navajo Mountain for many years, and got to know those people well, as I feel I know the Hopis."

Yet Goldwater revealed he did not understand the issue as well as he should have, given the time he claims to have spent with the Navajos and Hopis. He misunderstood the significance of the ruling in *Healing v. Jones* that stated the two tribes had equal, undivided, and joint interest in the JUA. Goldwater told a House subcommittee during debate: "I was instrumental in getting the special court set up which first heard this problem, and this court, as have two since that time, ruled that the Navajo were in error, and they should get off." The court had ruled no such thing.

Goldwater's grasp of the issue he influenced so powerfully remained vague. In 1978, four years after the Settlement Act became law, he tried to tell a group of Navajos that they didn't have to move off their land. Jerry Kammer recorded that meeting in his book, *The Second Long Walk:*

> At the end of July, Goldwater cleared room in his busy Washington schedule and flew by helicopter from Phoenix to Big Mountain for a four-hour meeting with some 220 Navajos under the shade of a brush shelter. The senator, without whose support the land dispute legislation probably would not have passed in 1974, showed an almost total lack of awareness of what the bill was doing. "There has been no decision that says you have to move or what you have to do," he said, unmindful of the partition order. "And until that happens, and I don't think it's very close to happening or the way it looks now will happen. I won't say don't worry, but nobody can push you around."
>
> As the Navajos who understood English shook their heads and muttered disbelief, the senator compounded his mistakes. The relocation commission had been receiving funding for more than three years, but he insisted, "No money has been appropriated for relocation." The BIA had removed over half the Navajo stock from the JUA, but the senator said he knew of no federal stock reduction program since the one organized by John Collier in the 1930s. Goldwater said the major thrust of the land dispute legislation was to establish a commission to develop a plan for partitioning the JUA. He said he would talk with Rev. Paul Urbano, one of the commission members, about the hardships of the people at Big Mountain. . . .
>
> The elderly Navajos received Goldwater with elaborate courtesy. They served him lunch of mutton stew, peaches, and fry bread, and when they came up to the front of the brush shelter to speak, they shook his hand gravely. Translation into Navajo was spotty, so most of the people there did not understand what Goldwater was saying. But the English-speaking young expressed exasperation. "So what you are saying is that Public Law 93-531 is no good, or it's vague, or *what is it?*" Annie Holmes said. Percy Deal, new director of the Navajo's Land Dispute Commission, got down to specifics. "Sitting here among my people and listening to you this morning, it became apparent to me that either your staff down here in Phoenix or up there in Washington is not doing their homework," Deal said. "I can tell you right now that relocation is in progress, livestock reduction is in progress, fencing is in progress, and you are here telling us that this has not come about yet. I would suggest that you go back to the Phoenix

office or your D.C. office and tell your staff to get on the ball and keep you current on information going on out here."

The senator responded defensively. "Well, for your information, I helped write that act. I sat through the debate in the Senate, I listened to the debate in the House." Obviously knocked off stride now, he tried to recover his balance, acknowledging that, yes, partition had occurred, but still, relocation was a remote prospect. Then he added, "If you people are willing to force your tribal government to accept the court decision that they don't like, then you can live with it. But it is not my decision to tell your tribal government what to do."

It was a baffling, disturbing performance. Senator Goldwater was absolutely out of touch with the consequences of the Land Settlement Act. Apparently he was suggesting that the Navajos didn't have to go along with the court decision if they didn't want to. Daniel Peaches, a Navajo member of the Arizona Legislature, and a Republican, suggested sarcastically that Goldwater's statements were up to the usual level of Washington's understanding of the land dispute. "The people here have suffered because the politicians in Washington, especially our Republican leaders from the state of Arizona, failed to understand, failed to recognize, failed to see that if the land was to be divided fifty-fifty, it was inevitable that tragedy was going to fall on the shoulders of the Navajo people."

Goldwater departed soon after, pushing himself through a crowd of elderly ladies who hung on to him and urged him to stay on for a few days and learn about how they lived. Roberta Blackgoat asked him to stay for three days, as he'd promised, and sleep on the hogan floor and eat their food. "I even washed out a sheepskin for him and set it out to dry," she remarked wryly to an observer. Before Goldwater dragged himself out of the crowd and into the waiting chopper, he told a reporter, "I've lived here fifty years, and I probably know this land better than most of these Navajos here today do."

Again, in 1982, Goldwater showed himself embarrassingly ignorant of the subject about which he professed to know so much. He had introduced a bill to swap sixty-two acres of Big Mountain back to the Navajos in exchange for coal royalties. Hearings on the proposal were widely attended. Commissioner Sandra Massetto recalled, "TV cameras were rolling, and people were snaked out the door of the hearing room down the hall waiting to get in because it was so packed. It was incredible, it was wall-to-wall Indians and crazy wannabes. Then Goldwater gets up with his big map and says he wants to save Big Mountain because he's so close to the people and he points to a spot on the eastern edge of the reservation, somewhere around Window Rock. The Navajos in the room all started laughing. It was hysterical. It was sad in the sense that he didn't know where Big Mountain was, but it was funny because he was up there saying how well he knew the area, and he'd been there since he was a boy and all that. Typical white guy who says he knows everything about Indians but when he gets to show what he knows, he shows he doesn't know anything."

Goldwater, as might be expected, was not happy when he learned that someone else—William Clark—wanted to see if any changes might be made in his program. And, since Clark had approached the President to discuss his concerns about Navajo-Hopi, so did Goldwater. Only his message was a very different one. Goldwater aide Twinkle Thompson told House Minority Counsel Gregg Houtz that Goldwater had gone to the President to ask his help in hurrying up the pace of the relocation before he left the Senate. When Goldwater learned of Clark's mission, he said he hoped Clark would support his own position that "the law is the law and the Navajos should get off the land."

One Navajo lobbyist with ties to the White House pointed out that the Morris-Clark mission was a very low-profile effort as far as the administration went. He surmised that its response had been carefully adjusted to accommodate the opposing desires of both Clark and Goldwater. Clark was an old friend of the President's, and the administration would need Goldwater's help in the Department of Defense reorganization in the coming year.

Goldwater was not pleased with what he saw of Morris and Clark's work. In fact, he was so unhappy that on July 5, 1985, he summoned Morris and Clark to his office. He had also assembled there Relocation Commission lawyer Fred Craft, Goldwater aide Twinkle Thompson, and Harrison Loesch, Craft's new law partner, and an old player in the land dispute. In 1972, Loesch had broken Interior's neutrality on the partition legislation by coming out strongly in favor of the division of land. In 1974, he had helped draft the bill, and in 1976 had left the government to become a vice president for Peabody Coal Company. Fred Craft had worked as Loesch's deputy minority counsel on the Senate Interior Committee when the bill passed, and he had also helped draft the Settlement Act.

Goldwater asked Morris and Clark for a report on their progress. They informed Goldwater that their attempts to accomplish a settlement had been made difficult by the Hopis' determination not to discuss an exchange of land. Goldwater, according to Morris, then abruptly asked Clark why he didn't just tell the Navajos to get off. Morris remembers being unsure of just where Goldwater stood. He had originally felt that Goldwater "was very anxious to see a resolution [and] would support any agreement." Later on, Morris acknowledged that "Goldwater said conflicting things." Said Morris, "My perception was that Goldwater had misunderstood our mission. I think he understood it to be one that required us to make an effort to get the Navajo and the Hopi to conform to what the law was. We didn't see it that way. Our mission was to determine whether or not we could make some kind of agreement, if possible, to change that law."

Goldwater's position that day disturbed Morris. And Morris had no idea why Harrison Loesch was still in the picture. But another issue raised at the meeting horrified him. Fred Craft proposed folding up shop at the Relocation Commission, halting the federal program, and instead, paying each Navajo family $75,000 to depart from the HPL. Craft happily announced that his plan would save the government a lot of money and time.

Morris was speechless. "Craft said, 'Just take out a roll of bills and start peeling them off and the people will get interested,' " he recalled. Although Craft, on behalf of relocation commissioners Ralph Watkins and Hawley Atkinson, had been trying to get support for the so-called buy-out plan on the Hill all summer, he had failed to get anyone's attention except Goldwater and Senator James McClure, the Republican chairman of the Senate Subcommittee on Interior Appropriations.

The buyout proposal had never been formally acknowledged by the Commission. Craft's suggestion of evicting the Navajos with their pockets full of cash left a bitter taste in Morris's mouth however, and he urged Clark to make one last stab at negotiations, which they did, with no greater success.

Goldwater's top aide, Twinkle Thompson, was closely allied with Craft, a peculiar liaison for an aide to a senator who saw himself as a friend of the Indian. Said Morris, "I always saw her and Fred together. And I got to the point where I knew if something was happening with Fred, why it was probably happening with Twinkle."

The question begs to be asked: How did Senator Goldwater manage to have such a big effect on a law he seemed to know so little about? "Senatorial courtesy," answers James Abourezk, the former senator from South Dakota. "People generally do not go against home-state senators." That is, if there is a problem the Senate is called upon to address that only affects one state, the Senate will usually go along with the senators of that state, whatever they say.

And why was Goldwater so determined to support the Hopis? Abourezk attributes Goldwater's tenacity to one thing: "Goldwater was antagonistic to Peter MacDonald. He didn't like Peter MacDonald. And he had tried to get Peter MacDonald indicted a couple of times, but he beat the rap."

George Vlassis, the former general counsel of the Navajo Tribe under Peter MacDonald, remembers precisely when Goldwater turned against the Navajos: it was immediately following MacDonald's decision to support organized labor in exchange for help fighting the partition bill. Before then, says Vlassis, "Goldwater was very friendly with the Navajos."

The approach to organized labor came in 1973 after Vlassis realized that his lobbying efforts with a large delegation of Navajos and the traditional Hopis was a failure. He had come to the conclusion that "we can't swing this by ourselves. We're going to have to get some help." The Navajos began to forge a relationship with the AFL-CIO.

The time was ripe for the Navajo courtship with labor to succeed. Labor unions were interested in organizing on the huge Navajo reservation as well as making an inroad in Arizona, which was, like Goldwater, staunchly conservative. Labor was interested in the big plans for coal gasification plants on the New Mexico side of the reservation, and the AFL-CIO proposed to set up schools to train Navajos to work in the plants. The labor union also planned to help organize a voter registration drive on the reservation.

Several of the labor lobbyists, according to Vlassis, "took the problem to heart" and launched a spirited campaign against partition. And the voter registration efforts brought record numbers of Navajos to the polls; in the 1974 elections, the Navajos for the first time in their history established themselves as an effective voting bloc. Navajo votes were perceived as having clinched the victory of Democratic gubernatorial candidate Raoul Castro of New Mexico. Although Goldwater won reelection, ninety percent of the Navajo vote went against him.

But MacDonald's first misstep with Goldwater may have taken place even earlier—in 1972. MacDonald threatened to support George McGovern for president if the Republicans didn't work to stop the partition bill then making its way through Congress. McGovern, chairman of the Senate Subcommittee on Indian Affairs, in which the partition bill rested, pledged his opposition to relocation. Goldwater was furious at the insubordination of MacDonald, a Republican Indian leader, a "Goldwater conservative" who had worked on Goldwater's own 1964 run for the presidency. Wayne Sekaquaptewa, Abbott's late brother and then publisher of the Hopi newspaper, believed this was the event that turned Goldwater against the Navajos. Said Sekaquaptewa, "He was sitting on the fence before that."

Abourezk and the Navajos managed to achieve a softening of the partition bill Goldwater advocated and won quite a few concessions during the extended congressional battle. As the debate heated up, Goldwater and Arizona Senator Paul Fannin tried to regain control of the issue. Recalls Vlassis, "Goldwater and Fannin were standing up red-faced on the floor of the Senate shaking their fists, saying, 'This is a matter of senatorial courtesy, gentlemen, this is a problem that occurs in our state!' " After the passage of the bill, which included far more compensation than Goldwater had originally wanted, says Vlassis, "it was a matter of embarrassment to the Arizona senators. If there was a little bad blood before, there was a lot [then]."

Vlassis feels the Navajos' association with labor significantly improved their effectiveness. "We fought a hell of a battle and changed things around a very substantial amount and whatever was to come in the future, we had a lot more cards to deal with." Although the Navajo strategy to go head to head with Goldwater may have gotten them a better deal with PL 93-531, the battle left them permanently bloodied.

The Navajos lost the battle of images, and they alienated their two senators. Their choice to wage an all-out power battle matched the image of them the Hopis wanted to advance. After the campaign, they were perceived as "obnoxious, not law-abiding, and unreasonable." The Navajos won a piece of the battle but lost the war. Goldwater's dislike of Peter MacDonald would permanently hinder the Navajos' efforts to alter the relocation law, long into the term of MacDonald's successor, Peterson Zah. Morris Udall observed in 1986, "Barry's still cursing him."

(14)

The Relocation Commission

> A certain rich man was enjoying a
> banquet. As he sat at the groaning
> table he could see an old woman,
> half starved, weeping. His heart
> was touched with pity. He called a
> servant to him and said, "Go out
> and chase her away."
>
> FELIX S. COHEN

By fall 1985 the relocation program had been extraordinarily influenced by two men. The first, as we have seen, was Barry Goldwater, who, driven by his antagonism toward the former Navajo leader Peter Mac-Donald, shepherded the Settlement Act through Congress and jealously guarded its integrity ever afterward.

The other was Hawley Atkinson, the only commissioner of the three originally appointed in 1975 who was remaining at the agency in the fall of 1985. His influence on the Commission was profound. Like Goldwater, he distinguished himself with his ignorance of the land dispute and particularly the Settlement Act, a twelve-page document that outlined the Commission's duties and responsibilities. An Interior Department lawyer observed about the Commission, "These people do not know the law, they never took the time to read it over or listen to those who had. They perceived that they lived in a protected kingdom in which they could not be disturbed."

Atkinson also distinguished himself by his antagonistic relations with the Navajo Tribe and the tenacity with which he held on to his job in spite of repeated calls for his removal. He had devoted himself to carrying through Goldwater's vision; and Goldwater rewarded him for it, stepping in to save his hide in 1976, when the Secretary of the Interior investigated the Commission and Atkinson. Unable to comprehend the complexities of the program he was overseeing, and therefore unable to develop his own vision of it, Atkinson had allowed himself to be directed by what he thought his political mentor wanted. To carry out Goldwater's wishes was to Atkinson a noble endeavor. He likened Goldwater's imminent departure from government to "a star that's collapsing." However, Atkinson's view of his job as Goldwater's right hand led to constantly changing directives and a pattern of crisis management at the Commission that marked its entire history.

Atkinson not only admired Goldwater, he even resembled him, with a flat, slightly ski-chute nose, chiseled features, lean frame, and western swagger. He wore heavy framed black glasses and liked to shoot from the hip like Goldwater, except that he didn't have as much in his six-gun. He was a rough-hewn version of Goldwater without the style or talent. But history has not been kind to Hawley Atkinson. Morris Udall summed up that "Hawley has been a disaster from the beginning. This was just a little lark that he got for his own pleasure, going up to Flagstaff and making trips everywhere." Richard Ivey, who once worked with the Commission, is blunter: "Hawley is a mean, vicious old man. Mean, vicious, and ignorant."

In 1975, three men were appointed by the Secretary of the Interior to be Commissioners for the new Navajo and Hopi Indian Relocation Commission located in Flagstaff, Arizona. Atkinson's two colleagues were Father Paul Urbano, an Episcopal priest and rector of All Saints Episcopal Church in Phoenix, and Robert E. Lewis, former governor of the Zuni Pueblo, and the only Indian ever appointed as commissioner. At first, as government employees at the GS-18 level, they were remunerated $138 for every day or portion of a day they worked, including travel days. By 1986, the commissioners received $263.36 per day—generous pay for the area.

Atkinson was not prepared for the reaction he got from the Navajos once the program got underway. "When I got on the Commission," he recalls, "I was woefully ignorant of the emotional nature of the dispute between the two tribes." Atkinson had not given much thought to the concept of trust responsibility either, nor was he a student of native cultures or psychology or anthropology. "I never got emotionally involved," he says. "I never questioned whether it was right or wrong. That was not my job. My job was to carry out the law as best as I could." Unfortunately for everyone, he had not even read the legislative history of the bill. One of the biggest shocks he had, he says, was learning that the Navajos he was to relocate didn't speak or write English. He blamed the Navajo Tribe for not telling him this fact. Instead, "it was always confrontation at the chapter houses. . . . It was a great crime that those people slipped through the system and never went to school," says Atkinson, heaping invective on "those responsible." Yet the legislative and court records are replete with testimony from anthropologists and Navajos themselves saying they would never survive in the white man's world and that they had no skills except those associated with raising livestock.

The three commissioners' first contacts with the Navajo relocatees took place at chapter meetings in the summer of 1976, one year after their appointments to the Commission. On June 12, Atkinson and Father Urbano arrived at the Coal Mine Mesa chapter house in Urbano's red Mercedes sports car to speak with a group of sixty elderly Navajos. Lewis came by himself. The *Gallup Independent* reported that the meeting "provided an intense first chapter in the relationship between Navajo residents . . . and the three-man Commission that will administer the relocation of several thousand Navajos currently living on lands to be partitioned to the Hopis. The relationship is certain to be a long one. And, if Saturday's meeting is any indication, it will be a stormy one." Several issues were discussed over the course of the five-hour meeting among the Navajos themselves and between the Commissioners and representatives of the tribe. Translations were made from English to Navajo and back again after each statement, and the Navajos, as they would do over the next twelve years, listened carefully and patiently to the words and concepts they didn't understand.

At the Coal Mine meeting, the discussion turned to whether the Commission would help the Navajo tribe acquire the House Rock Valley–Paria Plateau land on the Arizona Strip. Atkinson told the gathered Navajos that the Commission had no role in the selection, and, as he spoke, he gestured at the crowd, "his right hand punching the air before him on every third or fourth word." Atkinson spoke as if he were fighting the Navajos, talking "at the people rather than to them, in the manner of a rigid school principal." The audience didn't know what to make of this, since the Settlement Act had directed the Commission to "identify the sites to which [the Navajo] households shall be relocated," and this was the land the tribe had chosen. Joe Dayzie, a councilman from Tonolea, criticized the commissioners for not supporting the application for land and said, "You people shouldn't pass the buck that way. I'm getting to think that the white man won't help us much. That's the way I feel now. I think an Indian would have a feeling for what's inside us. We're having a hard time, and we're sore inside."

Percy Deal asked a question that was on everyone's mind. "How have you people been appointed? Do you have any experience in this type of situation where people have to be relocated?" Only Father Urbano answered, saying, "I suppose my only qualifications are love for the people, some experience with human beings in my work, fairness, and objectivity."

Robert Lewis, the former Zuni governor, quickly revealed himself to be at odds with his two colleagues. He complained to the people at Coal

Mine that the first year of the Commission's life had been taken up with meetings between federal agencies. He told them that as an Indian, he knew that they must take part in planning for their futures. "Too often other people have been making plans for us without our input," he said. "Many times they do not know our ways, our culture and do not have an understanding of the way we think. And so they bring in a plan, ask for their money, and leave, and their plan doesn't work. That is why it is vitally important that your input be obtained. We go into this job with compassion for those who will have to move."

After the Coal Mine Mesa meeting, the commissioners were asked to meet at the Forest Lake and then the Hardrock chapters. Only Lewis showed up. Atkinson was in Phoenix, campaigning for a seat on the Maricopa County Board of Supervisors. At Forest Lake, Joe Biakeddy spoke to the absent commissioners and was unable to control his tears. "We don't believe you have the qualifications to understand the under-developed Navajo people," he said. "We are suspicious that you will treat us unfairly. We are suspicious of your thoughts and your ways. I say this with all apology." Biakeddy, who spoke in the English he had learned working for the railroad, also had thoughts about the difficulties the Navajos were having in getting land for the relocatees. "We feel and we understand that nobody wants us anywhere out of the executive-order reservation. There is no place for us. Even though we suffer here, we like it. We don't want to suffer anywhere else. . . . We don't want to leave here. Wherever you take us, it's wrong. That's the way I feel. We don't want to push anybody and we don't want anybody pushing us."

Two days later, at Hardrock, the HPL chapter that includes Big Mountain, several Navajos stood up and said they might just refuse to move off their land. Again, Robert Lewis was the only commissioner there. Taja Begay, who walks with crutches as the result of injuries to his back and legs he received fighting with the U.S. Army in 1944 in France, said the financial benefit was not enough to convince him to move from his home. "Many Navajo men were drafted by the army some thirty-three years ago," said Begay, "and some did not return. I did return and am standing here before you on a pair of crutches. I feel that we have done valuable things for the country and now they want us to move from this simple piece of land."

Tribal official Samuel Pete stated his disappointment that all three commissioners were not in attendance, and he made it clear why it was important. "By not attending these meetings they will fail to understand the Navajo culture and values as expressed here. Moving Navajo families who are predominantly uneducated is not at all comparable to moving non-Indians for highway rights of way. Our problems are unique in that the Navajo people have a strong attachment to the land."

Robert Lewis tried to reassure Pete and the group that he wanted to include the Navajos in planning an appropriate new home. "We want this plan to be your plan," he told them. "We want you to give us some idea of what you want us to do and how you would like to have it done."

Unfortunately for the Navajos, Lewis had little sway over his two colleagues. The Commission from its earliest days was torn with conflict over how to proceed. Commissioner Lewis felt that his ideas were not considered by the other two, and that the hiring of the Commission staff was proceeding badly. On April 30, six weeks before the chapter meetings, he had typed a memo to his fellow commissioners in which he implored them to cooperate "so we can try to catch up on all the time we have wasted so far." Lewis suggested that the Commission become fully staffed immediately to facilitate the writing of the Report and Plan for Relocation, which was due to Congress in two years. He also outlined a chain of command that gave the commissioners "an executive role of policy making and evaluating progress" and the executive director "an administrative role of developing procedures and supervising the staff."

Atkinson and Urbano disagreed with Lewis on every point of his memo, and let Lewis know this during a conference call on the evening of April 30. They wanted the "management officer," a redundant administrative position occupied by a real estate man named Bob Sharp and a personal friend of Atkinson's (whom Atkinson had hired before his résumé had even arrived at the Commission office) to report directly to the commissioners, bypassing the executive director. Atkinson and Urbano did not want the executive director to hire or supervise staff; they wanted to do that themselves. Atkinson, according to a summary of the conversation written by Lewis, also wanted to maintain control of the Commission's finances.

Atkinson's determination to run the staff instead of delegating authority to an executive director crippled the Commission for its lifetime. His immediate purpose in hiring Bob Sharp was to weaken the position of the executive director, John Gray, a former BIA official who was close to Robert Lewis. Although Gray wrote intelligent and sensitive memos containing suggestions that, if followed, could have made the Commission's efforts more successful, they were vetoed by Atkinson and Urbano.

The commissioners were supposed to be part-time policymakers who oversaw and evaluated the progress of the relocation. The law specified that the day-to-day operation of the Commission would be run by an executive director. But Atkinson would not stand for this, and with Urbano's vote in his pocket, he interfered in the daily staff activities and disrupted the management functions that should have been carried out by the executive director. In the view of an Interior Department official who has long observed the Commission, the commissioners succeeded in "emasculating" every executive director they hired to run the agency.

Because there was not a distinct line of authority or an effective manager, the character of the Commission evolved as an idiosyncratic reflection of the personality of Hawley Atkinson. Paul Urbano followed Atkinson's directions. The third member ran the risk of becoming irrelevant if the other two agreed.

When Lewis returned to the Commission after his trip to the chapter meetings, he found that there had been very negative press reports concerning Atkinson's and Urbano's absences. The Navajo Tribal Council had passed a resolution requesting that the Commission seek the aid of Thayer Scudder as an expert on relocations and David Aberle, an anthropologist who has written about and lived with the Navajo. The commissioners (except Lewis) continued to be unresponsive to the Navajos and their concerns, and by the end of June, the tension was so high that Navajo councilman Marlin Scott asked Urbano and Atkinson to resign.

The Commission's executive director, John Gray, tried to suggest ways to control the damage created by the commissioners' absences at the chapter meetings. The tone of his memo suggests the atmosphere at the Commission: "It is written as a suggestion only. It is not written to disagree with prior decisions or to question your judgment. Whatever decision you make will be supported by the staff and carried out enthusiastically. Please feel free to accept or reject all or parts of this without explanation." The emasculation of John Gray had clearly begun. However, he continued to make intelligent suggestions—among them, that the commissioners should attend at least two chapter meetings in all affected areas, that a professional planner should be hired to help with the Report and Plan, that Scudder and Aberle should be given consultation contracts, that the staff should be enlarged, and that field offices be opened with Navajos chosen as liaisons to keep the Commission informed of developments on the JUA and vice versa.

But Atkinson refused to budge. On August 2, Robert Lewis walked out of the Commission's public meeting and informed his colleagues he planned to resign. On November 15, he sent a letter, handwritten in a graceful script, to Atkinson, explaining that "My leaving of that meeting represented the sum total of frustration, desperation, and actual disgust over the actions taken by you and Commissioner Urbano." The letter went on to say, "As you well know, I feel that the last year and a half of activities of the Commission have been a total waste. Far worse is the fact that the Commission's policies, which have been dominated by you and Commissioner Urbano, have proven totally ineffective in bringing about an orderly approach to our mission."

On August 3, the day after Lewis walked out of the meeting, Atkinson and Urbano fired John Gray. Two days after that, Atkinson wrote letters to the Hopi and Navajo tribal chairmen, the Secretary of the Interior, and Deputy Undersecretary Ickes, informing them of Lewis's departure, although Lewis had not announced his resignation to the Interior Secretary and his status remained unclear.

Atkinson's response to Lewis's letter was typically off the mark. He said, "I question his motivation in this. The individual Navajo and Hopi relocatee is not served by this type of letter, particularly because it is based on either ignorance or Zuni Governor Lewis wanting to satisfy his voracious appetite for publicity at the expense of the facts." But the editorial pages of Arizona's newspapers filled quickly with words of support for Lewis. The *Gallup Independent*, in an editorial titled "Lewis Belongs on Commission," described him as a "wise leader," "soft-spoken and contemplative." The editorial stated that the *Independent* "never found him to be overeager for publicity" and that Lewis was known to be "a courteous gentleman." A Letter to the Editor in the *Arizona Republic* written by a chaplain at the Phoenix Indian School stated it was with "dismay and disgust" that he read of Atkinson's determination to remain on the Commission. "My question is this," wrote Father James F. O'Brien (who praised Lewis as "highly acceptable to the people involved"), "what are two white people, a minor politician, and a nonresident clergyman doing on a Commission that purports to decide the fate of 3,500 Indians? The history of U.S. government and Indian relations is full of politicians and clergymen who thought they had a firm grasp of the 'problem' and knew just what the Indians needed. They didn't."

The Interior Department, chagrined by events, dispatched an investigator to the Commission. Meantime, Atkinson and Urbano, showing a disturbing bit of paranoia, made a Freedom of Information Act request for any documents in the Interior Department that mentioned the two of them. They requested letters, interoffice memoranda, legal opinions "either in draft or final form," notes of telephone conversations, and minutes of meetings. The Interior Department politely responded in the negative, saying that no such documents could be found.

A look at Atkinson's employment history suggests that had anyone known anything about him, they might have guessed he'd wreak havoc at the Commission. Hawley Atkinson moved to Phoenix in 1965 from Boise, Idaho, where he had run his family's building supply business, and had been active in right-wing politics. He believed that Senator Joe McCarthy was "more right than he was wrong." In an interview, he confessed that in the 1950s, he was so "consumed" by his "intense dislike" of Communists in the United States that he developed ulcers.

In Phoenix, he found himself without a job when a business merger he'd counted on fell through. "It was a long, hard summer," Atkinson recalled twenty years later in his office at the Relocation Commission, a converted icehouse, a photograph of General Douglas MacArthur on the wall across from his desk. Atkinson, who didn't have a college degree, sought the help of an employment agency, and was told that the Navajo

Tribe needed a buyer in its Department of Construction. He took the job, and eventually reorganized the tribal warehouses and put them on computer inventory, "not a high-level, high-visibility position," said Atkinson. During the two years he worked for the tribe, he lived in Window Rock alone. His wife and four children remained in Phoenix, because, Atkinson said, the two-bedroom house he was given in the Navajo capital was too small. He didn't stay on with the tribe, and in August 1967, he returned to Phoenix, finding himself again unemployed. "After I left the Navajo Tribe, I did anything, even mowed lawns, and I was an old man then." He was fifty-one years old, and it was two years before he got another steady job. In 1969 he applied for an opening at the Indian Development District of Arizona (IDDA), a group funded by the federal government through the Economic Development Administration under the Public Works Act of 1965 to help distribute federal public works funds to the then seventeen tribes in Arizona. Atkinson got a job as an economic planner, and was based in Prescott. He worked with the Walapai, Havasupai, and Yavapai–Prescott and Camp Verde Yavapai–Apache tribes, helping them find public works monies. Grace McCullough, who worked in IDDA's Manpower Division when Atkinson was there, was puzzled over how Atkinson got the job. "Everyone thought that because he had worked with the Navajos he was an Indian expert, which was not true."

Atkinson developed a reputation for being combative and short-tempered. In his own words, "I'm antagonistic and bombastic, and I don't have a brilliant mind." At IDDA, he showed an intolerance for strong personalities. He had trouble with Grace McCullough, an erudite Navajo woman, because, she surmises, she was an outspoken advocate of the Indians' desire to govern themselves. She later served as IDDA's executive director.

After working at IDDA for one year, Atkinson got a job on Arizona Governor Jack Williams's staff as a special assistant for economic development for Indian tribes. Again, the fact that Atkinson had previously worked with Indian tribes was considered evidence that he was knowledgeable about Indian affairs, says Paul Klores, a former vice-president of Phoenix-based Valley National Bank. "Atkinson was perceived by Williams as an Indian expert because he had worked at IDDA," Klores recalls. Yet when he met Atkinson on the Papago reservation, he sensed right away something was wrong. "I assumed that since he was the governor's man, he must have known a lot of people, but I was surprised to see that I had more contacts there than he did," he said.

Although he may have benefited from being misperceived as an Indian expert, Atkinson did not promote the notion, and even after eleven years on the Relocation Commission, has never claimed to be particularly knowledgeable about Indian Affairs. "I was a fluke, politically, in Arizona," he said. Hawley Atkinson found the opportunity to advance from a warehouse organizer to a member of the governor's staff to a federal employee with a congressional appointment. He is a twentieth-century example of nineteenth-century political patronage in Indian country. "I was very grateful to get a job with the Navajo Tribe," he said two decades later about his first job in Arizona, because it led directly and indirectly to all of his other employment and his political career.

Atkinson, Klores observed, was of the mind that Indians should adapt to the wishes of the U.S. government and Anglo ways. Atkinson's attitude, shared by Governor Jack Williams, was, as Klores recalls it, "We live in a world of opportunity and the Indians should be encouraged to pull themselves up by their bootstraps. Atkinson felt concern for Indians and had credibility with some, but there was no doubt in his mind that they had to adapt to the white man's ways." This was not an unusual point of view. Atkinson was only one in a long line of Anglos, going back to General James H. Carleton, who wanted to "civilize" the Indians by teaching them the white man's ways. Grace McCullough suggests that this attitude led to her difficulties with Atkinson at IDDA. He went far enough, McCullough later learned, though he was not her senior at the agency, to try to have her removed from her Manpower job. He was unsuccessful.

Atkinson's job with Jack Williams ended in 1974 when Democrat Raoul Castro beat Williams for the governorship. He tried unsuccessfully to work for Senator Paul Fannin, and then did some consulting for IDDA while, McCullough thinks, he lobbied for the job of commissioner of the newly created Navajo and Hopi Indian Relocation Commission. On July 1, 1975, Atkinson was appointed by Secretary of the Interior Hathaway at the request of Senator Fannin to be one of three federal relocation officials.

Two years after his appointment to the Relocation Commission, Atkinson again had job trouble. Early in December of 1976, the investigator dispatched by the Interior Department to look into the Commission's affairs reported difficulties at the agency. Deputy Undersecretary of the Interior Dennis Ickes traveled to Phoenix to meet with the three commissioners. At that meeting, all three agreed to try to work out their differences. Navajo official Samuel Pete, who attended the meeting, doubted there would be any improvement. "I don't see how this reunification can last," he said. "The basis for Governor Lewis leaving the Commission in the first place was that the other commissioners did not share his philosophy that the Commission must be the advocate for the Navajo people who will be relocated. They made it plain Wednesday that they still do not share this philosophy."

The Navajos remained concerned about how Atkinson, who had just been elected to the Maricopa County Board of Supervisors, could properly perform his duties for both jobs. Residents of the Joint Use Area sent a petition to the Secretary of the Interior urging him to remove Atkinson and Urbano. However, Atkinson was getting some behind-the-scenes support from Barry Goldwater, who wrote to Interior Secretary Thomas Kleppe stating, "I urge you to the point of being insistent that these two men not be terminated because, frankly, you are not going to be able to get the kind of thinking provided by these two gentlemen anywhere else." What kind of thinking he meant is unclear. Maybe tough-minded, as Atkinson says of himself: "We had a hard job to do and I intended to see that we got it done. The Navajos felt that if I hadn't been there, that they could have controlled the Commission." After a second letter from Goldwater, blaming the Commission's troubles on former Governor Lewis, and a promise from the three commissioners that they would try to work together, Kleppe decided to take no action. He wrote to Atkinson: "Investigative findings do suggest a history of delays, personality clashes, petty bickering, and poor judgment in personnel matters and in delegation of responsibility, which in its accumulative effect raised questions as to the potential effectiveness of the Commission in carrying out its mission." He went on to caution the commissioners that "evidence of continued internal frictions within the Commission, allegations of ineffectiveness . . . or claims of conflict of interest [would] lead to re-evaluations of the Commission."

The three commissioners ceased their public displays of friction. However, the problems that drove them apart still simmered. Atkinson repeatedly criticized the Navajo Tribe for the Commission's lack of progress. The Navajo Tribe continued to want to know where the relocatees were going to live, and to press the Commission to support the tribe's choice of House Rock as replacement land. William Simkin, the federal mediator who led the Navajo and Hopi teams to draw the partition line, himself urged the Department of the Interior in 1975 to " 'bite the bullet' and make the House Rock Valley–Paria Plateau lands available for purchase by the Navajo Tribe." The mediator stressed that " 'time is of the essence' in the acquisition of new lands on which to relocate Navajos." It had been two years since the mediator had made his plea, however, and no land was yet available.

The day after his election to the Maricopa County Board of Supervisors, Atkinson suddenly decided that the Commission should support the Navajos' selection of land. As soon as he no longer stood to be hurt politically by supporting the controversial Arizona Strip acquisition, he changed his tune. When asked what had led to his change of mind, Atkinson replied, "It just dawned on me."

It was too late, however. The Save the Strip Committee had made such a fuss about the loss of their hunting grounds that it held up the selection of new land until Congress passed the 1980 Amendments to the Settlement Act which included a proviso forbidding the purchase. The problem of where the Navajos were to relocate was still not settled.

Atkinson repeatedly criticized the Navajo Tribe for not finding room, even though anthropologist Thayer Scudder, whose help Atkinson eventually solicited, made it clear that there was no room on the existing reservation if the relocatees planned to support themselves with livestock.

The Commission continued to ignore this problem and accomplished little else in its first two years. Although Hawley Atkinson wrote a five-page memo and seven letters extolling the virtues of a waterless toilet he had examined, the Commission had still not decided who was going to write its Report and Plan for Relocation, where the relocatees would be settled, who was eligible for benefits, and how many people were actually living on the HPL.

Atkinson was largely preoccupied with getting legal opinions from the White House about whether the Secretary of the Interior had the power to fire commissioners and criticizing the Interior Department for the Commission's own failings. He repeatedly rebuked Interior for a purported lack of cooperation and attributed the problems to "old bureaucrats" who "have been entirely resentful of the independency of the Commission."

The Interior Department, for its part, indicated that problems arose between the two agencies largely because none of the Commission staff were knowledgeable about government practices. "I have concluded," wrote Deputy Undersecretary Dennis Ickes to the BIA commissioner, "that most of the problems caused are due to an unfamiliarity by the Commission and its employees with Federal regulations and other requirements." He urged Atkinson to help the Commission establish its needs regarding procurement, disbursements, personnel, and expenditures so the local BIA administrative office can "provide them with the appropriate forms, assist them in filling out the forms properly and to give them good advice as to what the Commission can and cannot do under current law and regulations." Ickes was quite worried in 1976 about the Commission's ability to carry out its mandate, largely because it didn't have staff with the requisite skills. Atkinson's dislike of "bureaucrats" painted him into a corner when it came time for his agency to mesh with other federal departments. The Commission eventually encountered severe financial problems. A budget analyst brought in from Interior informed the commissioners that a memo written by Atkinson demonstrated "a very basic misunderstanding of the Federal budget process and related financial management activities." The Commission was warned that if it didn't watch out, it would be guilty of violating the Antideficiency Act, which prohibits government agencies from encumbering money they do not yet have. The Commission eventually did violate the Act, and negotiations with Interior were necessary to provide the Commission with a clean bill of health. Atkinson had an answer for this as well. He bitterly criticized Congress for not giving the Commission enough money.

Atkinson's trouble with federal regulations should have come as no surprise; his politics were virulently antigovernment. In a survey he completed for the *Arizona Republic* before his campaign for County Supervisor, he stated his position:

> I believe we are on the threshold of a radical change which threatens the very fabric of our Republic. Government at all levels burdens our industry, saps our initiative, and taxes us into literal submission; and very simply I am running to seek a change. "Fiscal responsibility," "limits on government," "priorities," "local control," can no longer be campaign slogans or politicians' promises; they must be the touchstones of any government which aspires to rule a free People. I am seeking election to restore these fundamentals to our local government, in hopes that the fire which will start by our example will shed it's [sic] light all the way to Washington with one clear, resounding message—here the people are once again sovereign.

In 1977, the Commission finally moved its first family—to a house in Gallup, New Mexico. Commission records show that seventy-five percent of the first moves were of relatively well-educated younger people who had already moved off the reservation by the time they were relocated. (This means that when the Commission bought them a house, they were already living in Flagstaff and going to school, or renting a trailer or apartment or living with relatives in another border town because of a job. The younger generation is often in flux, moving between the reservation and the border towns for work and schooling. Although they speak English, most still know little about taxes, utility bills, and so forth because they grew up on the reservation. And the reservation remains home; most Navajos, no matter what their jobs or ages, return home for extended periods of time before moving on to the next stage of their lives.)

In 1979, a staff survey showed that twenty-five percent of Navajos who had relocated were already in poor shape; they had either already lost their houses after putting them up as collateral for loans they couldn't pay or, as predicted, were experiencing family instability, health problems, depression, and suicide attempts. By 1983, half of the relocatees who had moved into border towns had either lost their homes by defaulting on loans, falling prey to unscrupulous loan sharks and real estate agents, or had encumbered themselves with significant debts. Although the Commission had been repeatedly warned by the Navajo Tribe and the relocatees themselves that they were not able to live in a world of steady utility bills and taxes, the Commission had developed no other options.

According to Leon Berger, who was the Commission's planning director in 1976, and who eventually wrote the Report and Plan and then became executive director, getting the first families moved had been a "political deal." He recalls that the commissioners were in Washington and called him in Flagstaff. They told him "we've made a commitment that we'll have a family moved in one week." Berger says that "there was little thought involved in getting that family moved." Even after the reports that the first moves had not gone well, the attitude at the Commission, according to Berger, was "we will ignore the problem and hope it goes away or [we'll] deal with it when we absolutely have to."

The problem they hoped would go away was that their clients were suffering from the difficulties that had been foreseen by anthropologist Thayer Scudder before the Act was passed, which he clearly stated in congressional testimony, and which he repeated numerous times to the commissioners. The Commission even acknowledged his findings by publishing excerpts from his work in the Report and Plan. Nevertheless, it did nothing to provide the Navajos with the guidance or counseling that they needed. Says Christine Chisholm-Tures, chief of social services at the time, "In the very beginning, the first moves, there was no counseling program, nothing. There wasn't even an illusion of giving people preparation. They simply believed that they could buy a person a house and put them in it."

One of the Commission's first errors was in not moving extended families together. "One of my deepest regrets about that whole period of time was that people were moved in nuclear family units," explained Chisholm-Tures. "You're not just taking a family and putting them in a setting where they can't comport themselves, but you have taken away the support system that *might* have enabled them to make it—the grandmother who might have been there for child care, somebody who could have gotten a job as a maid or a dishwasher or whatever. I think it's the splintering of the families that was the real downfall of the relocation. And there was no excuse for it, because before the Commission began moving people, they had the Thayer Scudder report, which said, loud and clear, to move people together, keep extended families intact."

As more and more relocatees moved to Flagstaff, the local real estate men smelled easy prey. "Consumer loan problems are the largest factor in relocatees' loss of homes," says Lee Phillips, who in addition to his work for the Big Mountain people, represents relocatees who get into financial difficulties in town, or whose houses, many of which are of substandard quality, need major repairs (which of course the Indians can't afford to make). Most Navajos, and most relocatees, don't have steady jobs. But living in town requires the regular payment of water and electricity bills and taxes, not to mention home maintenance. When the Navajos get behind on their bills, they try to take out loans. Legitimate banks and finance companies won't help them, because their incomes aren't steady, so the relocatees find their way to unscrupulous loan sharks who give them loans with their houses as collateral. Most Navajos do not know this means they could lose their houses if they get behind on their payments, which is almost inevitable. Says Phillips, "These people are the poorest and the least educated consumers and are in the unique position of having an asset [a relocation house] worth fifty or sixty thousand dollars. This makes them easy prey for any conceivable swindle or rip-off."

The Relocation Commission not only knew about the problems, the agency actually repurchased sixteen relocation houses from those who had lost or sold them, and sold them to other relocatees. Yet the Commission still refused to help people who had lost their houses in this way, maintaining that their responsibility ended after they had supplied the relocation house—a strong echo of Atkinson's pick-yourself-up-by-your-bootstraps philosophy. The Commission did not institute a post-move counseling program until 1986, after receiving pressure from a House investigation, news reports, and the Big Mountain Legal Defense/Offense Committee.

Getting behind on bills seemed almost inevitable for relocatee families. Says Charlotte Beyal, a counselor at the Flagstaff Indian Center, called Native Americans for Community Action (NACA), "There are so many more expenses. In public schools, the children want to dress like the other kids. Also, entertainment is available and parents have to come up with money for movies and sports equipment. On the reservation, in BIA schools, the BIA paid for everything." Beyal says that relocatee families have to change their entire way of living and thinking about the world in order to survive. They must budget money—a foreign concept —to pay for the costs that never existed on the reservation, such as taxes, home insurance, auto registration, water, school books, and meal tickets. Many relocatees are not employable, and the $40 bimonthly welfare check that got them somewhere on the reservation is almost useless in town.

Counseling was not the Commission's only oversight. Internal memos between Urbano and Atkinson show that they were considering hiring an outside consultant to write the Report and Plan. According to the Settlement Act, and apparently contrary to what Atkinson believed, the Report and Plan was meant to be the heart and soul of the Commission's work. It was to be the blueprint for the relocation and, according to the law, was to be presented to and accepted by Congress.

The Report and Plan was to be developed "to the maximum extent feasible in consultation with the persons involved in such relocation" [the Navajo and Hopi relocatees], and was to consider and minimize the "adverse social, economic, cultural and other impacts of relocation."

Thayer Scudder felt very strongly that the Commission should develop the Report and Plan itself, not subcontract it out. He said to a local newspaper reporter at the time, "If they just bring in a third party which stays in its offices and develops a plan which it superimposes on the relocatees, the plan will probably fail. I feel that for this to succeed there has to be a fantastic amount of input from the Navajo people in the area and from the Tribal Council. I told the commissioners they must seek much more actively the Navajo perception of their needs and desires. If you bring in an outside firm, you decrease the chances of that happening."

So vital a document was the Report and Plan to the future of the Commission, that even Father Urbano, who seldom opposed Atkinson, felt compelled to warn him that in contracting out this piece of work, the Commission would run the risk of "abdicating its responsibilities."

Atkinson relented on this point, but proceeded to fire a second executive director and give greater responsibilities to his friend, the real estate man Bob Sharp, a man so ignorant of the law and the land dispute that his appearance on a radio show provoked a BIA employee, Bill Benjamin, to send him a short, written history lesson.

Meanwhile, Atkinson dismissed overtures from those who were qualified and had offered to help out. He wrote a brusque letter to anthropologist David Aberle, telling him the Commission had no use for his services. Atkinson, however, did meet with Thayer Scudder, and Scudder followed up their meeting with a letter that recommended material to read and people to contact about rural relocations. According to former staffers, Atkinson's decision to consult with Scudder was made to appease the Navajo Tribe, but the Commission took no heed of his recommendations. "They used him and threw him away," said a former high-level employee who requested anonymity. And the relocatees were left to move off the reservation, not because of a policy decision to that effect, but rather, by default. "Moves were made off-reservation," said the senior staffer, "because no other arrangements were made."

Other staffers and planners were kept from performing their jobs as well as they might have by the fear of Atkinson's wrath. He responded to challenges defensively, and earned a reputation as disruptive, argumentative, and addicted to underhanded power politics to destroy anyone who crossed him. David Shaw-Serdar, research officer at the Commission in 1985 and a long-time employee, confirmed that no one survived in that agency if he or she angered Atkinson. Shaw-Serdar said, "Working here in the administrative levels is like being a courtier." A great deal of everybody's time is spent "courting for continued employment." He said that the words "You let me do this or I'll quit" were scarcely ever heard, for one reason: "the high pay." Upper-level employees at the Commission (most of them greatly underqualified) were earning almost double what they would have earned at other jobs. The catchwords, said Shaw-Serdar, were " 'alliances' and 'working relationships' in an extremely personal setting."

Atkinson disrupted the staff's attempts to help the relocatees; after a plan had been worked on for months, a single objection from Atkinson, who never hesitated to object, could scuttle it. Shaw-Serdar said, "If whatever was going on didn't match [Atkinson's] opinion or intuitive feel, he'd ask for an explanation of what was being presented." This often led to the end of whatever was "being presented." Leon Berger was a little blunter. He recalled the Commission as a "wacko, crazy environment" where "Atkinson would stand up one week and say something and the next week he'd contradict himself just as forcefully." Atkinson also kept "shit lists," according to Christine Chisholm-Tures, the former director of social services. He kept a "real bad list and a sort of bad list." She was told she was on one of those lists because she was seen accepting a ride from Sandra Massetto. Said Chisholm-Tures, "I had taken a ride with somebody who was seen by one of the commissioners as an enemy—namely, one of the other commissioners."

The Relocation Commission was provided with all the information it needed to perform its tasks properly. But because the Commission's leader, the executive director, was hamstrung by the commissioners— rather than guided and supported by them—the Commission was never able to become the powerful and effective planning agency it should have become. And the reason it didn't was largely the result of the influence of Hawley Atkinson, working under the self-imposed mission of satisfying Barry Goldwater—to punish the Navajos.

Congress must bear primary responsibility. It never faced the evidence that relocations of rural populations are as a rule disastrously disruptive to the populations in question. Aside from that, Congress never adequately addressed the problem of where the Navajos would go. Manuel Lujan, representative from New Mexico, made a public statement about this issue during House hearings regarding the passage of the 1974 Act. He asked,

> Mr. Chairman, we know that H.R. 10337 will result in the moving of families, but what we do not know—because there are no provisions in the bill that would let us know—what we do not know are the answers to these questions. First: How would these eight thousand people be moved? By bus, by train, by cattle car? How do you propose to move these people who have said they will die before they move? Second: Where do you propose to move them? Does the bill say, we will pick them up from here and set them down there? No, it does

not. I have read the bill line by line, and I have not seen one single reference to a destination for these people. . . . Third: What right do we have to treat these people different from other Americans? Would any single member of this body sit here quietly while we passed a bill that would move eight thousand of his constituents out of their homes to an undisclosed destination? What gives us the right to say to these people that we are going to settle their problem in a way that we would never dream of settling it if it were between two factions of non-Indians instead of between two Indian tribes?

By the summer of 1978, lawmakers involved in the relocation issue had decided among themselves that Atkinson "had to go." Onto a bill authorizing an increase in the Commission's budget, Senator Dennis DeConcini attached an amendment aimed specifically at removing Atkinson. It prohibited a commissioner from holding public office.

Atkinson claimed the legislation was a "sour grapes" reaction. "They've got a history of two hundred years of failure," he told a reporter. "Now three private citizens are going to accomplish what they couldn't do. If there's one thing the bureaucrats in Washington can't stand, it's a small, independent Commission achieving success."

The House and Senate agreed on the authorization bill, which also put a ceiling of $28,000 on the yearly salaries of commissioners, and allowed either house of Congress to veto the Report and Plan for Relocation within ninety days of its submission.

Atkinson was not just under fire for his work at the Commission. As a Maricopa County supervisor, he had earned a reputation as disruptive and hotheaded. He was also criticized in the Arizona media for using his office to benefit his friends and for "double dipping"—taking home two governmental salaries. In 1977, Atkinson earned $31,190 as salary for Commission work, pocketed $9,917 for expenses, and also earned $19,600 as county supervisor. For someone who was so antigovernment, he was making a pretty good living from Uncle Sam. An *Arizona Republic* editorial, entitled "Mr. A Blows Smoke," read: "Atkinson is grumbling that because he is a Republican, Democrats want to deprive him of his seat on the Navajo-Hopi Relocation Commission. That's Atkinson's tale. We prefer to sit on ours. The fact is, Atkinson is about to lose a cushy side income for which he does precious little." The editorial concluded, "Of course, if Atkinson wants the Indian Commission job so badly, he can always resign as a county supervisor. Your move, Atkinson." A week later, Caleb Johnson, a Hopi who headed the Navajo-Hopi Unity Committee, a group opposed to relocation, wrote a Letter to the Editor answering the editorial, saying simply, "We Indians would rather have him remain as a county supervisor so that he will stay out of the Navajo-Hopi relocation business."

But that was not to be. Atkinson was saved when Jimmy Carter vetoed the bill on constitutional grounds relating to the separation of powers. Carter disapproved of the one-house veto of an executive branch agency's plan, and also to the provision preventing public officials from serving on the Commission because it "has constitutional implications since it would allow for Congressional removal of officers in the Executive Branch." Carter concluded that "the Commission needs to operate more effectively" and promised to work toward that end through legislation in the next session.

Atkinson once again demonstrated his uncanny knack for surviving attack. At the turn of the new year—1979—he dictated a querulous letter to Senator Goldwater. In spite of mounting evidence to the contrary, Atkinson claimed the Commission had done an "outstanding job to date" and complained about his old nemesis, the Interior Department. Atkinson's letter took on a desperate tone: "What exactly did you personally want from me as a member of this Commission? I would greatly appreciate your writing me and telling me where you think that this Commission has failed. . . ." He admitted having made some staffing errors, but claimed they were "minor when compared with the overall achievements."

Although Congress directed the Commission to identify relocation sites, and although Atkinson was criticized for not supporting the Navajos' land selections, he once again excoriated the Navajos for not accepting relocatees onto the existing reservation. "Now isn't that heartbreaking and mystifying," he sneered, "that the Navajo leadership has so little compassion for their own people they will make no room for them!"

Atkinson refused to acknowledge the truth: that the relocation shouldn't go on without replacement lands. The Commission would not accept the facts of the Navajos' lives. As former Executive Director Leon Berger said in an interview, "The Relocation Commission could never understand that as Navajos accepted relocatees onto other parts of the reservation, they were destroying the existing agribusiness. They thought the Navajos' reluctance was totally political."

At the end of January 1979, Robert Lewis resigned his position to serve his sixth term as governor of the Zuni Pueblo. Two weeks later, Paul Urbano died. It was a Democratic administration, so the ranking Democrats suggested replacements. Senator DeConcini recommended Sandra Massetto, a thirty-three-year-old Phoenix attorney. Representative Udall recommended Roger K. Lewis, who had been Udall's administrative assistant for seventeen years. Massetto made it clear on accepting the position that she disapproved of relocation as a policy. However, she emphasized that the only proper way to plan relocation was with the full involvement of the relocatees and their tribal representatives—a refrain oft heard and little heeded.

The new commissioners faced some formidable problems. In addition to the lack of replacement land, an active resistance to the relocation effort had grown among the Navajos of Big Mountain, and the Report and Plan had not yet been written.

Massetto and Lewis realized that the 1974 Act needed to be amended. Through negotiations between the Commission, the Navajo and Hopi lawyers, and the Arizona delegation, a bill was written and passed in July 1980 that addressed some of these problems. The new law, PL 96-305, known as the 1980 Amendments, prohibited the Navajos from acquiring the House Rock land, but compensated the tribe by giving it the 250,000 acres the 1974 Act had authorized it to purchase, and allowing it to purchase 150,000 additional acres of land. The Amendments also provided for life estates to those people older than forty-nine or over fifty percent disabled. A life estate would allow elderly Navajos to live in their homes until they died, but would not allow their children to live with them. The Act provided for a total of 120 life estates of not more than ninety acres.

The Amendments also included provisions that made Atkinson happy. The new law allowed the Commission to hire its own attorney and take care of its own housekeeping duties. It included a passage that made the tribal lawyers happy: the government agreed to pay the tribes' legal fees, up to certain limits, arising as a result of the 1882 case and the 1934 area case. And there was something that made Lewis and Massetto happy: the amendments gave authority to the Commission to initiate land exchange negotiations between the two tribes. These negotiations, aimed at reducing the number of Navajos required to relocate, became the focus of Massetto's and Lewis's energies over the next two years. The idea of life estates never materialized. The Navajos considered the concept as "death estates" because they couldn't imagine living out their lives without the prospect of passing their land and ways on to their children.

But while the negotiations to amend the law were underway, a crisis had developed at the Commission. Sandra Massetto recalls,

> It was in 1979. I had been on the Commission only a short time. I was sitting at home on a Saturday night at about 11:30 and I received a telephone call from a man who said his name was Dave Williams, and he identified himself as a Commission employee. He said he was in San Diego and had something important to tell me. He was coming to Phoenix the next morning and wanted to meet me at the Phoenix airport on his way back to Flagstaff.
>
> I was a little stunned by the telephone call and I asked him what the problem was and could he discuss it with me. He said it was of such a sensitive nature that he didn't want to discuss it over the telephone. He also indicated that he wanted to meet me in a kind of secure place where we could talk without people hearing us. I agreed

to meet with him and suggested we meet at the Phoenix executive airport. By this time, I thought it was maybe a funny call. So I said, 'I don't know you, how would I recognize you, would you be wearing a trenchcoat?' He said no, that he'd be wearing civilian clothes and he knew what I looked like so he would approach me. And then he hung up the phone.

We met the next morning at about 10:30 and spoke for about an hour at the airport. During the conversation, he made some general allegations about contractor kickbacks to relocation staffers. At that point I wasn't real knowledgeable about who did what at the Commission. [Real Estate Director] Bob Sharp's name came up, and [Executive Director] Leon [Berger]'s name came up. We had a general discussion about how the real estate section functioned. I was flabbergasted by all of it. I remember getting in the car to take him back to the main airport. While we were in the car, he told me he didn't want me to tell the other commissioners about this. I asked him specifically was Hawley involved. He said he wasn't telling me that, but he didn't want me to discuss it with the other commissioners or with Leon. I told him that put me in a terrible position. He said the Commission was very small and that if any investigation was initiated, and people were told about it, it might have an impact on the investigation. He didn't use the word cover-up. I thought it would cause a real credibility problem for me with the other commissioners. I told him that I would get back in touch with him. I could not believe what he had told me. And I was particularly concerned because Hawley and I—although we weren't buddy buddy—we had at least developed something of a working relationship and Hawley was not exhibiting as much paranoia about my appointment and my relationship with DeConcini as I had expected.

Massetto had worked with Senator Dennis DeConcini's brother Dino on Governor Raul Castro's staff, and had been involved in the senator's first Senate campaign. She had also been chosen for the job by DeConcini. Atkinson didn't like DeConcini, who had lobbied to have Atkinson removed from the Commission. Massetto decided to call the U.S. Attorney in Phoenix. "I felt uncomfortable about not informing the other commissioners," Massetto says, "but I didn't want somebody leveling obstruction of justice criticism against me either. I decided to call the U.S. Attorney on Monday morning. Then I made the decision to go ahead and call [the other new commissioner] Roger Lewis. I told him what had happened and that Williams had told me not to tell anybody and that I felt real uncomfortable about it. I don't remember exactly what Roger's comment was, but he wasn't very helpful about it."

Massetto heard nothing else about the affair for a while. She was on her way to Washington to begin discussions about the Amendments bill when she got a telephone call "that Leon had gone berserk about this, that he was just livid at me. Apparently the FBI agents came and started talking to people."

In February 1980, an FBI investigation was opened to investigate charges that Commission employees were receiving bribes for steering relocatees to a contractor called Village Homes. In addition to monetary bribes, it was alleged that favors received by Commission employees included prostitutes, motel rooms, and gasoline for personal vehicles. There also was evidence that a list of relocatees had been made available to Village Homes. That list was protected under the Freedom of Information/Privacy Act.

At the beginning of 1980, eighty percent of the Commission's housing contracts had gone to the one firm, Village Homes. Almost immediately after the first houses were constructed in 1977, the Commission knew that they were of unacceptably poor quality. Says Leon Berger, "We knew after the first few moves there were problems with the houses, one of the reasons why some of Lee Phillips's cases have merit. They [the commissioners] wanted to keep moving people. The Commission *knew* about all the problems."

The investigation revealed a consistent pattern of Indian families being persuaded to sign contracts with Village Homes and discouraged from pursuing contracts with other builders. The Indian families were told by Commission realty staff that Village Homes would build them houses that were less expensive, better, and completed faster. The Village Homes houses were constructed by Tummurru Trades Corporation, a Utah corporation owned by a Mormon separatist group in Hilldale, Utah, and Colorado City, Arizona. FBI documents showed that this Mormon group "consists of some 4,000 Mormon individuals believing in polygamy and who are an extremely reclusive group. This group does not consider the twelfth article of faith of the Mormon Church, which states that Mormon followers should obey the law of the land. This group operates outside the law of the land and has been known to be highly violent and anti–law enforcement." The FBI report indicates that there were minor children working in the plant. Relocatees reported observing children on the job repairing houses.

At the center of the investigation was Bob Sharp, Hawley Atkinson's friend and personal hire, the man whom Atkinson promoted through the hierarchy, who prompted an unsolicited history lesson from a BIA official, who set up the Commission's realty department and served as its director until the summer of 1979, when he was demoted to "realty specialist." He was responsible for purchasing relocation houses both on and off the reservation. One other man was targeted; his name was Ted Namingha, and he worked for Sharp. He was a Hopi and he primarily handled on-reservation moves. (Namingha helped several Hopi relocatees; most of the Hopi relocatees moved onto the Hopi reservation.)

Steve Goodrich, assistant to Berger, told the FBI agents in a memo that Ted Namingha had come to see him at his home "and alleged that Bob Sharp, his supervisor, was supplying names and addresses of prospective buyers to Village Homes in anticipation of the relocation process and, further, that Sharp was probably accepting kickbacks or 'commissions' of some sort for each sale." Goodrich, however, felt that Namingha's suspicions were "just that, just suspicions. There was no substantive evidence over and above weak allegations," Goodrich said. "Since that time, there have been numerous events which have strengthened my suspicions and fears that staff in our realty section may have been compromised by Village Homes, Inc."

The FBI report shows that all of the relocatee families interviewed—both Hopi and Navajo—indicated that they had been persuaded to sign contracts with Village Homes, even after some specifically stated they did not want to use that contractor because of reports from relatives that their own Village Homes were of poor quality. An FBI document relating a conversation with one Hopi relocatee family states that "Namingha was really pushing them to buy a Village Home." Another document, also about a Hopi family, said, "At times Namingha got rather pushy about going with Village Homes and then would back off. Namingha would say things and then would deny them." A Navajo who was aided by Bob Sharp told the FBI agents that "Sharp never mentioned any other building contractors to him or gave him any other choice." Several other relocatees related the same story, that they "never even realized that possibly there were other contractors available." Some Navajos specifically asked for other contractors and were discouraged by Sharp, who then persuaded them to sign contracts with Village Homes.

Sharp told relocatees that the builders they had selected were not "reliable" or "wouldn't do a good job" or "would take too long." He was observed by Commission staff ushering the Indian families over to the Village Homes office, which was across the street from the Commission. On several occasions, Village Homes representatives came into the Commission offices to conduct business with relocatees, and at Christmas 1979, Village Homes representatives distributed holiday bottles of liquor to Commission employees. The Commission staff was later directed to either return the bottles or reimburse Village Homes for their cost.

The problem with the Village Homes buildings was that they fell apart. From the very first houses that were built, relocatees complained to the Commission that the construction was poor, that building materials were left lying on the ground for long periods of time, and that the relocatees' requests for certain building specifications were ignored. Several relocatees complained that although they informed the Village Homes builders that they would only be able to use butane in the remote areas where their houses were built, the houses were supplied with regulators that only worked with natural gas. Families who couldn't afford to change the regulators themselves were reduced to living in their new homes without a stove or heat. One man paid three hundred dollars out of his own pocket to get the regulator changed.

Many problems in the houses arose from poor foundations that cracked almost immediately after the houses were built. According to David Williams, who established a housing repair program for the Commission after the Village Homes scandal, about thirty Village Homes were built on the reservation, all of which had serious problems relating to "faulty foundation work." In addition to these construction flaws, the houses were equipped with used appliances even though the Commission had paid the contractors for new appliances. "Those homes were *terrible,*" says Williams, who left the Commission in early 1985 for another job.

One relocatee complained to the FBI agent that Sharp talked them into having a wood floor "and that it was not level and very unstable. In fact, everything in the house jiggled when you walked across the floor. [The relocatee] said he noticed the material that was used in the building of the house was of very poor quality, that lots of the boards were split and full of holes. He said that due to this, at one point, he inquired about buying his own materials, but Mr. Sharp discouraged him and just told him to go to Village Homes." When the relocatees suggested another contractor, Sharp told them "they would not be satisfied" if they used the other contractor. Several relocatees complained that the steps out front were uneven, that doors and windows didn't fit, and that walls peeled and carpets came up.

Christine Chisholm-Tures says that houses built for several Hopi families and also for some Navajos who relocated onto the reservation were built with appliances for electric heat even though electricity was not available in the area. They were also provided with gas stoves that they could operate with a propane tank but which had "a pilotless ignition for the ovens, so you have to have electricity to use your oven."

"You really have to see a Village Home to believe it," says Peter Osetek, who, as a lawyer for the Navajo-Hopi Legal Services in Tuba City, tried to get the Commission to fix the faulty houses. "They cut every corner there was to be cut." Looking under the house from the crawl space, Osetek noted that the nail gun used to fasten the plywood subfloor and linoleum surface to the joists beneath had missed the joists on almost every nail. The floors were not properly supported and therefore bounced. "If you were a ballerina, you'd think they were great," says Osetek, who developed a sort of gallows humor trying to negotiate with the Commission to build these families new houses, in 1985, six to eight years after they had been built. In addition, the two sides of the house—they were modular, prefabricated in two pieces—"never got closer than a few inches apart" on some houses. The support piles were not sunk in cement but into the ground, and then packed in with some cement poured in around them, according to Osetek, so the houses had "literally no support."

The FBI investigation did not find evidence that bribes were paid. The primary informant refused to cooperate with the FBI, stating that he belonged to the same small polygamist Mormon community as the defendants and had to see them in church on Sundays. The FBI hadn't sufficient information to compel him to testify.

During the course of the investigation, Namingha left the Commission and moved to Salt Lake City, Utah. Bob Sharp remained at the Commission until he retired in 1984. He later opened up a realty office in Flagstaff. When approached by a reporter, he said he had "never taken any relocatees over to Village Homes."

The FBI report was initiated in February 1980 and closed on October 1, 1981. It consists of pages of notes and interviews, but does not attempt to reconcile conflicting statements nor does it indicate any independent investigation was made of the veracity of personal statements. No conclusions were drawn except that no evidence of bribery was collected. Sandra Massetto, who was Commission chairman at the time the investigation was completed, felt that the FBI's job was inadequate. She says, "Apparently they used FBI agents in Flagstaff who were not experienced with white collar crime. They had done rapes and murders and robberies. And I think the investigation became bogged down because they didn't have the capability or tools to investigate a potential bribery and kickback matter."

Said an official from the Solicitor's Office, "Do you think you'd get a report like that if the FBI was investigating an organized crime figure? No. The agents assigned to Flagstaff, Arizona, are not exactly top of the line."

In August 1981, the FBI informed the U.S. Attorney in Phoenix of its findings. The U.S. Attorney determined there was insufficient evidence to prepare any indictments. The FBI investigators were very upset. According to Dave Williams, who worked closely with the agents, "The FBI guys wanted to prosecute and were angry the U.S. Attorney decided not to subpoena witnesses for a grand jury." It seemed they didn't know what evidence they should have produced to get indictments.

Perhaps the deeper problem with the investigation was that it was looking for the wrong thing. The FBI was investigating charges that bribes were paid to relocatees or to Commission employees to sign contracts with Village Homes. However, bribes paid to relocatees were hardly likely; as the so-called realty specialists knew so well, all they had to do was persuade the relocatee that Village Homes would make them a better house and the relocatee would not argue. The families were so bewildered in their passage through the Commission's bureaucracy, and so traumatized by the necessity of leaving their old homes, that they simply did as they were told. Indian people, both those who do not speak English as well as those who have been to school, will rarely argue with a white person about something in the Anglo world.

Says Ella Bedonie, "A lot of Indian people don't feel right in talking to white people, because all their lives they've been looked down upon by white people. They feel like that." One relocatee said in the FBI report that "Sharp never seemed to go along with [the Indians] on anything that they suggested; however, they felt they had to deal with him because they were assigned to him by the relocation office." The Commission was synonymous with Washindone, the Great White Father, whom they trusted, and felt would deal with them fairly, though he would break their hearts.

The FBI investigation was looking for something it would never find. The real crime was that the realty section, which operated as an autonomous entity within the Commission, had no regulations, adhered to no building codes, and had not provided for any building inspections until 1980, after approximately 189 relocatee families had been supplied with bad houses.

"It's an indication," says Sandra Massetto, "of how the three original commissioners weren't controlling one of the most important tasks they had to perform. They spent a lot of time yelling at each other up on the reservation instead of writing regulations and setting up standards. It shows the lack of sophistication and experience that the Commission had to deal with its fundamental charge of providing people with a safe, decent, sanitary house. Never mind the counseling they never provided and everything else, the housing program is the fundamental program and they couldn't even do that right."

The Commission's aversion to governmental controls and its lack of understanding of the concept of trust responsibility always came back to Atkinson. It was he who placed a small-town real estate man—Bob Sharp —in charge of buying houses for relocatees. Dave Williams says of Sharp, "He came from the real estate world, he had never worked under federal regulations or known what was involved in the duties of a public servant." Williams says that Sharp "operated the shop as if it were a real estate agency, and there was a strong aspect of 'Caveat emptor'—Buyer beware."

How had this happened? According to Berger's assistant Steve Goodrich, there was "a lot of pressure on the Commission staff [from the commissioners] to relocate families from the former Joint Use Area." Also, the housing benefit levels were so low in the early days, according to Williams, that it was difficult to get builders to build houses for the money the Commission was offering. In 1974, the benefit level for a family of three or fewer was $17,000. For four or more, $25,000. In March

1977, benefits were raised to $21,250 and $31,250. By 1979, the levels were increased to $26,520 and $39,000. In 1980, after the problems with housing had been forced to the surface by the FBI investigation, the benefit levels jumped to $44,800 for a family of three or fewer and $66,000 for more than four.

Village Homes, according to Goodrich, "was the first with the most." The company was willing to build on the reservation, unlike some other firms, and it "saw a good market and went after it." However, according to Williams, there were several other contractors who were offering to build better houses than Village Homes for the same prices. Goodrich told the FBI agents that "after competitors entered the field it appeared that Village Homes was still getting the majority of the business."

Sharp was not only pressuring relocatees to sign up with Village Homes, but he also put pressure on the Commission so that Village Homes got as many houses built as possible in as short a time as possible. Christine Chisholm-Tures told the FBI agents that several of her clients were told by Bob Sharp that "if they didn't hurry up with Village Homes, they wouldn't get a house." Some were threatened with losing their benefits if they didn't sign a contract by a specific date.

Chisholm-Tures also told the agents that in ten instances, "Sharp had attempted to hurry social services through their processing." Also, Village Homes was repeatedly issued draws for work that was not yet completed. Bob Sharp was found, on at least one occasion, to have possession of a purchase agreement between a relocatee and Village Homes that was missing from the client's file. When questioned, he replied that he had taken it to get the signature of the relocatee. However, sixteen thousand dollars had already been released to Village Homes to build a house that the relocatee in question had yet to agree to purchase by signing the agreement.

Georgia Nagel, who worked at Nagel Homes in Winslow, told the FBI agents that "she was told by Bob Sharp on one occasion that if a relocatee did not go with Village Homes, they conveniently lost the [relocatee's] file." There was further evidence that "losing files" of relocatees who had signed with other builders had been feared by other contractors and by Executive Director Leon Berger. Nagel "lost" a contract to build a house for a relocatee when she was told that her company would have to absorb the expense of electrical wiring. Village Homes charged less than other contractors for this service, and many relocatees chose Village Homes because they were the only ones they could afford to contract with. In 1986, when electricity was finally brought in to the Hopi relocatees, it was found that all the electrical wiring in the houses built by Village Homes had to be torn out and installed again.

Sharp told the FBI agents that he signed contracts almost exclusively with Village Homes because they were a "dynamic group and they take care of their product." When asked whether other contractors did not do the same thing, Sharp "related that he had limited experience with other contractors."

In August 1980, after several staff members complained about Sharp's "overall pattern of poor service," Goodrich told staff that "at the minimum, Bob Sharp was guilty of poor judgment in his handling of cases, but that the problem would resolve itself with Bob's scheduled retirement early in 1981." Unfortunately, he did not retire until February 24, 1984.

"There were some real, real funky things going on with Village Homes," says Christine Chisholm-Tures. "I don't believe Bob Sharp was just ignorant." What distressed Chisholm-Tures the most was that Village Homes representatives apparently had a list of the relocatees and knowledge of their financial situation. "There were relocatees at that time that Village Homes would offer money. Let's say someone was having financial problems. Maybe they're going to have their car repossessed or something. Village Homes would come in with that information somehow, which was interesting, and offer them a couple of thousand dollars, offer to loan money, saying, 'Look, when you get your bonus, you can pay us back.' " (Relocatees got cash bonuses for signing up early. They usually used the money to buy furniture.)

Village Homes representatives even traveled to the reservation. "They had a van out there, going door to door. And they would knock on the door and say, 'Hi, I'm here from Flagstaff, from the Flagstaff office, and I want to talk to you about your new home.' To a relocatee back then—it's probably even true now—they didn't know that wasn't a representative of the Relocation Commission." Chisholm-Tures found out about this when "clients would come in and say, 'So and so was out at my house yesterday, so I came in to talk about the new house.' And they gave me this brochure with pictures of my new house. 'Oh, they don't work here? They said they came from the Flagstaff office.' "

A year after the FBI investigation was ordered and several months before it was concluded, Village Homes went out of business and was resurrected under the name of High Country Homes. The employees were the same, but the president, Boyd Dockstader, was replaced by his attorney, Tony Cullum. But, even after the FBI investigation and the commissioners' knowledge about the poor quality of Village Homes, the Commission honored nine contracts signed with Village Homes that had been taken over by High Country Construction, the building arm of the realty office High Country Homes. The name Village Homes on the contracts was simply crossed out and High Country Homes typed in.

In March 1979, Dave Williams had recommended that the entire realty department be overhauled. He suggested that proper construction inspections be performed by qualified technical personnel. Up until that time, houses were basically inspected to see if they conformed with the floor plan ordered, not whether the insulation was adequate, the foundation proper, the walls sturdy. Williams also wrote that "considerable redesign is in order" regarding the houses they were building for relocatees. "We are building Anglo homes which are not practical on the reservation, especially when heated with butane." While preparing his recommendations, he had visited the home of Louis and Myra Begay in White Cone. "They were sold a four-bedroom house by Village Homes for two old people living alone," recalls Williams. "It was a two-story house with substandard insulation built on a foundation that was improperly built and had cracked. I went to see them a year after they relocated. It was an electric house, but there was no electricity in the area, and no contract with the Navajo Tribal Utility Authority to provide electricity. The people had no money to pay for it. They had an ornamental fireplace. These old people were wrapped up in clothes and blankets in front of the fireplace in a 2,000-square-foot home with less insulation in it than required by any other federal agency for that climatic location. Snow was blowing in the door and some windows. Snow was piled on the floor. There was no running water, though the house was plumbed for running water." Williams was told by a housing inspector that the Begays later brought their sheep into the house to help keep themselves warm.

Williams suggested that a better effort be made to attract other builders, and he also suggested a training program for the Indians to help build their own homes. These recommendations were made before the Village Homes scandal erupted, and the recommended changes were not made.

In February 1980, as the FBI investigation got underway, Williams again recommended a complete overhaul of the construction program. Over the next four years, most of his recommendations were gradually adopted. Building codes were finally written in 1980 and 1981. It wasn't until 1982 that inspections and contracting standards were imposed. Williams was appointed head of the housing department in January 1983. His selection reflected a profound change in the Commission's philosophy. His predecessor had resisted housing inspections and building codes, perceiving them as an impediment to speedy implementation of the law. With Massetto and Roger Lewis as commissioners, the program was starting to become more responsive to the relocatees' needs. As Williams put it, in the housing area, at least, things had "changed fundamentally—no more 'Caveat emptor.' "

In 1984, Williams made a presentation at a public Relocation Commission meeting about repairing faulty houses. He knew at the time the program would cost many millions of dollars, but he was instructed by the executive director not to announce the extent of the problem.

In March 1982, inspections of houses built before 1980 had begun. However, the men who worked in the new housing repair program had formerly worked under Bob Sharp and had a built-in allegiance to the realty department's work. So the repair program was booby-trapped. A member of the repair and appraisal staff was reported to have said that "he didn't think the Indians deserved the houses then, and he doesn't think they deserve to have them fixed now." Between January and March 1983, nineteen cash settlements with unhappy relocatees were made. According to Williams, cash settlements were "supposed to be for small items, grievances between the Commission and relocatees, not for items violating the 'safe, decent and sanitary' housing stipulation." However, according to Williams, the employees of the Commission repair department "went too far" and paid relocatees $500 to $3,000 for problems that should have been fixed, not paid off. In May 1983, the Navajo Tribe discontinued settlement negotiations because they objected to the cash payoffs that relocatees were accepting. In 1986, the Commission offered to make repairs on twenty-eight houses averaging $20,000 to $30,000 per house, but most of the relocatees wanted new houses, as they didn't feel the old ones could be fixed.

"After so much misunderstanding," says Williams, "after those families had been treated so badly by the Relocation Commission—they felt they were cheated and abused—getting an agreement with them on repairs was very difficult. The clients don't bear goodwill toward the Commission."

Another problem the relocatees faced was deciding on an appropriate housing design. The lack of standard housing packages allowed builders the freedom to sell "extras" to relocatees such as veneers, carports, and ornamental add-ons, which have a high profit margin and little value to many of the relocatees. As the problems were revealed, the Commission was eventually forced to increase controls. So Hawley Atkinson's aversion to standards and controls accomplished one thing—relocatees got bad homes. No one gained, the relocatees suffered, and the Commission, eventually, had to pay.

In 1986, even with standards and inspections in place, however, houses were still being built by incompetent contractors. A story in the *Navajo Times* on February 10, 1987, describes a family who had not been able to move into their relocation house because of extensive repairs needed on the brand-new structure. A Commission inspector had determined that "the original contractor didn't have the skills to build a house." The only remedy the Commission offered in these cases was to put the name of the contractor on a list, to prevent them from building another relocation house. However, in this case, which received a lot of media attention, Assistant Director for Operations Paul Tessler told a reporter, "We're going to get this taken care of, believe me. Hawley directed me to take care of it and he'll have my ass if I don't. They're going to get the [media] attention and we're going to do it."

That family was lucky. According to Barry Paisner of the Navajo-Hopi Legal Services Program, by 1987 the Commission had only repaired 17 of the 189 inadequate houses since the repair program was authorized in 1982.

Eventually, even more restrictions would be placed on the relocatees' choices. After it was found that many lost their homes after offering them as collateral on loans they couldn't pay, the housing contracts forbade encumbrances and resale for a period of two years. Also, relocatees were not allowed to move into border towns unless they earned a steady income. This brought up issues of paternalism that some at the Commission were uncomfortable with. Christine Chisholm-Tures recalls, "I was a very staunch advocate of people being given total autonomy in the decision-making process. I believed that the Commission had additional responsibilities because of that approach, and the responsibility was to prepare them for that autonomy. That was naïve on my part because I did not reckon with the kind of pressures that were being placed on people which made education just a farce." Relocatees were being pressured by the realty office at the Commission, pressured by overcrowding at home on the HPL, by reduced livestock herds, and by growing families and increasing poverty. "You don't sit down and 'seminar' people and talk taxes, utility bills, and all those brand-new concepts when somebody is feeling traumatized, stressed, and feeling 'I've got to move, I've got to move now and I don't care about the consequences,' " Chisholm-Tures says. She feels that the relocatees did not understand the consequences of moving off the reservation. The consequences "were not real."

In the spring of 1986, having already shored up the process of building houses, the Commission decided to reorganize the process of repairing defective houses. It approached the tribe and asked for recommendations on how to proceed with the stalled repair negotiations. Barry Paisner, from Osetek's Navajo-Hopi Legal Services office, prepared detailed suggestions, which, according to Osetek, were ignored. Instead, the Commission decided it would conduct new inspections and decide how much it was willing to pay for repairs in each case. Osetek was optimistic with what he had heard about the offers being made. They seemed to be generous and to exceed estimates made previously. However, Osetek had only heard of the estimates through clients. The Commission refused to send him the documents pertaining to his own clients; he was told to request the information through the Freedom of Information/Privacy Act requests.

Louis and Myra Begay's faulty 2,000-square-foot house stands empty on the reservation near White Cone and the couple live in a hogan with relatives. Although the Commission finally got the Begays hooked up to electricity, their house had not yet been repaired, eight years after it was built, seven years after Dave Williams observed the two old people huddled before their ornamental fireplace, wrapped in blankets, surrounded by drifts of snow.

On May 21, 1982, Sandra Massetto and Roger Lewis commenced land-exchange negotiations, whose authorization they had fought for and won in the 1980 Amendments to the Settlement Act. Massetto and Lewis had already worked for a year to develop a framework for negotiations that was acceptable to both tribes. They had also produced three possible land-exchange proposals to begin discussions.

One was a modest acre-for-acre exchange within the JUA that would have reduced by thirty-six the number of Navajo families subject to relocation. The second proposal involved more than three times the acreage of the first, and traded 86,100 acres of HPL for 86,000 in the 1934 reservation area. It was estimated this exchange would save 372 families from relocation. The third proposal was the most comprehensive—140,000 acres of HPL would be turned over to the Navajos and the Hopis would receive 23,066 acres from the NPL, the 100,000-acre Bar-N Ranch in Chambers, Arizona (part of the New Lands), and 100 percent of the mineral royalties earned on the 1882 reservation for ten years. This proposal would also have settled the 1934 area litigation, giving the Hopis 65,000 acres of land linking Moencopi with the HPL. It was estimated that this plan would reduce the number of Navajos to be relocated by 795 families.

These latest attempts at negotiation seemed to be taking place at an auspicious moment. Barry Goldwater appeared at least tacitly to support the effort and had even introduced his own plan to reduce relocations in the Big Mountain area. And Senator James McClure, usually a supporter of relocation, had told the Commission at a recent appropriations hearing that Congress didn't think relocation was a good solution.

Nevertheless, the negotiations ran immediately into bad luck. Four days after the proposals were offered to the tribes, Commissioner Roger Lewis resigned. He told the *Arizona Republic* that he no longer believed in the relocation program and therefore didn't think it was fair to the Hopis if he stayed. He said his Commission post was "the worst job I ever had."

He called relocation "a tragic, tragic thing." In an emotional speech at a public Commission meeting, Lewis said, "I feel that in moving some of these elderly people, I almost feel—and I think that our staff sometimes feel—that we are as bad as the people who ran the concentration camps in World War II." Hawley Atkinson sensed the agitation and confusion in the air and used it to his advantage. Since he was the chairman of the Commission at that time, he led the first meeting of the negotiating teams, which took place in June 1982, in Albuquerque. He had not been active in the preparations for negotiations or the negotiations so far, and had let Massetto and Lewis take the lead.

The meeting was scheduled to begin at 9:00 a.m. The Hopi representatives were in the meeting room at the designated time, as were the federal mediator and the two commissioners. But there was no sign of the Navajos. Atkinson recalls that after five minutes he asked Abbott Sekaquaptewa if he was willing to wait. Abbott said yes, another five minutes. After five more minutes, at about 9:15, Atkinson decided enough was enough. He adjourned the meeting.

"I have to tell you, the Navajo leadership came unglued," recalls Atkinson in an interview. "But I had pledged my word to the Hopi people, I had pledged my word to the Navajo. [I had told them,] 'If you're not there, we're going to adjourn the meeting.' "

Atkinson says that the Hopis had repeatedly complained about the Navajos' rudeness by "sauntering in a half hour late." So Atkinson was determined that both teams be on time in Albuquerque. "I told Chairman MacDonald, and I told Leon Berger, 'This meeting is going to start right on the nose, because the Hopis won't come in and be treated rudely by you.' "

The Navajos have a very different version of events. According to Leon Berger, who had left the Commission six months before and was then heading the Navajo Tribe's land dispute task force, the Navajo delegation had been praying. A few minutes after Atkinson adjourned the meeting, the Navajos were found in their hotel rooms, waiting for one of their lawyers to give them the cue to enter the meeting room. The lawyer had lost track of the time. Massetto and the mediator tried in vain to get everybody back together, but, according to Massetto, Hopi lawyer John Paul Kennedy didn't answer the phone in his room and later left the building.

"I still think about that meeting to this day," she said four years later. "I have always admired Abbott [Sekaquaptewa] because he was eloquent and spoke for his people. He never was devious. We had grave disagreements, but they were all professional. I had seen MacDonald and the Navajo leadership treat the Hopi leadership badly; they often arrived late to meetings and would grandstand. That day, as Abbott waited at the table and the Navajos didn't come, he was humiliated. And I felt for him, and I was embarrassed myself after having put so much effort into setting up the negotiations. I felt I couldn't stand up and ask everybody to stay [after Atkinson adjourned the meeting] because I'd seen this thing before."

But Navajo general counsel George Vlassis made it plain to Massetto that he was very angry she had doubted their intentions. The Navajos were taking the negotiations very seriously, he insisted. And Massetto knew they had brought copies of the third and most comprehensive land-exchange proposal to all of the chapters. Every chapter but one had passed a resolution supporting it. Vlassis made it clear that he was furious at the member of his staff who had not called the Navajos to the meeting. Massetto felt the miscue had given the Hopis "a perfect excuse" to back away from the negotiations. Peter MacDonald had taken a political risk to enter into negotiations as well, for by taking the proposals seriously, MacDonald had reversed his position up to that point of fighting for repeal of the law.

The negotiations, still technically continuing, took a bizarre turn when Hawley Atkinson offered his own proposal to the negotiating teams a month after the June fiasco. Atkinson offered a change in the Commission's regulations which would have reduced the number of Navajos eligible for relocation benefits. He claimed the change would effect a savings of $100 million. The new regulation would have denied eligibility to all those Navajos who were not then living on the HPL—who had already moved off because of job opportunities, schooling, or because they could no longer live in their HPL houses for want of repair. Atkinson explained that his proposal "should help convince the tribe of the need for cooperating with the program in order to assure the best possible deal for the Navajos who must relocate."

Leon Berger said that Atkinson's proposal "can only be viewed as what it is—vindictiveness and spitefulness toward the Navajo people." George Vlassis said Atkinson's proposal was "retaliation" for the Navajo Tribe's criticism of Atkinson for adjourning the negotiating session.

The situation took an even more bizarre turn soon afterward, when Atkinson and Massetto were in Washington, and Atkinson seemed to have completely forgotten that the negotiations had ever been undertaken. Massetto recalls, "We were right in front of Barry Goldwater's door and Hawley said that the Commission had never really endorsed the land-exchange proposals. I got so mad I had to hold myself back to keep from slapping him." She attributed the confusion to his "typically selective amnesia."

After returning to Flagstaff, Atkinson asked a staffer to look up any records of the Commission endorsing land exchanges. He couldn't remember being at a meeting in the spring during which the proposals had been adopted. Atkinson's request states, "I wish the records searched for the minutes of the alleged spring meeting. If such records are in existent [sic], then I have made quite an error. If there are no records, then Sandra has made quite an error." Steve Goodrich sent Atkinson copies of the statements made by Massetto and Lewis when the proposals were introduced as well as a press release, which had been sent out under Atkinson's name, announcing the introduction of the proposals to the negotiating teams.

There was great disappointment on the Navajo side and among members of the Commission that the land negotiations had dribbled away in such ignominious fashion. Further, Atkinson's bizarre behavior set everybody on edge.

In October 1982, Ralph Watkins, a Phoenix Chevrolet dealer and businessman who had headed "Democrats for Goldwater," a group credited with helping Goldwater squeak through his last election, was appointed commissioner to replace Roger Lewis. The patterns of the Commission's first years were quickly reestablished. Watkins and Atkinson formed a quorum and gradually pushed Massetto out of the picture, as Atkinson and Urbano had excluded Robert Lewis.

Winter 1986

A lot of our ancestors, they had Hopi blood. We're part of the Hopi people. And the Hopi people, they're also part of us, too. And we have a lot of intermarriage. It's really hard for us to say anything bad about the Hopi people because we would just be hurting one of our own relatives. But this law is destroying us. It is too much for the old people to bear. I think something must be done to stop it. It should be up to the old traditional people. They should get together and settle it, and leave everybody else out of it.

ELLA BEDONIE, NAVAJO

(15)

Washington Gets Involved

Every four years they have elections from Washington all the way down to Navajo and Hopi land. But these people that are elected just bring more problems. They tell us, "I'll protect you when you vote for me." But once they get in office, they turn around and do the most harsh things to us.

KEE SHAY

As Richard Morris's attempts to bring the tribes to the negotiating table faltered in the fall of 1985, and the July 1986 deadline loomed ever closer, a wide variety of government officials began to sit up and take notice. Senators and representatives, Interior Department lawyers, commissioners, and officials of the Navajo Tribe all began to realize that something had to be done to avert what could become a disaster of national proportions. Everyone imagined different scenarios, but most feared that the Hopis would take some legal action to remove the Navajos from the land, and might even find a way to forcibly evict Navajos from their hogans.

Commissioner Sandra Massetto began to fear what the Relocation Commission, her own agency, might do as the July 7 deadline neared. For more than a year, she had been effectively excluded from the decision-making process; her two colleagues, Ralph Watkins, who had been appointed in 1982 to replace Roger Lewis, and Hawley Atkinson failed to inform her of all their meetings and consistently voted as a bloc against her.

Over the summer, unbeknownst to her, Atkinson and Watkins, along with Commission lawyer Fred Craft, had conceived the buyout plan that had so disturbed Richard Morris when he learned of it in July. Both Watkins and Atkinson were becoming increasingly agitated as the dead-

line neared, particularly Atkinson. Said Massetto, "There was this craziness on Hawley's part that he wanted to get the job done. He was
obsessed with getting the job done on time."

But Atkinson and Watkins both knew that if the Commission continued at its own pace, the deadline would not be met. According to the
Commission's own numbers, in late 1985, more than three hundred families were still living on the HPL, and twelve hundred families had vacated the HPL but were waiting for their relocation houses. At the rate
the Commission was going, about 220 relocations a year, the job would
not be completed until 1993.

So Watkins and Atkinson, along with their resourceful attorney, devised the buyout plan, and spent time over the summer in Washington
(paid for by taxpayers) lobbying for it. Fred Craft, in spite of the poor
reaction with which it met in some quarters, still believed that the buyout
was the best deal for the government. He said, "If the Commission builds
houses, it will cost $22 million to move 105 families." If the families were
simply given $55,000 each and told to build their own houses, "$88
million would build 1600 houses." Added Craft, "We would have met
the obligation for all the families. Eighty-eight million. That's what it
would have cost the government to wash its hands of its obligation."
Craft went so far as to convince the Senate Subcommittee on Interior
Appropriations to prepare an appropriations bill that authorized an $88
million budget for the Commission for calendar year 1986.

Massetto was horrified to learn of the buyout. She recalled, "In July
and August, Ralph and Hawley were on the Hill lobbying for the buyout
plan, which they never publicly acknowledged. During the Commission's monthly public meetings I kept saying, 'We have no plan to move
people' and they were saying there was. I kept asking them what they
were doing in Washington. I tried to get them to admit in a public meeting that there was a buyout plan. I think Ralph got so upset he wanted
to stop me, so he put the letter in my file."

In August, Watkins, frustrated over negative press reports about the
relocation effort, had accused Massetto of malfeasance and misfeasance
of office, and placed a letter of his complaints in her personnel file.
"Before then, I tried to appeal to their sanity and good nature," said
Massetto. "I tried to appeal to their humanity to get the relocation done
right. I realized after that these people were not rational, they would not
listen to me, and they were going to do things that were irreversible
before anybody knew."

Finally, one day in early October, after discovering that her colleagues
had conceived of a second, secret plan to clear the HPL, Massetto decided
that radical action was required. She called her friend Dan Jackson, staff
attorney for the Department of the Interior's Field Solicitor in Phoenix.
She asked him to meet her at the bar of the old Adams Hotel in down-
town Phoenix. Massetto was terribly agitated. She pulled a set of blue-

prints from her bag and set them on the table between them. Jackson unrolled the papers and what he saw made his stomach lurch. The maps detailed Watkins and Atkinson's plans for a four-hundred-unit housing development on the New Lands. Massetto told him she feared that her two colleagues had plans to slap up high-density housing (which she dubbed "Hawley Acres"), move the Navajos remaining on the HPL into it, and declare the relocation of Navajos complete. Jackson "became unglued."

"When I saw the Commission's plans for these rural communities along the highway, I just had apoplexy, because there are no jobs," he said later. "You're not going to put people on two to five acres—'Here's your house and your electricity bill'—when they can't pay anything and they can't have any animals." To a friend he said, "This is horseshit. This cannot and will not happen."

Jackson was a study in contradictions. Although a boyish-looking forty-two in 1986 and a marathon runner, he had deep lines in his face. A Vietnam veteran, at times he was officious, soldierly, and carried himself as if he were on active duty. At other times he stood with his shoulders folded together as if he were waiting out a storm. Tall and lanky, with gold-rimmed spectacles, he wore his straight brown hair an inch or so over the collar. He arrived at work in jeans and short-sleeved golf shirts, yet for hearings or court appearances was impeccably dressed. Jackson was—and is—intense, dedicated, with a fundamental belief in the letter of the law. He was an obsessive worker who often woke at two or three a.m. and worked through the next evening. A legal services lawyer for four years, including two on the Navajo reservation, he had dedicated much of his professional life to defending the rights of "the little people," as he put it, those people at the bottom of the socioeconomic order.

But now he was working for the government. He lost so many of his legal services cases, he liked to joke, that he decided to work for the other side, so at least his losses would benefit the underdog. In the office of the Field Solicitor, he had been the government's chief legal adviser on the Navajo-Hopi issue for the past six years, and on numerous occasions involving the myriad legal actions between the tribes, he had stepped forward to prevent the little people from getting crushed in the crossfire between the tribes.

After meeting with Massetto, Jackson got on the telephone and made an extraordinary series of calls to associates at the Justice Department and the Solicitor General's office. He requested a meeting. Jackson wasn't sure what would happen in Washington, if anything, but he knew he had to let the appropriate people know about the rogue plans for the New Lands, a proposal that both he and Massetto felt would be a complete disaster.

Earl Gjelde, assistant to Interior Secretary Donald Hodel, was the top policymaker at the meeting Jackson arranged. Jackson told the assembled lawyers and Interior officials what he knew of the plan for the large subdivision and explained his fears that the Commission, in an attempt to meet the upcoming deadline, would slap up housing and begin forcible evictions. He was so determined to get across the insanity of the plan that Gjelde said later, "We heard about the housing development, and we were incredulous as it was described to us. We thought maybe it was an overstatement on some level." But the other men at the meeting, some of whom had kept up with the issue over the years and others who had been briefed by Steve Carroll, a Justice Department attorney and a close associate of Jackson's, backed up Jackson's story and agreed that something had to be done. "Jackson was deeply concerned," said Gjelde, "not necessarily from a legal standpoint, but from a moral standpoint. The meeting itself provided clear agreement between Justice and the Solicitor that even if it was a close call [whether we were responsible] legally, we were morally responsible to proceed."

Congress had decided, in 1974, to make the Relocation Commission an independent agency within the executive branch. Congress did not want the Commission to be a part of the Interior Department (in which the BIA finds its home), since Interior, by action and inaction, had played such a large role in the creation of the Navajo-Hopi problem. In addition, Hopi attorney John Boyden argued that the Relocation Commission should not be within the BIA since the Navajo Tribe, as the largest tribe in the country, could unduly influence the BIA. He argued that placing the agency in charge of relocating Navajos in the BIA would be like putting a fox in the henhouse.

Since Interior had no role in relocation, it had unclear legal responsibilities toward the relocatees. So, to Jackson, having moved the lawyers and policymakers in the room to feel they had some responsibility meant he had overcome the first big hurdle—getting Interior involved. The specific problem now was a strategic one: how to prevent the Commission from building inadequate houses and forcing evictions. After the meeting, Gjelde met in his office with Jackson and Tim Vollmann, the associate solicitor for Indian Affairs. Jackson repeated that something had to be done. Gjelde asked Vollmann if he had any suggestions. Vollmann said, "What about noneviction language?" Gjelde turned to Jackson and asked, "Would that satisfy you?" Jackson, running the consequences through his mind, and wondering how the language might be enforced, hesitated for a second, then said yes.

He and Vollmann left Gjelde's office and worked out some bill language. An attorney in the Justice Department was consulted, and did not object. The legislation was to be slipped into the Relocation Commission's appropriations bill in December. It would protect Navajos currently domiciled on the HPL from eviction unless an adequate replacement home had been built for them.

Gjelde recalled later that although Interior had been watching from the sidelines since the Morris-Clark mission, Jackson's presentation had spurred the agency to get involved. "It was very important that Dan Jackson came and met with us," said Gjelde. "He clearly believed what should be done for these people was to have a comparable but workable living arrangement." What was clear to Gjelde was the "need to work with these people, with concern about the people, the land and within budgetary restraints" rather than making decisions about the people, as the Commission was doing, without consulting them. "We are concerned," said Gjelde, "and we will remain concerned." As for Jackson, he was pleased and surprised that Interior picked up the ball so quickly. There was no hemming and hawing, no requests for further study, no bureaucratic sloughing of responsibility. "We were very lucky," he said later, looking back on the meeting, "that the people in that room were sensitive, cared, and carried their weight."

Jackson didn't know it, but the appropriations bill onto which he added the noneviction language was to change the career of the Relocation Commission. And it was to change his own. How that happened is a lesson in budgetary politics. The laws we live by are seldom coherent documents that reflect one point of view. They emerge as a mishmash of different, and sometimes completely opposed positions. As Arizona Representative John McCain said, "No one should know how their laws or how their sausages are made."

Appropriations bills are prepared separately by House and Senate committees and are hammered into a single entity during the period of conference meetings, when negotiators from each chamber meet. In December 1985, the two houses of Congress had different agendas for the relocation program. The Senate Appropriations Committee, aware of Barry Goldwater's desire to get the problem solved before he left office, and open to Craft's buyout plan, wanted to give the Commission enough money to complete the program in one year. The House negotiators, Democratic Representative Sidney Yates's staff, had a different agenda. They had lost confidence in the Commission. They felt that the BIA, particularly because of its new commissioner, Ross Swimmer, former chief of the Cherokee Nation, would be better than the Relocation Commission at furthering the program.

Before the conference meetings, the Senate's appropriations bill had been discussed in subcommittee and on the floor of the Senate. Dennis DeConcini, Democrat of Arizona and a longtime opponent of relocation, had offered several amendments. In subcommittee, he tried to slash the appropriation to the Commission by $65 million, returning it to its normal yearly amount—about $22 million. He also offered a stipulation that would require the Commission to supply Congress with a detailed report regarding its planning for the New Lands. He also tried to slip in a year's extension of the deadline. His amendments were killed.

When the appropriations bills were in full committee conference, the one-year extension was reintroduced. Morris Udall had indicated to DeConcini that he would not oppose the one-year extension, so Yates concurred with it. Yates, Udall, and DeConcini brought their weight to bear against Republican James McClure, who acquiesced on the year's extension and also returned the year's appropriation to $22 million.

After the committee had apparently reached a consensus, but before it had taken a final vote, DeConcini's press assistant prematurely released word of the one-year extension of the deadline to the press. The news immediately reached Barry Goldwater, who was attending his wife's funeral in Phoenix. He was outraged. Says Fred Craft, "Goldwater, even in his moment of distress, was pissed. He felt it was a total affront that this should happen while he was gone." According to Craft, Senators Hatfield and Stennis objected to the underhanded treatment of their colleague, and the issue was reopened. The year's extension was removed and the yearly appropriation was raised to $44 million. The Navajo Tribe was devastated.

But the authorization for $44 million opened a new can of worms. The Relocation Commission had an authorization limit. It could not accept an appropriation of more than $22 million in any year, so the extra $22 million was added to the BIA budget with directions that it should be used to build houses for the Commission.

When the appropriations bill in the form of a Continuing Resolution was passed on December 19, 1985, the new head of the BIA, Ross Swimmer, was effectively thrust into the middle of the century's most contentious Indian problem. Only a few months before, Swimmer, forty-two, a quarter-blood Cherokee, had been about to start his third term as principal chief of the Cherokees, when Secretary of the Interior Donald Hodel asked him to accept the post as head of the Bureau of Indian Affairs. At first, Swimmer was reluctant. He had just produced a document calling the BIA a "Byzantine system of overregulation" that is "designed for paternalistic control and . . . thrives on the failure of Indian tribes." That report had been prepared by the Presidential Commission on Reservation Economics in 1984, which Swimmer cochaired. A lawyer and banker, Swimmer had grown up in an unusual family; his father had been one of the first Indians to make use of Indian education grants to go to law school. Swimmer had distinguished himself at Cherokee by stimulating on-reservation business such as poultry and cattle ranching. He guided the Cherokees' investment in local companies and increased the tribal coffers by 250 percent. He had also overseen a mutual-help housing program for about twenty-five families, and had learned from his own mistakes that one must involve people in planning the building of their own homes. When Hodel asked Swimmer to take the job, Swimmer was looking forward to an end to politics and concentrating on his business career. Although his report to the President had stated that the BIA's problems were so entrenched that they couldn't be "overcome by entrusting to the Bureau's bureaucracy the responsibility of reforming itself," he accepted the job as its new head.

Swimmer immediately impressed his colleagues with his ability to absorb information and understand problems. "He's clearly the brightest person that's ever had that job," said a Republican staffer on the House Interior Committee. Swimmer also impressed people with his independence. "He infuriates the control types in the Department and the tribal leaders because he is so independent," said the staffer. "He just does his own thing."

Although Interior's role in the relocation program had been limited up to this point, when Swimmer arrived, the department was in the process of reexamining the issue as a result of the Morris-Clark mission, Dan Jackson's trip to Washington, threats of violence in the Big Mountain area, and a legal decision handed down by Ralph Tarr, then acting assistant attorney general of the Office of Legal Counsel at the Justice Department. That opinion stated that although the Interior Department had a limited role in the relocation program, it had some potential liabilities. Interior Secretary Hodel could ultimately be held responsible for the actions or defaults of the Commission. Tarr also determined that Interior had the power to fire commissioners.

"The Secretary was not too concerned about going to jail," said Swimmer in an interview. "As he said, it would be a new experience." But Hodel realized that if Interior had some liability, then it had better take a role in assuring that the program got onto a better track. He assigned that job to Swimmer. "As the new kid on the block, I was kind of asked to take a look at what was going on," Swimmer said later, ruefully.

Ironically, Tarr's far-reaching decision that Interior held some liability for the potential failures of the relocation program had not been solicited by the Department, but by the commissioners themselves in the service of advancing Ralph Watkins's personal ambitions. Commission attorney Fred Craft poked around Interior trying to get career senior executive service status for Watkins, a job description that both Massetto and Atkinson held. The difference between Watkins's status and that of the other two was a subtle one relating to the grade of service. A person with noncareer status, which Watkins had, could be fired, while those with career status theoretically could be transferred to another position of similar standing if their jobs ended. Watkins wanted an opportunity to slip into a highly paid situation in the Interior Department where his employment was virtually guaranteed. In trying to make a decision on that, Tarr's opinion on the Commission's relation to Interior came up collaterally. According to Interior sources, Craft tried for months to get career senior executive service status for Ralph, but failed. Massetto bitterly opposed the work Craft did for Atkinson and Watkins, which benefited them personally, and which was paid for by tax dollars. Between 1982 and 1986, Craft billed the Commission for a total of $321,716 for legal work and help as a "liaison" in Washington. In 1985 alone, Craft billed $108,335, part of which included work concerning Watkins's career status and the so-called buyout plan, which seemed to serve very little except Watkins's and Atkinson's own anxiety to get the job done on time.

In his first weeks on the job, Swimmer read everything he could get his hands on about the Navajo-Hopi question. He read the now-familiar litany: after twelve years, one thousand families had been relocated, but many had already lost their homes, or were having trouble staying afloat. Another twelve hundred families had moved off the reservation and were still waiting for their replacement houses. No one knew where they were living. And three hundred or so families still lived on the HPL. "I'm just going around scratching my head wondering what in the world is going on," said Swimmer. "This was about the craziest thing I'd ever seen."

After learning as much as he could in Washington, Swimmer flew to Flagstaff, Arizona, to visit the Relocation Commission. On January 29, Swimmer was taken on a quick tour of the New Lands, and then met with the Commission staff. "Well, I walked into this room," said Swimmer, "and all over the walls they've got these beautiful plans that are colored and here we've got rural developments. It looks like Reston, Virginia, with these huge cul-de-sacs, and I think, Gee, I wonder what we're doing, are we in the wrong office?" He listened dumbfounded as Commission staffers said they didn't know how many people were still living on the HPL. He also wondered about the twelve hundred families living with relatives or in border towns, waiting for their houses. He asked, "Well, what are we going to do about those other families that have signed up, been certified, moved off the land, and are out there in limbo somewhere?" It became a Kafkaesque nightmare when the Indian Health Service engineer at the meeting told Swimmer that the IHS couldn't construct water systems on the New Lands for another couple of years. Swimmer was saying to himself, "I thought we had a July deadline, what is this talk about two or three years?" Later, after looking over the appropriations bill, and realizing that the BIA had been drawn into the program through a funding arrangement but had no authority to plan the house building, he realized that unless some changes were made and made quickly, he'd be overseeing the building of the cul-de-sacs for Navajo sheepherders.

Although Ralph Watkins publicly denied plans for a large subdivision, Swimmer was looking at it—he was staring at pictures of the plan the Commission staff called "Hawley Acres." According to a member of Swimmer's staff, the Commission "put on a dog and pony show about how well things were going."

That wasn't the only surprise Swimmer would have. Toward the end of the meeting, the Commission staff pulled out a Memorandum of Understanding they had prepared—a document outlining the ways the two agencies would work together. But Dan Jackson had already gotten hold of the document, had prepared a critique of it, and had presented it to Swimmer. The document stated, according to Jackson, that "in very broad strokes, Interior was to be their handmaiden."

That was about the last thing Swimmer planned to be. "I will not build another urban ghetto out there," he said angrily. Atkinson then said, "It's not a ghetto, what do you mean, a ghetto?" Swimmer replied, "It will be an economic ghetto. What are those people going to do when they're moved into those subdivisions?"

It was clear that the Commission didn't much care. Fred Craft said in an interview, "It was never the intent of the Act to meet the relocatees' psychological needs, medical needs, social needs, or economic needs. It was only after Congress started playing with it that some of these were addressed." Craft further stated, "This is a benefits program, an inducement program, not a housing program." However, PL 93-531 includes an explicit directive to "avoid or minimize" the "adverse social, economic, cultural, and other impacts of relocation" and to "assure that housing and related community facilities and services, such as water, sewers, roads, schools, and health facilities for such households shall be available at their relocation sites." Nevertheless, Craft's opinion reflected the attitude of Atkinson, Watkins, and the Commission senior staff, who tried to ignore this directive.

Swimmer was infuriated. "I'm not going to do it," he told them. He proceeded to tell the Commission what he expected. "He outlined, bang, bang, bang, what he expected them to do—go out there and start working with those relocatees, find out who they were and what they wanted and where they wanted to go and to get as many of them out on the range as they could and then to begin planning for the people who can't fit on the New Lands in locations where they could be close to relatives or jobs. He insisted that they start looking at them as individuals instead of something else." And then he got up and left. Atkinson was still sputtering.

Swimmer, whose position as head of the BIA made him an Assistant Secretary of the Department of the Interior, had come to depend on Jackson for briefings regarding the issue. Jackson knew more about the pertinent laws than probably anyone else except the Hopi lawyers. Swimmer asked him to draft another Memorandum of Understanding, one that suited Swimmer's plans. Jackson's version of the memorandum was subtly crafted, and the meat of it rested in the definitions of terms. Innocuous-seeming enough, what it did was bring Assistant Secretary Swimmer into the planning process without stating it as such. They believed it was essential that the BIA should have control over the planning. Without a role in the planning, the BIA would be forced simply to build houses at the Commission's direction.

The memorandum was delivered to Fred Craft a week later, on February 4, 1986, the day Sidney Yates called the Commission to Washington for an early and unusually thorough budget hearing.

Sidney Yates had been appropriating money to the Relocation Commission for twelve years. In 1986, as a result of the volume of mail he had received from supporters of the Big Mountain Legal Defense/Offense organization all over the world, calling for repeal of the law and an end to relocation, as well as the negative reports about the program's results, he had decided to get tough. He said about the Commission, "Here we are, twelve years after the fact, and they still haven't been able to put anything into shape. Twelve years into the future, they still won't know what to do with it." He said he had scheduled a meeting early, before the usual spring round of budget hearings, "because I want to find out what the hell they're doing. I have a feeling that what they're going to do in view of the deadline and in view of Goldwater's pressure . . . is move them into one of these housing communities.

"I'd like to get out of [the relocation program], but Congress is apparently committed to going through with it. The problem I have is Goldwater."

The senior senator from Arizona apparently was also having second thoughts about the program, although for the most part he was keeping those thoughts to himself. He did, however, break his code of silence on the issue (a position he maintained throughout the last year of his term) to speak to a reporter for CBS's "West 57th Street" during the third week of January 1986. Researcher Ty West says that Goldwater told him that in hindsight relocation had been a mistake. Yet Goldwater went on to say that he was still adamant about meeting the July 6 deadline. When reminded by West that that was a practical impossibility and that the appropriations language forbade removal of Navajos until they had houses to live in, Goldwater seemed confused. West says, "Goldwater was very cavalier. In effect, he said, 'Yeah, I fucked up in 1974, so what?' " When asked about the terrible cost of the program, Goldwater replied, "Money? That's nothing compared to what we waste around here." West says, "I kind of admired the guy for his honesty, but then I thought about how horrifying his statement was and what it meant [to the people out there]."

When West told Yates of the conversation (the segment on the land dispute was never aired), Yates observed, "The whole thing is just kind of a monstrosity that's been built up and they [Goldwater and Udall] don't know how to get out of it now. And we, who are trying to find some way to get out of it, haven't got the cooperation of the Commission because the Commission doesn't know what the hell it wants to do." Yates felt that getting Swimmer involved was the only available path. "I told [Swimmer] I thought I was going to try to turn the whole thing over to him and get the Commission out of there."

Yates added, "There's a great question whether the legislation is working. We could terminate the Commission by cutting off funds, but that in itself would not satisfy the intent of Congress." The right thing to do would be well-nigh impossible. Nevertheless Yates said what was on his mind: "There ought to be a land switch here."

In February 1986, while Sidney Yates was trying to figure out how to get the business of moving people out of the Relocation Commission's hands, his colleague Arizona Representative Morris K. Udall was also rethinking relocation. Since 1974, Udall had maintained a consistent but quiet position in support of the Hopis. His mother, Louise, had been a very close friend of Abbott Sekaquaptewa's mother, Helen. Udall recalls in an interview, "I was close to my mother and dad and I'd go to Phoenix frequently as a student and a young lawyer and the Sekaquaptewa family was there periodically as well as other Hopis and Mother would repeat stories about the fights in and among the traditionalists and against the others, and the disputes with the Navajos."

On her deathbed, Louise asked her son to promise to side with the Hopis in the land dispute. This position was problematic for Udall, since most of his fellow liberals sided with the Navajos. "I always sympathized with the Hopis," Udall says about that time, "and got indignant when some of my bleeding-heart left-wing liberal [friends] who were always for the underdog went out and took sides with the Navajos against the great big oppressors, the little Hopi Tribe that was up there on the mesas behaving itself."

Because Udall took some heat for his position, he decided to maintain a low profile during the debate over the partition bill. He explains: "It was a no-win situation for me. . . . I recall I didn't take a great part in the debates but I was quietly there and working for a fair settlement. My feeling was, let's get it settled and I'm going to protect the Hopis if I can so they get a fair shake."

In 1974, with his mother's request in mind, he voted in favor of the passage of the Settlement Act. And in 1980, he bowed to the pressure of Anglo interests, and introduced amendments to the Settlement Act that prevented the Navajos from choosing the House Rock Valley–Paria Plateau land.

Over the years, as the bumblings of the Relocation Commission became grosser and of greater consequence, Udall had second thoughts about the wisdom of relocation. And when he saw the Senate Appropriations subcommittee report published in October 1985, with $88 million targeted for the Relocation Commission, almost four times its annual appropriation, he leapt to action. First, he fired off a letter to Sidney Yates. He was quite concerned that the Senate's intention was only to clear the land by July.

Moreover, Udall was no longer content to remain silent while Barry Goldwater controlled discussion of the issue. He was undergoing a change of heart. "Relocation, in hindsight," said Udall on February 4, 1986, as Yates prepared to grill the Relocation Commission, "may have been one of those good ideas that wasn't appropriate in an Indian setting. If I got ten thousand people together in Phoenix and I said, 'We're going to have to move you and we've got houses with plumbing in a subdivision outside of Flagstaff and Winslow,' I think most people would have gone along. But to tell Navajos who are attached to the land 'You've got to go to Flagstaff and settle down in a white man's subdivision,' it wasn't as easy as some thought. I thought there would be more integration into the remaining Navajo villages and areas rather than sending them off to other little cities, ghettoes in Flagstaff, and so on. Relocation at best is a difficult thing, but dealing with these people and their sensitivities was tougher than I thought."

After inquiring about the appropriations bill, Udall's next move was to contact Representative John McCain and discuss how they might approach Goldwater about rethinking the law. Both agreed that any attempts to change the law without Goldwater's support would fail. Said McCain in an interview, "The problem is, the key to it is Barry Goldwater. If Barry Goldwater doesn't want a piece of legislation going through the U.S. Senate, I promise you, Barry Goldwater can keep a piece of legislation from going through the U.S. Senate. He's just too powerful."

John McCain wasn't about to cross Goldwater, because he was preparing to run for the Senate seat Goldwater was vacating at the end of the year, and had received his blessing. At the same time, McCain felt he might have some influence over the senior senator. "[It would take] Mo and me together. Mo couldn't [sway him] by himself and I couldn't by myself. The reason why I have the leverage is because Barry views me as his successor. He's my honorary campaign chairman, and I have no primary opposition." But McCain was skeptical about their chances for success: "Whether Mo and I together [will be successful] is not clear to me. Part of it has to do with his staff and the other part of it has to do with the fact that he thinks the issue is simple. He thinks it's just Big Mountain. It's not just Big Mountain, it's a whole lot of other places, like Teesto and Coal Mine Mesa."

But McCain felt that he and Udall had to try something. "I have every reason to believe that the long and close relationship those two guys have had [Udall and Goldwater] will indicate that there's a possibility or a probability that Mo and I can sit down with him and talk sense. I think we can do that. If we can't, then God only knows what's going to happen."

Udall agreed that Goldwater could keep any legislation from moving through the Senate if he wanted to. Said Udall, "Here's a very popular man who's in his last year as U.S. senator. He knows the Club. The Republicans control it, it's his pet baby in his home state and I can't see the old guy up there running a filibuster and his friends trying to cut him off over some goddamn Indian dispute that no one takes the time to get into."

Over the Christmas holidays, the Udalls had had a family discussion about the Navajo-Hopi problem. They felt prodded by the increasing media attention brought to bear on relocation, and a desire to help Peterson Zah win his reelection battle against Peter MacDonald. Also, Mo was thinking about his upcoming election, and Stewart, the former U.S. representative and Interior Secretary, had some thoughts about reviving his own political career. And Navajo-Hopi was sure to become a volatile campaign issue. Stewart had also played a minor role in facilitating the Morris-Clark venture and felt an investment in its continuation.

Mo Udall had also become very fond of Peterson Zah, the soft-spoken Navajo leader. "Peterson Zah is a prince of a guy," he says. "You need an Anwar Sadat to go to the other side and say, 'We've had enough killing, let's talk.' He told me he didn't want his kids fighting the same fight thirty to forty years from now. So he wanted a two-year extension [of the deadline] to try to work something out. And it appeared to me not to be the way to go. But the more I studied his position, the more I came to the conclusion it might be possible to craft a different type of approach."

Udall let Zah know he was prepared to discuss his ideas. In the fall of 1985, Zah returned to him with a plan for land exchanges that would reduce the number of Navajos who had to be relocated. Zah and his advisers had begun conceiving the plan during the Morris-Clark mission. Zah offered Udall not just a proposal for reducing the number of relocations, he offered a comprehensive settlement of the tribes' disputes, much like what Richard Morris had wanted to achieve. It proposed to settle the 1934 area litigation as well as the handful of related claims the Hopis had brought against the Navajos and the U.S. government for damages and adjustments resulting from partition and their loss of use of the HPL. The Hopis' suits requested damages of up to $100 million.

The Navajos offered to give the Hopis 79,000 acres in the form of a corridor from the mesas to Moencopi—finally connecting that outlying Hopi village, which had been left out of the 1882 area reservation, with the rest of the Hopi reservation—to settle the 1934 area case. In the 1882 area, large chunks of the HPL would be returned to the Navajos to reduce the number of families to be relocated, and the Hopis would receive the New Lands near Sanders—350,000 acres of ranch land.

Udall and his staff assistant for Indian Affairs, Frank Ducheneaux, examined the proposal. They accepted its terms and added one item. The Navajos would give the Hopis $300 million in royalties over the next hundred years from the tribe's Black Mesa mine and also from the future proceeds of the Paragon Ranch (an undeveloped coal-rich 35,000-acre tract in New Mexico, chosen as part of the New Lands the Navajos were authorized to acquire by the 1980 amendments), where the Navajos had planned to build a mine. In all, the Hopis would be giving up 350,000 acres of HPL land, and receiving 350,000 acres of the New Lands plus the 80,000-acre corridor to Moencopi. On top of that was the $300 million cash settlement. A deal generous enough, Udall thought, that the Hopis might go for it.

Said Udall, "The 1974 act was premised on relocation. That was the way we were going to resolve it—everything else was secondary, but relocation was the way to go. The Navajos were going to have more land and we were giving them great chunks of public land and the where-withal to buy some ranches. This bill suggests that we abandon that approach and we stop relocation to a large degree. There'd still be some of it that would have to go on. Stop relocation and give the Hopis a big set of goodies to compensate them for the land they would lose, so they'd end up with land and with money and there'd be a big economic package. We would take care of three to four hundred families that way—most of the remaining people on the JUA would be able to stay there. The boundaries of the reservation would be redrawn to include that as Navajo, not Hopi."

As Udall and McCain waited for a sign from Goldwater that he wouldn't work to kill the bill, the two Arizona representatives, Udall and McCain, met on February 4, 1986, with the Hopi and Navajo tribal chairmen, Ivan Sidney and Peterson Zah, in a closed-door session.

Ivan Sidney "was indignant and said no. And that was about the end of that," reported Udall just after the meeting. John McCain recalled, "Ivan went around saying, 'It's a done deal.' And I said to him, 'What's a done deal?' And he said, 'The proposal of Mo's.' And I kept saying to him, 'It's not a done deal. You got a better idea? Have you got an input to make? You've got a proposal to try to make this situation better? Then tell us, give us your input.' But he didn't have any. He just said, 'Nope, I'm not going to do it and that's it.' He said, 'I guess maybe I shouldn't have come here.' "

Udall says that Sidney seemed to be under great pressure. Udall feels that he wanted to be able to step forward and participate in a historic compromise, but that forces at home prevented him from doing so. Said Udall, "He implied to me that he recognizes the realities and would like to be a leader, but that the traditionalists on the Council have a veto and the elders won't let him do this and they won't recognize anybody's title but their own." Who the traditionalists were on the Council was unclear, because the so-called traditionalists have always boycotted the Council. It is possible that Sidney used the term to ward off further inquiry, because Anglos are loath to question the legitimacy of the views of Indian "elders" or "traditionals." The words have been used by both sides to at once clarify and obscure the issue. For example, Ivan Sidney didn't recognize Roberta Blackgoat as an elder because she had no religious position or authority. Thomas Banyacya does not recognize the authority of Ebin Leslie, a Hopi from First Mesa whom Sidney presents as a Kikmongwi, when he brings Leslie with him to Washington—for example, to Yates's hearing. And Ivan Sidney does not recognize Banyacya as a leader or spokesman, but sees him as a Hopi with a personal agenda. Indians have come to arguing about who is the more legitimate Indian.

McCain surmised that Sidney's determination not to negotiate was the result of his recent bad loss to Abbott Sekaquaptewa in the Hopi primary. (Sidney eked out a victory in the November 20, 1985, general election by forty votes.) McCain thinks that Sidney visited the villages trying to find out why he had done so badly and he was told, as McCain put it, " 'You're getting in bed with Peterson Zah and you aren't standing up for us Hopis.' " George Vlassis, the former Navajo counsel, thought the problem was that Sidney simply couldn't command the respect—or fear—his predecessor, Sekaquaptewa, did. Said he, "Ivan stepped into shoes much too big to fill." And he was not about to give away the store while in that position.

Udall observed that during the meeting, Sidney seemed unable to speak his own mind. "I couldn't fully fathom what pressures were on him, but Ivan said to Zah, or said to me for Zah's consumption, that he has to be tough and hard-boiled publicly. Particularly when Zah says anything about staying on the land, he'd have to hit back."

During the meeting, Sidney also threatened to take the law into his own hands if the government wasn't prepared to move the Navajos off by the deadline. Recalled Udall, "He made what Zah thought was a very arrogant statement that if the government wouldn't do it, he'd have the Hopi police evict those people." Later, privately, Sidney acknowledged that he didn't have any police who could do so. "He was doing this for show," said Udall. What Sidney proposed was to let the law run its course, and that after the deadline passed, "he would be very magnanimous. He implied all the Navajos had to do was lift sovereignty and sign a lease, a life estate or whatever."

Not only was Sidney responding to pressure from his constituency, he was also being pushed by John Paul Kennedy, the Hopi tribal lawyer. The influence of the Hopi lawyers on the Hopi chairman and Tribal Council had been an issue since John Boyden became the tribe's first general counsel. John Paul Kennedy is Boyden's son-in-law. By February, Udall and McCain had both voiced concern about the extent of Kennedy's influence. McCain felt that Sidney was being pressured by the attorneys not to agree to any comprehensive plan that would settle the outstanding suits, which the Udall-McCain bill proposed to do, because the lawyers stood to gain from protracted litigation. In a letter to Sidney dated January 22, 1986, even Barry Goldwater wrote, "I have had a hunch for a long time [the attorneys] are too intimately and intricately involved in your tribal decisions."

Hopi aide J. C. Smythe offered a different view of the Hopi lawyer: "John Paul Kennedy still treated Abbott as the chairman after Ivan was elected. . . . He was a very divisive force in Ivan's first term—pitted people against each other. . . . It was no longer an attorney-client relationship, it was parent-child. Kennedy thought he was part of the family. Hopis wanted to take on their own leadership, they didn't want the surrogate of Kennedy." Kennedy interfered in tribal politics and backed Sekaquaptewa in the election, even campaigned for him in the village of Moencopi. This infuriated Sidney, who eventually did take steps to sever the tribe's relationship with Kennedy. He refused to sign a new contract with him for services as general counsel. This prevented Kennedy from being paid on a fee schedule. The 1980 Amendments to the Settlement Act guaranteed that the government would pay the tribes' legal fees, up to certain limits, for litigation connected with the 1934 case, as well as any litigation associated with the 1882 case. Even though the government was paying Kennedy's fees and expenses for those cases, Sidney was holding up the government vouchers so Kennedy couldn't get paid for his work there, either. Eventually, Kennedy gave notice that he was withdrawing from all Hopi cases, and asked for $30 million in expenses and anticipated fees for the 1934 litigation. The pressure took its toll on Sidney. Says Vlassis, "He's a well-meaning guy who's been jerked around so many times he's being spoiled and will turn into a jackass, I'm afraid."

So Udall and McCain waited for Goldwater to make his move. "Goldwater is pretty cool on this sort of thing," said Udall on February 4. "He wants Ivan to give Big Mountain to the Navajos and he thinks everything will be all right. That's as far as he wants to go—then let the law take its course."

Goldwater had long maintained that he had special feelings for the people of Big Mountain. In a late January 1986 letter to Sidney, Goldwater roundly scolded him for his tough talk of threatening to use his own police to remove Navajos from their homes. Goldwater wrote,

I have just finished a conversation with Jack Casserly [an editorial writer at the *Arizona Republic* generally considered a mouthpiece for Goldwater] and I am going to put it to you in a straight, honest way.

I am shocked. I am shocked almost beyond my ability to express it to you.

Goldwater went on:

> If what I heard is true, and I have every reason to think it is true, you have been influenced to say that there will be no settlement of the Big Mountain issue when those people have lived up there for hundreds of years with your people and there has never been any problem.

Goldwater warned Sidney that he was asking for violence. The senator wrote that he had alerted the governor and the National Guard of Arizona.

> You cannot do this, Ivan. You cannot do it as a religious Hopi. You cannot do it as a religious American. You cannot do it for any moral, sane, or intelligent reason. If you want to lose the complete support of what you have in Congress, this is just about the best way I know of doing it.
>
> So, I implore you, once again, tell those Big Mountain people they can stay where they are because you are going to wind up having them whether you like it or not, and I would rather have you do it in a peaceful way than have you do it at the point of a gun. I don't know who gave you this advice. If it came from your attorneys, my next step would be to fire the attorneys.

Why Goldwater believed that the people of Big Mountain deserved to stay on the land more than any other Navajo on the HPL is unclear. They had been the most vocal opponents of relocation, however, and had developed an effective public information campaign. Goldwater told Udall that if Ivan would just agree with a Big Mountain swap, they'd "pull the teeth out of these radicals who come out and try to agitate, because they've made Big Mountain a symbol."

"Goldwater's erratic," admitted Udall. "His attention span isn't all that long anymore. He wants to deal broad-brush in blacks and whites, no shades of gray. If I got him to sit down long enough to try out this concept [of a comprehensive settlement], he might come around, I don't know. I've found that if I don't push him, I get further."

Udall told how he once managed to get Goldwater's ear: "We got the best wilderness bill in Arizona I ever thought we'd have . . . that was two years ago. I finally decided to take Barry head on and I asked for an appointment and said he and I were going to be here forever. I said, 'You are one of the few people who knew Arizona before Lake Powell and up to Rainbow Ridge when you were two, and one of the first hundred people to see that. Let's save a little chunk of wilderness.' He started yakking about World War II, the Udalls, the Goldwaters, and I kept trying to bring the thing back. And the bells rang and I thought, 'Oh, hell, we've lost this.' He said, 'Come on, walk with me, are you going back to the House?' I said yes, so we walked back to Senate chambers. I was trying to get in a word or two about my wilderness bill, the doors swung open for him to go to the chamber. He put his arm around me and said, 'I'm going to cosponsor your bill.' But if I had tried to use logic and reason to get him to sit down and go over the complexities of the bill, I'd never have gotten anywhere, but some bullshit and friendship. . . . I've thought if I could get this bill introduced and get everybody to focus on it, then maybe someday he'll come around. You never know."

Udall was discouraged that his attempts to get the tribes together to talk had proved so difficult: "I think it's like Northern Ireland where you'll never settle it. It pains me. After [Peterson Zah and Ivan Sidney] were elected, I remember the great good feeling between them. They married sisters or married cousins and went to school together and all this. . . . So different from the hostility now. Apparently you can't break through it, a wall of hostility so old and tight that you can't loosen it up."

For three weeks after his meeting with Peterson Zah and Ivan Sidney on February 4, Udall performed a shadow dance with Goldwater, trying to coax him toward a position that was, if not supportive, at least neutral toward the Udall-McCain bill. As Eric Eberhard, the director of the Navajos' Washington office, put it, "They're trying to flush him out."

Word from Goldwater's office was confused and contradictory. On February 4, Goldwater sent McCain a letter that began: "There are about five hundred things that run down between members of a delegation and 499 of them are, in effect, running around the end." Goldwater accused McCain of going behind his back in an attempt to win the Navajos' support for his Senate bid. "I was quite upset that you and Mo have been trying to solve this on your own when it is not even in your district." He also warned that something had to be done quickly, because "Peter MacDonald is running for Pete Zah's seat and the chances are very good he will win, and you can then forget about any progress that has ever been made in this whole matter." He didn't suggest what that solution might be, except that the law should be enforced. He concluded: "I hope you will get the gist of this letter. I have only ten months to go and I don't want to find things being done without my knowledge of them." The letter bewildered Udall and McCain, who had kept Goldwater informed of their every move.

Barry Goldwater had made no public statement about the bill. But on February 7, his aide Twinkle Thompson was quoted saying that Goldwater thought the bill was "a vehicle for discussion." The next day, Goldwater aide James Ferguson said, "He is adamantly against it."

Five days later, on February 13, J. J. Casserly published an editorial in the *Arizona Republic* declaring that Goldwater had rejected the Udall-McCain bill. Casserly quoted Goldwater saying, "I can't buy this . . . I'm not going to stand still for extending the deadline."

Then six days after that, on February 19, when contacted by the *Gallup Independent*, Twinkle Thompson read directly from Casserly's week-old editorial to answer the reporter's questions. And on February 21, Goldwater aide Earl Eisenhower said that Goldwater had rejected the bill, and would fight it if it was introduced. "It has no future," said Eisenhower. "It's time to clear up all these rumors. The July 6 deadline is still on."

Peterson Zah tried on three occasions in February to meet with Goldwater, twice in Washington and once in Phoenix, but was unsuccessful. "He is the key player," Zah said. "That is why we need to see him. I still like to believe he is a just man. If we can just explain our position to him, he will make a just decision."

A week later, Goldwater, or his aides, sent the Navajo Tribe a letter stating, "You may be assured that I am opposed to any extension of time on this hundred year dispute between the Navajo and Hopi." The Navajos wondered if Goldwater had ever seen the draft bill. Zah's press spokesman said, "Staff members are shielding us from the senator. We don't even know if he has studied it."

Udall told Ivan Sidney at the end of their February 4 meeting that he would not introduce the Udall-McCain bill until the beginning of March so that Sidney would have time to "initiate proposals" he felt were "important." However, during the third week of February, Sidney sent a telephone message to McCain stating that the Hopis opposed any change in the Navajo-Hopi Land Settlement Act. "Senator Goldwater has chosen the stand on principle and is doing what is right. We are in agreement with Senator Goldwater's opposition to any legislation. He is the greatest statesman Arizona has ever produced. He is the champion of Native American causes for the nation."

When McCain showed Ivan Sidney's message to Udall, they concluded that there was no longer any reason to hold up the introduction of the bill for Sidney's benefit. Neither Udall nor his aide Frank Ducheneaux wanted to force a solution on the Hopis. Yet they felt that some pressure was necessary to get the Hopis off dead center, and the introduction of the bill, they hoped, might provide the needed impetus.

Although Goldwater's public posturing suggested he was opposed to the bill, he had not informed either Udall or McCain of his position. According to Udall's press aide, Matt James, "He and Barry know what each other are doing on this. Barry told Mo to go ahead and do whatever he had to do." Udall and McCain still hoped that Goldwater would come around. McCain acknowledged that Goldwater "has told us that he is not happy with the proposal, but I don't think he's made up his mind about it yet."

On February 27, Udall introduced his bill "with extraordinarily little fanfare." In his comments before the House, he stated, "While it is clear that the Hopi Tribe has a legal entitlement to the lands partitioned to it under the 1974 act, it is also clear that the ten-year process of relocation has caused extreme hardship, trauma, and bitterness among the Navajo families that have relocated or are facing relocation." Udall suggested that the circumstances had changed sufficiently to warrant Congress to take a new look at the law. He noted that among those circumstances was the threat of forcible removal of Navajos from their homes and the "potential for violent confrontation." He also cited the escalating costs of relocation, whose final costs, approximately $300 million, might not be available because of "the severe budget constraints now in place." Udall noted that the "great pain and suffering caused by relocation" was also a reason for Congress to rethink the issue.

Udall told his colleagues that he did not feel his bill was the final word, but hoped it would "be the beginning of a process which may lead the Congress, the two tribes, and other concerned parties to an enlightened resolution of these very knotty problems associated with the land dispute." Udall said he thought the best solution would be one accomplished by the two tribes, but he noted he didn't think that would be possible without the presence of "some outside factor." In conclusion, he pointed out that the bill would extinguish five ancillary lawsuits brought by the Hopis against the Navajos that were then in federal court. He stated that although he felt his bill might "cause some unhappiness and disappointment in some quarters," he hoped it would lead to a proposal that would finally bring a conclusion to the divisive battle.

Unfortunately, Ross Swimmer had embarked on his own plan to improve the relocation effort. And his charge was to develop the New Lands. He was set on a collision course with the Navajo Tribe, which wanted the Udall-McCain bill to move forward. Not only did the tribe think it was the best solution to the problem, but movement on the bill could help Peterson Zah in his upcoming election battle with Peter MacDonald. Since every member of Zah's administration would have to look for work on a reservation with few jobs if MacDonald won, every member of the tribal administration was pushing for the Udall-McCain bill with all the energy and investment of a personal crusade.

(16)

Sandra Massetto's
Last Act

This was her last act, and Sandra Massetto knew it. In a couple of hours, she and the two other relocation commissioners would sign the Memorandum of Understanding, which would formalize the entrance of the Bureau of Indian Affairs into the relocation program. Because of Dan Jackson's clever wording of the memorandum, a cursory reading didn't reveal it as the first drumbeat of the Commission's funeral march. But Massetto knew that was precisely what it was. So did Fred Craft. Hawley Atkinson and Ralph Watkins hadn't a clue.

The memorandum placed the responsibility for planning in Swimmer's hands. This meant that the myriad decisions and details necessary to fashion a community out of empty rangeland—for people who would have few resources outside that community—would not be mangled by the Commission. It would still be a difficult challenge—creating a community for people who lived in the nineteenth century that has enough flexibility to grow into the twenty-first century.

Although Massetto supported the memorandum, she felt the warning signs of an impending loss. She had been deeply involved, both professionally and emotionally, in this problem for eight years. She wanted out, but it was hard to let go. She thought about the 2:30 a.m. wake-up, an affliction she shared with Dan Jackson, in which they sat bolt upright in bed, terror-stricken, thinking about what might have been happening out on the HPL, wondering what they had forgotten to do, who might have been hatching what plan.

As she dressed on the morning of February 25, 1986, everything seemed ironical to her. She brushed her short brown hair, recently overwhelmed with gray, pushed it into shape, and smudged eyeshadow onto her upper lids. She had been living at her parents' house for the past few months, stopping by her condominium only to feed the cats. As she looked around her place, she thought about changing it, making a break, starting again. "I'm tired, I want to get on with my life," she mumbled to herself. "I don't want to wake up every morning and step onto a roller coaster." She gave her hair a last nudge, then stepped into her champagne-colored Mercedes and drove off to Ralph Watkins's house for a breakfast meeting and the signing of the memorandum.

Watkins's huge Paradise Valley house was surrounded by a wooden fence. Massetto parked the car out front and walked up to the heavy wood door. She rang the bell. No answer. She rang again. No answer. She smiled to herself and felt the rise of hysteria she had come to expect when dealing with Atkinson and Watkins. She stepped away from the front door and walked to the garden gate. She had to reach way up to the latch set absurdly high in the gate. She felt like Alice in Wonderland quickly shrinking in size, as she squeaked with the effort of opening the gate. Suddenly the latch gave, the door swung open, and Massetto tumbled straight into a flower patch.

"So," she said, brushing herself off, as Watkins appeared anxiously at her side. "You were kind enough to invite me, but you wouldn't let me in." Even dour Swimmer chuckled at short, chubby Massetto struggling out of Watkins' garden plot; her joke gave them license. They had been sitting in the backyard—Fred Craft, Swimmer, Watkins, Atkinson, and Watkins's wife, Patty.

Breakfast was soon ready, and Watkins led his guests through the living room, where elephant and buffalo hooves were set into the plush carpet in a winding track to the dining room. Animal heads decorated the walls, as did several stuffed fish. Watkins guided Massetto through the maze of hooves, prompting her to crack, "I always knew you were quite a hoofer, Ralph," which elicited a laugh, but by now, everyone was getting a bit tense. Fred Craft had flown out from Washington for the day (at taxpayers' expense) to oversee the signing, and Mrs. Watkins had prepared a large ham, which she served with eggs and miniature bagels. "What are these?" Watkins asked, holding a bagel up in his fingers. "You know I don't like them." Massetto reached over and took one, thanking Patty. Atkinson looked grim. Somewhere in his scowling, refractory, sixty-nine-year-old countenance, Massetto felt, was a glimmer of understanding about the import of today's signing. Serving on this Commission for the past decade had formed the backbone of his political life and the largest part of his yearly income. Once Swimmer got authority to plan the New Lands, the Commission would no longer have control over the major decisions.

Over breakfast, attempts were made at chatter. Watkins spoke a bit about his bank in Sun City. A self-made millionaire who started out as a Chevrolet dealer and wore a gold Rolex watch, Watkins liked to find points of common interest between people. When he first met Swimmer at the Commission offices, he shook the hand of the man who had led the Cherokee Nation for twelve years and said in a drawl that sounded like J. R. Ewing of "Dallas," "Well, hello. You know, I'm part Cherokee too." Swimmer spoke briefly of the bank he had once owned in Tulsa, saying he had sold it and gotten out of banking just in time, before the oil market began to fall.

After the ham and eggs, the group followed the trail of hooves back to the living room. Swimmer reiterated what he had said at the Yates hearing, that he felt the work must begin with a survey of all the people left out on the land.

Massetto wanted to talk about the fast-approaching deadline. She reminded them that the term "eviction date" had been repeated so many times by the Hopi Tribe that it had taken on its own life. She suggested that in fact, the deadline was a legal fiction; the law stated only that the Relocation Commission should be finished with its job by that time, not that the Navajos were then legally required to leave their homes. She felt the Interior Department had to formulate a position about the deadline and inform both tribes. She believed they had a right to know if the government was prepared to evict them.

Fred Craft agreed that the deadline was simply a target completion date for the Commission. He told the group he also thought that some-one had to make clear to the tribes what would happen on July 7. There developed in the room a sudden sense of common purpose, an ease, a point on which all felt the same, and a shared concern for the Navajos who waited in terror.

But then Atkinson piped up. "I'm tired of hearing that the deadline doesn't exist," he said. "The Hopis won in the District Court, the deci-sion was affirmed in the Court of Appeals. The land belongs to the Hopis, and when are they going to gain possession? They have waited long enough."

"You are straying from the point," Massetto told him brusquely.

"You are trying to break my train of thought," he retorted. He fin-ished, no one responded, and Massetto asked for the agreement to be brought out.

They signed it with little discussion. Swimmer wanted to discuss one more crucial point. He had learned from Dick Ivey, project manager of the engineering firm, CH2M Hill, that Commission assistant director Mike McAlister had used his position to try to control the technical con-tracts and in so doing had severely hampered progress. Swimmer wanted the engineering and planning contracts to be controlled by the BIA. Atkinson objected. Fred Craft told Atkinson it was an insignificant point, and they should go along with Swimmer's request. Craft under-stood that they must work with Swimmer. Craft also knew that as they spoke, Yates's staff was investigating his own activities, particularly charges that he had been paid government funds for lobbying activities.

He wanted no trouble with Swimmer. The Commission had to work with him because as the implications of the memorandum emerged, it was clear that the Commission still had significant responsibilities in relocating people. The BIA would develop the New Lands and settle on it those three hundred or so families living on the HPL—mostly traditional families who had livestock. The Commission was still responsible for building houses for twelve hundred families who had moved off the HPL and were still waiting, some for as many as twelve years, for replacement houses. The Commission didn't know where most of them lived. The Commission would build them houses in border towns, or on homesite leases (if they could secure them) near relatives on the Navajo reservation. At that point, no one knew if they would be allowed to go to the New Lands, which weren't big enough for all the relocatees. This would be an area over which there would be difficult coordination between the two agencies. Many of the older Navajos who were still on the HPL likely would not move to the New Lands without their children. In many cases, their children were among the so-called twelve hundred. Swimmer would have to develop a policy on whether the family members would be able to get houses near their parents. And then, the question remained, who would build them, the Commission or the BIA? Such were some of the complications of the biggest federal housing program in the country.

Toward the end of the meeting, it became clear to Atkinson and Watkins that Swimmer and Massetto seemed to be saying the same things and communicating on the same level. As they walked toward the front door, everyone was thinking of who would drive Swimmer back to his hotel. When it seemed that Swimmer might actually leave with Massetto, Watkins playfully threw his body against the great wooden door, blockading it with outstretched arms. He roared, "I'll drive you." They all stood in shocked silence beneath the ferocious claws of a great stuffed brown bear. Then Atkinson drawled, "Well, I drove him down here." Right on the beat, Massetto said, as she might have expected the Mad Hatter or the Queen of Hearts to rejoin, "But I want to drive him home."

Swimmer was aghast. He asked Massetto if she would take him to his hotel. They said their good-byes and walked to the champagne Mercedes.

(17)

Ross Swimmer Travels
to the HPL

Dennis Bedonie sits on the living room floor of his and Ella's campus apartment in Flagstaff. He is completely absorbed by a huge map of the 1882 area, which is spread across his knees. He is also examining a copy of the Udall-McCain bill, and he is trying to decipher from the descriptions in the bill which pieces of HPL land would be returned to the Navajos. When he is able to identify a square on the map from the written quadrant locations in the bill, he colors it in with light blue pencil. He is coloring in boxes all around Coal Mine Mesa, trying to find out whether his in-laws' place would be spared under the proposed law. But every time he matches the quadrant locations with the grid on the map, he gets a different answer about the Hatathlie house.

Ella is not examining the map. She doesn't want to get her hopes up. She has different plans today. Lee Phillips told her that Assistant Secretary Swimmer is headed up to the HPL to visit some families and to begin to learn about the land dispute. Swimmer plans to spend the night at the Hopi Cultural Center. Ella decides to spend the night there as well, in hopes that she will have a chance to talk to Swimmer herself.

As Ella steps out the door to go, Dennis is mumbling to himself, engrossed in the notations, thinking that at this point the house would be saved. Ella says to him, "Why are you so worried about the boxes? We'll be in no matter if we're in or out." Dennis is a bit more skeptical. Having spent most of his life in border towns, he is less Navajo-minded than she. He says to Ella with a tip of his head and an understanding smile, "Sometimes I think you depend a little too much on your faith."

Ella drives over to the elementary school a few blocks from the apartment. Nell is playing with some other children on swings in a playground beside the large stone schoolhouse that both she and Buzz attend. Nell sees her mother and runs over, her pink snow jacket flapping. Buzz stands alone; when he sees the truck, he walks slowly over. Ella asks him if he would like to go up to Hopi. Buzz scowls and says, "I'll go up to Hopi after they give the land back to my grandma."

As she heads north to the reservations, Ella says that her father helps out her brothers and sisters financially. She speaks with a mixture of jealousy that he doesn't give her money and pride that he feels she doesn't need it. In the traditional Navajo way, if an individual needs something—food, shelter, a blanket, money for a ceremony—and asks a relative for help, the relative is obligated to do what he or she can. There is no shame attached to asking for help. However, Ella's Anglo and Mormon teaching has introduced her to the world of self-sufficiency. She often feels torn between the two value systems. She accepts school clothing from the tribe for her children, but will criticize its quality and pooh-pooh the program, implying it is only for poor people. She criticizes the quality of food in the government's commodity program, which distributes cheese, canned meat, and vegetables to Indians, but she accepts the food anyway. She gives it to her mother who feeds it to the goats. She resents accepting handouts from the government, but her tuition is paid for by a tribal scholarship, which also provides her with a living stipend and access to student housing.

"My dad told me that the reason he [helps her brothers and sisters out financially] is that they're not ready to take care of themselves and they don't have any way of making money. He said he wanted me to be an example to them, that I've always managed to provide for my family without any financial assistance from them. And I've always been able to make it on my own because of my weaving and my beadwork and things that I know how to do that I can sell.

"He told me I have more than my brothers and my sisters because my grandmother passed some medicine bundles down to us and my mother has some medicine bundles that she had that I have now and they had other medicine men come to our house and had some medicine bundles made for me and my children.

"He told me that those were more valuable than things that money can buy. And also some of the traditions that have been in the family for a very long time, my parents gave to me because they think that I can take care of them, that I can carry those things on. And the moccasins that my great-grandmother used to have. Those were given to me by my mother and I'm supposed to pass them on to my little one, Nell.

"My dad said those things I got from my grandmother, the songs that she gave me, the things that I really need in life—I guess more or less how to survive in this life—those were more valuable than what he was giving his other children, which was just money."

Ella's grandmother had a large role in telling Ella the old stories and instructing her in the ways of Navajo women. Ella recalls, "My grandma used to talk to me. Sometimes I'd fall asleep and she'd talk on and on.

She'd take me out and tell me about the stars—if the moon was at a certain place, the women are supposed to have their babies, or women are supposed to have their period. I guess everything that Navajos did, they did according to the stars. Before she died, I spent several nights with her and I asked her about things I'd forgotten. I told her one night about the observatory [on campus at Northern Arizona University], and she said a lot of things people are just now discovering, we had it before. We've always had it.

"She planted according to the stars, she had sings and made offerings according to the stars. Certain times when the sheep were having babies she'd say when they would come by the stars. When I was carrying my babies she'd tell me I'd have them at a certain time according to the moon and I better start preparing.

"She said there were certain times when certain stars were in a certain place, when the Big Dipper was in a certain place, you should not have sex with your husband, she used to tell me. Just before she died she told me the stars, the whole solar system, seems like it had shifted, that the world is going to shift, is going to turn. She says there are a lot of things that were predicted that today are happening. She said one time in our legends, the world was turning in the opposite way. She said it's happening again. Even the stars aren't in their right places. The earth is going to shake a lot and there's a lot of things going to happen with the water. When she tells me these things, I tell her about the news, what's been happening in different places, and she says everything's happening because the people are lost."

Ella's grandma had certain idiosyncrasies. "When I used to take my kids over there," she recalls, "she would look in her big suitcase, she'd look in her boxes and flour sacks searching for things, all the time she'd be talking to herself saying, 'I know I bought some and I put it in this bag.' She'd be looking in there and she'd say, 'Maybe my other grandkids came and were digging in my stuff,' and [finally] she'd bring out her Saltine crackers and open up her fruit can—a can of fruit. She'd open them up and give them to the kids to eat. When we were leaving, she'd always give us another box and several cans of fruit to take along for the kids to eat, peaches or apricots or pears.

"She used to always tell us we should have something for the kids to eat because you never know when you might break down somewhere in the middle of nowhere and the kids wouldn't have anything to eat." Ella laughs, a bright tinkling of notes, a shy, happy appreciation of her grandmother.

"She used to say, when you go to the store, buy these kind because the cans open easily. She always carried a pop opener too, in her purse. She used a pop opener, she'd just make holes in it and pop it out. She couldn't see too well and she'd always feel you. Buzz was always real bony and she'd feel him and say, 'You probably fed him too much white man's food.' She said if you feed your kids that food they'll never get fat. She used to tell me Buzz needed to eat more mutton. She said when you have fat on your bones you were healthy. She said men like fat ladies. But she was never fat. She was on the slim side."

Talking about her grandma makes Ella feel serious about the land and what it means to her. "If you're brought up in a traditional family, you're taught that the land is going to be your mother for life, that she provides for you, she takes care of you, she's the one that lays out the lesson plan daily so you can learn from her. If you go and accept money for her, it's like accepting money for your own mother. Relocating is like selling out on a people, selling out on your people, running out on your people. Giving up."

Ella says, "I go to a lot of peyote meetings and I go to a lot of ceremonies for the land. I see the old people there, they sit in there and they cry. And it seems like if I ever went around and just accepted money for it, I would be sort of like giving up on them and giving up on what they believed in. It would be like I never witnessed their crying for the land. It would just be like turning my back on them.

"Some people say they were forced to leave the land. I think with an education you can make a living almost anywhere. Especially if you're married to a family where they don't have a land dispute and you can always move over there, but not accept money for the land that you've been chased off of.

"That's just like giving up your way of life, selling your way of life, selling your religion, selling everything that you believe in, the things your parents taught you. It's like selling it all and turning around and accepting the white man's way. Accepting his bribe, which comes in the form of money. I think even white people will put their mothers or their sisters on the streets just to get some money.

"I relate to it that way, selling my own mother, so I don't think I would ever accept money, because I know I can make it in the white man's world. And I know I can always keep my traditional teachings even though my children will be brought up in a white man's environment. I know they can make it. But those old people. You go to meetings, all they talk about is how their relationship is with the land and they have a lot of faith in that piece of land that they were raised on.

"The way I look at it, all the relocatee families I know, it seems they have given up something that's very special to them. Most all of them have lost life in their family.

"I think about that a lot. It scares me. Sometimes I think I should just relocate, because it's going to take me years to pay for a house. I should just go, but then I think of that. What good am I if I want to teach Navajo culture and I turn around and accept money for my way of life and the teachings that were handed down to me?

"I would be giving up, living like a white person in the dominant society. It's hard living in the Anglo world and trying to keep your cultural identity. It's really hard.

"I want the things that I was raised with, I want my kids to have those kinds of things, and I don't intend to keep my kids in the city, trying to make them little white kids."

Ella is not only afraid of retribution from the gods, of feeling she has betrayed her own people, and taken away her children's identity, she also fears what might happen to herself and her family if she were to move permanently from the reservation. She says that she had never heard of a Hopi or a Navajo going senile—until the people were forced off their land. She fears senility is caused by separation from what is most important. She says, "I went to a mental home in Phoenix where I did some volunteer work. The Indian people I saw were retarded or handicapped. None were senile. It was the white people who were senile."

Ella sees that leaving the land makes people lose their minds. "Four years ago," she says, "my grandmother passed away. I still remember her during my wedding when she came and brought bread and things like that. I never thought she would get into a condition, but it seems slowly she started losing herself. She talked mostly of sheep, the land. A lot of times, people go to chapter meetings and talk about the land dispute. She never wanted to go where people were talking about the land dispute, about the Hopis taking the land. She used to cry all the time. As the months went by she started going down, but she talked continuously even though she wasn't aware of where she was or what she was doing. She had to be taken care of all the time. If you put her in a sitting position, she'd keep talking about the land, being out herding sheep in the Big Mountain area, where her people were from.

"Just recently, we lost my grandfather too. He was over eighty. He got like that last summer, he started losing himself. He just talked about the land dispute all the time. He worried more about what would happen to his grandkids, that they would have no land to pass on; he worried about the kids not having enough to eat because the sheep would be gone. He worried about the kids not being able to learn how to herd sheep, how to take care of horses. He was very good at tanning hides. He would get hides that other people butchered during the winter or he would trade with the Hopis. He would cut them in strips and make horse whips or horse bridles and ropes. He would trade these with the Hopi people.

"He worried that his kids wouldn't be able to learn this kind of trade and keep it within the family because it was really sought after—those kinds of things. He was really worried about that."

. . .

Ella arrives at Hopi in the late afternoon. She drives past Oraibi and sees the sign asking visitors to park and register with the village leader, Stanley Bahnimptewa. Ella knew Stanley many years ago, when she was in Mormon placement in California. Stanley was a Mormon then. "He felt the Mormon Church was the true church," says Ella. "When he used to bear his testimony, he said he realized that what he'd been brought up with was the ways of Satan. Now, he talks about his Hopi ways. I don't think he even remembers about his Mormon teachings."

She turns into the Hopi Cultural Center and sees that the parking area is crowded. Ella apparently is not the only person driving up to Hopi in the hopes of bending Swimmer's ear. The cultural center is filled with individuals trying to pitch their cause, advance their franchise to the new man in charge. Dick Ivey, project manager of the Commission's planning and engineering firm, CH2M Hill, is one. He has suffered through years of dealing with the Commission and is excited at the prospect of actually building good houses in well-planned areas under a leader who understands the issues, a man like Swimmer. He wants to convince Swimmer to keep using his firm, though he knows that Hawley Atkinson wants him gone. Dan Jackson called Ivey the day before, and told him to get up to Hopi because the Assistant Secretary wanted to meet with him.

Ivey, a well-spoken, cultured man, pulls into the parking lot of the attractive pueblo-style cultural center about seven p.m., checks into a simple double room with green floral bedspreads and a broken black and white television, and washes up. He walks from his room to the restaurant, admires the brilliant stars and the sweet dry smell of creosote bushes in the crisp air and enters the restaurant, where he meets Jim Stevens, director of the BIA Phoenix area office. Stevens is waiting for Swimmer to return from his day out on the land.

Ivan Sidney is also waiting, sitting impatiently on the ivory cotton couch just inside the doors. "Ivan was giving Stevens the business," recalls Ivey, "that this was goddamn *his* reservation and what was Swimmer coming out here and spending time with the Navajos for and not telling him what he was doing. He was really mad. He said, 'This is my reservation.' " Ivey says, "Ivan was really pissed. He wouldn't look at me. I know Ivan pretty well and he wouldn't even speak to me."

At about 7:30 Swimmer arrives at the restaurant wearing a golf shirt and jeans. He looks tired and a bit bewildered. His light complexion and small features make him look more like one of the tourists frequenting the restaurant than one of the Indians. He tells a throng of reporters who meet him at the door that he doesn't want to say anything on the record, that this is a "learning experience" for him. He says he isn't ready to come to any conclusions, he is just looking and listening.

A small crisis is waiting to happen as Swimmer tries to make his way to the dining room. The waitresses and cooks, used to closing up promptly on schedule, have to be convinced to stay in the restaurant to serve the Assistant Secretary, the press corps, the BIA officials, Navajo tribal officials, and Hopis waiting to see and hear what happened today. Alf Secakuku, BIA superintendent for Hopi, walks into the kitchen to try to convince the cooks to remain at their stations. Alf's brother is a part-owner of the restaurant, yet it requires plenty of cajoling from Secakuku to persuade the workers to stay.

As soon as it is clear that food will be provided for the unusual array of guests, BIA director Stevens arranges for Dick Ivey to sit with Seca-kuku, Ray Smith, who oversees livestock on the HPL for the BIA, and Kathy Helmer, Swimmer's assistant. It is believed, largely through lob-bying by Sandra Massetto, that Ivey's firm should have a prominent role in planning the New Lands. The other commissioners, loath as they are to plan a complete community, dislike the firm, which has come out as a strong advocate for the relocatees. Atkinson, in particular, can't abide Ivey. Atkinson calls him "intellectually arrogant."

Stevens asks Ivan Sidney if he wants to have dinner with Swimmer and himself or meet with Swimmer alone. Sidney says, "I want to meet with Swimmer alone and tell him what I think of him."

Percy Deal, president of Hardrock chapter which Swimmer and en-tourage visited today, eats with Navajo Attorney General Claudeen Bates-Arthur and Peggy Scott, a Navajo married to a Hopi man, and the newly appointed head of the Navajo Land Dispute Commission. They order mutton stew and fry bread. They sit in a booth and carefully watch the goings-on. Later in the evening, Percy finds Ella and recounts the day's activities.

Percy says that a large contingent of people drove out on the land with Swimmer. There was Claudeen and Peggy Scott and himself for the Navajos, then Swimmer, Kathy Helmer, and Ray Smith for the BIA, and three other Hopis with Don Ami, head of the Hopi Department of Eco-nomic and Natural Resources. On top of that was a clerk from the Keams Canyon BIA office, who served as interpreter.

The day had started off badly for the Navajos. They had expected to take Swimmer around themselves, a comfortable number of people in one or two vehicles visiting in a not too obtrusive way with the families. But that was not to be. Peggy, Percy, and Claudeen waited in the parking lot of the cultural center from noon until 2:30 p.m. when the BIA contin-gent finally showed up. The Navajos joked that they would sit under the tree and maybe Ivan would come by. They were echoing Pete Zah's current joke about the period of great good hopes after his and Ivan's election, that he went out and sat under the tree by himself, and that Ivan never came to sit with him.

"Just when we were about to leave with Swimmer," says Percy, "Don

Ami came up with three Hopis. Ivan said, 'You've got four Navajos, it's only fair that we have four Hopis.' Claudeen told him she thought that was totally unnecessary. Ivan offered to withdraw his four if they withdrew theirs. So they all went.

"Apparently, Ray Smith had a list of families," says Percy. "I think what Smith had in mind was that the families he'd chosen would say they were willing to go if the planning was adequate. It worked with the first family. After the first family, the BIA and the Hopis were really smiling."

But the second family offered some resistance, and the third, the Clinton family of Teesto, "was really harsh." "We don't trust you," they told Swimmer, according to Percy. They said they had eight kids. Three had relocated, but they weren't any better off and were all having problems. The children came home constantly and the parents had to keep supporting them. "If things don't improve," said the mother, "we don't see any reason why the other five should relocate." They followed Swimmer out to the vehicles as he departed, saying, "You're not the first person to come out from Washington and promise us things. We don't trust Washington. We're not going to relocate."

By this time, the Navajo interpreter was having some difficulty. She had trouble understanding the Navajo of the people on the HPL, and at one point, asked Peggy Scott to help her, saying she didn't understand the issues. According to Deal, by the time the party had reached the Clintons, the family members themselves announced she was not interpreting properly. So Peggy and Claudeen took turns interpreting. By the time they had reached the fourth family, the interpreter had backed off completely. The BIA officials, irritated that the clerk had been intimidated by the Navajo tribal officials who questioned her competence, were also uncomfortable having such political Navajos interpreting; they wondered if Peggy and Claudeen were unduly coloring the words they translated.

Percy realized what was happening, and regretted it deeply. The Navajos had wanted to do everything to avoid just this situation—Swimmer feeling suspicious of them. The Navajos' first sign that this might happen had come two days ago, when the Navajo Washington office learned that Swimmer would not go out to see families that Percy had chosen. Originally, Percy had thought he'd take Swimmer around himself, as he had shown Richard Morris the HPL. The Navajos learned that Swimmer would use an interpreter from the BIA area office and visit families identified by Ray Smith, whom the Navajos knew as the Anglo with the baseball cap who drives out and counts their sheep and tells them to conform to stock regulations.

This was a bad omen for the Navajos. The Zah administration had worked hard to undo the tribe's reputation as aggressive, untrustworthy, and manipulative, a reputation that was in large measure the result of the techniques used by Peter MacDonald, who had been known to bring an entourage of his own medicine men into meetings with government officials. Says Eric Eberhard, head of the Navajo Washington office, "It will take a few more years to change the perception generated over twenty years with MacDonald and [MacDonald's predecessor Raymond] Nakai that Navajos are dirty, greedy, land-grabbing, unreliable people."

For their part, the Navajo leadership in Window Rock feared that Ray Smith would take Swimmer only to families who wanted to relocate. They were afraid that what had promised to be a courageous and important trip by Swimmer to examine life on the HPL could turn out to be a charade. The Navajo Tribe was convinced that if Swimmer visited a Navajo family determined to stay on the HPL, really listened to them and thought about their lives, he would be convinced that relocation was wrong, and he might slow down his plans long enough to allow the Udall-McCain bill a chance.

The Reagan administration, however, was apparently cool on the Udall-McCain bill. And BIA officials had gotten the word that Swimmer "wanted this project." Not only did the chance of turning around a bad program appeal to him, but also, his boss, Interior Secretary Donald Hodel, apparently was quite upset with an Inspector General's investigation of the Commission's procedures, which, among other problems, revealed deficiencies in the Commission's procurement of goods and services.

Percy tells Ella he's still hopeful, that he believes Swimmer will see. And there's always tomorrow, when Swimmer will go out again.

The next morning, breakfast at the Hopi Cultural Center is an exercise in frantic maneuvering. The object is to press the flesh with the Assistant Secretary. Dick Ivey breakfasts with Swimmer, then gets up to speak to Peggy, Percy, and Claudeen. Ivan is standing sentinel by the door with Pat Dallas. After certain members of the press make contact with Swimmer and Helmer, Ivan loses his cool and orders the entire press corps off the Hopi reservation.

As Dick Ivey leaves the restaurant, he meets Ivan by the door. "Ivan told me that he had thrown out the press. Ivan was very pleased with himself. He asked me what I was doing there. I said I'd been asked to come up and meet with the Secretary. That sort of made him stop and think and he turned nice. And he said, 'No one will talk to me. The Secretary comes to my reservation and he goes off with the Navajos.' He said, 'Will you talk to me? Tell me what's going on?' He was like a little boy."

Swimmer heads back to his room at the motel before leaving for the HPL. Ella and he cross paths in the courtyard. She hesitates for a moment, then, Nell by her side, walks up to Swimmer and stops him. "I don't plan on relocating and I don't plan on advocating relocation," she says. Swimmer looks at her with a pained expression and says, "Well, you're going to have the kind of house that you want, the kind of house that you want built for you is the kind of house you're going to have."

Ella retorts, "The houses are already falling apart, what about that, and there's never been any response from the Relocation Commission. I think we've been promised too many things. Why is it that bureaucrats from Washington come down here and think that they can do something in two or three days? Why don't you try living with us, living among us and find out what it's like?"

Swimmer replies that the New Lands are very nice, that he's visited them. "The land can give you a good life," he tells her. "You can have your sheep again and your livestock again. You can continue your life as it is." This doesn't satisfy Ella. She asks him what the Hopis had said to him, are they going to move onto the land, or is it just going to be for cattle? He tells her that it may be true that they will graze cattle, but the Hopis have a right to make some type of a living.

Ella says, "You're taking a bunch of cattle over human life, you're willing to sacrifice human lives over a bunch of cattle."

"I'm not saying that," he replies. "The land doesn't belong to the Navajos. It belongs to the Hopis. The Navajos keep encroaching on them. And now they outnumber the Hopis."

Swimmer tells her the Udall-McCain bill isn't going anywhere—it won't even get out of the House of Representatives.

Ella says, "I want to ask you to think about it for several days. I hope you support the McCain bill because I think it is the only solution to this whole thing. Or else, come July 7, I don't know what's going to happen."

Ella goes on. "You've given a death sentence to my family, especially my mother. My mother has no plans after July 7. She feels her life is going to end on that date. I think you should look at both sides, our side and the Hopi side. Are you willing to let this land go for cattle and let human beings suffer and human beings die because of this land dispute? I know you have a hard choice, but I want you think about it, taking human lives over cattle."

Swimmer replies, "I never heard it put that way, but I'll think about it." Swimmer asks her where she is from. She says she is from Flagstaff, that she is a student there. "I know how to live in both worlds," she tells him, "but I don't intend to let my children go into the Anglo world." He tells her he isn't asking her to do that. She says, "No, you're not asking me that, but those are the kinds of plans you have. If I move out to the New Lands, you're going to have modern housing, school facilities. What kind of plans do you have to keep the culture alive? Are you going to teach it in classes?"

But Swimmer won't address the deeper issues of relocation, won't admit that it is severing the Navajo relocatees from their families and culture, that it has already disrupted their social and economic system to the point they might never be the same again. Ella wants him to recognize that she and others like her value their old ways, and don't want to become assimilated because someone else has ordered them to.

"How is my mom going to survive on the New Lands?" Ella asks Swimmer. "All of her relatives are in Coal Mine Mesa. My mother will go out there and be lonely, probably die of loneliness. What will she do about squaw dances?"

"What's a squaw dance?" Swimmer asks.

Ella looks at him in disbelief, then she gets angry. How can a man who is planning her future not even know about one of her people's most important ceremonies? "I don't have time to explain all that to you," she snaps. "If you'll stay for at least a week, then maybe we'll be able to talk about it."

He asks her, "How can your mother not want to go to a place where she'll have sheep and a nice home that she wants, the way that she wants it? How could she not want that? Having the life she used to have?"

Ella says, "There's more to life than that, and it's relatives and friends and where she's rooted in the land. It's like a tree, it grows someplace. If you dig it out and try to transplant it, it will die."

Today, Swimmer's entourage will be smaller. Ivan Sidney asserts himself and insists that no Navajos travel with Swimmer. Swimmer is not up for a fight and says okay then, no Hopis, but Pat Dallas is determined to accompany him. Dallas is director of the Office of Hopi Lands, and as the top administrator for the HPL, believes he should be included.

The Navajos are told they aren't wanted, and that the BIA will use its own interpreter. "They felt Peggy was too biased and confrontational. They were sort of afraid of Peggy." The Navajos are bewildered and hurt. Claudeen came in by plane from Window Rock at the crack of dawn and Peggy drove up from Teesto.

"If Swimmer didn't want us here, he could have told us before we traveled all that way," mumbles Scott in the parking lot, where Peggy, Claudeen, Percy, and Ella stand and talk. "Ivan's actions speak for themselves," says Percy. "He's afraid Swimmer will see the truth." Percy still believes that Swimmer will see through all the games. The four stand in silence for several minutes and watch Swimmer leave. Ella laughs and says to Percy, "You have a lot of faith."

On the way back to Flagstaff from the reservation, Ella is quiet for a while, then she begins to talk. "My mom always says, 'Never trust a white person.' And then my dad says, 'There are a lot of white people that have deep hearts and they know how to think with their hearts.'

And then my mother tells us, 'When you go to school, the white man teaches you to think with your head and then you eventually forget how to think with your heart. And when that comes about, that's when you start losing your identity as an Indian. And you start feeling ashamed of your own people and ashamed to speak your own language.'

"And sometimes I wonder, how does she know all these things? How does she know these things are being taught in school? And I asked her that. And she says, 'I hear you talk about them when the children bring their homework home, and just by looking through the pages, and I ask them what is this? And they'll respond and say that was a certain war that happened here in the United States.' She says to me, 'I see the things the white man teaches in you, I see it in my other children too, a lot of the things they do and the way they act, I see it in you. So that's how I know.'

" 'Maybe the white man's way of teaching is not for the Indian people,' my mother says to me. 'Someday I would like to see a school,' she says, 'maybe since you want to be a teacher, maybe you can start a school where you teach white children how to be Indian children. When you start teaching white children how to think like Indians, maybe we'll have human beings again,' " she tells me.

"And then I thought about it. What is a human being? What do you mean by that? Aren't we all human beings? And she says no. 'A human being thinks with his heart, a person who thinks of the good all the time, that has respect for life around him, that has respect for even the smallest rock. A human being is a person that talks to rocks, a person that thinks the rock will talk to him and teach him a lesson. The smallest thing that Mother Nature has made available for us. A human being must understand why we are here on earth, why the plants are growing, why we have the four seasons. Why we have the heavens, that is a human being, somebody that understands nature. Somebody that thinks he's not any better than anybody else. That thinks everybody is equal no matter what color they are or what language they speak. That is a human being.' She says, 'I don't want life to end. I want my children to grow and reproduce. And I want my children to get along with the white children, learn how to share and live like human beings.' "

(18)

Peterson Zah Brings
His Plan to Hardrock

We are suffering very much right
now. It is like being tied up. I feel
very much like a dog being tied to
a pole and then somebody comes
out with food and acts like they are
going to give it to them and then
they don't. It feels like this day and
night. We don't like it. I want to see
the day that I will be happy again.
I want to see that day very soon. I
always look forward to that day.

HARRIET WILSON, NAVAJO

So far 1986 has been a mild winter. The red graded roads leading to Big
Mountain are soft and lined with tracks from heavy traffic. Soon, after
the rains, the roads will become like soup, the mud so loose that tires
will roll through it like egg beaters. Some of the roads become impassable. When the mud finally dries, the ridges will be hard as cement and
deep enough to break an axle.

But today, February 10, the roads are the finest they will be all year,
still supple, like the texture of spring leaves. The residents of Hardrock,
which includes Big Mountain, have come from all directions, leaving
curlicue paths behind in the vermilion dirt. They are congregating at the
Hardrock Chapter House to hear Peterson Zah explain the new bill that
may save their homes.

The parking lot is filled to overflowing with pickups. Inside, almost
four hundred chapter residents have just finished a meal of mutton stew,
salad, and fry bread. Salad is a new element in the Navajo diet, introduced by tribal nutritionists and encouraged by some of the younger

Navajos, who encountered leafy vegetables while living off the reservation. The Navajos eat the salad—iceberg lettuce and bottled red salad dressing—but find it somewhat strange. They are used to eating meat and bread and corn. A good bowl of stew and a few mutton bones have made the crowd here happy. If they don't get a chance to eat it for a while, they say they have "mutton hunger." Mutton means contentment. Mutton means home.

Some of the people still eat quietly from their cardboard plates and bowls as Peterson Zah starts to speak. One old lady rests her hands over her bowl of cleaned bones. Grease from the meat has run over the swollen, bony joints of her hand, and she has no napkin. She waits patiently for her hands to dry. The elderlies sit in the first rows of folding chairs, close to Zah. Behind them sit the middle-aged, and the back of the room is filled with the young people, some of them standing. Navajo meetings always seem to form a similar pattern.

Katherine Smith sits in the front row, picking her nose thoughtfully. When she is done, she rubs her nose with bag balm, an ointment for veterinary and human use. Mae Tso and Roberta Blackgoat sit near each other. Mae is quiet and attentive; Roberta kibitzes with her neighbors. Kee Shay sits along the right-hand wall, cowboy hat resting on his bony knee, head lowered, listening carefully. Percy Deal sits behind the dais, facing the crowd with other chapter officials.

Zah, in a maroon velour shirt, wears a heavy turquoise belt buckle, a silver and turquoise bow guard (once used to protect the wrist from the sting of the bow string), and ring. He is tall and handsome, and his most striking quality is the aura of quiet strength and dignity he conveys. But he appears grayer than he did when he met with these same people six months ago, vowing to do "anything" to prevent further relocations. Today, he tells them of his accomplishment. It took two years for the lawmakers and their staffs in Washington to consider his proposal, he explains in Navajo. Still closed-minded and uninterested after the treatment they received from the MacDonald administration, the people of Capitol Hill were slow to open up to Zah, slow to give him the chance to show he was a very different leader and was willing to give in order to receive.

After months of quiet discussion on the idea of a land exchange, he was able to convince Morris Udall to rethink his position. Zah explains to the rapt audience that Udall's mother, Louise, was very close to the Sekaquaptewa family and helped Helen, Abbott's mother, write a book. But, Zah says, the Udall family has had second thoughts about relocation, and while gathered over the Christmas holidays, they discussed the possibility of another solution. Soon after the New Year, "the time they go and shoot"—Navajo men welcome the New Year by firing a few rifle shots into the air—Udall invited Zah down to Phoenix to discuss the idea of the bill. Peterson Zah speaks with old Navajo expressions, without notes, in a rich, mild voice.

Behind the podium is a blackboard, across which are strung the words of Barboncito, the Navajo leader who led his people home from Fort Sumner after negotiating the release of the Navajos with the cavalry in the summer of 1868, saying, "Do not ask me to go to any land but my own." Beneath the hand-lettered sign are maps of the 1882 area, marked in colors to explain the land exchange.

More and more people try to jam into the room as Zah speaks. They whisper greetings to each other as they squeeze through the swinging doors. Elderly ladies sit with gaily colored kerchiefs on their heads, full skirts and velveteen or cotton blouses under their wool plaid jackets or Pendleton shawls. Men dressed in jeans and cowboy boots fidget with their felt hats. There are young people too, who have come from chapters far away from Hardrock to hear what their leader has to say. They listen with intense concentration. Many of the younger ones take notes; some even run tape recorders so they can retell the happenings to those who couldn't come. Navajos take notes assiduously, and they take great store by records; years from now a Navajo family might point to these notes in a dresser drawer and recall the hope of Zah's visit.

Zah gives a detailed history of the land dispute and describes the many lawsuits still outstanding. He summarizes the Morris-Clark initiative and winds up with a description of the Udall-McCain bill. Zah inspires confidence because he speaks as one of the people. He tries to address the elderlies; when it comes to technical sections, he speaks in English first, then explains as best he can in Navajo. He tells them that the bill would give to the Navajos 350,000 acres of land in the HPL, land on which live the greatest concentration of people. Navajos whose homes won't be saved would be offered 160-acre allotments on which they could finish out their lives. If they chose, they could be relocated instead. In return, the Hopis would receive the 350,000 acres of New Lands, plus 79,000 acres of land connecting Moencopi to the rest of the Hopi reservation. The Navajos would also pay the Hopis $300 million in coal revenues over a period of years. All remaining suits relating to the 1882 area as well as the 1934 area would be extinguished and the Bennett Freeze (which has halted construction and limited livestock on the 1934 area, where another suit is pending) would be lifted.

Zah tells the crowd that people frequently ask him why he doesn't respond to Ivan Sidney's threats of violence against the Navajos. He says that Ivan Sidney has been going around in Washington saying that he would use "Hopi police" (Zah uses the English words, because there are no Navajo words for the concept) to evict Navajos come the deadline, and that he would send in bulldozers to destroy Navajo dwellings. Zah says Sidney put off a lot of people in Washington with that kind of talk.

Zah says he refuses to act on the same level; he doesn't think that rough talk and unpleasantness dignify the office he holds, an office for which he swore a sacred oath. He says it disturbs him that some Navajos speak that way about each other, especially around election time.

Larry Anderson, a Navajo leader involved with the Big Mountain defense group, stands in the back. His long hair is pulled into a ponytail and he sports an AIM T-shirt (he was formerly treasurer of AIM). His Fu Manchu mustache hangs from a chin that is generally thrust upward in an attitude of defiance, although his forbidding expression can easily break into warm laughter. Lew Gurwitz sits near Roberta and Mae, but with his back against the podium, facing the audience, as if a bodyguard for his contingent here, the Big Mountain people.

When Zah finishes, a woman from Jeddito takes the microphone. She says that she is the last one left where she lives—everyone else has moved. She begins to cry as she speaks, and she continues, sobbing, expressing her gratitude to Peterson Zah for doing what he can, even if the bill never becomes law. The crowd surrounds and embraces her with its acceptance. The people are no longer made uneasy by these displays of emotion. After years of these meetings, the Navajos have become more accustomed to expressing tears and pain in public. They help the Navajos, much as a therapy session might; they have a chance to explain how they feel and they receive unconditional support from their neighbors.

Mae Tso steps to the front of the room and takes the microphone in her hand. Five years ago, she didn't know what a microphone was. Today, she holds it with the ease of a talk show host as she voices her fears of the lasting effects of the ten years of fighting and stagnation. "The struggle has been long and hard," she says. "The people are tired. I'm tired. Relocation has caused a lot of sickness, mentally and physically, among the people. And it also has affected our children, because our children will not listen to us. They're going into drugs and alcohol. Maybe if this bill goes through, maybe the tribe can do something to help our young people."

Another woman says, "None of the senators or congressmen who have written this law have come out here to visit us, talk with us, stay in our hogans and sleep on our sheepskins. Richard Morris is the only white man who took the time to listen to us and see how we live." She says that she told him, "The white man has taken from behind me, in front of me, underneath me, and over my head [the moon]. I'm now afraid he'll take my dog." She tried to make light of her fears, but the people here, who have so little control over their daily existence, feel that dislocation from their land is the final incomprehensible act. As one elderly woman said about moving to a new place, "The wind won't know me there. The Holy People won't know me, and I won't know the Holy People. And there's no one left who can tell me."

This meeting gives the Navajos hope again, hope that the cloud which has hung over them for so many years will disappear, as they have dreamed it might in the deepest part of the night when wishes are painted strong and reality rides a light brush. An elderly man expresses the feelings of many when he tells Percy Deal, "This bill is like a visit from the medicine man. This bill is a step toward restoration of harmony; harmony between ourselves, our neighbors, between ourselves and the land, and between ourselves and the Hopi Tribe." The old man hopes that, as in a ceremony, "through this legislation, beauty will be all around us. Beauty will be with us. Beauty will be among all of us, and we will walk in beauty again, and we will walk in beauty forever."

After all the people have spoken (they exasperate the chapter officials because their statements drift to other topics and back and forth from the issues), Zah gets up and responds to questions they have raised. One of them has been asked by many Navajos. Why must the Navajos pay $300 million of their own mineral revenues over the next hundred years to make up for a mistake made by the federal government? Zah answers simply, "Money is replenishable, always available, but there is no land like your own. How much does a life cost?"

When he is finished, he walks through the crowd. Elderly women surround him; some shyly shake his hand, others throw their arms around his neck. Navajo Attorney General Claudeen Bates-Arthur passes a note to Duane Beyal, the tribe's press officer. "It's a love fest," it reads. On her mind is the upcoming election battle and the bitter fight she expects against Peter MacDonald. Peterson Zah is not a political animal and his staff must think for him in these matters. He is honest, straightforward, cares deeply for his people, and is prepared to take political risks to do what is right. He is taking a risk here today, telling the people about a bill that could simply disappear and never be heard of again.

The tribe is hoping for support from the Big Mountain group, whose voice has become loud on Capitol Hill. But it seems the tribe won't get it. Lew Gurwitz files out of the chapter house and expresses concern about certain aspects of the bill. He is disturbed that the exchange will make for an even stranger boundary line, which may leave some Navajos very close to Hopi land. He says he is afraid someone like Roberta Blackgoat will find herself right next door to a strip mine. When asked what would keep the Navajos from making a mine next to her themselves, he says, "This right here," pointing to the clamor of the meeting behind him. "This is what will keep the Navajo Tribe from doing something like that." He is moved by the outspokenness of the people, the way they've taken to participatory democracy. In fact, the Navajos have adopted with great enthusiasm the concept of self-government. Although they voted down the Indian Reorganization Act in 1934, they were nevertheless organized according to its general principles.

At first, the idea of a tribal government caught on slowly, in large measure because until recently the Navajos didn't consider themselves part of any grouping larger than family or clan, and had a general aversion to the idea of representative government. As one anthropologist put it, "The native way of deciding an issue is to discuss it until there is unanimity of opinion or until the opposition feels it no longer worthwhile to urge its point of view."

But in the last twenty years the Navajos have begun to see themselves more as a tribal unit, though the people of Big Mountain were quick to declare themselves a separate nation when the tribe proved unable to help them.

Since 1938, the Navajos have tinkered with the structure of their tribal government, enlarging it to include a Department of Justice and other branches, but they have yet to write a constitution. Unlike the Hopis, however, the Navajo people have lost their apprehension about expressing themselves in public, and these gatherings have become an important part of their lives. And Navajo leaders understand the vital importance of these chapter meetings to their own careers. The Navajos insist on hearing their leaders. And they don't hesitate to let them know what they think, with their voices or their votes.

It appears that the Navajos here like Zah's land exchange proposal, and they seem not to share Gurwitz's skepticism about the bill. The Hardrock chapter votes 386–2 for a resolution "supporting and endorsing the concepts embodied in the purposed [sic] Navajo-Hopi Land Exchange Act of 1986 and requesting the Navajo Tribal Council and chairman of the Navajo Tribal Council to ensure enactment."

(19)

Askie Throws Mae Out

Soon after the Hardrock chapter meeting, Mae Tso's husband Askie returns home from the railroad and throws Mae out of the house. Picks her up and throws her out.

He throws Mae out because he is lonely, he feels abandoned by her, he feels fractured by the land dispute and feels he is losing control over his own life and his family. In the past year, Mae has been traveling more and more, going off to strange cities to speak about the land dispute. Oftentimes when Askie returns home after months on the road, Mae is not there, and he misses her. He starts thinking of his wife in foreign places talking to other people. When he thinks about Mae talking with strange men, he gets angry. Several times he returns home and goes back to work without seeing her. When they finally find themselves at home together, Mae is exhausted and absorbed with the land dispute and the Big Mountain meetings and all she is learning about the outside world.

Askie doesn't understand any of this. It defies his sense of life. Finally, he can no longer contain his anger and his jealousy. The children are home, Mae is there, but he is overwhelmed with the shame of his own ineffectiveness. He starts to shout at his wife, shouting about his fears, accusing her of being with other men from other tribes and nationalities. "Look at the children," he cries to her. Some aren't in school, others have no jobs, a few are getting in trouble with drugs and alcohol. "What is to become of them?" he asks her, overwhelmed with grief. Askie, a husky man, finally unnerved to the point of violence, grabs Mae and dumps her outside the door of the house. She falls in a heap at his feet. He tells her, "This is my house. I will stay here with the children. Never come back." Mae picks herself up, wraps her arms around her body, and runs, bent at the waist, to the pickup truck and drives off.

For the next month and a half, Askie stays at home, thinking about the family and Mae, wondering where he has gone wrong. Soon after

Mae leaves, he starts to drink. The children watch as he drinks himself into a stupor day after day. Sam and Hoskie stay away at the survival camp. Betty stays in Flagstaff. Earl tries to busy himself with the sheep. At other times he sits in the hogan and listens to tapes. The little children, Frances, Timothy, Calvin, and Juanita, lose interest in school and stop going. Earl tries to talk to his dad but it doesn't do any good. "The only thing that will make him feel good," he says, "is for my mom to be here with him."

After Mae drives off, she heads over to the Tuba City Hospital. She is afraid she is having another heart attack, like the one she had when the rangers impounded her horses and put her in jail. At the hospital, she sees a psychiatrist. She explains what has happened. Then she sees social workers, who tell her she should get a divorce. She asks, how can she get a divorce? She doesn't have a marriage license. She's had eight children with Askie without ever having a ceremony or a paper drawn up. She doesn't think that her problems can be solved by ripping up a paper that doesn't exist. The people at the hospital tell her it is her house and they can order Askie to be removed from it. She tells them she doesn't think that is the way to do it. She tells them that she looks at it differently. Then she leaves and drives to her son Larry's house. Larry had a different father from the other children's. He died while his son was still an infant. Larry and his wife take Mae in. She thinks about home, about Askie, about her battle with the world. She is ashamed about being apart from her husband. She thinks with embarrassment of what her relatives and neighbors must think. Mae hears that Askie is drinking and in a bad way. Mae loses weight, a bad sign with Navajos, but continues going to meetings and trying to do what she can to save her land and her place there, though now everything is all mixed up. She is defending a home she has been expelled from. She is defending her right to bring up her family in the way she knows, but which seems to be failing. Her world is turning upside down.

(20)

Indian Anger, White Guilt

Goose was once a roadie for the Grateful Dead. At least, that's what everybody says about her. Actually, she was a cook at the Hog Farm, a commune associated with the rock group. She also cooks at the Big Mountain survival camp; she orchestrated the feeding of the seven hundred spectators at last year's sun dance. She is a small owlish woman in her fifties, with short gray hair, bangs, and bookish plastic-framed glasses.

Goose is one of the founders of the Big Mountain defense group, whose first chapter opened in Berkeley in 1979. She had learned of the land dispute through the International Indian Treaty Conference and from an AIM group in Oakland whose meetings she attended. Goose became involved, eventually helping to build the camp, which consists of a wooden cookshack and bunkhouse, the sun dance arbor, and the log roundhouse, where public meetings are held. The bunkhouse is dark, with a dirt floor. The bunks will sleep a handful of people; the walls are hung with AIM posters, and a small wood-burning stove heats the room. Shelves lining the walls are stocked with provisions, and a small Buddhist altar is maintained by some of the support group members. It was erected by a Buddhist monk, who, with silver staff, flowing black robes, and bells, chanted prayers from a hilltop at last year's sun dance.

The chill of February winds cuts through winter clothing. Goose walks back to her brown van, in which she lives most of the time. It is parked by the bunkhouse. Goose tapes a sheet of heavy plastic over a broken window. She asks a passerby to hold the plastic while she cuts a piece of thick silver tape. Goose recently organized a Grateful Dead concert in San Francisco through the group's charitable arm, the SEVA Foundation, which also funds an eye clinic in Nepal and a health clinic on the Pine Ridge Sioux Reservation in South Dakota. The concert produced ten thousand dollars, which Goose has given to Larry Anderson, the former

AIM activist to whom the Big Mountain ladies originally turned for help in 1977. After Anderson brought in Lew Gurwitz a few years later, he was only periodically active in Big Mountain politics, but now he is assuming a larger role.

Down a short incline from Goose, in a clearing by the roundhouse, are parked a half-dozen pickups. Navajo ladies dressed in shapeless wool plaid jackets or windbreakers chat with each other beside their trucks. After a while, they walk with a wide hip-rolling stride into the roundhouse. The ladies solemnly shake hands with those they know as they pass inside, place blankets on the dirt floor, and sit with their legs curled underneath them. The men take their places on the few seats and the rest sit on their haunches against the octagonal walls.

Anglo supporters of equal number fill the roundhouse across from the Navajos. The Navajo women sit on the south side. The men and the Anglos sit on the north side. The Anglos are here for different reasons and with varying comprehension of the land dispute, but their body language indicates an awkward, reverential attitude toward the Indians. One young German couple sport hair dyed purple and orange and cropped short about their faces and long in back. They wear multiple earrings, flowing, chiffonlike tunics and jodphurs, and leather jackets. A Navajo lady points at them and giggles with a friend over the strange apparitions. The young couple maintain distracted, intense expressions. Indian lore is very popular in Germany.

Aside from the few flashy dressers, most of the Anglos look as if they had popped fully dressed out of the 1960s. The men wear jeans, wide belts, and T-shirts, and their hair is long. The women, imitating Navajo women, wear skirts, beads, solid shoes, and kerchiefs over their heads. Most of these people either live with a family on the reservation and help out with chores, or they volunteer their time to the Big Mountain Legal Defense/Offense Committee office in Flagstaff and live in communal houses rented by BMLDOC in town. They support themselves with part-time jobs, savings, or by "dumpstering" (searching out edible food from dumpsters). Oddly enough, many of the whites associated with the struggle have the names of birds, like Pelican, Goose, Raven, Robin, and Swan Eagle. There is also a Feather and Kodiak.

The idea of sending Anglos out to the reservation to live with families was conceived by members of Clergy and Laity Concerned (CALC), a Berkeley-based interfaith organization whose literature describes it as having "a history of challenging racism and supporting Indigenous [sic] struggle." The purpose was to generate a group of "witnesses" who had seen firsthand how the Navajos live and how the dispute affects their lives. Many had come out and passed on the word. Other left-wing organizations, from the International Indian Treaty Council to Peoples

Anti-War Mobilization/All-Peoples Congress to local Democratic party organizations, antinuclear activists, and environmentalists have joined in the protest. Momentum began to build in 1983, when Navajo women started traveling to California selling rugs and giving speeches about the dispute.

In 1986, the growth of the support network has exploded. In May 1985, BMLDOC had thirty support groups across the country. In February 1986 it boasted two hundred domestic support groups from Tucson, Arizona, to Venice, California, to Lavergne, Tennessee, to Hancock, New Hampshire, and fifty-five chapters abroad. BMLDOC informed its members about the dispute and coordinated its congressional letter writing campaign with photocopied newsletters. The newsletter, which when it was inaugurated in June 1985 was mailed to thirty-five people, had by February 1986 reached thirteen hundred. The recipients then generated hundreds of letters to members, urging them to write to Congress, prompting Senator Daniel Inouye of Hawaii to refer to "the overwhelming lobbying effort" aimed at stopping relocation. Senator Alan Cranston's office was reportedly receiving eighty letters a week from California constituents alone. The Berkeley support group also published a quarterly newspaper called the *Big Mountain News*, whose first printing in 1984 was 3,000 copies and by 1986 was 50,000. One hundred copies of a slide show called "In Defense of Sacred Lands" was distributed by local defense groups, a "resistance art network" had been set up, and handbooks and audio-tapes were offered for sale. With these resources, word about relocation had spread quickly in radical "movement" circles. Donations were beginning to pour into BMLDOC coffers and the mailing lists were growing rapidly. In the next few months, $10,000 a month in small denominations would flow into BMLDOC coffers.

Although the newsletters, generated in Flagstaff and supervised by Phillips and other leaders of the resistance, stuck to reports of legislative activity, posted the voting records of congressmen, and attempted to organize letter writing campaigns, many other fliers sent out by local support groups or individuals were less sober. Because each group operated autonomously, different versions of the land dispute and its causes were disseminated.

In spring 1985, BMLDOC's Flagstaff office, the brain of the nationwide organization, occupied a one-room office and boasted a half-dozen dedicated workers and "maybe ten or twelve others, who were sort of marginal, part-time people who were sort of hanging out for a month or two." By February the office had been expanded to nine rooms, and the staff accordingly.

Not everyone who arrives on the Navajo reservation to observe and help is capable. But such are the vagaries of a grass roots organization. Along with the able-bodied and committed are drifters, lost souls, and nuts. The previous summer the Rainbow Tribe, a fellowship of Anglos who travel in buses and commune with nature, created a furor when they paraded naked at the survival camp and were found in flagrante delicto by several very offended Navajo ladies. Navajo men and women rarely show affection in public, and they dress modestly. One of the Big Mountain matriarchs, when at a relative's house, was horrified by a spectacle she saw on television. What were those two people doing, she asked— eating each other's faces? "Old Navajos," explains Dennis Bedonie, "don't much go in for making out. They just get down to the nitty-gritty."

The incident at the camp deepened a split long brewing between the Indians and Anglos in the defense group. The Indians need the supplies and monetary support brought in by the Anglos, but resent being led by whites. And they have yet to come up with a Navajo to lead the resistance.

Larry Anderson sits on a broken-down green couch at the western end of the roundhouse, the position of honor. He is a tall, heavyset man with a countenance that could stop a locomotive. Anderson was one of the leaders of the 1975 AIM takeover of the Fairchild semiconductor plant in Shiprock, New Mexico, to protest wages and working conditions. But in the last few years, he has traded his sword for a pen and decided to fight within the tribal system. Anderson is now president of the Navajo Nation's Fort Defiance chapter on the Arizona–New Mexico boundary near Window Rock. His presence here today marks a symbolic first step toward assuming more leadership in the antirelocation movement.

Although Anderson did not grow up in the Big Mountain area, he is the only Navajo with enough stature and political knowledge to be a leader of the resisters here in the heart of Navajoland. Ironically, he is married to a Hopi and has several Hopi children. Gurwitz and Phillips feel that they can guide the political struggle in Washington and the courts, but the movement needs and wants an Indian with the personal charisma to become a symbol. Says Phillips, "The single biggest obstacle we have on this issue is the lack of Indian leadership. We should really be technicians helping Indian leaders get where they want to be. What we have is a lot of technicians running around making decisions. It's like running a political campaign without a candidate. There is no symbol."

This problem points out a peculiar fact of present-day Navajo culture: the men have no well-established role models. The raiders and warriors of days gone by, the traditional models, are no longer appropriate or relevant, and men have not yet developed a new, powerful role in Navajo life. The women are the ones associated with the land and livestock and have come to represent the land dispute, but even they have no role models for aggressive, outspoken female leadership. As Phillips says, the media loves good-looking, well-spoken symbols, and the Big Mountain Navajos have not come up with one who can carry their message, in large measure because the idea of a leader speaking for a large group is still very new. Navajos believe in consensus; the idea of choosing a leader and giving him or her one's vote is a foreign idea. And in this isolated area, it is even more foreign than it is on the rest of the reservation.

Larry Anderson is trying to play the part, but again he has significant responsibilities elsewhere, and his image is highly colored by his angry, violent days with AIM. Gurwitz's and Phillips's effectiveness in running the resistance has been slipping, not only because activist Indians in other parts of the country from whom they could receive support look warily at a traditionalist movement run by whites, but also because Gurwitz and Phillips themselves are fully mindful of the awkward paternalistic issues that are raised by their leadership.

Larry begins the meeting in Navajo, offers a prayer, and introduces Jake Swamp, a Mohawk from New York State. Swamp is here to conduct a small ceremony for the Navajos. He leads everybody up to the sun dance circle, where the cottonwood tree has been taken down, and the boughs are gone from the arbor. Swamp burns some tobacco, says prayers in his native language. The Navajos join in a circle around him. Most of the whites tentatively take their places in a second ring around the Indians. A few straggly Anglos, eyes closed, brows turned to the sky, really get into the prayer and rock back and forth on their feet. The wind swirls off the rocks into the protected niche of the arbor and picks up Swamp's unfamiliar language. It seems that if the Great Spirit were to hear anything, he would hear the sounds from this wind-torn spot. After the ceremony, Swamp passes around a coffee can for donations to help defray the cost of his trip. The white visitors dutifully dredge bills and change from their pockets. Few Navajos do likewise.

Back in the roundhouse, Larry holds up a chart that indicates how the ten thousand dollars in proceeds from the Grateful Dead concert will be handled and spent. Half the money will go to the legal office. The other half will be put in the "land fund," and used to fix up the camp, to sponsor the International Treaty Conference in the spring as well as July's sun dance, and to allow some elderlies to return the sun dance pipe to South Dakota. The division of the money was decided after long negotiation between Larry, Lee Phillips, and Bahe Katenay, who represents the young men who stay year-round at the camp to patrol the area.

Decisions about money here are fraught with jealousies. Katenay, whose family lives within a couple miles of here, and some of the other young men who live at the camp would like more of the money to go for trucks, radio communication, food, and medical supplies in preparation for the siege they anticipate come July 7—the congressional deadline for relocation. They are supported by the more radical white members of the Berkeley support group who believe that warfare is the way to win. Says Lee Phillips, "They feel [Peterson Zah's] congressional route is hopeless. They are interested in sovereignty and direct resistance. They want to stick to the PLO approach." Phillips maintains the argument on the other side, that if the Navajos want help from him, it will have to be for political and legal reasons.

But there remains a major split within the Big Mountain community between those who opt for violent resistance and those who want to fight within the system. Because there is no precedent for political activity among these people, it is hard for them to decide on a coherent political strategy. The families around Big Mountain maintain control over their livestock and their customary use areas, yet decision-making rarely stretches beyond family problems. So when the leaders of the resistance, the older people like Kee Shay, Roberta Blackgoat, and Mae Tso looked for help, all they could ask was, "Please make the law go away." When they told this to Lee Phillips, he thought of political strategies. When they approached Bahe Katenay and Larry Anderson, the men filtered the elders' wants through their AIM ideals. Phillips says the older people had no way of determining which route would be most effective, so they were pulled back and forth between the adherents of peace and violence. "They are basically anarchists," says Phillips, and conceiving of a strategy to help them meant imposing leadership on them, imposing decisions from outside. "There was no mechanism for decision-making on a community-wide basis," says Phillips, "so decision-making was left unfortunately to outsiders." Outsiders like him, Anderson, and some of the more active whites from the support groups. Phillips and Gurwitz were the ones to develop a workable political strategy. Says Phillips, "We told them that the idea of sovereignty—a declaration of independence from the tribe—is an ideal goal, but it won't work to stop relocation." Trying to make the people understand the twists and turns of the law and the political process when the whole system makes no sense is very difficult. The idea of violent resistance is at least comprehensible.

After Larry Anderson explains the money distribution in English and Navajo, a young Anglo woman steps away from the wall of the hogan where she has been standing. In a loud voice, tinged with painfully inappropriate self-assertiveness, she says, "We have a problem out here at the camp. There are people who are racist and sexist out here. Anglos and women are treated like slaves. One woman was raped. If we are going to carry out a resistance against oppression and imperialism, we'd better start right here. That's all I have to say."

Larry's impending explosion is palpable before he utters a word. He gets to his feet quickly and paces the front of the room, gesticulating. "We hear a lot of accusations—all are deceptions—about the camp and who is at the camp, why they are at the camp," he says, his voice rising. "The camp is this and that. If you don't like it, don't be around us, don't be around here. Go home. Go home!" he shouts. "Maybe you are useful there. But don't come around here using your mouth to say what we should do or how we should do it!" Larry's body is tensed, ready for attack. "The camp has already been done, it's practical and it's happening right now. And it's what the elders are saying—'No way are we going to move or are we going to take sides with what the relocation is saying.' "

Fear flashes through the roundhouse. Anderson's voice cracks and roars, contracts to soulful reflection, snaps so quickly the audience starts at his words. The whites are visibly shaken. "Let's shape up, man. Let's get our heads together. If your mothers and fathers were under the same conditions as these elders and many of these women that are sitting here, if *your parents* were under that situation, I'm sure damn well you'd be doing something too.

"That is what is happening today, my brothers, my sisters, my grandmothers and grandfathers. That's why we bring many other Indian people of different nations, who want to come and be a part of this struggle here even though they have other responsibilities at home. But they want to come and participate in something that is very, very dear to them. This is it, man, this is 1986. A few months from now, July, that's just going to come overnight like that. You're going to go to sleep tonight and you're going to wake up July seventh. Deadline. And you're going to be running around with your heads chopped off, asking, 'What shall I do?' But it's too late then. It is *now* that you have to make that commitment. I see many brothers and sisters coming to the sun dance ground last year making a commitment and putting war paint on themselves or by Leonard Crow Dog. Hey, when you come out into the sacred sun dance circle and make a commitment to the people and to the land, you are making that commitment. I remember who was all out there. I know who they were. After July seventh, when I'm here and if you're not here, then I'm going to think twice about it. I'll probably say, 'That old redneck did not come back.'

"But the camp here needs a lot of support. We need food, we need tools. We need people coming here to at least keep the morale going. We've got a radio house being built up on the top of the hill there. That has to be finished. Look at this roundhouse here. The logs that we were going to use to make the walls is only partly built. It's got to be *completed.*

"But again," says Larry, his voice low, "it's very difficult." His words come out like a chant, a poem. "Whatever you hear about the American Indian Movement, I wish you would reconsider your thoughts. Whatever you heard about the American Indian Movement, erase that from your mind. Because you've been watching TV too long. You've been watching John Wayne too long. You've been reading all of this trash that's been coming out by the news media, talking about a totally different story about what is happening here between the Hopi and the Navajo. You heard here in the newspaper and TV stations that the Hopis and the Navajos are still fighting. They're at each other. And you're still putting that in your mind. Then when you hear about the American Indian Movement, that's the same thing, man, as a bunch of hotheads, radical, militant Indians.

"Hey, I'm a hothead. I'm a radical. I'm a militant. Whatever they call me, that is what I am. And I can't ever erase that. But you as non-Indian people, you better start learning, because you are still learning, about who we are as native people, who our mothers and grandmothers are, our children and our grandfathers are here. I don't want you to come back after July seventh crying, saying that you're here and you want to help the Indian people. It's a bunch of bull.

"If you want to be involved, you better be here. You better be with the women, with the children, with the grandmothers, with the grandfathers. Don't put fear into them. Continue to build the love, the way *you* want it, the way you want to express it. That's what we want to see. And if I go to jail after July seventh, I want to see some of you pink faces in jail with me!" The room is silent. Everyone reels with the anger in Larry's heart. None of this has been translated for the Navajos, but some are nodding and softly echoing "oh," the Navajo word for yes. Others— those who understand that Larry's anger is directed at the whites, or bilagaanas, "those with whom we fight"—look uncomfortable. They have just participated in a sacred ceremony, and angry words are not appropriate after such a blessing.

Larry senses disapproval. He looks around the room and sees whites who have devoted much energy and time to this cause, who have remained year after year: Lew Gurwitz, Lee Phillips, Jay Mocilnicar, a teacher from Berkeley. They look confused, embarrassed at the unclear logic of Anderson's diatribe. Ella, who is here, looks perturbed. Nell has moved closer to her mother and looks around the roundhouse in fear and exasperation. Ella had earlier in the day wished she'd sprinkled Nell with herbs to protect her from any anger that might be expressed. "I hate to say these words in front of my elders here," Anderson says, "but sometimes, you know, I have to say this. This has built up in me *so much* I have to release the energy."

Suddenly, he stops, remembering his guest. He reintroduces Jake Swamp, whom some of the Big Mountain elders met during the Longest Walk, a protest march from Alcatraz to Washington, D.C., in 1978. The marchers, explains Larry, "took a detour to Onondaga where the Six Nations were in council." The Navajos entered the Long House and a ceremony was undertaken. "That day, the people of the JUA and the people of the Six Nations agreed to help each other," says Anderson. Swamp rises and offers a prayer in Mohawk. Then, in English, he tries to address what he saw here in the roundhouse. "Our young people and elders do not think the same today. We have to work on the young people to sway their minds back to the important things in life, to the oneness of the earth and the Creator. When your spirituality is complete, it is easier to come to decisions."

Swamp returns the room to calm with his soft words. He tells of his own experiences living in a camp in the Six Nations, under siege for a whole year as a protest against the U.S. government's policies toward the Mohawks. He tells the Navajos it was the most difficult yet the happiest time of his life. "We had to take care of each other," he says. "When my brother speaks of the dissensions that come about in these camps, it was just like I was at home a few years back." Swamp explains that divisions within his community are even greater than they are here, since the Indians of his community do not share common traditions, but are members of eight different Christian denominations. "Only a few people know the traditional ways," he says. "I can't blame those who never learned the old ways, but for them we have to hold on. For the whole world we have to hold on. Each individual person has a purpose in life. We told them we would never give in. If we give in, who will bring change to our people in the future? We'll never give in."

Swamp also tries to address the issue of the treatment of women that came up today. He tells the crowd, "The ones who kept us going were the women. The women are the strongest because in their hands was placed the power to bring life. And they are connected to the earth and to the moon." Swamp speaks calmly, hypnotically, of the need for unity in the struggle. They must keep their aims clear and their hearts in the right place. They must remember their culture. "Here we are, the people, trying to express our culture the best way we know how," he says. And echoing what the Navajos here believe is at the root of the land dispute, he says, "The big corporations, they are in control."

When he is done, two Anglo women carry in steaming pots of mutton stew and boxes of fry bread. Before eating, the Navajos file past Larry and shake his hand, a respectful thanks for running the meeting. Larry makes a point of offering firm and overly friendly handshakes to the Anglos who approach him. He looks relieved by his outburst and slightly sheepish. The Anglos hang back to let the Navajos eat first. Everyone grabs greasy utensils and is served some stew, a piece of fry bread, and a cup of sugared coffee. The Anglos get in line behind the Navajos and after receiving their bowl of stew return to their places on the floor. They eat enthusiastically, as if the thin stew of old sheep bones were the most wonderful thing they had ever tasted.

Lew Gurwitz, who has been quiet throughout the meeting, makes a sandwich of sweet potatoes from the stew and a piece of fry bread. "This is why I have ulcers," he says, holding up the sandwich and walking out of the roundhouse, laughing in self-deprecation. That is hardly the reason. This meeting has revealed all the anger, confusion, and irony of the movement Gurwitz is trying to build. It will take all his energy to keep the fragile alliances from bursting apart as tensions increase toward the deadline and to help the area return to its natural order—families looking out for themselves in whatever way they can.

It pains him to know how the efforts he has encouraged—getting the women to go out on speaking trips—have led to family difficulties. It is problematic for women like Mae Tso to do what he asks of her, because by traveling to the outside world she threatens the order she is trying to protect. Nevertheless, without these trips, their political efforts are weakened. It pains him that he and Lee have been left to make decisions about strategy because it continues old patterns of paternalism. Yet Larry Anderson, in one meeting, has frightened and alienated people gathered here as the result of years of grass roots organizing.

Anderson is not the only angry Indian here. He is just one of the handful of younger Navajos schooled in AIM ways who are full of rage and have put off some of the people who have come to the camp to help. It is Gurwitz's job to use Indian anger and Anglo guilt to fuel this political movement. But these deep-seated emotions and their trying dynamic are not easily or predictably controlled.

Annie Oakley's Hopi Friends

Dennis Bedonie is negotiating his truck down a rocky, washed-out path into Coal Mine Canyon, a deep, snaking, rainbow-colored gulch across the highway from the Hatathlies' camp. The vehicle shudders through the deep ruts of the road and progress is slow. The rattling is not helping Ella, who is suffering a pounding headache, the result, she believes, of Larry Anderson's outburst at Big Mountain yesterday. "After offering your prayers, your sacred tobacco, you are not supposed to pass angry words like that," she says. "Larry should know better." She is disturbed that the sacred offering had been sullied with violence, and the balance that Swamp attempted to achieve with the gods upset.

But off they go to attend another rite. Down in this canyon live some of Dennis's relatives, one of whom, Annie Begay, is having a curative ceremony tonight. In addition to Dennis and Ella, Annie's guests include Ella's parents, Billy Yazzie (Jack's neighbor with the red tractor), and Ethylene Samea, a Navajo who now lives at Hopi. Annie, who is known as Raggedy Ann or Annie Oakley because of her fierce independence and quirky personality, routinely negotiates this hair-raising trip backwards. The transmission on her truck is broken, and though she has tried to fix it, the truck will only drive in reverse.

Coal Mine Canyon was named for the thick coal deposits that stain the outcroppings of rock that twist and fold to form the canyon walls. One can see the areas that have been mined with picks and hands and sticks over the years. The endless lines of coal ribboning the canyon cannot fail to call to mind the interests that fueled the government's intrusion into these people's lives. Here is the coal, the powerful energy source that the Indians use to heat their homes and cook their food and which is desired by others who have a say over their lives.

Though Dennis grew up in the city, his father's relatives come from the canyon. He was chosen as a suitable mate by Ella's grandmother.

Says Ella, "It wasn't really up to my mom and dad. It was my grand-mother. She knew Dennis's father's family down in the canyon. I knew that family too. I had gotten a marriage proposal from one of Dennis's cousins down there. We kind of grew up together and had horse races. My parents said no because those people gambled."

Apparently Dennis's branch of the family was more acceptable. "[My grandma] told me Dennis seemed like a good man. He comes from a good family, they raise a lot of corn, they have a lot of sheep, they have real big cornfields and lots of singers in the family. She didn't mention anything about love, you know. It was just that the family was good and they were always helping people.

"My grandma and I talked," says Ella. "She told me it was best like that [for her marriage to be arranged]. She said if I had any problems, nobody could blame me. Sometimes you marry somebody you like and the marriage doesn't work out. Better if you marry someone you don't know. If you marry someone from far away, she said, if you start having problems, you've got nobody to turn to. She said it's really hard to help each other from a long distance like that."

Dennis's relatives live in several different clusters of hogans and at different points along the path to the canyon bottom. Those who live at the bottom live in the most primitive way, inhabiting old-style hogans that are dug into the ground. When Bessie brought her grandchildren down with her once to visit, she scolded them for staring. "These kids are running around with their eyes so wide they look like little white kids," Bessie told Ella.

There are advantages to living so far away from civilization. Neither the Hopi rangers nor the BIA livestock officers venture the several miles down a virtually impassable road, and the families still have substantial livestock herds, which they run in the canyon bottom. Also, because of their isolation from the effects of the land dispute and the bitterness that has developed between the tribes, the people still freely trade with the Hopis, who live very close by. "We don't think anything will happen to us. We'll always be here," they say, noting that they feel safe as long as their Hopi friends still come down to barter with them. They still believe and live in the old way, where alliances between families and trading agreements form the basis of their lives.

Dennis reaches Annie's cluster of dwellings on a wide plateau. He sees that the medicine man is already here, preparing the ceremonial mud hogan. Annie and some friends and relatives are in another, larger hogan, situated next to a ramada filled with car parts and odds and ends. Annie has scandalized her relatives by donning jeans and working on cars, one of the ways she has supported herself over the years. Out in front of the ramada is an old kitchen cabinet, in which a dozen chickens are roosting. When a human passes near, they peck furiously at their shelves, setting up a sound that succeeds in scaring him or her away.

Dennis parks the truck and walks with his daughter Nell to the corral, which is filled with over thirty sheep and goats. Dennis stands by the fence, a big smile on his face, remembering when he spent the summers out here herding sheep. It had been a big change for him, a city boy, herding sheep, hauling water. He remembers how different it was for him. But like any Navajo, the sight of a good-sized flock brings feelings of happiness and well-being. Annie Oakley also has burros and mules way down in the bottom of the canyon where one can go only by foot. Dennis shakes his head and says, "I remember herding sheep all over this area and into the next canyon when I stayed out here with my grandma. And I remember when we used to ride over to the trading post in an old wagon with rubber tires. We used to sit in the back with our feet hanging out. Sometimes we'd fall out and run along beside and jump back in." Dennis shakes his head again with restrained excitement as Nell reaches over the fence to pat a little lamb. It is an ironic picture. Nell is dressed from head to toe in fashionable pink clothes, with a small pink handbag over her shoulder.

They walk into the hogan to greet Annie, who is dressed in traditional Navajo skirt and blouse with moccasins and concho belt and a Pendleton shawl over her shoulders. She is a thin, athletic woman with a girlish body and pretty face. She trudges back and forth across the hogan, checking that everything is in place, and repeating over and over a story about a sheep that a relative brought over for the ceremony. Annie, whose eccentricities are variously ignored and appreciated by her relatives, explains that the sheep wouldn't join her herd but repeatedly ran away. Annie kept getting on her horse and chasing it back. Annie takes a few athletic, impulsive steps across the room, then tells the story again, until people start to ignore her. Annie is in her sixties and walks with the energy and menace of a black bear.

Annie has several blankets laid out on the floor. Ella says that her father always teases Annie about them, asking her who they're for, asking her whether she is expecting anyone. She tells him that she doesn't expect anyone, but she puts the blankets out for the Holy People to come in and rest on. Jack often asks her if she gets lonely. She says she's never lonely. Jack asks her why she has so many livestock and such a big cornfield, who's she going to leave it to since she has no kids. She tells him that if she had to do it all over again, she would have had kids for any man. She says she wasted her best years with the wrong man, with whom she had no children.

Ethylene Samea is an old friend of Dennis's father. She has been married to a Hopi for thirty-seven years, lives in the Hopi village of Polacca, and has adopted Hopi ways. Unlike the other women here, who are all dressed in Navajo garb, Ethylene dresses like a Hopi in a flowered print cotton dress with white cotton bib apron. Her hair is cut short and waved about her face.

Ethylene sits on a bed near the wood stove. She giggles often, she seems happy to be here with the women she grew up with. She says she's had a lot of ceremonies herself lately, Navajo ceremonies. She was recently having trouble breathing and she went to a medicine man who helped her recall a childhood game in which she filled up a wind hole with rocks. He told her that that game was the cause of her breathing difficulties, that she had angered the Holy People by filling up that hole. He instructed her to travel to another wind tunnel. She did. She found a place where the gusts were so strong blowing down through a hole worn in the rocks that she could hardly stand up. But she walked forward, closer to the hole, struggling to stand up straight, hardly able to breathe. She pushed on, followed the directions of the medicine man, and now her problem has gone away. She beams as she tells the story, absolutely delighted. Although she lives with the Hopis, at times of great stress she returns to Navajo ways. She seems contented and at peace.

When asked about how the land dispute and the friction between the tribes affects her, she answers quietly. "The Hopi Council is very eager to get the land from the Navajos," she says, "but there are so few of them, only a handful!" Nine members of the Tribal Council are listed in the fourth issue of *Hopi Tutu-veh-ni*, the Hopi newspaper. These individuals make the decisions for fourteen autonomous villages and for the entire Hopi Tribe. "I don't think they represent the feelings of the people," she says, before looking at her hands and changing the subject. This, clearly, is painful for her.

In the mud hogan about three hundred feet from Annie's house, Annie's brother, Billy Yazzie, helps prepare ashes for the ceremony. The medicine man is in the hogan too, preparing it for the sand painting he will make. Billy Yazzie comes into the house and chats with his sister. He is agitated about the land dispute and makes some disparaging remarks about the Hopis.

Moments after he leaves and goes back to the mud hogan, two carloads of Hopis arrive with fresh baked bread, pies, and cakes for the ceremony. They are Ethylene's Hopi relatives. After they have delivered their gifts and driven away, Billy Yazzie reenters the house. Annie strides up to him and chides him, "See, here you come empty-handed and saying bad things about the Hopis and they come with their arms full."

Billy is so upset by his sister's words that he climbs into his truck and drives home, abandoning the ceremony. It seems there is nothing easy about this land dispute, not even taking sides.

(22)

Two Faces of Relocation
in Hardrock

Percy Deal steps out of his trailer, which is set on a neat, well-kept tract in Tuba City, not too far from Dennis Bedonie's relatives who live in a dugout as they wait for their relocation house. Although Percy's own trailer is built on a legitimate homesite, all around him is a mass of shacks, trailers, and hogans stuck up by relocatees awaiting new houses, or families who have lost their relocation houses and moved back to the reservation. Since they can't go back to their old homes, which they gave up to the government, they head for Tuba. There, because it is something of a city, they can fit in, or, if they prefer, remain inconspicuous.

Tuba City is one of four urban areas on the reservation where there are stores, tribal and BIA offices, jobs, and some land for urban-type living. In addition to Tuba City, the Navajo Tribe has identified three other "growth centers." Kayenta is northwest of Tuba, near the Utah border, Chinle is at the edge of Canyon de Chelly near the New Mexico border, and the Window Rock–Fort Defiance area is southeast of Chinle. These are the only urban areas on the entire reservation. Most of the people affected by the land dispute originally lived closest to Tuba, so they gravitate there for work, for housing, to hide.

Percy Deal is chapter president of Hardrock, where he grew up and where his parents still live. But Percy stays in Tuba City now, so he can have a telephone, so he is close to the paved roads, since his work for the tribe takes him to Washington, Flagstaff, Phoenix, Window Rock. Hardrock is so remote that at times during the winter, no one can drive in or out. If the snows are bad enough, it becomes a disaster area and hay and medicine must be dropped in by helicopters. No one can live in Hardrock who must be able to leave.

Percy has held many different jobs in the tribal government, through different administrations. But all of his positions have involved the land dispute. He knows the land and its people profoundly, and maintains close contact with them. In fact, he is headed to Hardrock this morning. He speaks movingly about his people in English that tries to reveal the Navajo language and thoughts he interprets. His speech is heavily accented in characteristic Navajo fashion, with glottal stops and climbing rhythms that express an unstoppable hopefulness.

Percy Deal is a tall man with wavy hair and a broad, friendly face. He has a ready smile and a hearty laugh. His front teeth are filled with gold. He wears light blue corduroy Levi's pants and a nylon shirt with a loud pattern of blue swirls.

He heads east out of Tuba City past Moencopi and the grassy plateaus of Howell Mesa and Coal Mine Mesa, past the Hatathlies' house and the Coal Mine Chapter house. "One hundred percent of the area of Coal Mine Mesa within the 1882 reservation has been awarded to the Hopis," says Deal. "And one hundred percent of the rest of the chapter lies within the Bennett Freeze. The chapter has nothing to do."

The chapter of Coal Mine Mesa had the bad luck to find itself half in the 1882 Executive Order Area and half in the 1934 area—also called the Bennett Freeze area because of a building freeze ordered in 1966 by then Indian Affairs Commissioner Robert Bennett. The Bennett Freeze area extends west from the western edge of the 1882 area to the Navajo reservation's western boundary, and its north and south boundaries are the same as the north and south boundaries of the 1882 area. The Navajos and Hopis are still battling in court over their rights to the Bennett Freeze area, and for twenty years, the people living on this land have not been able to improve their homes, nor have they had the benefit of new roads, schools, or hospitals. All the residents of the Bennett Freeze area are Navajos.

Thirty miles farther on, Percy skirts the boundary of District 6 and then heads south again and up through the Hopi mesas. Before Hotevilla, he turns off onto a graded dirt road toward the Dinnebito trading post and on to Hardrock.

Percy motions to a camp on the north side of the road. He pulls off and follows the driveway back past a series of houses. He parks and walks toward a round hut, about six by eight feet, dug partly into the ground and covered with cardboard Pampers boxes. Smoke curls from the smoke hole. Next to the makeshift hogan is a three-sided ramada covered with juniper boughs. And beside the ramada is a small cave, a doghouse, dug into the ground and covered with an earthen dome. Inside, a rangy dog peers out from its rag bed. It is drizzling—what the Navajos call a female rain—and the dog looks out with only moderate interest through the drips falling from his doorway.

Percy knocks on the door of the shack. A small woman in her late fifties pushes it open and greets him with a smile. Her name is Bessie Yazzie (no relation to Billy) and she asks him in. On her stove is a pot with water and a few mutton bones. The stovepipe is held in place in the ceiling with wire and pieces of towel. Bits of plastic keep the rain from dripping in the smoke hole. Along the back wall of the hogan is a bench that serves as Bessie's bed. Behind it she has stacked her blankets, wool, and yarn. A loom is set up on the floor. Hanging on the walls are her essentials: little bits of herbs and tea, pots, an ax. A sack of Blue Bird flour is propped on the floor. There is hardly enough room for Percy and Bessie to stand. The two of them speak in Navajo. Bessie used to live up on the hill behind her, she tells Percy, but her hogan got old and needed repairs. She couldn't get permission from the Hopis to rebuild, so she moved down here near some relatives and built herself this shack. Bessie made her cardboard hogan thinking the Hopis wouldn't bother her about it because it is so "shabby," as she puts it.

Percy says, "She does not want to relocate. If the time comes and she has to go, she will go a short distance, because of the trading post, because of the security of the trust she has built in that trading post. And the trust works vice versa. For as long as she is around, she is a human being who will work hard to make another rug and try to make ends meet." Bessie supports herself by weaving. She also gets eighty dollars a month in support from a government check. She survives on credit extended to her by the trading post, whose owners she has known for decades. Anywhere else, she would be a stranger without help. She does not want to move to the New Lands. "She's afraid that the people who own stores over there on the New Lands won't know her. She doesn't know them. Not knowing each other, they would just reject her credit out of hand, just simply by looking at her."

Bessie tells Percy that here she can always get a lift to the trading post. Everybody knows her and all she has to do is walk to the road and someone will stop for her. "On the New Lands, when she gets out on the road, she will just be an old woman out on the road to those people on I-40. She wonders who would give her a lift."

The Dinnebito Trading Post, a one-story building with groceries, wool, jeans, kerchiefs, shoes, guns, and some small appliances, as well as a check casher, telephone, and mail boxes, is the center of Bessie's world. She goes there to visit with friends, check for mail, cash the $40 check she receives every two weeks. Then she fills up her paper sack and catches a ride back home.

She doesn't think she would survive in a new environment. "On the New Lands she would be a total stranger, not only to the land and the environment out there, but also to the social part of what makes a community," says Percy. Last week, she visited her children in Tuba City. She went there for a birthday party, but felt ill as soon as she arrived. She insisted that they take her home and now she feels much better. "A piece of me starts to die when I go to Tuba City," she tells him. It is too noisy, there are too many people. Out here she can hear the sounds of the wind and plants and animals that she has known all her life.

A photographer from the *Navajo Times* arrives to take pictures of her for an upcoming hearing in Washington, D.C. A Japanese man married to a Navajo woman, he takes several pictures and then hesitantly, quietly, hands her some money. Bessie rolls it into a ball in her fist. "I feel so bad," he says later, after he leaves Bessie's hut. "She could be my grandmother. I never give money, but this is so sad."

Percy tells Bessie there will be hearings soon in Washington, and she tells him she is waiting for something to break, for land exchanges or something that will allow her to stay. She likes it here—it is her home, and the reservoir of all her memories. Percy tells her he will try his best. He says good-bye and moves to the door. Bessie grabs his arm. "Whatever you do," she tells him, "do it right. And those pictures that you take of me, don't let them blow around in the wind and let them get into crazy and unthinkable people's hands. Then they laugh at me. They think I'm a funny."

Percy climbs back in the truck and drives to the dirt road. "I've been dealing with this issue officially since 1978 [it is now early 1986]. And I've probably submitted, within that time period, a large number of requests to repair homes from individual families residing out here to Abbott Sekaquaptewa and Ivan Sidney. To my knowledge, in the last eight years, I do not remember even one approval. Instead, what we get from the Hopis is, okay, you do have a problem out there, we will agree to set up a process and procedures that will respond to those types of things. However, before we even attempt to set that up, you must do the following, one, two, three, four, five, six. Major things." This is how the Hopis respond to Navajo requests. They say they'll think about letting a particular person repair her hogan if the Navajo Tribe dismantles every other hogan that has been repaired without the Hopis' permission.

"The Hopis never respond to people like the Yazzies," he says. "They'd much rather respond to the Navajo Tribe in general and only under pressure.

"The people in Congress and at the Commission have no idea whatsoever about what these people are made of," says Percy. "Each soul out here strongly believes they have a purpose, they have a purpose in *life*. And they're trying to discover that purpose. They're trying to find that purpose and when they do find it they want to hang on to it and carry it out to the fullest. And many people, particularly those that are so dependent on the land, strongly believe that they have found their purpose and now their purpose is being taken away by somebody who is blind and simply refuses to understand them."

Bessie Yazzie feels she is better off in a cardboard shack than she would be in a new house away from here. She knows what she needs, and it is to be where she is. "She possesses everything that a human being is made out of," Percy says. "There isn't a thing that she physically doesn't have that [Relocation Commissioner] Ralph Watkins or [Commissioner] Hawley Atkinson has. But one thing that is unique about her is that she is very strong inside. She is happy, very happy with what she has or doesn't have. But another person who may come and cast his eyes upon her condition could think, 'How can anybody live like that?' It's not really her choosing, she was forced into that condition, but she's making the best of it. She is a condition right now, the condition of a governmental decision. She's only a case number to them, that's all she is to the U.S. government.

"These people out here are more than numbers," Percy says angrily. "They're human beings. They're somebody that has religion, they're somebody that has children, they're somebody that's going to have more children. They're somebody that has livestock, they're somebody that has to eat, that has to survive, that looks for security. That's what people are. That's what human beings are. They're more than numbers."

Percy drives across the line into the Navajo Partition Lands. "Hardrock is the other chapter that is so adversely affected by relocation, both geographically and populationwise," he says. Before partition, the chapter had a total of 305,000 acres. After the line was drawn, only thirty percent of the chapter was left on the Navajo side. Seventy percent became part of the HPL. But since there was some part of the chapter still left for the Navajos, the Relocation Commission conceived of a plan called the Hardrock group move. It decided to move as many people as possible from the HPL side of the fence to the NPL. The Commission has built about fifty houses by 1986. But there were already many people living on the thirty percent of the chapter that stayed Navajo land, so the area is very crowded. There is little room for livestock and little remaining arable land. As Percy puts it, "You're moving hundreds of people onto seventy thousand acres of a behavioral sinkhole."

We approach the group-move area and see modern, stucco houses reinforced with fiberglass set in clusters of two and three on the rocky hills. The houses are beautiful, with high windows and overhanging roofs—houses beyond imagining in these parts. But the road is almost impassable. Percy grinds into first gear. The rains finally came, and these tracks, soupy a week ago, have now hardened into deep ruts. The Relocation Commission hails the Hardrock group move as one of its greatest accomplishments, but for a good part of the year, residents cannot enter or leave this area.

The truck shimmies and rattles over the tough washboard. The average Navajo family spends thirty-five percent of its income on maintenance and purchase of vehicles alone. This figure does not include gas or depreciation. The majority of people in Hardrock who have vehicles log over thirty thousand miles a year, about twice the average for non-reservation cars in Arizona.

Percy pulls up to the house of Mattie Yazzie (no relation to Bessie or Billy), who lives in a grouping of fine modern houses. Her daughter Beulah lives in another of the homes. Solid, rectangular dwellings sit on raw dirt lots, where the marks of the land-moving machines are still clear. Percy knocks on the door, but no one is home. The house, with curtains and modern furniture, looks abandoned. A bucket is set under the house gutter to collect rainwater. A kitten sleeps atop the propane tank attached to an outside wall.

"The last time I was here," he says, "I brought [Relocation Commissioner] Sandra Massetto to visit Mattie. Mattie told her, 'The house that was built for me by the Commission isn't me. That house just isn't me, isn't meant for somebody like me accustomed to living in a hogan with plenty of area to plant their corn and plenty of area to graze their livestocks. The house is good, but the furniture and all the rooms under that roof, I'm not comfortable in.' "

Percy points to a half-finished hogan beside the house. "Her grandkids made her that hogan, and she plans to move into it. Although she relocated a short distance, she is still lonely for the area that she left. In order to get away from that loneliness, she has to wander away from the house daily. She was telling me that if the sun lasted eight hours during the day, a good six hours she would spend away from the house, just wandering around, either up in the hills or among neighbors, trying to escape that misery she knows she's going to be in for the rest of her life."

He drives to the neighboring house, about two hundred yards away. Beulah and Beulah's daughter and granddaughter live here. Outside the house is an old outhouse. These houses were built with bathrooms, clothes washers, and dryers. But there is no electricity or running water in Hardrock, nor do these people have enough money to pay for the utilities every month if they were available. A camper shell is propped on rocks near the outhouse. Underneath it is a pile of coal chips the Yazzies picked up for free at the Peabody Coal Mine, which they burn for heat. Percy pushes open an aluminum storm door that doesn't latch. He steps into a breakfast nook with Formica table and chairs. The table is separated from the rest of the kitchen by a counter. Over the counter are heavy, walnut-stained cabinets with ornate brass-colored hinges and handles. Behind the kitchen table, a huge floor freezer is stacked with soda pop empties. The freezer runs on propane, but the Yazzies usually don't have enough money to replace the tanks. As a temporary measure, the houses have been supplied with cisterns and photovoltaic cells, but each family had to pay extra for these in addition to the twelve thousand dollars deducted from their house benefits to pay for the water and electricity that will eventually be provided.

Beulah's daughter flips on a light, which doesn't glow. It has been cloudy and the photovoltaic battery is drained. When it's working, the system lights one bulb per room, she says. The bathroom is currently a storeroom, the sink and toilet never used. A wood- and coal-burning stove heats the living room, where a large loom is set up, and propane heaters in each room supplement the heat from the stove. If they can't afford to buy more gas, they must make do with the wood stove.

Beulah walks slowly into the kitchen from her loom. She sits down at the kitchen table and slowly brushes crumbs from the oilcloth. Percy asks her in Navajo if she is comfortable in her new house. She speaks just above a whisper, runs her hand over her forehead slowly, fatigued. Percy translates: "She says living over here is quite different from where they used to live on the HPL. Everything in general is just slightly different."

Beulah's daughter walks into the kitchen. She is short and strong-looking. Her own daughter, a toddler, stands next to her. She speaks English. "I was happier down there, myself. This is just a house, you know. Where you grow up and spend all your life, that's home. You move up here and you just don't have anything to show for it. Seems like we just got ripped off."

They are allowed four sheep. "My grandma's always talking about going back and living down there. She said we used to have fat sheep, we don't have fat sheep anymore. The sheep taste different. They eat the brush off the mountain, you can taste it in the meat. There's no grass up here, it's already overgrazed. And my grandma doesn't even have a cornfield. There's no earth to grow anything."

Beulah speaks again. Percy translates: "She says, 'We were told we were going to have water and other things. Those are not to be seen for a while. I have to rely on my kids to bring me firewood and haul water. When they're not around, I just run completely out of them. I have to go to my mother's and get water from my mother.' "

Several of Beulah's sons enter the house and stand quietly beside their sister. The Yazzies were lucky; their new homes were built on a piece of their former customary use area. That means they are at least familiar with the land; the kids used to ride horses up here and they once had a winter camp nearby. However, the horses they once rode here are gone. "We used to have horses, but the Hopis took them and sold them without telling us," says Beulah's daughter. The Yazzies are also fortunate because part of their customary use area fell on the NPL. This allowed them to bring some stock over, but there's only forage enough for four. Most relocatees who move onto somebody else's customary use area cannot have *any* animals. Their livestock permits are for a specific piece of land. Once off that land, they have no rights to livestock. Even though the Yazzies have some token animals, they can't make a living off the land. They depend on wages of family members who live off the reservation and on the money from the rugs Beulah weaves and sells in Sedona.

"They deducted twelve thousand dollars from our benefit money for plumbing and water, and they said there was going to be roads, hospitals, a store," says Beulah's daughter. Percy asks her who promised them this. She answers, "Ralph Watkins. We went and brought him back one time to the chapter house, that's where we talked to him. We asked how long it would take for the water to come. And he said within the next three years. That was two years ago now. I said to him, 'You deducted twelve thousand, thirteen thousand dollars from each of these houses.' I asked where's the money at to do these projects. And they just started blaming each other, he said that, he said this.

"My grandma now more than ever wants to move back down there. You go over to her house any time of the day and she's not going to be there. She goes around visiting other people. She used to have a garden, a big cornfield, but she says she can't. There's no place to grow. We're going to try, though. We're going to try peach trees and apple trees through the Hardrock Coop Farm Program."

Back outside, the houses have the uncomfortable look of housing projects the world over. There is nothing to do here. The kids sit around with no livestock to tend, no cornfield, and too far away from jobs. One can see immediately what this house will look like in ten years. It will have fallen into disrepair. Roofs will leak, rot will develop, and the Navajos will not be able to repair them. They were just able to afford the repair of a hogan, to disassemble it and rebuild it with some new logs. Who will repair these houses, or will they eventually melt back into the earth?

A report prepared by CH2M Hill, the Commission's planning firm, points out the economic realities of this area. Unemployment is over fifty percent, most people receive some welfare assistance, and there is little arable land. Yet the Commission continues to move people into this region with promises of water and electricity. Percy drives back to Mattie's house. She has not returned. He drives the truck back out the deeply rutted single-track path and thinks aloud about Bessie Yazzie and Mattie Yazzie. Bessie, living in a shack of Pampers boxes, is self-sufficient, happy, and in control of her life. Mattie, who has a multiroom, elaborate house, cannot stand to be in it and wanders around outside all day. It is clear who is in better shape. Bessie has a will to live because she depends on herself; her life is still in her hands and she is firmly planted in the community where she is known. Mattie wanders, because as Percy says, "There's nothing else left for her to do. Everything has been taken away from her. All she has are those four walls. And she's not comfortable inside them."

. . .

The Navajo Gospel Mission School sits on a twenty-acre square of land that has just made it onto the Navajo side of the wildly zigzagging partition line. "This is where I went to school," says Percy, laughing, looking around at the compound of small stone houses that includes a chapel, student dormitories, teacher housing, and classrooms. Here and there, huge piles of juniper boughs are stacked for burning. It is quiet, serene, a little haven in Hardrock for students whose parents are inclined toward Christianity. In the old days, before the Rocky Ridge School was built nearby, it was also for students whose parents couldn't bear to send them all the way to boarding school in Tuba City. Tuition is a hundred dollars a year; room and board is an extra hundred. There are thirty children enrolled now in the elementary grades.

Director Strickler is an angular, soft-spoken man who looks like Abraham Lincoln. He sits at a table in a small room in the main school building with Linda Wisdom, a teacher of first and second grades. Wisdom's gray hair is coifed into a round dome about her face and her glasses cast a rose-tinted glow onto her fragile-looking, cream-colored skin. Wisdom says that her students are usually excited about moving into a relocation house. Strickler scowls at the table and listens. "They get all excited about having carpeting in their house and a room of their own. But one girl told me her mom yells at her a lot more about getting the house dirty. I have the feeling some of these mothers aren't completely prepared to take care of that kind of house." In a hogan with a dirt floor, or a frame house with cement or linoleum, one has only to sweep. A carpet requires a vacuum, but there isn't electricity. Walls must be repainted and repairs made. The cost of that maintenance is usually more than a family can bear.

"Some of the little ones say they're glad they're moving because they don't have to work anymore with the livestock," says Strickler. But the children have absorbed their families' turmoil. "We took a trip to the Hopi mesas," says Wisdom. "And the kids said, 'We don't want to go there. They're our enemies.' But we spent the day with a Hopi family that was very hospitable and friendly to the children and when we got back, one little girl said, 'They're just like us. They were really nice to us.' It was a shock to her."

"We haven't seen too many success stories," pipes up Strickler in a deep-voiced drawl. "For one, they're still sitting here and they still don't have water; they still don't have electricity and they don't have livestock or employment. So where have they been bettered, really? Except they're in a nice house and half of that they block off so they don't have to have all that heat in the wintertime." Wisdom breaks in, "Or they leave two of the houses empty and they all live in one." Despite the fact that the hogan is the most practical design for the open range, the Commission maintains that hogans don't satisfy the law's requirement that replacement houses be "decent, safe, sanitary," and consequently they won't pay for them.

"The shepherds are feeling the crunch," says Strickler. "They're not geared to thinking that from now on they're going to pay taxes and pay water and pay electric bills. All those things are perfectly foreign to them. Now, all of a sudden [if they move into a house off the reservation], they're paying that and if they don't have a job they're going to lose that house. It's happened several times. And then they come back out here and there's nothing left for them to do. That's a tragic thing."

Wisdom says that of their thirty students, only one or two have fathers who are not alcoholics. "Most of them are alcoholics because they don't have jobs. There aren't enough jobs here. And if they find work on the railroad or in another town, they are gone for six or seven months at a stretch. That's no family life. And if they move their families close to them at their work, their houses stand empty." The families don't like to leave the houses unattended, because then they are likely to be vandalized by drunks. And they cannot simply sell their house and purchase others near work. Individuals do not own land on the reservation; the government owns the land and holds it in trust for the Indians. And even if they owned their reservation houses and could legally sell them, they'd be hard-pressed to find many Navajo families with sixty thousand dollars to fork over for them.

The Mission School suffers with the rest of the community in the winter when the roads become impassable. Last year, the area was determined a disaster area, and helicopters dropped emergency supplies. "We really need a road, yet it seems like there's some kind of friction going on there," says Strickler. In 1984, Congress appropriated $5 million to construct a road from the Rocky Ridge boarding school out to state Highway 264. But the Hopi Tribe withheld approval of an easement. Strickler says, "It's not right. If money's there, why don't they go through with it?

"You know," says Strickler, leaning over the table and folding his hands, "all this land that the Hopis are going to get. What are they going to do with it? I mean, they're village dwellers. So what are they going to do with the land?" He looks about the table, as if he were expecting a reply. He continues. "I think it's too bad that somehow, if it was a matter of trying to get money, if they just wanted to get in on the royalties of some of the coal and stuff like that, why didn't they just say, 'Okay, let's not worry about relocating everybody. Let's just give them royalties, and let the people live where they were living. It's just too bad they did this to all these older people. It's just a tragedy in their lives.'"

Spring 1986

It's fine to say that we can all live on the land together. The only problem with that is we've tried that for over one hundred years and the conflicts are still there. If one tribe would not try to dominate the other, that would be a step in the right direction.

ABBOTT SEKAQUAPTEWA, HOPI

(23)

The Fence

They wake just before dawn on the morning of April 4. Reggie Deer, Willie Lonewolf Scott, Thomas Katenay, and Sam Tso pull on camouflage fatigues, strap on their belts and knife sheaths, step into their boots. It is cold at the survival camp, the wind is gusting up to fifty miles an hour on Big Mountain and the bare trees do little to cut the chill. There will be no breakfast this morning; the young men (who have garnered the appellation "the bros") fried up the end of the potatoes for dinner last night. Then they had taken a sweat and sung some AIM songs.

The stores are low at the camp. The periodic delivery of food and clothing from the support groups is going directly to the families at Big Mountain, not to the people living at the camp and readying it for the International Treaty Council in May and the sun dance in July.

They set out toward Dove Springs on foot, heading north of the camp past the sun dance arbor. Reggie, sad-faced and quiet, Thomas angry, his aviator-frame glasses growing dark in the bright light, and Sam, at twenty-three, the youngest in the group, his hair braided high on his head, his features small, almost feminine, his jaw set more against fear than in determination. Willie, twenty-five, the eldest, calm, self-possessed, throws some cedar on the fire before they leave and claps some of the smoke onto his chest.

The smell rests in their noses, clean, warm, strengthening. Without speaking, they walk four abreast, shifting to a line when the road narrows or they head out through a break. As the sun rises, they see that spring is fast approaching; the dried undergrowth shows green, the juniper trees are budding. They climb to the top of the ridge to the west of the camp and head down toward the Dinnebito Wash before the sun breaks over the horizon.

The bros are heading out to Sam Tso's aunt Bessie Begay's house in Dove Springs, a few miles north of Mosquito Springs, where Mae lives.

Bessie sent a message that a fencing crew was near her place, ripping out cottonwood trees and constructing a fence. New dirt roads had been cut in the dry underbrush for the work trucks and Bessie was frightened by the traffic and commotion. The Hopi Rangers and the BIA police who were supervising the fence work didn't speak Navajo, so she couldn't ask them what they were doing.

Bessie drove over to her sister Mae Tso's house and told Mae she was frightened. After getting the message, Sam Tso immediately drove to the trading post and placed a call to Willie Scott in Fort Defiance, told Willie to meet him at the camp, where they would be joined by Thomas and Reggie.

About noon the bros see the fence crew at work. Sam's blood boils at the sight of the raw swaths cut through the land so near his aunt's place, to see that fence going up right through her customary use area. There is no such thing as an Indian fence. Used to be the horses could run for miles in any direction, coming home at night on their own, or staying on the range if they chose. Now there is the fence that divides the HPL and NPL as well as other so-called interior fences put up by the BIA for the purpose of managing the range—keeping certain areas free of livestock for a while so they can rest, and alternatively guiding the animals to less popular grazing areas to keep the range uniformly used. These fences infuriate the Navajos, because they make it difficult to travel to neighbors or gather herbs and firewood.

The bros kneel down and rest for a few minutes, then offer a prayer. Willie repeats the decision they had made earlier that they would remain nonviolent. They take off their knives and hide them beneath a snake-weed tuft. With Willie in the lead, they walk toward the fencing crew. There are three Hopi Ranger vehicles, a Bronco belonging to the BIA police, and the trucks holding the fencing materials. Willie walks up to the crew and asks, "What are you doing here?"

"What do you think, man," one replies.

"This land belongs to someone," Willie says. "It belongs to Bessie Begay, and she's upset that you're building this fence here, disturbing her livestock and cutting all these roads."

A burly BIA policeman walks over and places himself between Willie and the Hopi he is addressing. Willie remembers the policeman as big, wearing a blue jumpsuit, and standing about six foot two and 220 pounds. Willie doesn't know what tribe he belongs to, thinks maybe a Papago or Pima. He has close-cropped hair, a light mustache, and is dark complected.

"What is your business here?" the policeman asks, stepping right up to Willie, a slender man, less than six feet tall, with fragile-looking hooded eyes and a long braid that reaches to the middle of his back.

"We're here to register protest for the family whose land you're running this fence through," Willie says. "You can arrest us if that is what you want." Willie steps forward, grabs one of the metal fenceposts and pulls it out of the ground. He flings it as far as he can, then grabs another. Thomas and Sam follow suit, until the policeman grabs them, handcuffs their hands behind their backs, and takes them to the Hopi Tribal Jail.

Later that night, Lee Phillips succeeds in getting the four released. It requires a telephone call to the chief Hopi judge, who is in California for the weekend. "On Friday," recalls Phillips, "they wouldn't let them out on their own recognizance. I asked the clerk if I could make a motion to the chief Hopi judge. She said I could do whatever I wanted, but that she was going home and I could get them out on Monday. I had to get the judge, who was in California, to order her to stay while he heard my motion. He did, she did, and we finally got them out."

The arraignment is scheduled for the following Monday. Phillips meets the four defendants at the Hopi Cultural Center at eight a.m. to confer about the proceeding. He explains their rights, and they all agree to plead not guilty. They discuss their apprehension about Reggie's case, because he is not a Navajo but a Winnebago. They fear the Hopis will use this incident as an excuse to evict everyone from the camp. Ivan Sidney has been very vocal recently about foreigners congregating at Big Mountain.

The Hopi Tribal Court is a new building, set right beside the police station, several miles from Kykotsmovi. The courtroom is designed to look like a pueblo structure; raw logs jut from an adobe facade around the perimeter. Hopi design elements are painted behind the bench. Hopi Tribal Judge Delfred Leslie hears dozens of drunk and disorderly charges against Hopis before the four Navajo men are called. By that time, half the spectator area is filled with Navajos. Kee Shay and Roberta Blackgoat are here, as is Mae Tso, and her sister, whose property the men were defending. Phillips is here with Matt Strassberg, a law student who helps him out with some of his cases. They are accompanied by a representative of Church and Laity Concerned, a group that has been making regular trips out to the Big Mountain area to gather information with which to keep its members informed of developments. Betty Tso sits in the visitors' section with her mother Mae, who wrings her hands. Mae maintains her sense of humor, however, joking that she hopes everyone will be there when her own trial comes up. She faces charges stemming from her attack on two BIA police who had impounded her horses.

The bros' names are called, one by one, and the charges against them read. The young men rise and plead. Willie Scott pleads not guilty to charges of injuring public property. Reggie pleads not guilty to resisting arrest, Sam and Thomas plead not guilty to injuring public property and resisting arrest.

To the Navajos, intrusion into their customary use areas is as shocking as a physical assault. The land and livestock are part of a whole that includes mother, family, and the Creator. The hogan is a sacred place not only for its walls and inhabitants, but for the floor itself.

One of the fence crews, while digging out a juniper tree, uncovered a cradleboard that had been returned in a Navajo ceremony to the tree from which it had been cut. This intrusion was a sacrilege to the Navajos, intolerable. They didn't understand why the fence was being built and assumed the purpose was to frighten and offend them.

It turns out that the fence the bros pulled out was a range management fence used to control livestock and help range restoration. It was being put up by the Hopi Tribe under contract to the BIA. "As far as I know," says Dan Jackson, the lawyer who decides the legality of the decisions of the BIA, "there is no 'conspiracy' to build fences out there or harass the people. It is simply a management decision made by the BIA to prevent livestock from crossing from one grazing unit into another. The purpose, presumably, according to the science of range management, is to allow certain areas to rest and recover by keeping animals off."

The courts have affirmed the Hopis' rights to manage the lands on the HPL. The Navajos lost an appeal of the Writ of Assistance and Order of Compliance delivered in 1972 by District Court Judge James Walsh. On September 12, 1974, Circuit Judge M. Oliver Koelsch of the Court of Appeals affirmed the decision of the District Court that "plaintiff tribe (Hopi) had been ousted from lands and that tribe in possession had wasted the lands." He wrote in his decision: "[Grazing] districts are a recognized land-management device which may cut across or combine parcels of land under separate legal ownership in order to regulate range for grazing purposes. . . . A grazing district does not alter either tribe's rights in the land—it simply facilitates government regulation of the land to protect it from waste."

"It turns out," says Jackson, "that an interior fence had been installed in the wrong place. The BIA ripped it out and put it in again at the area of the recent dispute. But Judge Koelsch's opinion clearly indicates that actions such as that are within the law and purely management decisions." Fences are usually placed on ridges, and a grazing unit must include at least one source of water. The location of range fences is determined by experts, who base their decisions on natural resources and the condition of the grazing. People's houses or customary use areas are considered irrelevant. Although it has legal justification, Judge Koelsch's decision that "members of one tribe may appropriately live in the exclusive grazing district of the other, gather wood there, or do anything else there, except use the land for grazing livestock" does not reflect the realities of the Navajo lifestyle. Sheep corrals are located within a stone's throw of the place of residence. And since it is believed

by Navajos that one's soul wanders at night near the place where the
umbilical cord is buried—usually, the sheep corral—a range fence that
cuts the house off from the sheep corral will have dramatic impact on the
family. When the four young men confronted the fencing crew, they
wanted to communicate what that fence meant to the Begay family. The
BIA police, trying to protect the crews who were just implementing ju-
dicially mandated range management techniques, were operating within
their own framework of law and imperatives. There was no effective
communication. "No matter where you put a fence, you're going to gore
somebody's ox," says Jackson. "The location, timing, and method of
constructing fences requires wisdom. Unfortunately, one person's wisdom is another's folly."

At the time of the arraignment at Hopi court, another drama is taking
place at Hopi, at the tribal headquarters in Kykotsmovi. A note is found
pinned to the car of a BIA policeman stating that bombs have been
planted in the Hopi offices. Ivan Sidney clears the government building
and locks himself in his office, insisting that no one and nothing will
intimidate him or drive him from his office, even a bomb threat. The
offices are searched and no bomb is discovered. But Sidney decides the
threat is the opening salvo in the violence he has expected as the relocation deadline approaches.

Later on in the afternoon, after the arraignment, Mae Tso, her sister,
Lee Phillips, and the defendants, accompanied by a vanload of CALC
people who had driven in from San Francisco, all drive to the Hopi
Cultural Center for lunch. Sidney greets the group but doesn't let on that
he wonders whether the bomb threat was tied to the arraignments that
morning. "Ivan was very friendly to me," recalls Phillips. "He called me
over to his table as we walked in and asked me how everything had gone
that morning. I joked with him that I had expected him to be there, and
in fact was prepared to ask him to appear as a character witness for me
at the Hopi court."

Phillips notices that a local reporter has just left the cultural center
and assumes she must have completed an interview with Sidney. Phillips
is yet unaware of the bomb threat. The next morning, a story by that
reporter appears in the *Arizona Republic*. It quotes Sidney as saying, "I
feel that the action today was a planned attempt to generate publicity for
Big Mountain Navajos. . . . When the weather gets nice, a lot of non-
Navajos travel to the Big Mountain area. They try to stir up trouble. I
would like to call on Chairman Zah to join me in getting rid of the non-
Navajos that are behind these tactics. I've seen a lot of outsiders around
lately, but Zah should do something about that."

When Phillips learns of Sidney's comments, he says, "Well, people
will probably try to link us with that. When I heard about it last night, I
didn't give it a second thought, it seemed so ludicrous." But Sidney is

convinced this is just the beginning. In fact, everyone is worried about the actions of the people at the survival camp as the deadline approaches.

The bomb threat catches quite a few people in its web. Abbott Sekaquaptewa sets off for his ranch but is prevented from passing the government offices while police search for a bomb. He wonders whether the threat hasn't been concocted by Ivan himself. "I wouldn't put it past Ivan, creating the problem himself to make a smoke screen to deflect attention from the fact that he is about to lose lots of things."

Sidney has reason to be worried. The Udall-McCain bill is gaining momentum as the Navajo chapters review it and as media attention increases. An Academy Award–winning documentary on the land dispute, *Broken Rainbow*, highly sympathetic to the Navajos, has just been released nationwide, accompanied by star-studded news conferences and demonstrations. And Gurwitz's repeated visits to Washington seem to be finally paying off. In the wake of the introduction of the Udall-McCain bill, other lawmakers are stepping forward to introduce their own ideas. Representative Bill Richardson, Democrat from New Mexico, has a bill in the works to put a moratorium on further relocations until July. And Representative Mickey Leland, Democrat of Texas, is drafting a bill at Gurwitz's urging to repeal the Settlement Act. The tide seems, for the moment, to be turning.

The fence that the boys had tried to stop on April 4, two weeks ago, and for which they were arrested, is being continued through Mosquito Springs (an area about fifteen miles west of Big Mountain) directly toward the camp of Mae Tso's sisters Sara and Bessie Begay. Hopi trucks and police vehicles are parked in the center of huge ruts and gouges that the activity has made in the soft red earth.

Sara and Bessie and Mae sit on sheepskins under a large juniper tree exactly in the path of the incomplete fence. Beside them, a line of green fence posts wind up over a rise toward Dove Springs, where the boys had been arrested. Several young Navajos are gathered near the sisters. They have covered up the license plates of their trucks with cardboard cutouts that read BUZZ OFF! At the peak of the hill, a Hopi police truck is parked, snaked into the rise as if it were an animal lying in wait. Inside, a Hopi policeman in aviator glasses peers down over the Navajo gathering. Occasionally he lifts a small automatic camera and snaps photos. Fear and paranoia envelop the air here.

Soon Mae and her sisters are joined by other women, and the camaraderie of the women eventually dispels the gloom. They card chunks of gray wool into strands and then spin the flaxen wisps into yarn on handmade spindles. Young men drive up to the gathering in trucks, pass a few words, and take off again. Sam Tso stays near his mother and his aunts. Bags of groceries surround the women. A package of cinnamon rolls peeps out from the top of one paper sack. A stained fry pan and plastic bowl of dough lie close to a pile of wood. The ladies appear prepared to stay for a week if necessary. Lee Phillips arrives, late as is his pattern, in response to a summons from Mae. Mae jokes that he has come only because of the chance of a free meal.

A trim man with short wavy hair approaches the women. He stands around them for some time, listening to them speak to each other and to Phillips. Phillips recognizes the man as Don Ami, head of the Hopi Department of Economic and Natural Resources, and part of the Hopi contingent that showed Ross Swimmer around the HPL in January. Phillips asks him if he knows who is doing the fencing. Ami tells him the Hopi Tribe is doing it. The ladies become silent and listen to the conversation, some understanding only a few of the English words, others understanding more.

Phillips points out that the women are terrified. They don't know what the fence is or why it's headed straight for their houses. They can't cross the work lines to go to the outhouse for lack of privacy. Ami says, "We're taking that into consideration. We're not here to bother anybody." He explains that the fence is not a boundary marker nor a change in the line dividing the Hopi and Navajo Partition Lands. "We are doing cross-fencing," he explains to Phillips, "which is a management practice put in place to expedite range practices on the land. We sector out range units within ecosystem types. This area doesn't have high carrying capacity. This is a way of conserving resources."

Ami points out that a sector fence to the east has been removed and the fencing crew is correcting its boundary based on maps of the vegetation and lay of the land. He does not reply to questions about how the fence wound up heading straight through the ladies' camp. Phillips listens to him and nods. He wears a gray woolen coat over his jeans, and cowboy boots. He stands with his hips tipped, one leg straight out in front of him. He looks out from under his light brows with the bathos of a fifteenth-century rendering of a Christian martyr. He speaks in a high pitch, asking a question he seems to have his own firm answer to. "Why now?" he asks. "How did you arrive at your timing, three months before the deadline?"

Ami replies readily, a smile on his lips. "The timing was off, I must admit. The timing was not meant to coincide with the deadline." Ami wears new calfskin cowboy boots, jeans, and a light jacket. He wears a belt of heavy turquoise stones and a white cowboy hat. He is friendly and open, his appearance ostentatiously fashionable for this remote locale.

"Why is fencing required?" asks Phillips. "There are hardly any animals left out here." The livestock reductions have brought the residents' herds down below ten sheep. Ami concurs. "You're right, there aren't many animals here, but there's the potential that more will be put on." Ami says that there are applications pending from Hopis who want to graze animals out in the Big Mountain area.

Phillips points out that the issue now is that the residents of the area are frightened and upset at the fencing, which is uprooting trees and coming dangerously close to burial sites. Ami tells Phillips that he has already told the people that he will not continue if they have a problem with it. "I don't think there will be any further activity here," he says. "I've instructed the guys to pull out." Phillips looks surprised at the quick decision. He suggests that some of these people could meet with representatives of the Hopi Tribe and discuss their fears. "These people feel left out," he says. Ami says he will bring the message back to Ky-kotsmovi. "We'll leave the posts in place until we are able to discuss it. If they want the whole thing moved, we'll have to discuss that." Ami is standing easily now beside the group of ladies. His hands are still crossed protectively high on his chest, but he appears more relaxed.

One of the elderly ladies calls out to him in Navajo with an accusing shrillness. Ami looks embarrassed for a moment and replies in English, "I'm Hopi and Tewa." The woman is quiet and then, in English, says, "I thought you were Navajo. I didn't understand why you would be doing these things to your own people." Ami turns to her and says, "I grew up in Low Mountain, so I understand some Navajo." The woman sinks down to her sheepskin. Ami grew up on the Navajo reservation, in the same area in which Peterson Zah was born. It is hard even for the people of this area to know who is Hopi and who is Navajo, who is friend and who is enemy. But one thing is clear: that which has introduced divisions between them is the law.

Ami leaves and Mae Tso lights a fire and starts frying bread. She stirs a large iron pot of beans and sets a coffeepot on the fire. The ladies still talk to each other about their surprise that Ami was a Hopi.

Mae's niece changes the subject and says, "This fence is disrespectful to the land." She points out the deep ruts formed in the earth by the trucks. Large circular tracks have been cut in the soil by the tires, making roads in an area that was formerly untouched. Several cedar trees have been pushed over, as if a truck had carelessly backed into them. "The cedar trees are juniper-related trees," Mae says. "They are people too, women and children. They live as they are. When we need wood to cook we give them corn pollen. In return, they give us warmth. We do not like what they did to the trees. Only tornadoes and hurricanes destroy trees. Who do they think they are, ripping out the trees?"

Jenny Manybeads, Mae's hundred-year-old grandmother, whose Navajo name means Lady Lefthand, joins her younger relatives under the tree and talks excitedly with great spleen. She says in Navajo that *her* grandmother is buried here somewhere, that when she was a little girl, she used to tend a cornfield up over the hill and wander down here to the shaded grove to rest. She says she thinks the fences are the first bad sign. What will come next are the trucks for the livestock and then the trucks for them. "Where am I going to go if they move me off?" she asks. The answer in her mind is obvious. There is no place but here.

The women think the fencing is being done at the behest of the government. "Altogether, they're trying to cheat us in one way or another, trying to pick on us to make some kind of a conflict," they say.

Phillips believes the work is Ivan Sidney's doing, or the idea of the Salt Lake City lawyers. He surmises they think that provoking the Navajos to violence will play into their hand, reinforcing the idea of law-breaking, violent Navajos in an attempt to scuttle the Udall-McCain bill and any other modification of relocation. "There are two purposes for the Hopis' coming out here," Phillips says. "The tribe is trying to put pressure on the last resisters when tensions are already high. And secondly, the Hopi Tribe wants to establish a physical presence out here to scuttle any land exchange proposal."

The Begay sisters are not as concerned with the political implications as with their fright. "I'm sick and tried of their creeping around our houses, showing off their vehicles," they say. "I'm afraid to get the firewood or go to the bathroom. When we see them over the hill, they are looking at us with binoculars. We do not look at them when they're going to the bathroom."

The ladies explain that they asked the four boys to go to the fence construction site when it was farther away from them because they were scared. "For that they arrested them. But why? They did nothing wrong, they only did what their elders told them."

Bessie Begay says, "Last night I went to sleep past midnight. I am sleepy now. We are still expecting them to come back. It is tiring waiting for them, it makes us ill. We are afraid of them, they have weapons. We don't. We have our spindles and our yarn to make our livings with." Her sister Sara butts in. "Last night there was one looking at us, a BIA police. He came by last night when it was dark. Left around one a.m., spying around, so I didn't have enough sleep. Yesterday, I was here with my mother. She got tired, sick, got a headache. This makes people sick."

Bessie's son, a soft-spoken young man, says the workers first came out near their house a week ago. "The elderly people have really been harassed," he says. "They don't speak English and didn't know what happened. Four rangers came by. I told them we don't destroy things over on your side, but you come over here and cut our trees. We use trees as offerings." He speaks with a tired incredulity. "We've been told to keep our patience for the last twenty-one years," he says, his eyes growing wide. "This really made us angry." In this area he can feel the presence of his ancestors who are buried here. He has associations with offerings he and members of his family have made here. It holds his memories. And the sudden intrusion and destruction has thrown him into a confusion.

Later, he confides that he has accepted the Mormon faith, which he was introduced to at boarding school. He is disturbed about something, though. He has heard that the Mormons were involved in the relocation scheme; the Big Mountain group, for instance, refers to a Mormon conspiracy to get the minerals out of the ground. He saw a paper describing it. He wants to know if it is true. His eyes are troubled as he asks Lee Phillips. Phillips doesn't see the pain in the boy's face or hear what he is really asking. Phillips replies yes, that it seems the Mormons were involved in trying to take the minerals out of the ground, a simplification of a very complex problem that involved some Mormon individuals. The boy walks along silently, trying to digest what he has heard and measure it against his faith.

Later on in the day, Ivan Sidney agrees to meet with the women from Mosquito Springs. He announces that the fencing will not continue until he speaks to them in one week, Thursday, April 17. The women are also concerned about the construction of an earthen dam and some water pipes in Teesyatoh—another name for the area near Mosquito Springs. From the look of things, the women figure the Hopis are creating water ponds for cattle, but they are diverting the water from springs the Navajo families use. The Hopis, under the law, have every right to prepare the land for their future expected occupancy, but to the people who live in the area, and who pray that the law will simply evaporate, the presence of the trucks makes real what they have all hoped would disappear. And they wonder why it is happening so abruptly and in the tense months before the deadline. Some of them agree with Lee Phillips that the Hopis are trying to make a presence on the land so as to discourage land exchanges of the sort offered in the Udall-McCain bill. However, Ivan Sidney's offer to talk to them about their concerns heartens them.

But not for long. Sidney lets the ladies know that he only wants to meet with two of them, and asks them to decide on the two to send as representatives. All the Teesyatoh women are very independent and don't believe anyone can speak for them. Each has her own mind and will express it. After a meeting at the Hardrock chapter house, the ladies decide that, with those preconditions, they will not go at all.

Lee Phillips is in Washington, D.C., when he hears about their decision not to go. He has met with some of the traditional Hopis—Will Mase, Byron Tewa, and Earl Pela—in hopes of broadening the resistance. The Hopis have told him that if he wants their support in the fight against relocation, then the elderly Navajos should not meet with Ivan Sidney, whose legitimacy as a leader they reject.

Phillips calls Annie Holmes, sister of Kee Shay and an outspoken opponent of relocation who nevertheless is viewed with some suspicion by the other Big Mountain Navajos because she appears to be allied with the Navajo tribal government. The Big Mountain Navajos feel that the tribe has abandoned them—in large measure because the tribe hasn't been able to do away with relocation. Although the Zah administration has worked tirelessly and at great peril to its own political future to come to their aid, the people want results. The tribe's interests are not always exactly the same as the interests of the Big Mountain residents. For example, when the tribe is slapped with fines of five hundred dollars a day for illegal construction on the HPL, it must eventually discuss the construction with the Navajo owners. The tribe has incurred almost a million dollars in fines already. Gurwitz and Phillips have the luxury of standing firm in their push for repeal of the law, and they can fight every action of the government and the Hopis; the tribe has to respond to realities. It has already lost many battles defying the law. The ladies approached some tribal representatives after the boys had been arrested for damaging the fence and they had been told that the Hopis were within their rights to construct improvements on the HPL. Although this was correct, the women didn't want to hear it, and it confirmed their view that the Navajo Tribe has turned its back on them.

So, in addition to all the other stresses, the law has caused the Navajos affected by relocation to view their own government as their enemy. And Annie Holmes, one of their own, is viewed skeptically because she talks with the tribal government.

Lee Phillips tells Holmes on the telephone that Mae Tso and the others have decided not to meet with Sidney. In spite of Phillips's call, Holmes wants the meeting to go on. The day of the scheduled meeting, Ivan Sidney flies back from Phoenix and waits for the Navajos to arrive. He arrives to find out that "Lew Gurwitz had canceled the meeting." A few hours before the 1:00 p.m. scheduled start of the talks, Annie Holmes calls Sidney's office. She is told the meeting has been canceled, but that the Hopis were all there. Ivan tells her he is there with some council members and religious leaders. Annie and her niece Nancy Walters decide to go up themselves.

As Mae and others boycotting the meeting had feared, the meeting that ensues does not focus on the fencing, disruption of burial sites, and water development in Mosquito Springs. Apparently Ivan Sidney wants to lecture the women about the law. He tells a reporter while waiting for Nancy Walters and Annie Holmes that he doesn't think the Navajo leadership has informed its people about the reasons for relocation. "For this reason, we are always willing to meet with Navajos from the affected area," Sidney said. "That is why we are here today." However, Sidney says that he and the religious leaders who support him are willing to discuss the possibility of some Navajos remaining on the HPL. "Any request made by Big Mountain Navajos living on Hopi lands to remain on our lands would be seriously considered. So far, no Navajos have come and asked this, but if they did, we would have to consider it." He says that the elders "want to listen to the Big Mountain people and explain to them the conditions under which they may stay." Sidney says he is entertaining the possibility of allowing some of the Navajos to stay under certain circumstances in part because Senator Barry Goldwater has asked him to.

It later becomes clear that the Hopis want to meet with elderly Navajos who remember the legends. The Hopis want the Navajos to try to prove that the land they are living on is theirs. The Hopi elders feel that if confronted face to face, the Navajos will *have* to admit that they are in fact on Hopi land. Once they admit that, then the Hopis are prepared to tell them the conditions under which they may be allowed to stay.

Ivan Sidney's offer to meet with the Navajos is really a carefully constructed political move—just what Mae had feared. By stating that the Hopi elders are willing to accept requests from the Navajos to stay, Sidney is satisfying the demands of some of the Hopis to have it out with the Navajos and force them to admit they are wrong in law and legend. At the same time Sidney is satisfying the demands of Goldwater to be generous to the Big Mountain people.

Above all, Sidney wants nothing constructive to happen, nothing that could be interpreted as showing weakness on his part. So Sidney announces that he wants to speak to the "religious leaders." But the Navajos don't have anything like the Hopi hereditary religious leaders who speak for their communities. When that is pointed out to Sidney, he replies that that isn't his problem. "The traditional people told me it is up to those people to come to us. They are the newcomers." We have returned once again to the Hopi imperative: the primacy of law. "The Hopis aren't going to force the Navajos to move. They should move out of respect for the law."

But going to the Hopis and asking permission to stay under Hopi jurisdiction is unthinkable for Mae Tso and her relatives. They didn't wrest the land from anyone as far as they can remember. It was empty and they made use of it. As Kee Shay has asked, "Whatever did we do wrong for these things to happen here? We have never stepped on anybody's toes."

Nancy Walters and Annie Holmes meet with Sidney and other residents of First Mesa—his political base—for three hours behind closed doors. At a press conference following the meeting, Nancy Walters makes her own concerns clear. She wants to set up some contact between the resisters and the Hopis, hoping that some private accommodations might be made. "My Navajo people are very shy and very patient," she says. "All this time, they have been thinking something has been done for them by the tribe and the attorneys. But they are saying right now that it is about time that they put us traditional people together and let us talk."

Walters's words reveal another deep division among the Navajo resisters. One part of the Big Mountain people supports the efforts of Gurwitz and Phillips. Staunch supporters include Mae Tso and Ella Bedonie and her family. But some others are having second thoughts. They haven't seen any results. Where is the repeal bill that Gurwitz has supposedly been working on for the last four years? Some of the ladies are panicking, feeling they had best take matters into their own hands.

Everything is getting too complicated. Gurwitz and Phillips have not yet come out with a position on the Udall-McCain bill. By all measure, the Navajos are for it; they want to be saved. But Gurwitz and Phillips, instead of seizing the opportunity for some reduction of relocations, are still holding out the unlikely hope for repeal of the law. Gurwitz and Phillips are even divided on this matter between themselves, Phillips leaning toward supporting the bill, Gurwitz wanting the whole pie. This, of course, causes further confusion among the Navajos.

This uncertainty is making the idea of cutting individual deals with the Hopis more enticing. Mae hears that a second meeting with Sidney is in the works. She drives to the trading post and calls her daughter Betty at the BMLDOC office in Flagstaff. Betty agrees to come home and help her mother decide what to do. They meet with Percy Deal, who, according to Betty, "really lobbied my mom to go." He shows Betty a newspaper article in the *Navajo Times*, in which Ivan Sidney said he was disappointed that the Navajos didn't keep their appointments with him. Nevertheless, after a discussion, Mae, her mother, and sisters decide not to go. Mae, still loyal to Phillips, is swayed by what he has told her, that they shouldn't deal with Ivan Sidney, so as not to threaten Phillips's pact with the Hopi traditionalists.

On the appointed date, still determined not to go herself, Mae drops off her grandmother Jenny Manybeads at Ivan's office. Mae sees that mostly old people are there. After struggling with herself, she goes in, and she tells some people that it is better that they go home. Also, she tells them, "Ivan Sidney is treacherous in many ways." A group of people leave with her and they go to the trading post at Kykotsmovi and discuss the situation. Then they decide to go back. Mae has grave doubts, however, and returns reluctantly.

When the group arrives back, they are asked who their representatives are. Betty stands up and says they are all there representing themselves and that they are not being represented by Percy or Annie or anybody else. It seems that Ivan wasn't expecting them on that day, because no Hopi elders are there. Percy tells Ivan they had heard about the meeting on Navajo Nation KTNN radio. Ivan replies that he had only discussed "tentative dates" with Annie Holmes, and that somehow that date had mistakenly been broadcast.

According to Percy Deal, Ivan then proceeded to "recount his view of the events leading up to the fencing incident and said he didn't want to have a discussion with the Navajo ladies until the Hopi and Navajo elders could get together." Ivan then told them they had better choose who their leaders are. "Now, it's getting more confusing as who do we listen to," he says. "But it is something for you people to decide, not me." Percy Deal tells Ivan, "The people are here *now* and they want to discuss the issue of daily harassment." Ivan Sidney replies that he has ordered all work in the area stopped for the time being, and that "it wasn't the Hopi position to violate anyone's civil rights."

But Ivan insists again that he doesn't want to talk about the fencing with the women until the Hopi elders are present. Percy recalls, "It was then Mae started getting excited. She said, 'We are here to talk to you today. If you don't want to hear us, let us tell you what is bothering us, you might as well just tell me to die. Just tell me to die.'" Mae recalls later, "All this time I had hurting within me and I started perspiring and my pulse was going rapidly because of the commotion in the office and because I felt I was deceived. I didn't think Ivan was there to get things straightened out." And she felt no one was there to explain, properly, in English so Ivan could understand what they objected to. "I wanted to be represented by Lee," she said later.

Then, some of the women of Mosquito Springs speak up against the fence and the disruption of burial sites. Bessie Yazzie stands up and makes a comment that shocks the assembled Navajos. She says she is glad about the fence because it keeps the stock away from her cornfield. Several people remark that she shouldn't have said that and then Mae starts to shout. She feels everything falling to pieces around her. "This is too frustrating for me," she says. Mae begins to cry and feel ill. Betty yells for a paper bag and Percy helps her outside. Annie Holmes and Betty follow her, putting a Pendleton blanket over her shoulders. She is hyperventilating. When Mae gets outside into the air, the press corps surrounds her. Eventually, Mae is taken to Keams Canyon Hospital to make sure she hasn't had another heart attack. Later, Ivan Sidney, through his press spokeswoman, accuses Mae of getting sick "so she could have her picture taken."

(24)

Small Victories

In April 1986, Hopi stock pens, range fences, and livestock ponds appeared in Coal Mine Mesa as well as in Teesyatoh. These developments seriously unnerved the Navajos, because they were proof of the Hopis' intentions to ready the land for their own livestock. And the Hopis' unspoken message was clear: it is time to get your things and leave, because our stock will soon live where you do.

The tensions over the range improvements reflected and intensified other anxieties. It was three months until the deadline. No one knew what the deadline really meant. No one knew if there would be violence and if so, what it would lead to.

The Navajo Tribe still had high hopes for the Udall-McCain bill. They could do little but wait, however, since the bill's fate rested with Barry Goldwater, and Goldwater refused to meet with them.

The Relocation Commission had been beaten up pretty badly, but any slack that shake-up might have had on the program's forward march seemed to be taken up by Assistant Interior Secretary Ross Swimmer, whose activities now appeared to be on a collision course with the Navajos, who wanted the New Lands to remain empty and a bargaining chip in discussions with the Hopis.

Lew Gurwitz and Lee Phillips were floundering, trying to keep together their alliance of traditional Hopis and Navajos and still produce a plan in a reasonable amount of time. Their actions were puzzling. Instead of joining with the Navajo Tribe to back an effort put forward by Mo Udall, the powerful chairman of the House Interior Committee, they found a low-ranking House member, Mickey Leland, to draft a bill to repeal the law—not much of a solution.

The Navajos affected, fearing that no one was helping them, had started taking matters into their own hands. As we have seen, part of that involved the violent resistance to fencing from the young men at the camp; the other was the fledgling effort begun by Annie Holmes for Navajos to cut individual deals with the Hopi Tribe to allow them to live out their lives on the land.

Peterson Zah, in an effort to protect the Navajos from further stress, wrote Ross Swimmer on April 10, asking for his help. He pointed out two specific incidents in which elderly Navajos had been disturbed by Hopi rangers or BIA police. Zah explained that two unidentified men presented themselves to Mary Begay at her house and "taunted her, using their own version of sign language to inform her that she should pack all her belongings on her back and hike down the road." In another case, an elderly couple was frightened by "BIA employees or Hopi Rangers, [making] repeated requests to loan them a spare tire from a broken-down car (which had no tires) parked at [their] residence."

Zah wrote, "Mr. Swimmer, you and I cannot comprehend the anxiety and frustration faced by the Navajo relocatees, individuals who have been without a homeland since the date of partition of the Joint Use Area. By their own words, they presently live under 'duress and fear.' " Zah concluded, "The Navajo Nation strongly objects to the shameful treatment of these individuals, especially at this point in time, approximately three months before the expiration of the relocation deadline, by persons subject to your control." He explained that the Navajos had no one to protect them against the harassment, since the Navajo police had no jurisdiction over the HPL, and the Hopi and BIA police were involved in the objectionable activity.

In Washington, too, nerves continued to fray over the upcoming deadline. Most focused their apprehension on the sun dance, which they feared would attract thousands of people to Big Mountain. Some worried that the slightest provocation from the Hopi police would spark a conflagration. The concern was not so much with the sun dancers, for they would be absorbed in a grueling and essentially spiritual activity. Interior officials, congressional staff, and members of the tribes worried about the observers, many Anglo, who had varying degrees of understanding of the dispute, and who would likely be worked into a frenzy by provocative literature from the various support groups. The Big Mountain Legal Defense/Offense Committee made it clear that the threat of violence would work in its best interest. In the past months, it had opened additional offices in Atlanta, Kansas City, St. Louis, and Washington, D.C., and was stepping up its activities across the country. On March 27, BMLDOC organized a rally in Griffith Park in Los Angeles to protest relocation at which actor Jon Voight had made an emotional plea to protect the Indians from what he described as the government's determination to clear the land for strip mining. Singers Stevie Van Zandt, Connie Stevens, and Buffy Sainte-Marie also denounced the relocation program. And on April 10, BMLDOC organized a twenty-four-hour sit-in at the Department of the Interior in Washington to protest relocation.

The Hopis were the wild card. No one knew if they would go out on the HPL with their tribal policemen and try to evict Navajos from their homes. For the Hopis, any violence on the part of the Navajos would feed into their hand, for it would simply confirm the image of the violent neighbor on which the Hopis had based their case. On the Navajo side, a shedding of blood would bring in hoards of press with stories of government officials dragging Indian people from their homes—which could work to the Navajos' advantage. The chance of violence, since it would seem to serve both sides, appeared high.

Concerned about this issue, which would of course look very bad for Congress, Sid Yates summoned Ross Swimmer and Wayne Nordwall, an attorney from the Solicitor General's office, to a meeting in his office on April 21. Yates asked Nordwall whether the Hopis might try to initiate eviction proceedings against the Navajos on the HPL once the deadline had passed. Nordwall told him it was unlikely that any court would order eviction because of the limiting language, which prohibited federal monies from being used to evict Navajos, inserted in the 1986 appropriations law by Dan Jackson on his extraordinary trip to Washington in the fall of 1985. Nordwall told Yates that the Secretary of the Interior would uphold his duty to protect those Navajo persons and property on the HPL until they were relocated. At the same time, however, BIA officials were selecting twenty-five officers from around the country for special riot training in case violence should erupt. Yates wanted to know if the appropriations language aimed at preventing evictions superseded the 1974 Act's deadline. Nordwall thought that the appropriations language was "obviously a binding limitation on the use of federal funds."

There were actually two possible interpretations of the July 7 date in PL 93-531. One was that Congress had decided that all Navajos must be off the HPL by that date. The other was that the deadline was conceived as a target date for the accomplishment of the Commission's duties. Around April, the idea of the July 7 date as a "target" for completion of relocation emerged from the Solicitor General's office, traveled to Yates in this meeting, and eventually made its way to the Relocation Commission. This idea evaporated the notion of a deadline and the problems that might ensue from it, and was quickly adopted by all concerned. This was the second piece in Dan Jackson's carefully laid plan, the first of which was the limiting language in the appropriations bill. Without the acceptance of the "target date" concept, said Jackson, "we didn't have a real good case against the Hopis if a court decided the government's [responsibility to protect the Navajos] had passed."

Yates asked Ross Swimmer, "Tell me what you're doing on relocation. You were regarded as the savior. Are you?" It was Yates who had dubbed Swimmer the savior two months ago. Swimmer, a tall, lanky man with a dignified but friendly manner, brushed aside the left-handed compliment and responded in his comfortable drawl. He told Yates about his trip to the HPL, during which he met families and representatives from the tribes. "I'm now familiar with the deficiencies of the Commission and the fact that the Navajos on the HPL are confused," he said. Swimmer told Yates about the signing of the memorandum and his entrance into the planning process for the New Lands, yet he noted that the Commission was dragging its feet about getting him the funds to conduct a thorough survey of the people on the HPL. In addition, he felt that the introduction of the Udall-McCain bill had "greatly undermined our efforts. The Navajo Tribe told families not to move." Swimmer said, "It's too late for Udall-McCain. We only have two hundred fifty families left on the HPL." Swimmer said that in spite of the Navajo Tribe's efforts to scuttle what he called his "pilot project"—the first effort to get a few Navajo families moved to the New Lands—he thought he would find enough to go.

Yates concluded his meeting by asking about the harassment of Navajos by Hopi work crews. He told Swimmer to make sure the activity stopped. Swimmer said he would do so.

The day after Yates's meeting with Swimmer, the Relocation Commission assembled in a conference room on the ground floor of the Rayburn House office building. Yates had called them for another grilling. The Commission senior staff and Ross Swimmer sat across a large oval conference table from Yates. The day's business was the Commission's annual budget hearing, during which the Commission had to account for its use of last year's money and try to defend its requests for next year's funding. A group of schoolchildren was assembled in the rows of leather-seated chairs behind the conference table. Ross Swimmer had just finished giving them an impromptu history lesson about the Cherokee Indians' trek from their eastern homelands to Oklahoma, a long, sad journey known as the Trail of Tears. The children filed out, the meeting began, and Ralph Watkins said to Yates, "Thank you for the history lesson. I was unaware of that." Yates shot him a look of disbelief. "The Trail of Tears?" Watkins repeated, "I wasn't aware." Yates's eyes glazed over and he told Watkins that if he had any good things to report, "I suggest you get them into the record quickly."

Before Watkins could reply, Yates deftly changed the subject and began asking questions. He wanted to know about the "twelve hundred Navajo families who voluntarily agreed to move from land assigned to the Hopi and departed from their homes, and who are now living in circumstances that I will describe as very bad for the most part. They don't have homes of the kind that were originally ordered by Congress: safe, sanitary, and comfortable."

Yates asked, "What is the status of the relocation effort, Mr. Watkins?" Watkins replied that he and his staff had done everything they could to help Mr. Swimmer in his task to take care of those people still left on the Hopi Partition Lands, but he didn't mention the twelve hundred families Yates had just referred to, and whose moves were still the Commission's responsibility. "We are attempting to get everybody off the HPL with the assistance of the BIA and Mr. Swimmer, and hopefully we will be in a position in the not-too-distant future to come to you and say it looks like we have completed our task, let's go out of business."

Yates replied, "We would like to see you go out of business, too."

Yates asked Watkins, "Does the Commission know where all of the twelve hundred families are located?" Watkins turned his head left and right over his shoulder at his staff. "Give him a direct answer," he said to no one in particular. Newly selected Executive Director Chris Bavasie answered, "Yes." Yates asked, "Do you know how they are living, what their needs are?"

Bavasie: "We can't be specific about all their needs."

Yates: "How do you know where they are? Do you have them on a computer?"

[Operations Director] Tessler: "Yes."

Yates: "Could you furnish the committee with a printout of where they are located?"

Tessler: "Yes."

Yates: "Incidentally, what was your last contact with them? What did you do with the twelve hundred? Did you tell them, 'We are going to take care of you' and then sit back?"

Tessler: "To some extent, that is what we did. . . . We have a bi-monthly newsletter that goes out to everyone who applies for relocation and everyone who moves—"

Yates: "Can all of them read?"

Tessler: "No."

Yates: "What do you do, print it in Navajo?"

Tessler: "No. There are usually members of the household who will read that letter to them. There is not a written Navajo language."

After a few minutes, Yates returned to the location of the twelve hundred.

Tessler: "Our addresses in most cases are post office boxes in Tuba City, they aren't house addresses."

Yates: "Then you don't know where they are living."

Tessler: "Of course we do. We have a mailing address for all of them."

Yates: "It is a post office box. You go to a post office box, they are not living in the box. . . ." Yates was now furious. He barked, "You don't know what their condition is, you haven't looked at them. You know when you want to get in touch with them, you send them a letter to a post office box. You don't know what they are like, where they are living, or anything else."

Yates paused for a moment, and pulled out a handful of photographs taken by a member of his investigative staff. He set them on the table. They showed Navajos living in shacks in south Tuba City and in condemned buildings near an abandoned uranium processing plant in an area known as Rare Metals. He said, "They are living there at the present time while they are waiting for new homes." He added dryly, "If this keeps up and they are living on radioactive land, they may not be able to enjoy their new homes."

Watkins started sputtering. He bounced in his seat, angrily denying that any relocatees lived in Rare Metals. He said he'd sent up some staff to take videotapes of the area to prove his point. Yates repeated that *his* investigator had found people there, and had identified them by name. He asked the Commission why they hadn't made use of money for emergency moves to help them.

Suddenly, Watkins pleaded ignorance of the situation, though he had just claimed to have sent staff up to videotape the area. Watkins asked, "Why did we just find this out? I don't know why we are just finding this out." Eric Eberhard, head of the Navajo Washington office, said that he thought the tribe had indeed informed the Commission that families forced from their homes on the HPL had moved into the condemned area. Eberhard said he would try to provide that information to the Committee. Watkins then raised his voice and said, "I resent his implication to you, sir, and to the people here, about the Commission. I think it is a real injustice to us, and it is a real injustice to the relocatees who are our clients. It is a real injustice, and he cannot furnish that material."

But he did. Eberhard found and sent to Yates a letter dated a year previously, written by Louise A. Linkin, the director of the EPA at Window Rock, to a caseworker at the Commission, saying that a man named Thomas Yazzie was awaiting his benefits and living in Rare Metals. Linkin informed the caseworker that the area in question was a mile north of a site that was presently being cleaned up by the Department of Energy. "There is a strong possibility," she wrote, "that the housing compound will be included in the remedial action." Linkin wrote further, "It is our strongest and highest recommendation" that Yazzie be relocated promptly.

Eberhard also provided Yates with an affidavit from Yazzie, saying he had been told by the Commission that he was unable to qualify for emergency moving funds because of a technicality. Yazzie stated that the Commission had informed him that his "situation was not critical enough, and that the temporary emergency housing funds were only for elderly or handicapped persons currently living on Hopi Partitioned Lands. I was therefore denied emergency housing benefits." Yazzie had a young son who was born in Rare Metals and had lived there all his life.

Yazzie explained he had also been told by the Commission that since the Commission had been directed by Congress to relocate those families

still on the HPL, and since he wasn't living on the HPL, he would probably not be relocated for another four years.

After Yates's hearing, the Commission made emergency funds available for Thomas Yazzie and another family found to be living at Rare
Metals.

Yates acknowledged that the Congress had given contradictory directions to the Commission about whom to relocate, and that this, unfortunately, was a problem of politics. He said, "I am going to change the law
if I can, but unfortunately I think this is the Senate's view, they want the
people off the HPL before anything happens. They are trying to get the
people off the HPL as quickly as possible, regardless of how the other
twelve hundred are living."

Yates questioned Swimmer about the feasibility of Swimmer taking
over the whole project and expanding his survey of the 248 families on
the HPL to include the twelve hundred as well. After the hearing, Yates
decided he would like to turn over the entire job to Swimmer, but the
Senate Committee did not agree. It was left to the Commission to conduct
a survey of the twelve hundred.

At this point, more investigation of the Commission had revealed that
its record-keeping had been so sloppy and its rules so lax that one third
of the people it had relocated to date were not eighteen years old—adults
—in 1974. The law specified that Navajos would be determined eligible
for relocation benefits if they were adults in 1974. The Commission just
kept certifying individuals as they turned eighteen, even if they turned
eighteen in 1985. This, of course, benefited the Navajos, but greatly
increased the cost of the program.

The Senate Appropriations Committee, upset that the Commission
had certified so many ineligible Navajos, wanted the Commission to
begin decertifying people. So, suddenly, the Navajos, on top of everything else, were facing decertification.

"It's inhumane pushing these people through the gate," said an Interior Department official who had long observed the program. "To get
the twelve hundred in to the Commission so the staff can find out where
they're living, we're threatening them with losing their benefits if they
don't make contact. At the same time the Commission is trying to take
their benefits away through decertification."

But there was some good news for the Navajos. A month after the
hearing, Swimmer replied to Peterson Zah's letter about harassment on
the HPL. He wrote that the incidents Zah described in his earlier letter
had been confirmed by the Navajo Area and BIA criminal investigators,
and that the harassment had been caused by Hopi tribal rangers and the
fencing crews. Swimmer informed Zah that he would "issue a directive
to all Bureau of Indian Affairs field personnel, including law enforcement
officers and fence crews to halt the on-going harassment." Also, Swim-

mer wrote that he "[would] mandate" that any further fencing be performed in accordance with the National Historic Preservation Act and
the American Indian Religious Freedom Act. The Hopi fencing that disturbed Mae Tso and her sisters, and that the four Navajo men were
arrested for, would now have to be undertaken with greater care. The
Hopi fencing crews couldn't run over graves, drive rapidly through Navajo homesites, or harass the residents. At this point, even small victories
were sweet ones.

(25)

The Rug Sale in Tucson

In 1985, Goose won the hearts of the Big Mountain ladies by organizing a rug sale that earned them fifteen thousand dollars. It took place at the Sheraton El Conquistador Hotel in Tucson, a sprawling tennis and golf resort at the foot of the dramatic Catalina Mountains. On these two April days in 1986, she is trying to do as well by them. Half a dozen ladies from the disputed land drive down in the back of a covered pickup with sixty rugs. The ladies also agree to speak at a Tucson BMLDOC support group meeting. Goose arranges for them to stay in the presidential suite at the El Conquistador.

Dennis, Ella, Buzz, and Nell Bedonie decide at the last minute to drive down with an extra rug from Ella's sister in California. The rug was driven to Flagstaff by a support group member who was heading this way. They pick it up at the Turquoise House, where many of the BMLDOC volunteers live. Out front there are four bulbous 1940s trucks and stacks of tipi poles for the Native American Church ceremonies the volunteers help set up for the Navajos. Inside, the floor is scattered with bedding and various radical political manifestos and declarations about the environment. Shoes are forbidden in the house, whether for reasons of hygiene or religion is unclear. A bearded man strums on a guitar. Despite their thoughtfulness on certain issues, someone carelessly left Ella's sister's rug in a plastic bag outside overnight. Moisture from the dew has rendered the rug shapeless.

As the Bedonies pull into the luxury complex of El Conquistador, they find themselves in a lush compound of bungalows, swimming pools, volleyball and tennis courts, and golf courses set beneath mammoth volcanic mountains. The kids are silent until Buzz cracks, "I'll bet old Grandma Scratch is out there on a volleyball court running around with her skirts all pinned up." Six-year-old Nell groans at the folly of her twelve-year-old brother. She says, "Buzzo, Grandma doesn't know how to play volleyball."

Dennis parks the car and the family walks to the front entrance. Young men in uniform swing open the tall wooden doors, and the Bedonies enter a plush lobby of fountains, exotic plants, and small seating arrangements of earth-toned velvet furniture. Up thirty feet on the mezzanine, hanging over the balustrade, are several Navajo rugs, which are a stunning addition to this pricey vacation resort. After climbing the curved staircase to the mezzanine, the Bedonies see that a loom has been set up, but none of the ladies are about. Goose is there, however, manning the booth, dressed in a purple jumpsuit with turquoise jewelry. Her gray hair is in a pageboy cut and her large purple glasses partially conceal the effects of decades of sun on her face. A tall, bearded man stands next to her behind a table of rugs. She is not too happy; sales are slow. She tells the Bedonies the ladies are at the nearby San Xavier reservation at a powwow.

Ella recognizes her mother's work on the loom and sits herself down in front of it. She pushes the wool down briskly with a wooden tool, and with great speed and efficiency, adds to the design, pulling and pushing warp and weft, evening out the strands with a flick of her fingernails, threading colors, tying knots. Several middle-aged guests stop and watch in silence. Nell wants to go out to the swimming pool. People are sunning themselves in pool chairs. Young men wear long bathing trunks in loud Hawaiian prints. Women with well-kept figures wearing fashionable pool wear rest in graceful positions; young couples timidly eye each other's bodies. Nell looks around, identifies the deep end of the pool, notes that no one is swimming, wishes she could go in and show off her new swimming skills. Then, she says, "Not many Indian people, here, huh?"

The Bedonies head off to the powwow. One enters the Papago's San Xavier reservation on Mission Road, which winds down through a narrow strip of land that eventually opens into the reservation proper. On either side of Mission Road are houses, small cinder block dwellings surrounded by junked cars and trailers. From every house on that narrow neck, Tucson can be seen, growing closer with every housing development and shopping mall.

The San Xavier del Bac Mission is an eighteenth-century Spanish church with an elaborately carved and painted nave. Beside the great white building is a mission school. The size and construction of these buildings completely overwhelm everything around them. The rest of the reservation seems to be in the wrong century. This reservation is small: a little over one hundred square miles. There is a larger Papago reservation to the west. Papago culture has been profoundly affected by Catholic missionaries, and many tribal members speak Spanish.

Inside the mission, in the chapel, a monk delivers a speech to the visitors, many of them wide-eyed Indian children. They squirm in their mothers' arms, look about with fright, impatience. "This is scientific fact," the monk says of various feats ascribed to a saint whose likeness lies in a glass-covered sepulcher on the north side of the chapel. "This is a matter of scientific fact." A worn sign on the wall asks for donations to help restore the chapel and its badly faded cherubs, saints, and gargoyles.

Dennis, Ella, and the kids wander through the booths of Indian silver and sand paintings at the crafts display. Most of the crafts are not handmade; some are stamped Hong Kong. Concessionaires sell stuffed animals, white cowboy hats with purple feathers, neon hula hoops, snow cones. As they head out across the asphalt parking lot toward the powwow dance on the grassy lawn behind the mission, Dennis calls out, "There's Roberta." Sure enough, Roberta Blackgoat, her daughter, and some other women are crossing the street. Roberta points across the parking lot to a pickup where Dennis sees Bessie Hatathlie just climbing in the back of the camper. They walk over. Inside are six elderlies, crosslegged in the bed of the truck. Annie Holmes' eighty-five-year-old mother is lying on a bed platform; the others sit with their knees folded beneath them, dignified, eager to get on with the next item on the agenda and then home. Ella shakes hands with the ladies and her mother. She never shows overt affection to her mother, approaching her instead with ritual protocol. With her daughter, Nell, Ella is sometimes different, hugging her or stroking her. Kisses, however, are few. And with her husband, no public displays of affection.

The ladies are all dressed up today, with their best jewelry on. Now they are going back to the hotel to rest for a bit, and then on to dinner and the support group meeting, which will be held on the University of Arizona campus, at the ecumenical church center.

The ladies are late to the meeting. The room is already full of white sympathizers who are starting to eye the food preparations with intense interest. A small line begins to form near the table of food, when the elderlies finally file into the room, causing a hush among the spectators as if the godhead had arrived. The ladies are shown to the food table and they nod shyly and thankfully to the Anglos who direct them to the front of the line. Bessie Hatathlie finds Ella and brings her food to the table. Bessie seldom smiles, and she is deadly serious and very frightened about this land dispute. Roberta Blackgoat joins her and flashes a big smile, jokes that she is happy to have some good food after their experience at the El Conquistador Hotel. "They were served special meals there," Ella explains. "First, they were given a sit-down meal of fish. But Navajos don't eat fish, so the ladies picked at the potato and took some bites of the vegetables. The next day, Goose told the kitchen staff no more fish, so they came out with turkey, another Navajo taboo. So the ladies are hungry today." Roberta laughs, even Bessie cracks a smile as they dig into chili beans, salad, and fried chicken. In fact, boxes of commercially prepared fried chicken and packages of sliced ham were picked up at the last minute when organizers were told that the ladies would appreciate some meat. Many of the homemade dishes brought by support group members are what the ladies call "veggie"—organic lentils, noodle salad, soufflés, and vegetables—a cooking style that has yet to become popular on the reservation.

After coffee in Styrofoam cups, the ladies assemble themselves in the front of the room. The scent of orange blossoms floats in from the courtyard outside, the sun sinks rapidly, and the windows grow dark. Lee Phillips is here, dressed in jeans and a leather jacket. He wears a button that reads, "U.S. Out of Big Mountain." He begins the meeting with a brief statement. "Every effort must be made to stop this insane policy," he concludes, "which is just a variation of what Kit Carson conceived, eighty years before: starve or surrender."

Phillips introduces Roberta Blackgoat, the veteran speechmaker of the group, who speaks in the English she learned from her three years in BIA schools. "The reason for my going around," she begins, holding her strong hands before her, looking out comfortably to the crowd from behind her rectangular steel-rimmed glasses, "is for the youngsters, my grandkids. This is what will be destroyed when the mines start going. I don't want my kids to go to Washington, D.C., someday and see behind a glass wall in a museum the remains of their grandma's hogan and pieces of her sheep corral."

Roberta sits down and Ruth Benally walks slowly to take her place. She speaks in Navajo. Her voice breaks and wavers. Ruth has a fragile beauty that is emphasized by a blue film kerchief bordered with gold trim, which she wears tied under her chin. She gestures with her hands, turning up her palm and raising it, repeatedly, absently, as if gesturing, "What else can we say? With what words and to whom?" Danny Blackgoat, Roberta's son, interprets when Ruth is done. "I'm not an orator," he says for her, in his deep, rich voice, shaking slightly from nervousness. "Not a speaker. I wish I was educated so I could communicate convincingly and precisely what I think. I'm in staunch opposition to relocation. I'm staying. They tell us to relocate. If that happens, we'll be homeless. It's going to destroy us, this thing called relocation. That's why I'm here and also because I have some rugs that are for sale. They tell us we can't even plant corn, beans, squash, like in old times. We can't upgrade our dwellings. We have to get strong again. I brought my grandkids along with me. They should have been in school but I think they're receiving more education here.This is my first time. That is why I'm not that well acquainted with standing in front of an audience." Ruth sits down beside her two granddaughters, who wear their long shiny hair tied up in tsiyeels with bright white ties that are clearly new for the occasion. They wear cotton blouses and full skirts on their lithe, preadolescent bodies.

Bessie stands up next. Ella goes with her to interpret. Bessie has straight broad shoulders, low-hung breasts, a girlish tip to her hips. She wears a salmon-colored velvet blouse, a light blue printed cotton skirt with flecks of salmon in the design, strands of turquoise beads, two large bracelets, and rings. Her long black hair is pulled into a tsiyeel and she wears two beaded combs. After Bessie speaks, Ella begins with her own words: "My mom is fifty-six years old. She bore eleven of us and raised five others. Sometimes I wish that the ladies could speak English and really get across what they want to say. But then I think, it is hard to be educated and live in both worlds. It is hard to think in both languages." Ella wears jeans and a jean jacket whose pockets she beaded on the way down in the car. She looks off at the far end of the room as she speaks, her feathered haircut framing her wide face, her pink-tinted glasses slipping periodically down her fine nose. She stands with her hands in her jacket pockets, formal, serious.

"I get strength from these ladies," she says. "Seeing them get up every morning and get on with their lives when their very existence is threatened gives me physical and emotional strength." The room of about sixty people is dead quiet. The other ladies rest their chins on their hands as they listen. Ella begins to interpret. "My mom says she's been really enjoying herself down here, having a good time and meeting people who have good feelings in their hearts. She's been involved in this land dispute for a long time and is here to ask for help for herself and the other elderlies here and her kids. She hopes to sell some rugs so she can buy some food and groceries.

"The law had a big effect on her," Ella continues. "She doesn't feel good mentally or physically. She remembers when her grandma and grandpa had many sheep, up to a thousand. The sheep were everything to them. Because her mom died when she was young, she was brought up by her grandfather, who passed away when she was about eight. She then followed her livestock from relative to relative. Her sheep were her family, and she remembers those times. Now her kids are all in school or universities. One is studying to become an acupuncturist in California. But she brought her kids up to take care of the livestock. She says that she watches us kids, she watches us go to the places. . . ." Ella stops. She looks straight ahead. It is unclear for a few moments why she has stopped, and then it becomes clear she is fighting back tears. The room seizes. Bessie stands by her side, silently, full lips set, expressionless. Ella starts up again and her voice quavers. "She watches us go to the places where we used to take the stock." Ella's voice breaks again, and she stops. After a few seconds, she presses on, forces the words out through the tears. "To the water holes. She wonders what we're thinking then. She says that when we had stock, when we had those things, we had everything." The room is deathly quiet, tension runs through it like a high-voltage wire. "Now she says her kids have nothing to give to their kids or their grandkids. She feels she has nothing to give to us, no wool, no meat. She says today she has four cows, five goats, and two horses for her grandkids. She says for that reason, her eldest girls have gone out and met many people who care, and talked to them, encouraged them to tell other people, some are lawyers.

"She says her kids are at school but they can't concentrate there, they're thinking about the land. They come home on weekends. She tells them that they should go to school, that it is important. For herself, she says, 'I pray a lot of times, so that this injustice will not be carried out.' She says the people out there get up every day and make offerings in hopes that they'll be able to stay. She wants to thank you people for everything, the food, the lodging. She says there's been illness in the family, but she's going to stay strong for the people of the JUA and her family." Bessie sits down in a plastic chair with the other ladies. Ella comes back to the table. Nell climbs into her lap, puts her arms around her neck, and hugs her. Buzz stands by her side quietly. Ella keeps her eyes on the microphone, where Annie Holmes is introducing her eighty-five-year-old mother, Ashikie Bitsie. Annie Holmes says, perhaps remembering her recent meeting with Ivan Sidney, "When we go to Washington, the people we see ask us, 'Where is your leader?' That's one of the ways they avoid the issue. My mother is one of the people who go and speak."

Her mother steps up to the microphone. She wears a purple velveteen top, round turquoise brooch, and coral necklace with turquoise beads. She wears a purple silk skirt and stands sturdily, resolute. Her voice is deep, and her lower jaw is prominent; she looks twenty years younger than she is, and there is still quite a bit of black in her hair. She speaks in Navajo. Navajo oration is long and roundabout and interpreters are expected to remember the twists and turns of the talk without notes. Not everyone can interpret, and even with the best of them, much is lost in translation because of attempts to speed up the testimony, and also because a Navajo story is told by not quite getting to the point. Annie tries: "I appreciate all the people here, your concern for us, and also for the food. I have the same concerns as these ladies. Also, Big Mountain has shrines from way back when the Holy People first brought life to the land. Our grandmothers and grandfathers made offerings there and told us to protect the land. Us ladies—we have one another—every time the fencing comes we get together and sometimes get thrown in jail. The menfolks when they get involved, sometimes it gets out of hand, it's very hard to stay under control.

"I respect all of you as my children. You are born of a woman, even though you have different-colored skins. I call you my children and grandchildren. We don't speak English, so your people can tell the story in your words. I want to tell you that there isn't any dispute between the Navajo and Hopi traditional people, maybe just a lot of outside interference. Maybe both tribes picked up a lot of Anglo teaching. I have traded with the Hopis for eighty years. We the people of Big Mountain sent a letter to the religious leaders at Hopi. We got a letter back from the Hopi Tribal Council that the religious leaders have no business being in conflict with the Tribal Council. This makes me feel there is something behind all this. I consider the Hopis my brothers and sisters. We have strong ties with each other that are being greatly troubled by this.

"We have no land to go to, say we relocate. At night it is the worst. I wake up worried about my family—how will they survive this dreadful law? Too many drop out of school during the year, they have nothing to look forward to, they say. They have no future.

"I have no place to go and I'm staying for the younger generation, so they will know a home. And thank you for listening to me even though you don't speak my language; you are concerned enough to stay and listen to us."

When she's finished she sits down, and Danny Blackgoat moves to the microphone. He says, "You see, it is not only at Lake Wobegon that women are strong and men are above average." Danny is becoming a pro at these meetings. Six months ago, just recovering from alcoholism, he could barely speak before a crowd. Now he is growing back into his movie star good looks, a spark is returning to his eyes, and his smile is quickening.

Roberta approaches the microphone. "Uh-oh," says six-foot-two Danny, as his short, spry mother approaches him. "The boss has come." Roberta whispers in his ear, then walks back to her seat. Danny stands behind the microphone, resting his weight on one foot, then the other. He seems to be deciding whether or not to go on. He wears jeans and a denim shirt, his hair is pulled back in a tsiyeel. His face clears and he seems to have decided to tell his own story. "I'm an ex-relocatee," he says. "I lost my home, my family, any material benefits and all the prestige I had in the community as a result of this law. The Relocation Commission bought the house my wife and I moved into. I didn't see any money, or participate in the transaction at all, except I received the bonus payment, which I used to enroll at the University of Arizona to study political science.

"My problems started in 1981. I realized I had signed away my birthright. It's very embarrassing. It has taken me a long time to say that I was a relocatee and that I failed at that. I'm proud to realize, however, that my heritage and the pull of the land was stronger than my attempts to destroy myself. At the time, I tried to run away from my roots. I was looking for love in drugs and alcohol. I was enslaved. I had no values, no positive self-esteem. I was a street person for 1982, 1983, and part of 1984. I turned to friends and relatives and was tolerated. As soon as I walked in the door, my nieces and nephews asked me when I was going to leave and they called me 'Uncle-you-know-what.'

"I had nowhere else to go. I went back to my mom and my elders. It was a really heartwarming experience to be welcomed back. I had to lose everything to realize what I valued." As Danny speaks, his girlfriend, Annie, a white woman, leans forward and strokes Roberta's back. Roberta gets emotional listening to her son speak of his fall. She opens a small woven purse she carries in her handbag and takes out a crystal. She tumbles the crystal in her hand as Danny continues. "I had a lot of pride, a lot of ego. I didn't listen to my mother. I was not a loving father. Just because I had a college degree it didn't make me a wise man. In a certain respect, it put me a step lower. America prides itself on its diversity. If it forcefully removes these people, then we won't be able to boast about the land of the free. I was an Indian counselor. I was very good at giving other people advice while my own life was falling apart. We need to listen to our elders, not pollute the environment so we can have light at the flick of a switch. Technology is going to destroy man. That's one of the Hopi prophecies. We must listen to the elderlies. Relocation doesn't work, even for people who are educated, like myself. I attempted suicide twice. The second time I woke up with my finger on the trigger of a rifle whose barrel I was staring down. With a conscience strong and clear and a heart open, that's when healing begins. We don't need anything else." Danny looks around the room, catches his mother's eye and holds it. "We're going to go down in history," he concludes, "as the people who spoke."

The gathering slowly winds down. Some of the ladies leave before a slide show of pictures of the disputed land and its people is shown. Nell goes back with her grandma. After the slides and some more talk, Ella, Buzz, and Dennis drive back to El Conquistador and go up to the ladies' suite. There are two bedrooms, a bathroom with dressing area, kitchen, dining room, and living room. The decor could be described as upscale glass-and-chrome. The ladies who can't fit on the beds have spread Pendleton blankets out on the floor. Bags of oranges lie on the glass coffee table, some more fruit is on the kitchen counter. Bessie has put her sleeping gear down in front of the fireplace. Nell has fallen asleep on one of the matching love seats. Dennis picks her up and carries her to the car. The ladies are disappointed. On returning, they found that not many rugs had sold, and also that Goose expected them all to contribute to the cost of the room. The ladies had hoped to bring some money home with them, but many won't. Some of the ladies are already asleep. Bessie lies on her side, her back to the room, facing the unlit hearth. She opens her handbag, takes out a leather wallet. A couple of her rugs sold earlier, and she pulls out the cash she earned. She turns over the bills, scrutinizes them, counts and recounts them. She doesn't know Ella and her family are leaving, so occupied is she with those greenbacks. They tiptoe out.

In the lobby, the Bedonies pass young couples dressed for a fancy ball. Rock and roll music wafts from a distant function room. The party-goers are extremely well-dressed, the girls are svelte and tanned, their hair long and blow-dried. They all appear somewhat inebriated and world-weary. Outside, the air is warm. Nell shifts, calls out for her grandma in her sleep. They head back to Flagstaff, where the reports warn of snow.

(26)

The Messiah of Relocation?

As Ross Swimmer stepped forward into his new role as "the messiah of relocation," the mantle he reluctantly received from Sidney Yates, he ran full tilt into several determined roadblocks. The Relocation Commission fought with him over matters of authority; the Navajo and Hopi BIA area offices fought over jurisdiction; the Senate Appropriations Subcommittee objected to his sudden entry into the program; and the Navajo Tribe, which considered Swimmer's initiative a threat to the Udall-McCain proposal, fought vigorously to slow him down.

The Navajos were heavily invested in the idea of a comprehensive solution, even if it meant waiting for Goldwater to retire and reintroducing the idea the next year. The tribe's position was "to load the record with information that the present law [was] not a comprehensive solution. Then we will come back next session and try for more."

The Navajos had so much invested in a comprehensive settlement for several reasons in addition to the obvious one of limiting the number of Navajo relocations. The Navajos were also concerned about the upcoming trial over the 1934 area, which could lead to another round of relocations. And the most pressing issue to the Zah administration heading into the summer of 1986 was Peterson Zah's reelection. Peter MacDonald was already revving up his political machine, distributing bumper stickers saying RELOCATE ZAH, and Zah had placed a lot of political capital on the hopes of a comprehensive solution. It was John McCain's opinion that Pete Zah's reelection rested on what happened in the next few months.

Swimmer's surprise entrance into the arena threatened to destroy the Navajos' hard-won advances, and his involvement deepened quickly. He formed a task force to plan for and direct the survey of the relocatees and the planning for development of the New Lands. It included Kathy Helmer, a social worker who had helped him with a housing program at the Cherokee Nation; Dan Jackson; Ray Smith, the BIA livestock chief; and two BIA employees in Phoenix, Tom Davis and Tom Tippeconnic. As they began to sort out the issues, they discovered for themselves what others had known for a long time: the Commission not only didn't have a plan for the development of the New Lands, it had not even made the most basic determinations about relocating Navajos there; it didn't know how many people actually were left on the HPL, or who was legally eligible to move to the New Lands, or if the relocatees would have running water and electricity, or who would pay for these services.

The first issue to be determined, and the one endlessly debated, was how many Navajos were to be moved. The Commission's numbers suggested there were approximately three hundred Navajos certified as eligible for relocation benefits living on the HPL and sixty-five to seventy families who had not signed up for relocation but who were full-time residents of the HPL. The BIA's numbers were lower: the Bureau knew of 238 full-time HPL residents.

During the week of January 21, 1986, staff from the Bureau and the Commission tried to reconcile their numbers by going on a house-to-house check. The fieldwork turned up forty-four household heads on the Commission's list that the BIA didn't know about and twenty-two families the BIA knew about and the Commission didn't.

Sandra Massetto believed that both agencies' counts were low. She said, "Ray [Smith of the BIA] only knows those people who come forward and identify themselves to him," for livestock permitting. "The same problem occurred during the [Commission's] enumerations in 1974. Anglos only know about those people who make themselves known."

The Navajo Tribe conducted its own count throughout the summer and fall of 1985 and the winter of 1986, arriving at the figure of 828 "full-time resident households," which included 1,130 adults and 525 children —more than double the Commission's figure. The tribe counted people, not grazing permittees or those who had gone through a bureaucratic system and had been determined "eligible." It counted bodies. The tribe's point of view was that if the land was to be cleared, those people would have to be taken care of and the government had better know how many there were.

In April, before Yates's budget hearing, Swimmer announced that he had revised his list up ten families to 248—a fourth of the Navajos' figure. And he maintained that the Commission, the BIA, and the Navajo Tribe were basically in accord; they were just using different terms. The attitude of Swimmer's staff was that the numbers supplied by the Navajo Tribe were unreliable, even though every body it counted could be attached to a census number. "Hell, they'll truck in people," one official said. "They'll truck in people to raise the count."

The government felt the numbers had to stop somewhere. Each year that the program went on, more individuals turned eighteen and the Commission certified many of them as eligible for benefits. Where would it end? There were many meetings and discussions on the matter. The conflicting figures were not resolved. Swimmer decided he would relocate the 248 on his list.

Other issues came up whose resolution by Swimmer's task force infuriated one party or another. Dan Jackson made a legal determination that the New Lands were meant solely for the benefit of Navajo families who resided on the HPL as of July 6, 1980. That meant that anyone who had moved off before or after 1980 for work or school would not be eligible. Conversely, the Commission had decided the New Lands were open to any eligible relocatee.

The task force eventually accommodated the wishes of the tribe and the Commission to settle some additional people on the New Lands. Priority for grazing would be given to those actually resident on the HPL, and depending on how many actually wanted to move, other people, such as those who had moved off since 1980, and families of the HPL residents, could get a homesite on the New Lands. Later, if there was still room, others could receive homesites near relatives on the New Lands. The BIA also decided that there would be some form of housing for people who did not want to graze; that would allow more people to settle in higher-density communities in certain areas of the New Lands.

Another brouhaha emerged over how much the BIA would spend building each house. The government felt it could build better houses for less money than the houses the Commission was buying. Then, claimed some, why would the Navajos move to the New Lands if they could get a more expensive house built by the Commission? The obstacles to Swimmer's effort seemed endless. Yet, with the loyal aid of Dan Jackson, who knew the related laws better than anyone else, Swimmer pressed forward, shedding one problem after another.

Swimmer's task force was faced with some stark realities. Since it still had not conducted a survey, it didn't know who wanted to move and with which family members, so planning roads, housing sites, and wells was like putting together a puzzle whose pieces they hadn't received yet. They were trying to put together a program to accomplish a goal, but as they tried to make it move forward, "the mass kept changing," said a participant. "It was like solving a three-dimensional puzzle that was constantly moving."

Eventually, decisions had to be made just so the project could advance to the next problem. Areas of possible development were laid out based on grazing capacities, water potential, and natural boundaries. Possible road sites were established. Using the best available U.S. Geological Survey maps, likely water supplies were hypothesized. And then the other pieces started to fit in, each new element depending on the preceding decision. The first decisions were made with the least information. And into these plans were supposed to fit human beings who had very little hand in their futures. The task force members were aware of this; they even knew they were guilty. Said Kathy Helmer, "Over time, the number of decisions that can be made become fewer and fewer and less and less significant. It's like a funnel or a cone. When I'm feeling the worst, I think I'm right down in the narrowest part of the cone. Other days, I get hopeful."

As Swimmer's task force tried to make sense of what it did and didn't know, it was besieged with criticism from all sides. A steady stream of letters from Window Rock registered extreme displeasure about the way Swimmer was going about his project. The Navajos questioned his motives. Some of the tribal lobbyists felt he had indeed become "messianic" in his determination to settle the problem. John McCain was put out that Swimmer refused to take the Udall-McCain bill seriously. "It's natural to want to fix things and make them better," said McCain. "Ross appears to be a very sharp guy. But to jump into this thinking he can solve it flies in the face of the efforts of many other people including [Judge William] Clark and [Richard] Morris." McCain's feeling was that Swimmer was "trying to please" too many people. He felt that Swimmer's idea was to relocate all those people from the HPL who were willing to go and then find a compromise between the tribes about the rest. "I think the deal [Fred] Craft and the Commission and Swimmer are trying to cut is one that would be very acceptable to Goldwater—take care of the Big Mountain issue and let the rest fall through."

McCain felt that Swimmer's desire to build houses quickly was ill advised. "Swimmer isn't the only one to run into quicksand. He's going to find some other bodies down there."

And so he did. What disturbed the Navajos most was the "pilot program" that Swimmer wanted to accomplish quickly, to prove to Congress and to the relocatees that he could do what he'd claimed. Swimmer's task force had met with the handful of families that Swimmer had visited during his February three-day visit to the HPL. These families were the focus of Swimmer's pilot project. Zah wrote Swimmer that the tribe was very concerned that families had been chosen "with no in-place criteria or standards." Zah also pointed out his concern about grazing regulations, that from what he had heard, the HPL residents' current permits, "which are not adequate to sustain them economically," were being used as a standard for permits on the New Lands. Zah called that plan "ludicrous." Zah argued that if the tribe worked more closely with Swimmer, these problems could be worked out as they went along.

Swimmer's plan, which Yates had endorsed heartily, was to conduct a thorough interview with every family to find out where people wanted to live, and with what family members, with livestock or without. This knowledge was essential to his moving forward with development plans. But because of the increasing tension on the reservation, the survey was put off until after the deadline.

Swimmer was left to work with the families chosen for the pilot project. The BIA presented its first compilation of plans in April in a paper called "The New Lands Project—Project Structure." It later became known as "the blue sheets" because when it came time to copy them, there was no more white paper in the BIA office. Navajo officials Claudeen Bates-Arthur and Roger Boyd met with Kathy Helmer and the task force on April 11 to discuss the blue sheets. The meeting was a fiasco. The task force felt later that they had been "criticized mercilessly" by Bates-Arthur. They felt she had expressed her displeasure so strongly that "she had overstepped her bounds and really attacked [us]. That's not the way to keep up a working relationship," one said. But Bates-Arthur remembered the meeting differently. She felt she and her staff had made "a lot of suggestions." Later, she said, "We were told they had no intention of changing anything they were doing and they were going to go forward."

The Navajos' criticism was indeed sharp and it questioned many of the decisions made by the BIA group in an effort to deal with the limitations of space and money. Although the Navajos complained that they weren't a part of the day-to-day workings of the task force, their views were aired, both through periodic meetings, letters from Zah to Swimmer, and through the grapevine from the Navajos through Sandra Massetto to the task force. Ultimately, the task force adopted plans that respected tribal regulations. And it compromised on matters involving eligibility and grazing. Communication took place, but through the back door.

The problem, Bates-Arthur felt, was Swimmer's attitude toward them. "Suggestions we made were rebuffed because they were not what [Swimmer] had in mind," she said. "There has never been throughout this whole process any real discussion that was on a give-and-take basis. The first time he came to Window Rock to meet with Mr. Zah, he *told* Mr. Zah what he was going to do. He didn't ask him if he thought it was a good idea. He didn't say, 'Do you have any ideas about this?' He came into a meeting and he said, 'This is what I'm going to do and I expect your cooperation.' " The Navajos found Swimmer "arrogant," said Bates-Arthur, who felt he was telling them, " 'If you don't agree with me, you are simply delaying and refusing to cooperate and you can't possibly have any good ideas because I have the whole answer.' It's virtually impossible to work with that kind of a person."

Swimmer, for his part, had been advised that the Navajos, following their pattern since the passage of the 1974 Act, would do everything to obstruct him. The Zah administration understood that the tribe's historical position not to aid the relocation process had resulted in hurting the relocatees, but the tribe found itself in a very awkward position. Any sign that it was aiding relocation would be used by political opponents as proof that the administration had caved in. In fact, MacDonald supporters accused Zah of capitulating by choosing the parcels of land that became the New Lands. Said ex-commission director Leon Berger, a MacDonald sympathizer, "Now that Zah has accepted the land, [there's] very little reason for this thing not to continue on to some horrible conclusion. . . . I think Zah will go down in history as the man who accepted relocation."

So, although Zah and his staff understood that delays wound up hurting the relocatees, they found themselves in the painful political situation of not being able to cooperate openly with Swimmer's initiative. Claudeen Bates-Arthur conceded that the tribe's adamant refusal, under the previous administrations, to aid in the relocation process "was a calculated mistake. . . . The tribe let those folks be out there on their own while taking the position that no one's going to move, and it's our land and we're going to get it back." Yet the Zah administration was being pressured to make the same mistakes.

Although Swimmer received a lot of criticism in the first months of his initiative, he pushed ahead, most of the time successfully. He shed light on issues that had remained murky for years, and made true progress where the Commission had failed. He did make one resounding error, however, and that was his pilot project. Although Swimmer envisioned the pilot project as a means of working out the bugs in the system he had developed, the Navajo Tribe, as well as the individual relocatees, wanted to see a plan in place first. Where would their children go to school? Would there be a hospital nearby? What about stores or trading posts? What kind of a life would they have? With all the problems of insufficient space, how could Swimmer allow ten families or so to pick sites, without planning in advance who would live around them? If there was going to be cooperative grazing, where herds of different families would run together, where was the planning to get compatible families to live within a cooperative grazing unit? All of the positive preparations that Swimmer had outlined and that had been cheered by Yates seemed to have been abandoned for the purpose of showing he could produce quick results.

Claudeen Bates-Arthur recalled that "Bureau employees used the word 'entice' for Mr. Swimmer's program. 'We're going to entice a few families down there because then we can show them what we can do and then it'll all fall into place.' "

The tribe, infuriated by Swimmer's determination, did what it could to derail the pilot project. After pressure from relatives, and chapter and tribal officials, most of the families Swimmer had chosen backed out. The only Navajo who finally agreed to be a participant was a single ex-marine named Alfred Yazzie. Yazzie chose a site in the Parker Draw area near Sanders, Arizona. The area consisted of softly rolling green pasture land studded with stark juniper trees. Many trees around the building site were dead, making a stark, Georgia O'Keeffe–like backdrop for Yazzie's new house.

But a comedy of errors followed. First, to comply with federal regulations, the area had to be walked for possible archaeological sites. However, the archaeologist inspected the wrong site. Then, Yazzie was to show the contractors how he wanted his house positioned. But the contractors poured the cement slab foundation before Yazzie got there. Then, the BIA built a road. Since the funds came from the BIA roads budget, the road followed the regulations necessary for using federal highway funds. Hundreds of trees were bulldozed to clear its path. But the gigantic asphalt road stopped a half mile before the house because of restrictions on federal road money being used to build driveways or access roads to houses. Even worse, the BIA drilled two wells and both came up dry. Total cost of the effort: $300,000.

The errors were splashed all over the local papers. "First BIA Bid to Transplant Navajos Flops" read the headline on page one of the *Arizona Republic*, with the subtitle "$300,000 spent on one house on wrong site, with dry well." Swimmer was brought to task in Washington, and received a predictable tongue-lashing from the Navajo Tribe and the Commission. However, the press and the Navajo Tribe made more of it than was necessary. The site would eventually serve thirty houses, so the cost of the road ($165,000) wasn't as outrageous as it seemed. And later test wells did produce water. The ground in the area was mostly shale, and layers of shale had fallen down into the holes as they were dug. This meant the sides of the holes had to be packed. Eventually, after the well had been properly handled, water was found.

But Swimmer had learned his lesson. He needed somebody in charge who could handle the Relocation Commission, knew the law, and could oversee the whole project. At the time the errors were made, the task force was run by committee, with different people in the BIA responsible for contracting out different tasks. Kathy Helmer, an academician by training, had no experience dealing with bureaucracies and no knowledge of construction schedules or contracts. On May 30, Swimmer selected Dan Jackson to be the New Lands project manager. Swimmer gave Jackson authority to issue verbal and written directives as his "personal representative." The Navajo and Phoenix area offices were instructed to "render any and all assistance" to Jackson in accordance with "this extraordinary detail."

Ironically, Jackson was the man who had gone to Washington in October 1985 to tell people in the departments of Justice and the Interior that he was afraid of what the Commission might do on the New Lands. Now, eighteen months later, he was in charge of the development himself. As a legal adviser for the government on this issue for six years, and two years prior to that working for Navajo Legal Services on the Navajo reservation, as well as being a contracts lawyer for the Department of Land Management, Jackson was certainly qualified to take charge. While sensitive to the needs of the relocatees, he was a man who got a job done. The program needed to get off the ground, take a new direction, and be executed speedily but competently. Jackson could be authoritative and abrasive and appear to be unbending, but behind the scenes, often working twenty hours a day, he laid out a workable plan that eventually incorporated the views of the relocatees and considered the needs of the tribe. His dictatorial style was not greeted with much affection, but he almost singlehandedly created a coherent basis and schedule for development of the New Lands. Kathy Helmer remained in charge of counseling and the creation and application of the survey.

The centerpiece of Ross Swimmer's initiative to settle the New Lands was his idea to involve the relocatee families in planning their future communities. He had learned through his own mistakes as chairman of the Cherokee Tribe that Indian people must be involved in the plans for their own futures if those plans are to work. This idea was not new to the Navajo-Hopi relocation. In 1984, the Commission's planning firm, CH2M Hill, had begun just such meetings with Navajo extended families. The effort had been aborted, however, when the Commission ordered the planning stage ended—prematurely, in the view of the firm, which tried to walk away from its million-dollar contract. The Commission, instead, ordered engineering plans made for the high-density housing arrangement—"Hawley Acres"—the sight of which had spurred Dan Jackson to fly to Washington in October 1985.

In the Southwest, water is a matter of first priority when housing, agricultural developments, or livestock operations are planned. The New Lands are semiarid, made up of rolling rangeland interrupted by bluffs, ridges, and badlands. Average precipitation varies from nine to twelve inches per year. In its most preliminary studies of the New Lands, CH2M Hill had indicated that tests for water quality and quantity would have to be undertaken before any other planning was possible.

However, when Dan Jackson took over the reins for Swimmer in May 1986, the necessary tests had not yet been performed. The studies on water had been hung up by Hawley Atkinson, who, according to Sandy Massetto, had a penchant for "removing the technical people and replacing them with those who didn't know anything." According to Massetto, "Hawley didn't want to make decisions based on facts and he didn't want to deal with technical people."

But technical people were desperately needed to determine the effects of the largest known uranium tailings spill, which had occurred in 1979 when a dam at United Nuclear Corporation's Church Rock Mine broke, sending 1,100 tons of tailings and 94 million gallons of toxic waste water gushing into the Puerco River, a waterway that passes through the New Lands.

In July 1985, Robert Brown, a young law student working for the Big Mountain Legal Defense/Offense Committee, found that the Arizona Department of Health Services had made a statement to the EPA in July 1983 reporting that "waters collected from the Puerco River at Chambers, Arizona, and the Little Colorado River at Cameron, Arizona, contained levels of gross alpha and gross beta particle activity that were far in excess of EPA-approved Arizona State surface water quality standards."

The statement argued that "levels of radionuclides in surface water in the Puerco River are currently high enough to pose a health hazard in terms of excess cancer risk to those persons employing this water for long-term use for drinking." The high levels were the result of the 1979 spill and also United Nuclear's repeated discharge of polluted effluent subsequent to the spill.

The report stated that through 1982, uranium and radium levels in the effluent water running out of the Church Rock mine were in excess of approved conditions. The statement also noted its concern that the contamination could eventually enter the Arizona groundwater. In fact, one well in Lupton, Arizona, had already shown signs of contamination.

Brown also discovered a letter from the Northern Arizona Council of Governments to the EPA dated March 4, 1984, asking the EPA not to renew its discharge permits for the uranium mines because of repeated violations and pollution of the Rio Puerco. The letter pointed out the group's worries about contamination of wells along the river in Apache County. The executive director of that group was Chris Bavasie. Now, as executive director of the Relocation Commission, Bavasie stood behind Atkinson and Watkins's denials that the water supply on the New Lands was dangerous in any way.

Watkins and Atkinson, over Massetto's objections, relied on a determination of safety made by Larry Agenbroad, a hydrologist at Northern Arizona University. Agenbroad, who said he'd never seen the Arizona Department of Health Services report, said that in spite of the danger, he thought that avoiding the area for the sake of the river pollution would mean "giving up some of the best rangeland in the area for the sake of a five-mile stretch of water." He suggested fencing off the river. He did not explain how he would plan to keep children and sheep from breaking through the fence along that five-mile stretch, or explaining the contamination to non-English-speaking Navajos who would be living at its banks. The fact was that many Navajos were already using water from the Puerco to water their livestock. A public education project, aimed at teaching residents about the dangers of the river, noted that many residents of the area felt that payment of the out-of-court settlement of a 1980 lawsuit filed by them against United Nuclear meant that the problem had been taken care of. They were surprised to learn that that was not true. The river, which had once been called Toinjoni, "the beautiful river that flows," was now referred to as Tohchooi, "the river that is harmful."

In the summer of 1985, after Robert Brown's discoveries, Lee Phillips and Lew Gurwitz brought the issue up at the Commission's monthly public meeting. The response from Atkinson and Watkins was irritation, then outrage, then finally a refusal to respond. They had satisfied themselves that there was no danger after hiring a firm, Western Technologies, Inc., in a noncompetitive bid arrangement, to prepare a report that cost $3,500. The president of the firm, James Warren, was a personal friend of Ralph Watkins.

The report concluded, with no argument presented, that "water quality in the study was good, [and] that groundwater contamination from the spill of six years ago was no longer evident." The results of the 1985 report by Western Technologies were contradicted by tests conducted by the Arizona Department of Health Services in 1986, and the Western Technologies report was immediately criticized as "inaccurate and poorly conceived."

During the Relocation Commission's September 1985 monthly meeting, Hawley Atkinson criticized Lee Phillips for bringing up the issue of water once again, telling him he was "plowing nothing but dust" and making remarks "simply for the television people that are here." He concluded the water discussion with an ominous accusation, stating that discussion of the water was in fact hurting the potential residents of the New Lands. "Mr. Chairman," he said, "we've got two gentlemen here, who, I think, are far more interested in disrupting this meeting and trying to spread rumors and fears amongst the relocatees. And the fears simply aren't there." Chairman Watkins echoed, "It's not there."

Unfortunately for everyone, the problem had not gone away. When Dan Jackson took over as New Lands project manager, his first concern was water. "I always understood this to be the most difficult issue," he said. He told the Commission that the Puerco must be studied. The BIA contacted the U.S. Geological Survey and a meeting was set up between the Commission and the USGS on July 15, 1986. USGS said it would come up with a proposal for a "reconnaissance level" study of the Puerco.

On September 19, the proposal was sent to the Commission. Swimmer was also sent a copy of the USGS outline. The Commission announced it didn't want to pay for the study, so Swimmer contacted the

USGS headquarters and personally ordered the study anyway. Swimmer promised that he would find funding if the Commission refused to foot the bill. In early November, the USGS presented a slide show to the commissioners and senior staff of how it planned to proceed.

The effect of the slide show was chilling. Aside from showing the immediate effects of the spill, referred to as the "largest single release of radioactive waste in United States history," it explained how the drilling and pumping of water from wells on the New Lands might draw the radioactive particles in the sand and alluvium of the river into the underground water supply ducts, known as aquifers. The Commission was also told of the dangers of livestock eating plants that had assimilated radionuclides, as well as the danger to humans of inhaling dust carrying the radioactive particles. When the presentation was over, Hawley Atkinson exclaimed, "Why didn't anyone ever tell me?"

During discussion about funding after the presentation, Chris Bavasie, the man who, three years before, as executive director of the Northern Arizona Council of Governments, had written Environmental Protection Agency Director William Ruckelshaus to express his concern about the effects of the contamination, yet who had gone along with Atkinson and Watkins when they repeatedly told the public there was nothing to worry about, argued that the Commission ought to pick up the tab. He felt it would be advantageous for "political purposes."

There were many other water issues that had yet to be answered. No one knew for sure whether the quantity of water available on the New Lands would be sufficient to support the people Swimmer planned to move there.

The day Jackson was appointed New Lands project manager, he wrote to Chris Bavasie urging him to initiate tests for the location and quantity of groundwater for the interim wells that would serve the relocatees until a larger, community water supply could be built by the Indian Health Service. Swimmer had made the policy decision that no one would be relocated into a house that didn't have running water. The Commission thought it was adequate to set up cisterns and let the relocatees haul water, but Swimmer decided that he was not going to sanction the practice that led many Navajos to haul water in old oil barrels and, in times of difficulty, to take unhealthful water from livestock wells.

Jackson wrote that an immediate study of water availability was needed because "if there does not exist a sufficient amount of potable groundwater underlying the New Lands to supply the needs of the persons to be settled thereon, we as well as Congress need to know that information as quickly as possible."

The Commission was subdued by the logic of this request, and in July entered into an agreement with the USGS to dig twenty-one test wells. Drilling the test wells turned out to be an arduous task. Dealing with the shale meant that well-drilling, instead of taking one day per hole, wound up taking three and four days until the drillers learned what to expect. Well-drilling in the West is very complicated. Sometimes several different strata of water-bearing areas must be crossed before one with sufficient supply is reached. Sometimes a drill can hit a cave, or empty cavern of air, and then the hole must be abandoned. Also, a driller must be careful that water tainted with, say, arsenic is not dragged into a pure supply at a different level. Locating the source of the contamination is often difficult. Then, after a well has been abandoned, it must be capped and sealed with cement so that runoff or surface pollutants don't seep down the well hole and contaminate the whole supply.

When the test wells dug at Alfred Yazzie's new house came up dry, the press, the Commission, and the Navajo Tribe jumped all over Swimmer. The holes that were dug and presumed dry had in fact hit good water. As soon as the walls were properly packed with mud, the well was found to yield seventy-five gallons per minute. The house itself was not finished until six months after Swimmer had hoped his pilot project would be completed. Yazzie still couldn't move in, however, because the Navajo Tribe refused to allow electrical lines to be brought in. Swimmer was not going to move anyone in until he could turn on the faucet and have water. Having water in this case, because of electric pumps, meant having electricity.

The Commission staff, irked that Swimmer was doing what they should have done, battled him on every point. In perfect character, Watkins suggested that the relocatees be moved without water. In a letter to Swimmer, he suggested it would be better to abandon the interim system because of its cost. "Considering the problems encountered to date we believe that it may be necessary to reexamine the policy of individual interim water systems for the families moving to range clusters on the New Lands." He suggested that the problems associated with finding water be used as a reason to deny relocatees a water supply until a community supply was established—years hence. This is what the Commission had done in the Hardrock group move—promised the relocatees water at a future date. The situation at Hardrock had disturbed Swimmer enough that he made public comments about it on several occasions. Swimmer's reply to Watkins's suggestion not to provide an interim water supply was, "Unfortunately, water, in general, on the New Lands appears to be a problem and I do not see any way we can move people to new homes without a source of water identified."

Watkins had bragged earlier of knowing exactly where the water was on the New Lands, and blamed Swimmer's pilot project difficulties on Swimmer's failure to ask the Commission where the water was. "We've got plenty of water," he said in a June 1986 interview. "Nobody asked us. We know where it is, we know exactly where it is." Watkins was asked if he could have pointed Swimmer to the proper sites. "Yes," he replied. "The water's good. We've got an adequate, abundant supply. Honest Injun."

(27)

"All This Madness
Building Inside"

Mae Tso sits at her kitchen table rolling small lumps of blue corn mush sweetened with honey into dry corn husks and tying them into tight packets the size of a cracker. The Navajo word for these morsels is "the one you tie up." Mae is making them for Askie to take back to work in Needles, California. Mae and Askie have just reconciled after a two-month separation.

Mae has the look of a teenage bride on her face, soft, new, unprotected. Her husband is less expressive, more closed. But he is trying to look friendly to visitors who have come by to talk to Mae.

In the cement hogan a stone's throw from the house sits Mae's son Earl. Earl lived in this hogan with his wife Helena and daughter Fiona until his wife left him for another man a year ago. Now he lives here alone. The walls are finished with plasterboard and wood-looking paneling. The dirt floor is swept clean and the double bed is neatly made with a quilted comforter. Framed school photos of Mae's children hang on the walls, as well as a poster of a Navajo elder with her head in her hands titled REPEAL PL 93-531—GENOCIDE and a poster celebrating the treaty of Guadalupe Hidalgo. A black and white photo of protest marchers heading to Washington is marked "Trail of Broken Treaties." Several bureaus line the octagonal walls, and a tapestry of Jesus Christ surrounded by a flock of sheep hangs over the bed. Eagle feathers with beaded handles and a flute are hung on the wall, and shelves are filled with rock and roll tapes including Judas Priest, Black Sabbath, and other heavy metal bands. An old black-and-white television which works when hooked up to a car battery sits on a dresser.

A sheet hangs over the doorway and rustles in the breeze. The goats are just outside, ringing their bells and bleating. Earl wears a red T-shirt and denim overalls and black and red leather high-top sneakers. Earl has a knife wound by his eye and a nasty gash on his nose, both the result of a fight with a man he accused of stealing his wife. Earl and his brothers Sam and Hoskie have all been through periods of trouble with alcohol and drugs. Hoskie was arrested and jailed several times for alcohol-related incidents. Since their mother's arrest, the boys have rallied around her and tried to curtail their wild ways. But alcohol remains a problem among youth all over the reservation and the Tso boys are not immune to its appeal. They get into trouble when they drive to Tuba City or Piñon. But now, Mae and Askie are stricter and forbid the boys from driving the truck unless they are asked to run an errand for their parents.

Earl's four-year-old daughter Fiona is here to visit. She runs in and out of the hogan, chasing after the sheep and saying *"naaa-naaa."* She is a beautiful child. She likes to be home with her grandma and father. There is a chance she'll stay on and go to school at Rocky Ridge this fall. Earl and Helena have another child, a boy, just over a year old, who lives with his mother. Earl has struggled to maintain a life at home and in the modern world. It hasn't worked out well. It was while he was away working that his wife ran off. Now, since his mother's arrest, he has taken it upon himself to stay home. Sometimes at night he and a friend practice drumming for peyote meetings.

"I feel I have to be here at all times," says Earl. "I respect my mom and my father for giving me this wonderful life here on earth. I just can't abandon them with all these things going on. I guess some other people are like that . . . they're out supporting themselves and they don't really worry about their mothers and fathers, you know, what they're going through. I feel I have to be here to be strong. I feel it makes me strong, makes my parents strong. We have to be here *together* to solve all this hardship. We have to pray that one day we will be able to go on with our lives."

Earl stays home while Sam and Hoskie are preparing the camp for the sun dance. Although some Navajos still object to having a sun dance on the Navajo reservation, Earl says he feels good about the Sioux bringing the sun dance here to help them. "At least some other tribes, they're concerned about this whole thing, and want to help. It's not our way. I wouldn't dance because it's not my religion." Earl motions to the tipi ground—a circle of stone markings laid out in front of Mae's house. "I participate in peyote meetings. I help with the drum, or cedar, or help out with the fire."

Earl would like to study to be a medicine man. But he knows he can't leave home and travel around with a medicine man to learn to perform ceremonies now. For one, it costs a lot of money. And second, he feels he must take care of the cornfield and the livestock. The Tsos are over their permit levels with sheep and cattle and they have received warnings to get their livestock down. Earl feels he must be here in case there is another confrontation. "I don't want *anybody* to be telling us what to do, how to live and whatnot. It's not right. I thought America was supposed to be a free country and here I'm a Native American and I'm getting this kind of treatment. It's not right." Mae's attitude toward the BIA's permitting system is simple. As she often says, "When the BIA shows us that they make the rain fall and the grass grow, then we'll consider paying livestock fees."

Earl has been tempted by the outside world, but he is now struggling to live simply, as his parents did when they grew up. "I try my best to be a Navajo, traditional Dine. I try my best to think of things to help my grandfather like digging out roots, herbs, stuff like that." But even his religion is influenced by the Christian world. The peyote meetings are a pan-Indian rite tinged with Christian elements—more or less according to the particular leader's, or roadman's, orientation. The Tsos observe the traditional Navajo ceremonies and also attend peyote meetings. They choose roadmen who make little reference to Christ to lead their own ceremonies. "A lot of traditionals follow the fire, the herbs, the medicine, but now there's a lot of Christianity involved. I disagree with that," says Earl.

Mae walks over from her house and sits beside Earl on a metal cot. She proudly points out that a photographer from the *Washington Post* slept on that very cot the night before. Mae sits forward on the edge of the bed and speaks about her reconciliation with Askie. She flutters her hands in the air to accentuate her words. She places her hand on her chest, over her eyes, sets them in her lap.

It is not typical for Navajos to talk about private matters, but Mae has made a decision that she will do so in hopes it will help outsiders understand what the land dispute has done to her and her family. Lately, she's even come to believe that talking is good for the family. Her daughter Betty has said that one of the reasons her family has had so much trouble —the boys drinking, her parents fighting—is that they were never encouraged to air their feelings. It is not the Navajo way to pour out one's heart about personal things, although many have done so over the last ten years in chapter meetings and antirelocation meetings. Mae is changing, starting to express her feelings and to understand them, and also to try to understand what emotions underlie the actions of her family. While she was separated from Askie, she thought over and over about what he had said to her. She couldn't believe that he was really jealous about her being with other men. In fact, she told him, "I only speak Navajo and I don't understand [other] languages. There really was no reason for you to be jealous about my travels and my speaking." After six weeks of separation, Askie went to Mae's parents and apologized for what he had done and said he wanted her to move back with him. The family arranged a large meeting, with relatives from all sides. Mae and Askie each told their stories and then the families decided what should be done. They decided that the two should try to work out their problems.

Mae learned quite a bit at the family meeting and from subsequent talks with Askie about what had happened. She said that she felt he was using the argument about jealousy as an excuse for what he was struggling with inside. "He wanted his kids to go to school and to get jobs and hold jobs and make a life for themselves," she says. "Because of the land dispute, the kids weren't happy at their jobs and their schools and they always just came back here without finishing anything. He wanted better things for his family, but because of what's happening here, he can only go so far. He can't plan ahead, he can't do anything. He felt incompetent with what he was doing, he felt real incompetent about how he was trying to raise his family."

He had many frustrations. He sold his livestock in despair over the struggle it was to keep them. But Mae told him, "We've just got to be strong together and overcome these obstacles. We still have to look forward to old age and we want to get old together and we still have that to attain before we can go through another life." Mae says that is what she said to him and how she felt about it. She thinks maybe he doesn't really understand what the struggle is all about, because he isn't involved in it like she is.

Earl interrupts and comes to his father's defense. "He doesn't have time. He's off working all the time. Other times when he's here, he'd get involved pretty good in it, but it's just that he's really quite frustrated about this whole thing, and then he's got all this madness building inside of him. It's pretty hard for him to be away from his family while all this is going on here, you know. So with all that and my mom traveling and whatnot, you know . . . they couldn't be together when he wanted to be together and all this kept them separated. . . . All this, it builds up inside him."

Earl continues in English, so his mother doesn't understand. "It was us, the children, that got hurt. I couldn't stand seeing what my father was going through," he said. "I couldn't, you know, go on my mom's side, because they're both my parents and I love them very much. I wanted to work things out for them, try to help so they could be together, so we could be happy and so they could be happy. I couldn't take sides, you know."

Now Earl is taking on some of the traveling for his mother. Recently, while she stayed home, he went to San Francisco on a speaking tour in her place. "I liked it, because talking about the whole problem made me feel good. It's that way in everyday life, if you have a family problem, you talk about it and afterward you feel good. So for that reason, talking about it, helping the people by publicizing the whole issue, made me feel good, made me feel I was doing something for the people."

Despite the moments of catharsis, Earl is still angry. And his anger is directed at "Washindone," the government, which Earl refers to as "he." Earl says, "What he's got to learn is, he's the one who created this whole problem here. The government, he's the one who made boundaries on the maps, he's the one who created it, not the people here. He's going to have to correct his own mistake because of that mistake he made there. The people are suffering here. We're human people. We have feelings just like them, we've got feelings. Why can't he understand?"

(28)

The International Indian
Treaty Conference

It is June 3. Ella heads up to Big Mountain to attend the eleventh gathering of the International Indian Treaty Conference. The conferences, organized by the International Indian Treaty Council, are sponsored by AIM; the first one took place in 1974 at Mobridge, on the Standing Rock Reservation in North Dakota. The purpose of today's conference, according to the Treaty Council's literature, is to "provide an essential opportunity for representatives of Indigenous Nations from all over the world to gather together, build unity, share information, present documentation, discuss issues of common concern, and have input into the priorities and direction of the International Indian Treaty Council." Information gathered at the conference regarding the land dispute will be used "for the formulation of interventions to be submitted to the United Nations Commission on Human Rights and the Working Group on Indigenous Populations." The men and women of Big Mountain don't know very much about what this means or what the Treaty Council does, but they accept any gestures of help, and they welcome the opportunity to meet with Indians from other tribes.

The roads are newly graded and Ella and Nell drive quickly from the Dinnebito Dam up toward the survival camp. The day is clear and the foliage green from recent rains. The land looks and smells lusty with the new season. "When I told my dad we were going to the treaty conference," says Ella, "he told me to remember my smoke, my corn pollen, and my bitters. Before we left this morning I sprinkled Nell with bitter herbs to protect her from any bad feeling there might be up there. Young mothers, a lot of them, don't realize their young kids must be protected. Their hearts are still small and their minds tender. She needs to be protected from the harsh words, or anger and strong feelings that are present at these gatherings."

Nell turns to her mother and asks, "Mom, when am I going to get real big?"

Ella answers, "It takes a long time to grow. Every year you grow a little bit until you're big."

Nell thinks about this for one second. Then she says, "Oh, Mom. I don't have time to wait that long. I want to be big now." Ella bursts out laughing, a tinkling, musical laugh.

At the place where the road branches—right to Big Mountain, left to Teesyatoh—there is a new, neatly lettered white sign with INTERNATIONAL TREATY COUNCIL boldly stenciled on it. The sign is commanding, authoritative, and it is Indian, prepared by the Indians from the Treaty Council. It is not BIA—like most every other signpost here. Down the road, at Kee Shay's house, there is another sign, one arrow pointing the way to the survival camp and the other pointing to the treaty conference meeting. Five miles up the road on Alice Benally's land is another small sign and arrow for the conference. In a clearing of juniper trees, on a hilltop, sits a huge blue and yellow striped tent.

Before the first checkpoint is a sign reading ALL VEHICLES WILL BE SEARCHED. A shack has been constructed out of new lumber for the security people, and five AIM guards approach the vehicle. They ask for identification and write names and addresses on a pad of yellow paper attached to a clipboard. The guards are very polite as they check for guns and alcohol, and say that all cameras must be registered at the next checkpoint.

Sam Tso comes over and says hello. He looks happy, confident. He enjoys the respect he has as a member of the security force, and the authority he commands with the long knife he and the other AIM members wear sheathed and strapped to their legs. Most of the guards are not from the area but from other tribes. Ella drives farther up the road and parks the car. A newly built hogan is labeled with a sign reading INFORMATION BOOTH. Inside, newspapers and fact sheets are passed out. Special packets have been prepared for the press. Both the treaty council and BMLDOC distribute their own material.

Ella's sister Lenora Hill is helping out in the press hogan. She has short wavy hair and glasses, and is petite, not strong like Ella, who has her mother's broad shoulders and solid hips. "She's a veggie," says Ella, laughing again, about her sister who lives in California and is married to the Indian comedian Charlie Hill. "That's my sister who eats grass," she says.

On her way up to the tent, Ella sees her mother. Ella says Bessie is feeling strong these days after their last peyote meeting. Bessie and Jack will leave in a week for Texas, where they will collect some more peyote. The meetings, which are intensely personal all-night talks about feelings and fears—aided by the tongue-loosening effect of the peyote—help her family deal with the increasing stress.

Ella walks under the tent. Willie Lonewolf Scott sits in the back with some other AIM members. Roberta Blackgoat is here, as are Mae and Betty Tso. The ladies, as a rule, greet each other with solemn hand-shakes. Mae Tso, however, gives bear hugs in her shy yet impulsive way. Dennis Jennings, an Indian activist and poet, is leading the discussion. Jennings makes a short presentation in which he reads from various letters and documents dug up by a BMLDOC researcher. He concludes, "There were water, energy, and bank interests that wanted this land. I bring this up just to start things off." He announces that the afternoon's business will be devoted to "conflict resolution." All sides will have a chance to air their views, especially those who feel their views have not been heard. Members of the Big Mountain office assemble on stage. Lee Phillips wears a large straw cowboy hat with a dramatically curved "potato chip" brim. Lew Gurwitz jokes later that it is a ten-gallon hat on a five-gallon man. Lew himself looks tired, gray. His face lights up as he speaks to people and shakes their hands. Yet as soon as he is alone again for a moment, melancholy creeps over his features and he seems ten years older. He has lost favor among some of the Navajos lately. They want to see results, and there have been few. The Udall-McCain bill, the only concrete accomplishment, is being hemmed and hawed over by Lew. The leadership of the office is in upheaval, and Lew and Lee are trying to get Danny Blackgoat into a position of greater visibility and activity. Especially here, at a conference sponsored by Indians whose major message is self-determination, Lee and Lew feel awkward presenting themselves as the leaders of the Navajos.

The floor is open for questions from the audience. Just before the questioning gets underway the skies open up to a torrential downpour. No one can be heard over the din. The rain turns to hail and Jennings shouts over the crowd that the generators running the microphones will be turned off until the rain and lightning stop. "This is a good sign," he says.

The hail pounds down on the tent. People run in from outside covered with slush. Two people run out and make an offering to the rain, which is desperately needed. "This is a male rain," says Ella, a "hard rain. A sign the men have been bad," she giggles. In a few minutes the downfall subsides and Louise Benally, daughter of Alice, on whose land this tent is set, steps up to the podium and poses a question to Lew. Her voice is harsh and unforgiving. "We would like to see a copy of the repeal bill you have prepared. Can you supply me with a copy?"

Lew stands up and walks to the microphone. He pushes his long gray hair behind his ears and gestures with his hand. "We can't give you a copy because a final bill does not yet exist," he says in his sincere, weary Boston accent. "We are having a meeting this evening at the Hopi village of Shongopavi to discuss the bill in its present unfinished form. We don't intend to introduce a bill until it receives the approval of the Hopi and Navajo elders." He sits down. Gurwitz's efforts are slowed by his desire to get full support and consensus from all concerned—the traditional Indian way—before proceeding. This is important for his clients, the older, traditional people. Louise has different ideas. She approaches the microphone on the center aisle facing the stage. "We have been hearing about repeal for five years. Why is it that we haven't seen a bill yet?" The audience stirs uncomfortably. Ella whispers, "She's just trying to stir up trouble and get attention for herself. She doesn't know what she's talking about." Louise translates her question into Navajo. She poses another one, this time addressing it to Lee Phillips. She asks him where the First Amendment suit is. In addition to the repeal bill, the BMLDOC office has long been preparing a suit which claims that the Settlement Act violates the Navajos' First Amendment rights to practice their religion. Phillips stands up, removes his hat. Eyes shaded behind aviator glasses, he explains what the suit means and who is working on it. Louise steps up to the microphone and interrupts. "I'm not asking what the suit is about. I want to know when it will be filed."

Ella and Mae Tso and Roberta Blackgoat support the efforts of Lee and Lew, although sometimes the ladies wonder why their efforts have brought them no relief. Others, notably the Benallys and Biakeddys, are impatient. Louise has formed her own group called Youth for the Future. She has asked Ella to join it, but Ella told her that she supports Lew and Lee. For her part, Louise in frustration has criticized Lew for making all the decisions; she calls him the "Great White Father" with derisive irony, although he sees himself as trying to be exactly the opposite—bringing to the American people the ideas of the traditional Indians.

But Louise is expressing fears that are on every Navajo's mind. What is really being done to help them? Has there been any progress? What can they hope for? Ivan Sidney declared in May that there would be no forced evictions come the deadline, but can they believe it? Ross Swimmer has said the BIA will not move to evict either, but what will be their fate? Is there anything to hope for?

The rain begins again, creating a tremendous noise and interrupting the proceedings once more. Monsoon season is starting early this year. In front of Ella sit four elderly ladies, one of whom is Mae Tso's grandmother Jenny Manybeads, who sat in at the fence a month ago. One of her great-grandsons, who has accompanied her and her other relatives here, tells her to go up and ask her questions. The four ladies look at each other, stir, but don't get up. They concentrate on the words of the speakers, waiting patiently through the English for the Navajo translation. They have listened to a bewildering array of viewpoints this morning. They have been told the radical view that energy and banking companies conspired to steal their land. They have been told a very different and detailed history of the legal aspects of the dispute by a representative of the Navajo tribal government. They have been told that the Big Mountain group is trying to save their homes with elaborate suits and attempts to repeal the law, but so far they have seen nothing. They have heard the Udall-McCain bill discussed and have wondered why the Navajo Tribe is required to pay the Hopis $300 million. Yet, in spite of all the conflicting, sometimes misleading information, in their own intuitive way they understand that the mood here is bad. The chairs in the tent are half empty. The Hopi tribal chairman, who, it was believed, would come and talk to them, did not show up. The Navajos are divided against themselves and pushing away the people who have come here to help. "I really feel bad about this whole thing, about what's happening up here," says Ella. "The Benallys are four-sided," says Ella. "That means that one minute they'll speak from the east, then from the west, another day from the north and then the south.

"My parents and grandparents taught us to think the good way, the Navajo way. Anger and dissatisfaction are not good. One must think the good way and then one will walk the good way, walk in beauty. We young people are still green and still growing. We have a lot of places to go and a lot to see yet. The old people have traveled a long road. They know how to speak, they use the right words, they can make people understand. We young people get angry and hurt, instead of fighting what the white people are trying to do to us."

The Hopi traditionalist leader Thomas Banyacya heads up to the podium to make his presentation. He is a fixture in antirelocation meetings, because he opposes the government's involvement in any Indian affairs. But many Hopis are bewildered about what he really thinks about the land. And they wonder if the Hopi traditionalists like Banyacya and David Monongye are activists for the same reason Sekaquaptewa is involved in the Council—to seize a role in Hopi life they have been barred from because of a lack of religious training. Banyacya, like Sekaquaptewa, has only been initiated into the Kachina Society and holds no priestly position. Sensitive to criticism about his lack of religious training, Banyacya declares his religious situation from the start.

"I am not a member of a high religious society," Banyacya begins, "only the Kachina ceremony. But when I listened to those elders talk in 1948 [at an unprecedented gathering during which Banyacya and four other interpreters were asked to spread the word of the religious leaders opposed to the Tribal Council], I felt very proud and deeply impressed by the message they brought for the first time to the public.

"They spelled out many prophecies at that time, but two main ones. White brother was going to create things, invent things, and bring them back to his younger brother, the brown people. They exchanged tablets when they parted company many, many years ago. They each were given two tablets. Two are still at the Hopi villages of Oraibi and Hote-villa. The other two were taken by the white brother.

"Massau [the Hopi god of fire and death] told us that as long as we followed the Way the land would be protected. We must maintain our belief in the sacred circle, symbol of Hopi life. If the white brother should return with a cross, he told us, beware. He will tempt us with sweet invention. And he will ask us to sign papers. Old people do not sign papers if they don't understand them.

"Other forces are watching us: rain, clouds, water, wind. It makes me think how we are all related to each other. The blades of grass are with us, trees are with us, and the animals are with us. I firmly believe they have sent us a message today with the rain and the hail."

The old ladies in front of us are fidgeting. They are awaiting the Navajo translation, which won't come until Thomas is finished. Ella giggles. "Jenny Manybeads just said she wanted to go home. The lady next to her said, 'Whenever I take you anyplace, you want to go home as soon as we get there. Why don't you stay at home? Why don't you just sit there, you might learn something.'" Ella giggles again. "They're so cute," she says.

Banyacya continues: "I have gone out for six years meeting native people all across the country, talking about the spiritual things old people know. By singing, dancing, we can keep this land in balance.

"I'm the only one left of four people originally chosen to go out and explain these things. We original native people know what the supreme law of the land is. It is the Great Spirit. It is not written down. Hopi people don't want fencing, they don't want livestock permits. Those laws are from Washington. I tell white people across the country that this is their law, from their congressmen. 'With your taxes and your votes,' I tell them, 'you are doing this to us.' It is like a hatchet. This is a genocide bill. We have no place to go. If the bill goes, the land will fall to mineral development. If this happens we will all find ourselves with our bedrooms on our backs. The law is doing this to all native peoples."

What exactly is Banyacya's message? He believes the native people can work their problems out their own way. But in what forum? Who are the native people he wants to include? Does Ivan Sidney count as a native person? How about Abbott Sekaquaptewa? Who is traditional enough? And the Navajos—who would they choose? The ladies of Teesyatoh made it clear they didn't want anybody representing *them* in talks with Ivan Sidney, even traditional ladies from Big Mountain. Who has the authority to speak for other Indians? Is everyone speaking from the four sides of their mouths? Is discussion possible, or a dream? Can discussion bring compromise? Will anyone accept compromise?

Jenny Manybeads and her relatives get up at the supper break and walk down to the cookshack. Their great-grandson tells them he is going home to water the sheep. He carries one of the old ladies into the truck. He says, "When I come back, I want you to tell me that you asked someone your questions." One of the ladies asks if the people to ask speak Navajo. The great-grandson says, "There are a lot of interpreters around, find an interpreter and go ask those people your questions." The ladies mill about until their great-grandson is gone. After eating, they saunter back up to the tent for the evening activities. One turns to the other and whispers, "I brought a sack of bread that we didn't eat before. If you get hungry, just let me know, and I'll give you a piece." They sit, huddled in their winter coats, their tsiyeels pushed awry by their coat collars, waiting to hear more.

Later, the announcement is made that the Hopi Tribe has dropped all charges against Mae Tso stemming from her fight with BIA officials trying to impound her horses. Mae jumps up and down, clutching and unclutching her fists. She beams and hugs the ladies who congratulate her. After a while, they take the stage and sing songs about their land and animals. Mae's face alternates between expressions of reckless joy and worry. Singing with her friends and being surrounded by these other Indian people makes her feel strong, puts out of her mind, for a while, the harsh reality of her world.

And what do the Indians from the International Treaty Council think of this? Whose side do they take in a conflict between two Indian tribes? They take the side of the "Navajo and Hopi traditional leadership." The Treaty Council supports repeal of PL 93-531, the bill that divides the land; it opposes the compromise efforts of the Udall-McCain bill. The group opposes any effort supported by the Navajo or Hopi tribal councils.

The poet Dennis Jennings, in an interview, vigorously denies that Hopi people want the Navajos off the land. "Only the so-called progressives, who are ranchers and businessmen who benefit from U.S. government policies, want the Dine off," he says a few days after the conference. "Because of destructive policies of the U.S. government, the economy of the Indian tribes has been ruined, and the only economy left is the exploitation of their own minerals, resources, and human beings. Only that element with a particular self-interest" wants the Navajos off.

He emphasizes that the Treaty Council's position is self-determination. "Instead of working from the top down, through the tribal government, let the people work out the problem themselves in their own way," suggests Jennings. He points to documents written by the traditionalists of Mishongnovi and Shongopavi villages, the heart of old Hopi, which state that the Hopi people have never supported and still do not support their tribal government. "Nine percent of the population votes in the elections," says Jennings, who adds that the progressive element is "collaborating with the economic interests of the U.S." and is not representative of the Hopis' own "ceremonial people." "There is a lot of contradiction in Indian societies," says Jennings, "but there is a thread that goes back tens of thousands of years. It is not a question of numbers, how many support the progressives, how many are traditional. As long as that flame, the tie to the land and the ceremonial ways, is kept alive, there will be Hopi, there will be Dine, there will be human beings. This thread of life has to be maintained because the industrialized, materialist, dominant society is trying to cut that thread. And they do this through the use of patsies, Indians who have been torn from their culture. This is not just a struggle between traditional and progressive people. It goes to the very heart of Indian culture: whether that thread will be cut and the flame stamped out."

(29)

Udall Pulls Out

On the morning of June 4, 1986, Morris Udall placed a call to Paul Brinkley-Rogers, the *Arizona Republic* reporter who covered the Navajo-Hopi land dispute. Udall told Brinkley-Rogers that he wanted to give him an exclusive story. He said that he was abandoning his efforts to move the Udall-McCain bill through Congress. Udall said he felt it was "futile, misleading and cruel" to hold out any hope of a compromise settlement in light of the stiff opposition his bill had received from the Reagan administration, the Hopis, and Barry Goldwater.

"As far as I am concerned," Udall told the reporter, "Ross Swimmer is in charge of this thing now, and I expect him and [Interior Secretary Donald] Hodel to ask for more money and to do the job right."

Udall then called Peterson Zah, read him a statement he had prepared for the *Congressional Record,* and then called Ivan Sidney and did the same.

Udall's abandonment of the bill shocked the Navajos and left them scrambling for direction. Peterson Zah was deeply hurt. He told Udall, "You dropped me off a cliff on top of my head. If you were going to do that, you could have at least told me so that I could have put my feet down first."

There had been little warning. The tribe had followed every twist and turn of the maneuvering to persuade Goldwater not to obstruct the bill, and they believed they were winning the effort to keep Goldwater from openly opposing the bill. In the beginning of April, one Navajo lobbyist, flush after the successful introduction of the bill, said, "Udall said he's waiting to hear from Barry about the bill. If he doesn't hear anything, he'll go ahead with the hearings."

John McCain, the bill's co-sponsor, had said in early spring, "The only thing that's stopping the bill is Barry Goldwater. A lot of things are going to happen between now and July and we want to be ready and

Barry's been known to change his mind." McCain had even held out hope for action in the next session, adding, "Mo and I have to do what we think is right. A lot will change. I don't think relocation will be over even next year and by then, there'll be a new senator in Washington."

And in the middle of March, John McCain had called Ross Swimmer and "disabused him of the notion that the bill is a political move," according to the Navajos' top Washington lobbyist, who had announced confidently, "The bill will move."

But, in his announcement that he was dropping the proposal, Udall suddenly referred to the bill as a "phony bill" that was never meant to go anywhere, but had been intended to "stimulate debate." Although it was clear from the beginning that Udall would not openly oppose Goldwater, most observers felt that Udall was committed to pushing it through the legislative process, or, at the least, picking it up again after Goldwater left office. "We were all surprised," says Claudeen Bates-Arthur. "Some of us were even angry. I was angry. We always expected that he would see it through." Sandra Massetto said she had "never" heard the bill referred to as "phony" until Udall abandoned it.

Stories flew across the country following Udall's announcement. One ominous report was repeated with enough regularity to warrant attention. "Supposedly Mo had a meeting with Goldwater two days before he dropped it," Sandra Massetto said. "The rumor was that Goldwater had threatened him, said he would go back to Arizona and tell people Mo was sick."

Udall suffers from Parkinson's disease, a degenerative disorder of the central nervous system marked by motor problems, slurring of speech, and sometimes a shuffling gait. Udall has fought the disease since 1974. But in 1986, he has become increasingly stooped and weakened by his illness. Many of his constituents were not aware of the extent of his condition, which was of constant concern to his aides. Claudeen Bates-Arthur had also heard about the reported visit with Goldwater. "I know he went over to see Goldwater and when he came back, the word that I heard was that he was shaken. Whether that had to do with a threat or whatever, I don't know." Said Massetto, "Something bad happened that scared him. His actions after that are not understandable. It's another one of those unexplainable events that have marked this entire process."

Udall stated for the *Congressional Record* that Goldwater's opposition was key to his abandonment of the bill. He wrote, "Early on in this process, I made it clear that distinguished senior senator Barry Goldwater would be essential to any legislative action. He has made clear his opposition to our comprehensive bill and I must keep my word to him."

But he was also disturbed by the opposition to the bill expressed at a one-day hearing in May. He later joked, "We raised a proposal up the flagpole, and we're still picking the buckshot out of our pants from it." Udall heard strong objections to the bill from the administration and from the Hopis. Ivan Sidney, in an emotional plea, said, "You are going to see one day the Hopis sitting on their mesa tops with their feet dangling down, because that is all we're going to have left."

Swimmer had also raised legal and constitutional questions about whether the government had the right to swap the lands, raising questions of "taking," though privately he still seemed to support some kind of small-scale accommodation for the people of Big Mountain. Swimmer also noted that the government had binding contracts with twelve hundred families to build them houses. The administration's view was that the "contracts could not simply be canceled." Swimmer had earlier stated his position that had he become involved earlier, he would have opposed relocation as a solution to the land dispute, but twelve years into the process, with legal contracts signed with Navajos and the machinery in full operation, he felt he had no choice but to move forward.

The administration's opposition to the bill was the crushing blow. Said McCain, "The person who really hurt us was Swimmer, who said the administration couldn't support the bill." Swimmer was the factor that neither Udall nor McCain had anticipated when they conceived of the legislation. As long as the Commission had been in place, fumbling and bumbling along, they had time to wait out Goldwater. But with Swimmer determined to get the move accomplished in eighteen months onto the very lands the Navajos hoped to trade, the bill was on a collision course with the administration. Swimmer's arrival on the scene, though hailed as a saving grace by Yates, flummoxed the possibility of a compromise.

And the Navajos doubted that Swimmer would be able to accomplish all he thought he could. Said Navajo attorney Peter Osetek, "The BIA is dashing full speed ahead without even opening its eyes. Ross Swimmer thinks he's going to do this in eighteen months and walk away the hero. I think he's dreaming."

Added McCain, "Swimmer came into this with a lot of enthusiasm and has gotten himself in very deep. One thing Swimmer said that I found interesting was that he claims the New Lands are better for the people, they'll be able to have livestock and better grazing. He ignores the tie these people have to their old land. They don't care if it's dried lava."

John McCain acknowledged a few days after the hearings that Udall was "depressed" about what had happened. "He still doesn't know what to do," he said. His aides were "trying to figure out the next move"— perhaps a "dramatically reduced proposal" involving life estates or a "Moencopi settlement." McCain said at that point, "I don't know if we can force a compromise."

In an interview a few days after his abandonment of the bill, Udall was asked if he had made it clear to the Navajos that his proposal was a "phony" bill. Udall did not answer directly. He said he felt Zah had "got his hopes up. A lot of Indians did. The public relations apparatus they've had has been pretty good. And we were starting to get quite a volume of letters and I think they may have convinced themselves that something could be done."

Udall explained that the idea of the bill being a "concept" bill occurred to him after he wrote it but before he introduced it. He said, "When I produced that bill, [Ivan] Sidney and his friends were just apoplectic almost. Sidney got me to delay it two or three times. I was going to come out with it and get it done. Finally, to pacify Senator Goldwater and some of the others here, I had to make it very clear in the story when we filed the bill that this was a concept bill, that it was simply to get discussion going. It contained ideas and we hoped it would generate counterproposals." Udall believed that Zah understood this change. "Maybe he didn't believe it. He thought the snowball would begin to roll." When Udall announced to the Congress that he would no longer push the bill, he expressed "profound regret" to Peterson Zah. When asked if he realized he might have dealt a death blow to Zah's reelection hopes, Udall waffled. He said, "It's been obvious that he is in a tough fight. I've developed a great admiration and affection for the guy. He's a fighter and he feels that doing something right is more important than winning. And he's tried to do the right thing and pushed his Council as far as some of them wanted to go. But I never conceded the election to the other side. I hope he wins. He's got a good chance."

Udall may have been put off the effort by something other than Goldwater's opposition. He expressed uncharacteristic anger and bitterness about the Big Mountain support group in his June 4 call to reporter Paul Brinkley-Rogers. "He mouthed off about the Big Mountain group very angrily," said Brinkley-Rogers, "how they were causing a great deal of trouble because they were falsely raising the people's hopes." In his statement for the *Congressional Record*, Udall wrote, "I especially call on outside groups, such as the Big Mountain Legal Defense Fund, to cease their misinformation and distortion campaign and allow the principals to work out their differences without the threat of violence and disruption of the lives of two peaceful peoples."

After Udall's abandonment of the bill, the Navajo Tribe also turned its anger against BMLDOC. Just as the tribe had watched every move and whisper coming from Goldwater to try to fend off active opposition from him, so too had they courted BMLDOC, first to try to win Lew Gurwitz's and Lee Phillips's support of the bill, and then to try to soften their opposition. Phillips had acknowledged at the end of February: "The Navajo Tribe is lobbying us on this issue as if we were a congressional office. Not that they're afraid of us as any powerful force, but because we're sort of uncontrollable and could muddle the issue. And they can't afford to fight people on their own side about whether Udall-McCain is good or bad or whether the traditional people oppose it or support it or whether the traditional Hopis would come in as part of a deal, and then what about our office, and who knows what else. The tribe had to make sure they didn't have us creating brush fires on this issue."

But that was exactly what BMLDOC had done. Phillips did not understand quite how much influence BMLDOC's letter-writing campaign had had. Not only was BMLDOC's opposition to the bill causing brush fires, it had caused a conflagration that burned Udall badly. Before Udall's one-day hearing on the bill in May, BMLDOC supporters waged a very heavy letter-writing and telephone campaign. While some supported the bill in concept but had criticisms of certain provisions, others angrily denounced the settlement attempt, arguing instead for repeal. And as emotions rose and the issue intensified around the day of the hearings, someone from a Pacific Northwest support group had called Udall's office and physically threatened the congressman. It is not clear what was said, but Udall was deeply offended by it. It wasn't clear why he had reacted so strongly, but he voiced angry words about BMLDOC immediately following the incident. Sandy Massetto said, "He's run for President and had been in politics for a long time. I don't understand how a call from a nut at that point would have upset him so much." But it did.

Unable to compromise with their allies, and suddenly defeated, all sides turned against each other. Udall, frustrated that the Hopis, with the support of Goldwater, refused to negotiate, turned against the BMLDOC group. The tribe, confused and feeling betrayed by Udall, also turned against BMLDOC, which itself began to break apart. The younger Navajos, led by Louise Benally, turned against Lee and Lew. Some of the Navajos started calling the group Bumbledoc. The deadline was fast approaching, and the resistance was falling apart.

The BMLDOC group had grown to ten thousand members in the months before the deadline, with three hundred support groups in the United States and fifty-five abroad, but it was riven with divisions. Lee Phillips complained, "There has been so much hatred and disrespect in our organization, typical of [movements of] the left." Gurwitz told him at one point, "Forget the government, God save us from our friends." Phillips found the effort to direct a movement made up of very different people—all of whom wanted a voice—a discouraging task. Gurwitz sustained himself through some of the rough spots by remembering his successes in the seventies with AIM. For Phillips, his career had "started and finished with this issue. I haven't the memories to bolster my spirits."

Hobbled by internal dissent, the group also suffered from a complete

shut-out by the Navajo Tribe after the Udall-McCain hearings. Peter Osetek, one of the tribe's attorneys who focused on relocation issues, said
angrily, "The Big Mountain group's activities are hurting the tribe.
There's too much rhetoric and some untruths. When the tribe has to
explain they're not associated with them, it takes a lot of time and resources and is not productive."

For his part, Lee Phillips couldn't understand why the tribe's anger
fell so heavily on himself and Gurwitz. "I've never understood why they
took an angrier position toward us for advocating no relocation than
against the government [after Udall-McCain was dropped]." Phillips
adds, "There was a real anger directed toward us behind the scenes
about the failure of Udall-McCain. They allowed emotion to interfere
with business. To deal from a position that they're not going to talk to us
about anything was not helpful. We sent them our testimony on Udall-
McCain. We would have been willing to work with the tribe where we
could."

Phillips said that he had made BMLDOC's mailing lists of ten thousand people available to the tribe. "We supported the concept of Udall-
McCain, and made specific recommendations: one, that the allotments
[for Navajos who would still remain on Hopi land even after the ex-
changes] be increased to 640 acres [from 160 acres] because of livestock;
two, we felt the numbers [describing the people still resident on
the HPL] supplied to the House Committee were underestimated; and
three, that the cost shouldn't be borne by the tribe. Also that the
Hopis shouldn't be burdened with the New Lands if the water was
contaminated."

These objections had seriously undermined the bill. Phillips and Gurwitz never understood that the moment for compromise was at hand. In
fact compromise was never a part of Gurwitz's vocabulary. And Phillips
realized too late that the moment had passed. Nevertheless, Phillips
remained perturbed about why the tribe condemned BMLDOC so strenuously. He says, "It's like we were at different hearings after listening to
Eric [Eberhard] and [Navajo tribal official] Roger [Boyd] retell the events.
It was almost as if we had burst into the hearing room and thrown blood
all over Udall."

Claudeen Bates-Arthur said that BMLDOC's determination to fight
for repeal of the law and its unwillingness to compromise was unrealistic
and eventually fatal to the tribe's efforts. She said in an interview at her
office in Window Rock,

> We asked them from the beginning to work with us. I had a meeting
> in this room with Lew and asked them to work with us, asked them
> to concentrate their efforts in a way that would help the people, that
> we could not be destructive of each other's efforts. And over time, we
> tried to do that. We didn't take on Lew or his people or his cause in
> public in a way that would be harmful to them. After the Hardrock

chapter meeting, in which all of his clients that I know about voted to support the Udall-McCain bill, I personally asked him if they wouldn't direct their letter-writing campaign to help in that effort, now that their people had voted for it. And he said, "I don't know, we'll have to think about it." And he later got back to say, "We can't do it because of the power-line issue and coal issues." And I said, "What does that have to do with this? The real issue is the people, and if we have something that will allow the people to stay in their homes, we can deal with those other issues at a later time. The issue is not coal development and power lines. The issue is whether human beings can stay on the land of their ancestors." And he said, "No."

This decision had surprised the tribe. Said Bates-Arthur, "From that time on, I determined that his real agenda was not the people, his real agenda was something else which I see as . . . [a] personal need to have a cause. I equate Lew Gurwitz with Ross Swimmer, they [both] have their own agenda[s]. They know better than Navajo people what is good for them and they go down that path, regardless of what the Navajo people themselves say."

Bates-Arthur felt that Gurwitz had a need to feel he was the Navajo people's savior. She said, "I know for a fact that he does not wish to talk to Roger Boyd or Claudeen Arthur or any other educated Navajo who can question what he's doing. He wants to talk to Navajo people who haven't the experience or the background to question what he's doing."

(30)

Violence Erupts in Teesto

Window Rock was in turmoil, and the tribe was scrambling to regain control. After Udall's withdrawal of the bill, "everybody on Zah's staff was going around kicking the walls," said Duane Beyal, Zah's press spokesman. Instead of thinking up aggressive strategies with which to fight Peter MacDonald in the upcoming primary battle, Peterson Zah was trying to console his staff. He told them, "Let's pull ourselves together and find a creative solution. There's always a positive side to setbacks."

Zah is not an aggressive politician, but rather a conciliator concerned about doing the right thing. Those around him feel compelled to heat up the political machinery for him. Peter Osetek made the first move. On June 11, one week after Udall had withdrawn his bill, Osetek filed a class action lawsuit on behalf of seven relocatees in U.S. District Court seeking to halt the BIA's settlement of Navajos on the New Lands. "Our position is that there is no plan," said Osetek, "and they shouldn't spend any money doing what they've been doing in the past few weeks."

What they'd been doing in the past few weeks was the comedy of errors surrounding the building of the first house in the BIA's pilot project—pouring the foundation slab in the wrong place, approving the wrong site for archaeological clearance, and building a huge, highly-engineered road that stopped several hundred yards short of the house. The only aspects of the project that appeared to be flowing easily were the jokes. As Sandra Massetto quipped about the road, "Every pilot project needs a landing strip."

Osetek's suit charged that the BIA was violating the law by not following a proper plan. The suit also alleged that to get the project off the ground, the BIA was offering preferential treatment of certain relocatees over others who had long awaited relocation. The plaintiffs included Navajos who had moved off the HPL, but had yet to receive relocation homes. The suit named as defendants Interior Secretary Donald Hodel,

Assistant Secretary Ross Swimmer, project manager Dan Jackson, and the Relocation Commission and its three commissioners, Sandra Massetto, Ralph Watkins, and Hawley Atkinson. It infuriated the defendants, since it named them in their personal capacities (suggesting that their actions were illegal or capricious and outside their statutory responsibilities) as well as in their professional roles (which questioned the legality of the laws under which they were operating). The suit served to further convince the BIA that the tribe was determined to disrupt the relocation efforts.

The action was more a nuisance suit than anything else, because the 1974 Act limits the rights of individual Navajos to sue the government over issues related to relocation; only the tribe has the standing to initiate legal action. (Osetek's suit was a class action suit brought on behalf of individuals; it was not brought by the entity of the Navajo Tribe.) This limitation in the law was highly objectionable to the Navajo Tribe and to BMLDOC's Phillips and Gurwitz. It would be the most difficult hurdle for Lee Phillips to overcome when he filed his First Amendment suit. Consequently, he had assembled a team of constitutional lawyers to help him produce a strategy—one reason why the suit had been so slow in coming. The effect on the relocatees of the limitation was twofold: it further alienated them from the tribe, since the tribe could only act legally on their behalf if the tribe's interests were the same as the resisters', which they invariably were not; and it further reinforced the feeling that the Navajos had lost control of their destinies. It had deprived them of a voice.

Emotions were running high all over the affected areas of the reservation in the last weeks before the deadline. Leroy Morgan observed, "Jealousies and fights are splitting people all over, in the Teesto group, at Big Mountain, all through the chapter houses." Ella reported that Roberta Blackgoat told her, "People are mad and getting very frustrated. They want to just fight it out and get it over with with the Hopis. People have been told to be patient. How long can they be patient?"

The Hatathlies were trying to cope by concentrating on prayer and ceremonies. But the tension in the family couldn't be overlooked. On June 17, in the middle of a peyote meeting, Felix suffered another grand mal seizure. His eyeballs rolled up into his head, his body jerked in frightening spasms, and someone stuck a wallet in his mouth to keep him from chewing on his tongue. After the seizure, Felix was exhausted and his eyes were black.

The day after Felix's seizure, the first act of the long-dreaded and long-awaited violence erupted in Teesto. Two Hopi BIA officers and a Hopi tribal ranger checking a damaged fence were roughed up by a group of Navajos, who also took away their guns. Early BIA reports stated that one officer was stabbed. The officers, who, according to the

BIA, were surrounded by forty to fifty Navajos, managed to escape in one of their police vehicles. The other car at the scene was "disabled" by the Navajos.

After hearing of the incident, Ivan Sidney canceled press conferences he had scheduled in Los Angeles and San Francisco to remain on the reservation and investigate. He told one reporter, "We have been worried that the Navajos would create any kind of violence in order to attract press coverage as the relocation deadline draws nearer. They want to change the law and will do anything to get their way." The Navajos, particularly those aligned with the Big Mountain group, believed that the Hopis had again stepped up their construction activities on the HPL just to provoke the Navajos to violence, and to give Ivan Sidney the opportunity to remind the world that Navajos were lawless bullies.

If that was the Hopis' purpose, they succeeded very well. Said Eric Eberhard, head of the Navajo Washington office, "The Teesto incident hurt us badly. The great majority of people believe the Hopi-Swimmer-Craft line that Navajos are the big bad guys trying to steal the land. That's why we're telling the people to turn the other cheek."

The people of Teesto were as radical as the people of Big Mountain, but more unpredictable. Not only were they not a part of the BMLDOC hierarchy, they also opposed Peterson Zah and were fierce supporters of Peter MacDonald. They were considered rogues in the resistance effort, and the BMLDOC group didn't know them well. Nevertheless, after the incident, the resisters in Teesto called Lew Gurwitz, and he agreed to advise them. The guns the Navajos took from the policemen were still missing.

June 18 breaks hot and the sun is high in the sky by seven o'clock. Teesto is a verdant area of volcanic buttes and rolling flatlands. One feels close to the history of the earth out here, confronted as one is by the ancient geology. The largest buttes are Horse Spring Butte, Star Mountain, and Seba Dalkai Mountain, which the Navajos consider a sacred shrine. Finger Point and Little Star Mountain fill out the range that circles the area. Star Butte is a large, messily shaped explosion of craggy surfaces. A soft rise just near the chapter house and trading post has the name Teesto carved out of it into white rock.

The people involved in the confrontation with the police yesterday have scheduled a press conference here. Press conferences are becoming as common on the reservation these days as coralling sheep. The meeting is going on at Alvin and Ida Clinton's house, ten miles away from the chapter house, between Star Butte and Fingerpoint. The road is badly damaged by rains and is a shattering washboard. An elderly man and two young girls walk along the road. When the car stops, the girls run over and ask, "Where are you going?" "To Alvin Clinton's," comes the answer. The girls dance away from the car and toward their dad, turn excitedly, and say, "That's where we're going, too."

Their father comes over, and they climb in. He introduces himself as Harry Nelson. He is wiry, with short, black hair. He has a sad, nervous expression, and begins to speak in English. He points out the fence that divides the HPL from the Navajo reservation. He takes out a little black notebook and flips the pages to a map of the executive order area. He points out the location of the fence where he was told the trouble broke out, and he points out the HPL fence and motions with his hand where it goes off toward the mountains. He notes that the boundary fence was moved once, after an adjustment in the partition line. To the people who live on the affected area, fences are like trees struck by lightning. They are feared, they are closely observed. The Navajos know everything about them, when they appeared, where they are, what changes they have undergone.

Harry Nelson says he worked on the track crew of the Santa Fe Railroad for twenty-one years, with a short break between 1971 and 1974, when he came back to the reservation and lived at home. He says he eventually became restless and returned to the railroad in Phoenix, Flagstaff, and Gallup, until he was disabled by an injury. He began work in 1954 on a gang, mostly in California, near Barstow. He and his family moved around, to Los Angeles, Needles, Pasadena. He has a wife and ten kids. He points out his house as the car bumps down the road. The kids in the back whisper. They imitate their father and point out the fence to each other. The elder of the two, who is around ten, has a voice like Carol Channing's.

Seba Dalkai Mountain rises to the right. Harry Nelson points out a fence running from the road up toward the summit. The fence posts have been bent and some of the wires torn off. Harry Nelson gets very excited, rising from his seat and speaking to the girls in Navajo, pointing out the fence and saying that that was the site of the disturbance yesterday. He has only heard stories of what happened. He is eager to attend the meeting.

Nelson says that he doesn't want to relocate. He shakes his head, says with emotion, "There is no place to go. I will not move anywhere." What about the New Lands? He says, "There is nothing there. There are no schools, no hospitals, no stores. There is nothing there. It is too far away," he says. "My chapter house is over here," he says, motioning toward the Teesto chapter house with his mouth. It is inconceivable to him that there might be a new chapter house on the New Lands. This is his community, where he has friends and relatives and elaborate systems of communication and mutual help.

About ten miles down the road Nelson sees a house surrounded by a dozen pickup trucks. A group of people are assembled under a large ramada. The girls scamper out of the car. Thomas Katenay, Reggie Deer, and Sam Tso are here. They say they came down last night from Big Mountain after they heard about the trouble. A few minutes later, Danny Blackgoat arrives with his girlfriend Annie. Lew Gurwitz is here, sitting with Dave Clark and Anderson Tulley, the leaders of the Teesto resistance, who have been active for years in tribal politics. They are speaking to a reporter from the *Navajo Times*. They speak both Navajo and English. Anderson Tulley is a handsome man who wears a black golf shirt and blue jeans. He looks a bit agitated, unlike his friend Dave Clark, who, in blue slacks, white shirt, and maroon baseball cap, appears as comfortable as a man in front of his television watching Sunday football. Ida Clinton speaks rapidly in Navajo to the reporter, gesturing with her hands. Geraldine Clark also speaks, adding to what her neighbor Ida has to say. The four of them retell their story, interjecting, clarifying the testimony of the others.

Dave Clark repeats over and over that no names are to be used in the newspaper story, and Gurwitz, their attorney, sits there to advise them about whether they should speak about certain subjects. It becomes clear that there is part of the story they are not telling.

The group explains that for the last year, they have suffered from the harassment of Hopi fence and water crews. "About two years ago," says Clark, "Hopi cattle were driven into this area, about a hundred, two hundred head. They need water, so they want to use ours. We have only one water source, Fingerpoint Pond." The Hopis built pipes and storage tanks to siphon off the water. "That's why the tension developed." On Monday, a couple of Clinton children went down to the well to draw water. The Hopi rangers told them they had no right to use the tap, that it belonged to the Hopis. The children ran back to their parents with the story, upset and angry.

The Clintons went over to the chapter house, they told some of the people there what had happened, that the Hopis had told them not to take water. The next morning, Clark and Tulley and some others drove back to the Clintons'. They talked about the problem and decided to drive over to the newest fencing site, on the side of Seba Dalkai Mountain. They expected a fence crew to be there. When they arrived, they found Hopi members of the BIA police instead, looking over the fence that had been damaged the previous evening. (They do not say who damaged the fence.) They saw two vehicles and three officers. One officer remained in his truck. Ida Clinton walked over to one of those standing on the hillside and asked him what they were doing there, why were they building fences and taking away their water? As she approached him, the rest of the Navajos climbed up the hill behind her forming a ring around the officers. There were about thirty people, they say, as many as there are now, under the shack, including elderlies and children. One of the police officers reached for his billy club. Ida Clinton says she grabbed his arm to prevent him from striking her. He in turn grabbed her arm. Before anyone knew what was happening, the crowd rushed the two policemen and accosted them. The two officers drew their guns. The Navajos quickly disarmed them and took the guns. The Hopis were terribly frightened. The Navajos deny having approached with any weapons; they say they announced to the officers that they were unarmed. The BIA later corrected the report that there had been a stabbing. Even Ivan Sidney conceded that the supposed stabbing victim had a superficial cut near his belt. The Navajos surmise he may have been cut on the barbed wire fence, which ran right beside the area where the scuffle took place. Says Clark, "We didn't see anybody get stabbed. Nobody was armed."

The Navajos shouted that they wanted the Hopis off their land. And they wanted them to take away the bulldozers they were using to rebuild a dam near Fingerpoint Pond. The Hopis climbed back into their vehicles and drove off. One of the officers sat in his vehicle for a long time, trying to regain his composure. Clark said the man looked very scared. Clark said he let the police know they'd be at the Clintons' house later in the day.

And, sure enough, in a few hours, according to Clark, "a whole police force came, about eighteen units with three or four police in each unit and reinforcements down the road." Clark claims, "All told, there were thirty police units, BIA, Hopi, and Navajo police wearing bulletproof vests."

Everyone in the shack laughs when Clark recounts this detail. The police asked for the officers' guns back. "We told them they better go knock on doors to find out. We don't know where the guns went." David Clark adds, "Gramm-Rudman must be really bad, going through all that to get two guns back," joking about the government's budget-balancing efforts.

What the people in the ramada don't know is that another woman in the area, fearful of the violence, yesterday called Peggy Scott, a tribal official, who grew up in Teesto. Scott then called the Navajo police and told them that Teesto residents were upset over the militants' actions. But to the Navajos under the ramada, the arrival of the police was proof that the Navajo Tribe is also the enemy. Geraldine Clark says, "We asked for a resolution to be introduced at the Tribal Council on a moratorium [on relocation]. It was never acted upon by the Council when the Udall-McCain bill was on the floor. We have requested a lot of things through Teesto [chapter officials] but nothing is ever done for us."

The ramada is covered with cedar boughs. In it is a large double bed covered with a Pendleton blanket. At the other end is a stove, where some ladies are preparing food. An old bridle with rusty bit hangs from a post. Someone carries a couple of sides of mutton into the house. Trucks come and go. Sam and Thomas use binoculars to watch the BIA police vehicles that have been circling the area. At one point, they catch sight of an unfamiliar vehicle and jump into their truck, dashing after it. They think it contains an "informer." It turns out to be a relative of one of the families.

Danny Blackgoat intones with melodrama, "The Public Law is moving toward us in the shape of bulletproof vests and hollow points." There is silence for a few moments. Lew Gurwitz says for the benefit of the press, "What we heard out here was that it was a question of self-defense. Mrs. Clinton, who has lived her life here, has every right to ask and find out why the Hopis are building fences and tapping water. It is absurd for the police to feel they have to grab her arm and twist it rather than simply answer her questions. The pressure has built up to such a point here that it brings these people to rage. It takes a lot to bring Navajos to the point of yelling and defending themselves, a lot of pent-up frustration. I believe that Ivan Sidney is trying to exacerbate the situation and provoke just such situations. They're making the range war now that never existed before."

Gurwitz adds, "I think this provocation is part of a plan by the Hopi Tribal Council to discredit all the peaceful methods of settling this issue that we're trying to accomplish, the moratorium and the repeal bill that are doing so well. The traditional Navajo and Hopi people combined their efforts to ask Congress for a moratorium bill. It is the peaceful way to handle this."

The bills Gurwitz refers to are actually *not* doing well. Representative Bill Richardson, Democrat from New Mexico, introduced a bill on May 21 that would have placed a one-year moratorium on relocation. But after Udall dropped his bill, Richardson agreed that he "[would] not push the measure without Udall's consent." The hopes for another bill, a repeal effort, being drafted by Representative Mickey Leland, Texas Democrat, also dimmed with Udall's action. Udall said, "I don't think there is going to be any serious attempt by anybody to repeal or drastically modify the law."

Gurwitz's efforts to keep up the hopes of these people are coming to be an exercise in self-deception. The people in Teesto still cling to the hope that if they can only get their message out, people will understand and the tide will turn. Says Clark, "The people in Washington and the Tribal Council are listening to someone else. They are listening to Goldwater and Udall. They don't ask us, the people who live here. They listen to other people who are deciding what is good for us. That is where the misunderstanding comes in."

The meeting winds down around lunchtime, and on the way back to the Teesto chapter house, a small car passes and stops. Peggy Scott, director of the Navajo Land Dispute Commission, steps out of her vehicle and says she is a little scared to go over to the Clintons'. She says that Peterson Zah warned her not to come, claiming that the people were emotional and irrational and would most likely perceive her as an enemy, a representative of the Zah administration, rather than a Teesto resident and relative.

Scott then says she has just come from the house of one of her relatives, which was attacked by the band of Navajos. Scott fills in a section of the story that the Navajos in the ramada failed to mention. After confronting the policemen, the Navajos drove to a trailer owned by Alf Secakuku, Hopi agency superintendent, and a cattleman who runs his animals near here. They set fire to his trailer and left it to burn. Then they went to the site of a relocation house just over the line in the Navajo Partition Lands. The house was being built for Scott's uncle. The Navajo gang set fire to the lumber stacked on the site. Her relatives were very upset, and her aunts were crying when she left them.

Scott decides to head on to the Clintons' in spite of Zah's warnings. As it turns out, Zah's predictions are correct. As soon as Scott arrives, Anderson Tulley tells her she is not welcome. She speaks to some people there, including her mother, and is addressing a Phoenix television crew when she is told again to leave by a man she doesn't know. The man then twists her arm in an attempt to escort her away. Her mother steps in and pushes the man away from her daughter. Scott is hurt and frightened. She climbs into her car and drives home. She fears what is yet to come. Later that day, Lew Gurwitz returns the officers' guns to the BIA's Hopi area law enforcement section. He does not say where he got them.

It appears that the violence the tribe believed would be so detrimental to the Navajo cause was not being roundly discouraged by BMLDOC. As Lee Phillips said once, "It only takes one Stokely Carmichael," suggesting that a movement can be crystallized by violence. Navajo Washington office director Eric Eberhard said, "The assumption in Congress is that Lew and Lee are actively and purposely provoking violence, spreading misinformation. And the government will not respond sympathetically to that. They're doing incredible damage to the people they're claiming to help. I never thought I'd come to say that."

A week previously, members of the BMLDOC support group occupied and shut down the Oregon office of Representative James Weaver, demanding that he support a moratorium bill. "The [Big Mountain] Committee is the biggest flim-flam since the 1974 Act was rammed through the Congress," said Eberhard bitterly. "At least Goldwater is honest and up front about his intentions."

And Goldwater had not let up on his determination to protect the

Settlement Act. His grudge seemed still to burn white hot. After learning that Senator Alan Cranston of California had just introduced a bill authorizing an eighteen-month moratorium on relocation, Goldwater blasted Cranston with an "unusually strongly worded letter for one between senators," according to Cranston aide Hal Gross. Goldwater had let Cranston know "we had our facts *all* wrong, and he would resist our efforts." Goldwater wanted Cranston to know that "there was only one person living on Big Mountain."

Cranston was quite concerned about the issue since so many of the BMLDOC letters came from his constituents in California, and because he felt somewhat guilty about his yes vote for the 1974 legislation, according to Gross. But until the recent heavy lobbying from the Navajo Tribe and BMLDOC, he had little idea what the dispute was about. Said Gross, "For years, people were persuaded to stay out of this because it was a simple Arizona problem between two tribes. [We were told it involved] the aggressive Navajo Tribe choking out the meek Hopis. People were skeptical, but stayed aside. Now, our sophistication has grown."

That may be, but it was now a bit late. Little seemed to make sense any more. Gurwitz, at Teesto, said, "We're trying to maintain a peaceful, spiritual defense," yet his clients had disarmed police. Gurwitz's group was falling apart over the "semidictatorship going on," according to one supporter, who added, "People are going around doing things independently because they don't want to go to the Great White Father of the Big Mountain Group, Lew, for approval."

For his part, Eberhard couldn't believe that Gurwitz was still advocating repeal of the law. "Do they know what repeal means? Repeal means the Hopis and Navajos have joint and equal use of the JUA. That means the Hopis can come down and camp right next to a Navajo family. I don't like what I hear from the people on that. They say, 'The land is ours.' "

The Navajo Tribe was still hoping that a compromise bill might be passed after Goldwater left the Senate. "I think we're at the point now where things just have to play out. I really regret that." Eberhard, however, was still hopeful, and the tribe intended to do everything it could to prevent Swimmer from hastily settling Navajos on the lands they hoped to exchange with the Hopis. On June 18, the Navajo Tribe joined Osetek's suit against the BIA, hoping to lend weight to the plaintiffs' attempts to slow down relocation. Eberhard said, "All things being equal, we'll have a settlement bill through Congress in twelve to eighteen months. But then, in this issue, things are never equal."

(31)

July 4, Independence Day

Although they fear violence, the most debilitating force operating on the Navajos has nothing to do with violence. It is fatigue.

Says Sandra Massetto, "The BIA is dealing in this issue with the Indians exactly as it has throughout history. They work with the ones who agree with them, who are open to the goods and incentives they offer, who are cooperative, and they slowly chip away at the rest until they are defeated."

The Hatathlies are wearing down. "My mom is very depressed," says Ella. "She says she just wants to be left alone. After a lifetime of hard work, she has nothing to show for herself. She doesn't want a white man's house. She doesn't want handouts. She doesn't want to hear about relocation, or talk about it. It makes her sick. She just wants to be left alone now, she's so tired. She told me I should move, that Dennis and I would never survive on the reservation, that there are no jobs for us. She told us we should take advantage of the relocation benefits. I didn't say anything," says Ella. "You don't argue with your elders," says Dennis. "But we're not going to go," says Ella.

It is July 4, 1986, and Jack and Bessie's wedding anniversary. Thirty-six years ago, at the Flagstaff powwow they decided to "be together," as Ella puts it. They didn't get a marriage license until some years later, when the census takers drew up marriage licenses for Navajos who didn't have them.

Ella makes a feast to celebrate. Dennis barbecues large, meat-laden ribs and steaks. Ella makes tortillas and corn and salad and iced tea seasoned with a citrus-like berry her mother picked in Sedona, where they traveled yesterday and sold two of Bessie's rugs.

Bessie sits in the living room, repairing the boundary of another rug. Jack catches a nap in one of the bedrooms, and Felix sleeps in the cab of the truck. His seizures have worn him out. Dennis, tending the meat on the grill, says he thinks the family has exhausted traditional forms of healing for Felix and that they may now be forced to seek modern medical care. Dennis, of course, won't suggest it, because it is not his place. Though the family thinks the problem may be the result of repeated falls from the horse, Dennis thinks any brain damage Felix may have suffered is the result of Felix's former habit of sniffing gasoline. "I used to see him walking around, all glassy-eyed. Who knows what he damaged inside there?" he says.

Dennis wears white pants, a Hawaiian shirt, gray loafers, and a fedora. He looks like he's stepped out of an episode of "Miami Vice," one of his favorite shows. Dennis is enjoying his new life as a social worker. He has been employed by the tribe for almost six months now, in one of the tribe's programs for handicapped youth. He has a newfound self-respect, and a healthy appetite for the material world which he now has license to enter by virtue of his steady income.

Dennis graduated from NAU a year ago, and Ella will graduate soon. The two will no longer be a part of the university, where they have lived for the past half-dozen years, able to ignore, for a time, the fact they have no place to live. They know it is unlikely that they will again become what Buzz calls "reservation Johnnies." But the decision to relocate, to take advantage of a once in a lifetime offer to be given a house, is a difficult one. Dennis says that despite Ella's protestations to the contrary, the deadline is bothering her a great deal. The pressure on them is great and growing. Their two-bedroom apartment is too small for the five of them (including Ella's son Kimo who has just returned from California), particularly when relatives visit, and they need a house. Dennis is ready to relocate, but it is Ella's decision, one she must make and be able to live with. Dennis says, "I really like Flagstaff. You know, if it weren't for Ella's mom, we'd probably relocate there, but until she makes a decision to relocate herself, or tells her kids to go ahead, and Ella is comfortable with it, we're going to stick with her." Ella is ambivalent, unable to make any decisions regarding her life. The Navajo Tribe's housing repair program has denied them help repairing the hogan in Coal Mine, eliminating the possibility of moving back there. Dennis was turned down for housing in Tuba City, and they have no homesite lease on another part of the reservation.

Bessie senses Ella's confusion. She tells her, "You're not the girl we once knew." She tells Ella she should be weaving, that weaving would restore her thoughts to order. Jack's opinion is that she should let her hair grow long and tie it up like her mother's. "Your thoughts are all tangled with your hair like that," he tells her about her short cut and perm.

Bessie asks, "How can you think clearly when you walk around on cement all day?" She also objects to Flagstaff. Says Bessie, "They even have reservations for trees out there." The television is another object of Bessie's ire. She thinks it causes the young ones to have nightmares, and confuses adults because she says they pattern their lives on the soap opera plots they watch. Jack is not so orthodox. Ella says, "He likes the cartoons, because a lot of the characters are animals and they remind him of our winter stories."

Ella is becoming increasingly unnerved at school. She says she has caught herself dressing down Hopis in class, and she is no longer able to say hello to Hopis she knows when she bumps into them at the supermarket in Tuba City. She keeps wanting to ask them, "Why don't you say anything to your Tribal Council? Why don't you tell them you don't think relocation is right?"

July 4 is America's day for cookouts, and while Dennis turned ribs, contemplating his family's future, several other Arizonans were celebrating Independence Day, planning their own futures. A political barbecue, complete with hamburgers and hot dogs and potato salad, was taking place in the Fairfield Continental Country Club in Flagstaff for senatorial aspirant John McCain, gubernatorial hopeful Burton Barr, and U.S. Representative Bob Stump. Ralph Watkins, the peripatetic politico was also there, quite concerned about his own future, since the results of a highly critical audit of the Commission by the Inspector General's office of the Department of the Interior had recently been released. Also looming over the Commission were oversight hearings called by Udall and scheduled for the end of July. Watkins recently asked Sandra Massetto to call John McCain and ask him to prevail upon Udall to cancel the hearings. Massetto refused.

Watkins approached John McCain and McCain's wife Cindy. McCain asked, "How are you, Ralph?" Watkins, eyes glinting like paint on the hood of a new silver car, head set into his shoulders on a short, stout neck answered, "Wonderful. Just wonderful. I'm earning a lot of money. I'm happy, and we're solving this Indian problem. This Indian thing is easy." To a stunned silence, he repeated, "Oh yes, we're moving right along with it, the Indian problem is easy. It really is, it's easy." He announced that he had just bought a radio station in Flagstaff, a Christian station that would feature light rock music. "If they don't cover the Indian problem the way we like," he chuckled, "then we'll just tell the story ourselves." He smiled brightly and bobbed his head. John McCain and his wife walked quietly away.

(32)

The Sun Dance, Big Mountain

Dawn breaks over the sun dance camp as it might have broken over another sun dance camp a century ago. The scene is composed like a nineteenth-century Ben Wittick photograph. Smoke rises from small campfires and hovers in a low cloud about the tipis and igloo-shaped sweat lodges just emerging from the black of night. Horses, tethered around the camp, snort, stamp their feet in the quickening light. Slowly, the sun dancers emerge from their bedrolls, hungry, exhausted, some in great pain from their wounds. Men lounge in their long skirts, brushing, braiding, and tying their hair. The women gather at their own tipis, adjusting their skirts and blouses, arranging their hair. The sun rises warm and golden, spreading its rays slowly across the valley.

Today is the fourth and final day of Big Mountain's fourth sun dance. Tonight will be a great feast. Tomorrow is the deadline.

The only sound that makes this sun dance different from those of days long gone is the eerie drumbeat and wailed prayer of a Buddhist monk chanting from a camp high on a ridge. The chanting filters through the mist that swirls about the camp. The monk will chant from dawn until dusk, keeping his song aloft throughout the trial of the dancers.

Away from the arbor, observers also begin to stir, light their own fires, and gather over coffee. Trailers, tents, and pickups dot the hillsides as far as the eye can see. The camps are again segregated—at the request of the Indians—into Indian and non-Indian sites. Estimates suggest there are a thousand people here from all over the world. There are Scandinavians, Germans, Indians from twenty-five different tribes, and an RV full of Black Muslims. Perhaps another one or two hundred people, mostly Navajos, will stream in and out of the carefully guarded camp during the day. AIM guards search cars and write down names and addresses of all visitors to the sun dance. Several members of the media are turned away. Some are allowed to enter, but are compelled to leave their camera equipment behind. A reporter and photographer from the *Atlanta Journal and Constitution* are thrown out after the photographer insists it is his First Amendment right to photograph the ceremony.

The AIM security guards are strict, quasimilitary in appearance, and intimidating. A sign on the graded road by Kee Shay's house at the turnoff to the survival camp reads "Big Mountain Sundance July 3-6 1986. No guns, drugs, alcohol. Not responsible for accidents." The last line is new.

Lew Gurwitz is around and about, but keeping a conspicuously low profile. He wears a red headband, says hello, greets people. He has been relegated to directing traffic. He appears weary but good-humored. Today, everything is run by the Indians, and no acknowledgment is made of the white attorneys or supporters. Gurwitz accepts this state of affairs with grace.

Sam Tso works security, sometimes at the entrance gate signing people in, or back around the sun dance arbor, making sure that people don't step inside the arbor with shoes on, checking that no water is brought in to the area, making sure nobody crosses the eastern entrance of the dance circle.

At one point, he and Thomas Katenay drive back to the base camp. They drive in a large green pickup truck that has been lent to them. Plowing up rocky slides of shale and down into sandy valleys, the truck struggles and shakes. At the first campsite, where the support groups have been encouraged to stay, Sam finds potsherds around some of the camping areas. The ceramic pieces are porous, unexpectedly delicate; the faded pastel colors of the clay are decorated with black brush strokes.

Sam picks up some fragments and says, "My elders told me not to bother those things, not to camp there, but to let them alone. My great-grandfather, before he died, told me that at one time the Anasazi people lived around here. But it was a period of incest and breaking of taboos. A terrible tornado struck one of the hills of Big Mountain, sending a message to the Hopis' ancestors that they didn't belong there." According to Sam's grandfather, the gods made a circle with arrowheads around Hopi and told the Hopis to live within the boundary.

This is a story the Hopis probably haven't heard. The story they tell is that after the Navajos returned from Fort Sumner, several of their leaders approached the Hopis for permission to live near them. The Hopis assented, telling the Navajos they could stay as long as they didn't revert to their former raiding ways. The Navajos gave the Hopis small doll-like figures, called tiponi, which the Hopis have kept. With the gift, it is said, the Navajos gave the Hopis power to hurt them. Ivan Sidney has on occasion threatened to destroy the tiponi, suggesting that with their destruction would come the destruction of the Navajo people. The Navajos believe their stories. And the Hopis believe their stories. The government writes its own stories, which, in the scheme of things, tend to overrule the more poetic ones.

Back at the sun dance arbor, two hundred Indians including five Hopis have resumed their dancing. When entering or leaving the arbor, the dancers raise their arms to the sun and turn in a circle. On the backs of many of them is painted a star and crescent moon to reflect the present position of Venus and the moon in the night sky. Sage, tied with red ribbon, circles the dancers' ankles and heads. Some wear sprigs on their foreheads. Others wear eagle feathers sticking from the sage rings circling their heads. Willie Lonewolf Scott carries a staff hung with eagle feathers. At certain times, during piercing of the men, or later, breaking, the dancers form a tight circle around the affected dancer, dancing mesmerizingly, whistling to the intensifying beat of the drum.

Most of the dancers are now oblivious to the pain. The burning sun, the red-hot sand, and the fatigue produced by hunger and thirst help the dancers to forget their bodies, leaving them with only their faith and hopes for a vision.

Willie Scott is tied to the tree today, as he was yesterday, the day before, and the day before that. He has decided to endure this for the sake of the people here. His skirt hangs off his hips, his ribs stick through his skin like odd pieces of firewood, and his tsiyeel hangs in disarray. Yet he whistles and dances with a regular beat, and is even able to adjust the ropes tied to the pegs in his chest as he moves forward and away from the cottonwood tree.

The drummers, sitting around a single large drum, are becoming hoarse, but as the ceremony advances and those still pierced must break, the energy of the dancers and singers swells.

When the time comes, at the climax of this ceremony, Willie breaks his skin himself, throwing himself backward, offering, with his own will, his skin to the Creator. He flings himself with such force that he falls to the dirt. He picks himself up and runs tentatively around the arbor. Betty Tso steps out to embrace him and many tears are shed.

The next morning, July 7, opens to a dark sky. At the Rocky Ridge School, about 50 Navajo veterans, and 250 other protesters, including many sun dancers, begin a three-mile walk south over the dusty road to the place where the partition fence passes near the road, two miles south of the Dinnebito Trading Post. Veterans from World War II and the Korean and Vietnam wars march with flags raised, singing chants. Behind them march women from Big Mountain, led by Roberta Blackgoat carrying a sign saying "The Creator is the only one who's going to relocate us." Mae Tso carries the Stars and Stripes upside down.

The veterans are upset that Mae carries the flag this way, and it leads the marchers to separate into two groups. One veteran, Chester Morris of Indian Wells, says that peace might come if all the protesters agreed to raise the flag properly. "Our government is splitting us apart," he says. "This was not what we fought for."

As the marchers reach the partition fence, Percy Deal addresses them. The mood is somber. The people are exhausted. Deal says, "The American nation in the last four or five days has been celebrating the restoration of the Statue of Liberty. But if the Statue of Liberty were to turn around and look over her shoulder, she'd be disappointed. Justice and peace have not been given to Native American people and particularly the Navajo people."

At the fence, the people offer their own prayers into the wind, toward the threatening sky. Then, protesters step forward and clip the fence with wire cutters. Mae Tso tries to explain to the veterans why she resisted their call for the group to recite the Pledge of Allegiance, and why she carries the flag on her stick with its blue field down. She tells them that the government has tried to make her feel worthless, that it has taken away most everything she holds dear. She tells the veterans that she respects them for what they have done, but she cannot respect the government for what it has done. She reminds the veterans that the Indians have their own flag, and it is the eagle, and it flies all by itself, up in the air, without staffs, without poles, and even sometimes upside down.

Epilogue

Ella and Dennis Bedonie relocated in December 1988 to a house the Commission built for them in Flagstaff.

Although the house is beautiful—"it has everything," as Dennis puts it—tragedy soon struck the family. A year after they relocated, Ella was diagnosed with breast cancer. In the fall of 1989, the Bedonies rented out their house and moved back to the reservation to be closer to the Indian Health Service Hospital in Tuba City.

The cancer seemed to confirm Ella's worst fears about her decision to relocate—that it would lead to a catastrophe. Although her mother told Ella she must make her own decision after considering the needs of her family, one can hardly keep from recalling Ella's own thoughts: "Our traditional teaching tells us that if you ever accept payment for your land, it's going to take a five-fingered human from you."

Ella underwent two lumpectomies and was put on a course of chemotherapy, which she stopped after three months. Cancer was still in her system, and the doctors recommended a mastectomy. But Bessie stepped in, forbade further operations as well as the chemotherapy, and orchestrated a year's worth of traditional healing, including a Chinese acupuncturist. At the end of the year, Ella was pronounced free of cancer by medical doctors. She and Dennis live in a trailer in Tuba City, near Dennis's work as a counselor for "at risk" children in the Tuba City primary school.

In April 1992, a tree beside the Bedonie's relocation home was struck by lightning. Ella consulted her father, Jack, about what to do, and he told her that according to Navajo ways, they must stay away from the strike. In May 1992, the Bedonies put their house up for sale.

Lee Phillips's First Amendment suit was filed January 26, 1988, in U.S. District Court for the District of Columbia. The National Council of

Churches and other national religious groups joined with him by filing an amicus brief. The Navajo Tribe filed an amicus brief as well, arguing that individual Navajo tribal members should be able to bring suit apart from the tribe.

Phillips filed the suit in Washington in hopes of getting a hearing with a judge more sympathetic to his clients. But at the request of the government, the case was transferred back to Arizona, to Judge Earl Carroll, before whom the other related suits are being and have been argued since Judge Carroll took over the Navajo-Hopi cases from Judge Walsh of the *Healing v. Jones* panel.

From October 4 to 7, 1988, Judge Carroll heard Lee Phillips's request for a preliminary injunction to halt relocation and related activities such as stock impoundment, fencing, and the construction freeze. Carroll also heard the government's motion to dismiss.

On September 20, 1989, the court granted the government's motion to dismiss and denied Phillips's request for relief.

Judge Carroll based his ruling on the findings of a recent case, *Lyng v. Northwest Indian Cemetery Protective Association*. He wrote, "The holdings of *Lyng* are the law of this country—whether or not personally acceptable to plaintiffs or those who espouse their cause." The issue in *Lyng* was whether the "Free Exercise Clause prevented the government from constructing a road through a portion of a National Park 'that has traditionally been used for religious purposes by members of three American Indian Tribes.' " The U.S. Supreme Court determined that the Free Exercise Clause "neither restrained the government in such instance nor required it to demonstrate a compelling need to use its property for building a road." Judge Carroll concluded, "The fact that [people's] ability to practice their religion will be virtually destroyed by a governmental program does not allow them to impose a religious servitude on the property of the government [much less property which the government holds in trust for another sovereign Indian Tribe]." He also wrote, "The nature of the religious rights claimed cannot create a de facto beneficial ownership of public (or private) property, in order to practice one's religion."

Judge Carroll made it clear that the laws of the United States do not protect the exercise of religion if that worship is tied to a particular physical site. Our legal system is not constructed in such a way as to protect Bessie Hatathlie's or Mae Tso's way of life, though that way of life existed here long before the laws were written.

Phillips filed an appeal on December 18, 1989, with the Ninth Circuit Court of Appeals. And on May 10, 1991, the court issued an unexpected and extraordinary order stating that "the panel believes that the best interests of the parties would be served if the case were settled." Toward that end, the court ordered negotiations with the help of a mediator. Negotiations began in June 1991, and they continue to the present.

The Hopi Tribe listed ten conditions that had to be met for it to consider negotiating with the Navajos under orders from the Ninth Circuit Court of Appeals. One was tearing down the survival camp, which was done in December 1991. Another was tearing down a hogan near Mae Tso's house that had been used for a meeting place and as a residence for various Tso family members. The Navajo Tribe had incurred fines of $1,000 a day since May 15, 1990, on this illegal construction. (The first fines levied against the tribe in the 1970s were $250 a day, the next round were $500, then $1,000.) In December 1991 Peterson Zah, Lee Phillips, and the mediator convinced Mae Tso to let the tribe take down the hogan. The third condition was that the partition fence be completed through Big Mountain. In February 1992, the people of Big Mountain agreed. As a result, negotiations continued.

Says Lee Phillips, "To make mediation work we have to make the people out on the land willing to make concession after concession, and it's so hard to do. We're asking them to trust in a legal system that has never been willing to recognize what is most important to them—their religious view—and trust a system that has treated them with such disrespect and dishonesty. It shows how desperate the people are for them to make concessions to that system, holding out one last hope to be able to stay on the land. They're slowly suffocating the people out there. It is the same policy of a hundred years ago, surrender or starve, that Kit Carson used to round up the Navajos."

After listing the preconditions for mediation talks in the winter of 1992, the Hopi Tribal Council disbanded, no longer able to achieve a quorum. Although the federal mediator continued his efforts, there was no Hopi entity to sign binding agreements. The Hopi Tribal Council reacted the same way in 1985 during the Morris-Clark mission. This kind of passive resistance has roots deep in Hopi history.

Mae Tso is healthy and happy. In defiance of the law, she has increased her herd to a healthy number. In a recent visit, she expressed guarded hope for the mediation efforts and stated that whatever the outcome, she would stay. "This is our home," she said simply.

Betty Tso is working for the Navajo Tribe in Tuba City in the Navajo-Hopi Legal Services Office. She has a one-year-old son named Gerard.

Lee Phillips left a job with the Public Defender's Office in Flagstaff to work for the Navajo Tribe, representing his clients in the mediation effort. For the first time in almost a decade of fighting, he expressed fears of defeat: "I was happily in the Public Defender's Office, with a weekly paycheck, health insurance, and now, the relocation issue has all come washing back over me like a huge wave. When you represent child molesters and you lose they're taken away, there's a sense of justice. But here, fearing I will lose, I can anticipate no sense of justice. These people are not criminals. If we lose, and they're taken away, I don't know what I'll do. Their loss will represent a terrible injustice. Yet winning seems so unlikely.

"The people out there are driven and guided by their belief. The actions of the government don't violate that belief. They have somehow found it within themselves to believe that they will survive, that they will be protected by the Great Spirit. I don't have that same sense of faith, so it's much harder for me sometimes. My faith in being a lawyer is that you can make a difference and that the law will do what's right and just. The betrayal in this system takes away everything I believe in. They at least have a different system in which to place their hopes."

Abbott Sekaquaptewa was killed in an automobile accident near Keams Canyon on August 7, 1992. He was sixty-two years old.

Grandfather David Monongye died in April 1988. He was 101 years old.

Earl Pela died in July 1988.

Thomas Banyacya lives in Kykotsmovi and continues to disseminate the words of the traditional Hopi religious priests.

Dan Jackson still holds the position of staff attorney for the Office of the Field Solicitor, U.S. Department of the Interior, in Phoenix. He continues to serve as the government's legal adviser in the Navajo-Hopi dispute and to handle contract matters for the Department of the Interior.

The three relocation commissioners were removed from their positions by an order of Congress. PL 100-66, the Navajo-Hopi Relocation Amendments of 1988, were signed by President Reagan on November 16, 1988. The Act replaced the three commissioners with a single commissioner authorized to hold a two-year term. Carl Kunasek, a former member of the Arizona State Legislature, was confirmed by the U.S. Senate on May 22, 1990. The Commission is once again solely in charge of relocation. On January 31, 1989, the 1988 Amendments transferred responsibility from the BIA to the Commission for building houses on the New Lands.

. . .

Sandra Massetto was transferred to another job in the Interior Department doing heirship determinations for the White Earth Chippewa Land Settlement case, in which the government is paying individual allottees or their heirs for loss of allotments that occurred in the early part of the century. She also hears other appeals dealing with land for the Office of Hearings and Appeals, Department of the Interior, in Phoenix.

Hawley Atkinson is retired and living in Sun City, Arizona.

Ralph Watkins suffered major losses in the Arizona real estate crash of the late 1980s. He now works for a real estate auctioneer in Phoenix.

Barry Goldwater is retired and living in Phoenix.

Morris Udall retired from the U.S. House of Representatives in 1990.

John McCain was elected to the U.S. Senate in 1986.

Jack Hatathlie retired in 1989 from the Navajo Power Plant in Page. In the summer of 1992, he was busy planting corn, melon, and squash. He was doing more than his usual amount of farming to take advantage of the generous spring rains.

Bessie Hatathlie has aged considerably. But, like Mae Tso, she has increased her herds to take advantage of the lush grasslands produced by the rainfall. Bessie's daughter Lenora Hill lives with her, as do Lenora's three children. Bessie's daughter Lula lives in Tuba City with her own children. Bessie's youngest daughter, Brenda, the bookworm and flute player, was offered college admission by George Washington University, Georgetown University, the University of Arizona, Arizona State University, and Northern Arizona University. She wants to pursue a Ph.D. in engineering. Although Ella encouraged her to take advantage of the opportunity to study in the East, Brenda doesn't want to leave Arizona. "It's too far," she says. She'll miss home. She decided to enroll at the University of Arizona.

Felix attended trade school to learn how to operate heavy machinery, but his seizures prevented him from completing the program. Glenn is repairing computers and office equipment in Phoenix. He is married to Vida Mae and they have a son named Dexter. Freddy served in Saudi Arabia during the Gulf War. When he was gone, Bea gave birth to a boy, whom they named Bradley, after the tank. Levonne is attending Northern Arizona University. Genny works for the tribe, placing Navajo children in foster homes. Budge has three children and lives with her new boyfriend in Tuba City.

Bessie says, "I'm going to be here as long as the sun rises and sets. Everything's here."

. . .

Danielle Bedonie (Nell) is a very grown-up twelve-year-old who has had the first of two puberty ceremonies (Kinaalda). One of the stages of the ceremonies requires the young girl to lie down and be "molded" by an older woman. Nell was "molded" by Ann Begay (Annie Oakley). Nell does very well in school and has been placed in an accelerated program. She is also a prize-winning powwow dancer, and an avid student of Navajo traditions. She must learn many different things because she is the heir to the Hatathlie clan. Although she will have no land or any claim to a home on the Navajo reservation by the time she marries, she will be richly endowed with traditional religious and cultural teachings. It will be Nell's challenge to show her own daughter the traditions without benefit of the land and sheep with which to teach her.

Ella's son Kimo completed one year at Pima Community College in Tucson and has transferred to the University of Arizona. Buzz is finishing high school in Tuba City.

Ann Begay (Annie Oakley) has fixed the transmission on her Ford pickup so that it now drives forward and back. In fact, she changed the entire transmission from an automatic to a manual. She also recently replaced all the valves in her engine, which she called "changing the engine's bracelets." "It was easy," she said. "I looked at the repair manual and followed the pictures."

Peterson Zah lost to Peter MacDonald in 1986. Peter MacDonald was subsequently removed from office for accepting bribes, and Peterson Zah was elected president of the Navajo Nation in 1990. The tribe reorganized its government in December 1989 to better define the separation of powers (executive, legislative, and judicial). The former position of chairman of the Tribal Council was replaced with president of the Navajo Nation.

Ivan Sidney was beaten by Vernon Masayesva in his 1989 reelection bid. Sidney now serves as a special assistant to the president of Northern Arizona University for Native American programs. Sidney raises funds from corporations and federal and state programs for the university.

Vernon Masayesva, the current Hopi chairman, is an educator. After receiving degrees in political science and public administration from Arizona State University in 1968, he earned a Masters in Administration at Central Michigan University. He ran the Hotevilla-Bacavi Community School for thirteen years. He became a Tribal Council member in 1984 and was then elected vice-chairman in 1988 in a special election after the former vice-chairman died. He defeated Ivan Sidney for the chairmanship in 1989. He has made a priority of trying to end the use of precious

Hopi water for the slurry pipeline that transports coal from Peabody's Black Mesa mines to the Mohave plant in Bullhead City.

Eight hundred of the twelve hundred Navajos who have moved off the HPL but who have not been built houses by the Commission are still awaiting relocation houses.

Ross Swimmer practices law in Tulsa, Oklahoma.

Peter MacDonald was removed from office after being indicted by the Navajo Tribal Court for ethics violations stemming from the tribe's purchase of a 491,000-acre ranch near the Grand Canyon during his tenure as chairman. He is serving 5 years, 335 days in tribal jail for his convictions on multiple conspiracy and bribery counts. In May 1992, MacDonald was also convicted of sixteen federal counts of racketeering, extortion, fraud, interstate transportation in aid of racketeering, and conspiracy. He was accused of using his position as tribal chairman to enrich himself by accepting bribes and kickbacks at the expense of the tribe.

Percy Deal serves as staff assistant to the Speaker of the Navajo Nation Council.

Claudeen Bates-Arthur serves as counsel to the Navajo Nation Council.

After much Sturm und Drang, the New Lands have become home to about 225 Navajo families. In 1991, the New Lands became the 110th chapter on the reservation. Its name is Nahatazhil [Strong Planning] Chapter.
    Percy Deal says that residents of the New Lands tell him, "We like our house, the road, the water. We like it here Monday through Friday. On the weekends, we go home."

Three hundred Navajo families (about a thousand people) remain on the HPL, according to Percy Deal.

A total of twenty-six Hopis have moved onto the HPL vacated by the Navajos. Nine of them are Hopi relocatees from the NPL, whose homes were built for them by the Relocation Commission. Another fifteen Hopis have built houses or bought trailers and live full time or part time on the land. Seventy-three Hopis currently use the HPL for grazing. And ten Hopis use the HPL for agricultural purposes.

In the spring of 1992, Judge Earl Carroll made the first round of decisions in the 1934 area case. He determined that the Hopis have exclusive rights to approximately one hundred thousand acres directly surrounding

Epilogue

Moencopi and partial interest in an additional one hundred thousand acres in the immediate area. The Navajos considered this a victory, as it will not likely require additional relocations. The Hopis had claimed rights to about 1.25 million acres. Further litigation on the 1934 area case and on money matters continues.

Chronology

1882   President Chester A. Arthur sets aside a rectangle of land in Arizona, seventy miles north to south and fifty-five miles east to west, "for the use and occupancy of the Moquis [Hopis] and such other Indians as the Secretary of the Interior may see fit to settle thereon." It becomes known as the 1882 Executive Order Area.

1934   The Navajo reservation boundaries are extended, including land that the Hopis later claim is rightfully theirs. As part of the Indian Reorganization Act, passed in 1934, a Hopi exclusive livestock district, called District 6, is established. It is the first de facto partition of the disputed land.

1958   Congress passes Public Law 85-547, which authorizes the two tribes, through their respective tribal chairmen, to defend or commence a legal action against each other to determine their respective rights to the 1882 Executive Order Area. The Hopis file suit; the case is known as *Healing v. Jones*.

1962   A three-judge panel of the U.S. District Court of Arizona issues its decision on *Healing v. Jones*, determining that the Hopi Tribe, subject to the trust title of the United States, "has the exclusive right and interest, both as to the surface and subsurface, including all resources" to District 6. Also, that the Hopi and Navajo tribes, subject to the trust title of the United States, "have joint, undivided and equal rights and interest both as to the surface and subsurface, including all resources" to the 1882 area outside of District 6. This shared area is known as the Joint Use Area (JUA).

1972   The U.S. District Court of Arizona orders the Navajos to reduce drastically the number of livestock on the JUA and imposes a construction freeze on all building that does not meet the approval of the Hopi Tribe.

1974   Congress passes Public Law 93-531, the Navajo-Hopi Indian Land

Chronology

Settlement Act, "to provide for final settlement" of the Navajo-Hopi land conflict. It is also known as the Settlement Act and the Act.

1977   The U.S. District Court of Arizona partitions the former Joint Use Area into the Navajo Partition Lands (NPL) and the Hopi Partition Lands (HPL).

1980   Congress passes Public Law 96-305, which consists of amendments to PL 93-531. Referred to as the 1980 Amendments Act, the Amendments, and the Amendments Act.

1985   Departing Secretary of the Interior William Clark initiates an effort to bring the tribes to a negotiated settlement that would limit the number of Navajo relocations. His longtime counselor, Richard Morris, does the legwork. It is known as the Morris-Clark Mission.

1988   Lee Phillips files a suit in Federal District Court claiming that the 1974 Settlement Act violates the Navajos' rights to exercise their First Amendment rights to worship. It is referred to as the First Amendment suit.

Notes

Unless otherwise noted, quotations were made at the places and times indicated in the text.

1. SUN DANCE

p. 5 "This ceremony was originally" to "and the gods": Jamake Highwater, *Ritual of the Wind* (New York: Alfred Van der Marck Editions, 1984), p. 152.
"The sun dance is also" to "transcend pain": ibid., p. 152.

6 "So great was their faith" to "in captivity": Dee Brown, *Bury My Heart at Wounded Knee* (New York: Washington Square Press, 1981), p. 413.

10 "The fencing is hurting": Roberta Blackgoat, affidavit for Lee Phillips's First Amendment lawsuit collected by the Big Mountain Legal Defense/Offense Committee, 1985–86.
"I thought I'd arrived": Lee Phillips interview, July 1985.

11 "tried to figure out": Lew Gurwitz interview, December 16, 1986.
"It was clear to the people": Lew Gurwitz, telephone interview, December 16, 1986.
"straight" practice: ibid.

12 "We are going": This and following quotations from Lew Gurwitz were made July 7, 1985, at Big Mountain, Arizona.

2. THE HATATHLIES, COAL MINE MESA

Bessie Hatathlie's thoughts in this chapter were translated and told to the author by her daughter Ella Bedonie.

22 "We do not want to go": Gerald Thompson, *The Army and the Navajo* (Tucson: University of Arizona Press, 1976), pp. 153, 155.

23 "The next year" to "1,000 goats": Raymond Friday Locke, *The Book of the Navajo* (Los Angeles: Mankind Publishing Co., 1976), p. 395.
"They had learned" to "modern clothing": G. Thompson, op. cit., pp. 158–65.
"When we saw the top": As quoted in Locke, op. cit., p. 387.

3. THE COMPLICATED WORLD OF THE HOPIS

25 about 4,500 of them: Figures from an analysis of 1980 census data supplied by Ronald G. Faich, Ph.D., demographer for the Navajo Tribe, August 1985.

p. 29 "This is very discouraging," "I'm just frustrated," "I don't know if," "I was elected": Ivan Sidney interview, July 1985.
"If Thomas or David": ibid.

30 "never worked," "the conscious and unconscious": John Collier, *From Every Zenith*, (Denver: Sage Books, 1963), as quoted in *Report to the Hopi Kikmongwis and Other Traditional Hopi Leaders on Docket 196 and the Continuing Threat to Hopi Land and Sovereignty* (Washington, D.C.: Indian Law Resource Center, March 1979), p. 66.
"However, every Hopi": Ivan Sidney interview, July 1985.
"If we had had cameras": ibid.

4. THE LAW: *HEALING V. JONES*

32 "the Hopis were grouped": Stewart Udall interview, September 8, 1986.
"My thought was that": ibid.
"I realized there was this": ibid.

33 "In 1882, agent J. H. Fleming" to "boarding school": *Report to the Hopi Kikmongwis*, op. cit., p. 11.
"On November 11, 1882" to "two Anglos": ibid., p. 10.

34 "reservation that will include": *Healing v. Jones*, 210 Fed. Supp. 125 (1962), p. 136.
"for the use and occupancy": ibid., p. 129.
"would become so friendly": ibid., p. 156.
"quite frequently trifling": *Report to the Hopi Kikmongwis*, op. cit., p. 6.

35 "offered suggestions" to "joint use reservation": 210 Fed. Supp. 125, op. cit., pp. 135–37.
"to remove all Navajo Indians": ibid., p. 146.

36 "should not be permitted to eject": Leo Crane, letter to the Commissioner of Indian Affairs, June 22, 1914.
"They are strictly a community people": Inspector H. S. Traylor, report to the Commissioner of Indian Affairs, June 6, 1916.
"A survey in 1965" to "650,013 acres": Jerry Kammer, *The Second Long Walk* (Albuquerque: University of New Mexico Press, 1980), p. 41.
"for the purpose of determining": Public Law 85-547, the Act of July 22, 1958, as cited in *Healing v. Jones*, op. cit., p. 129.

37 "the greatest title problem": ibid., p. 129.
"has the exclusive right": *Healing v. Jones*, No. Civil 579 Prescott, U.S. District Court for the District of Arizona, Judgment, filed September 28, 1962, p. 7.
"have joint, undivided": ibid., p. 8.

5. A BRIEF HISTORY OF THE HOPIS

43 "Learning is the wrong word": Ruth M. Underhill, *The Navajos* (Norman: University of Oklahoma Press, 1956), p. 50.
"The Navajos are aggressive": Abbott Sekaquaptewa interview, Flagstaff, Arizona, February 27, 1986.

44 "Hopi means different things": ibid.
"I think over the years": ibid.

46 "Down on the bottom": Frank Waters, *Book of the Hopi* (New York: Penguin Books, 1963), p. 20.
"It is a Road of Life": ibid., p. 26.
"The three narrow mesas" to "high desert": For more, see J. O. Brew, "Hopi Prehistory and History to 1850," in *Handbook of North American Indians*, vol. 9 (Washington: Smithsonian Institution, 1979), p. 515.

p. 47   "the cultural remains": ibid., p. 514.

"Ten thousand years ago" to "turtles": Cynthia Irwin-Williams, "Post-Pleistocene Archaeology, 7000–2000 B.C.," in *Handbook*, op. cit., p. 31.

"three basic economic propositions" to "clan ties": For more, see Richard B. Lee and Irven DeVore, eds., *Symposium on Man the Hunter, University of Chicago* (Chicago: Aldine Publishing Co., 1966). Also: Paul S. Martin and Fred T. Plog, *The Archaeology of Arizona: A Study of the Southwest Region* (Garden City, N.Y.: Doubleday Natural History Press, 1973).

"has been judged": Richard B. Woodbury and Ezra B. W. Zubrow, "Agricultural Beginnings, 2000 B.C.–A.D. 500," in *Handbook*, op. cit., p. 43.

48   "Around A.D. 500" to "was in use": ibid., pp. 43–44.

"Hopi is a Uto-Aztecan" to "Anasazi culture": Kenneth Hale and David Harris, "Historical Linguistics and Archaeology," in *Handbook*, op. cit., p. 177.

"ancient people" to "enemy ancestors": Fred Plog, "Prehistory: Western Anasazi," in *Handbook*, op. cit., p. 108, note.

"Between A.D. 600 and 1000" to "food production": ibid., p. 129.

"One anthropologist" to "Four Corners region": Waters, op. cit., p. 118.

"the tail wagging": ibid.

49   "It is not clear why" to "Hopi and the Zuni": Plog, op. cit., p. 129.

"But they also had the advantage" to "ditches": Brew, op. cit., pp. 515–16.

50   "Had the Spanish not interrupted": Plog, op. cit., p. 130.

"the principal motif": Waters, op. cit., p. 121.

"one of the three major centers": Brew, op. cit., p. 514.

51   "enthusiastic if exaggerated": Marc Simmons, "History of Pueblo-Spanish Relations to 1821," in *Handbook*, op.cit., p. 178.

"three hundred men" to "friars," "the conquest might be": ibid., p. 178.

"Whatever the origin" to "twenty years late": Waters, op. cit., pp. 251–52.

"To tell the truth": George Parker Winship, trans., "The Narrative of the Expedition of Coronado by Castaneda," *Annual Report* 14 (Washington, D.C.: Bureau of American Ethnology, 1876), pp. 488–89.

52   "Bear Clan leader": Waters, op. cit., p. 252.

"extravagant and unprofitable": Brew, op. cit., p. 519.

"a cosmopolitan, sophisticated": Frederick J. Dockstader, *The Kachina and the White Man* (Albuquerque: University of New Mexico Press, 1985), p. 6.

53   "By 1674" to "Mishongnovi": Waters, op. cit., p. 253.

"the finest examples": Brew, op. cit., p. 520.

"The Hopis also modified" to "on the walls": Brew, op. cit., p. 520.

"However, the rains didn't come" to "Rio Grande": Waters, op. cit., p. 253.

"Enforced labor not only": ibid.

"vented their fury on": Frank Waters, *Masked Gods* (Athens, Ohio: Swallow Press, 1950), p. 42.

54   "The Hopis remained" to "rebuild their mission": Edward H. Spicer, *Cycles of Conquest* (Tucson: University of Arizona Press, 1962), p. 192.

54ff.   "the Awatovis possessed" to "all the Hopis": Waters, *Book of the Hopi*, op. cit., p. 263.

55   "the most famous 'apostates' ": Spicer, op. cit., p. 188.

"in order to keep": ibid.

"The people of the Hopi villages": Albert Yava, *Big Falling Snow* (New York: Crown Publishers, 1978), p. 137.

56   "The stereotype of the Pueblo Indian": Simmons, op. cit., p. 189.

"For the Hopis were": Waters, *Book of the Hopi*, op. cit., p. 266.

Notes

6. A BRIEF HISTORY OF THE NAVAJOS

p. 58 "They led a wandering life": Underhill, op. cit., p. 5.

58ff. "The earliest known site" to "1541": ibid., p. 18.

59 "They started to walking": Clyde Kluckhohn, *Navajo Witchcraft* (Cambridge, Mass.: Peabody Museum Papers, 1944), p. 98.

"walk over every stone": Underhill, op. cit., p. 24.

"Anthropologists do not agree" to "after the Spanish": For a detailed discussion, see David R. Wilcox and W. Bruce Masse, eds., *The Protohistoric Period in the North American Southwest, A.D. 1450–1700*, Anthropological Research Papers, no. 24 (Tempe: Arizona State University, 1981).

"It is not clear" to "became empty": Brugge, op. cit., p. 490.

"expansion was really": Wilcox and Masse, op. cit., p. 228.

"largely based on": ibid.

60 "shrinkage and inward collapse": ibid., p. 214.

"living in skin tents": Herbert E. Bolton, *Coronado, Knight of the Pueblo and Plains* (Albuquerque: University of New Mexico Press, 1949), pp. 246–47.

"A buffalo village is mentioned" to "buffalo scrotum": Underhill, op. cit., p. 24.

"In 1583" to "Mount Taylor": Locke, op. cit., p. 154.

They grew corn: ibid.

"They traded meat" to "ceremonial cultures": Brugge, op. cit., p. 491.

"The meeting of these people" to "by a Hopi": Locke, op. cit., p. 154.

"that the Querechos": George P. Hammond and Agapito Rey, *The Rediscovery of New Mexico, 1580–1594: The Explorations of Chamuscado, Espejo, Castaña de Sosa, Morlate, and Leyva de Bonilla and Humana* (Albuquerque: University of New Mexico Press, 1966), p. 26.

"the trade or sale of slaves" to " 'wild' tribes": Brugge, op. cit., p. 491.

"In 1630, Fray Alonso de Benevides" to " 'very great farmers' ": ibid., p. 496.

61 "In 1626" to "San Juan River": ibid.

"It is not clear" to "Hopi villages": Spicer, op. cit., p. 210.

"The Apaches de Navaju" to "(*muy grandes labradores*)": Brugge, op. cit., p. 496.

"The Navajo words for gourd dipper" to "food of the strangers": Underhill, op. cit., pp. 4–5.

"This 'age-old device' " to "mother-in-law joke": ibid., p. 9.

"highly composite": Clyde Kluckhohn and Dorothea Leighton, *The Navaho* (Cambridge, Mass.: Harvard University Press, 1960), p. 4.

62 "The name Navajo": Ruth Underhill, "Ceremonial Patterns in the Greater Southwest," *Monologues of the American Ethnological Society*, vol. 13 (Seattle and London: University of Washington Press, 1948), p. x.

"The Pueblos have not discarded": ibid.

"many marks of the": ibid., pp. 37–38.

63 "The Navajos are descendants" to "Yurok in California": Underhill, *Navajos*, op. cit., p. 6.

"In fact, these colonizing": ibid.

"It has been suggested" to "Pueblo refugees": Karl Luckert, *The Navajo Hunter Tradition* (Tucson: University of Arizona Press, 1975), p. 14.

"Undoubtedly, among the refugees": ibid.

"Also, at this time" to "revived, among the Navajos": ibid.

64 "To the Navajo": Underhill, *Navajos*, op. cit., p. 62.

"The Navajos quickly learned" to "political purposes": Kluckhohn and Leighton, op. cit., p. 7.

"Navaho 'nomadism' ": ibid.

p. 65   "The Navajos retaliated" to "Jemez from raids": Spicer, op. cit., pp. 212–13.
        "They lived in bands" to "families": ibid., p. 215.
        "the temporary associations": ibid.
        "ran wild," "Warfare had": ibid., p. 213.
        "By 1860" to "Navajo slaves": ibid., p. 217.
   66   "Between 1846 and 1850" to "New Mexico": ibid., p. 216.
        "Instead of bowing" to "fight back": ibid., p. 217.

7. THE TSOS, MOSQUITO SPRINGS

   70   "This dispute": Kammer, *Second Long Walk*, op. cit., p. 193.
   71   "We would have been like a road sign": Betty Tso interview, Flagstaff, Arizona,
        March 1, 1986.
        "I think it is important": Hearings before the Subcommittee on Indian Affairs of the
        Committee on Interior and Insular Affairs, House of Representatives, 93rd Congress,
        First Session. Hearings held on May 14–15, 1973, Washington, D.C., p. 68.
        "The hogan has": Mae Tso, affidavit for Lee Phillips's First Amendment suit, collected
        by Betty Tso for BMLDOC.
   72   "I think from the beginning": Betty Tso interview, March 1, 1986.
        "My mother was sick": ibid.
        "Our roof was leaking": ibid.
        "At the beginning": ibid.
        "Uncle, you are breaking," "Uncle, why should I": ibid.
   73   "In our traditional tongue": Pauline Whitesinger, as quoted in "The Big Mountain
        Peoples and Other Land-Dispute Navajos," a pamphlet produced by the Navajo Land
        Dispute Commission, Window Rock, Arizona, 1980.
   75   One day in 1983: Events retold by Mae Tso, August 1985, Mosquito Springs.
   78   "Our Creator has placed us": Mae Tso, affidavit for Lee Phillips's First Amendment
        suit, collected by Betty Tso for BMLDOC.

8. THE HATATHLIES AND THE OLD WAYS

   84   "Navajo livestock had increased" to "to 433,000." Ruth Roessel and Broderick H.
        Johnson, *Navajo Livestock Reduction: A National Disgrace* (Chinle, Ariz.: Navajo Com-
        munity College, 1974), p. 222.
        "In percentage terms": David Aberle, *The Peyote Religion Among the Navajos* (Chicago:
        Aldine Publishing Co., 1966), pp. 72–73.
        "Before stock reduction": Roessel and Johnson, op. cit., p. 159.
        "In my long life": Collier, op. cit., p. 252.
        "the most devastating experience": Aberle, op. cit., pp. 52–53.
  104   "My grandfather knows": Ella Bedonie interview, March 1, 1986.
        "They'd run out at dusk": ibid.
        "Raiding was common": ibid.
        "The Navajo 'economic theory' ": John Ladd, *The Structure of a Moral Code* (Cambridge,
        Mass.: Harvard University Press, 1957), p. 244, as quoted in Gary Witherspoon, *Navajo
        Kinship and Marriage* (Chicago: University of Chicago Press, 1975), p. 97.
        "[The Navajos have] no Christian": Friedrich Abel interview, Flagstaff, Arizona, April
        1986.
        "I think I know who it is": Albert Francis interview, Teesto, Arizona, February 22,
        1986.
  105   "One of our horses": Ella Bedonie interview, March 1, 1986.
        "In my lifetime": Abbott Sekaquaptewa interview, March 18, 1986.

p. 105 "It's as if": ibid.

"If nobody does anything": ibid.

"Our ranch was right": Helen Sekaquaptewa, *Me and Mine* (Tucson: University of Arizona Press, 1969), pp. 198–99.

106 "I had the first real": ibid., p. 184.

"We used to have a bull": Ella Bedonie interview, February 26, 1986.

"One time they beat him": ibid.

107 "If horses ate the corn": Sekaquaptewa, op. cit., p. 187.

"Chairman Abbott": Richard O. Clemmer, *Continuities of Hopi Culture Change* (Ramona, Cal.: Acoma Books, 1978), p. 8.

"There was never any problem": The Hopi man quoted insisted on anonymity.

9. THE AMERICAN ASSAULT ON THE HOPI SPIRIT

109 "The Hopis have been": Oliver LaFarge, *Running Narrative of the Organization of the Hopi Tribe of Indians* (LaFarge Collection, Harry Ransom Humanities Research Center, University of Texas at Austin, 1936), p. 5, as quoted in *Report to the Hopi Kikmongwis*, op. cit., p. 46.

110 "As I understand it": Abbott Sekaquaptewa interview, March 18, 1986.

111 "The traditional enemy": ibid.

112 "I lived out": ibid.

"A former church leader" to "the reservation": Kammer, *Second Long Walk*, op. cit., pp. 63–64.

113 "a cotton dress": Helen Sekaquaptewa, op. cit., pp. 237–38.

"Tu-bee, formerly a chief": *Report to the Hopi Kikmongwis*, op. cit., p. 9.

"The lands most desirable": 210 Fed. Supp. 125, op. cit., p. 137, note 7.

114 "And the Americans" to "in 1848": *Report to the Hopi Kikmongwis*, op. cit., p. 3.

"An unconfirmed executive order": 210 Fed. Supp. 125, op. cit., p. 126.

"Throughout the period": Spicer, op. cit., p. 344.

"This curious paradox": ibid., p. 346.

115 "the treaty was sealed by": Waters, *Book of the Hopi*, p. 275.

"About the destruction": ibid.

"We are still": Letter from the traditional Hopis to Harry S. Truman, March 28, 1949.

"The idea of the treaty": Vine Deloria, Jr., and Clifford Lytle, *The Nations Within* (New York: Pantheon Books, 1984), p. 8.

116 "When the law was passed": Ella Bedonie, telephone interview, January 26, 1986.

"would gradually be absorbed": S. Lyman Tyler, *A History of Indian Policy* (Washington, D.C.: U.S. Department of the Interior, Bureau of Indian Affairs, 1973), p. 71.

"a tendency to further": ibid., p. 91.

117 "It is plainly the ultimate": ibid., p. 96.

"The Curtis and Dawes Acts" to "Five Civilized Tribes": ibid., p. 97.

"From 1881 to 1900" to "77,865,373 acres": ibid.

"By 1934" to "48 million acres": *Report to the Hopi Kikmongwis*, op. cit., p. 18.

"Furthermore": ibid., pp. 18–19.

"replace tribal culture": Tyler, op. cit., p. 96.

"These first white": Waters, *Book of the Hopi*, op. cit., pp. 307–8.

118 "When we were five": Helen Sekaquaptewa, op. cit., pp. 8–12.

119 "If you do": ibid., p. 13.

120 "The Third Mesa Hopis' ": Laura Thompson, *Culture in Crisis* (New York: Harper and Brothers, 1950), p. 197.

The trip had been arranged: James, op. cit., p. 130.

"On June 16, 1890" to "Washington": Waters, *Book of the Hopi*, op. cit., p. 289.

"the most pitiable": 210 Fed. Supp. 125, op cit., p. 186.

"Were he otherwise": ibid., p. 186, note 83.

p. 121 "heard the rumble": ibid., p. 186, note 84.

"When they returned" to "some missionaries": James, op. cit., p. 131.

"Loloma took his son" to "the Americans": Waters, *Book of the Hopi,* op. cit., p. 289.

"Upon his return" to "Bahana": James, op. cit., p. 131.

"The latter rallied" to "sacred tablets": ibid., pp. 131–32.

"In 1899" to "ceremonies": ibid., p. 134.

"In 1898" to "to 1,832": Waters, *Book of the Hopi,* op. cit., p. 292.

121ff. "In 1904" to "men were arrested": This version culled from James, op. cit., pp. 135–39.

122 "Days dragged": Helen Sekaquaptewa, op. cit., pp. 81–82.

123 "Not even the size": Waters, *Book of the Hopi,* op. cit., p. 309.

"I do not know": ibid., p. 310.

123ff. "The children" to "Phoenix Indian School": ibid.

124 "I shall go home": ibid., p. 311.

"He was squatted": ibid.

"When he returned" to "Christianity": James, op. cit., p. 142.

"Eventually, Tewaquaptewa's" to "temporary basis": ibid., p. 144.

125 "Loloma's receptiveness": Mischa Titiev, "Old Oraibi," *Papers of the Peabody Museum of American Archaeology and Ethnology,* vol. 22, no. 1 (Cambridge, Mass.: Harvard University Press, 1944), p. 75.

"It is believed": F. E. Leupp, Annual Report of the Commissioner of Indian Affairs (Washington, D.C.: 1906), as quoted in Titiev, op. cit., p. 75, note 60.

"The Oraibi split": Waters, *Book of the Hopi,* op. cit., p. 306.

126 "Largely because of" to "principles of the Act": Tyler, op. cit., p. 132.

"I do not mean to say": *Report to the Hopi Kikmongwis,* op. cit., p. 31.

"Smarties, Christians": Letter from Oliver LaFarge to John Collier, September 21, 1934. At the Colton Research Center Archive, Flagstaff, Arizona.

127 "are not clearly drawn": ibid., p. 5.

"a total of": ibid.

"Some of them wear": ibid., p. 4.

"made a speech": ibid.

"We must take account of": ibid., p. 8.

"allowing the Christian," "abandoned": ibid.

128 "The name Hopi": LaFarge, *Running Narrative,* op. cit., p. 3, in *Report to the Hopi Kikmongwis,* op. cit., p. 34.

" 'good manners' " to " 'wrongs received' ": LaFarge, *Running Narrative,* op. cit., p. 3, in *Report,* op. cit., p. 35.

"The Hopis fight": LaFarge, *Running Narrative,* op. cit., p. 35, in *Report,* op. cit., p. 35.

"I told them": LaFarge, *Running Narrative,* op. cit., p. 13, in *Report,* op. cit., p. 37.

"It is alien": Oliver LaFarge, *Notes for Hopi Administrators,* on file at the Interior Department library, p. 8, in *Report,* op. cit., p. 48.

129 "No amount of explaining": LaFarge, *Notes,* op. cit., p. 9, in *Report,* op. cit., p. 51.

"deeply dishonest": LaFarge, *Notes,* op. cit., p. 35, in *Report,* op. cit., p. 40.

"a low character": LaFarge, *Running Narrative,* op. cit., p. 4, in *Report,* op. cit., p. 40.

"Here at Kiakuchomovi": LaFarge, *Running Narrative,* op. cit., p. 8, in *Report,* op. cit., pp. 39–40.

"These people": LaFarge, *Notes,* op. cit., p. 14, in *Report,* op. cit., p. 40.

"In this organization": LaFarge, *Running Narrative,* op. cit., p. 17, in *Report,* op. cit., p. 37.

"The Hotevilla leaders": LaFarge, *Running Narrative,* op. cit., p. 13, in *Report,* op. cit., p. 41.

p. 130   "Entirely governed": LaFarge, *Running Narrative*, op. cit., p. 3, in *Report*, op. cit., p. 42.

"gutless": LaFarge, *Running Narrative*, op. cit., p. 52, in *Report*, op. cit., p. 42.

"rigid attitude," "grabbing every benefit": LaFarge, *Notes*, op. cit., p. 18, in *Report*, op. cit., p. 42.

"The main theme": LaFarge, *Running Narrative*, op. cit., pp. 59–60, in *Report*, op. cit., pp. 44–45.

131   "Progressive and Conservatives": *Report*, op. cit., p. 46.

"which discounted": ibid., p. 56.

"the Washington office": ibid., p. 59.

"In 1943" to "opposition to it": Clemmer, op. cit., pp. 65–66.

"The tribal council": Waters, *Book of the Hopi*, p. 317.

132   "Hopi political organization": Fred Eggan, *Social Organization of the Western Pueblos* (Chicago: University of Chicago Press, 1950), p. 106.

"On the whole": Titiev, op. cit., p. 65.

10. COAL

133   "Coal was discovered" to "executive order area": John Redhouse, *Geopolitics of the Navajo-Hopi Land Dispute* (Albuquerque: Redhouse/Wright Publications, 1985), p. 8.

"In 1933" to "minerals in the 1882 area": ibid., p. 9.

134   "One estimate suggests" to "ancestral lands": Peter Wiley and Robert Gottlieb, *Empires in the Sun: The Price of the New American West* (New York: G. P. Putnam's Sons, 1982), p. 228.

"developed a close": *Report*, op. cit., p. 90.

"Before setting out" to "taking": ibid.

135   "As an example" to "9 votes": ibid., p. 92.

"In this play": ibid., p. 93.

"[Boyden] pointed out," "Further than this": ibid., p. 102.

136   "The Bureau of Indian Affairs": ibid., p. 106.

"novel attempt," "the exciting new prospects," "within the foreseeable future,": Redhouse, op. cit., p. 10.

137   "So few villages" to "a quorum": *Report*, op. cit., p. 119.

"Littell seemed so eager" to "the two tribes": Redhouse, op. cit., p. 11.

"Never until now": "Littell Reports to the Council," *Navajo Times*, June 13, 1963.

138   "What has evolved": Transcript of the Hopi-Navajo Conference, Valley Ho Hotel, Scottsdale, Arizona, August 6–7, 1963, U.S. Department of the Interior, Bureau of Indian Affairs, p. 169.

"Now if we just": ibid., p. 143.

"was speaking against them": Kammer, *Second Long Walk*, op. cit., p. 137.

"Definitely. I think not just": ibid., p. 136.

139   "Between 1974" to "their lawyers": Letter from Ross Swimmer to Barry Goldwater, May 22, 1986.

"one of the hottest," "have been licking their chops," "the ripest wildcat target": Redhouse, op. cit., p. 13.

"In 1974" to "in New Mexico": Kammer, *Second Long Walk*, op. cit., p. 136.

139ff. "Harrison Loesch" to "Peabody Coal vice-president": ibid., p. 134.

140   "Wayne Owens" to "in 1976": ibid., p. 166.

"Jerry Verkler" to "Bureau of Reclamation": ibid., pp. 135–36.

"We all know": Leon Berger interview, Williams, Arizona, June 1985.

141   "Now, how is it": George Vlassis interview, Phoenix, Arizona, June 12, 1985.

"Little did" to "Kennecott Copper": Wiley and Gottlieb, op. cit., p. 233.

"The Navajos" to "strip-mining it": John Farrell, "The New Indian Wars," *Denver Post*, November 21, 1983 (special supplement), p. 20.

"Comparable coal" to "from others": Peter Matthiessen, "Battle for Big Mountain," 2 *Geo* 9, 19, March 1980.

"The Peabody Mine" to "precious water": Alvin M. Josephy, Jr., "The Murder of the Southwest," *Audubon*, vol. 73, no. 4, July 1971, p. 57.

"The Hopis are paid" to "acre-foot": Mark Panitch, *The Washington Post*, July 21, 1974. "The relationship between": ibid.

p. 142　"was a routine": Lawrence Kelly, *The Navajo Indians and Federal Indian Policy* (Tempe: University of Arizona Press, 1976), as quoted in Jerry Mander, "Kit Carson in a Three-Piece Suit," *CoEvolution Quarterly*, Winter 1981, p. 57.

"rubber stamp an agreement": Peter Iverson, *The Navajo Nation* (Albuquerque: University of New Mexico Press, 1981), p. 19.

"In 1921" to "to the BIA itself": Mander, op. cit., pp. 57–58.

"government aid": Kelly, op. cit., in Mander, op. cit., p. 58.

"This is a fight": Larry Nez interview, Tuba City, Arizona, June 6, 1986.

11. PUBLIC LAW 93-531: THE SETTLEMENT ACT

143　"The well-off Hopi": Yava, op. cit., p. 137.

144　"Our lives were a combination": Helen Sekaquaptewa, op. cit., pp. 186–87.

145　"When the tribal council": Clemmer, op. cit., p. 39.
　　　"The Sekaquaptewa family": ibid., p. 38.

146　"We feel that it is imperative": Hopi-Navajo Conference, Scottsdale, Arizona, 1963, op. cit., p. 160.
　　　No Hope Area: Kammer, *Second Long Walk*, op. cit., p. 75.
　　　"My grandfather used to say": Abbott Sekaquaptewa interview, February 27, 1986.

147　"I've never showed a profit": Abbott Sekaquaptewa interview, May 29, 1986.
　　　"The BIA had determined" to "overstocked by 400 percent": Kammer, *Second Long Walk*, op. cit., p. 81.
　　　"full and peaceable possession": *Writ of Assistance*, No. Civil 579, Prescott, Arizona, October 14, 1972.

148　"BIA figures showed" to "sheep or goats": Kammer, *Second Long Walk*, op. cit., p. 84.
　　　"The Hopis had built": This lobbyist insisted on anonymity.
　　　"The Navajo people": George Vlassis interview, June 12, 1985.
　　　"The next extraordinary thing," "Steiger arrives in," "get on the horse": ibid.

149　"While the Navajo": Kammer, *Second Long Walk*, op. cit., p. 120.

150　"relentless Navajo dominance": Hearings Before the Subcommittee on Indian Affairs of the Committee on Interior and Insular Affairs, House of Representatives, 93rd Congress, First Session, May 14 and 15, 1973, Washington, D.C., p. 28.
　　　"onslaught of Navajo trespasses": ibid.
　　　"Violence and destruction": ibid., p. 29.
　　　"It should be remembered": ibid., p. 30.
　　　"We began to take": George Vlassis interview, June 12, 1985.

151　"just making a nuisance": ibid.
　　　"The Navajo now seeks": Hearings Before the Subcommittee on Indian Affairs of the Committee on Interior and Insular Affairs, House of Representatives, 92nd Congress, Second Session, April 17 and 18, 1972, Washington, D.C., p. 186.
　　　"John Boyden set": This lawyer insisted on anonymity.
　　　"Only three senators" to "Interior Committee": Kammer, *Second Long Walk*, op. cit., p. 122.

p. 151   "Basically, Congress has": James Abourezk interview, Washington, D.C., April 21, 1986.

152   "virtually stage-managed": Panitch, op. cit.

"A routine problem": *Arizona Republic,* April 16, 1972.

"The profound shock," "Violence, alcohol abuse": Thayer Scudder, *No Place to Go, Effects of Compulsory Relocation on Navajos* (Philadelphia: Institute for the Study of Human Issues, 1982), p. 10.

153   "It is not the will": *Navajo Times,* August 1, 1978, in Kammer, *Second Long Walk,* op. cit., p. 203.

"emotional campaign": Goldwater-Fannin letter, November 25, 1974, in Kammer, *Second Long Walk,* op. cit., p. 203.

"so as to include": 25 USC 640d-5.

"a surveyor's nightmare": *Navajo Times,* January 24, 1972.

"just and fair": Act of July 22, 1958 (72 Stat. 403).

153ff.   "in such manner," "requiring the courts": Richard Schifter and W. Richard West, Jr., *"Healing v. Jones:* Mandate for another Trail of Tears?" *North Dakota Law Review,* vol. 51, no. 1, Fall 1974, p. 94.

154   "consistently have refused," "patterns of use": ibid., p. 96.

"A few had homes": 210 Fed. Supp. 125, op. cit., p. 169.

"wood cutting": ibid.

the Hopis have 342 acres: Figures from an analysis supplied by Ronald G. Faich, Ph.D., demographer for the Navajo Tribe, August 1985.

"The enactment by Congress": Schifter and West, op. cit., p. 103.

155   "I would simply tell": HR 10337, 93rd Congress, First Session, unpublished mark-up of session of December 11, 1973, in Kammer, *Second Long Walk,* op. cit., p. 109.

"I think the Navajos," "giving the Hopis," "Peter [MacDonald]," "[Back in 1974]," "The Navajo tribal": This former staffer and current lobbyist insisted on anonymity.

155ff.   "unbelievable strain," "They just break down": Kammer, *Second Long Walk,* op. cit., p. 218.

156   "At Hopi" to "from a Navajo": ibid., p. 217.

12. TRADITIONAL HOPIS TRY TO HOLD ON

158   "When a Hopi": Letter from Oliver LaFarge to John Collier, op. cit., p. 6.

13. HOPE FOR CHANGE: THE MORRIS-CLARK MISSION

174   "The Navajo-Hopi" to "state court cases": Whitson, op. cit., p. 371.

"In 1974" to "jump of 824 percent": Surveys and Investigations Staff, Report to the Committee on Appropriations, U.S. House of Representatives, on the Navajo-Hopi Indian Relocation Commission, January 1985, p. 9.

"They learn": Scudder, op. cit., p. 10.

175   "eight times": Martin Topper, "Mental Health Effects of Navajo Relocation in the former Joint Use Area." Report submitted to the Mental Health Branch, Navajo Area Office, Indian Health Service, 1979.

"The Commission's mentality": Leon Berger interview, Williams, Arizona, June 1985.

"omission": This official requested anonymity.

"the epitome of": Leon Berger interview, Williams, Arizona, June 1985.

"trial and error," "conflicting goals": Surveys and Investigations Staff Report, op. cit., p. 11.

175ff.   "Counseling is a misnomer": Aric Press and Emily Benedek, "Two Tribes, One Land," *Newsweek,* September 23, 1985, p. 78.

176   "a planning agency": ibid.

"By 1985" to "greater than $10,000": Report to Congress in opposition to the NHIRC budget request, March 1985, submitted by BMLDOC.

"There's a slaughter": Press and Benedek, op. cit., p. 78.

"questionable, non-discounted": Surveys and Investigations Staff Report, op. cit., p. 16.

"Although each sale": ibid.

"a number of real estate licenses": ibid.

p. 177   "The relocatee Indians": ibid.

"minimize the adverse": Senate Committee on Interior and Insular Affairs, deliberations on PL 93-531, as quoted in *Report and Plan,* Navajo-Hopi Indian Relocation Commission, April 1981, p. 1.

178   "and such other Indians": Act of June 14, 1934 (48 Stat. 960).

"He felt when he went": Richard Morris, telephone interview, August 1987.

"He had some personal concerns": Richard Morris interview, Washington, D.C., February 12, 1986.

"that have consumed": Letter from Ronald Reagan to Ivan Sidney, February 8, 1985.

"important need": ibid.

"I am very hopeful": ibid.

179   "It's *their* land": Ralph Regula interview, Washington, D.C., February 5, 1986.

"The land is theirs": ibid.

"We just want to see": Pat Dallas interview, Kykotsmovi, July 1985.

180   "Like I say": ibid.

"Most people do that": ibid.

"The Hopis were not prepared": Richard Morris interview, February 12, 1986.

"I have tremendous compassion": Richard Morris, telephone interview, August 1985.

"In 1971" to "turned down": John Orr, "Navajo Tribe to Lobby for DeConcini JUA Bill," *Gallup Independent,* September 23, 1978.

181   "Let's take it away": Dale Russakoff, "Two Indian Friends Move to Resolve a Centuries-Old Tribal Land Dispute," *The Washington Post,* April 15, 1983.

"I remember the great": Morris Udall interview, Washington, D.C., February 4, 1986.

"The book shows": Russakoff, op. cit.

"I kept thinking": Morris Udall interview, February 4, 1986.

"a series of resolutions," "I actually believe": John Farrell, "The New Indian Wars," *Denver Post,* op. cit., p. 20.

182   "The Hopis don't": Richard Morris, telephone interview, August 1985.

"turn back the clock": Stewart Udall interview, September 8, 1986.

188   "came out here and": Claudeen Bates-Arthur interview, Window Rock, July 17, 1986.

"they [would] *not* exchange," "[would] not enter into": Richard Morris, telephone interview, August 1986.

"Certainly, you would," "As a matter of fact": Richard Morris interview, February 12, 1986.

"I realize that those": ibid.

"The Hopis are very": Abbott Sekaquaptewa interview, March 18, 1986.

"The great emphasis": Titiev, op. cit., p. 65.

189   "If you were a Hopi": Sandra Massetto, telephone interview, September 22, 1985.

"In the Hopi perception": Richard Morris interview, February 12, 1986.

"By the end of 1985" to "$4.26 million": Letter from Ross Swimmer to Barry Goldwater, May 22, 1986, op. cit.

"The Hopis are in a position": Richard Morris interview, February 12, 1986.

"Perhaps they could": ibid.

"I am here," "I'll never forget": Percy Deal interview, January 30, 1986.

190   "They see their mission": J. C. Smythe interview, Flagstaff, Arizona, September 22, 1986.

p. 190   "Did [the Hopi lawyers] ask": ibid.

"The Council tried," "a way to work": ibid.

191   "They are so absorbed": ibid.

"in good faith," "resources having values": Letter from William P. Clark to Peterson Zah, July 30, 1985.

"the Hopis were unable": Statement prepared by Richard Morris for William P. Clark relative to their investigation of differences confronting the Hopi and Navajo Indians, October 21, 1985.

"If Chairman Sidney knew": Peterson Zah, press release, August 23, 1985.

192   "Chairman Zah is saying": Ivan Sidney interview, Kykotsmovi, July 1985.

"compassion is more important": Richard Morris, telephone interview, September 9, 1985.

"Whatever the conduct": Statement prepared by Richard Morris, op. cit.

"Judge Carroll urged": ibid.

"should not look": ibid.

"We, but not both Tribes": ibid.

"Unless a comprehensive plan": ibid.

"Pleased?": Richard Morris, telephone interview, October 22, 1985.

192ff.   "anyone who reads it": ibid.

193   "some kind of credibility": ibid.

"Congress doesn't really know": ibid.

"Goldwater's pride": Lee Phillips, telephone interview, July 23, 1986.

Note: Senator Barry Goldwater refused repeated requests to be interviewed for this book.

"I do not think": Hearings before the Subcommittee on Indian Affairs of the Committee on Interior and Insular Affairs, House of Representatives, Washington, D.C., May 14–15, 1973, pp. 42–43.

"My interest in this matter": ibid.

193ff.   "I was instrumental": ibid.

194   "At the end of July": Kammer, *Second Long Walk*, op. cit., pp. 164–65.

195   "Goldwater departed" to "how they lived": Leroy Morgan interview, May 1986.

"I even washed out": Matthiessen, op. cit.

"I've lived here fifty years": Kammer, *Second Long Walk*, op. cit., p. 165.

"TV cameras were rolling": Sandra Massetto, telephone interview, March 18, 1990.

196   "the law is the law": Gregg Houtz, telephone interview, August 28, 1986.

"was very anxious": Richard Morris, telephone interview, August 1985.

"Goldwater said conflicting things": Richard Morris, telephone interview, September 1, 1985.

"My perception was": Richard Morris interview, February 12, 1986.

197   "Craft said, 'Just take' ": Richard Morris, telephone interview, July 1985.

"I always saw her": Richard Morris interview, February 12, 1986.

"Senatorial courtesy": James Abourezk interview, Washington, D.C., April 21, 1986.

"Goldwater was antagonistic": ibid.

"Goldwater was very friendly": George Vlassis interview, June 12, 1985.

198   "we can't swing this": ibid.

"took the problem": ibid.

"He was sitting on the fence": Kammer, *Second Long Walk*, op. cit., p. 99.

"Goldwater and Fannin": George Vlassis interview, June 12, 1985.

"it was a matter of embarrassment": ibid.

199   "We fought a hell of a battle": ibid.

"obnoxious, not law-abiding": Claudeen Bates-Arthur interview, July 17, 1986.

"Barry's still cursing him": Morris Udall interview, February 4, 1986.

14. THE RELOCATION COMMISSION

p. 200 "These people do not": This lawyer requested anonymity.

201 "a star that's collapsing": Hawley Atkinson interview, Flagstaff, Arizona, September 4, 1986.

"Hawley has been a disaster": Morris Udall interview, February 4, 1986.

"Hawley is a mean": Dick Ivey [project manager for CH2M Hill, the commission's planning firm], telephone interview, January 30, 1986.

"When I got on the Commission": Hawley Atkinson interview, Glendale, Arizona, January 20, 1987.

"I never got emotionally involved": Hawley Atkinson interview, September 4, 1986.

"it was always confrontation": ibid.

202 "provided an intense": Jerry Kammer, "Navajo Relocation Talks Begin," *Gallup Independent*, June 14, 1976.

"his right hand punching": Kammer, *Second Long Walk*, op. cit., p. 175.

"at the people": ibid., p. 174.

"identify the sites": 25 USC 640d-12.

"You people shouldn't pass": Kammer, "Navajo Relocation Talks Begin," op. cit.

"How have you people": ibid.

203 "Too often other people": ibid.

"We don't believe you have": Kammer, *Second Long Walk*, op. cit., p. 176.

"We feel and we understand": ibid.

"Many Navajo men were drafted" Jerry Kammer, "Navajos May Defy Relocation Order," *Gallup Independent*, June 30, 1976.

"By not attending": ibid.

204 "We want this plan": ibid.

"so we can try": Memo to commissioners and executive director from Chairman Robert Lewis, April 30, 1976.

"an executive role," "an administrative role": ibid.

"emasculating": This official requested anonymity.

205 "It is written": Memo from Executive Director John Gray to the commissioners, July 8, 1976.

"My leaving of that meeting": Letter from Robert E. Lewis to Hawley Atkinson, November 15, 1976.

206 "I question his motivation": "Relocation Commission Is Attacked," *Arizona Republic*, November 28, 1976.

"wise leader," "soft-spoken and contemplative," "never found him to be," "a courteous gentleman," "Lewis Belongs on Commission": *Gallup Independent*, December 1, 1976.

"dismay and disgust," "My question is this": *Arizona Republic*, November 16, 1976.

"either in draft": Letter from Hawley Atkinson and Paul Urbano to Thomas S. Kleppe, Secretary of the Interior, November 5, 1976.

"The Interior Department" to "could be found": Memo from William Benjamin, Project Officer, Joint Use Area Administrative Office, U.S. Department of the Interior, to Hawley Atkinson, December 17, 1976.

"more right than he was wrong": Ward Harkavy, "Special Report: Hawley Atkinson," *Arizona Republic*, January 15, 1984.

"consumed," "intense dislike": ibid.

"It was a long, hard summer": Hawley Atkinson interview, September 4, 1986.

207 "not a high level": Hawley Atkinson interview, January 20, 1987.

"After I left": Hawley Atkinson interview, September 4, 1986.

"Everyone thought": Grace McCullough, telephone interview, December 1986.

p. 207   "I'm antagonistic": Hawley Atkinson interview, September 4, 1986.

"Atkinson was perceived": Paul Klores, telephone interview, January 21, 1987.

"I assumed that since": ibid.

"I was a fluke": Hawley Atkinson interview, September 4, 1986.

208   "I was very grateful": Hawley Atkinson interview, January 20, 1987.

"We live in a world": Paul Klores, telephone interview, January 21, 1987.

"I don't see how": Jerry Kammer, "Navajo Expresses Doubts About Relocation Board," *Gallup Independent*, December 10, 1976.

209   "I urge you": Letter from Barry Goldwater to Interior Secretary Thomas Kleppe, November 17, 1976.

"We had a hard job": Hawley Atkinson interview, January 20, 1987.

"Investigative findings," "evidence continued": Letter from Interior Secretary Thomas Kleppe to Hawley Atkinson, January 19, 1987.

" 'bite the bullet' ": William E. Simkin, "Navajo-Hopi Land Dispute, Public Law 93-531, Mediator's Report and Recommendations," vol. 2, p. 23.

" 'time is of the essence' ": ibid.

"It just dawned": Kammer, *Second Long Walk*, op. cit., p. 175.

210   "old bureaucrats," "have been entirely resentful": Letter from Hawley Atkinson to Barry Goldwater, November 7, 1980.

"I have concluded," "provide them with": Letter from R. Dennis Ickes to BIA Commissioner, December 22, 1976.

"a very basic misunderstanding": Memo from Steve Goodrich, Liaison, U.S. Department of the Interior, to Commission members and acting executive director, March 14, 1978.

211   "I believe we are": Phoenix Newspapers Primary Candidate Survey, July 12, 1976, in clip files in the Arizona Room, Phoenix Public Library.

"In 1979" to "suicide attempts": Navajo and Hopi Indian Relocation Commission, *Report and Plan*, April 1981, p. 139.

"By 1983" to "significant debts": Report to Congress in Opposition to the NHIRC budget request, March 1985, submitted by BMLDOC.

212   "political deal": Leon Berger interview, Williams, Arizona, July 1985.

"we've made a commitment": ibid.

"there was little thought," "we will ignore the problem": ibid.

"In the very beginning": Christine Chisholm-Tures interview, Hardrock, February 13, 1986.

"One of my deepest regrets": ibid.

"Consumer loan problems": Lee Phillips interview, July 1985.

213   "These people are the poorest": ibid.

"There are so many more expenses": Charlotte Beyal interview, Flagstaff, Arizona, August 1985.

"to the maximum extent": PL 93-531, 86 Stat. 1717, Section 13 (c) (1), (25 USC 640d-12).

214   "If they just bring in": Jerry Kammer, "Need to Develop Use Area Cited," *Gallup Independent*, December 13, 1976.

"abdicating its responsibilities": Memo from Paul Urbano to NHIRC chairman, November 29, 1976.

214ff.   "Working here," "courting for continued," "You let me do this," "the high pay," " 'alliances' and 'working relationships' ": David Shaw-Serdar, telephone interview, January 21, 1987.

215   "If whatever was going on": ibid.

"wacko, crazy environment," "Atkinson would stand": Leon Berger, telephone interview, January 28, 1987.

"real bad list," "I had taken a ride": Christine Chisholm-Tures interview, February 13, 1986.

"Mr. Chairman, we know": Debate on passage of HR 10337, *Congressional Record*, U.S. House of Representatives, May 29, 1974, p. 4506.

p. 216   "had to go": Lisa Shepard, "Locally-Based Relocation Commission a 'Political Football,' " *Arizona Daily Sun*, August 20, 1978.

"sour grapes," "They've got a history of," "Now three private citizens": Laurie Wegner, "Bureaucrats Jealous, Says Tribe Relocator," *Arizona Republic*, September 1, 1978.

"He was also criticized" to "as county supervisor": Tom Fitzpatrick, "Bridge to Nowhere Offers 4 Million Reasons to Vote Out Atkinson," *Arizona Republic*, November 1, 1984.

"Atkinson is grumbling": "Mr. A Blows Smoke," *Arizona Republic*, September 5, 1978.

"We Indians would rather": Letter to the editor, *Arizona Republic*, September 12, 1978.

217   "has constitutional implications," "the Commission needs to": Memorandum from President Jimmy Carter released November 2, 1978, on HR 11092, as reprinted in *Qua Toqti*, November 23, 1978.

"outstanding job to date," "What exactly," "minor when compared": Draft letter from Hawley Atkinson to Barry Goldwater, January 19, 1979.

"Now isn't that heartbreaking": ibid.

"The Relocation Commission": Leon Berger interview, July 1985.

218   "It was in 1979": Sandra Massetto, telephone interview, May 9, 1990.

219   "I felt uncomfortable": ibid.

220   "that Leon had gone berserk": ibid.

"We knew after the first": Leon Berger interview, July 1985.

"consists of some 4,000": FBI field file #58-355, Phoenix, Arizona.

221   "and alleged that Bob Sharp," "just that, just suspicions," "Since that time": Steve Goodrich memo, February 14, 1980, included in FBI file, ibid.

"Namingha was really pushing": ibid.

"At times Namingha," "Sharp never mentioned," "never even realized": ibid.

"reliable," "wouldn't do a good job," "would take too long": ibid.

222   "faulty foundation work," "Those homes were *terrible*": David Williams interview, San Diego, California, August 5–7, 1986.

"and that it was not level," "they would not be satisfied": FBI file, op. cit.

"a pilotless ignition": Christine Chisholm-Tures interview, February 13, 1986.

"You really have to see": Peter Osetek, telephone interview, September 23, 1986.

"If you were a ballerina," "never got closer than," "literally no support": ibid.

223   "never taken any relocatees": Bob Sharp, telephone interview, July 1985.

"Apparently they used": Sandra Massetto, telephone interview, May 9, 1990.

"Do you think": This official requested anonymity.

"The FBI guys": David Williams interview, August 5–7, 1986.

224   "A lot of Indian People": Ella Bedonie interview, May 19, 1986.

"Sharp never seemed": FBI file, op. cit.

"It's an indication": Sandra Massetto, telephone interview, February 2, 1987.

"He came from," "operated the shop": David Williams interview, August 5–7, 1986.

"a lot of pressure": FBI file, op. cit.

224ff.   "In 1974, the benefit level" to "more than four": *Report and Plan*, op. cit., p. 173.

225   "was the first," "saw a good market," "after competitors entered": FBI file, op. cit.

"if they didn't hurry up": ibid.

"Sharp had attempted": ibid.

"Also, Village Homes was repeatedly" to "signing the agreement": David Williams, memo for the record, February 12, 1980.

"she was told," "losing files," "lost": ibid.

p. 225 "In 1986, when electricity" to "installed again": Sandra Massetto, telephone interview, September 15, 1987.

"dynamic group," "related that he had": ibid.

226 "overall pattern," "at the minimum": David Williams, memo for the record, August 4, 1980.

"There were some real," "I don't believe," "There were relocatees": Christine Chisholm-Tures interview, February 13, 1986.

"They had a van," "clients would come in": ibid.

227 "considerable redesign," "We are building": David Williams, "Thoughts on the Realty Audit," memo to the Commissions, NHIRC, March 2, 1979.

"They were sold," "It was a two-story house": David Williams interview, August 5–7, 1986.

"changed fundamentally": ibid.

228 "he didn't think": This informant requested anonymity.

"supposed to be," "went too far": ibid.

"After so much misunderstanding": ibid.

"the original contractor": Betty Reid, "For Relocatees, the Dream Is Elusive," *Navajo Times*, February 10, 1987.

"We're going to get this taken": Mary Tolan, "Many Relocation Homes Not Livable," *Arizona Daily Sun*, February 8, 1987.

229 "According to Barry Paisner" to "in 1982": Barry Paisner, telephone interview, March 17, 1987.

"I was a very staunch," "You don't sit down," "were not real": Christine Chisholm-Tures interview, February 13, 1986.

230 "the worst job": "Navajo-Hopi Relocation Panel Member Quits," *Navajo Relocation Review* (a publication of the *Navajo Times*), July 1982.

"a tragic, tragic thing": ibid.

"I feel that in moving": "Relocation Is Like Nazi Concentration Camps," *Navajo Relocation Review*, July 1982.

231 "The meeting was scheduled" to "adjourned the meeting": Hawley Atkinson interview, September 4, 1986.

"I have to tell you": ibid.

"sauntering in," "I told Chairman MacDonald": ibid.

"According to Leon Berger" to "the time": Leon Berger, telephone interview, January 28, 1987.

"I still think about": Sandra Massetto, telephone interview, September 3, 1986.

232 "a perfect excuse": ibid.

"should help convince": "Atkinson Proposes to Limit Relocation Benefits Eligibility," *Navajo Times*, July 21, 1982.

"can only be viewed": ibid.

"retaliation": ibid.

"We were right in front," "typically selective amnesia": Sandra Massetto, telephone interview, August 28, 1986.

"I wish the records": Memo from Hawley Atkinson to Steve Goodrich, July 27, 1982.

15. WASHINGTON GETS INVOLVED

238 "There was this craziness": Sandra Massetto, telephone interview, January 14, 1986.

"If the Commission," "$88 million," "We would have met": Fred Craft, telephone interview, September 22, 1986.

"In July and August": Sandra Massetto, telephone interview, January 14, 1986.

"Before then, I tried": ibid.

p. 239   "became unglued": Dan Jackson telephone interview, March 3, 1986.

"When I saw the Commission's," "This is horseshit": Dan Jackson, telephone interview, July 9, 1986.

240   "We heard about": Earl Gjelde, telephone interview, January 1986.

"Jackson was deeply concerned": ibid.

241   "It was very important that," "He clearly believed": ibid.

"need to work with," "We are concerned": ibid.

"We were very lucky": Dan Jackson, telephone interview, December 10, 1986.

"No one should know": John McCain, telephone interview, May 13, 1986.

242   "Goldwater, even in his moment": Fred Craft, telephone interview, January 1986.

"Byzantine system": Cass Peterson, "BIA Critic Takes on Job of Improving It," *Washington Post*, reprinted in the *Navajo Times*, February 11, 1986.

"He guided the Cherokees' " to "250 percent": ibid.

243   "overcome by entrusting": ibid.

"He's clearly the brightest," "He infuriates the control types": This staffer requested anonymity.

"The Secretary was not too concerned": Ross Swimmer interview, Washington, D.C., April 18, 1986.

"As the new kid": ibid.

244   "Between 1982 and 1986" to "job done on time": Department of the Interior and Related Agencies Appropriations for 1987, *Hearings before the Subcommittee on the Department of the Interior and Related Agencies, 99th Congress, Second Session, Part 9*, p. 129.

"I'm just going around": Ross Swimmer interview, April 18, 1986.

"Well, I walked into": ibid.

"Well, what are we going to do": ibid.

"I thought we had": ibid.

"put on a dog and pony": This staffer requested anonymity.

245   "in very broad strokes": Dan Jackson, telephone interview, March 3, 1986.

"I will not build another," "It's not a ghetto," "It will be an economic": Dick Ivey, telephone interview, January 30, 1986.

"It was never the intent": Fred Craft, telephone interview, January 1986.

"This is a benefits program": Fred Craft, telephone interview, June 9, 1986.

"avoid or minimize," "adverse social, economic, cultural," "Assure that housing and related": 25 USC 640d-12.

"I'm not going to do it," "He outlined": Dick Ivey telephone interview, January 30, 1986.

246   "Here we are," "because I want to": Sid Yates, telephone interview, January 27, 1986.

"I'd like to": ibid.

"Goldwater was very cavalier," "Money? That's nothing," "I kind of admired": Ty West, telephone interview, September 4, 1986.

246ff.   "The whole thing is just," "I told [Swimmer]": Sid Yates, telephone interview, September 1986.

247   "There's a great question," "There ought to be": ibid.

"I was close": Morris Udall interview, February 4, 1986.

"I always sympathized": ibid.

"It was a no-win situation": ibid.

248   "First, he fired off" to "Yates": June Tracy, telephone interview, December 13, 1985.

"Relocation, in hindsight": Morris Udall interview, February 4, 1986.

"The problem is": John McCain interview, Washington, D.C., February 5, 1986.

"[It would take] Mo": ibid.

"Whether Mo and I": ibid.

"I have every reason": ibid.

p. 249   "Here's a very": Morris Udall interview, February 4, 1986.
"Peterson Zah is": ibid.
250   "The 1974 act": ibid.
"was indignant": ibid.
"Ivan went around": John McCain interview, February 5, 1986.
"He implied to me": Morris Udall interview, February 4, 1986.
251   " 'You're getting in bed' ": John McCain interview, February 5, 1986.
"Ivan stepped into shoes": George Vlassis, telephone interview, February 24, 1986.
"I couldn't fully fathom": Morris Udall interview, February 4, 1986.
"He made what Zah," "He was doing this," "he would be very": ibid.
252   "I have had a hunch": Letter from Barry Goldwater to Ivan Sidney, January 22, 1986.
"John Paul Kennedy still treated Abbott": J. C. Smythe interview, September 22, 1986.
"He refused to sign" to "1934 litigation": Abbott Sekaquaptewa interview, Kykots-movi, May 29, 1986.
"He's a well-meaning guy": George Vlassis, telephone interview, February 24, 1986.
"Goldwater is pretty cool," "He wants Ivan": Morris Udall interview, February 4, 1986.
"I have just finished" to "the attorneys": Letter from Barry Goldwater to Ivan Sidney, January 22, 1986.
253   "pull the teeth out of": Morris Udall interview, February 4, 1986.
"Goldwater's erratic": ibid.
"We got the best wilderness": ibid.
254   "I think it's like": ibid.
"They're trying to flush": Eric Eberhard, telephone interview, February 21, 1986.
"There are about five hundred," "I was quite upset," "Peter MacDonald is," "I hope you will get": Letter from Barry Goldwater to John McCain, February 4, 1986.
"a vehicle for discussion": Anne Q. Hoy, "Udall-McCain Bill Aims at Navajo-Hopi Solution," *Arizona Republic*, February 7, 1986.
"He is adamantly": LeNora Begay, "Zah Still Hoping for Goldwater Support," *Navajo Times*, February 8, 1986.
255   "I can't buy this": J. J. Casserly, "Goldwater Rejects Udall-McCain Plan to Settle Dispute," *Arizona Republic*, February 13, 1986.
"Then six days after" to "answer the reporter's questions": Kim Oriole, "Barry 'Can't Buy' Land Swap," *Gallup Independent*, February 19, 1986.
"It has no future": Paul Brinkley-Rogers, "Goldwater Rejects House Panel's Hopi-Navajo Plan, Aide Says," *Arizona Republic*, February 21, 1986.
"He is the key player": ibid.
"You may be assured": "Relo Bill 'New Look'—Udall," *Gallup Independent*, March 4, 1986.
"Staff members are shielding us": Paul Brinkley-Rogers, "Goldwater Rejects House Panel's," op. cit.
"initiate proposals," "important": Letter from John McCain to Ivan Sidney, February 26, 1986.
"Senator Goldwater has chosen": Ivan Sidney telephone message to John McCain.
"He and Barry": Matt James, telephone interview, February 1986.
"has told us that": John McCain, telephone interview, February 1986.
255ff.   "with extraordinarily little fanfare": "Udall Introduces Land Exchange Bill," *Navajo Times*, February 28, 1986.
256   "While it is clear," "potential for violent confrontation," "the severe budget con-straints," "great pain and suffering," "be the beginning of": *Congressional Record—House*, H-724, February 27, 1986.
"some outside factor," "cause some unhappiness": *Congressional Record—House*, H-725, February 27, 1986.

16. SANDRA MASSETTO'S LAST ACT

This chapter is told from Sandra Massetto's point of view and with the use of her recollection.

17. ROSS SWIMMER TRAVELS TO THE HPL

p. 266 "Ivan was giving Stevens": Dick Ivey interview, February 27, 1986.
267 "intellectually arrogant": Christine Chisholm-Tures, telephone interview, March 6, 1986.
"I want to meet": Dick Ivey interview, February 27, 1986.
"Just when we": Percy Deal interview, Second Mesa, February 27, 1986.
268 "Apparently, Ray Smith": ibid.
"was really harsh," "We don't trust you," "If things don't improve," "You're not the first person": ibid.
269 "It will take a few": Eric Eberhard interview, Washington, D.C., February 12, 1986.
"Ivan told me": Dick Ivey interview, February 27, 1986.
270 "I don't plan": Ella Bedonie's version of this conversation was recorded immediately following its conclusion.
271 "They felt Peggy": Dick Ivey interview, February 27, 1986.

18. PETERSON ZAH BRINGS HIS PLAN TO HARDROCK

277 "This bill is like": "Hardrock Hopes Bill Brings Relief," *Navajo Times*, February 11, 1986.
278 "The native way of deciding": Clyde Kluckhohn and Dorothea Leighton, *The Navaho*, Revised Edition (New York: The Natural History Library, Anchor Books, Doubleday & Company, 1962), pp. 160–61.

20. INDIAN ANGER, WHITE GUILT

283 "the overwhelming lobbying effort": Letter from Senator Daniel Inouye to BMLDOC, as quoted in *BMLDOC Newsletter, 535 Update*, January 1986.
"maybe ten or twelve": Jay Mocilnikar interview, Flagstaff, Arizona, July 11, 1986.
284 "They are basically": Lee Phillips interview, December 1, 1986.
"There was no mechanism," "We told them": ibid.

23. THE FENCE

The events of this chapter were drawn from descriptions given by Willie Lonewolf Scott, Sam Tso, Thomas Katenay, and Lee Phillips on the Monday (April 7, 1986) following the altercation at the fence.

310 "As far as I know": Dan Jackson, telephone interview, April 7, 1986.
"plaintiff tribe (Hopi)," "[Grazing] districts": *Hamilton v. MacDonald*, 503 F.2D 1138, 1150–1151 (9Cir. 1974).
"It turns out": Dan Jackson, telephone interview, April 7, 1986.
"members of one tribe": *Hamilton v. MacDonald*, op. cit.
311 "No matter where," "The location, timing and method": Dan Jackson, telephone interview, April 7, 1986.
"Ivan was very friendly": Lee Phillips, telephone interview, April 8, 1986.
"I feel that the action": Catherine Feher-Elston, "Bomb Threat Closes Hopi Headquarters," *Arizona Republic*, April 8, 1986.

p. 311   "Well, people will probably try": Lee Phillips, telephone interview, April 8, 1986.

312   "I wouldn't put it past Ivan": Abbott Sekaquaptewa, telephone interview, April 7, 1986.

317   "Lew Gurwitz had canceled": Twinkle Thompson interview, Washington D.C., April 18, 1986.

"A few hours before" to "were all there": ibid.

"For this reason," "That is why we are here today": Catherine Feher-Elston, "Some Navajos May Stay on Hopi," *Gallup Independent*, April 19, 1986.

317ff.   "Any request made," "want to listen": ibid.

318   "The traditional people," "The Hopis aren't going to force": Ivan Sidney interview, Kykotsmovi, July 6, 1986.

"Whatever did we": Kee Shay, affidavit for Lee Phillips's First Amendment suit, op. cit.

"My Navajo people": Catherine Feher-Elston, "Sidney Sees Accord with Big Mountain," *Gallup Independent*, April 18, 1986.

319   "really lobbied my mom": Betty Tso interview, Flagstaff, Arizona, June 1, 1986.

"On the appointed date" to "Navajo Nation KTNN radio": This series of events told by Mae and Earl Tso, Mosquito Springs, June 25, 1986.

320   "tentative dates": Betty Reid, "Sidney Meets HPL Navajos Despite Mixup," *Navajo Times*, April 25, 1986.

"recount his view": Percy Deal interview, Hardrock, June 26, 1986.

"Now, it's getting," "But it is something": Betty Reid, "Sidney meets HPL Navajos," op. cit.

"The people are here *now*": Percy Deal interview, June 26, 1986.

"it wasn't the Hopi position": Betty Reid, "Navajo Elder Succumbs to Stress at Hopi," *Navajo Times*, April 25, 1986.

"It was then Mae": Percy Deal interview, June 26, 1986.

"All this time I," "I wanted to be represented": Mae Tso interview, June 25, 1986.

"This is too frustrating": Betty Reid, "Navajo Elder Succumbs to Stress at Hopi," op. cit.

"so she could have": ibid.

<h4 style="text-align:center">24. SMALL VICTORIES</h4>

322   "taunted her," "BIA employees or Hopi rangers": Letter from Peterson Zah to Ross Swimmer, April 10, 1986.

"Mr. Swimmer, you and I," "The Navajo Nation": ibid.

323   "obviously a binding": From notes taken at the meeting by Eric Eberhard, director of the Navajo Nation's Washington office.

"we didn't have a real good case": Dan Jackson, telephone interview, April 7, 1986.

"Tell me what you're doing on": Eberhard's notes, op. cit.

324   "I'm now familiar": ibid.

"greatly undermined our efforts," "It's too late for Udall-McCain": ibid.

"Thank you for the history lesson," "The Trail of Tears?," "I wasn't aware," "I suggest you get them": Author's notes of the hearing before the Department of the Interior and Related Agencies Appropriations for Fiscal Year 1987, for the Navajo and Hopi Indian Relocation Commission, April 23, 1986.

"twelve hundred Navajo families": This and the following quotations are from *Hearings of the Department of the Interior and Related Agencies Appropriations for 1987*, op. cit., pp. 174–233.

326   "There is a strong": Letter from Louise A. Linkin to Thelma Begay, June 3, 1985, as reprinted in *Hearings*, ibid., p. 197.

"situation was not critical": Affidavit of Thomas Yazzie, as reprinted in *Hearings*, ibid., p. 198.

p. 327 "I am going to change": ibid., p. 193.

"It's inhumane": This Interior official requested anonymity.

"issue a directive," "[would] mandate": Letter from Ross Swimmer to Peterson Zah, May 20, 1986.

26. THE MESSIAH OF RELOCATION?

338 "to load the record": Eric Eberhard interview, April 21, 1986.

Pete Zah's reelection rested: John McCain interview, April 23, 1986.

339 "The Commission's numbers" to "the Commission didn't": "Full-time Navajo Residents of the Hopi Partitioned Lands: A Comparison of BIA, Relocation Commission and Navajo Nation Estimates," prepared by Ron Faich, Navajo tribal demographer, undated.

"Ray [Smith of the BIA] only knows": Sandra Massetto, telephone interview, January 7, 1986.

"The Navajo Tribe" to "It counted bodies": Faich, op. cit.

"Hell, they'll truck in": Dick Ivey interview, January 30, 1986, quoting Jim Stevens of the BIA Phoenix Area office.

340 "the mass kept changing": This participant requested anonymity.

341 "Over time": Kathy Helmer, telephone interview, May 17, 1986.

"It's natural to want," "trying to please," "I think the deal": John McCain, telephone interview, April 23, 1986.

"Swimmer isn't the only one": ibid.

"with no in-place criteria," "which are not adequate," "ludicrous": Letter from Peterson Zah to Ross Swimmer, March 20, 1986.

342 "criticized mercilessly," "she had overstepped": This informant requested anonymity.

"a lot of suggestions," "We were told": Claudeen Bates-Arthur interview, July 17, 1986.

"Suggestions we made," "There has never been": ibid.

"arrogant," " 'If you don't agree with me' ": ibid.

343 "Now that Zah": Leon Berger interview, July 1985.

"was a calculated mistake": Claudeen Bates-Arthur interview, July 17, 1986.

"Bureau employees used": ibid.

344 "First BIA Bid," "$300,000 spent": Paul Brinkley-Rogers, "First BIA Bid to Transplant Navajo Flops," *Arizona Republic*, June 8, 1986.

"personal representative," "render any and all assistance," "this extraordinary detail": Memo from Ross Swimmer to Navajo Area Director, Phoenix Area Director, re: appointment of Daniel Jackson as Manager of New Lands Project, May 30, 1986.

345 "Average precipitation" to "planning was possible": *Planning for the New Lands*, CH2M Hill, 1984.

"removing the technical people," "Hawley didn't want to make": Sandra Massetto, telephone interview, December 7, 1987.

346 "the largest known" to "the New Lands": W. C. Weimer, R. R. Kinnison, and J. H. Reves, "Survey of Radionuclide Distributions Resulting from the Church Rock, New Mexico Uranium Mill Tailings Pond Failure," U.S. Nuclear Regulatory Commission Report, NUREG/CR-2449, 1981.

"waters collected": Statement by the Division of Environmental Health, Arizona Department of Health Services, before the U.S. Environmental Protection Agency public hearing, Gallup, New Mexico, July 27, 1983.

"levels of radionuclides in surface": ibid.

p. 346   "giving up some": Larry Agenbroad, telephone interview, August 1985.

346ff.   "A public education project" to "that was not true": Chris Shuey, "Report to the Public Welfare Foundation on the Activities of the Puerco River Education Project (July 1985–October 1986)."

347   "Toinjoni" to " 'that is harmful' ": Michael A. Brown, "An Analysis of Western Technology's Report, 'Water Quality Investigation,' and a Discussion of Water-Related Issues on the New Lands Acquired for Navajo Relocatees in Arizona," unpublished paper, February 1986.

"in a non-competitive" to "friend of Ralph Watkins": Sandra Massetto, telephone interview, August 19, 1986.

"water quality in the study": "Water Quality Investigation, Navajo-Hopi Indian Relocation Commission," Job No. 2175J266, by Western Technologies, Inc.

"inaccurate and poorly conceived": "Radionuclide Releases from Uranium Mining Activity and Ground Water Contaminants in the Puerco River," U.S. Department of the Interior Geological Survey, September 1986.

"plowing nothing but dust," "simply for the television": Navajo and Hopi Indian Relocation Commission, minutes of the September 1985 public meeting.

"Mr. Chairman," "It's not there": ibid.

"I always understood this": Dan Jackson, telephone interview, July 9, 1986.

348   "largest single release": Chris Shuey, "The Puerco River: Where Did the Water Go?" in *The Workbook*, vol. II, no. 1, Southwest Research and Information Center, Albuquerque, New Mexico, January/March 1986.

"Why didn't anyone": Sandra Massetto, telephone interview, December 7, 1986.

"political purposes": From notes taken by Sandra Massetto at the meeting.

"if there does not exist": Letter from Daniel L. Jackson to Chris Bavasie, May 29, 1986.

349   "Considering the problems": Letter from Ralph Watkins to Ross Swimmer, August 8, 1986.

"Unfortunately, water": Letter from Ross Swimmer to Ralph Watkins, August 26, 1986.

349ff.   "We've got plenty of water," "Nobody asked us," "The water's good": Ralph Watkins interview, Flagstaff, Arizona, June 10, 1986.

28. THE INTERNATIONAL INDIAN TREATY CONFERENCE

362   "Navajo and Hopi traditional leadership": Dennis Jennings interview, Flagstaff, Arizona, June 9, 1986.

"Only the so-called progressives": This and the following quotations from Dennis Jennings are from an interview that took place in Flagstaff, Arizona, on June 9, 1986.

29. UDALL PULLS OUT

364   "futile, misleading and cruel": Paul Brinkley-Rogers, "Udall Quits Bid to Aid Navajos in Relocation," *Arizona Republic*, June 5, 1986.

"As far as I am concerned": ibid.

"You dropped me off a cliff": Claudeen Bates-Arthur interview, July 17, 1986.

"Udall said he's": This Navajo lobbyist requested anonymity.

364ff.   "The only thing," "Mo and I have to do": John McCain interview, February 26, 1986.

365   "disabused him," "The bill will move": Eric Eberhard, telephone interview, March 12, 1986.

"phony bill," "stimulate debate": *Congressional Record*, Proceedings and Debates of the 99th Congress, Second Session, House of Representatives, vol. 132, no. 74, June 5, 1986.

"We were all surprised": Claudeen Bates-Arthur interview, July 17, 1986.

"never," "phony": Sandra Massetto, telephone interview, June 26, 1986.

"Supposedly Mo had a meeting": ibid.

"I know he went over": Claudeen Bates-Arthur interview, July 17, 1986.

"Something bad happened": Sandra Massetto, telephone interview, June 26, 1986.

"Early on in this process": *Congressional Record*.

p. 366   "You are going to see": Transcript of Hearings on HR 4281, House of Representatives, May 8, 1986.

"contracts could not": ibid.

"The person who really hurt us": John McCain, telephone interview, May 9, 1986.

"The BIA is dashing": Peter Osetek, telephone interview, May 9, 1986.

"Swimmer came into this": John McCain, telephone interview, May 9, 1986.

"depressed," "He still doesn't know," "trying to figure out," "dramatically reduced proposal," "Moencopi settlement," "I don't know if": John McCain, telephone interview, May 13, 1986.

367   "got his hopes up": Morris Udall, telephone interview, June 19, 1986.

"concept": ibid.

"When I produced that bill": ibid.

"Maybe he didn't believe it": ibid.

"profound regret": *Congressional Record*, June 5, 1986, op. cit.

"It's been obvious": Morris Udall, telephone interview, June 19, 1986.

"He mouthed off": Paul Brinkley-Rogers, telephone interview, June 4, 1986.

"I especially call": *Congressional Record*, June 5, 1986, op. cit.

"The Navajo tribe is lobbying us": Lee Phillips interview, February 22, 1986.

368   "He's run for President": Sandra Massetto, telephone interview, July 31, 1986.

"There has been so much hatred," "Forget the government": Lee Phillips, telephone interview, August 2, 1986.

"started and finished": ibid.

369   "The Big Mountain group's activities": Peter Osetek, telephone interview, May 9, 1986.

"I've never understood," "There was a real anger": Lee Phillips, telephone interview, July 1986.

"We supported the concept": ibid.

"It's like we were": ibid.

"We asked them from the beginning": Claudeen Bates-Arthur interview, July 17, 1986.

370   "From that time on," "I know for a fact": ibid.

30. VIOLENCE ERUPTS IN TEESTO

371   "everybody on Zah's staff," "Let's pull ourselves together": Duane Beyal, telephone interview, July 3, 1986.

"Our position is": Paul Brinkley-Rogers, "Navajos File Suit to Halt Relocation," *Arizona Republic*, June 12, 1986.

372   "Jealousies and fights": Leroy Morgan interview, June 5, 1986.

"People are mad": Ella Bedonie, telephone interview, June 24, 1986.

373   "We have been worried": Catherine Feher-Elston, "Hopi Officers Hurt in Fight," *Gallup Independent*, June 18, 1986.

"The Teesto incident": Eric Eberhard, telephone interview, June 20, 1986.

377   "[would] not push the measure": Anne Q. Hoy, "Udall Retreat Stalls Other Moves to Alleviate Relocation of Navajos," *Arizona Republic*, June 7, 1986.

"I don't think there is going": ibid.

378   "It only takes one": Lee Phillips interview, February 1986.

Notes

p. 378   "The assumption in Congress": Eric Eberhard, telephone interview, June 20, 1986.
"The [Big Mountain] Committee is the biggest": ibid.

379   "unusually strongly worded letter": Hal Gross, telephone interview, June 20, 1986.
"we had our facts," "there was only one person": ibid.
"For years, people": ibid.
"We're trying to maintain": Lew Gurwitz interview, Teesto, Arizona, June 18, 1986.
"semidictatorship going on": This support group member requested anonymity.
"Do they know": Eric Eberhard, telephone interview, June 20, 1986.
"I think we're at the point": ibid.
"All things being equal": ibid.

31. JULY 4, INDEPENDENCE DAY

380   "The BIA is dealing": Sandra Massetto telephone interview, June 19, 1986.

32. THE SUN DANCE

386   "Our government is splitting": LeNora Begay, "Following the Beat of Different Drummers," *Navajo Times*, July 8, 1986.
"The American nation": Paul Brinkley-Rogers, " 'No Relocation': Navajos Slice Fence Separating Their Nation from Hopis," *Arizona Republic*, July 8, 1986.

Index

A NOTE ON THE TYPE

The text of this book was composed in a film version of Palatino, a type face designed by the noted German typographer Hermann Zapf. Named after Giovanbattista Palatino, a writing master of Renaissance Italy, Palatino was the first of Zapf's type faces to be introduced in America. The first designs for the face were made in 1948, and the fonts for the complete face were issued between 1950 and 1952. Like all Zapf-designed type faces, Palatino is beautifully balanced and exceedingly readable.

Composed by Dix Type Inc.,
Syracuse, New York

Printed and bound by Arcata Graphics,
Martinsburg, West Virginia

Typography and binding design by
Dorothy Schmiderer Baker